To Cornflake

Modern Land Law

Eleventh Edition

Martin Dixon
Professor in the Law of Real Property,
University of Cambridge,
Honorary Bencher of Lincoln's Inn

Routledge
Taylor & Francis Group

LONDON AND NEW YORK

Eleventh edition published 2018
by Routledge
2 Park Square, Milton Park, Abingdon, Oxon OX14 4RN

and by Routledge
711 Third Avenue, New York, NY 10017

Routledge is an imprint of the Taylor & Francis Group, an informa business

First edition published as Principles in Land Law by Cavendish Publishing 1994
Tenth edition published by Routledge 2016

British Library Cataloguing-in-Publication Data
A catalogue record for this book is available from the British Library

Library of Congress Cataloging-in-Publication Data
Names: Dixon, Martin (Martin J.), author.
Title: Modern land law / Martin Dixon.
Description: Eleventh edition. | Abingdon, Oxon : Routledge, 2018. | Includes
bibliographical references and index.
Identifiers: LCCN 2017057690| ISBN 9781138555853 (hbk) | ISBN 9781138555860
(pbk) | ISBN 9781351237321 (epub) | ISBN 9781351237314 (mobipocket) |
ISBN 9781351237345 (master) | ISBN 9781351237338 (web pdf)
Subjects: LCSH: Land tenure—Law and legislation—England.
Classification: LCC KD833 .D59 2018 | DDC 346.4204/3–dc23
LC record available at https://lccn.loc.gov/2017057690

ISBN: 978-1-138-55585-3 (hbk)
ISBN: 978-1-138-55586-0 (pbk)
ISBN: 978-1-351-23734-5 (ebk)

Typeset in Joanna
by Wearset Ltd, Boldon, Tyne and Wear

Visit the companion website: www.routledge.com/cw/dixon

Printed and bound in Great Britain by
TJ International Ltd, Padstow, Cornwall

Outline Contents

Detailed Contents

List of Abbreviations

Terms

AGA	Authorised Guarantee Agreement
CRAR	Commercial Rent Arrears Recovery

Legislation

AJA	Administration of Justice Act
CCA	Consumer Credit Act
CLRA	Commonhold and Leasehold Reform Act
ECHR	European Convention for the Protection of Human Rights and Fundamental Freedoms
FLA	Family Law Act
FSMA	Financial Services and Markets Act
LA	Limitation Act Land
LCA	Land Charges Act
LPA	Law of Property Act
LP(MP)A	Law of Property (Miscellaneous Provisions) Act
LRA	Land Registration Act
LRR	Land Registration Rules
LTCA	Landlord and Tenant (Covenants) Act
SLA	Settled Land Act
TOLATA	Trusts of Land and Appointment of Trustees Act

Journals

CLJ	Cambridge Law Journal
CLP	Current Legal Problems
Conv	Conveyancer and Property Lawyer
LQR	Law Quarterly Review
LS	Legal Studies
MLR	Modern Law Review
SLR	Student Law Review
SLRYB	Student Law Review Yearbook

Preface

Approaching land law for the first time can seem a daunting prospect. A major aim of this text is to dispel fears and to explain land law in an understandable and logical way. No attempt has been made to minimise the complexities of the subject simply to make it attractive or readable, for that benefits no one. However, the text is designed to explode the myths and mysteries of land law and substitute instead a picture that is both detailed and comprehensible. There is no denying that land law is different from other subjects, not least because its language is unfamiliar at first. But different does not mean difficult. Similarly, there is a common belief that land law is boring, not as sexy or apparently relevant as other legal disciplines. This too is misplaced, for land law remains at the heart of the legal system and is the vehicle for so much that concerns our everyday lives, both at home and at work. Seen in context, the issues raised in land law are as challenging and as topical as any that other law courses have to offer.

Land law is also a subject steeped in history. Many of the concepts and much of the language have their origin in centuries-old legal tradition. However, the historical dimension of land law – which in its own right is a fascinating topic for those with a passion for social and legal history – should not blind us to the reality that we live in the twenty-first century and that the principles of land law that touch us all in our everyday lives have moved on. The great reforms of 1922–5 that gave birth to the reforming property law legislation of 1925 no longer seem radical and unfamiliar, has been in force for nearly 15 years. Of course, what we have now owes much to what we once had, but land law is a modern subject and it has embraced the modern world, both in its substance and in its form. Land law deals as much with human rights as it does with land ownership and as much with electronic transactions as it does with paper deeds tied up with pink ribbon. Land law is about the life of a community. That said, I have resisted the temptation, which was never very great, to present land law as some kind of modernist social construct. The need for modern teaching of a modern subject does not mean the abandonment of a method of analysis that has stood the test of time. This is a book about law, based on our traditional understanding of the foundations of property law, albeit that concepts, principles and rules which are of purely historical interest have been omitted.

Land law is like a jigsaw and this book aims to explain the rules and principles and how they fit together to form a coherent whole. The arrangement of the chapters is intended to facilitate the growth of a steady understanding of each topic and its place within the jigsaw. Many pieces are needed before the jigsaw shows a picture, so the text aims at an accumulation of understanding rather than dropping the reader in at the deep end. However, while the overall picture remains essentially the same, some of the pieces have changed shape since the last edition of this book. There have been – as always – developments in the case law, and the Land Registration Act 2002 has been in force long enough for there to be consideration of whether it needs fine tuning. The Supreme Court and the Court of Appeal have been active, particularly in the general area of land registration and co-ownership, but other subjects like easements, covenants and estoppel have seen significant developments in the case law. I have also taken the opportunity to re-write large sections of the text to recognise that what was 'new' in the first edition is now no longer novel. Some outdated sections of the book have been omitted altogether and the overall aim has been to present the material in a fresh way without making the book larger. All that said, my aim has remained the same as when the first edition appeared: to help the reader swim with the subject, rather than let them drown in the detail.

As ever – and I mean it every time I say it – I am grateful to many current and former students, at home and abroad, who continue to raise questions about land law that require thought and reflection. They have done much to sharpen my thoughts and to save me (I hope) from serious error. Students are never shy in making it obvious when the text is unclear and that is right and proper. A textbook is a tool, and it must be fit for purpose. I still live in hope that my family will one day share my fascination with this subject. As I write, Biden is slumped next to the sofa, waiting to go for a walk across the wild and beautiful flatlands of the Fen. His love of land law knows no bounds, for he never complains as I explain it to him.

Martin Dixon
Cambridge
Winter 2017

Guide to the Companion Website

www.routledge.com/cw/dixon

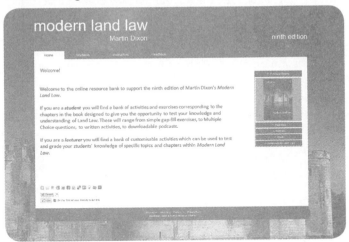

Lecturers

Testbank
Download a fully customisable bank of questions which test your students' understanding of land law. These can be migrated to your university's Visual Learning Environment so that they can be customised and used to track student progress.

For Students

Multiple Choice Questions
Test your understanding of land law with more than 150 online questions, including statute and case law quizzes.

Essay Questions
Over 30 open essay and problem-based questions for exam practice and to help deepen your understanding of complex issues and perfect your exam technique.

Podcasts
Thirteen podcasts divided by topic and updated with any land law cases, complex topics or issues in the news.

Additional Reading
Stay up to date with the latest developments in Land Law by downloading Martin Dixon's latest articles from the *Student Law Review*.

Table of Cases

Table of Statutes

Table of Statutory Instruments

Table of European Legislation

Chapter 1
An Introduction to Modern Land Law

Introduction

Land law is a subject steeped in history. It has its origins in the feudal reforms imposed on England by William the Conqueror after 1066, and many of the most fundamental concepts and principles of land law spring from the economic and social changes that began then. However, while these concepts and the feudal origins of land law should not, and cannot, be ignored, we must remember that we are about to examine a system of law that is alive and well in the twenty-first century. It would be easy to embark on an historical survey of land law, but not necessarily entirely profitable. Of course, the concepts and principles that were codified and refined in the years leading up to 1 January 1926 – the effective date of the first wave of great legislative reforms[1] – were themselves the products of decades of development, and every student of the subject must come to grips with the unfamiliar terminology and substance of the common law. Yet the purpose of this book is to present land law as it is today without obscuring the concepts and principles on which it is built. Indeed, as we move speedily forward in our electronic age, there is a need to constantly reassess and revise the system of land law that came into effect on 1 January 1926 in the light of all that has happened to society and our world since then. Consequently, although the substance of modern land law is still governed by the structure established by the Law of Property Act 1925 (LPA 1925), over 90 years of social and economic changes, inventive judicial decisions and further legislation have all played a part in moulding the substantive law to the needs of the modern age. In this respect, the most significant legislative development in recent times was the enactment of the Land Registration Act 2002 (LRA 2002). This came into force on 13 October 2003[2] and replaced entirely the Land Registration Act 1925 (LRA 1925). It heralded a new era for the law of real property, and its full effect is still being worked out in the case law.[3]

The LRA 2002 was the product of years of consideration and consultation by the Law Commission in conjunction with HM Land Registry. The reforms – the development of which is chronicled in detail in Law Commission Report No. 271, *Land Registration for the Twenty-first Century: A Conveyancing Revolution* – are designed to provide an efficient, clear, reliable and modern mechanism for the regulation of land of registered title. Many of the changes made by the 2002 Act remain controversial, even though nearly 15 years has passed since its entry into force. The most controversial proposal of all – the introduction of a system of paperless, electronic dealings with land (e-conveyancing) – would have revolutionised the way in which land is sold or transferred, marking a sharp break with the feudal past and the ancient origins of land law. However, even though the 2002 Act

---

1 In particular, the Law of Property Act 1925, the Land Registration Act 1925 (now the Land Registration Act 2002), the Trustee Act 1925, the Administration of Estates Act 1925 and the Land Charges Act 1925 (now the Land Charges Act 1972).

2 This is an unusual date for such momentous legislation. It appears to have been chosen so as to give enough time for the reforms to take effect before another piece of amending legislation – the Commonhold and Leasehold Reform Act 2002 (CLRA 2002) – was brought into force. In the event, the entry into force of the CLRA 2002 was delayed. Coincidentally – perhaps – the date was also 100 years after the opening of HM Land Registry HQ in Lincoln Fields, London.

3 The Law Commission is currently considering whether the Land Registration Act 2002 itself needs modification in the light of case law and practice. See e.g. *Updating the Land Registration Act 2002, A Consultation Paper* No. 227 (1916).

established the legal tools for e-conveyancing to operate, this has not yet taken place and it looks unlikely that the full scheme as originally envisaged will be implemented.[4] A more likely scenario is the introduction of targeted tools and processes designed to facilitate electronic dealings with land as befits the reality of land transactions in our property market.[5] However, even without full e-conveyancing, it is fair to say that the reforms of the system of land registration achieved by the LRA 2002 already have altered fundamentally the nature of land law in England and Wales. Modern land law has echoes of the past, but it looks to the future.

1.1 The Nature and Scope of the Law of Real Property

The 'law of real property' (or land law) is, obviously, concerned with land, rights in or over land, and the processes whereby those rights and interests are created and transferred. One starting point might be to consider the meaning of 'land' itself or, more properly, the legal definition of 'land' as found in the Law of Property Act 1925. According to section 205(1)(ix) of the LPA 1925:

> Land includes land of any tenure, and mines and minerals ... buildings or parts of buildings and other corporeal hereditaments; also a manor, an advowson, and a rent and other incorporeal hereditaments, and an easement, right, privilege, or benefit in, over, or derived from land.

Clearly, this is complicated and the statutory definition assumes that the reader already has a working knowledge of the basic concepts of land law, such as 'land of any tenure' (e.g. a 'freehold' or 'leasehold') and 'incorporeal hereditaments' (e.g. 'easements'). In essence, what this statutory definition seeks to convey, and what is at the heart of land law is the idea that 'land' includes not only tangible, physical property such as fields, factories, houses, shops and soil, but also intangible rights in the land, such as the right to walk across a neighbour's driveway (a practical example of an easement), the creation of a 'charge' on land to secure a debt (a 'mortgage'), the right to control the use to which a neighbour may put his land (a 'restrictive covenant') or the right to take something from another's land, such as fish (being a 'profit' and another example of an 'incorporeal hereditament'). As a matter of legal definition, 'land' is both the physical asset and the

---

4 Full e-conveyancing means, in simplified terms, that rights and interests cannot be created or transferred other than by making a direct, electronic entry on the land register, with paper documents having no legal effect and 'registration' being carried out by the parties to a transaction over e-networks. When the project was put on hold in 2011, HM Land Registry thought that it would be possible to implement full e-conveyancing when economic and technological conditions permitted, but the Law Commission (and probably HM Land Registry) now recognise that the ambitious original scheme needs to be re-evaluated and more realistic targets set: see *Updating the LRA* at para. 20.10 a 'new vision for electronic conveyancing'.

5 Some ancillary aspects of electronic dealings with land are in operation already, particularly in relation to the creation and discharge of mortgages (i.e. when a loan is taken out and then repaid) and the transmission of forms electronically rather than on paper. It is likely that the adjusted vision of e-conveyancing will include developing and enhancing these electronic services.

rights that the owner or others may enjoy in or over it. Consequently, 'land law' is the study of the creation, transfer, operation and termination of these rights and the manner in which they affect the use and enjoyment of the physical asset.

It is also important to appreciate why land law is fundamentally different from other legal disciplines, such as the law of contract or the law of tort. As we shall see, very many transactions concerning land or intangible rights in land take place through the medium of a contract. Thus, land is sold through a contract and a mortgage is also a contract of debt between lender and landowner. Similarly, the right to enjoy the exclusive possession of another's land for a defined period of time (a 'lease') may be given by a contract between the owner of the land (technically, the owner of an 'estate' in the land and in this context the 'landlord') and the person who is to enjoy the right (in this context the 'tenant'). Obviously, the conclusion of such a contract would bind the parties to it as a matter of simple contract law and the contract might require one of the parties to 'complete' the transaction by executing a 'deed' that formally 'grants' the right to the other.[6] In such cases, the contract is said to 'merge with the grant', and the contract ceases to have any separate existence as a legal concept.[7] Indeed, in everyday conveyancing practice, the parties to such a transaction may choose to proceed directly 'by grant' (i.e. by deed) without first formally concluding a separate contract. Clearly, however, whether the parties are bound by a 'mere' contract, or by the more formal 'deed of grant', they may enforce the contract or deed against each other: in the former case, by an action for damages or specific performance; in the latter, by relying on the covenants (i.e. promises) contained in the deed. In fact, if it becomes possible to create property rights electronically without a paper deed or a written contract, it will remain true that the parties to the 'electronic bargain' will be bound to each other. Yet the thing that is so special about 'real property rights', whether created by contract, by grant, or by some other method,[8] is that they are *capable* of affecting other people, not simply the parties that originally created the right. To put it another way, 'land law rights' are capable of *attaching* to the land itself so that any person who comes into ownership or possession of the land may be entitled to enjoy the benefits that now come with the land (such as the right to possess the land exclusively, or the right to walk across a neighbour's land to get to the highway), or may be subject to the burdens imposed on the land (such as the obligation to permit the exclusive possession of another person, or not to interfere with the neighbour's right of way). This is the 'proprietary' nature of rights and interests in land and it is very different from the merely 'personal' obligations that an ordinary contractual relationship establishes. In fact, another way of describing what land law is about is to say that it is the study of the creation and operation of *proprietary* rights, being rights that become part of the land and are not personal to the parties that created them. This is represented diagrammatically in Figures 1.1 and 1.2.

---

6 A deed is a formal written document, executed, signed and delivered as such by the grantor of the right and witnessed as such by a third person – see section 1 of the LP(MP)A 1989. It is no longer necessary to fix a red seal to a deed, but the document must declare itself to be a deed and be witnessed by a disinterested person as a deed. If e-conveyancing comes into force, deeds may be executed electronically without paper, section 93 LRA 2002.

7 But if the lease as such fails to be created out of the contract, it is possible that the parties could still enforce the contract between them: Berrisford v. Mexfield Housing Co-operative (2011) (see Chapter 6).

8 For example, by long use (prescription – see Chapter 7) or through proprietary estoppel (see Chapter 9) or perhaps in the future by electronic bargain.

Figure 1.1

Where A and B have entered into a contract for the creation of a proprietary right in favour of B, over A's land, the contract is enforceable between A and B like any other contract:

A – landowner: the grantor of the right

B – a person to whom A has granted a lease, easement or some other proprietary right in A's land: the grantee of the right

Figure 1.2

Where A sells his land to X (or, more accurately, sells his right of ownership or estate in the land), the proprietary nature of B's right means that it is *capable* of 'binding' X. The proprietary right is enforceable beyond the original parties to the contract (A and B) and so B's right is potentially enforceable against X, even though X had no part in the creation of the right:

B – the person with a lease, easement or some other proprietary right in A's land, and who may be able to enforce that right against X, the transferee or purchaser of A's land, even though X had no part in the creation of the right

The intrinsic ability of a proprietary right to affect a person in his capacity as an owner or occupier of land, as well as the person who originally created the right, means that the proper identification of what amounts to a 'proprietary right' is of particular importance. The categories of proprietary right must be defined with some care, and their creation must be established with a large measure of certainty, because not every right that has something to do with land can be proprietary. If that were the case, then the practical use and enjoyment of land by the owner would become extremely difficult, if not impossible, and the value of his land would fall. For example, in Chapter 9, we examine whether a 'licence' over land (being a permission given by the owner to another person allowing use of the land for a specific purpose, such as permission to hold a party) is proprietary or merely personal. This is especially important given that licences may arise in a huge variety of circumstances and sometimes they are given voluntarily (e.g. to a friend who is visiting) and sometimes in return for a payment (e.g. on the purchase of a cinema ticket). If licences as a category were proprietary (and they are not), then the owner of the land affected would find that his land was so overburdened by other people's rights that it became difficult to use it for his own purposes. Consequently, it became less valuable on sale because a purchaser might also be bound to permit the licence-holders to use the land. Necessarily then, it is not all rights merely connected with land that are 'proprietary', and a proper understanding of land law must encompass an understanding of how we distinguish between proprietary rights in land and merely personal rights to use land.

The traditional starting point in a search for the 'proprietary' character of rights is the a priori definition of 'an interest in land' put forward by the House of Lords in *National Provincial Bank* v. *Ainsworth* (1965). In that case, the essential point was whether a wife's *right to live* in the former matrimonial home could be regarded as a proprietary right given that she did not actually own a share of the property. If it could, the right might bind a third party such as the National Provincial Bank, which had a mortgage over the land and whose claim to possession might be defeated if a proprietary right existed. If, however, the right was purely personal – that is, enforceable by the wife only against the husband personally – it could never bind the land and the bank's mortgage would necessarily take priority. The bank could take the house. In deciding that the wife's right to live in the property could only ever be personal (assuming she had no actual share of ownership), Lord Wilberforce stated that:

> [b]efore a right or an interest can be admitted into the category of property, or of a right affecting property, it must be definable, identifiable by third parties, capable in its nature of assumption by third parties, and have some degree of permanence or stability.

So it is, then, that rights to use land must, apparently, satisfy this four-fold test before they can be regarded as 'proprietary'. As a general indication of proprietary status, this 'definition' has merit, but it is susceptible to criticism. For example, not only are 'definability', 'identifiability' and 'stability' inherently open-ended (how definable, identifiable and stable must a right be?), the definition is clearly circular, for only if a right is *already* proprietary is it *capable* of assumption by third parties (that is, of affecting people who did not create it). After all, the search for an answer to the question – does it bind third parties? – is often the very reason why we need to establish the proprietary or personal nature of the right in the first place. Nevertheless, perhaps we should not seek to pick over Lord Wilberforce's words as if they were enshrined in legislation or were intended to be cast in stone. What he is trying to identify are those attributes that mark out candidates for proprietary status from those rights to use land that are clearly personal, 'however broad or penumbral the separating band between these two kinds of rights may be' (*per* Lord Wilberforce in *Ainsworth*). After all, proprietary rights should – indeed *must* – be definable, identifiable and stable precisely because they can affect the land for considerable periods of time irrespective of who now might own or occupy it. The definition tells us, in other words, that proprietary rights have a certain quality other than merely being connected with the use or enjoyment of land and it is this quality that makes them fit to endure beyond changes in the ownership or occupation of the land. Necessarily, this leaves room for argument and perhaps the only really certain way of identifying all proprietary rights is to make a list – to have a so-called *numerus clausus*[9] – but English law has not trodden this path and so we are left with useful, but not definitive, judicial dicta and a wealth of case law that has examined the proprietary status of rights to use land on a case-by-case basis.[10]

---

9 See e.g. Rudden, B (1987) 'Economic theory versus property law: The numerus clausus problem', in Eekelaar, J and Bell, J (eds) *Oxford Essays in Jurisprudence*, 3rd series, Oxford: Clarendon Press.

10 It is not only case law that can settle the matter. Sections 115 and 116 of the LRA 2002 confirm the proprietary status of previously disputed rights. Thus, rights of pre-emption, equities by estoppel (proprietary estoppel) and mere equities are confirmed as proprietary.

1.2   Types of Proprietary Right

Generally, and with some necessary simplification for the purposes of exposition, 'proprietary rights' fall into two categories: estates in land and interests in land.

1.2.1   Estates in land

The 'doctrine of estates' forms one of the cornerstones of the law of real property, and this is as true today as it was in feudal times, even with the introduction of near universal registration of title. Theoretically, all land in England and Wales is actually owned by the Crown[11] – and all other persons may own 'merely' an 'estate in the land', rather than the land itself.[12] In this sense, an estate confers a right to use and control land, being tantamount to ownership, but with the important difference that the type of estate that is owned will define the time for which the use and control of the land is to last. In this sense, an estate in land is equivalent to ownership of the land for a 'slice of time'.

1.2.1.1   *The freehold estate (the fee simple)*

When people say that they own their land, usually they mean that they own this estate in the land: 'the fee simple absolute in possession', usually referred to as the freehold estate. The freehold estate comprises the right to use and enjoy the land for the duration of the life of the grantee and that of his or her heirs and successors. Furthermore, the freehold is freely transferable ('alienable') during the life of the estate owner (i.e. by gift or sale), or on his or her death (i.e. by will or under the rules of intestate succession when there is no will), and each new estate owner is then entitled to enjoy the land for the duration of his or her life and that of his or her heirs and successors. Consequently, although the freehold is, at its legal root, a description of ownership for a limited duration – as are all estates – the way in which the duration of the estate is defined and its free alienability means that, in most respects, the freehold is equivalent to permanent ownership of the land by the person who is currently the estate owner. In practice, the paramount ownership of the Crown is usually irrelevant. Each freehold owner has it within their own power to transfer the estate to another (even on death), and because the full duration of the estate may be enjoyed by a new estate owner and he or she may then transfer it (and so on), the estate can, and usually does, survive through generations. However, in one situation the true nature of the freehold estate is revealed and the land will revert to the Crown as ultimate absolute owner. If the current owner of the freehold estate has not transferred the land during their life and then dies leaving no will and no next of kin to inherit under the rules of intestate succession, the estate has run its course and the land reverts to the Crown. This is uncommon for natural persons (but more common where an estate is held by a company that dissolves with no successors), but it does illustrate the inherent nature of

---

11 The 'Crown' is neither the Government, nor the reigning king or queen in a personal capacity, but a legal entity in its own right, which can be regarded as the repository of the sovereignty of the nation as expressed through a constitutional monarchy.

12 Under section 79 of the LRA 2002, the Crown may now grant itself a freehold estate so that it may be able to register its title.

the freehold as 'ownership for a slice of time'. As we shall see, a freehold may be either 'legal' or 'equitable',[13] although the former is much more common and the latter will arise only in special circumstances (e.g. see Chapter 4 on co-ownership).

1.2.1.2   *The leasehold estate*

The leasehold estate comprises a right to use and enjoy the land exclusively as owner for a stated period of time. This may be one hour, two days, one year, three months, 99 years or any defined period at all. Somewhat misleadingly, the leasehold estate (however long it is stated to last) is frequently referred to as a 'term of years' even if the 'term' is shorter than a year. The owner of a leasehold estate may be referred to as a 'leaseholder', 'lessee' or 'tenant' (sometimes 'underlessee' or 'subtenant') and the leasehold estate is carved out of any other estate (including itself), provided that its 'term' is fixed at less than the estate out of which it is carved.[14] For example, a leasehold of any duration (say, 999 years) may be carved out of a freehold, the latter being of greater duration because of the principles discussed earlier. However, in the very unlikely event that the freehold estate should actually terminate before the end of the leasehold period that is carved out of it, then the lease also terminates. Again, a leasehold can be carved out of a leasehold of longer duration. For example, X, who holds a lease of seven years from the freehold owner, may grant a lease of three years to Y, in which case X can be regarded as the tenant of the freeholder but the landlord of Y, and Y is the subtenant in actual possession of the land. In fact, as will be discussed in Chapter 6, the fact that a lease can be carved out of any estate of longer duration means that a plot of land may have several different 'owners', each enjoying specific rights in relation to the land: for example, there may be a freehold owner, a lessee, a sublessee, a sub-sublessee and so on. As with freeholds, a leasehold may be 'legal' or 'equitable',[15] although equitable leases tend to occur more usually in a residential rather than a commercial context.[16]

1.2.1.3   *The fee tail*

Although originally an estate in land, the *fee tail* is more properly regarded, since 1 January 1926, as an 'interest' in another person's land.[17] However, it is considered here because of its feudal origins as a true estate. The fee tail is an interest permitting its

---

13 Technically, because of section 1(3) of the LPA 1925, an equitable fee simple is not an estate, but an 'interest', but nothing turns on this in the present context.

14 In the case of *Bruton v. London and Quadrant Housing Trust* (2000), the House of Lords suggested that a lease need not always be carved out of an estate in the land, but might, in some circumstances, be regarded as 'non-proprietary'. This interesting and controversial analysis is discussed more fully in Chapter 6.

15 See section 1.3.1.

16 Primarily because parties in a commercial relationship tend to use property professionals to organise their affairs and usually this leads to a lease that complies with the formalities necessary to create a legal estate.

17 Section 1(3) of the LPA 1925 provides that the only estates capable of existing as legal estates are those identified in section 1(1), being the fee simple absolute in possession (i.e. the freehold) and a term of years absolute (i.e. a leasehold). All estates and interests not listed in s.1(1) or section 1(2) – which concerns legal interests in land – 'take effect as equitable interests' only.

'owner' the use of land for the duration of his life and that of his lineal descendants (not *all* heirs). A lineal descendant is a person who can show a parental, grandparental, great-grandparental (and so on) link to the person who was originally granted the fee tail. As with the freehold (the fee simple), a fee tail (or 'entail') may turn out to be of very long duration indeed, save that an 'entail' may be curtailed in practice by restricting the qualifying successors to either male or female lineal descendants. For example, the fee may be 'entailed' from father to son and so on, to the exclusion of daughters.[18]

At the death of the last lineal descendant (e.g. the current interest-holder who has no sons or daughters, as specified in the entail), the land will revert either to the person entitled to the estate in fee simple[19] or to the Crown if there is none. More importantly, although existing entails are unaffected, since 1 January 1997 it has been impossible to create any new interest in fee tail (see Schedule 1 to the Trusts of Land and Appointment of Trustees Act 1996 (TOLATA 1996)). This legislative prohibition of the creation of new fee tails, coupled with the fact that it has been, and still is, possible to turn an existing entail into a freehold (by a process known as 'barring the entail'), means that the interest in fee tail rarely survives as a feature of modern land law. Where it does exist, it may do so only as an 'equitable' interest (section 1 of the LPA 1925).

1.2.1.4 *The life interest*

As with the fee tail, the *life interest* was once an estate proper (i.e. prior to 1 January 1926 and the entry into force of section 1 of the LPA 1925), and it is considered here because of that history. A life interest (or 'life estate') gives the holder the right to use and enjoy the land for the duration of his life. On death, the life interest comes to an end and the land reverts to the superior estate owner, who is usually a long leaseholder or freeholder. Somewhat confusingly, the owner of a life interest is frequently referred to as a 'life tenant', although this has nothing to do with the leasehold estate. Again, like the estate in fee tail, the life interest today may exist only as an 'equitable' interest (section 1 of the LPA 1925).

All of this may seem complicated, but the important point to remember is that an estate effectively means ownership of the land: either of virtually permanent duration (freehold), or limited by agreement to a defined period (leasehold). The other two interests (fee tail and life interests) represent ownership for different slices of time, but are relatively rare in practice. They will be discussed in the text where appropriate. Of course, all four types are 'proprietary' in that they are capable of being sold or transferred during the time period for which they exist. Thus, in common parlance, the freehold or the leasehold may be sold or transferred by the current owner at any time, provided that the estate has not terminated. So, A may sell his freehold to B and C may sell ('assign') his 999-year lease to D, provided that there is still time to run.[20]

---

18 This was the conventional pattern. Such a fee tail is at the heart of Jane Austen's *Pride and Prejudice* – the estate owner (Mr Bennet) has no son and, on his death, the surviving women will have to leave the land because the estate in tail will terminate, having been limited to male heirs.

19 Mr Collins in *Pride and Prejudice*.

20 If X is a life tenant, thus holding an estate for life, it may be sold to Y, but Y's estate will last only for so long as X is alive. Y's interest is then said to be *pur autre vie* – for the life of another.

1.2.2   Interests in land

The above section considered those rights in land that give the holder the equivalent of a right of ownership for a defined period of time. By way of contrast, 'interests in land' may be used to denote those proprietary rights that one person enjoys in the land (technically, in the 'estate') of another. Good examples are the right of way over someone else's land (an easement), a debt secured on the debtor's land (a mortgage), the right to prevent an owner carrying on some specific activity on his own land (a restrictive covenant) and the right to buy another's land within a fixed period of time (an option). These are all proprietary interests in the land (in the estate) of another person and this is not an exhaustive list. As proprietary rights, they may be transferred or sold to another person (often, but not always, as an incident of the land benefited by the right)[21] and may be binding against a new owner of the 'estate' over which they operate, as illustrated by Figure 1.2 (page 5).

1.3   The Legal or Equitable Quality of Proprietary Rights

In the discussion of estates in land in the previous section, reference was made to whether the estate could be 'legal', or 'equitable'. In fact, it is important to determine of all proprietary rights (i.e. of both estates and interests) whether they are *capable* of existing as a legal or equitable right, and whether they do *in fact* exist as a legal or equitable right in any given case. To discuss whether a proprietary right is legal or equitable is to consider its *quality* as opposed to its content: the question is *not* 'What does the right entitle a person to do on the land?' (content), but 'What is the nature of the right?' (i.e. is it legal or equitable?). Moreover, although the distinction between 'legal' and 'equitable' proprietary rights became less important as a result of the changes made by the 1925 property legislation, it is impossible to come to grips with modern land law without an understanding of (a) how the distinction between legal and equitable proprietary rights is to be made, and (b) the significance of the distinction.

1.3.1   The origins of the distinction between legal and equitable rights

Historically, the distinction between legal and equitable rights was based on the type of court in which a claimant might obtain a remedy against a defendant for the unlawful denial of the claimant's right over the defendant's land. Thus, the King's Court (or court of common law) would grant a remedy to a claimant who could establish a case 'at law', usually on proof of certain formalities and on pleading a specified 'form of action'. The court of common law was, however, fairly inflexible in its approach to legal problems and would often deny a remedy to a deserving claimant simply because some small part of the proper formalities had not been observed. Consequently, the Chancellor's Court

---

21 For example, the benefit of an easement – such as the right to walk on a neighbour's land – will be sold as part of the benefited land, but the right to an option to buy may be sold independently of any land.

(or Court of Chancery) began to mitigate the harshness of the common law by giving an 'equitable' remedy to a deserving claimant, even in the absence of the proper formalities required for a remedy 'at law'. This led to many clashes of jurisdiction where a claimant would be denied a remedy 'at law' in one court, but was able to secure a remedy 'in equity' in a different court, although eventually it was the Court of Chancery, administering the rules of equity, which was to prevail. In other words, what started out as a different procedure for the administration of justice eventually developed into two different sets of substantive legal principles: the common law courts dealing with 'legal rules' and the court of equity dealing with 'rules of equity'. Since the Judicature Act 1875, all courts have been empowered to apply rules of 'law' and rules of 'equity', and clashes of jurisdiction no longer occur. However, this historical diversity still resonates in the modern law. In modern land law, the distinction between legal and equitable *proprietary* rights no longer rests on which type of court hears a case, but it still has a flavour of the old distinction between the formality of the common law and the fairness of equity.

1.3.2 Making the distinction between legal and equitable rights today

In order to determine today whether any given proprietary right is 'legal' or 'equitable', two issues need to be addressed. First, is the right *capable* of existing as either a legal or an equitable right? Second, has the right come into existence in the manner recognised as creating either a legal or an equitable right? As we shall see, there are certain rights that may be *either* legal or equitable, depending on how they have been created, and some that are capable of being only equitable (there are none that are capable of being *only* legal).

1.3.3 Section 1 of the Law of Property Act 1925: is the estate or interest capable of being either legal or equitable?

The starting point is section 1 of the LPA 1925. This defines conclusively those rights that are in principle *capable* of being legal. Necessarily, therefore, any rights not within this statutory definition can only ever be equitable. According to section 1:

(1) The only estates in land which are capable of subsisting or of being conveyed or created at law are –

(a) an estate in fee simple absolute in possession;
(b) a term of years absolute.

(2) The only interests or charges in or over land which are capable of subsisting or of being conveyed or created at law are –

(a) an easement, right or privilege in or over land [held as an adjunct to a fee simple or leasehold absolute in possession];
(b) a rentcharge;
(c) a charge by way of legal mortgage;
(d) [not relevant for present purposes];
(e) rights of entry [annexed to a legal lease or legal rentcharge].

(3) All other estates, interests and charges in or over land take effect as equitable interests.

In simple terms, this means that, in the language of the distinction between *estates* and *interests*, the only *estates* that may be legal are the fee simple (the freehold), provided that it gives an immediate right to possession of the land ('absolute in possession') and the leasehold (whether giving possession immediately or on the termination of a prior right, i.e. in 'possession' or 'reversion'), and the only *interests* that are capable of being legal are easements (and associated rights to enter another's land and take some produce of it, such as wood, being *profits à prendre*), mortgages, rights of entry contained in a legal lease and the (now relatively rare) rentcharge. Given, therefore, that in the words of section 1(3), 'all other estates [and] interests … take effect as equitable interests', such rights as the life interest and fee tail and such other interests as the restrictive covenant, the option, the right of pre-emption and proprietary estoppel will always be equitable. However, let us be clear about what this section says: it does not say that such estates and interests as are listed in section 1 *must* be legal; only that they *may* be *capable* of being legal. In addition, therefore, it is vital to understand the ways in which potential legal estates and interests may actually come into existence.

1.3.4   The manner of creation of the right

As noted above, section 1 of the LPA 1925 tells us only what rights *may* be legal; it does not say that they *always will* be legal. In other words, even the estates and interests specified in section 1 may be equitable in certain circumstances. If a proprietary right is capable of being, either legal or equitable, then its final quality depends on the circumstances in which it has come into existence and, in particular, whether the formality requirements for its creation (which are established by statute) have been observed. Generally, full formality is required for the creation of legal estates and interests, and more informality is permitted for the creation of equitable rights. Here, then, lies the heart of the legal/equitable distinction in the current law, and it has echoes of the historical division between law and equity that originated in a dispute between two sets of courts, one of which was prepared to enforce rights only if they were accompanied with the proper formality (courts of law), the other of which was prepared to enforce rights when it was equitable to do so (courts of equity), notwithstanding the lack of proper formality.

1.3.4.1   *When is a proprietary right legal in practice?*

Assuming it falls within section 1 of the LPA 1925, a proprietary right (estate or interest) will be 'legal' if it is created with proper formality. This has two aspects.

1   Subject to only limited exceptions, the proprietary right must have been created by deed. A 'deed' is a written document of a special kind and it goes beyond a mere written contract.[22] According to section 1 of the Law of Property (Miscellaneous Provisions) Act 1989 (LP(MP)A 1989), an instrument is not a deed unless it makes it clear on its face that it is a deed (either by such words or otherwise) and it is executed as a deed (commonly by a signature, that is witnessed

---

22 *Eagle Star Insurance Company v. Green* (2001).

with delivery of the deed). Usually, a document intended to be a deed will declare itself to be a deed (it will say 'this is a deed' or similar) and will state that it is 'executed as a deed by X and Y' and will be witnessed as such by another.[23] As indicated, however, in special circumstances, certain proprietary rights can be legal without the need for a deed. For our purposes, these are when there are certain leases for three years or less (the 'short lease exception' – see sections 52(2)(d) and 54(2) of the LPA 1925, and see Chapter 6),[24] or where an easement arises by 'prescription' (long use – see Chapter 7). These special cases will be considered where appropriate.

2   In addition to the use of a deed, *certain* potential legal estates and interests must also be 'registered' in the manner required by the LRA 2002. In this context, 'registered' means entered on the register in order to create the legal estate or interest (sometimes called 'substantively registered'), rather than registered (i.e. recorded) to protect the interest.[25] Failure to substantively register will render the relevant estate or interest equitable even if it has been created or transferred by a deed – sections 7 and 27(1) of the LRA 2002. These registration requirements are considered in detail in Chapter 2, but (briefly) they require the following: all potential legal freeholds must be registered as a title; all potential legal leaseholds of over seven years' duration must be registered as a title;[26] all potential legal mortgages must be registered as a 'registered charge' against the title of the freehold or leasehold that they affect; all potential expressly created legal easements must be registered against the title of the freehold or leasehold land they affect, if so created on or after 13 October 2003.[27]

To sum up then: proprietary rights will be legal where they fall within section 1 of the LPA 1925, provided that they originate in a deed (with limited exceptions) and so long as they are substantively registered, where such registration is required. This means that even a potentially legal estate or interest may fail to be legal because either no deed has been used where required, or a deed has been used but registration has not occurred where required.

When is a proprietary right equitable in practice?

A proprietary right has the potential to be 'equitable' for *any* one of three reasons. First, it may be excluded from the definition of a legal estate or interest found in section 1 of the LPA 1925. Such rights can only ever be equitable because they cannot be legal, as with a life estate, a restrictive covenant, a claim in proprietary estoppel, an option to

---

23 Land Registry transfer forms (e.g. for the sale or gift of registered land) are deliberately cast as deeds for this purpose.

24 Leases for three years or less, giving an immediate right to possession for the best rent reasonably obtainable, provided that no lump sum is payable at the start of the lease as a condition of it being granted.

25 The different meanings of 'registered' are explained more fully in Chapter 2.

26 In certain exceptional cases, legal leases for a term of less than seven years may require substantive registration, but these are of an individual and special character – see sections 4(1) and 27(2)(b) of the LRA 2002, and also Chapter 2.

27 Impliedly created easements are not caught by section 27(2), neither are those special easements that fall under the Commons Registration Act 1965 even if expressly created.

purchase, a right of pre-emption and so on. Second, despite being within section 1, no deed may have been used where such is required. Third, despite being within section 1 and the use of a deed (if required), substantive registration has not occurred (where required).

However, even if a claimed proprietary right is potentially equitable, that is not enough for it to exist. Even equitable proprietary rights are required to be created in an appropriate manner before they may exist as such. After all, let us not forget that *all* proprietary rights – be they legal or equitable – have the capacity to affect land for many years irrespective of who owns that land and so it is important that we can be reasonably certain that alleged proprietary rights do in fact exist. The formality rules provide that certainty. In the majority of cases (there are some exceptions), the relevant formality for the creation of an equitable property right is the use of a written instrument, either a comprehensive written contract signed by, or on behalf of, the parties to the contract, as required by section 2 of the Law of Property (Miscellaneous Provisions) Act 1989 (LPA(MP)A 1989), or by a written instrument signed by the person creating the equitable right, as required by section 53 of the LPA 1925.[28] In the event of a failure to use a written instrument where required, the intended right does not exist at all *as a right in property*.[29] Of course, the unwritten agreement may still be enforceable between the parties to it (e.g. it might be a contract), so as to permit the person to whom the right is given to exercise the right against the person who gave it – but *only* against that person for the right is now merely personal. It would then be a 'licence', the generic name given to personal rights to use land.

Of course, the requirement of a written contract or instrument for the creation of an equitable proprietary right is relatively formal, but there is a clear distinction between such a written contract/instrument and a deed, not least that the latter must be witnessed. What it does mean, however, is that, in the normal case, merely verbal agreements or promises cannot create property rights or obligations. Note, however, that, in *exceptional* circumstances, the courts will recognise the existence of an equitable proprietary right arising from an oral contract, agreement or promise, provided that the conditions for proprietary estoppel or implied trusts (resulting or constructive) have been fulfilled.[30] As will be seen in Chapters 4 and 10 respectively, the creation of equitable rights by purely verbal dealings between the parties can occur only in defined circumstances, usually where this might be thought to achieve fairness – or 'equity' – between the parties. The reason for these exceptions is that it is offensive to the law that a person should be able to deny that they have granted a proprietary right

---

28 The written contract will be used where the creator of the right receives a benefit in return for burdening his land; a written instrument under section 53 of the LPA 1925 is more appropriate for a voluntary grant of an equitable right, often using a trust. Note also that under section 53(1)(b) LPA 1925 a valid trust of land may be evidenced in writing, if not actually made in writing: *Kaki v. Kaki* [2015] EWHC 3692 (Ch).

29 It may be possible to save part of a written instrument by separating a valid clause from an invalid one and giving proprietary effect to the valid part: *Murray v. Guinness* (1998).

30 By section 53(2) of the LPA 1925 and section 2(5)(c) of the LPA 1989, implied trusts are a statutory exception to the formality requirements found in section 53 of the LPA 1925 and section 2 of the LPA 1989, respectively. Proprietary estoppel is an invention of equity and is justified on a policy basis in order to prevent unconscionability – see *Taylor Fashions v. Liverpool Victoria Trustees* (1982).

to another by pleading non-compliance with statutory formalities (such as the need to use a deed or written instrument) where this is unconscionable, such as where they are seeking to rely on their own fault to take advantage of the other party to the transaction. Nevertheless, the creation of equitable rights by proprietary estoppel or implied trust (i.e. verbally or by conduct) are exceptions to the rule that equitable rights should be created in writing and, consequently, the relevant principles must not be so widely interpreted so as to destroy the primary rule itself.[31] Finally, for completeness, it should also be noted that proprietary rights arising before the entry into force of the LP(MP)A 1989[32] can be equitable even if created by an oral contract, without the need to plead proprietary estoppel or implied trust, provided that the oral contract was supported by some 'act of part performance' in pursuit of the right, as in *Thatcher v. Douglas* (1996), applying the now repealed section 40 of the LPA 1925.[33] This is now of largely historical interest, although it is possible for property professionals still to encounter a valid equitable right created before 1989 under the old regime of oral contract plus 'part-performance'.

1.3.5 Impact of e-conveyancing on the distinction between legal and equitable property rights

If electronic, paperless conveyancing were ever to be introduced, it could make the distinction between legal and equitable property rights largely redundant, or certainly less significant. This is because e-conveyancing as originally conceived would have required specified property rights to have been created only by electronic entry on a register, with deeds and written contracts having no effect.[34] Obviously, in such circumstances, there is no room for legal rights (created by deed) and equitable rights (created by written instruments) as either a right would be created electronically and exist, or not exist at all. Perhaps there might have been a 'safety net' role for proprietary estoppel, and so some residual 'equitable' status, although this is unclear.

As noted above, however, it now seems unlikely that this ambitious scheme will come into effect.

1.3.6 The division of ownership and the 'trust'

Although the distinction between legal and equitable property rights turns, primarily, on the definition in section 1 of the LPA 1925 and the manner in which the right is created, there is a third way by which the distinction can arise. This is where enjoyment of the land is regulated by use of the 'trust'. In English law and systems derived from it, it is perfectly possible for a single piece of property (any property) to be owned by two or more people at the same time. This is not simply that two people may share ownership; it is, rather, that two or more people may have a different quality of ownership over the

---

31 Auction contracts are also excepted from the need for writing (section 2(5)(b) of the LPA 1989), as are short leases (section 2(5)(a) of the LPA 1989).

32 That is, before 27 September 1989.

33 Repealed prospectively by section 2(8) of the LPA 1989.

34 This would have been achieved under section 93 of the LRA 2002.

same property at the same time. In other words, one person may have the legal title to the property, and another may have the equitable title. Of course, in the normal course of events, when a person owns an estate in land (or any other property), this legal and equitable title is not separated, and the person is regarded simply as property), this legal and equitable title is not separated, and the person is regarded simply as 'the owner', or sometimes the 'absolute owner'. However, the ability to 'split' ownership is a distinctive feature of the English legal system and other common law jurisdictions, and has many practical applications. So, for land, it is possible to have a legal owner and an equitable owner: one with legal rights of ownership; the other with equitable rights. Necessarily, these two owners must stand in a relationship to each other and this relationship is known as a 'trust'. This is what is meant when it is said that A holds land on trust for B: A is the legal owner (and trustee), and B is the equitable owner (and beneficiary), as illustrated by Figure 1.3.

The 'trust' that exists between A and B can take many forms, and different rights and duties can be imposed on A (the trustee) for the benefit of B (the beneficiary), depending on how the trust was established and any relevant statutory provisions (e.g. the TOLATA 1996 – see Chapter 4). In some circumstances, a trust will be imposed on a landowner without a deliberate act of trust creation, thus creating by force of law a distinction between the legal and equitable titles.[35] Finally, it is also important to appreciate that the creation of legal and equitable proprietary rights through the use of a trust requires compliance with a different but complementary set of formality rules to those discussed above: that is, rules similar to (but not identical with) those required for the simple creation of proprietary rights. Unless there is a 'constructive trust', 'resulting trust'[36] or a successful claim of proprietary estoppel, a trust concerning land or any right therein must be 'manifested and proved by some writing', as required by section 53(1)(b) of the LPA 1925. This means that the existence of the legal and equitable interests under a trust concerning land depends on the trust being created in the proper manner, although the requirement here is that the trust of land must be *evidenced* by some written document (perhaps one drawn up later), rather than actually be in writing itself.

Figure 1.3

Legal owner (trustee)		Equitable owner (beneficiary)

Land, or rights in land, are held by A on trust for B

---

35 As with implied, resulting and constructive trusts.

36 Both are exempt from formality by section 53(2) of the LPA 1925 and section 2(5)(c) of the LPA 1989.

1.4 The Consequences of the Distinction between Legal and Equitable Property Rights

It is apparent from the above that whether a proprietary right is legal or equitable may tell us many things: for example, how the right was created and whether there is any possibility of the existence of a trust. However, in times past, one of the most important consequences of the distinction, albeit much modified by statute, was the different way in which legal or equitable rights could affect the new owners or occupiers of the land over which such rights existed.[37] As noted at the outset of this chapter, the peculiar quality of proprietary rights is that they attach to the land itself, and thus the right to enforce them and the obligation to honour them is *capable* of passing to new owners of the benefited or burdened land. This is the situation represented by Figure 1.2 above. So, before the advent of land registration, the precise effect of a proprietary right on a third party (in the sense of the third party's obligation to honour it) depended crucially on whether the proprietary right was 'legal' or 'equitable'. However, while this is not yet entirely a matter of history, it must be appreciated that, in modern land law, the effect of a proprietary right on a new owner of the land burdened by it depends much more on the effect and interpretation of statute than it does on the nature of the proprietary right. This is the impact of the Land Registration Acts, originally the LRA 1925 and now the LRA 2002. Indeed, even in respect of the relatively small number of titles that remain unregistered (i.e. outside the LRA and known as 'unregistered land'), the relevance of the legal or equitable distinction between proprietary rights is much reduced by the Land Charges Acts, originally the Land Charges Act 1925 (LCA 1925) and now the Land Charges Act 1972 (LCA 1972). That is not to say, of course, that we must not spend some time understanding the distinction between legal and equitable rights, not least because even now it is impossible to understand modern land law without an appreciation of the historical importance and limited present impact of it. Yet we must understand that its relevance today is much less than it once was.

1.4.1 Legal property rights *before* the 1925 legislation

Before 1 January 1926, if a proprietary right was *legal*, it would always bind every person who came to own or occupy the land over which the right existed. As was commonly said, 'legal rights bind the whole world', and the person entitled to enforce the legal proprietary right could exercise it against any purchaser of the land, a recipient of it as a gift or under a will, a squatter and all others. So, for example, the person entitled to a legal right of way (an easement) would have been able to enjoy that right of way no matter who came to own or occupy the land over which it existed.

---

37 The distinction between a 'legal' property right and an 'equitable' property right may have other limited consequences. For example, the rights of the parties under a 'legal' mortgage are marginally different from those under an 'equitable' mortgage, and there may be some circumstances where the 'legal' or 'equitable' quality of a right will affect the remedy given if it is infringed. These differences – which are not large – are discussed in the text when dealing with the individual property rights.

1.4.2   Equitable property rights *before* the 1925 legislation

Prior to 1 January 1926, if an existing property right over land was *equitable*, it would bind every transferee or occupier of that land *except* a bona fide purchaser for value of a legal estate in the land who had no notice of the equitable right. This appears to be a complicated rule (and bear in mind that it is hardly ever relevant in modern land law), but it can be broken down into its constituent parts. Thus, under this rule, an existing equitable right over land *would* be binding on a transferee or occupier of that land (that is, enforceable against them) in *all* the following cases:

1   where the transferee or occupier was *not* a purchaser for value, as where he received the land by will, or as a gift, or under the rules of adverse possession (squatting);
2   where the transferee did *not* purchase a legal estate in the land, as where he purchased an interest in the land by taking an equitable lease;
3   where the transferee was *not* bona fide, as where he acted in bad faith; and
4   where the transferee or occupier had notice of the equitable right, as where he either knew of its existence (actual notice) or knew of circumstances from which a reasonable person would have been aware of its existence (constructive notice) (*Hunt* v. *Luck* (1902), *Kingsnorth* v. *Tizard* (1986)), or where the transferee's agent (e.g. his solicitor) had actual or constructive notice of the equitable right (so-called imputed notice).

In all these cases, the equitable right would have been binding on a transferee of the land. However, it is important to realise that, in the great majority of cases, the transferee of the land would easily have fulfilled the first three requirements of the 'bona fide purchaser' rule, and so very often any dispute would turn on whether the bona fide purchaser of the legal estate had 'notice' of the equitable right. In practice, this was usually the only real question. Consequently, the rule about equitable interests came to be known as the 'doctrine of notice', because it was usually the transferee's 'notice' of the equitable interest (bound by it) or lack of notice (not bound by it) that was the real issue. However, such were (and are, in those rare cases when it still applies) the vagaries of the doctrine of notice that neither the transferee of the affected land nor the owner of the equitable right that was alleged to bind the land could ever be certain whether his land or his right (as the case may have been) was secure. Was there 'notice' or not? Indeed, in many cases, the 'owner' of an equitable right over land could do little to ensure its survival should the burdened land be sold, and, conversely, a purchaser might find that the land they had just purchased was encumbered by an equitable right of which they were deemed to have 'constructive notice', even though in truth they knew nothing about it. In short, the operation of the 'doctrine of notice' was so uncertain that the 1925 property legislation modified the rule in a radical way and thereby substantially reduced the importance of the legal/equitable distinction.

1.5   The 1925 Property Legislation and the Land Registration Act 2002

All that we have considered so far forms the basis of the modern law of real property. However, the start of the twentieth century brought with it fundamental social and economic changes, and when these were allied to the defects, mysteries, vagaries and plain injustices of the law before 1 January 1926, it was clear that wholesale reform was necessary. The detail of the legislative changes that came into effect on 1 January 1926 is considered later in the appropriate chapters, especially Chapters 2, 3 and 4, but for now it is important to realise that both substantive and structural changes were made by the 1925 property legislation, particularly regarding the question of ownership of land and the way in which proprietary rights could affect 'third parties' – being persons who came to the land after the proprietary rights affecting it had been created. The main legislative enactments of 1925 are considered briefly below. It should be noted at this early stage that the LRA 2002 has remodelled parts of the original 1925 scheme substantially.

1.5.1   The Law of Property Act 1925

The LPA 1925 made very significant substantive changes to the law of real property, including, as we have seen, a redefinition of what rights could be legal or equitable. It also has much to say about joint ownership of land, the creation of proprietary interests, the nature of the freehold and leasehold estates, and much more. Although amended in parts, it remains the governing statute for modern land law.

1.5.2   The Settled Land Act 1925

The Settled Land Act 1925 (SLA 1925) is a complicated statute, designed to regulate the creation and operation of 'successive' interests in land, as where a house is given to A for his life, and then to B for her life and then to C absolutely. It is considered in Chapter 5. Its importance is very much diminished by the abolition of 'settlements' for dispositions taking effect on or after 1 January 1997 – see section 2 of the TOLATA 1996. It would be unusual to come across a settlement governed by the SLA today.

1.5.3   The Land Registration Act 1925 and the Land Registration Act 2002

The machinery originally established by the (now repealed) LRA 1925 and now found in the LRA 2002 is examined in detail in Chapter 2. The LRA 2002 is fundamental to the modern law of real property. It creates a system whereby title to land (being the estates of legal freehold or legal leasehold) and many other rights in that land are entered on a register maintained by HM Land Registry. The 'register' itself used to comprise a series of file cards (a physical register), but it is now held largely in electronic form. In essence, each title (i.e. right of ownership) is assigned a 'title number' linked to a physical plot of land. Under each 'registered title', there are then recorded details about the type of estate (e.g. freehold or leasehold) and who owns it, as well as many other rights affecting the land, such as any mortgages. These provisions replaced the haphazard system of conveyancing that existed before 1 January 1926 and are designed in particular to bring certainty and stability to the question of who owns the land and how proprietary rights binding the land affect third parties. This is what we mean when we say the LRA 2002 governs 'registered land', or more accurately, land of registered title.

As indicated briefly, the system introduced by the LRA 1925 was ripe for reform, and that reform was carried out by the LRA 2002. Although many of the central principles of land registration have remained the same under the LRA 2002 as they were under the LRA 1925 (albeit 'tidied up' to reflect modern circumstances), there is also much that is different. The 2002 Act came into force on 13 October 2003 and the LRA

1925 is no more. Not all of the provisions of the new legislation are in force yet (e.g. section 93 and e-conveyancing), but most are and the LRA 2002 has had a significant impact on the way modern land law operates.[38] It is simply not possible to understand modern land law without a thorough understanding of the LRA 2002 and what it means to say that the land (i.e. its title) is 'registered'.

1.5.4   The Land Charges Act 1972

The LCA 1972 (originally, the LCA 1925) is also examined in detail later – see Chapter 3. Once again, it establishes a system to regulate the transfer of land and is also designed to bring certainty to dealings with land affected by the proprietary rights of other people, particularly if those rights are equitable. Importantly, land that is covered by the LCA 1972 is not 'registered land', and it falls outside the scope of the LRA 2002. Thus, the LCA 1972 concerns what is called 'unregistered land', this being land to which the title is not entered on a register but is proved by the title deeds to the property and any related bundle of documents. If the land is 'registered', there are no title deeds because the title is found on the register. Today, less than 15 per cent of all titles to land are 'unregistered' and clearly the scope of operation of the LCA 1972 is very much reduced.

1.6   The Distinction between Registered and Unregistered Land

The fundamental distinction that every student and practitioner of property law must draw since 1 January 1926 is between registered and unregistered land. Registered land – more accurately, land of registered title – is governed by the LPA 1925, the common law and the LRA 2002. Unregistered land is governed by the LPA 1925, the common law and the LCA 1972. Most importantly of all, the registered land system and the unregistered land system are *mutually exclusive*. Land either falls into one system or the other, but never both at the same time. Land is either 'registered land' or 'unregistered land' but never both. As explained in Chapter 2, the great majority of titles are already registered (well over 85 per cent of all titles) and in due course virtually all land will become registered – it will move from being 'unregistered' and become 'registered', a process that has been speeded up by the entry into force of the LRA 2002. However, at present, two systems of land conveyancing are in operation in England and Wales, side by side, albeit that unregistered land is becoming rarer and rarer. What follows is an outline of the two systems, and the detail is provided later in Chapters 2 and 3. Particular attention should be paid to the way in which both systems deal with the question of the effect of proprietary rights on third parties: that is, the issue that was once governed by the distinction between legal and equitable rights and the doctrine of notice. That said, it is also of paramount importance to appreciate that 'registered land' is the system intended to govern land law into the twenty-first century and beyond, and that it is already by far the predominant system. Unregistered land is of diminishing importance, legally and practically.

---

38 For example, the strengthening of 'title guarantee', the reform of the law of adverse possession (squatting) and the introduction of the electronic creation and discharge of mortgages.

1.6.1 Registered land

1   Registered land is land to which the title is substantively registered in a register. Every title is given a title number and the details of the current owners are registered against it. Once a person is registered as estate owner, that ownership is guaranteed,[39] and prospective purchasers may buy the land in the certainty that the title has been thoroughly investigated and approved before it was first registered (e.g. as in *Habenec* v. *Harris* (1998)). A title that is registered under the LRA 2002 is a strong, marketable title.

2   A second category of right in registered land is the *registered charge*. These are essentially legal mortgages, used to raise money for the estate owner by offering the land as security for a loan. Legal mortgages are registered against the estate they affect either a freehold or leasehold title. If so registered, they are guaranteed (*Swift 1st Ltd* v. *Chief Land Registrar* (2015)).

3   There is another group of proprietary rights in registered land, central to the operation of the LRA 2002, called *unregistered interests which override*. These property rights, conveniently called 'overriding interests',[40] are *automatically* binding on any transferee or occupier of the land, without the need for any kind of registration. They have priority over all owners, whether the transferee was a purchaser or not.[41] Importantly, unregistered interests which override include both some legal rights and some equitable rights. This is because they are defined in the LRA 2002 – in Schedules 1 and 3 to the Act – and these definitions are conclusive. In fact, it is a right's status as an 'interest which overrides' that is important, not its legal or equitable quality. It is this statutory status under the LRA 2002 that makes such rights binding on a third party. The list of overriding interests looks long, but the actual number in practice is small.

4   A fourth category of right in registered land is the *protectable registrable interest*. These rights include all other proprietary rights not included in the above categories, be they legal or equitable. The fundamental point about these interests is that they will only bind a *purchaser* of the land if they are registered (that is, recorded) against the title that they affect.[42] In this sense, 'registration' preserves the status of an existing right, rather than creates the right: it is 'recording' registration rather than 'substantive' registration.[43] This registration is by means of a Notice.[44] If these rights are not so registered, they have no priority over a purchaser of the affected land, meaning that they cannot be enforced against him. They may be effective against a non-purchaser, even if not registered, such as a person who inherited or was given the land.[45]

---

39 Section 58 of the LRA 2002 provides that registration as proprietor (owner) of an estate is conclusive, even if there were defects in the title prior to registration. See *Walker* v. *Burton* (2013) and *Swift 1st v Chief Land Registrar* (2015).

40 As they were known under the LRA 1925.

41 Sections 11, 12, 29 and 30 of the LRA 2002.

42 They will bind a non-purchaser, whether registered or not. See Chapter 2 and section 28 of the LRA 2002.

43 If the right is registered (i.e. recorded) but it was not actually valid, registration does not make it valid: section 32(3) LRA 2002. This is why it is not 'substantive' registration which does confer validity.

44 The 'Notice' is the name given to the register entry. It is not the doctrine of notice.

45 See section 28 of the LRA 2002.

To conclude, three points about registered land bear repetition. First, in registered land, the effect of a proprietary right on a transferee of the land is determined by its status under the LRA 2002, especially whether it is an interest which overrides or a protectable registrable interest. Its legal or equitable quality is relevant, but not crucial. Second, under the system of the LRA 2002, the 'doctrine of notice' is *entirely* irrelevant and although certain provisions do make reference to the 'knowledge' of transferees of land, this is not the old-fashioned 'doctrine of notice'. Third, the concept of overreaching (see Chapters 2 and 4) may allow a purchaser of registered land to defeat *certain* equitable rights, even if they appear capable of being overriding or might otherwise thought to be protected. So, a purchaser who pays the purchase price of land to the co-owners of a legal estate (i.e. where there is more than one registered owner) will 'overreach' certain types of equitable interest, meaning that the equitable rights *cannot* bind that purchaser, whether or not the rights appear to fall within the definition of overriding interests or their registration by Notice has been attempted.[46] The equitable rights are, in fact, transferred to the purchase money that has been paid and the right holder is entitled to a share of that money. Overreaching is a limited, but powerful, 'trump card' and is explained in greater detail in Chapters 3 and 4.

1.6.2   Unregistered land

Unregistered land is land to which *the title is not registered*. The title is located in the old-fashioned title deeds (a bundle of documents), and a prospective purchaser must investigate 'root of title' through examination of the title deeds in order to be confident of obtaining a secure right to the land. Further, in unregistered land, it remains true that 'legal rights bind the whole world'. This aspect of the pre-1926 common law remains important and an understanding of how 'legal' rights come into existence is therefore crucial to understanding unregistered land. However, equitable rights in unregistered land fall into three distinct and separate categories.

1   Most equitable rights are 'land charges' within the LCA 1972. As such, they must be registered (i.e. recorded) as a 'land charge' against the *owner* of the land over which they take effect (*not* the land itself) in order to bind a purchaser of it. If they are not so registered (and registration must be against the person who owned the land at the time the right was created), they are not binding. They are void and the doctrine of notice is irrelevant. It should be understood that this is an *entirely separate* system of registration from that which exists in registered land. The two different systems of registration are mutually exclusive, and operate under different statutes. The equitable rights that are 'land charges' for the purposes of registration under the LCA 1972 are defined in the LCA 1972 itself: e.g. an equitable easement, an equitable mortgage, an option to purchase the land, a covenant preventing some specific use of the land.

2   There are a number of equitable rights that do *not* fall within the statutory definition of land charges. Consequently, they are not registrable under the LCA 1972 and are

---

46 Note, the common overreachable interests – equitable shares of ownership – *cannot* be registered by means of a Notice under the LRA 2002 (they cannot be a protectable registered interest) precisely because it is intended that they should be overreached: section 33 of the LRA 2002. In so far as other equitable rights are overreachable – see *Mortgage Express* v. *Lambert* (2016) and *Bakrania* v. *Lloyds Bank* (2017) – it is likely that protection by a Notice would not stop overreaching, although this is not absolutely certain.

not 'land charges'. Their effectiveness against a purchaser is decided by the application of the old doctrine of notice. This is a very limited class of right and provides the only circumstance in modern land law where the doctrine of notice remains relevant.

3   There are certain special equitable rights that are neither land charges nor always subject to the doctrine of notice. These are the rights that are overreachable. They are equitable rights of a special character, being rights capable of easy quantification in money (e.g. equitable ownership of a proportion of a house). They may be 'overreached' so as not to bind a new purchaser of the land. If this happens, the equitable owner must take the monetary value of the right (i.e. their share of the price paid) rather than enjoy the right over the land itself. This is explained more fully in Chapter 4, but its relevance here is to signpost the existence of equitable rights in unregistered land that are neither land charges under the LCA 1972, nor subject to the old doctrine of notice.

So, to reiterate with respect to unregistered land. First, in unregistered land, the distinction between legal and equitable rights is still of fundamental importance. Legal rights bind the whole world. Second, in unregistered land, the doctrine of notice is largely irrelevant, but may still play a part for those equitable rights that fall outside the definition of land charges under the LCA 1972 and which are not overreached. Third, the concept of overreaching (see Chapters 3 and 4) also applies to unregistered land, and may allow a purchaser of unregistered land to defeat certain equitable rights. Fourth, over 85 per cent of all titles are registered and unregistered land is slowly, but surely, disappearing from the map. As we shall see, land that is currently unregistered must become registered on the occasion of certain dealings with it. These 'triggers' for compulsory registration of title are discussed in Chapter 2. There are also procedures by which a freehold or leasehold owner may apply for voluntary first registration of their title, and the entry into force of the LRA 2002 has encouraged much greater voluntary registration. However, the important point here is the simple one: unregistered land is a fading system and soon will barely trouble practitioners and students alike. Figure 1.4 gives a diagrammatic representation of the 1925 property legislation.

1.7   Chapter Summary

The law of real property (or land law) is concerned with land, rights in or over land and the processes whereby those rights and interests are created and transferred. Rights in land are different from 'mere' contractual rights, in that 'land law rights' are capable of affecting persons other than the parties who created the rights. This is the 'proprietary' nature of land law rights and it is completely different from the merely 'personal' obligations that an ordinary contractual relationship establishes. Proprietary rights can 'run' with the land and can confer benefits and burdens on whomsoever comes to own or possess the land.

1.7.1   Types of proprietary right

Proprietary rights are either 'estates' or 'interests'. An 'estate' is a right to use and control land, being tantamount to ownership, but with the important difference that the 'estate'

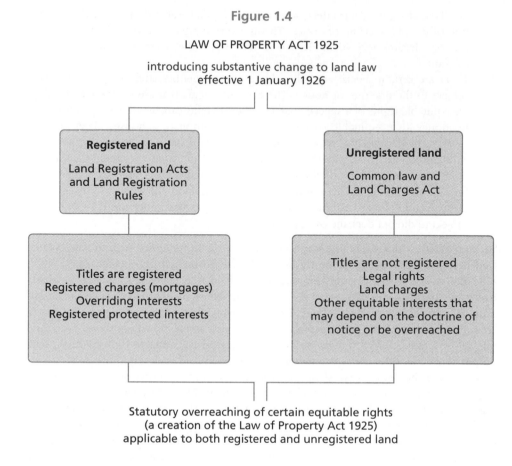

Figure 1.4

LAW OF PROPERTY ACT 1925

introducing substantive change to land law
effective 1 January 1926

Registered land

Land Registration Acts
and Land Registration
Rules

Unregistered land

Common law and
Land Charges Act

Titles are registered
Registered charges (mortgages)
Overriding interests
Registered protected interests

Titles are not registered
Legal rights
Land charges
Other equitable interests that
may depend on the doctrine of
notice or be overreached

Statutory overreaching of certain equitable rights
(a creation of the Law of Property Act 1925)
applicable to both registered and unregistered land

will define the time for which the 'ownership' lasts. An 'estate' is equivalent to ownership of the land for a slice of time. The two estates proper are:

1   the freehold (the fee simple); and
2   the leasehold (term of years or tenancy).

An 'interest' is generally a right that one person enjoys over land belonging to someone else; technically, an interest is a right in the estate of another person. These include two former estates (the fee tail and life interest), but also more limited rights, such as the easement (e.g. a right of way), mortgage (a debt secured on land) and restrictive covenant (a right to control a neighbour's use of land).

1.7.2   The legal or equitable quality of proprietary rights

Section 1 of the LPA 1925 defines which proprietary rights *may* be legal. These include the freehold (fee simple absolute in possession), the leasehold (term of years absolute), the easement, mortgage and right of re-entry. An estate or interest not falling within section 1 must necessarily be equitable. For estates and interests that *do* fall within the section, they may be legal or equitable and their legal or equitable status will be determined by the manner of their creation.

Assuming the estate or interest falls within section 1 of the LPA 1925.

1   A right will be 'legal' if it is created with proper formality, which usually means by deed. Note that, in special circumstances, certain proprietary rights may be legal without the execution of a deed, such as where there are certain leases for three years or less at the best rent etc., or an easement is generated by prescription (long use). Many potential legal rights must also be substantively registered under the LRA 2002 in order to achieve 'legal' status.

2   A right will be 'equitable' if it is created by a written contract or written instrument within section 2 of the LP(MP)A 1989 or section 53 of the LPA 1925. In exceptional circumstances, an equitable right can arise from an oral contract, promise or agreement, provided that the conditions for proprietary estoppel or implied trusts have been fulfilled.

3   A right falling outside section 1 of the LPA 1925 may only ever be equitable, but must still fulfil the formality requirements necessary to establish an equitable proprietary right (as 2 above).

4   The distinction between legal and equitable proprietary rights also can arise through the use of the 'trust'. One person may have the 'legal' title to property and another may have the 'equitable' title. This is common in co-ownership situations, as where Mr X may own the legal title, but Mr X and Ms Y may share the equitable title to the house they live in.

1.7.3   The original significance of the legal/equitable distinction prior to 1926

As well as indicating how a proprietary right came into existence and whether any trust is involved, a significant reason for distinguishing between legal and equitable proprietary rights *before* the 1925 property legislation was that this could determine their effect on third parties.

1   If the right were legal, it would always bind every transferee, owner or occupier of the land over which it existed.

2   If the right were equitable, it would bind every transferee or occupier of the land *except* a bona fide purchaser for value of a legal estate in the land who had no notice of the equitable right.

These principles have been replaced by requirements of registration except in isolated cases of unregistered land.

1.7.4   The 1925 and 2002 property legislation

The LPA 1925 made substantive changes in the law of real property, including a redefinition of what rights may be 'legal' or 'equitable'. It applies in equal measure to registered and unregistered land.

The LRA 2002 governs the system of registered land whereby title to land is entered in a register administered by HM Land Registry. Provision is made for the registration of other rights affecting the land. 'Registered land' now accounts for over 85 per cent of all titles. The original land registration system under the LRA 1925 has been thoroughly overhauled by the LRA 2002.

The LCA 1972 (replacing the LCA 1925) establishes a system of registration (record-ing) of equitable interests in unregistered land, being land where title is not entered on a register but is found in title deeds. The LCA has no impact on registered land. Unregis-tered land is now much less important, given that most titles are registered under the LRA 2002. Unregistered conveyancing will largely disappear as more titles become registered.

The SLA 1925 controls dealings with 'successive' interests in land, but only in respect of settlements in existence before 1 January 1997. Thereafter, any new successive inter-ests are controlled by the TOLATA 1996. Issues involving the SLA are very rare.

The distinction between 'registered land' and 'unregistered land' is as follows. Regis-tered land is land to which the title is registered: for example, the legal freehold or the legal lease of over seven years' duration. Other categories of right in registered land are, registered charges (e.g. mortgages), unregistered interests which override (being rights that automatically have priority over the land without the need for any kind of registra-tion) and protected registrable interests (being rights requiring registration to bind a purchaser of the land). Overreaching applies in registered land.

Unregistered land is land to which the title is not registered. The title is located in the title deeds (or sometimes the fact of possession) and a prospective purchaser must inves-tigate 'root of title'. In unregistered land, it remains true that 'legal rights bind the whole world', although the validity of equitable rights against a purchaser depends on their status as either land charges (requiring registration under the LCA 1972), rights dependent on the doctrine of notice or overreachable rights.

 ## Further Reading

Battersby, G, 'Informally created interests in land', in Bright, S and Dewar, J (eds) Land Law: Themes and Perspectives, Oxford: OUP, 1998.

Dixon, M, 'Proprietary and non-proprietary rights in modern land law', in Tee, L (ed.) *Essays in Land Law*, Cullompton: Willan, 2002.

Jackson, P and **Wilde**, D (eds), *The Reform of Property Law*, Aldershot: Dartmouth, 1997.

Now visit the companion website to:

* test your understanding of the key terms using our Flashcard Glossary;

* revise and consolidate your knowledge using our Multiple Choice Question testbank.

www.routledge.com/cw/dixon

Chapter 2
Registered Land

Introduction

The system of registration of title was perhaps the greatest of the reforms that came out of the wholesale restructuring of English property law in 1925.[1] While the original system of land registration inaugurated by the LRA 1925 had many flaws, it served well for nearly 80 years and was able to cope with the fundamental economic and social changes that took place over that time. It was not perfect,[2] but judicial management through sensible interpretation in cases ensured that it worked on an everyday basis. Today, the majority of land in England and Wales is 'registered land'[3] and is now governed by the LRA 2002. The LRA 2002 entered into force on 13 October 2003 and significantly amended the original scheme. This legislation replaced the 1925 Act in its entirety. While some aspects of the old law remain operative through transitional provisions,[4] it is to the 2002 Act and the Land Registration Rules (LRR) that we must turn for the detail of the system. Consequently, this chapter will concentrate on the law of land registration as it exists today – that is, under the LRA 2002. Reference will of course be made to the 'old' law of land registration under the 1925 Act, especially where its provisions have been given longer life through the transitional provisions of the LRA 2002. However, the LRA 2002 is the controlling statute.

The 2002 Act was the product of years of consultation and evaluation and it was a joint project between the Land Registry[5] and the Law Commission.[6] The draft Bill was virtually unamended during its passage through Parliament and it is a work of clarity and principle. As well as ensuring that the substantive principles of land registration were brought up to date and expressed in clear language, the 2002 Act is also designed to facilitate e-conveyancing: that is, the holding and transfer of estates and interests in land electronically. This goal of a virtually paper-free conveyancing system has not yet been achieved because the e-conveyancing provisions of the LRA 2002 have not yet been triggered and the move to full e-conveyancing is 'on hold', with some uncertainty about what the next steps will be.[7] However, e-conveyancing or not, the 2002 Act is designed to ensure that e-conveyancing will work when the remaining technological and legal issues have been resolved. In this sense, the 2002 Act is 'transaction-driven' – its primary aim is to ensure

---

1 It is a common misconception that land registration in England and Wales is a relatively modern phenomenon. In fact, the first legislation was enacted in 1862, with further statutes in 1875 and 1897, although it was not until the entry into force of the LRA 1925 on 1 January 1926 that giant steps were taken towards a nationwide system of title registration.

2 See Law Commission Report No. 271, note 6.

3 See below for a more accurate description of what it means to say that land is 'registered'.

4 That is, the 2002 Act necessarily has to preserve the pre-existing situation in some instances and does this by incorporating some of that law through transitional provisions.

5 The state agency responsible for administering and operating the system of registered land.

6 In July 1998, the Law Commission published its Report No. 271 entitled *Land Registration for the Twenty-first Century: A Conveyancing Revolution*, on which the 2002 Act is based.

7 A pilot scheme was completed in 2007/08. It is not clear when the move towards e-conveyancing will be resumed, but it may be tied to the volume of land transactions and income earned, relative to the cost of moving to an electronic system. Law Commission Consultation Paper No. 227, 31 March 2016, *Updating the Land Registration Act 2002*, suggests that the goal of simultaneous registration and completion of transactions through electronic means should not be pursued in its original form, but it is not yet clear what this means.

the quick, efficient and inexpensive transfer of estates and interests in land while ensuring that third-party interests in land (the proprietary rights of others in the registered estate) are properly protected. To further this in a practical way, the 2002 Act seeks to implement a number of policies through changes to the substantive law. First, it seeks to ensure that as many estates in land as possible become registered. Second, it seeks to ensure that as many third-party rights as possible are recorded on the register of title of the estate that is affected by those rights. The necessary corollary is, of course, that failure to protect rights by registration when required may well mean that the interest ceases to affect the estate when it is sold. Third, it seeks to minimise the number and effect of those third-party proprietary rights that can be effective against the new owner of land even without being registered ('unregistered interests which override'). In turn, this will do much to ensure that the register provides a very clear picture of the legal state of the land. Fourth, if e-conveyancing materialises, it would provide that the effective transfer and creation of most proprietary rights in land could not occur except through an electronic entry on the e-register.

At this early stage in the analysis of land registration, these policy goals may appear difficult to understand, but the point of importance is that the LRA 2002 is designed to promote the efficient transfer of land by bringing certainty both to the question of who owns the land and protection for those who have rights in that land. That said, it would have been foolish for the framers of the 2002 Act to ignore what had gone before, so necessarily the 2002 Act builds on the principles of the 1925 Act and its fundamental architecture is the same as that of the 1925 Act. There is still a register of titles, there is still a Chief Land Registrar and district registrars,[8] and under the 2002 Act there are concepts, ideas and distinctions that are to be found in the 1925 Act. The difference is in the detail, not the basic structure, at least prior to the introduction of full e-conveyancing. The 2002 Act represents evolution not revolution.[9]

2.1 The Basic Concept of Title Registration

Simply put, to describe land as 'registered' means that the title to it (the estate, a right of ownership) is entered in a register maintained by HM Land Registry and accessed through a number of district land registries around the country or, increasingly, online. Each title is referenced by a unique title number. In addition to information about the title itself (e.g. quality of title, general description of land and identity of estate owner), other rights and interests affecting the title may be recorded on the register against the title number. Thus, while it is convenient to talk of registration of 'land', in fact the system is built on registration of title and it is not a 'cadastral system' (in which it is the land itself that is recorded and described in the register).[10] The fact that our system depends on registration of title, not of land, also means that it is perfectly possible for one plot of land to have more than one type of title registered in respect of it. Where this

8 The Chief Land Registrar is also the Chief Executive of the Land Registry, the administrative head of the agency in its day to day running.
9 The Law Commission Report is entitled *A Conveyancing Revolution*, but I am grateful to Professor Edward Burn for this pithy turn of phrase when commenting on the 2002 Act.
10 Of course, under the LRA 2002, the physical land to which each title relates is described in the register.

occurs, it is clearly identified on the register and a suitable cross-reference is made. For example, a person might be registered as having the freehold title (a registered fee simple) to a parcel of land, and a different person might be registered with title to a long lease over the same parcel (and so will be the freeholder's tenant). These will be cross-referenced to each other so that a person dealing with either title will be able to identify all registrable estates (titles) over the land that he is purchasing.

As things currently stand under the LRA 2002, not quite every 'estate' in land is a 'registrable title' because some estates are excluded from registration for practical or legal reasons (e.g. they may be of too short duration to require the protection of registration). Currently, a registrable estate – being an estate that must be registered on its transfer or creation[11] – is either a *legal freehold* (being the fee simple absolute in possession) or a *legal leasehold* of over seven years' duration (or with over seven years left to run if it is sold by one tenant to another[12] or some specialist and uncommon leases of shorter duration). All other estates cannot be registered in their own right but, as discussed in the previous chapter, these two 'qualifying' titles are for all intents and purposes the most important indicia of land ownership in modern land law.[13] The Land Register is thus intended to provide a comprehensive picture of title ownership in England and Wales, and 'registration of title' has replaced 'title deeds' as the proof of that ownership. So, while the mechanics of the system are complicated, the central idea is simple enough. There should exist an accurate and reasonably comprehensive record of title to land and of third-party interests in that land in order that dealings with the land can be accomplished safely and quickly. In pursuit of this, on 1 December 1990, all land in England and Wales became subject to compulsory first registration of title, although, at that time, there were already some 13 million registered titles. Today, HM Land Registry estimates that over 85 per cent of all titles are registered.

The consequence of the introduction of nationwide compulsory first registration of title on 1 December 1990, now continued under the LRA 2002, is that certain transactions concerning what is currently 'unregistered land' require the new owner to apply to the Land Registry for 'first registration of title'. On such application, the Land Registry will investigate the title, will register it and will assign a unique title number. The LRA 2002 specifies the transactions that trigger compulsory first registration of a qualifying title (i.e. a freehold or lease of over seven years) and essentially these encompass all significant dealings with land. These 'triggers' for compulsory first registration of a previously unregistered title are:[14]

---

11 Sections 4 and 27 of the LRA 2002.

12 The limitation to legal leases of over seven years is a practical one to ensure that HM Land Registry does not get swamped with applications to register titles. In due course, the trigger for registration will fall to legal leases of over three years, thus matching the trigger for the use of a deed to create a legal lease. Under the LRA 1925, the trigger for registration was legal leases of over 21 years, and so the LRA 2002 already has brought more leasehold titles on to the register than its predecessor.

13 Under the LRA 2002, it is also possible to register rights of ownership of other types of real property, not being estates. These 'franchises', 'rentcharges' and 'profits à prendre in gross' give their owners specialist and limited rights over the land they are registered against. A 'manor' – an old feudal property ownership right – may no longer be registered, but can continue to be registered if it was registered under the LRA 1925.

14 See generally section 4 of the LRA 2002.

1   the transfer ('conveyance') of an unregistered freehold estate to another person, whether for valuable consideration (e.g. a sale), by gift, on death, by way of trust or under order of the court;

2   the transfer of an existing lease in the land to another person, with more than seven years left to run at the date of the transfer, whether for valuable consideration (e.g. a sale of the lease), by gift, on death or under order of the court;[15]

3   the grant of a legal lease of more than seven years' duration, either out of an unregistered freehold or out of an unregistered leasehold of more than seven years' duration (in this case, the lease will be registered, even if the estate out of which it is granted is not);[16]

4   the creation of a first legal mortgage over an unregistered freehold or unregistered leasehold with more than seven years left to run, which will trigger registration both of the mortgage and of the title over which it is created.[17]

Clearly, the great majority of transactions concerning unregistered land will be caught by these triggers with the consequence that, as HM Land Registry estimates, the vast majority of titles to land should be registered in the near future.[18] In addition, the 2002 Act also provides for voluntary first registration of title[19] and for registration by the Crown of title to its land.[20] So, for example, an existing owner of an unregistered freehold can apply for voluntary first registration and thus 'convert' his land from 'unregistered' to 'registered'. Indeed, the LRA 2002 provides powerful incentives to do this. There are reduced fees for voluntary first registration, subsequent dealings with the land are easier and cheaper to achieve and, as an added incentive, registered titles are also protected to a very great degree from claims of adverse possession.[21] For example, a large landowner, perhaps a farmer or local authority, who is unable to keep track of all of their holdings, might well apply for voluntary first registration of title in order to obtain the security offered by the LRA 2002.[22] Even then, however, some land will remain of unregistered

---

15 Certain shorter leases also require registration, but these are of a specialist kind. Perhaps the most important is the lease of whatever duration that gives a right to possession more than three months in the future: for example, a lease of six years' duration granted on 1 January 2018 to take effect in possession on 1 July 2018. This is registrable as a title irrespective of its duration because it cannot necessarily be discovered by inspection of the land because the possession might not have started at the time of the inspection.

16 Note the grant of a lease of more than seven years out of an *existing* registered estate of freehold or leasehold also must be registered. This is technically a 'disposition' of a registered estate, so is dealt with by section 27 of the Act.

17 Note the grant of a mortgage over an *existing* registered estate of freehold or leasehold also must be registered. This is technically a 'disposition' of a registered estate, so is dealt with by section 27 of the Act.

18 The happy consequence is that unregistered land conveyancing will be a rare event: see Chapter 3.

19 Section 3 of the LRA 2002.

20 Section 79 of the LRA 2002.

21 See Chapter 12.

22 In fact, several local authorities negotiated a block fee with HM Land Registry for the voluntary first registration of all of their holdings.

title even under these provisions, being land where the title is rarely, if ever transferred, and where voluntary first registration is not made.[23]

Finally, we should note that the idea (and language) of 'registration' in fact contains two separate ideas. First, 'substantive registration' refers to the situation where entry on the register actually creates or constitutes a legal estate or interest in land for the person so registered. This is what we mean by 'registration of title' and is the heart of our system. For example, as we shall see, the creation or transfer of legal freeholds, leases over seven years, mortgages and easements is not actually accomplished until the registration of the new owner as the new 'registered proprietor'. Without this 'substantive registration' the legal title to the freehold, leasehold, easement or mortgage cannot be created or transferred, but such registration guarantees that the relevant title is valid and secure, as well as protecting it if the title to which it relates is sold or transferred. Second, other peoples' interests in the land (in the registered title) might be recorded on the title register. This registration does not create the interest or guarantee its validity, but simply protects the interest if the registered title over which it exists should be transferred. This is 'protective registration',[24] because the registration of these interests (for example, options, covenants, estoppels) does not create the interest or guarantee that it was validly created, but it does ensure that an interest validly created under the general law continues to affect the land (the registered title) if the land is transferred.[25]

2.2   The Nature and Purpose of the System of Registered Land

The LRA 2002, and the LRR 2003[26] made thereunder, contain the details of the current system of registered land. Together, they provide a statutory code that seeks to regulate the transfer, use and enjoyment of registered land, and it is imperative to appreciate that an understanding of 'registered land' is indispensable before embarking on an analysis of the substance of modern land law. The 2002 Act (and the 1925 Act before it) represents an attempt to impose a self-contained structure on a vitally important area of social, economic, family and commercial activity – the sale and use of land – and in this it is largely successful. Of course, the system of registered land is not perfect, even though the 2002 Act has resolved many points of former difficulty,[27] but that does not detract from

---

23 For example, land held by the ancient universities or by the Church of England whose retention of land is central for their purposes. However, if this land is not transferred or dealt with, it being 'unregistered' is hardly an issue, because 'registered' or 'unregistered' status matters most when the land is dealt with.

24 The 2002 Act does not use this language, but it is a convenient description.

25 Substantive registration also has this effect e.g. a legal mortgage created by substantive registration over a registered freehold title is protected if the freehold title is sold.

26 As amended in 2008 and 2011.

27 As noted, although the 2002 Act replaces the 1925 LRA in its entirety, it nevertheless builds on its conceptual foundations. It has thus inherited much of its basic philosophy. In one respect, however, the 2002 Act deliberately departs from its predecessor in that it pays no regard to principles of unregistered conveyancing. The Law Commission Report is explicit that old principles of unregistered land (and those of the 1925 Act based on unregistered conveyancing) should not hinder the development of the modern law of land registration.

the importance of a thorough understanding of the 2002 Act and the principles that underlie it.

Land is one of the most important economic assets of any nation, but it is also used for a variety of social and domestic purposes that many would argue are at the foundation of a modern society. Land law has to reflect the needs of commerce, families, financial institutions, neighbours, purchasers and occupiers. It is in this context that the system of registered land must operate, for it is these masters that land law has to serve. Consequently, it is difficult to draw up a complete list of the aims and purposes of the land registration system of England and Wales, not least because the LRA 2002 is just one component of a complex system regulating land use and ownership. The introduction of near universal registration of title would not have been possible without the complementary changes in the substantive law of estates and interests that were brought about by the LPA 1925. These are discussed in Chapter 1 and contribute to the achievement of the objectives outlined below. It should be remembered that the 2002 Act (like its predecessor) is designed to be a practical tool to be used for the everyday business of land transfer and land exploitation and thus seeks to achieve the following:

1   To reduce the expense and effort of purchasing land by eliminating the lengthy and formalistic process of investigating 'root of title'.[28] If title is registered, the owners of land should be easily discoverable by a simple search of the register of title and the possibility of fraud should be reduced. Thus, land becomes much more saleable and alienable.

2   To eliminate the risk for a purchaser of buying a title that might be unsafe or difficult to establish. The purchaser can rely on the register of title, for this is a title that has been investigated by the Land Registry and whose validity is guaranteed. Thus, under the LRA 2002, the aim is to ensure that ownership of land in England and Wales takes the form of 'title by registration' instead of 'registration of title'. This means that title flows from *the fact of registration itself*, and is not found in the conveyancing documents that are sent off for registration – as made clear in section 58 of the Act. This is the effect of 'substantive registration'. As the Law Commission commented in Report No. 271, the 'fundamental objective' of the 2002 Act is that:

> the register should be a complete and accurate reflection of the state of the title of the land at any given time, so that it is possible to investigate title to land online, with the absolute minimum of additional enquiries and inspections.[29]

3   To ensure that a purchaser of land knows about the rights and interests of other persons over that land, thereby ensuring that the price paid reflects its true economic and social value. This can be done by ensuring that as many rights as possible must be entered on the register and by limiting those that need not be. This is an aspect of 'protective registration'. If the purchaser is able to discover these (usually) hostile interests by inspecting the register, the purchaser can make an informed decision whether to go ahead with the purchase at the agreed price or

---

28 As is necessary in unregistered conveyancing, see Chapter 3.

29 Law Commission Report No. 271, paragraph 1.5.

abandon it. Note, however, that not all interests will (or can) be recorded on the register, and so land registration must find a way to deal with these interests.[30]

4   To enable the purchaser to buy land completely free of certain types of interest over that land, those interests then taking effect in the money paid to the seller through the process known as 'overreaching'.

5   To provide a mechanism whereby *certain* third-party rights in land can be protected by entry on the register and so survive a sale of that land to a new owner. This is also an aspect of 'protective registration'. Therefore, the old unregistered land 'doctrine of notice' plays no part *at all* in the system of registered land, having been superseded by the operation of the register. In fact, the LRA 2002 adopts a threefold categorisation of third-party proprietary rights in land: those that are overreached,[31] those that are 'unregistered interests which override'[32] and those interests that must be protected by registration.[33]

6   Possibly, at a date yet to be announced, to introduce e-conveyancing whereby the transfer of land, its mortgage and the creation of many third-party rights will be required to be achieved by electronic entry directly on to the register of title. It is not yet clear whether this aim will be pursued in this form.[34]

As well as these major aims, which – as we shall see – have been achieved with varying degrees of success by the 2002 Act, widespread registration of title has brought other benefits. For example, more accurate plans are provided, standardised and simple forms and procedures have replaced bulky title deeds, disputes can usually be resolved more easily, transaction costs have been reduced and confidence has been brought to the conveyancing process.

2.3   The Three Fundamental Operating Principles of Registered Land

It is sometimes said that there are three 'principles' underlying the system of registered land against which we should judge the reality of the LRA 2002 (and the LRA 1925 before it). To some extent, however, these are no more than a restatement of what we have already noted: that land registration is about the easy, safe and efficient transfer of land and the appropriate protection of rights in land. Consequently, we should not regard these 'principles' as a substitute for a thorough analysis of the actual workings of the LRA 2002. They are a helpful guide to understanding the 2002 Act, but no more than that. The three 'principles' are the *mirror principle*, the *curtain principle* and the *insurance principle*, and they are discussed briefly below.

---

30   One expression of this is found in the 2002 Act's concept of overriding interests, see section 2.6 below.

31   As noted above, overreaching 'protects' the interest by converting it into its monetary equivalent.

32   These were called 'overriding interests' under the LRA 1925.

33   These were known as 'minor interests' under the LRA 1925, a description deliberately not repeated in the LRA 2002.

34   Its implementation is currently on hold. Law Commission Consultation Paper No. 227, 31 March 2016, *Updating the Land Registration Act 2002*, suggests that the goal of simultaneous electronic registration and completion of transactions should be re-thought.

2.3.1 The mirror principle

The mirror principle encapsulates the idea that the register should reflect the totality of the rights and interests concerning a title of registered land. Thus, inspection of the register should reveal the identity of the owner, the nature of his ownership, any limitations on his ownership and any rights enjoyed by other persons over the land. The point is simply that, if the register reflects the full character of the land, any purchaser and any third party can rest assured that they are fully protected: the purchaser knows what he is buying and the person with an interest in the land knows that it will be protected. Yet, as we shall see, the mirror principle does not operate fully in the system of registered land in England and Wales, even under the LRA 2002, and it was never meant to. This is mainly due to the existence of a category of rights that affect the registered title and which bind any transferee of it (including a purchaser) without ever being entered on any register. These are the 'unregistered interests which override' – found in Schedule 1 and Schedule 3 to the LRA 2002[35] – which although much reduced in scope by the 2002 Act (when compared with the 1925 Act) nevertheless contradict the idea that the register should be a 'mirror' of the legal status of the land.

In this sense, it is important to remember that 'unregistered interests which override' (still called 'overriding interests' for short) are not a mistake. Although the 2002 Act in particular intends to make the register much closer to a flawless mirror, it is recognised that it is simply impractical or undesirable to make absolutely everything subject to express registration. Indeed, registration of title is not intended to replace physical inspection of the land by the purchaser as a way of discovering whether there are any adverse rights over that land. Thus, the imperatives of the LRA 2002 are to ensure that as much as possible about the land is registered and, for those rights that are not registrable under the Act, to ensure that they are capable of discovery by a normal inspection of the land. Thus, the purchaser should inspect the register and the land and should thereby be able to discover all that he needs to know.[36] In this aim, the LRA 2002 largely succeeds.[37] Consequently, although the image reflected by the register under the LRA 2002 remains imperfect, the imperfection will not necessarily cause loss to a diligent purchaser.[38] Title registration exists to ease the purchaser's path, not to exclude his participation in the conveyancing process.

So, given that land registration is primarily a practical tool, not an academic concept, it is unlikely that the register will ever be a truly perfect mirror, as not everything can be expected to be entered on a register. For example, informally created rights where no property professional has been involved are unlikely ever to be registered by the parties, and short-term rights (e.g. a one-year lease) or rights necessary for the efficient use of land (e.g. rights benefiting the general public) are either too transient or too important to be subject to a registration requirement. That said, it is undoubtedly the case that the

---

35 Schedule 1 concerns first registration of title; Schedule 3 concerns dealings with titles already registered. However, the list of interests which override under the schedules is broadly similar.

36 Thus, for those rights not capable of registration, if they are discoverable, a purchaser who fails to inspect the land at all, or inspects badly, cannot claim unfairness if he is bound by rights not on the register.

37 See below for a discussion of the LRA's 2002 strategies in this regard.

38 As we shall see, however, if a right is registrable, then failure to register it (assuming it does not override) causes the right to be lost, even if the purchaser discovered it. This must be so, else there would be no incentive to register.

changes made by the LRA 2002 to the original 1925 scheme do much to improve the reflection of the mirror and this will improve further should e-conveyancing be implemented. Similarly, under the LRA 2002, fewer categories of rights are capable of overriding at all, irrespective of the circumstances in which they arise,[39] and the definition of those overriding interests that remain has been altered to give the purchaser a very real chance of discovering their existence before a sale is completed.[40] Further, there is now a general duty to disclose unregistered rights which override to the registrar so that they may be brought on to the register when a title changes hands.[41]

2.3.2   The curtain principle

The *curtain principle* encapsulates the idea that certain *equitable* interests in land should be hidden behind the 'curtain' of a special type of trust. Thus, if a person wishes to buy registered land that is subject to a trust of land, the purchaser need be concerned only with the legal title to the land, which is held by the trustees and reflected on the title register. He need not look behind the 'curtain' of the trust or worry about any equitable rights of ownership that might exist. The reason is that any such equitable rights will be 'overreached' if the proper formalities of the purchase are observed – see sections 2 and 27 of the LPA 1925. Consequently, these equitable rights will not affect the purchaser in his enjoyment of the land. However, although the interests of the equitable owners cannot affect the purchaser because of overreaching, they are not completely destroyed because the process of overreaching operates to transfer the rights of the equitable owner from the land itself to the money that the purchaser has just paid for it. Thereafter, the trustees (the legal owners) hold the purchase money in trust for the equitable owners. This doctrine of overreaching (which also operates in unregistered land) is discussed more fully in Chapter 4 on co-ownership, but for now the important point is that, once again, the aim is to facilitate the alienability of land by freeing the purchaser from the effort and worry of dealing with equitable owners. As we shall see, the 'curtain' principle operates effectively in the majority of cases, but when it fails (usually because the preconditions for statutory overreaching cannot be met), the purchaser is faced with considerable difficulties. It may then become necessary for the purchaser to look behind the curtain, as in the classic case of *Williams & Glyn's Bank* v. *Boland* (1981).[42]

The LRA 2002 does not alter the fundamentals of overreaching and so does not resolve most of the problems that arise when overreaching does *not* occur (i.e. when the purchaser has to look behind the curtain), save to the extent that the 2002 Act redefines what qualifies as an overriding interest.[43] The 2002 Act does, however, confirm that legal owners of land (the trustees) have all the powers of an absolute owner, subject only to

---

39 For example, equitable easements may not override at all.

40 For example, where there is 'actual occupation'. And note, as discussed below, on and after 13 October 2013, a number of rights ceased to override.

41 Section 71 of the LRA 2002.

42 See Chapter 4. The bank's failure to look behind the curtain meant that its mortgage lost priority to the rights of the borrower's wife.

43 This is done by redefining overriding interests in such a way as to exclude most interests that are undiscoverable. See below.

Restrictions on their powers placed on the register of title itself (see section 23 of the LRA 2002) and this will support the overreaching mechanism when there are the required minimum of two legal owners.[44] Similarly, the widespread use of the Restriction against a title of land when there is only one legal owner (but more than one equitable owner) is likely to encourage overreaching by ensuring that a purchaser is alerted to the existence of equitable interests and so alerted to the need to overreach (or to gain the equitable owner's consent) before he buys.[45]

2.3.3   The insurance principle

The *insurance principle* was one of the most ambitious of the motives underlying the LRA 1925 and it continues to underpin the operation of the 2002 Act. It encapsulates the idea that, if a title is duly registered, it is guaranteed by the State. This guarantee is supported by a system of statutory indemnity (i.e. monetary compensation) for any purchaser who suffers loss by reason of the conclusive nature of the register. The State insures against deficiencies, inaccuracies or other mistakes in the register.

The original scheme of indemnity provided by the LRA 1925 was quite narrow, but the (relatively) wider indemnity provisions of the 2002 Act are considered later in this chapter. The point to be grasped here is that any registration system that guarantees title effectively will need to provide a system of compensation for those persons who suffer loss by reason of the application of the system. A register of land titles, especially one that is designed to be conclusive for most purposes, will always generate cases in which loss is caused to innocent parties simply because of the way the system works. If A is the 'true' freehold owner of land, but B is registered with the title by mistake, and then C buys the land from B on the basis of his registered title as guaranteed by the LRA 2002, it is obvious that either A or C will suffer loss by reason of the application of the registration system. The 'insurance' principle stipulates that a registration system must provide compensation in such cases, irrespective of whether anyone was at fault for the error.

It is difficult to overestimate the importance of the insurance principle. It is not so much that persons who suffer loss are compensated – in reality, there are relatively few payments of indemnity because of the relatively few serious instances of loss caused by the registration system – but rather that the very existence of an indemnity provision gives confidence to those using the registration system and encourages reliance on it. By way of contrast with the system in England and Wales, the system of title registration introduced into Hong Kong has an 'indemnity cap' that limits the amount of compensation payable in the event of a loss caused by an error in the register. It is clear already that the absence of a provision providing for full compensation has eroded confidence in the system in Hong Kong and has put at risk the widespread adoption of land registration. After all, if the State is not confident enough to back its registration system by underwriting it, why should landowners?

---

44 Except in those cases in which the two legal owners attempt to commit a fraud by employing the overreaching machinery: *HSBC v. Dyche* (2009); see Chapter 4.

45 A standard Form A Restriction. Entry of this Restriction necessarily alerts the purchaser to the existence of an equitable owner because it requires purchase money to be paid to two trustees, an event that would be unnecessary if there were no equitable owners. Consequently, a Form A Restriction can effectively freeze transactions with the land until the issue revealed by the Restriction is dealt with. Its absence can be fatal for a claimant, *Haque v. Raja* (2016).

2.4   An Overview of the Registered Land System under the Land Registration Act 2002

As noted already, land is 'registered land' when title to it is recorded in the title register, provided that the title is either the legal fee simple absolute in possession (freehold) or the legal leasehold of over seven years' duration (or with over seven years left to run on assignment).[46] These are the two important titles in current land law that, when registered, are known as 'registered estates' and the owner is the 'registered proprietor'. Title is registered usually following some dealing with the land (e.g. a sale or mortgage) and after HM Land Registry has checked the validity of the title from the documents supplied by the person asking to be entered as the registered proprietor. Access to the register is through district land registries throughout England and Wales, or online, and the register itself is an open public document, searchable on payment of the appropriate fee.[47] Each registered title is given a unique title number and its entry is divided into three parts: the *property register* describes the land itself, usually by reference to a plan, and notes the type of title (i.e. the estate) that the registered proprietor has; the *proprietorship register* gives the name of the proprietor and describes the *grade* of their title and any benefits attaching to the title (the grade of the title varies according to the extent to which HM Land Registry is satisfied that the title has been established); and the *charges register* gives details of all third-party rights over the land (except unregistered interests which override) that detract from the registered proprietor's full use and enjoyment of the land. An illustration is given below. Although this illustration appears complex because of the unfamiliar language, it gives a flavour of the three-fold nature of the register and the degree of detail that may be found. Titles conveyed more recently than the one in this example may include a note of the purchase price and the identity of any lender (but not the amount lent).

Register extract
****
*Title Number: CB5341
*
*Address of Property: 16 Gunning Way, Cambridge
*
*Price Stated: Not Available
*
*Registered Owner(s): RONALD JOHN BUCKLEY of 16 Gunning Way, Cambridge
*
*Lender(s): None
****
TITLE NUMBER: CB5341

---

46 Note also the need to register certain specialist shorter-term leases.

47 A simple online search costs a few pounds.

A: Property register

This register describes the land and estate comprised in the title.

COUNTY: CAMBRIDGESHIRE DISTRICT:
CAMBRIDGE

1   (18 June 1955) The Freehold land shown edged with red on the plan of the above Title filed at the Registry and being 16 Gunning Way, Cambridge.
2   The land has the benefit of the rights of drainage under adjoining land with ancillary rights of access.
3   A Transfer dated 3 September 1956 made between (1) Albert Brian Clarke, Lawrence Martin Noakes, Quentin Pine and Gilder Pine and (2) Ronald John Buckley contains the following provision:

IT IS HEREBY AGREED AND DECLARED by the parties hereto that the Transferee and the persons deriving title under him shall not be entitled to any right of access of light or air to buildings to be erected on the land hereby transferred which would restrict or interfere with the free user of any of the land now or formerly comprised in this title number.

B: Proprietorship register – Absolute freehold

This register specifies the class of title and identifies the owner. It contains any entries that affect the right of disposal.

1   (18 September 1970) Proprietor: RONALD JOHN BUCKLEY of 16 Gunning Way, Cambridge.
2   A Transfer dated 11 April 1956 made between (1) The Mayor Aldermen and Citizens of the City of Cambridge and (2) Albert Brian Clarke, Lawrence Martin Noakes, Quentin Pine and Gilder Pine contains Vendors personal covenant(s) details of which are set out in the schedule of personal covenants hereto.

Schedule of covenants

1   The following are details of the personal covenants contained in the Transfer dated 11 April 1956 referred to in the Proprietorship Register:

THE Vendors hereby covenant with the Purchasers and their successors in title that if and when the local authority shall take over the highways upon which the red land abuts and intended to be known as Hurrell Road, Persey Way, Gunning Way and Harding Way or shall require any private street works (whether permanent or temporary) to be executed there the Vendors will pay the expenses thereof apportioned to the red land and will at all times save harmless and keep indemnified the Purchasers and their estate and effects from and against all proceedings costs claims expenses and liabilities whatsoever in respect thereof.

IT is hereby agreed and declared that the dropping of the kerbs to provide accesses for vehicles over the footpaths in front of the red land shall be carried out by the Vendors at the expense of the Purchasers.

C: Charges register

This register contains any charges and other matters that affect the land.

1   The land is subject to rights of drainage and ancillary rights of access.
2   A Transfer dated 11 April 1956 made between (1) The Mayor Alderman and Citizens of the City of Cambridge (Vendors) and (2) Albert Brian Clarke, Lawrence Martin Noakes, Quentin Pine and Gilder Pine contains covenants details of which are set out in the schedule of restrictive covenants hereto.

Schedule of restrictive covenants

1   The following are details of the covenants contained in the Transfer dated 11 April 1956 referred to in the Charges Register:

FOR the benefit of the owners occupiers and tenants for the time being of all or any of the Vendors adjoining land comprised in a Conveyance dated the fourth day of July One thousand nine hundred and forty seven and made between The Master Fellows and Scholars of the College of Saint John the Evangelist in the University of Cambridge of the one part and the Vendors of the other part the Purchasers hereby jointly and severally covenant with the Vendors that the Purchasers and the persons deriving title under them will at all times hereafter duly perform and observe all and singular the said conditions Restrictions and stipulations mentioned in the Second Schedule hereto.

THE SECOND SCHEDULE above referred to CONDITIONS and STIPULATIONS

1   NO building erected on the red land shall except with the consent of the Vendors be used for any other purpose than as a separate or semi-detached dwelling house.
2   NO portion of the red land shall be used for any trade or business noisy noisome dangerous or offensive pursuit or occupation or for any purpose which shall or may be or grow to be in any way a nuisance cause of grievance or annoyance to the Vendors or to the owners or tenants of any of the neighbouring property.
3   NO outbuildings other than a garage shall be erected on the red land without the written consent of the Vendors.
4   NO drains from any house erected or to be erected upon the red land shall be laid except in conformity with plans previously submitted to and approved in writing on behalf of the Vendors and such drains shall be connected to the main sewer at the Purchaser's expense.

2.4.1   Rejection of the doctrine of notice

At this early stage in our analysis of registered land, it is also critical to appreciate that the practical operation of the system means that the old distinction between legal and equitable interests as a method of regulating dealings with land is largely discarded. The LRA 2002 (as did its predecessor) also abandons the 'doctrine of notice'[48] as a method of

---

48 For a brief description of this doctrine, see Chapter 3 on unregistered land. Even in unregistered land, however, the doctrine has limited relevance.

assessing whether any third-party rights affecting land will bind a purchaser of it.[49] In fact, the LRA 2002 effectively establishes four categories of proprietary right[50] and the crucial issue in any given case is to identify the category into which a person's right falls and not to ask whether that right is legal or equitable, or (even more inaccurately) whether the 'doctrine of notice' applies. Not surprisingly, the 2002 Act, and the LRR made under it, occasionally utilise the legal/equitable distinction as a method of assigning specific rights to one of these four categories, but it is not the nature of the right that is ultimately important, rather it is the category identified under the Act into which it falls.

2.4.2   Registrable estates under the Land Registration Act 2002

Registrable estates are those that are capable of existing at law (i.e. as legal rights)[51] and which may be registered in their own right with a unique title number. Under the LRA 2002, there are two such estates (commonly called 'titles'), although we should note that the Act also makes provision for the substantive registration of three other types of legal registrable interest.[52] For present purposes, however, we are concerned with the two legal estates that most accurately reflect 'ownership' of the land. These are legal freeholds and, with some minor exceptions, legal leaseholds granted for more than seven years.[53]

These titles are registered for the first time ('first registration') on a transfer (or other trigger) of the previously unregistered estate. If the title is already registered (and most now are), there will be a 'registered disposition' transferring the already registered title from transferor to transferee (as on sale). The mechanics follow a well-worn pattern whereby the transaction is carried out by a deed and then the deed is sent to HM Land Registry for 'registration'. Failure to register a transaction when required means that the

---

49 Note that certain sections of the LRA 2002 refer to the 'knowledge' of a purchaser, or the discoverability of a proprietary right, but the Law Commission has made it clear that this does not import old doctrines of 'notice' in to registered land. The 2002 Act is to be interpreted afresh given its aims and purposes.

50 The Act itself does not specifically refer to four categories of property right, but this is the effect of its provisions.

51 Section 1 of the LPA 1925.

52 Being 'rentcharges' (an interest whereby land is charged with the payment of money by the owner to another person), 'profits à prendre in gross' (a right to take some commodity from another's land, such as fish or wood) and 'franchises' (a right granted by the Crown to hold a fair or market, etc.). These registrable interests may be registered with their own title number as befits their special character. 'Manors' may remain registered in this way under the LRA 2002 if they have been so registered under the LRA 1925, but no new applications for registration may be made.

53 Sections 2, 3, 4 and 27 of the LRA 2002. The Act gives power to the Lord Chancellor to change the leasehold trigger for registration (section 5). It is anticipated that eventually legal leases of over three years will be registrable with their own title as these are the leases currently required to be made by deed. In addition, some shorter-term leases are currently registrable as separate titles, but these concern special or unusual situations: sections 4 and 27 of the LRA 2002. Probably the most common of these is the legal lease of whatever duration that gives a right to possession more than three months in the future: sections 4(1)(d) and 27(2)(b)(ii) of the LRA 2002. Such a lease must be registered with its own title, otherwise a purchaser of the land out of which the lease is granted may not know of its existence, as the tenant may not yet be in possession.

transferee obtains only an equitable title to the land.[54] This is substantive registration. If e-conveyancing enters into force, these transactions will be carried into effect electronically rather than by deed (section 93 of the LRA 2002).

2.4.3   Registered charges

Registered charges derive from the power of the registered proprietor to mortgage the land in order to release its capital value. These are legal mortgages of registered land. Under the LRA 2002, the only way to execute a mortgage of registered land (leasehold or freehold) is by an instrument which takes effect as 'a charge by deed expressed to be by way of legal mortgage'.[55] Further, such a 'charge by deed' must then be entered on the register against the affected title in order to take effect as a legal interest.[56] This is another example of substantive registration. We should also note on a practical level that the 'charge certificate', which under the LRA 1925 was the mortgagee's evidence of a valid mortgage, was abolished by the LRA 2002. Under the 2002 Act, charge certificates are not necessary because the register itself is open to inspection. The creation of a registered charge over a registered estate is perhaps one area where e-conveyancing might work because most institutional lenders are geared up for paperless mortgage transactions and already operate an electronic system with HM Land Registry for the discharge of mortgages (i.e. removal from the register) after they are paid off. Mortgages are considered in more detail in Chapter 11.

2.4.4   Unregistered interests which override ('overriding interests')

Unregistered interests which override are those rights in another person's land (i.e. in their registered 'estate') that have priority to the registered title of the registered proprietor – that is, they are binding on the land without being entered on the register of title of the land they affect. They are, quite literally, *unregistered* interests which override the registered title and which thus permit the right-holder (the person who claims the overriding interest) to exercise the right against the land irrespective of who the registered proprietor is, and even though that right is not on the register.[57]

Under the LRA 2002, overriding interests may take effect against a first registered proprietor (after compulsory or voluntary first registration of title) or against a person who becomes the registered proprietor on the transfer of a title that is already registered. Interests which override at first registration are defined in Schedule 1 to the 2002 Act and interests which override following a transfer (e.g. a sale) of land that is already registered[58] are defined in Schedule 3. The scope of these two schedules is broadly similar,

---

54 Section 7 of the LRA 2002.

55 Section 23 of the LRA. For present purposes, 'charging the land by deed with the payment of money', which is also mentioned in section 23, is equivalent to a charge by deed by way of legal mortgage.

56 Sections 12 and 30 of the LRA 2002. See *Barclays Bank* v. *Zaroovabli* (1997), decided under the LRA 1925 but still illustrative, for an example of the consequences of failing to register a legal mortgage.

57 Sections 11, 12, 29, 30 of the LRA 2002.

58 This is known as a 'registered disposition' as it is a disposition – a transfer – of a registered title and is completed by registration of the new owner as proprietor.

but there are some important differences. In essence, Schedule 1 is wider in scope than Schedule 3 so that more rights may override under Schedule 1 against a first registration than may override under Schedule 3 against a registered disposition.

When compared with the LRA 1925, the LRA 2002 reduced the scope and range of overriding interests. The reason is to ensure, as far as possible, that a potential purchaser of the land is bound only by those unregistered interests that, for policy or practical reasons, should take effect against a purchaser without being entered on a register and then only in circumstances in which the purchaser had a realistic opportunity of discovering the existence of the interest by a physical inspection of the land or by making normal enquiries of the transferor. Moreover, in pursuit of this policy of protecting the purchaser, the 2002 Act encourages a person applying to be registered with a title (e.g. a purchaser) to disclose to the registrar any known overriding interest so that it may then be entered on the register.[59] Be that as it may, it remains true that overriding interests account for a significant number of rights affecting registered land and their importance stems from the fact that they have priority without being entered on the register. Their very existence was a cause of concern to the Law Commission and HM Land Registry when devising the LRA 2002, but their social and economic importance is such that, as a class, they cannot be dispensed with. What the LRA 2002 attempts to do is reduce their impact, redefine their scope, reduce their number and encourage their entry on the register.

2.4.5   Interests protected by registration

The LRA 1925 specified a category of property rights in another person's land that had to be registered against the burdened title if they were to be binding. Failure to ensure such registration meant that the interests generally were void (i.e. unenforceable) against a purchaser unless they could be saved (fortuitously) by falling within the category of overriding interests. These registrable interests were known as 'minor interests'. Under the LRA 2002, there is no specific category known as 'minor interests' and generally that terminology should be avoided.[60] However, the LRA 2002 does employ the same logic as that found in the LRA 1925 and so there is a general principle that third-party property interests should be entered on the register against the estate they burden. This is protective registration. Failure to make such an entry may mean that the property right loses its priority against the registered proprietor, unless the right falls within Schedules 1 or 3 (as the case may be) and so qualifies as an overriding interest.[61]

The broad and important principle of the LRA 2002 is, then, that unless the property right amounts to a registrable estate (in which case it should be substantively registered as a title), or a registrable charge (in which case it should be substantively registered as a

---

59 Section 71 of the LRA 2002 places a duty on an applicant to disclose such interests, although it is a 'duty' without a sanction. Once an overriding interest is registered, it ceases to be overriding and is protected by its registration. It cannot thereafter revert to overriding status, even if it is later removed from the register.

60 These interests are not 'minor' in the sense of being trivial or unimportant and a major aim of the LRA 2002 is to ensure that as many rights as possible are entered on the register. There is, then, nothing 'minor' or secondary about these rights.

61 Sections 11, 12, 29, 30. It is considerably less likely than was the case under the LRA 1925 that a right will override under the 2002 Act if it really should have been registered.

mortgage), or an overriding interest (in which case it has priority without registration), it has to be entered on the register of title of the burdened land by means of a Notice if it is to preserve its effectiveness against a purchaser.[62] Rights falling within this category may be known as 'interests protectable by registration' (i.e. protective registration applies) and they comprise the bulk of third-party rights, including the important categories of covenants, options to purchase and many easements. Indeed, these interests protectable by registration will, in time, become the major group of third-party interests in land. This is ensured under the LRA 2002 not only because the statute requires more rights to be registered than was previously the case under the LRA 1925,[63] but also because section 71 of the LRA 2002 provides for a general duty of disclosure whereby an applicant for registration of a title must disclose a range of overriding interests that affect his land so that they then may be protected by registration. In consequence, the group of interests which override under the LRA 2002 will shrink as more and more of these rights become protected by an entry on the register of title.[64]

The mechanics by which these third-party interests may be protected through registration is simpler under the LRA 2002 than it was under the LRA 1925. Under the LRA 2002, protection of an interest is achieved by the entry of a Notice – which may be 'Unilateral' or 'Agreed' – and the registered proprietor may be controlled in his ability to deal with the land by means of a Restriction. A Restriction indirectly protects an interest because it prevents a transfer of the land unless the terms of the Restriction are complied with.[65] These two register entries (Notice and Restriction) are discussed more fully below.

This classification of proprietary rights into four different statutory classes – estates, registered charges, interests which override and interests protectable by registration – is fundamental to the land registration system under the LRA 2002. It enables owners, purchasers and third parties to know in advance how to protect their rights and what will happen to those rights if the land over which they exist should be sold, mortgaged or transferred. Clearly, this is a radical shift away from the old legal/equitable distinction and it represents the abandonment of the doctrine of notice in registered land. It also brings certainty and stability for persons who have rights in land that is owned by someone else. It is a process that began with the LRA 1925 and has been enhanced by the LRA 2002.

2.5　The Operation of Registered Land: Titles

The registration of titles is the heart of registered land and this is what distinguishes it from unregistered land where title is found in the title deeds. Under section 58 of the LRA 2002, the registered proprietor 'shall be deemed' to have been vested with the legal estate (i.e. the freehold or qualifying leasehold) as it is noted on the register. This is irrespective of whether there has actually been any conveyance to him. Thus, a person

---

62　As we shall see, an unregistered interest remains valid against a non-purchaser of the land under section 28 of the LRA 2002.

63　With a corresponding shrinkage in the reach of overriding interests.

64　Of course, e-conveyancing depends on the register being as up to date as possible and the duty of disclosure is one method by which the register does become more mirror-like.

65　A Restriction can be used for many more purposes than simply indirectly protecting an interest.

registered as proprietor as the result of fraud or mistake has a valid title[66] and is able to rely on the provisions of the LRA 2002 as to the conclusiveness of his interest, albeit that they may be subject to a claim to have the register rectified against them.[67] Thus, in *Walker v. Burton* (2013), the registered proprietors had been registered in error with title to a large area of moorland. The register was not rectified so as to remove their ownership because there were no grounds to do so under the rectification provisions of the LRA 2002. The earlier registration, albeit in error, had given them title and the conditions in the Act for rectification had not been satisfied.[68] Further, although the conclusive effect of section 58 (and its predecessor under the 1925 Act) had been challenged in *Malory Enterprises Ltd v. Cheshire Homes and Chief Land Registrar* (2002) in relation to the 1925 Act[69] and then in *Fitzwilliam v. Richall Holdings* (2013) in relation to the 2002 Act, the Court of Appeal in *Swift 1st v. Chief Land Registrar* (2015) has decided that section 58 means exactly what it says. *Malory* was held to be per incuriam and wrong in relation to this issue and *Fitzwilliam* was overruled.[70] It is now clear that a person registered with a title to an estate or a charge has both legal and equitable title, even if there was some error in the transaction leading to the registration. Registration confers title and does not merely record the effect of some previous transaction. Consequently, because the register is conclusive even if there has been error or fraud leading up to it, any person contesting the title must use the rectification provisions of the LRA 2002 if they wish to recover their title. Such a request to rectify may be granted (see *Baxter v. Mannion, Gold Harp v. Macleod* (2014)) or may be refused (see *Walker v. Burton, Patel v. Freddy's Ltd* (2017)) but that is determined by the specific rectification provisions (Schedule 4 to the Act) and pending such determination the person registered is the title holder. This is what the Law Commission meant when it stated that the LRA 2002 signals a change from registration of title, to title by registration. The point is that the act of registration itself confers title and thereby permits the registered proprietor to exercise all of the powers of an absolute owner, subject only to entries on the register.[71] Further, as a counterpart to this, if the new owner of a registrable title fails to apply for its registration within the applicable time limit (currently

---

66 *Walker v. Burton* (2013). See *Argyle Building Society v. Hammond* (1984) applying the equivalent provision (section 69(1)) under the LRA 1925.

67 See below for a discussion of alteration and rectification. *Baxter v. Mannion* (2011) is an example of such rectification after a mistake – the mistake being that the adverse possessor should not have been registered with title at the expense of the paper owner (who secured rectification). Leave to appeal to the Supreme Court in *Baxter* was refused. Compare with *Walker v. Burton* (2013), where the fact of registration was recognised as conferring title and that it should not be disturbed by rectification even if there had been a mistake.

68 See paragraph 6, Schedule 4 to the Act. Note, the objectors were not claiming title for themselves but asserted instead that the proprietors should not have title. It is unclear whether the register would be rectified if the Crown – the only other possible owner – made an application for rectification.

69 In that case, Arden LJ had determined both that a registration following fraud is not conclusive as to the proprietor's title and, if title is innocently acquired from a fraudster, there was no 'disposition' within the meaning of the 1925 Act so as to confer title on the purchaser. The case was settled before its scheduled appeal to the House of Lords.

70 Another aspect of *Malory* – the existence and effect of a right to have the register rectified following a mistake is not affected by *Swift 1st*.

71 Sections 23 and 26 of the LRA 2002.

two months from completion of the transaction),[72] the transfer becomes a nullity as regards the legal title. This means that, in the case of an outright transfer to the new owner, the legal title actually remains in the transferor until registration, who will hold it on trust for the new owner,[73] and in the unlikely event of no proper registration of the estate taking place, the new 'owner' will have to rely on the other mechanisms of the LRA 2002 to protect his interest, such as relying on the category of overriding interests or interests protectable by registration.[74]

As indicated above, when a title is presented for first registration, HM Land Registry will investigate the 'root of title' and check the validity of the application to register. Obviously, this is vital given that registration can have a conclusive effect. There are, however, four possible grades of title with which a person may be registered and these reflect the fact that in some cases it may be difficult to establish a conclusive title due to the absence of relevant documents or other factual difficulties.

2.5.1   Absolute title

Absolute title is the highest grade of title possible and amounts to full recognition of the rights of the proprietor. It is available for freeholds and leaseholds, although less commonly for the latter because the registrar may not be in a position to validate the *lessor's* title to grant the lease (as required by section 10(2) of the LRA 2002) as well as that of the leaseholder who actually applies for registration.

Registration with absolute title to a freehold on a first registration has the effect ascribed by section 11 of the LRA 2002. This invests the proprietor with the full fee simple together with all of the benefits subsisting for the estate, but subject only to overriding interests within Schedule 1 of the Act, registered protected interests, rights of adverse possessors of which the first proprietor has notice and interests under trusts of which the proprietor has notice. These last two categories exist only to ensure that subsisting equitable ownership interests and the accrued claims of adverse possessors are not destroyed by the simple expedient of the landowner applying for first registration of title. After this event, 'notice' of these rights ceases to be important and a later transfer of the (now) registered title is governed by sections 28 and 29 of the LRA 2002.[75] A person first registered with absolute leasehold title is in the same position, save only that they are also bound by all express and implied covenants affecting the leasehold estate (section 12(1) of the LRA 2002).

---

72 And remembering that this will occur simultaneously with the purchase if e-conveyancing materialises.

73 See *Pinkerry Ltd* v. *Needs (Kenneth) (Contractors) Ltd* (1992) and *Leeman* v. *Mohammed* (2001), illustrating the position under the equivalent provisions of the LRA 1925.

74 An example under the 1925 Act is provided by *Brown and Root Technology Ltd* v. *Sun Alliance and London Assurance Co Ltd* (1998), in which the transfer of a long lease was not registered by the new tenant and the Court of Appeal held that the assignee had not acquired legal title. This had the consequence that the assignee had no power to give notice to end the lease as that power remained with the assignor (the original tenant), who still held legal title. See *Stodday Land Ltd* v. *Pye* (2016) and *Sackville UK Property Select II (GN) No.1 Ltd* v. *Robertson Taylor Insurance Brokers Ltd* [2018] EWHC 122 (Ch) for similar cases under the 2002 Act.

75 Section 28 provides that the transferee who is not a purchaser is bound by *all* pre-existing property rights; section 29 provides that a purchaser has priority over all interests except those entered on the register and those overriding within Schedule 3 to the Act.

2.5.2   Good leasehold title

As noted above, it is less common for a leasehold owner to be registered with absolute title on first registration simply because this requires the landlord's title to have been verified (section 10(2) of the LRA 2002). Thus, many proprietors of long leaseholds will be registered with *good leasehold title*. This invests the proprietor with the same quality of title as absolute title except that it is subject to any interests affecting the *landlord*'s freehold or other superior title (section 12(6) of the LRA 2002). In other words, the proprietor with good leasehold title has a strong title, every bit as marketable as an absolute title, save only that the validity of the freehold (or superior leasehold) out of which it is carved is not admitted. Should that freehold or superior title become registered with absolute title or should the registrar become convinced of the quality of the freehold or superior title, the good leasehold owner may apply to upgrade to absolute title under section 62(2) of the LRA 2002.

2.5.3   Possessory title

If an owner cannot produce sufficient evidence of title (freehold or leasehold) on an application for first registration, he may be registered with possessory title. This is available where the applicant is in actual possession of the land and there is no other title with which he can be registered.[76] This is effectively the position of someone who relies on adverse possession as the basis of his title or a person who is unable to prove their title formally at first registration because of some disaster with the title deeds. The possessory title is, however, subject to *all* adverse interests that exist at the date of registration, not merely those that are overriding or registered protected interests – see section 11(7) of the LRA 2002 for freeholds and section 12(8) of the LRA 2002 for leaseholds. This appears, then, to be a rather unattractive title with which to be registered because the proprietor may find the land burdened by undisclosed interests, even perhaps a superior title. However, the registrar may upgrade the possessory title under section 62 of the LRA 2002 if satisfied as to the validity of the proprietor's title[77] or if an adverse possessor is able to establish title under the provisions of the LRA 2002.[78] Note also that a person registered with possessory title because of some mishap with the title deeds usually takes out title insurance whereby the title is privately guaranteed. This should suffice for a purchaser interested in buying the land from a person registered with possessory title.

2.5.4   Qualified title

A person whose title is subject to fundamental defects that cannot be disregarded may be invested with a *qualified title*. However, qualified title is subject to the same interests as an absolute title *plus* any further interests that appear from the register to be excepted from the

---

76 Sections 9(5) on freeholds, and 10(6) on leaseholds.

77 For example, missing documents are found after registration.

78 On which, see Chapter 12.

effects of registration (sections 11(6) and 12(7) of the LRA 2002).[79] It is, therefore, of limited comfort to an estate owner and only rarely does HM Land Registry agree to a request for such registration. It will do so where there is the prospect of the qualified title being converted into an absolute or good leasehold title under section 62 of the LRA 2002.

Of course, once a person is registered as proprietor with one of the grades of title noted above, any subsequent dealings with that land will then be subject to the provisions of sections 28 and 29 of the LRA 2002 regarding the effect of registered dispositions – that is, transfer of land already registered. So, on a sale, mortgage or transfer of the now registered land, two issues arise: first, what is the position of the transferee (e.g. the new owner, purchaser or mortgagee); and, second, what is the position of a person with a 'third-party' interest in that land?

2.5.5   The new owner, purchaser or mortgagee under a registered disposition

According to sections 25, 26 and 27 of the LRA 2002, a transfer of a registered freehold or leasehold estate is not complete until the new owner is entered on the register as registered proprietor. This is substantive registration and is taken to occur when an application to register title is made. However, the penalty for failure to register (an unlikely event due to the involvement of property professionals) is that the legal estate remains in the transferor and the new owner receives an equitable estate only, even if all of the other formalities necessary for a transfer of the land have been observed.[80] This means that the new owner who fails to register his ownership is theoretically vulnerable to a subsequent sale of the land by the person from whom he took the transfer.[81] In practice, however, the transferee may well find their equitable interest protected as an interest which overrides under Schedule 3, paragraph 2 of the LRA 2002 if they are in discoverable actual occupation of the property. As we can see then, this is a good example of how the LRA 2002 has superseded traditional property law concepts because, under its system, the validity or otherwise of legal title depends crucially on the fact of its substantive registration, not on the method or manner in which that title was conveyed.

Once successfully registered, the registration is conclusive as to the title of the new owner under section 58 of the LRA 2002 and entitles him to exercise full powers to deal with the land under section 23 of the LRA 2002, even if there were errors in the transaction leading to the registration. Moreover, the LRA 2002 establishes exactly what types of proprietary interest affect the transferee when he becomes registered as owner. If the transferee is *not* a purchaser – perhaps he inherited the land under a will or received a gift – section 28 of the LRA 2002 provides that the new registered proprietor takes the land subject to *all* prior property rights, irrespective of whether those propriety rights were entered on the register or should have been entered on the register or would have been overriding interests. This is known as the 'basic priority rule' and simply says that a transferee, who has not paid for the land, should take it as it comes. If, on the other

---

79   This is a 'just in case' category that ensures that a qualified title is subject to those rights etc. that caused the registrar to have doubts about the title in the first place.

80   As illustrated by *Mascall* v. *Mascall* (1984) under the 1925 Act.

81   Of course, it would amount to a breach of contract.

hand, the transferee has given valuable consideration, section 29 provides that, when registered, he takes the land free from all pre-existing property rights *except* registered charges, overriding interests within Schedule 3 of the Act and protected registered interests. Any interests not protected in one of these ways lose their priority. This is known as the 'special priority rule', and in fact it will apply in most cases because most transfers of land are for value. It means simply that a purchaser should be bound only by those property rights actually entered on the register – and therefore discoverable by inspection of the register – and unregistered interests which override (which, on the whole, are largely discoverable by a physical inspection of the land itself). Note, however, that whether a transfer is for valuable consideration (and therefore subject to the basic or special priority rule) is a question of substance, not form. So, in *Halifax* v. *Popeck* (2008), the transfer was found to be *not for value* (and so within section 28), even though it was portrayed by the parties and the conveyancing documents as a sale/purchase.[82]

2.5.6   The third party with interests in the transferred land

It is inherent in what we have been considering so far that a major purpose of the land registration system is to ensure that land may be sold freely. Necessarily, this means that other people's rights over that land must be readily identifiable and their effect on the land must be known in advance in order to protect a prospective purchaser. As we have seen, when a registered title is transferred for value and a new proprietor is registered as owner,[83] that proprietor obtains the title free from all property rights except unregistered interests which override within Schedule 3 and interests entered on the register such as charges (mortgages) or protected registered interests – section 29 LRA 2002. All other property rights lose their priority against the new registered proprietor.[84] Importantly, the 'doctrine of notice' in its old, equitable sense plays no part in determining whether any third-party rights bind the purchaser because the matter is dealt with according to the statutory scheme established by the LRA 2002.[85]

2.6   The Operation of Registered Land: Unregistered Interests which Override

Much of the criticism of the operation of the system of registered land under the LRA 1925 was directed at the existence of 'overriding interests' as a category of right that bound the purchaser without a register entry. The basic principle was that a purchaser took the land subject to any existing overriding interests and these bound 'automatically' whether or not a purchaser knew about them. In fact, most of the interests that fell within the definition of overriding interests under the 1925 Act *should* have been obvious

---

82 See also *Gold Harp* v. *Macleod* (2014).

83 This will include a mortgage, and registration of the mortgage. If there is no transfer for value the basic priority rule applies and all pre-existing property rights have priority are binding.

84 Some are overreached and so take effect in the money paid by a purchaser: see Chapter 4.

85 The LRA 2002 does makes reference to the knowledge of the transferee when defining the scope of certain overriding interests within Schedule 3, but this is not meant to be a reincarnation of the doctrine of notice.

to a purchaser of land on inspection of the property, or were in the nature of public rights that did not seriously affect the registered proprietor's use of the land. Nevertheless, there were concerns about the potential for a purchaser to be bound by undiscoverable overriding interests[86] and also, of course, the very existence of the category appears to distort the 'mirror principle'. This in turn meant that there could not be an entirely 'register-only' system of e-conveyancing because not everything was on the register. Initially, the Law Commission considered abolishing the category of overriding interests altogether, but it soon became apparent that this was neither feasible nor desirable. Consequently, the LRA 2002 modified the operation and scope of overriding interests in order to minimise their impact on land and to ensure that as far as possible a potential transferee is aware of their existence before he completes the transfer.

2.6.1　　Strategies of the Land Registration Act 2002

In seeking to minimise and clarify the impact of unregistered but binding rights, the 2002 Act employs a number of strategies. First, overriding interests operate in different ways depending on whether the occasion is a first registration of a title or a disposition of an existing registered title. At first registration, overriding interests are listed in Schedule 1 to the Act and take effect against the first registered proprietor whether or not that first registered proprietor gave valuable consideration when obtaining the land (sections 11 and 12 of the LRA 2002). This is because the act of first registration does not involve a transfer of land – the applicant for first registration *already* owns it – and so whether they gave value is immaterial. Likewise, the list of overriding interests in Schedule 1 is more extensive than that operating in respect of a disposition (Schedule 3) precisely because the first registered proprietor should not be permitted to escape rights that bound him by the simple expedient of applying for first registration. If it were otherwise, a person bound by a right could apply for first registration to escape an adverse right. However, the transfer of an already registered estate (i.e. a disposition) is the occasion for a *new* owner to be registered and this person may well have given valuable consideration and *should* be given an opportunity to discover which rights might affect him. Consequently, the list of overriding interests in Schedule 3 is less extensive than those listed in Schedule 1.

Second, the number of potential overriding interests is now smaller than under the 1925 Act, both in respect of first registration and of subsequent dispositions of a registered estate. This has been accompanied by some redefinition of those that do remain in order to reduce their impact.[87] In this regard, we should note that, with effect from 13 October 2013, another group of rights ceased to be overriding interests under Schedules 1 and 3. This miscellaneous group of rights must now be registered by means of a Notice in order to bind a first registered proprietor or a new registered proprietor.[88]

Third, an applicant for registration – either for first registration or after a disposition of a registered estate – is required by section 71 of the LRA 2002 to disclose those overriding interests of which he is aware so that they may be brought on to the

---

86　Not *undiscovered*.

87　This is particularly marked in relation to Schedule 3. There is some redefinition in Schedule 1, but it is not as far reaching.

88　See below.

register.[89] These interests will already bind the applicant – being overriding – and so their protective registration by means of a Notice would simply confirm the priority that the right already enjoys. Obviously, the purpose here is to encourage the disclosure and registration of as many overriding interests as possible so that the register can become a clearer mirror of the land. If so registered, the interest necessarily ceases to be overriding and cannot recover that status if it is subsequently removed from the register.[90] Importantly, however, failure to disclose the existence of an overriding interest does not destroy the overriding status of the right.[91]

2.6.2 Unregistered interests which override a first registration under Schedule 1 of the Land Registration Act 2002

The unregistered interests listed in Schedule 1 to the Act will override the estate of a first registered proprietor – section 11 of the LRA 2002 (freeholds) and section 12 of the LRA 2002 (leaseholds). If these interests subsequently become registered, they cease to be overriding, but of course would bind because they would then be on the register. The categories of right listed in Schedule 1 are similar to those found in Schedule 3, save only that those found in Schedule 1 are marginally of wider scope.

2.6.2.1 Certain leases: paragraph 1 (legal leases for seven years or less) and paragraph 1A (relevant social housing leases), Schedule 1

With only limited special exceptions, legal leases originally granted for seven years or less will override a first registration.[92] Importantly, however, all leases that qualified as overriding interests under the old section 70(1)(k) of the LRA 1925 *before* the entry into force of the LRA 2002 will continue to override and no additional action needs to be taken to protect them while the current tenant remains the estate owner.[93] In other words, the current provision operates in respect of leases granted on or after 13 October 2003 and while a tenant under a seven-year legal lease (or less) may choose to register his lease against the burdened land by means of a Notice,[94] the lease will be fully protected as an overriding interest without such registration.

The three exceptions to the overriding status of 'short leases' are of a special kind and as such are required to be substantively registered as titles in their own right, irrespective

---

89 There is a special form – Form DI – that accompanies an application to register a title either on first registration or after a transfer.

90 Section 29(3) of the LRA 2002.

91 It is, after all, the applicant's land that is burdened and it would be strange if, by non-disclosure, he could destroy the priority of somebody else's right!

92 Legal leases *over* seven years are registrable titles. A lease granted originally for more than seven years that is transferred with less than seven years left is *not* an overriding interest and the transfer must be registered.

93 Schedule 12, paragraph 12 of the LRA 2002. These are legal leases of 21 years or less under the previous version of this provision.

94 Providing it is not granted for three years or less, as these cannot be registered by means of a Notice and must rely on their overriding status, section 33(b) LRA 2002.

of the length of the lease.[95] They cannot override even if of seven years or less. These are the grant of a lease out of unregistered land in pursuance of Part 5 of the Housing Act 1985 under the right to buy provisions,[96] the grant of a lease out of unregistered land of a dwelling house to a private-sector landlord where the tenant's right to buy is pre-served[97] and the grant of a lease out of unregistered land that is to take effect in posses-sion more than three months from the date of the grant.[98] The first two are special statutory creations and no more need be said of them. The third illustrates well the policy of the 2002 Act. A tenant under a short-term legal lease (i.e. seven years or less) is likely to be in possession and so his lease will be easily discoverable by an intending purchaser of the land and hence perfectly acceptable as an overriding interest – the purchaser will know of the lease. However, a lease where possession is 'delayed' may not be discovera-ble and hence is not suitable for inclusion as an overriding interest. It should be regis-tered with its own title. In addition, section 157 of the Localism Act 2011 added paragraph 1A to Schedule 1 and this provides that a 'relevant social housing tenancy' shall override irrespective of its length. These are specialised leases granted by private providers of social housing and were added to the list of overriding interests because it is important that they always have priority even if the superior title changes hands.

These provisions on leases carry into effect one of the main goals of the 2002 Act – the creation of a title register that is more comprehensive than its predecessor.[99] More-over, there is power under the legislation to reduce further the threshold for leases registrable with their own titles (to legal leases over three years), with a corresponding reduction in the length of leases that would qualify as overriding interests. This power has not yet been exercised but it would mean that there was symmetry between those legal leases that needed to be created by deed and those that were required to be substantively registered as a unique title. Finally, to emphasise, this category of overriding interest is concerned with legal leases (being leases that are *granted*). It should not be forgotten that an equitable lease – whether it is the result of an enforceable contract to grant a lease or the result of a failure to register the title to a registrable lease – does not fall within this paragraph but nevertheless might take effect as an overriding interest because the tenant is often in actual occupation of the land at the relevant time.[100]

---

95 Section 4 of the LRA 2002.

96 Schedule 1, paragraph 1, referring to section 4(1)(e) of the 2002 Act.

97 Schedule 1, paragraph 1, referring to section 4(1)(f) of the 2002 Act and a lease within the ambit of section 171A of the Housing Act 1985.

98 Schedule 1, paragraph 1, referring to section 4(1)(d) of the 2002 Act. Clearly, leases taking effect in possession three months or less from the date of the grant, if they also be of seven years or less, will be overriding interests.

99 Consequently, although it is not possible to apply for voluntary title registration of a lease granted for seven years or less, unless the lease is discontinuous (section 3(4) of the LRA 2002), it is possible to enter a Notice of such lease on the register of the superior title if the superior title is registered, at least if the lease was granted for over three years originally (section 33(b)(i) of the LRA 2002) and has more than one year left to run (Rule 57(2) of the LRR 2003).

100 The equitable lease must exist at the moment of first registration for this to be a possibility and most equitable leases should have been protected as a Class C (iv) land charge under the LCA 1972 to survive a transfer of the unregistered title to a purchaser. If they were not so registered, they would not exist at first registration.

2.6.2.2   The interests of persons in actual occupation – paragraph 2, Schedule 1

This is perhaps the most important of the overriding interests listed in Schedule 1. It echoes a concept found in section 70(1)(g) of the LRA 1925 and although the provision is not identical, the old case law on the meaning of 'actual occupation' has carried through to the 2002 Act. In particular, three points should be noted: first, there is no protection for the interests of persons in receipt of rent and profits of the land per se (i.e. if they are out of actual occupation) as there was under the 1925 Act; second, the enforceability of the interest protected is now to be limited to the land actually occupied by the interest-holder;[101] and, third, there is no qualification relating to disclosure of the interest under Schedule 1, as there is in relation to Schedule 3 (and as there was under the 1925 Act).

Schedule 1, paragraph 2, defines this overriding interest as an 'interest belonging to a person in actual occupation, so far as relating to land of which he is in actual occupation, except for an interest under a settlement under the Settled Land Act 1925'. In general terms, this means that a person claiming an overriding interest under this paragraph must prove that he holds a proprietary interest in the land that is about to be first registered and that he is in actual occupation of that land at the relevant time. Moreover, although occasionally the interests falling within this paragraph are mistakenly called 'occupier's rights', it is clear that any proprietary interest (unless specifically excluded) may gain overriding status through this provision provided that the interest-holder is in actual occupation of the burdened land.[102] In order to understand how the paragraph works, we can break it down into its components.

First, the proprietary interest to be protected must be enforceable against the land immediately before first registration of title: that is, the interest must subsist in reference to land at the time of first registration. Consequently, if for whatever reason the applicant for first registration can establish that the claimed right was not enforceable against the title immediately prior to the application for first registration, then the interest cannot be revived by the provisions of the 2002 Act. Actual occupation cannot protect that which does not exist. This is particularly important as it reminds us that, if a third-party interest did not survive a preregistration transfer or grant of title under the rules of unregistered conveyancing, then that interest has ceased to exist by the time of first registration and so cannot be revived as an overriding interest.[103]

Second, given that first registration involves no transfer of title (because the applicant already owns the land), there is no 'registration gap',[104] and the owner of the unregistered

---

101 This reverses *Ferrishurst* v. *Wallcite* (1999).

102 Often occupation will follow from the right itself, as with beneficial interests under trusts of land, but it need not. For example, an option to purchase given to a licensee of the land and who is in actual occupation would be overriding under this provision. Note, however, that it is the option that overrides; a licence per se cannot override under this section for it is not proprietary.

103 For example, an option to purchase should have been registered as a land charge in unregistered land. If the land is sold and the option was not registered, it ceased to bind the applicant for first registration *before* he applied for that registration and so it cannot override.

104 On which see below section 2.6.3.2.1.

interest that is alleged to override the first registration must be in actual occupation at the time the application to register the title is received at HM Land Registry.[105]

Third, to repeat, *any* proprietary right, provided that it is not specifically excluded, may qualify for overriding status by virtue of the interest-holder being in actual occupation of the affected portion of the burdened land. In many cases, the interest alleged to be overriding will also be the reason the occupier is entitled to be present on the burdened land (e.g. an equitable lease or a beneficiary's interest under a trust of land),[106] but there is no necessary reason why this should be so and there are a number of examples in which it was not.[107] In this regard, although there is no statutory definition of what amounts to 'a proprietary right', most instances will involve the familiar categories of leases and equitable shares of ownership, options and the like and includes rights of pre-emption, proprietary estoppels and mere equities.[108] Personal rights, such as contractual licences and bare licences, do not qualify. Other examples exist of rights that qualified under the previous law, despite being of uncertain character, and these include the right to seek equitable rectification of a document,[109] the right to seek alteration of the register[110] and the right to have a transaction set aside for undue influence,[111] provided of course there is the necessary actual occupation of the burdened land.

Fourth, in general terms, the meaning of 'actual occupation' under the 2002 Act is no different from that of its predecessor in section 70(1)(g) of the LRA 1925. However, Schedule 1, paragraph 1, does restrict the ambit of claims of 'actual occupation' so that the interest will override *only* in so far as it relates to the land actually occupied by the claimant. In other words, the legal reach of the overriding interest is limited to the factual reach of the occupation or, to use the words of Schedule 1, the interest overrides only 'so far as relating to the land of which he is in actual occupation'. This is an explicit reversal of the Court of Appeal's decision in *Ferrishurst Ltd* v. *Wallcite Ltd* (1999), in which Ferrishurst had been in occupation of part of the land as an underlessee but held an option to purchase the entire land comprised in the superior leasehold estate and, by virtue of that actual occupation, the right to purchase the entire land was held to override. Under Schedule 1, Ferrishurst's overriding interest would be limited to that part of the land that it did actually occupy.[112] With this qualification in mind, 'actual

---

105 See Rule 15, LRR 2003.

106 *Williams & Glyn's Bank* v. *Boland* (1981), now confirmed by section 3 of the TOLATA 1996.

107 For example, *London & Cheshire Insurance Co Ltd* v. *Laplagrene Property Ltd* (1971) in reference to a vendor's lien where the occupation was due to a lease.

108 Sections 115 and 116 of the LRA 2002.

109 *Blacklocks* v. *J.B. Developments (Godalming) Ltd* (1982).

110 *Malory Enterprises Ltd* v. *Cheshire Homes (UK)* (2002). This is not challenged by *Swift 1st* v. *Chief Land Registrar* which otherwise overrules *Malory*. The proprietary status of this 'right' is controversial.

111 *Thompson* v. *Foy* (2009), in respect of Schedule 3 to the 2002 Act, but the issue is the same. Other examples include a right to rectify a lease (*Nurdin and Peacock* v. *Ramsden* (1998)), an 'estate contract', being a contract to purchase a legal estate (*Webb* v. *Pollmount* (1966)) and an 'unpaid vendor's lien', being the seller's right to enforce any unpaid purchase price against the land itself (*Nationwide Building Society* v. *Ahmed* (1995), although no lien was found to exist in that case).

112 The same restriction, plus others, applies in relation to unregistered interests which override a registered disposition under Schedule 3 to the Act.

occupation' is a question of fact to be determined by reference to the circumstances of each case. In many (probably most) instances, it will be tolerably clear from the facts whether actual occupation exists, but the assessment should not be overly technical. According to Lord Wilberforce in *Williams & Glyn's Bank* v. *Boland* (1981),[113] interpreting the previous provision in section 70(1)(g) of the LRA 1925, these words:

> are ordinary words of plain English and should, in my opinion, be interpreted as such.... Given occupation, that is presence on the land, I do not think that the word 'actual' was intended to introduce any additional qualification, certainly not to suggest that possession must be 'adverse': it merely emphasises that what is required is physical presence not entitlement in law.

The meaning of actual occupation under the 2002 Act was considered at some length in *Thompson* v. *Foy* (2009), with the analysis further developed by the Court of Appeal in *Link Lending Ltd* v. *Bustard* (2010) and spelt out in the High Court decision in *Baker* v. *Craggs* (2017).[114] Although these cases concerned Schedule 3 to the 2002 Act (which does have an additional requirement of 'discoverability' – see below), the meaning of 'actual occupation' itself is not any different under Schedule 1. In *Thompson* v. *Foy*, Lewison J summed up the position in the following way:[115]

1   The words 'actual occupation' are ordinary words of plain English and should be interpreted as such. The word 'actual' emphasises that physical presence is required: *Williams & Glyn's Bank* v. *Boland* (1981).[116]

2   Actual occupation does not necessarily involve the personal presence of the person claiming to occupy. A caretaker or the representative of a company can occupy on behalf of his employer (*Abbey National BS* v. *Cann* (1991)),[117] and a builder can occupy on behalf of his client.[118] Likewise, in *Bustard*, the claimant was in actual occupation of her house despite being involuntarily detained elsewhere in a psychiatric unit. However, we should note that this does cut both ways. So, in *Lloyd* v. *Dugdale* (2001), Dugdale was unable to claim an overriding interest by virtue of actual occupation because even though he personally held a proprietary right in the land (in fact an estoppel lease), and even though he was physically present, his presence was deemed to be that of an agent for his company and so he did not have an overriding interest. Similarly, in *Hypo-Mortgage Services Ltd* v. *Robinson* (1997), it was held that children living with their parents – the estate owners – could not be said to be in actual occupation in their own right because their presence was wholly explained by that of their parents. Although this was an attractive solution on the facts of that case, and one that may well be followed, the decision must be approached with some care. It has long been accepted that wives do not occupy premises as a mere shadow of their

---

113 At pp. 504, 505.

114 See also *Thomas* v. *Clydesdale Bank* (2010) where, on a preliminary issue, the court made some observations on the meaning of actual occupation.

115 The analysis is adopted by Newey J in *Baker* v. *Craggs*.

116 Per Lord Wilberforce. See also *AIB* v *Turner* [2015] EWHC 3994 (Ch) emphasising that the occupation should be "actual".

117 Per Lord Oliver.

118 See the Court of Appeal in *Lloyds Bank* v. *Rosset*, and followed in principle in *Thomas* v. *Clydesdale Bank*.

husbands,[119] and while the *reason* for the occupation of children must be that they are with their parents, that does not explain why, factually, they too cannot be regarded as being in actual occupation. The issue is not, after all, by what right are they *entitled* to be in actual occupation, but whether they *are* in actual occupation on their own behalf, rather than as agent for another.

3   However, actual occupation by a licensee (who is not a representative occupier) does not count as actual occupation by the licensor: *Strand Securities Ltd v. Caswell* (1965).[120] Of course, however, a licensee can be in actual occupation on his own behalf, but would not gain an overriding interest unless he held a proprietary right in the land, such as option to purchase.

4   The *mere* presence of some of the claimant's furniture will not usually count as actual occupation: *Strand Securities Ltd v. Caswell*.[121] Note, however, Lewison J's reference to 'mere' presence and 'usually', because it is clear that the presence of furniture and the like can amount to actual occupation, especially if it reveals a sufficient degree of continuity and permanence of occupation: *Bustard* (2010), *Wishart v. Credit and Mercantile* (2015). In addition, it seems clear that the nature and extent of the physical presence required to constitute actual occupation can vary according to the type of property under consideration. In *Malory v. Cheshire Homes* (2002), the land was derelict and unusable, but the claimant established 'actual occupation' through acts of minimal use, particularly the erection of a fence around the plot to keep out intruders.

5   If the person said to be in actual occupation at any particular time is not physically present on the land at that time, it will usually be necessary to show that his occupation was manifested and accompanied by a continuing intention to occupy. What this seems to mean is that what is required is a physical presence on the land, not of a temporary or transient nature, but the absence of the claimant from the property for a period or periods of time does not of itself take the claimant out of occupation, nor does it imply abandonment of occupation once achieved. A person does not cease to be in actual occupation because they are away on business or on holiday or indeed in semi-permanent hospital care. However, they may not be in actual occupation if they have a residence elsewhere and the disputed property is visited only occasionally. The occupation must be 'actual', not notional (*AIB v. Turner* (2016)). It seems, however, that if someone is absent, they must have a continuing intention to return and this was one reason why, in *Thompson v. Foy*, the claimant would *not* have been in actual occupation. While one can see the attractiveness of this view (especially for a purchaser or mortgagee), it is not clear that previous case law supported it – see, for example, the discussion of actual occupation in the Court of Appeal in *Lloyds Bank v. Rosset* (1991). We should also remember that the rationale of the land registration system is to ensure that questions concerning the state of mind both of purchasers and of those claiming adverse interests are meant to be largely irrelevant. It is a functional system, based on facts, rather than a system based around the intentions of the parties. Likewise, how is a purchaser to

---

119 *Williams & Glyn's Bank v. Boland* (1981).

120 Per Lord Denning MR. See also *AIB Group v. Turner* [2015] EWHC 3994 (Ch).

121 Per Russell LJ.

know whether the person in actual occupation intends to return? The issues concerning actual occupation were *obiter* in *Foy*,[122] but they were material in *Link Lending Ltd v. Bustard* (2010), in which the claimant was absent from the land (her home) for lengthy periods while she was being looked after in a psychiatric unit. However, the land was effectively her permanent home, with all of her belongings and furniture there, and she visited from time to time and continued to pay the bills. She had a clear intention to return and thus was found to be in actual occupation, the Court of Appeal emphasising the degree of continuity and permanence of her occupation.

6   What is required is 'actual occupation', not actual *use*. Thus, using an easement does not amount to actual occupation of the servient land, because it is simply the exercise of the right granted: *Chaudhary v. Yavuz* (2011).[123] The same will be true of other limited proprietary rights to use the burdened land where, in the ordinary sense, the right-holder is not in occupation.

7   It is clear that more than one person may be in actual occupation of the relevant land for the purpose of establishing an overriding interest. This is seen most commonly in trust of land cases in which both the trustee (the legal owner) and the claimant (the equitable owner) are in actual occupation. In this sense, 'occupation' is not to be equated with 'exclusive possession'.

8   Finally, we might add that, for the purposes of Schedule 1, where the test of 'actual occupation' is not further qualified,[124] the occupation need not be discoverable in order to generate an overriding interest against an applicant for first registration (as it must be under Schedule 3).

Fifth, there are a number of interests that *cannot* override under this provision. We have seen already that the overriding status of the rights of persons in receipt of the rents and profits of the land has been removed by the LRA 2002, but also excluded are interests under a settlement governed by the SLA 1925,[125] the right of a tenant arising from the service of a notice seeking enfranchisement or the grant of a new or extended lease,[126] a spouse's statutory right of occupation of the matrimonial home,[127] the rights conferred on a person by or under an access order made under the Access to Neighbouring Land

---

122 The judge held that the claimant had no relevant property interest.

123 Note the apparently contradictory view in *K Sultana Saeed v. Plustrade* (2001), in which the Court of Appeal appeared to accept that the right to park under an easement amounted to actual occupation of the burdened land. However, this was following a concession from counsel and the point was not argued. Both the trial judge and Court of Appeal in *Chaudhary* regarded *Saeed* with suspicion.

124 Compare Schedule 3, paragraph 2, and the question of 'actual occupation' in respect of registered dispositions.

125 The appropriate form of protection is a Restriction controlling dealings. A Notice may not be used (section 33(a)(ii) of the LRA 2002).

126 Leasehold Reform Act 1967, section 5(5) as amended by paragraph 8, Schedule 11 of the LRA 2002; Leasehold Reform, Housing and Urban Development Act 1993, section 97(1) as amended by paragraph 30, Schedule 11 of the LRA 2002. A Notice may be used to protect the right and a Restriction to alert the interest-holder to any proposed dealing with the land.

127 FLA 1996, section 31(10)(b) as amended by paragraph 34(2), Schedule 11 of the LRA 2002. A Notice may be used.

Act 1992,[128] a right arising from a request for an overriding lease under the Landlord and Tenant (Covenants) Act 1995 (LTCA 1995),[129] and a pending land action, a writ or order affecting land issued or made by a court.[130] These are, of course, particular rights of a unique character and they cannot override because their protection is provided for in the special statutory regimes that created them.

2.6.2.3   *Legal easements and profits à prendre – paragraph 3, Schedule 1*

This category of overriding interest replaces the difficult section 70(1)(a) of the LRA 1925 and is simplicity itself.[131] Thus 'a legal easement or *profit à prendre*' will override. Indeed, prior to first registration, these rights would have bound the estate as 'legal rights binding the whole world' and so the fact that they override at first registration merely continues a priority they already enjoyed. Importantly, however, equitable easements will not override a first registration of title, once again because of the interplay between first registration and the rules of unregistered conveyancing. Quite simply, prior to first registration, an equitable easement should have been registered as a land charge under the LCA 1972.[132] On sale of the unregistered title, if registered as a land charge, it would have been valid and been apparent to HM Land Registry and would have been protectively registered by means of a Notice against the new registered title at first registration. If not registered as a land charge, it would have been void and so cannot be revived at first registration through the mechanism of overriding interests.[133]

The overriding status of all legal easements and profits at first registration is not controversial. Indeed, in many instances, these legal interests will in fact be entered on the register against the title at first registration (and so protected) and will then cease to be overriding. The burden will be noted against the servient title and an entry will be made on the title of the dominant land indicating that the right is a benefit to be enjoyed with the estate. This is because, at first registration, the registrar will examine the title documents in the normal way and will make appropriate entries in the register. Similarly, any other legal easement or profit not apparent from the documents of title may be disclosed at the time of application for first registration and so entered on the register.[134] As we shall see, the position of legal easements and profits on a subsequent dealing with an existing registered title is more complex.

---

128 Access to Neighbouring Land Act 1992, section 5(5) as amended by paragraph 26(4), Schedule 11 of the LRA 2002. A Notice may be used: paragraph 26(3), Schedule 11 of the LRA 2002.

129 LTCA 1995, section 20(6) as amended by paragraph 33(4), Schedule 11 of the LRA 2002. A Notice may be used.

130 Section 87(3) of the LRA 2002.

131 In relation to registered dispositions, Schedule 3, paragraph 3 (the equivalent provision) is narrower in scope.

132 Except equitable estoppel easements, which thus would appear to lose priority under this provision.

133 Note, however, that anything that overrode under the old law prior to the entry into force of the LRA 2002 will continue to do so. This could well include equitable easements (*Celsteel* v. *Alton* (1985)) the overriding status of which existed before the entry into force of the LRA 2002.

134 Using Form DI.

2.6.2.4   *Other overriding interests – paragraphs 4–9, Schedule 1*

The above three categories represent the most important overriding interests, with the 'actual occupation' provision being the widest in scope simply because, under it, *any* proprietary right can attain overriding status if coupled with actual occupation (unless specifically excluded). In addition, the Schedule lists further examples of less common overriding interests.

'Customary rights' are expressly preserved in paragraph 4 and encompass rights that are enjoyed by all or some inhabitants of a particular area. 'Public rights' also remain a category of overriding interest under the 2002 Act in paragraph 5, and include things such as public rights of way and rights of passage in navigable waters.[135] Paragraph 6 includes 'local land charges'. These are not to be confused with 'Land Charges' under the LCA 1972 but are instead rights within the Local Land Charges Act 1975 and relate to such matters as planning, highways and other local authority matters. Rights in relation to mines and minerals may also override under paragraphs 7, 8 and 9 of Schedule 1 and public–private partnership leases (PPP leases) may override under section 90(5) of the Act, even though they are not mentioned expressly in Schedule 1. These are contracts involving the provision, construction, renewal or improvement of a railway or a proposed railway where one of the parties is London Regional Transport, Transport for London or a subsidiary of either.[136]

2.6.2.5   *Miscellaneous, time-limited, overriding interests – now expired*

Paragraphs 10–14 and paragraph 16 of Schedule 1[137] contained a miscellany of rights and interests that originally override a first registration of title. As a group they had little in common save their feudal ancestry, but they shared the same fate in that they were to override *only for ten years* from the entry into force of the Schedule. Consequently, these rights ceased to override with effect from midnight 12 October 2013.[138] Thus, although they continue to bind the *unregistered* title pending its first registration – being legal interests – they will cease to bind on first registration unless protected at that time by the entry of a Notice.[139] Such an entry might be made if the interests are revealed in the documents of title sent in for first registration, or because they are disclosed by the applicant for first registration, or because they have been protected by a 'caution against first registration' lodged by the right-holder. While the desire to reduce the number of overriding interests is a major policy goal of the 2002 Act, there is a risk that right-holders will lose their interests because of this withdrawal of overriding status.[140] Perhaps, in such a case, the right-holder will be able to apply for alteration of the register in order to

---

135 See *Overseas Investment Services Ltd* v. *Simcobuild Construction Ltd* (1995).

136 See generally section 210 of the Greater London Authority Act 1999 and the other conditions specified therein.

137 Paragraph 16 was added by the LRA 2002 (Transitional Provisions) (No. 2) Order 2003. Paragraph 15 was inserted under the transitional provisions, Schedule 12, paragraph 7.

138 Section 117 LRA 2002.

139 Although factually unlikely, the right-holder could be in actual occupation of the burdened land so as to establish an overriding interest by that route.

140 This constitutes an exception to the general principle that first registration does not alter priorities of interests affecting the land.

correct a mistake and thereby secure the late entry of a Notice to protect his right.[141] Without such rectification, a right-holder who has failed to act to protect their right will lose it against the first registered proprietor and consequently against any subsequent transferee under a registered disposition.[142] Rights having lost overriding status under this provision include franchises, manorial rights, Crown rents, certain rights in respect of embankments and sea or river walls, tithes and liability to repair the chancel of a church.[143]

2.6.2.6 *Transitional and special provisions concerning the rights of adverse possessors*

Schedule 1 of the 2002 Act contains no specific saving for the rights of adverse possessors to override at first registration. There is no equivalent to the old section 70(1)(f) of the LRA 1925. However, three provisions of the 2002 Act will have an impact on the rights of adverse possessors. First, for a transitional period of three years from 13 October 2003 (now of course expired), title already acquired under the Limitation Act 1980 before the coming into force of Schedule 1 had overriding status against a first registration.[144] In effect, this meant that an adverse possessor who had completed the 12-year period of limitation under the old law of adverse possession enjoyed protection for that right as an overriding interest for three years from the entry into force of the 2002 Act.[145] Second, the interest of the adverse possessor will have priority as an overriding interest if supported by the adverse possessor's actual occupation of the land at the time of first registration, irrespective of when that registration takes place. This is likely to be the case in most situations. Third, the interest will have priority if the first registered proprietor has notice of the rights of the adverse possessor at the time of first registration, irrespective of when that registration takes place.[146] Taken together, these provisions mean that only rarely and in very unusual circumstances will an adverse possessor be denied priority for their possessory title against a first registered proprietor even though there is no dedicated category for the rights of adverse possessors. Note, however, that should this first registered proprietor sell the land, the purchaser under a

---

141 Schedule 4, paragraphs 2(1)(a) and 5(a) of the LRA 2002.

142 There might be room for the argument that the applicant for voluntary first registration is estopped from defeating the right by his own action.

143 This last was added to the list of time-limited overriding interests following the House of Lords' decision in PCC of *Aston Cantlow* v. *Wallbank* (2003) that the enforcement of such liabilities did not infringe the ECHR and so such rights remained valid. See LRA 2002 (Transitional Provisions) (No. 2) Order 2003.

144 Paragraph 7 of Schedule 12 of the LRA 2002, inserting a new paragraph 15 into Schedule 1.

145 An adverse possessor who has completed 12 years' adverse possession prior to the entry into force of the 2002 Act, and for whom in consequence the land would have been held on trust under section 75(1) of the LRA 1925 before the 2002 Act entered into force, 'is entitled to be registered as the proprietor of the estate' (paragraph 18 of Schedule 12 of the LRA 2002). Consequently, an adverse possessor who has completed the period of limitation should have applied within the three years' grace afforded by the transitional provision. Failure to do so now means that, on first registration, the title could be lost if the adverse possessor is not in actual occupation or the applicant for first registration does not have notice of the possessor.

146 Sections 11(4)(c) and 12(4)(d) of the LRA 2002.

registered disposition may well escape the claims of the adverse possessor if the possessor is not in discoverable actual occupation under Schedule 3, paragraph 2 of the LRA 2002.

2.6.2.7   *Interests removed from the category of interests which override a first registration of title: a summary*

Schedule 1 to the Act seeks to rationalise the types of interest that can override a first registration. There are some changes in definition, when compared to the 1925 Act, but also some exclusions. First, the rights of adverse possessors per se no longer qualify, but protection is available if the adverse possessor is in actual occupation, or if the first registered proprietor has notice of the claim – as discussed immediately above. Second, a person in receipt of rent and profits may not claim overriding status for their interest, although once again such landlords have other means of protection of their leases. Third, equitable easements will not override a first registration, although often this will simply reflect the priority already gained by the applicant for first registration. Fourth, in respect of possessory, qualified or good leasehold title, those matters 'excepted from the effects of registration' under the old section 70(1)(h) of the 1925 Act no longer override at first registration, which should be no surprise given that the land is unregistered immediately prior to the first registration. Fifth, a miscellaneous category of ancient rights ceased to have overriding effect at midnight on 12 October 2013.

2.6.3   Unregistered interests which override a registered disposition under Schedule 3 of the Land Registration Act 2002

As noted above, the range of unregistered interests which override a registered disposition of the land[147] are more restricted than those that may override a first registration. Even though they are *broadly* similar in scope, and many of the considerations discussed above in relation to Schedule 1 are relevant here also, Schedule 3 is narrower than Schedule 1. The principal reason for this difference is that Schedule 3 operates, by definition, when there is a *transfer* of land to a new owner and a primary aim of the LRA 2002 is to ensure that a transferee of a registered title is not compromised by hidden interests when he takes the title. In consequence, the Act seeks to ensure that as much information as possible is entered on the register of title of the burdened land and therefore it confines overriding interests under Schedule 3 to those that *could* be discovered by a reasonably diligent transferee making an inspection of the land before the transfer. The aim is to eliminate the 'undiscoverable' overriding interest. In this regard, always remember that overriding interests are directly related to the priority rules of the 2002 Act: by virtue of section 28 of the LRA, a transferee *not* for value takes the land subject to all pre-existing proprietary rights[148] but, under section 29, a transferee for value takes the land free from

---

147 That is, a transfer of the legal title, including sale, mortgage and the grant of leases, including leases for seven years or less, even though they do not generally require registration (sections 27 and 29(4) of the LRA 2002).

148 For example, *Halifax* v. *Popeck* (2008) in which the transferee was held not to have given value even though the transaction appeared to be a sale.

all pre-existing property rights except those interests entered on the register and overriding interests within Schedule 3 matters when – as is usually the case – the transferee is a purchaser, mortgagee or lessee of the land.

2.6.3.1   *Certain leases: paragraph 1 (legal leases for seven years or less) and paragraph 1A (relevant social housing leases), Schedule 3*

This provision is almost identical to the provision found in Schedule 1. Thus, with only minor exceptions, a legal lease originally granted for seven years or less will override a registered disposition.[149] It will bind the transferee automatically.[150] Legal leases for any duration longer than this are substantively registrable as individual titles. Likewise, equitable leases of any duration are excluded from this category of overriding interests and they must be protected by the entry of a Notice on the register or take effect as an overriding interest through the discoverable actual occupation of the tenant. It is also the case, as with Schedule 1, that certain specialist leases of any duration cannot qualify as overriding interests under paragraph 1 of Schedule 3 and must be registered as individual titles whatever their duration. These are: the grants of a lease out of a registered estate in pursuance of Part 5 of the Housing Act 1985 under the right to buy provisions;[151] the grant of a lease out of a registered estate of a dwelling house to a private-sector landlord where the tenant's right to buy is preserved;[152] the grant of a lease of any length out of registered land that is to take effect in possession more than three months from the date of the grant; the grant of a lease where possession is discontinuous;[153] and, finally, the grant of a lease out of registered land of a franchise or manor.[154] In addition, section 157 of the Localism Act 2011 also added paragraph 1A to Schedule 3 and this provides that a 'relevant social housing tenancy' shall override irrespective of its length. As noted, these are specialised leases granted by private providers of social housing and were added to the list of overriding interests because it is important that they always have priority even if the superior title changes hands. As with Schedule 1, the trigger for substantive title registration of a leasehold may fall below the current seven-year threshold and this will cause a similar reduction in the length of leases that could qualify as an overriding interest under this provision.[155]

---

149 As previously, a lease that qualified as an overriding interest immediately before the entry into force of the 2002 Act under the old section 70(1)(k) of the LRA 1925 – being a legal lease granted for 21 years or less – continues to override while the original tenant remains in possession. The 2002 Act is not retrospective.

150 Section 29 of the LRA 2002.

151 Schedule 3, paragraph 1(a) referring to section 4(1)(e) of the 2002 Act.

152 Schedule 3, paragraph 1(a) referring to section 4(1)(f) of the 2002 Act and a lease within the ambit of section 171A of the Housing Act 1985.

153 Schedule 3, paragraph 1(b) of the 2002 Act referring to section 27(2)(b)(iii). These are typically 'timeshare' leases where the estate owner is given the right to possess for a fixed period of time but only one week each year.

154 Schedule 3, paragraph 1(b) of the 2002 Act referring to section 27(2)(c). These are ancient estates of a specialist kind.

155 Section 118 of the LRA 2002.

2.6.3.2 The interests of persons in actual occupation, as restricted by paragraph 2, Schedule 3 of the 2002 Act

As with its counterpart in Schedule 1, this is probably the most important category of interest that can override under Schedule 3. However, two important general points must be noted at the outset. First, the actual occupation provisions of Schedule 3, paragraph 2, do not mirror the sister provision in Schedule 1 and Schedule 3 restricts, even more than Schedule 1, the circumstances in which a person may claim an overriding interest by virtue of their actual occupation. The reason is to ensure, as far as is possible, that a transferee for valuable consideration is not bound by an undiscoverable interest. In particular, under Schedule 3, we should be aware that: there is no protection for the interests of persons in receipt of rent and profits per se (i.e. if they are out of actual occupation), subject to transitional arrangements; the enforceability of the interest protected is now limited to the land actually occupied by the interest-holder; the provision in respect of inquiry and disclosure has been reshaped; the actual occupation must be discoverable or (if there is actual occupation) the interest must be within the actual knowledge of the transferee in order to qualify as an overriding interest; and there is no protection for tenants in occupation under a three-month reversionary lease.[156] The second general point is that actual occupation is likely to be most influential in elevating property interests into overriding interests against a registered disposition when those interests have arisen *informally*. This is not only because the 2002 Act expressly recognises the proprietary status of one type of informal interest whose status was previously uncertain (equities by estoppel),[157] but also because the way professional conveyancing is conducted means that most deliberately created rights will be entered on the register by protective registration as a matter of course.

2.6.3.2.1 General considerations

The general principle under paragraph 2, Schedule 3 is that a person claiming an overriding interest must establish both that he holds a proprietary interest in the burdened land and that he is in actual occupation of the land to which the interest extends within the meaning of the Schedule. The potential difficulty arising because of the time lag between the execution of a registrable disposition and its later registration (the 'registration gap') has been resolved judicially by *Abbey National Building Society* v. *Cann* (1991), and applied to the LRA 2002 in *Scott* v. *Southern Pacific Mortgages Ltd* (2014).[158] Consequently, actual occupation at the date of *execution* of the transfer is critical, not its later registration.[159] Note here that Lewison J in *Thompson* v. *Foy* implies that actual occupation must also exist when the disposition is registered, not only when the transaction is executed – i.e. at both

---

156 This exclusion is in addition to those types of interest that are specifically excluded from overriding status, either by Schedule 3 itself or under other legislation.

157 Section 116 of the LRA 2002. The Act also confirms the proprietary status of rights of pre-emption and mere equities although these are likely to be created formally, sections 115, 116.

158 In *Scott*, both the lender and the interest-holder were innocent victims of a well-organised mortgage fraud. The temptation to protect the weaker party – the occupiers – was strong, but the temptation to utilise the 'registration gap' was resisted by the Supreme Court.

159 Of course, also as explained above, the 'problem' will disappear come e-conveyancing because of the simultaneous execution and registration of dispositions.

moments. The judge based this on a forensic reading of the LRA 2002, but such a requirement makes no practical sense in that a purchaser will inspect the land prior to execution of the transfer and not again before the transfer is registered. Why then require actual occupation at that later date? Of course, this 'problem' will disappear under e-conveyancing, and Lewison J in *Foy* does recognise that his (*obiter*) conclusion is out of step with all major commentaries. Finally, for clarity, as with Schedule 1, it is clear that *any proprietary* interest (unless specifically excluded) may gain overriding status through this provision provided that the interest-holder is in actual occupation of the burdened land at the relevant time. Conversely, of course, if the person in actual occupation does not have a property interest at the relevant time – as was held to be true of Mrs Scott in *Scott v. Southern Pacific* – then simply being in actual occupation does not generate an overriding interest.

2.6.3.2.2 *Conditions shared with the similar provision in Schedule 1*

Many of the considerations relevant to the position under Schedule 1 are relevant here also and are noted below. Reference should be made to the discussion above for a fuller account. First, the interest to be protected must be in existence and enforceable against the land immediately before the disposition takes place, bearing in mind that actual occupation must have been present at the time of completion of the transfer or grant.[160] Actual occupation cannot protect that which does not exist at the relevant time.[161] Consequently, if a claimant acquires a proprietary right *after* the disposition, there can be no overriding interest, as in *Scott* where Mrs Scott's lease arose after the mortgage had been executed.[162] Second, as noted above, the relevant time for the interest-holder to be in actual occupation is at the moment the transfer or grant is executed under the general law and not (despite the contrary view expressed in *Foy*) the later date of registration. Third, any *proprietary* right, provided that it is not specifically excluded, may qualify for overriding status by virtue of the interest-holder being in actual occupation of the affected portion of the burdened land. Personal rights, such as licences, can never override simply because they are personal. Fourth, those interests that are excluded from qualifying as overriding interests under Schedule 1 are also excluded from qualifying as overriding interests through actual occupation under Schedule 3. Fifth, the meaning of 'actual occupation' as a state of affairs will be the same as that applicable to Schedule 1, including the fact that Schedule 3 also limits the effect of the overriding interest to the extent of the land actually occupied. However, of crucial importance is the *additional* requirements placed on 'actual occupation' before it can qualify under Schedule 3.

---

160 Note that the person claiming the overriding interest may have otherwise surrendered their priority, *Wishart v. Credit & Mercantile* (2015) and see note 161 below.

161 Such a right may be unenforceable for many reasons: perhaps it was overreached by the registered disposition; perhaps the right-holder has waived his priority or would be estopped from enforcing it by his conduct. However, the critical point is that the claimant must have an interest that has *potential* priority to the registered disposition before any question of an overriding interest arises.

162 Mrs Scott sold the house to the fraudster, who mortgaged it, before giving a lease back to Mrs Scott. At the time of the mortgage, Mrs Scott had no property interest in the land.

2.6.3.2.3 *Additional conditions for actual occupation under Schedule 3*

It is in respect of Schedule 3 that the Law Commission's policy of ensuring that 'actual occupation' operates as a warning to a prospective purchaser really comes to the fore. After all, registered dispositions involve a transfer of title and if the transferee cannot discover binding adverse interests from the register – especially in an e-conveyancing climate – then it must be made as easy as possible to discover them by other means. Consequently, as well as the issues discussed above about what *factually* amounts to actual occupation, and which are also relevant here, Schedule 3 introduces additional conditions that further restrict the circumstances that an interest-holder can claim to be in actual occupation so as to override a registered disposition.

The first additional condition is that the actual occupation must be capable of being 'obvious on a reasonably careful inspection of the land at the time of the disposition' or (providing there is actual occupation) the interest alleged to be protected must be within the 'actual knowledge' of the transferee at that time.[163] This is one of the critical provisions of Schedule 3 and it is not found in either the old law of section 70(1)(g) of the LRA 1925 or in Schedule 1 of the LRA 2002. It is a wholly new provision designed to ensure that a purchaser taking under a registered disposition cannot be subject to the priority of a third-party interest unless there is actual occupation and either that occupation is discoverable or the purchaser knows of the right. In essence, the overriding effect of 'actual occupation' is disapplied (no overriding interest) unless at least one limb of the qualification is established. The first limb prevents actual occupation triggering an overriding interest if the 'occupation would not have been obvious on a reasonably careful inspection of the land at the time of the disposition'. Clearly, this provision raises questions of fact because a purchaser – especially a mortgagee – is likely to reach for the 'undiscoverability argument' as soon as it appears that he is going to lose priority to an overriding interest through actual occupation. In that regard, the following now seems established. First, it is the *occupation*, not the right, that must be discoverable and so the purchaser should be concerned with signs of presence not entitlement, although of course the former should alert the potential purchaser to the possibility of the latter. Second, the Law Commission's view is that 'apparent' occupation is to be determined by reference to the law on latent and patent defects of title and not by reference to the principles of constructive knowledge or notice that so bedeviled the law of unregistered conveyancing.[164] Whether this real, but fine, distinction is fully implemented come judicial interpretation of the provision remains to be seen. Third, the relevant test is objective. The test is not whether the purchaser actually did or did not discover the occupation, but whether the purchaser *would have done so*, had he made a reasonably careful inspection of the property – *Wishart v. Credit & Mercantile*. In this sense, it is not necessary for the purchaser to make any additional enquiries and inspections other than those that he normally would have undertaken. In fact, the purchaser does not have to inspect at all to gain the benefit of this provision and he will be safe from the priority of the adverse interest if the actual occupation was not discoverable on a reasonable inspection whether

---

163 Schedule 3, paragraph 2(c)(i) and (ii).

164 Law Commission Report No. 271, *Land Registration for the Twenty-first Century*, paragraph 8.62.

he inspected or not. This illustrates well that the provision is designed to protect and not to catch out a purchaser. Finally, and obviously, the provision does not protect a purchaser just because he fails to discover occupation, even after inspecting, if the occupation was discoverable within the meaning of the Schedule. This is not protection for the indolent or incompetent and in particular the Schedule cannot be pleaded by a purchaser (e.g. a mortgagee) who fails to take routine precautions before advancing money under a registered disposition.[165]

The second limb of the exclusion is the necessary counterpart to the introduction of the discoverability condition. Thus, even if the occupation is undiscoverable (there must still be actual occupation), the third-party interest will still override if the transferee had 'actual knowledge' of the right. Again, there are some important points here. First, the issue of 'actual knowledge' is irrelevant if the interest-holder is in discoverable actual occupation of the land. This qualification only kicks in if the occupation is *not* apparent – and this is likely to be rare in practice because most occupation will be apparent. Second, it follows that the interest-holder *must still be* in actual occupation of the land (even if not discoverable) within the normal meaning of that term before the purchaser's actual knowledge becomes an issue. So, if the interest-holder is *not* in actual occupation, then the fact that the purchaser knows of the right is irrelevant. It is crucial to grasp this if the law of registered conveyancing is not to be undone by a secret reintroduction of the law of notice. Third, it is the *right* itself – not the occupation – that must be within the actual knowledge of the purchaser. Fourth, the provision requires 'actual knowledge' on the part of the purchaser and it is not intended that he could lose his priority to a third-party interest merely because he *ought* to have known of the existence of the adverse right.[166]

Clearly, this provision is more complex than its counterpart in Schedule 1. However, it is doubtful whether this definitional change in the scope of the 'actual occupation' overriding interest really will have much practical impact. It is unlikely that there will be many, if any, cases of actual occupation that is truly undiscoverable, rather than being simply undiscovered.

The second additional condition – additional to that required for 'actual occupation' under Schedule 1 – did in fact feature in a different form in the old section 70(1)(g) of the LRA 1925. This is the additional qualification that an interest will not override if inquiry was made of the right-holder and he failed to disclose the interest 'when he could reasonably have been expected to do so'.[167] The Law Commission took the view that this provision is simply a reformulation of the provision in the old section 70(1)(g) of the

---

165 Thus, it would not have helped the lender in *Boland*, for Mrs Boland was undiscovered, not undiscoverable. In fact, it is debatable whether there were many cases under the 1925 legislation in which the actual occupation was truly undiscoverable, as opposed to undiscovered. See M Dixon, 'The reform of property law and the Land Registration Act 2002: A risk assessment' [2003] 67 Conv 136. The 'discoverability' of the actual occupation appears to have been conceded in *Bustard* (2010) as there is little discussion.

166 The question arises whether imputed actual knowledge will suffice, as where the purchaser's solicitor actually knew of the adverse right (assuming undiscoverable actual occupation) but failed to tell his client. Issues of professional ethics and good practice aside, it appears that such knowledge cannot be imputed because Schedule 3, paragraph 2(c)(ii) talks of the actual knowledge of 'the person to whom the disposition is made'.

167 Schedule 3, paragraph 2(b).

1925 Act and that it operates by way of estoppel.[168] Thus, the inquiry must be directed towards the right-holder and it is his or her non-disclosure that is the key.[169] However, the provision is not identically worded to that in the 1925 Act, for the proviso is added that non-disclosure will only result in a denial of overriding status where disclosure could 'reasonably have been expected' to be made. This obviously accepts that there will be some circumstances in which it is reasonable not to disclose and in which such non-disclosure does not destroy the efficacy of the overriding interest gained through actual occupation. An example is provided by *Begum* v. *Issa* (2014) where the judge held that even if an inquiry had been made of the right-holder at a family party (which was not proven), it would have been reasonable for her to decline to assert her interest (i.e. reasonable for her not to reveal it). It was, simply, not the right time or place for such a discussion and the right-holder should not lose overriding status for failing to disclose in such circumstances. Thus, in addition to those obvious cases where it would not be reasonable to expect disclosure on inquiry – for example, when dealing with persons under a legal or mental disability[170] – *Begum* makes it clear that the general circumstances in which the inquiry is made is also relevant. Further, might it also be the case that it is reasonable not to disclose where the right-holder realises that to do so increases the chances that they might lose their home?[171] Evidently, this qualification to paragraph 2, Schedule 3 can work against purchasers (especially mortgagees), so it would be wise for purchasers to make inquiries in a relatively formal way in order to protect themselves.

2.6.3.3 *Certain types of legal easements and profits – paragraph 3, Schedule 3*

Paragraph 3 of Schedule 3 concerns legal easements but, unlike its sister provision in Schedule 1 of the Act, the provision in Schedule 3 is not straightforward and requires care in its application. The matter is not helped by the elliptical language used to express what is, in effect, a good practical solution whereby fewer easements and profits will override a registered disposition than will at first registration.

The first point to note is that any easement that qualified as an overriding interest prior to the entry into force of the LRA 2002 continues to override irrespective of the provisions of the LRA 2002.[172] The 2002 Act looks forward to easements created after it entered into force. That said, as a general principle, paragraph 3 of Schedule 3 provides, first, that no equitable easement or profit will override and, second, that only *certain types* of legal easements and profits may override. All other easements and profits outside this

---

168 Under the 1925 Act, the inquiry had to be both as to the occupation and the existence of the occupier's rights (if any) – see *Bank of Scotland* v. *Qutb* (2009). This is clearly the position under the LRA 2002, Schedule 3.

169 Thus, a lie given by the legal owner of land does not prevent the interest of an equitable owner from being overriding.

170 In any event, such disclosure/non-disclosure may be without legal effect due to the disability.

171 For example, in the context of co-owned land, by encouraging the transferee to overreach or by the intended transferee requiring the current registered proprietor to take action to eject the occupier before the transfer takes place.

172 Schedule 12, paragraph 9 of the LRA 2002. This will include all legal easements and some equitable easements in existence at that date.

regime require deliberate protection by an entry on the register if their priority against a registered disposition is to be preserved. The key to understanding this is to appreciate that legal easements and profits *expressly* granted or reserved on or after 13 October 2003 out of a *registered title* are excluded from the category of overriding interest because their creation amounts to a registrable disposition under section 27(2)(d) of the 2002 Act.[173] As such, they are 'required to be completed by registration' in order to operate as legal interests: they must be substantively registered.[174] This means, that every expressly granted or reserved legal easement or profit out of a registered estate can be created *only* by an entry against the burdened title, which of course means that the interest has no need of being overriding because they are by definition on the register and protected. If they are not so completed by registration, they are equitable and equitable easements and profits are excluded by clear words from paragraph 3.[175]

In its turn, this means that the *only new* legal easements and profits capable of being overriding are either those expressly granted out of an estate that is not itself registered (e.g. a lease of seven years or less) or, more commonly, those that are impliedly granted.[176] In the former case, there is no title against which to register the interest and in the latter there is no express grant to register. Even then, however, not all of even this limited class may override. In addition to being either expressly created out of an unregistrable estate or being impliedly created, the legal easement will override if, but only if, any *one* of the following additional conditions are satisfied. These additional conditions are either:

- the easement is registered under the Commons Registration Act 1965;[177] or
- the legal interest is within the 'actual knowledge' of the person to whom the disposition is made; or
- the legal interest would have been 'obvious on a reasonably careful inspection' of the burdened land, which, as with the similar provision on 'actual occupation', is an objective test, not necessarily requiring additional inspections and enquiries to be made, but designed to ensure that only 'discoverable' burdens override a registered disposition; or
- the person entitled to the benefit of the legal interest 'proves that it has been exercised in the period of one year ending with the day of the disposition' over which it is said to take effect as an overriding interest. In reality, this is a safety net for those impliedly granted interests that, while not being known of or 'obvious' on a reasonably careful inspection, are nevertheless used for the benefit of the interest-holder.

---

173 But excluding interests capable of registration under the Commons Registration Act 1965: see section 27(2)(d) of the 2002 Act.

174 Section 27(1) of the LRA 2002.

175 Hence the failed attempt to suggest that equitable easements could be supported by actual occupation in *Chaudhary* v. *Yavuz* (2011).

176 This means easements created by prescription, necessity, common intention, the rule in *Wheeldon* v. *Burrows* or by application of section 62 of the LPA 1925. These methods of implied creation are discussed further in Chapter 7.

177 This applies to easements supporting rights of common – such as pasture. They are subject to the special regime of the Act.

It is apparent that paragraph 3 of Schedule 3 is not the clearest provision of the LRA 2002. Its purpose is, however, clear enough. Its effect is to ensure that all newly expressly created legal easements or profits are substantively entered on the register. Then, for easements within Schedule 3, the Act attempts to reach a compromise between ensuring their protection in the face of a registered disposition and the need for the purchaser to be aware of such interests before he completes his purchase. The qualifications to Schedule 3 are designed to ensure that only those rights either known about (including those known about via commons registration), obvious or useful take effect as overriding interests. In truth, however, it is likely that, in practice, Schedule 3 will capture virtually all qualifying legal easements, for there will be few that fall outside its provisions.[178]

2.6.3.4 Public–private partnership leases

This provision mirrors the identical provision in relation to Schedule 1. A PPP lease is not found explicitly in Schedule 3 to the LRA 2002 but is made an overriding interest against a registered disposition by reason of section 90(5) of the Act.

2.6.3.5 Other permanent overriding interests – paragraphs 4–9, Schedule 3

This block of overriding interests is the same as those taking effect under Schedule 1. Thus, they include customary rights (paragraph 4), public rights (paragraph 5), local land charges (paragraph 6) and mines and minerals (paragraphs 7–9).

2.6.3.6 Miscellaneous, time-limited, overriding interests – now expired

Paragraphs 10–14 and paragraph 16 of Schedule 3[179] contained the same miscellany of rights and interests that once overrode Schedule 1 but no longer do so. Under the provisions of section 117 of the LRA 2002, they ceased to override with effect from midnight on 12 October 2013. This means: first, that they continue to bind the present owner of the land (they have not become invalid, merely no longer overriding); but, second, that they will need to be protected by the entry of a Notice[180] in order to be effective against a purchaser of the registered title – section 29 of the LRA 2002 – unless they qualify as an overriding interest through the actual occupation provisions; third, whether protectively registered or not, they will bind a person who takes a transfer of the land not for value – section 28 of LRA 2002.[181]

---

178 For example, given the nature of easements, especially those impliedly created, very few will not have been exercised within one year of the disposition. We might wonder, then, whether any practical purpose is served in excluding interests under this elaborate provision.

179 Paragraph 16 in respect of the liability to repair the chancel of a church having been added by LRA 2002 (Transitional Provisions) (No. 2) Order 2003.

180 Prior to 13 October 2013, no fee was charged for registration of a Notice.

181 It remains to be seen whether a person who loses their right through these provisions may nevertheless apply for alteration of the register to record a late Notice.

2.6.3.7   *Interests no longer enjoying overriding status under Schedule 3: a summary*

As is evident from the above analysis, Schedule 3 to the 2002 Act both rationalises and restricts those unregistered interests which may override a registered disposition, going even further in this respect than Schedule 1. In consequence, there are a number of matters that now do *not* qualify as overriding interests. First, the rights of adverse possessors per se no longer qualify, but an adverse possessor who has completed adverse possession prior to 12 October 2003 has an entitlement to be registered as proprietor and this entitlement can override through discoverable actual occupation. Second, a person in receipt of rent and profits may not claim overriding status for their interest, although there are transitional provisions for those holding overriding interests by virtue of such receipt prior to the entry into force of the Act. Third, equitable easements created after the Act enters force will not override, although those that existed as overriding interests under the old law on 12 October 2003 will continue to do so. Fourth, not all legal easements and profits granted after the Act entered into force will override.[182] Expressly granted interests out of a registered estate must be completed by substantive registration and so have no need to override. Failing such completion, they will subsist as equitable interests. Impliedly granted legal easements and profits (and those granted out of an unregistered estate, such as a lease for seven years or less) can qualify if they meet any one of the qualifying criteria. Legal easements that overrode under the old law on 12 October 2003 will continue to do so. Fifth, in respect of possessory, qualified or good leasehold title, those matters 'excepted from the effects of registration' under the old section 70(1)(h) of the 1925 Act no longer override a registered disposition. Sixth, a miscellaneous category of rights ceased to override at midnight on 12 October 2013.

2.6.3.8   *Transitional provisions*

For the sake of clarity, it is worth reminding ourselves that the 2002 Act is not retrospective. Thus, although the definition and scope of overriding interests has changed under the LRA 2002, there is no intention to deprive overriding status to those rights that were in existence and which qualified as overriding interests under the old law on 13 October 2003 when the 2002 Act entered into force. Consequently, if the right qualified under the old law *on this date*, then its overriding status is preserved in the following cases: the rights of persons in actual occupation and in receipt of rents and profits under section 70(1)(g) of the LRA 1925; legal and equitable easements within section 70(1) (a) of the LRA 1925;[183] and legal leases of 21 years or less within section 70(1)(k).

However, the transitional provisions regarding adverse possessors are a little more complex. It has been indicated previously that Schedule 3 of the 2002 Act contains no specific provision for the rights of adverse possessors to override a registered disposition.[184] There is no equivalent of section 70(1)(f) of the LRA 1925, although of course many such possessors will be able to rely on their discoverable actual occupation within paragraph 2 of Schedule 3. However, there is an important transitional provision

---

182 Those that overrode before the Act will continue to do so.
183 See *Celsteel v. Alton House Holdings* (1985).
184 The same is true under Schedule 1.

concerning adverse possessors operating under Schedule 3. By virtue of Schedule 12, paragraph 18, of the LRA 2002, a person who, prior to the entry into force of the 2002 Act, had land held on trust for him under section 75(1) of the LRA 1925 – that is, a person *who had completed 12 years' adverse possession by that date* – 'is entitled to be registered as proprietor of the estate'. In effect, this means that a possessor who has completed the 12-year period of limitation under the old law of adverse possession before the entry into force of the 2002 Act does not have to submit to the new scheme of the LRA 2002 but may achieve registration through a simple application to HM Land Registry. This is perfectly acceptable. However, if the paper owner sells the land before the adverse possessor's entitlement is realised, the adverse possessor is at risk of losing his right to be registered as proprietor of the estate. In essence, the adverse possessor must seek registration as the new owner before any sale or must rely on being in discoverable actual occupation so as to claim an overriding interest.[185] Failing this, the adverse possessor will lose priority to the new registered proprietor.[186]

2.6.4 The duty to disclose: entering overriding interests on the register

Overriding interests are, by their nature, unregistered. If the interest becomes registered, it ceases to be overriding and takes priority instead from its entry on the register. This is likely to occur by reason of the duty of disclosure found in section 71 of the LRA 2002 under which an applicant for registration must disclose overriding interests of which he is aware so that they may be entered on the register by means of a Notice. However, failure to disclose does not destroy the overriding status of the right.[187]

Importantly, however, the registrar will not enter a Notice in respect of *all* matters that are disclosed because some interests are incapable of being protected by a Notice and others do not amount to a disclosable overriding interest. The first group is found in sections 33 and 90(4) of the Act and comprises: interests under a trust of land or a settlement under the SLA 1925;[188] leasehold estates granted for three years or less of the kind that are not required to be registered with their own title; restrictive covenants made between a lessor and lessee so far as they relate to the demised premises;[189] interests capable of being registered under the Commons Registration Act 1965; interests in any coal or coal mine within sections 38, 49 or 51 of the Coal Industry Act 1994; and PPP leases.[190] These interests are all protected by other means and their entry on the

---

185 If the period of adverse possession would finish after the entry into force of the 2002 Act, then the scheme of the 2002 Act applies in full – see Chapter 11. There is no saving for partly completed adverse possession.

186 It is not clear whether the adverse possessor can apply for rectification of the register against the new owner in these circumstances.

187 The provision is intended to encourage registration, not to penalise the right-holder if the owner of the burdened land does not disclose it.

188 The former, but not the latter, may be an overriding interest through actual occupation but both may be protected to some degree by the entry of a Restriction against dealings.

189 Note this represents a change in the law for a leasehold covenant relating to land *outside* the demise may now be registered by means of a Notice.

190 This last is found in section 90(4) of the Act.

register would serve no additional purpose – except perhaps to clog the register. The second group is non-disclosable under Rule 57 of the LRR and hence does not fall within the registrar's power to enter a Notice. It comprises a public right, a local land charge and a leasehold estate within Schedule 3, paragraph 1, but with one year or less to run.[191] They are excluded from the duty to disclose because they also are otherwise protected and would clog the register for no practical reason.

2.6.5 The 'bindingness' of overriding interests under the Land Registration Act 2002

The existence of overriding interests remains a vital element in the system of land registration under the 2002 Act. As the above sections illustrate, their definition is reasonably clear but certainly open to interpretation in some areas, particularly the 'actual occupation' and 'easement' provisions of Schedule 3. However, we now come to another important issue concerning overriding interests. If we are satisfied that a right falls within Schedule 3 and qualifies in principle as an overriding interest, when *precisely* will it be binding against a purchaser? To put it another way, it cannot be true that a new registered proprietor will be bound by *everything* that could be an overriding interest whenever that interest came into existence or whatever the circumstances. It would be harsh indeed if, say, a new owner was bound by overriding interests that came into existence *after* he had purchased the land, or if the new owner were bound even if the right-holder had promised expressly to waive the bindingness of his overriding interest. Consequently, the following principles determine the time at which the overriding interest must exist in order to bind a purchaser automatically and the circumstances in which agreement between the parties can remove their effect.

For all categories of overriding interest, the crucial date for determining whether the purchaser is bound by an overriding interest is the date on which the purchaser makes an application to register his title, being the date of registration (section 29). This necessarily raises the possibility of a 'registration gap'[192] if the overriding interest arose after the purchaser had completed the purchase, but before he was actually registered with title. This is particularly acute in relation to the 'actual occupation' provisions – given that a person with an interest might go in to occupation after a purchase but before registration of the title. Consequently, it is now settled that, while an overriding interest established under the actual occupation provision of Schedule 3 crystallises at the date of registration, a person cannot claim the benefit of the Schedule unless he has a proprietary right and is in actual occupation of the land at the time of the sale to the new owner or when he was granted the mortgage (*Abbey National Building Society v. Cann* (1991)).[193] This pragmatic decision effectively eliminates the 'registration gap' for 'actual occupation' overriding interests. It means, in practice, that a purchaser will not find the value or use of his land diminished by the emergence of a powerful adverse right in the interval between his purchase and the application for registration as the new proprietor.

---

191 For example, a five-year lease that has already run for over four years.

192 See *Barclays Bank* v. *Zaroovabli* (1997) under the LRA 1925.

193 Applied to the 2002 Act by *Scott v. Southern Pacific Mortgages* (2014). Note also the view in *Thompson v. Foy*, criticised above, that actual occupation also had to exist at the date of registration.

The proprietary right, and the actual occupation that invests it with the status of an overriding interest, must exist prior to completion of the purchaser's transaction so increasing the chances that it will be discovered in time for the purchaser to react accordingly.[194]

Second, the 'owner' of an overriding interest that would otherwise take priority over a new registered proprietor is able to waive voluntarily the priority given to their right by consenting to the sale or mortgage of the land over which the right exists.[195] Indeed, in some cases, this consent will be implied because of the conduct of the holder of the overriding interest (*Paddington Building Society* v. *Mendelson* (1985)), or perhaps even because the right holder is deemed to have authorised the purchase/mortgage (*Wishart* v. *Credit & Mercantile*). In fact, a right-holder who has consented to a particular purchaser having priority over his otherwise binding right (e.g. a mortgagee 'X') may be taken to have consented to the priority of a different purchaser who steps into his shoes (e.g. a re-mortgagee 'Y', whose monies pay off the first mortgage), at least to the extent of the monies provided by the original mortgagee even if in reality the right-holder did not know of the substitution (*Equity and Law Home Loans* v. *Prestridge* (1992)).[196]

Although the precise circumstances in which a right-holder will be deemed to have consented to, or authorised, the sale or mortgage of the land over which the overriding interest takes effect are unclear, it was thought that mere knowledge that a transaction concerning the land was proposed would not be enough. So, for example, the person with the overriding interest need not volunteer information concerning their position and would not be taken to have consented simply because the transaction proceeds around them and they remain silent – having not been asked. The requirement was thought to be one of consent to the sale or mortgage, not simple knowledge of it (*Skipton Building Society* v. *Clayton* (1993)). However, this principled position has been challenged by a surprising decision in *Wishart* v. *Credit & Mercantile* (2015) where the Court of Appeal held that an equitable owner who might otherwise have had an overriding interest *must* be taken to have authorised the legal owner (their trustee) to deal with the land and to have given priority to the mortgagee, even though the equitable owner had no clue that a mortgage was even contemplated. With respect, this seems at odds with all of the previous case law (e.g. the House of Lords in *Williams & Glyn's Bank* v. *Boland*) and virtually wipes out any chance that the right-holder could have an overriding interest in those cases where they most commonly arise – in trusts of land (see Chapter 4). It is a decision that is difficult to explain in terms of previous authority and it appears wrong in principle that a right-holder could be deemed to have given away priority to a purchaser they never knew existed.

Of course, *active* participation in organising the mortgage or encouraging a purchaser is rightly regarded as deemed or implied consent, but the uncertainty as to the boundary between implied consent and 'mere' knowledge (or no knowledge but deemed authorisation – *Wishart*) has led many purchasers (especially mortgagees) to require all occupiers to sign express consent forms waiving such rights they *might* have in favour of the mortgage.

---

194 This convenient solution would not be required under e-conveyancing, when completion of the purchase and its registration would take place simultaneously and electronically. There would be no registration gap.

195 Note the connection with 'undue influence' cases in the law of mortgages.

196 This might now be better thought of as an example of subrogation rather than implied consent.

This would seem to be perfectly adequate to protect the priority of the mortgage and it was exactly what the lender failed to do in *Wishart*.[197]

Finally, for the sake of clarity, it is trite law that a proprietary right may qualify as an overriding interest only if it actually *exists* before the sale, lease or mortgage (as the case may be – see *Scott* v. *Southern Pacific Mortgages*). This is not startling news, but it does mean, for example, that if it turns out that the alleged overriding interest is, for example, not a lease at all, but a licence, this licence can never be an overriding interest because licences are not capable of binding any third party, being merely personal rights. Likewise, even if the alleged overriding interest does exist as a proprietary right, it may be ineffective against a particular purchaser because of circumstances wholly unrelated to the operation of overriding interests per se. One such case has been considered above as where the purchaser gains the consent or authorisation of the potential holder of the overriding interest so ensuring that that particular purchaser can never be bound. Also, therefore, if the alleged overriding interest is given by a landowner who had no power to give it, in such cases the right cannot bind the purchaser because, vis-à-vis the purchaser, it does not exist. An example is *Leeds Permanent Building Society* v. *Famini* (1998), in which the alleged overriding interest (a tenancy) was created by a landowner who had no power to create it, having promised the purchaser (the bank, his mortgagee) that he would not do so. The bank could not be bound by the alleged overriding interest.

2.7 The Operation of Registered Land: Protected Registered Interests under the Land Registration Act 2002

A major aim of the 2002 Act is to ensure that as many proprietary rights as possible that affect a registered title should be entered on the register. The category of protected registered interests – formerly known as 'minor interests' under the LRA 1925 – implements this policy. As such, these rights are not substantively registrable titles, or substantively registrable mortgages (charges) and, by definition, are not unregistered interests which override. In practice, then, this group of interests usually comprises the rights of persons other than the owner, being typical third-party rights such as easements, restrictive covenants or options to purchase, and they may be legal or equitable. This is important because it emphasises that the role of these provisions of the LRA 2002 is to provide a means whereby most third-party rights can be protectively registered, both for the benefit of the right-holder and in order to alert any prospective purchaser of the land. Consequently, these are interests that must be protectively registered if they are to take priority over a purchaser.[198] They comprise interests that *cannot* amount to unregistered interests which override in any practical circumstances,[199] as well as interests that could override but could also be

---

197 In *Wishart*, the lender was misled by their own agent into thinking that there was no one in actual occupation and so did not seek express consent. But that is not the fault of the right-holder.

198 Section 29 of the LRA 2002.

199 For example, freehold covenants.

protectively registered.[200] The latter group includes those rights that are either entered on the register by the registrar of his own volition after examining the conveyancing documents or those that are disclosed under the duty of disclosure when a transferee applies to be registered as the new owner.[201] In all cases, however, registration can protect only an interest which is valid under the general law – section 32(3) of the LRA 2002. This is protective registration, not substantive registration and the entry of a Notice does not make an otherwise invalid interest, valid.

2.7.1   The mechanics of registration of interests: Notices

Protective registration of third-party interests under the LRA 2002 is relatively simple. There is only one type of entry that can protect an interest, albeit that there are two variants.[202] This is the Notice. In technical terms, a Notice is 'an entry in the register of the burden of an interest affecting a registered estate'[203] and will be entered in the 'charges' section of the registered title affected by it.[204] The interest holder makes the application to enter the Notice, and the owner of the burdened land is under no duty to do so.[205] Notices may be of two types: an 'Agreed Notice' or a 'Unilateral Notice' and, if the former, the entry in the register must give details of the interest protected.[206] Importantly, both types of Notice confer priority on the interest to which they relate if the interest is otherwise valid (section 29 of the LRA 2002, *A2 Dominion Homes Ltd* v. *Prince Evans Solicitors* (2015)). In other words, a transferee takes the title subject to the priority of the interest protected by the Notice, whether the Notice be Unilateral or Agreed. This means that the choice of which type of Notice to use depends ultimately on the circumstances in which the interest arose and the needs of the right-holder. In particular, Unilateral Notices should not be seen as a weaker form of protection for a third-party right.

In fact, the 2002 Act does not offer an exhaustive list of matters that may be protected by the entry of a Notice, but rather it specifies what may *not* be so protected.[207] However, it remains true that most examples of classic third-party interests in land may be protected by the entry of a Notice against the registered title. This includes, for example, a contract for sale with the current landowner prior to completion, an option to buy land or a right of first refusal (right of pre-emption), a restrictive covenant, including a covenant in a lease not relating to the demised premises,[208] a deed supplemental to a lease, a charging order

---

200 For example, a six-year legal lease.

201 As discussed below, not all third-party rights need be disclosed and so there are some rights that may not be protected by the entry of a Notice.

202 One might argue that the registrar's Notice – considered below – is a third variant. The use of the Restriction is considered below.

203 Section 32(1) of the LRA 2002.

204 Rule 84, LRR 2003, except that a bankruptcy Notice will be entered in the proprietorship register (section 86(2) of the LRA 2002).

205 *Signature of St Albans* v. *Wragg* (2017).

206 Rule 84(3), LRR 2003. If the Notice is Unilateral, the entry may give such details as the registrar considers appropriate (Rule 84(5), LRR 2003).

207 Section 33 of the LRA 2002.

208 For example, in relation to other premises owned by the landlord, such as other shop units in a commercial development.

charging the legal estate[209] and an equitable charge of the legal estate, easements, claims in proprietary estoppel and some leases granted for seven years or less. Nevertheless, as indicated, there are a number of interests that *may not* be protected by the entry of a Notice at all. Generally, these are interests more appropriately covered by the entry of a Restriction or those which qualify as overriding interests not subject to the duty of disclosure. They are a beneficial interest under a trust of land,[210] a settlement governed by the SLA 1925,[211] a leasehold for three years or less unless it is one of the special class of such short leases that are registrable with their own titles,[212] restrictive covenants made between lessor and lessee relating only to the demised premises,[213] an interest capable of being registered under the Commons Registration Act 1965,[214] certain interests in coal and coal mines[215] and PPP leases.[216] In respect of these interests, the registrar is not permitted to enter a Notice of any kind and the right-holder must rely on other means of protection – either that found in Schedules 1 and 3 concerning unregistered interests which override, by use of a Restriction or under the special statutory regime applicable to certain of these rights.[217]

2.7.2   Agreed Notices

Subject to the exclusions identified above, a person may apply for the entry of an Agreed Notice affecting a registered estate under section 34 of the LRA 2002. The registrar may only enter such a Notice following an application in three circumstances: first, where the applicant himself is the registered proprietor or a person entitled to be registered as the proprietor; second, where the registered proprietor or person entitled consents to the entry of the Notice; or, third, where the registrar is satisfied as to the validity of the applicant's claim. Consequently, although an Agreed Notice will often be the result of the action of the registered proprietor or be with his consent, it may be entered even if the underlying right is contested. Of course, the applicant must furnish evidence to satisfy the registrar that such a Notice should be entered and this will usually be proof of the registered proprietor's consent, or of the instrument that created the right, or a court order giving rise to the interest protected. It can, however, be any other 'evidence to satisfy the registrar as to the validity of the applicant's claim'.[218] Consequently, if an Agreed Notice is entered in circumstances in which the proprietor has not actually

---

209 A charging order charging a beneficial interest in the registered estate cannot be protected by a Notice as it is not a burden affecting a registered estate per se. A Restriction may be used in that case.

210 For example, a share of the matrimonial home: section 33(a)(i) of the LRA 2002. A Restriction should be used.

211 Section 33(a)(ii) of the LRA 2002. The provisions of the SLA 1925 operate.

212 Section 33(b) of the LRA 2002. Likely to override either as a legal lease for a term of seven years or less or by reason of actual occupation.

213 Section 33(c) of the LRA 2002. Enforceable at common law or under the LTCA 1995.

214 Section 33(d) of the LRA 2002. It should be so registered and may then qualify as an overriding interest.

215 Section 33(e) of the LRA 2002, referring generally to an interest in coal or a coal mine and specifically to sections 38, 49 and 51 of the Coal Industry Act 1994. These may override.

216 Section 90(4) of the LRA 2002. These will override.

217 For example, with leasehold covenants under the LTCA 1995.

218 Land Registration Rule 81(1)(c)(ii).

consented, he may dispute the entry by applying for its cancellation only after it has been entered. However, while the entry of an Agreed Notice preserves the priority of a valid right against a transferee,[219] it does not guarantee the validity of an interest if it emerges that the interest is void as being contrary to the general law.[220] For example, the priority of an equitable easement will be protected by the entry of a Notice, but if it should appear that the alleged 'easement' was void under the general law, its entry on the register cannot clothe it with validity. One cannot protect what does not exist.

Finally, we should also note that certain third-party rights are protectable only by means of an Agreed Notice. This group is a mixed bag of third-party interests not truly proprietary in character – at least in a classical sense – but clearly requiring protection for the right-holder. They are found in Rule 80 of the LRR 2003 and comprise matrimonial home rights under the Family Law Act 1996, a Revenue charge in respect of inheritance tax liability, a customary right, a public right, a variation of a lease effected by section 38 of the Landlord and Tenant Act 1987[221] and an interest arising pursuant to an order made under the Access to Neighbouring Land Act 1992. These are clearly rights of a more limited and surgical effect and are 'agreed' in the sense of being indisputable by the registered proprietor whether he actually consents or not.

2.7.3   Unilateral Notices

An application for the entry of a Unilateral Notice by a person claiming to be entitled to the benefit of an interest affecting the registered estate or charge may be made under section 34(2)(b) of the LRA 2002. In essence, it is an application for the entry of a Notice without consent, although the applicant must furnish HM Land Registry with some evidence that the right exists. Assuming the registrar agrees to enter such a Notice (but not otherwise), the registrar must give notice to the proprietor of the land affected, thus affording him the opportunity of challenging the Notice and putting the applicant to proof of the existence of the alleged right, although the cancellation procedure operates only after an entry has actually been made. Again, as with Agreed Notices, although the entry of a Unilateral Notice confers priority protection on the interest claimed, it does not guarantee the validity of that interest under the general law.[222] Should the interest be found subsequently to have been invalid, its registration will not preserve its priority against a transferee. The entry of a Unilateral Notice will identify the land or part thereof affected by the interest and (unlike an Agreed Notice) it will also identify the person entitled to the right under the Notice.[223]

2.7.4   Registrar's Notices

Although an application by an interest-holder is likely to be the most common method by which a Notice is entered on the register, the 2002 Act also stipulates a number of

---

219 Sections 28, 29 and 30 of the LRA 2002.

220 Section 32(3) of the LRA 2002.

221 Including amendments made under section 39(4) of that Act.

222 Section 32(3) of the LRA 2002.

223 Presumably, this means the person entitled to enforce the interest.

circumstances in which the registrar may, or must, make an entry. These Notices are neither Agreed nor Unilateral Notices per se, although the circumstances in which such an entry is possible make them equivalent to Agreed Notices in the sense that there is usually no doubt about the existence of the underlying right they protect. They might be thought of as 'registrar's Notices' although that term is not used by the Act. They may be entered in a number of varied circumstances. First, certain transactions must satisfy specified registration requirements if they are to take effect as registrable dispositions under the Act and these entries are made by the registrar.[224] Second, under section 37 of the Act, if it appears to the registrar that a registered estate is subject to an unregistered interest which overrides at first registration, he may enter a Notice in respect of that interest provided that the interest is capable of protection by means of a Notice. Third, at first registration of a registrable estate, the registrar will note against the title any interest that burdens the land provided that it is capable of protection by a Notice.[225] Fourth, the registrar may enter a Notice in respect of overriding interests within Schedule 1 or Schedule 3 (assuming they are protectable by Notice) that are disclosed at first registration or on a registered disposition (as the case may be) under the applicant's duty of disclosure within section 71 of the Act. Fifth, it seems that the registrar may enter a Notice in pursuance of his general power to alter the register within Schedule 4, paragraph 5, of the Act in order to correct a mistake, update the register or give effect to a right or interest otherwise excepted from the effect of registration.[226]

2.7.5 Which type of Notice? Agreed or Unilateral?

As indicated above, certain special kinds of interest must be protected by means of an Agreed Notice and thus the right-holder has no choice but to adopt this route to protection. Yet in many cases there will be a choice, and the applicant has to consider which form of Notice – Agreed or Unilateral – is the most appropriate. Once again, however, we can remind ourselves that there is no difference in the level of protection offered by an Agreed or Unilateral Notice. Both confer substantive priority protection on the interest to the extent that the interest is valid under the general law. Thus, Unilateral Notices are not like cautions under the 1925 LRA, which gave only procedural protection. In deciding which version of the Notice to use, a number of factors may be important. First, is the applicant in possession of the consent of the registered proprietor or of sufficient evidence to prove the existence of the claimed interest so as to secure an Agreed Notice? Second, does the applicant wish to establish the existence of his interest at the time of application to HM Land Registry (Agreed Notice), or is he content to wait to see whether the registered proprietor decides to accept or challenge the claimed interest, if ever (Unilateral Notice)? Third, does the applicant wish the identity of the interest-holder to be revealed in the register – as is required for a Unilateral Notice but not for an Agreed Notice? Fourth, and perhaps of significant practical importance, an application for an Agreed Notice will usually be accompanied by documents proving the interest: for example, the deed of grant or contract. These documents will form part of the public

---

224 Section 27 of the LRA 2002.

225 For example, protectable former land charges.

226 Superfluous entries may also be removed.

record and will be open to inspection by any person.[227] They may, however, contain sensitive information of a commercial or other kind and, while it is possible to apply for documents to be given exempt status (an 'exempt information document'), a Unilateral Notice avoids this problem as documents do not need to be lodged and thus cannot form part of the publicly available register.

2.7.6 Removing and cancelling an Agreed Notice or a 'registrar's Notice'

By its nature, a right protected by an Agreed Notice or a Notice entered by the registrar under his various powers is not likely to be contested by the registered proprietor, even if it originally was made without his consent on the basis of submitted evidence or was the result of a court order. Consequently, the Act does not provide a specific mechanism for challenging such entries – any doubt should have been resolved at the time the making of the entry was considered. Nevertheless, it is apparent that there will be cases in which the removal of an Agreed Notice or registrar's Notice is justified: for example, if the right was time-limited or has been waived. Consequently, the LRR provide a procedure for the cancellation of such a Notice and the application must be accompanied by evidence to satisfy the registrar that the interest has come to an end. This is effectively an administrative procedure permitting the cancellation of entries by reason of the determination of the underlying right. It is not a procedure to challenge the *validity* of a third-party right or to challenge whether the original entry was properly made. No such provision exists under the LRA 2002 and this does much to explain the true nature of Agreed and registrar's Notices.

2.7.7 Cancelling and challenging Unilateral Notices

By its very nature, the entry of a Unilateral Notice is more likely to be contentious because the underlying right is not necessarily admitted. Even so, the entry will secure priority for the right (if it is valid) and potential purchasers of the land may well be concerned by the registration of burdens that appear to affect the utility of the land they are just about to acquire. Consequently, there are two principal means by which a Unilateral Notice may be deleted from the register. First, the Unilateral Notice may be *removed* under section 35(3) of the Act; second, the Unilateral Notice may be *cancelled* under section 36 of the Act.

Removal of a Unilateral Notice under section 35 is effectively a non-contentious process for its withdrawal from the register. Application may be made only by the person registered as the beneficiary of the Notice (or the personal representative or trustee in bankruptcy of such person) and the registrar must remove the Notice if he is satisfied that the application is in order. On the other hand, cancellation of a Unilateral Notice under section 36 of the Act describes the process whereby the validity of the underlying right is challenged and the registered proprietor seeks the elimination of the Notice from the register. It is, in essence, a 'prove it or lose it' process, but only the registered

---

proprietor or the person entitled to be so registered may make the application.[228] In general terms, the application to cancel will cause the registrar to notify the person identified as the beneficiary of the Notice and that person will have a period of time to object to the cancellation of the Notice. Failure to object within the required period means that the registrar *must* cancel the Unilateral Notice. Clearly, however, the person entitled to the underlying right protected by the Unilateral Notice may well object to its cancellation, in which case the registrar will seek to resolve the matter between the parties and this may result in either the cancellation of the Notice or its retention as an Agreed Notice. Where the parties cannot agree, the matter will be referred to the land registration division of the Property Chamber of the First Tier Tribunal (formerly the Adjudicator to HM Land Registry).[229]

2.7.8   Enforcing registered protected interests

The aims of the system of registration for third-party interests are two-fold: to protect the interest in the event of a transfer of the land and to alert a prospective purchaser before he buys. Consequently, if a valid interest is protected in the proper way by entry on the register, it takes priority over the interest of any subsequent transferee *and* purchaser of the registered land: sections 28 and 29 of the LRA 2002. For this reason, an intending purchaser will usually request a search of the register in order to discover whether there are any registered adverse interests. Following this search, the prospective purchaser will enjoy a 'priority period' in which to apply for registration of his title. If an application to register title is made within this priority period, any newly registered interest (i.e. registered after the search was made) will not have priority to the purchaser. Any interests properly registered at the date the new owner applies for registration and not excluded by the priority period will be binding. It must be remembered, however, that, unlike unregistered land, it is the register itself that is conclusive. Thus, any registered interest that is not revealed because of an inaccurate search of the register remains binding on the purchaser because it is still entered on the register. In situations where a purchaser is prejudiced by an inaccurate search not of his own making, he may be entitled to an indemnity or may sue the registry in negligence.

The converse of this is that any third-party interest that is not registered in the appropriate manner loses its priority over the interest of a subsequent purchaser of the land who registers their title, unless it is saved for some other reason (e.g. as an overriding interest). It is vital to appreciate that this is the case whether or not the purchaser knew or should have known of the existence of that interest. In other words, the doctrine of notice is irrelevant because loss of priority is the penalty for lack of registration.[230] Of course, in the great majority of cases, the new owner of land will be a purchaser (as opposed to a recipient of a gift or devisee under a will) and he will seek security in a search of the register for registered interests. However, this is not quite the whole story and some qualifications to the 'loss of priority rule' do exist, these being cases in which

---

228 Section 36(1) of the LRA 2002. A person entitled must adduce evidence of his entitlement: Rule 86(2), LRR.

229 With effect from 1 July 2013. The Adjudicator became the Principal Judge for Land Registration and all functions and staff were mapped across without change.

230 Sections 29 and 30 of the LRA 2002.

an *unregistered* interest does in fact enjoy priority over the interest of a new owner of the land. As explained below, these situations occur for specific rather than general reasons and, consequently, whenever it is alleged that an unregistered interest binds a new registered proprietor, the facts of the case are likely to be crucial.

First, an unregistered interest may nevertheless qualify as an overriding interest within Schedule 3 to the Act, typically under the actual occupation provision but not exclusively so. In such a case, it may well take priority over the interest of the new owner but only because it is an overriding interest. A typical example is an equitable lease, which could be registered by means of a Notice, but which will usually take effect against a purchaser as an overriding interest because the tenant will be a person in discoverable actual occupation of the land.

Second, an unregistered interest (not qualifying as an overriding interest) remains valid against a person who is *not* a purchaser for value of the land: for example, the recipient (donee) of a gift, the recipient (devisee) under a will. This is the effect of the basic priority rule found in section 28 of the LRA 2002 – see *Halifax* v. *Popeck* (2008). In essence, such transferees acquire no greater right than their predecessor: if he was bound, so are they, irrespective of registration.

Third, an unregistered interest (not qualifying as an overriding interest) remains valid against a purchaser who does not register their title. In such cases, the new owner has not completed a registered disposition within sections 25 and 27 of the LRA 2002. As such, he obtains an equitable title only and the unregistered interest takes priority under the basic priority rule of section 28 – the first in time prevails. For example, imagine that an equitable mortgagee fails to protect his mortgage by means of a Notice, but the land over which the mortgage exists is sold to X. If X fails to register her estate, she has only an equitable title created after the equitable mortgage and thus ranking behind it. Of course, should X seek registration of her new estate, the equitable mortgage will cease to be effective against the land, unless it has by that time been registered or otherwise qualifies as an overriding interest.

Fourth, an unregistered interest (not qualifying as an overriding interest) remains valid against a purchaser who has expressly promised to give effect to that interest and thereby gains some advantage: for example, a lower price. In such cases, if it would be unconscionable for the purchaser to deny the validity of the unregistered interest, that interest will be held binding on the purchaser by means of a personal constructive trust (see *Lyus* v. *Prowsa Developments* (1982), approved in general in *Lloyd* v. *Dugdale* (2001)). It should be noted that this is an exceptional way in which an unregistered interest will be held to have priority (as made clear in *Chaudhary* v. *Yavuz* (2011)[231] and *Groveholt* v. *Hughes* (2012)[232]) and it depends entirely on the conduct of the particular purchaser against whom a remedy is sought. If, for example, that first purchaser was to sell the land on, the interest would then need to be registered in order to take effect against the second purchaser. In other words, this is a personal remedy against a particularly unconscionable purchaser. What amounts to 'unconscionable' conduct, so as to deny a purchaser the benefit of the priority rule necessarily, will vary from case to case. As mentioned previously, a purchaser who promises the vendor that he will honour an unregistered interest, and thereby obtains a lower price, will be held

---

231 Where the claim was denied and in which *Lyus* was described as a very unusual case, albeit correct on the facts.

232 The claim was again denied and the very exceptional nature of the doctrine stressed.

to his agreement (*Lloyd* v. *Dugdale* (2001)). Again, however, it is important to emphasise that we are looking for 'unconscionability' on the part of the purchaser, not that he has old-style 'notice' of the interest, as explained in *Miles* v. *Bull* (*No. 2*) (1969). So, a purchaser who knows of an adverse interest that is not registered and is keen to complete the purchase before it is registered, thereby securing a bargain, is not acting unconscionably simply because they have been able to take advantage of the provisions of the LRA 2002.

Fifth, an unregistered interest (not qualifying as an overriding interest) remains valid against a purchaser where the purchaser has knowledge of the interest *and* is relying on the statute in order to perpetrate a fraud. This is similar to the situation outlined above and is an example of the old equitable rule that 'equity will not permit a statute to be used as an instrument of fraud' – *De Lusignan* v. *Johnson* (1973) – meaning that a person cannot plead the rule in section 29 of the LRA 2002 as justification for their own fraudulent use of the land.[233] Again, the emphasis is not on the purchaser's knowledge or notice of the existence of the unregistered interest, but that the purchaser is attempting to use the statute to further a fraudulent design. Knowledge or notice of the unregistered interest per se does not make a purchaser fraudulent. In short, 'fraud' means more than acting on one's rights under the LRA 2002. It appears to include schemes deliberately designed to defeat unregistered interests, as in *Jones* v. *Lipman* (1962), in which the new registered proprietor who claimed to be free from the unregistered interest was in fact a company controlled by the former proprietor who had been bound by that interest. Likewise, a promise given to the right-holder to respect the right and therefore to discourage deliberately its protection by registration will amount to fraud.

2.8   Restrictions

Restrictions were in use under the LRA 1925 and they have been given an enhanced role in the LRA 2002. Although not chiefly designed to protect third-party interests directly, the entry of a Restriction may well have this effect by controlling the registered proprietor's ability to sell the land or otherwise deal with it – see section 23 of the LRA 2002. In such cases, the third-party right is protected because the Restriction may prevent a disposition of the land. However, Restrictions are not chiefly about third-party right protection – that is what Notices are for – and are more directly concerned with preventing all manner of dealings with the estate by the registered proprietor by preventing entries on the register that do not comply with the terms of the Restriction. In essence then, the Restriction is a form of entry that places limitations on the registered proprietor's powers over the land. These limitations may be for specific events or specific periods, and may place the limiting power in the hands of others – as where another person's consent is required to a dealing with a registered title. Alternately, the Restriction can be of a general or universal nature.[234] A Restriction is entered in the proprietorship section of the register and will ensure that no dealings with the registered title can occur until the conditions specified in the Restriction are complied with.

---

233 See also *HSBC* v. *Dyche* (2009), in which the purchaser was relying on section 2 of the LPA 1925 to commit a
      fraud in the context of overreaching.

234 Section 40 of the LRA 2002.

Section 42 of the LRA 2002 sets out the registrar's general power to enter Restrictions[235] and section 43 establishes who may make an application for an entry. Given that Restrictions may be used in a wide range of circumstances, Schedule 4 to the LRR lists 'standard-form' Restrictions that are intended to cover the most common situations in which a Restriction might be required. HM Land Registry encourages use of standard-form Restrictions by making the application process smoother and cheaper than if a non-standard Restriction is applied for. Typical examples of when a Restriction might be required are where an equitable owner wishes to ensure that a sale of co-owned land is made by two trustees, thereby triggering overreaching,[236] or where a person with an option to buy the land wishes to control the registered proprietor's ability to sell the land to someone else. Restrictions are also vital in cases of bankruptcy to prevent dealings with the land that might defeat the interests of creditors. Importantly, a Restriction may be entered even though the substantive right is protected by a Notice. For example, a person with an option to buy the land might well protect that option by means of a Notice and, in addition, seek a Restriction to prevent the proprietor actually breaking the contract by selling to another.

2.9 The Operation of Registered Land: Overreaching

Throughout the above analysis, especially when considering whether and how a third-party right might be protected on a transfer of registered land, repeated reference has been made to the concept of overreaching. The following section will analyse the concept of overreaching and explain how it fits into the registration system. As will be seen, it is a process whereby rights that would otherwise be binding against a purchaser according to the rules of registered land will not be so binding because of this 'statutory magic'. As a preliminary, it is also important to realise that 'overreaching' is not actually a creation of the LRA 1925 or LRA 2002; it also operates in unregistered land and in a similar fashion. It will continue to operate in much the same way under the LRA 2002 as it did under the LRA 1925. This is explained in the following sections.

Overreaching is a process whereby certain *equitable* rights in land that might otherwise have enjoyed protection in the system of registration on the occasion of a sale of that land to a purchaser for value are 'swept off' the land and transferred to the purchase money that has just been paid. When this occurs, the equitable rights are said to be 'overreached' and no longer bind the purchaser, even though they might have fitted exactly into the category of overriding interests.[237] Overreaching is, in effect, a method of promoting the alienability of land by removing certain equitable rights from the land and recasting them as a monetary

---

235 In some situations, the registrar must enter a Restriction.

236 See below. Consequently, the application for a Restriction – standard Form A – can be used as a method of establishing an equitable interest in another person's land because such a Restriction cannot be entered unless such an interest exists. Likewise, it prevents a sole legal owner from disposing of the land to the potential detriment of the equitable owner. It is also likely to deter potential buyers until the underlying issue is dealt with, thereby indirectly protecting the equitable interest.

237 These rights cannot be protected by the entry of a Notice; see above.

equivalent. Note, however, that not all equitable rights can be 'swept off' the land by over-reaching. The rights that are capable of being overreached are: first, those equitable rights that exist behind a trust of land, being those equitable ownership rights that exist when the land is co-owned (see Chapters 4 and 5) and which have a readily identifiable monetary value. This is the main category. Second, as a result of clarification provided by recent case law, certain other equitable rights such as the equity to set aside a transfer as being uncon-scionable, some proprietary estoppels and possibly the alleged 'right' to have the register rectified in the event of a mistake.[238] The crucial point is, then, that if overreaching occurs, a right that would have been protected against a purchaser ceases to be so protected, irrespec-tive of whether it would have been an overriding interest under the LRA 2002. Overreaching is the purchaser's trump card, but conditions must be met before overreaching can occur.

2.9.1   The right must be capable of being overreached

The first condition is that the equitable right must be of the kind that is *capable* of being overreached. Not all equitable rights are 'overreachable' and so the trump card can be played only in defined circumstances. Overreachable equitable rights are defined in section 2 of the LPA 1925 and, in essence, are equitable co-ownership rights existing behind a trust of land – as in *City of London Building Society* v. *Flegg* (1998)[239] (including equit-able interests existing behind a strict settlement[240]) or certain other equitable interests as identified in *Mortgage Express* v. *Lambert* and *Bakrania* v. *Lloyds Bank* (the equity to have a trans-action set aside for unconscionability, certain estoppels and the alleged 'right' to have the register when there is a mistake). Consequently, equitable interests such as the equitable easement and equitable lease can never be overreached and will bind a purchaser of the registered land (or not) according to the rules of registered land just discussed.

2.9.2   The statutory conditions for overreaching must be fulfilled

The second condition is that the statutory preconditions for overreaching must be ful-filled. These are that there must be a conveyance of a legal estate made by those persons and in those circumstances that together constitute an overreaching transaction (section 2(1) of the LPA 1925). In general terms, the relevant 'conveyance' is either a sale, lease or mortgage of a legal estate that is completed by substantive registration, although recent case law may have extended this.[241] In terms of the relevant factual situations where overreaching may occur, we should consider four possibilities, although the first is the one most frequently encountered.

---

238 *Mortgage Express* v. *Lambert* (2016), *Bakrania* v. *Lloyds Bank* (2017). The identification of these rights as overreachable is relatively recent and not without difficulty. That they are overreachable seems justified on a careful reading of section 2 LPA 1925, but it is difficult to see how they can be expressed in monetary terms for the benefit of the right holder – which is one of the purposes of overreaching.

239 See Chapter 4.

240 See Chapter 5.

241 *Baker* v. *Craggs* (2016) decides that the grant of an express legal easement, properly substantively registered, counts as a conveyance of a legal 'estate'. This is based on a reading of the difficult section 1(4) LPA and is controversial, for an easement is not usually regarded as an 'estate'. The case is under appeal at the time of writing.

The first circumstance is that the transaction is made by at least two trustees (or a trust corporation being a limited company of £250,000 capital) exercising valid powers under a trust of land, usually in a co-ownership situation.[242] The trustees will be the legal owners of the land. The need for two trustees (legal owners) is a statutory requirement and has no relevance other than that this is the minimum number required. As we shall see in Chapter 4, the maximum number of trustees of land is four, so that if there are four trustees, all four must concur in the transaction (and likewise if there are three, etc.). The most common transactions effected by the trustees that will overreach any equitable co-owners are either the simple sale to a purchaser or the execution of a mortgage in return for funds. If there is a conveyance (e.g. mortgage or sale) the new registered proprietor will have overreached the equitable owners and may evict them; if there is a mortgage, the mortgagee's interest will have priority over that of the equitable owners and so, in the event that the land is sold, the mortgagee will have priority and be paid first.

As noted, the sale/mortgage in a co-ownership situation is the most common type of overreaching transaction and it will be discussed in Chapter 4. At this stage, it is noteworthy that section 2 of the LPA 1925 appears to assume that overreaching occurs when the sale proceeds (either from sale proper or monies advanced by mortgage) are *actually* paid to the two (three or four) trustees. This is quite natural as the rationale for overreaching and its ability to release a purchaser from otherwise binding rights is that the equitable owners take a share of the money in 'compensation' for the loss of their right to the land. However, as became clear in *State Bank of India v. Sood* (1997), many trustees will take out a mortgage of registered land not in order to receive immediate monies, but to guarantee future borrowings from the bank, perhaps to finance a business venture. In these cases, no money is actually paid over even though there is an overreaching transaction by two or more trustees. Consequently, the question that arose in *Sood*, apparently for the first time, was whether this type of transaction is an overreaching transaction so as to give the bank priority over any equitable rights. The answer is that it is. The Court of Appeal decided that, under section 2(1)(ii) of the LPA 1925, if capital monies were to be paid as a result of a conveyance by the trustees, those monies would actually have to be paid to two trustees to overreach. However, if capital monies did not arise on a transaction (as in the case of a mortgage to secure future borrowings), a conveyance by two trustees would overreach the equitable owners by mere execution of the conveyance. The Court reached this conclusion through a generous interpretation of section 2(1)(ii) of the LPA 1925 – the overreaching section. Effectively, the Court decided that if money is *payable* on the transaction, it must be paid to two trustees; if money is not payable, overreaching occurs so long as the mortgage is properly executed. This interpretation was bolstered by two policy considerations: first, that the aim of the overreaching machinery is to encourage the free alienability of co-owned land and this should be protected; and, second, that, although the point in this case had not been decided before, many lenders had agreed to these types of mortgages and to have held in this case that they did not overreach because no capital monies

---

242 Thus, overreaching will not occur, despite a transaction by two trustees, if this is to perpetrate a fraud – HSBC v. *Dyche* (2009), in which the 'sale' by A and B to A alone was in pursuit of a fraudulent design that if permitted would have destroyed the priority of C's equitable interest.

changed hands would be most unfortunate. These are compelling reasons because, although the argument that existing commercial practice assumed the law to be as stated in *Sood* is not an attractive one, it is realistic. On the other hand, apart from the absence of any authority for this decision, there are two real difficulties: first, that the words of section 2(1) of the LPA 1925 really do seem to contemplate the actual payment of money as a precondition for overreaching (even if they did not mean to); second, and more importantly, that overreaching can be justified as a matter of principle because the equitable owners' interests take effect in the money paid to the trustees. That is why the equitable interests can so easily be swept off the land. If overreaching can occur without the payment of such monies – because two trustees have charged the land for future debts – what protection/benefit is there for the equitable owners? Where do they get their *quid pro quo* for suffering overreaching? There is no capital money for them to take a share of, or if it was represented as credit at the bank, it is likely to have been spent by the time the case comes to trial. In other words, *Sood* is almost certainly correct, but for reasons of practice not principle.

The second situation in which overreaching can occur is where the transaction is made under the provisions of the SLA 1925 relating to the operation of strict settlements (Chapter 5). As we shall see, a strict settlement is, in simple terms, a device for ensuring that land is given to X for life, thence to Y. There are 'trustees of the settlement' who will not be X or Y, but X (the life tenant) or the trustees may have power to deal with the land (e.g. sell it) and this transaction can be an overreaching transaction, sweeping the interests of Y into the proceeds of sale. Settlements will become increasingly rare due to the inability to create new strict settlements after 31 December 1996.[243]

The third situation in which overreaching is possible is where the transaction is made by a mortgagee (e.g. a bank or building society) or personal representative of a deceased owner in exercise of their paramount powers to deal with the land, provided of course that the powers are indeed paramount to the interests of any co-owners.[244]

The fourth situation is that overreaching may occur if the transaction is made under an order of the court: for example, under section 14 of the TOLATA 1996. Any order of the court transferring the land to a third party, or directing that it should be sold, necessarily effects an overreaching transaction for the benefit of the transferee or purchaser, although the beneficial owner's interest is likely to be satisfied first out of the proceeds of such sale.

2.9.3   The consequences of failing to overreach

It is only if all of the above conditions are satisfied that an overreaching transaction occurs. The existence of an overreachable right is simply a question of fact and rarely gives rise to problems. However, what is more common is failure to ensure that a proper

---

243 Section 2 of the TOLATA 1996.

244 In this situation, the mortgagee must prove that its mortgage ranks first in priority, which means that it must either have the consent of the owners or have *already* overreached the equitable interests by being paid to two legal owners. If it does, then it may sell. This example of overreaching refers to a different situation – the sale by a mortgagee who already has the ability to sell and it overreaches both the legal and the equitable interests of the borrowers.

overreaching transaction has occurred, thereby denying the purchaser the trump card and preventing the overreachable equitable interests from being swept off the title into the purchase money. Usually, this is a result of a failure to pay the purchase money to two trustees as required in the most common type of overreaching transaction, as in *Boland*. Should there be a failure to overreach, there are two possibilities to consider.

First, if the equitable interest constitutes an overriding interest,[245] the purchaser will be bound by the interest and his use of land restricted accordingly (section 29 of the LRA 2002). Thus, a mortgagee may not be able to exercise their remedies and may not recover all of the money it has lent on the security of the land. In fact, as in *Boland*, on most occasions there will be an overriding interest because the equitable owner will be in discoverable actual occupation within paragraph 2, Schedule 3 of the LRA 2002. After all, the land is likely to be their home.

Second, if the equitable interest is not protected as an overriding interest, the purchaser who registers his title takes the land free of that interest (section 29 of the LRA), although a person who is not a purchaser remains bound by the interest (section 28 of the LRA 2002). This is not surprising, being simply an example of the priority rules referred to above. Note again, however, that it is possible for an equitable owner to enter a Restriction against the title – a standard Form A Restriction – preventing a sale by only one legal owner.[246]

It sometimes causes surprise that even a purchaser who fails to overreach may still take the title free from the priority of the relevant equitable interest. This can be understood more clearly if it is remembered that overreaching is an exceptional process – like a trump card – that frees the purchaser from the normal rules of registered (or indeed unregistered) conveyancing by providing an automatic priority over certain equitable interests. If the trump card fails, the normal rules of registered conveyancing come back into play. Hence, the equitable interest may still be unenforceable against the purchaser if it is not protected as an overriding interest. To sum up, then, overreaching is a special procedure and it can nullify the proprietary status of certain equitable interests in certain specified circumstances. When it works, these equitable interests are transferred to the purchase price of the land and cannot affect a purchaser. When it fails, the rules of registered land take effect in the normal way.

2.10 Alteration of the Register

It is a central tenet of the land registration system that the register should be as accurate as possible so that it can be relied on by all persons intending to deal with the land. Thus, the registration of persons as registered proprietors and the due entry of registered charges, Notices and Restrictions should be free from error. Of course, this is the ideal but, in practice, faults in the registration process and registrations based on incomplete

---

245 Remember, under the LRA 2002, a Notice cannot be entered in respect of such an interest.

246 It seems unlikely that an equitable owner can enter a Restriction preventing a sale by two legal owners because, if it were possible, it would provide a means of preventing overreaching. The author's view is that such a Restriction – a non-standard Restriction – is possible if ordered by the court under section 14 of the TOLATA. However, *Coleman v. Bryant* (2007) suggests that such a Restriction would never be ordered.

or inaccurate evidence do occur. Indeed, registrations based on fraudulent or negligent transactions are also a possibility.[247]

Consequently, the LRA 2002 establishes a statutory scheme to deal with changes to the register and the correction of mistakes. In broad terms, section 65 of the LRA 2002, operating through Schedule 4 of the LRA 2002, establishes the circumstances in which it is possible to make an 'alteration' to the register and this is complemented by a power to give an indemnity (compensation) under Schedule 8 of the LRA 2002 when a person suffers loss by reason of a mistake in the register, whether or not that mistake is corrected.[248] This scheme, which is a substantial improvement on that established by the LRA 1925,[249] allows alterations by either the court or the registrar (as the case may be) while at the same time seeking to ensure that the integrity of the register is not compromised by allowing widespread and wide-ranging alterations to be made. In this vein, it is important to appreciate that genuine errors by HM Land Registry in the input or understanding of information are rare, and that most claims for alteration arise from apparently proper applications based on false information offered by the applicant himself, either accidentally or deliberately. An example of the latter is *Gold Harp Properties* v. *Macleod* (2014), where the mistake in the register was caused entirely by the wrongful removal of a lease based on false information provided by an applicant.

2.10.1   General conditions for altering the register

Schedule 4 of the LRA 2002 establishes the circumstances in which the register may be altered either by the court or by the registrar. These are effectively four in number: first, in order to correct a mistake; second, to bring the register up to date;[250] third, to give effect to any estate, legal right or interest that is excepted from the effect of registration;[251] and, fourth (being a power exercisable only by the registrar), to remove superfluous entries.[252] The last three of these situations cover what might loosely be regarded as administrative alterations arising from the normal operation of the register or of property transactions. For example, the register might be brought up to date to reflect a change in the corporate name of the proprietor, to reflect a voidable transaction that has been avoided, or an entry relating to a good leasehold title might be added, or

---

247 See *Pinto* v. *Lim* (2005), in which a person got themselves registered as sole proprietor by fraud – a forged signature – and then sold the land to an innocent third party.

248 See section 2.11 below.

249 Under the LRA 1925, all cases of alteration were known as 'rectification'. Under the LRA 2002, 'rectification' means a special kind of alteration, being one that corrects a mistake and which prejudicially affects the title of a proprietor and so could give rise to an indemnity.

250 E.g. *NRAM* v. *Evans* (2017) where changing the register to reflect a voidable transaction that had been avoided was regarded as an 'updating' rather than the correction of a mistake. Contrast *Knightsbridge Property Development* v. *South Chelsea Properties* [2017] EWHC 2730 (Ch).

251 That is when the grade of title was good leasehold, possessory or qualified and so certain matters (according to which grade) were unaffected by the registration of the proprietor with this title.

252 Paragraphs 2 and 5, Schedule 4 of the LRA 2002.

time-expired entries might be removed as superfluous. Consequently, the most serious ground of alteration is really the first of these: the correction of a mistake.[253]

The LRA 2002 effectively introduces two categories of alteration that may be made in order to correct a mistake. First, there are those alterations that correct a mistake and that do not *prejudicially* affect the title of a registered proprietor. Applications for these 'harmless' corrections of a mistake reflect the idea that the register should be capable of being changed relatively easily if no-one would be prejudiced thereby. Where there is occasion to carry out a simple alteration, the court 'must' order the alteration unless the circumstances are exceptional,[254] whereas the *registrar* 'may' do so.[255] In contrast, the correction of a mistake that does or could prejudicially affect the title of a registered proprietor is much more serious. These are known as 'rectifications' and are subject to special rules. Both the registrar and the court have the jurisdiction to order a rectification and, *where the conditions of the statute are met*, both must do so unless there are exceptional circumstances justifying a refusal.[256]

2.10.2   Rectification

Rectification is a special class of alteration of the register and its importance lies in the fact that it is the principal ground on which an indemnity may be claimed. Rectification thus arises when there is (1) the correction of a mistake and (2) this would prejudicially affect the title of a registered proprietor.[257] Importantly, both limbs of the definition must be established before 'rectification' is possible.

First, in connection with the meaning of 'mistake', it is clear that a 'mistake' does not imply fault on any person's part, or on the part of HM Land Registry. It is used in a descriptive not a judgmental sense. So, if an innocent person is registered as a proprietor following a purchase from X, but it transpires that X fraudulently acquired the title from Y, there has been a 'mistake' in the register because Y should have been the proprietor and this 'mistake' existed not only when the fraudster acquired title through wrongful registration, but also when the innocent purchaser was registered with it.[258] The mistake

---

253 It seems that the 'mistake' to be corrected does not have to be in the register or be a consequence of the operation of the land registration system. Thus, in *Cygnet Healthcare v. Greenswan* (2009), the court ordered rectification where the 'mistake' was a failure in the parties' conveyancing transaction. HM Land Registry registered what it was given, but the parties had failed to ensure that an intended covenant was ever created. It is not clear if the power in Schedule 4 is meant to be available to deal with mistakes by the parties, as opposed to mistakes within the system. However, the statute itself is silent as to this.

254 Rule 126, LRR 2003.

255 See paragraph 5, Schedule 4 LRA 2002. Even though these are non-prejudicial corrections, a person may well wish to see the register altered and, presumably, if the registrar refuses to alter (but it is difficult to envisage why he would), an application can be made to the court.

256 Paragraphs 3 (court) and 6 (registrar), Schedule 4 of the LRA 2002. In *Paton v. Todd* (2012), Morgan J explains that the court or registrar must consider whether the circumstances are 'exceptional' first by identifying what those circumstances might be and why they are exceptional and, second, how they would impact on the parties if there were, or were not, to be a rectification.

257 Paragraph 1, Schedule 4.

258 *Pinto v. Lim* (2005).

is the error in the register that omits Y as proprietor – how it was caused or by whom does not stop it being a mistake. Likewise, there is a 'mistake' if the facts underlying an application to the registrar turn out to be false. So, in *Baxter v. Mannion* (2011), an adverse possessor was registered as proprietor following failure by the previous proprietor to object to his (the adverse possessor's) application. It transpired, however, that the adverse possessor had not in fact completed ten years' adverse possession[259] sufficient to justify an application to be registered in the first place.[260] Hence, there was a 'mistake' which could trigger rectification, even though the rules of registration themselves had been applied correctly.[261] Similarly, in *Gold Harp*, a lease was removed from the registered title of a freehold because of a false claim that it (the lease) had been ended by forfeiture. The absence of the lease from the register was a 'mistake' that could (and did) lead to rectification. Furthermore, it is now clear that a mistake in an earlier transaction necessarily means that later transactions concerning the same title are also, in this technical sense, 'mistaken' – *Gold Harp v. Macleod, Bakrania v. Lloyds Bank* (2017).[262] This, if B acquires A's registered title by mistake (say a fraud), B's later mortgage to C, or sale to D, is also mistaken for the purpose of the rectification provisions. This does not mean that the later transactions will be undone through rectification, only that the court has the power to do so if the appropriate conditions are satisfied. So, an initial mistake taints all subsequent dealings, although it does not necessarily mean that subsequent dealings will be 'rectified'. Note, in one respect 'mistake' is narrowly construed. If a voidable transaction is entered on the register, it is of course valid (it exists, but it is liable to be undone). If later, the voidable transaction is disavowed – that is it is 'avoided' by the person who has the right to do so – the register can be amended to reflect the fact that the transaction is no longer valid. However, this is not the correction of a 'mistake', because the transaction was valid when it was entered on the register. Rather, it is an example of bringing the register up to date – *NRAM v. Evans* (2017).[263]

Second, it is likely that any proposed correction of a mistake that affects the value of the land or removes land from a title or results in the removal or addition of a registered proprietor is 'prejudicial' within the meaning of the Schedule.[264] However, this will not be the case where the proposed changes merely recognise a pre-existing boundary that

---

259 See Chapter 11.

260 Leave to appeal to the Supreme Court in *Baxter* was refused. See also *Walker v. Burton* (2013) where the proprietors had been registered as owners of a large area of moorland (the 'Fell'), but this had been a mistake, because in fact the Fell probably 'belonged' to the Crown. No rectification was ordered, although the Crown was not party to the proceedings.

261 There remains controversy over what amounts to a 'mistake' and how far the mistake runs. Does an initial mistake operate to taint all subsequent transactions with the land, so that all could be rectified in favour of the original owner – *Baxter, Ajibade v. Bank of Scotland plc, Knights Construction (March) Ltd v. Roberto Mac Ltd* – or does it only concern the initial transaction and not taint all that follows so that the original owner cannot rectify against subsequent innocent transferees – *Barclays Bank v. Guy Stewart v. Lancashire Mortgage Corporation*?

262 As a decision of the property tribunal, *Bakrania* does not constitute binding precedent, but it contains a review of the relevant authorities.

263 Consequently, there is no power to 'alter' or 'rectify' the register and an indemnity cannot be paid.

264 See *Cygnet Healthcare v. Greenswan* (2009); *Walker v. Burton* (2013).

has been incorrectly shown on the register – *Drake v. Fripp* (2011).[265] Also, an alteration made to give effect to an existing overriding interest can never be a 'rectification' because it does not prejudicially affect the title of the registered proprietor, because it (the overriding interest) was already binding on that proprietor and the alteration merely openly recognises a pre-existing state of affairs.[266]

If these preliminary matters are resolved in the applicant's favour, it is then possible that the register can be rectified. But it is not automatic, because the register can be rectified against a registered proprietor in *possession* only in certain circumstances.[267] If those circumstances do not exist, rectification cannot be ordered against a proprietor in possession. This is a vital provision, for it demonstrates the fundamental policy of the LRA 2002 that, save in special circumstances, the register is conclusive and should protect the title of registered proprietors, particularly those in possession of the land. In this sense, possession means physical possession of the land,[268] although such possession may exist through the agency of others, such as where the registered proprietor's possession exists through the physical presence of his tenant, mortgagee, licensee or beneficiary.[269] It is also clear that the required degree of control necessary to qualify as 'possession' will vary according to the type of land – *Walker v. Burton* (2013), where possession was established over moorland by relatively low-level acts of use and control. The special circumstances in which a proprietor in possession can find themselves subject to a rectification are three-fold: first, if the registered proprietor consents; second, if the registered proprietor has caused or substantially contributed to the mistake because he has either been fraudulent or not exercised sufficient care; or, third, if it would be unjust not to order the rectification: paragraphs 3 (court) and 6 (registrar), Schedule 4. Importantly, these are now the only circumstances in which rectification may be ordered against a proprietor in possession.[270]

It is obvious that rectification may be ordered 'against' a proprietor in possession if he consents, and so too where he is responsible for the mistake on which the claim for rectification is based,[271] although it seems that the ground is still available even if the applicant for rectification was also partly responsible for the mistake.[272] The third

---

265 This echoes *Derbyshire CC v. Fallon* (2007), where the court decided that a proposed change to the register did not prejudicially affect the Fallons' title (and so was only an alteration) on the ground that if the land was not theirs on a 'true' appreciation of their title, any change to remove the land from their registered title merely reflected preregistration reality and so did not affect them prejudicially. We need to be careful, however, not to take this too far. We must not ignore the fact that the register is the conclusive title (section 58 of the LRA 2002) and that it is not permissible to introduce unregistered land concepts of title into decisions concerning registered title.

266 But note, if there has been a fraud, then the proprietor affected by the overriding interest may still be able to claim an indemnity, *Swift 1st v. Chief Land Registrar* (2015) and see below section 2.11.

267 The majority of applications for rectification will be against such a person. Where rectification is against a person not in possession, these additional conditions do not apply: *Farooq v. Kensington Mortgage Company* [2017] UKFFT 230 (PC).

268 Section 131 of the LRA 2002; *Walker v. Burton* (2013).

269 But not through an adverse possessor.

270 The arguably more flexible jurisdiction of the 1925 LRA has not been repeated – see *Kingsalton v. Thames Water* (2001) and *Pinto v. Lim* (2005).

271 *Rashid v. Rashid* (2017).

272 This appears to have been the reason in *Cygnet Healthcare v. Greenswan* (2009).

condition must, however, be approached with some care. Under the LRA 1925, a similar provision was held *not* to imply a general power to rectify merely because it was thought just and equitable to do so.[273] In one sense, it will always be 'unjust' not to correct a mistake in the register – after all, it is a mistake and this appears to be the view taken in *Baxter v. Mannion* (2011) where it was apparently a matter of 'simple justice' to order rectification. However, as *Walker v. Burton* (2013) and *Patel v. Freddy's* make clear, this is not a general power to disturb the title of a proprietor in possession and the existence of a mistake does not, itself, make it 'unjust' not to rectify. Rather, the applicant seeking rectification must show why it would be unjust not to rectify in light of the mistake.[274] It is relevant whether that applicant has themselves been dispossessed and the degree to which the registered proprietor has relied on the registration and dealt with the land. Thus, this provision can be regarded as a failsafe where, despite being in possession and *not* consenting and *not* contributing to the mistake, the registered proprietor's title might still be rectified. A good example is provided by *Rees v. Peters* (2011), whereby the mistake was in the omission of registration of a restrictive covenant against the title and mere compensation for losing the benefit of the covenant would not adequately protect those claiming rectification – hence it would be 'unjust' not to rectify.[275] On the other hand, neither must we forget that the registration system should protect the innocent possessory proprietor, or else what is the guarantee of title worth?[276]

Having thus established that there is a case for rectification, and that either the rectification is not against a registered proprietor in possession or that one of the three exceptions applies, both the court and the registrar *must* order rectification, unless there are exceptional circumstances that justify not making the alteration.[277] This is intended to ensure that, once the claimant goes through all of the hoops of establishing a claim for rectification, that rectification should normally take place. What 'exceptional circumstances' might be is as yet unclear, but the key word is 'exceptional' rather than 'unusual' or 'equitable' or 'fair'. It is a high hurdle and it is to be anticipated that most applications for rectification that progress to this point will be ordered.[278] If rectification is ordered, the court or registrar will do that which is necessary to correct the mistake. Thus, in *Gold Harp*, the court ordered that the mistakenly removed lease be re-entered on the register of the superior title. It did this – quite properly – even though it meant that a person who had acquired the land when the lease was not registered, now found themselves subject to the reinstated lease. Although this rectification altered the priorities – by giving

273 *Norwich & Peterborough Building Society v. Steed* (1992).

274 Perhaps *Baxter* is an unusual case – it would be very odd if the adverse possessor in that case could have kept title.

275 Leave to appeal to the Supreme Court in *Rees v. Peters* has been refused.

276 As in *Walker v. Burton*. So too, in *Pinto v. Lim* (2005), just decided under the old law, the court refused to rectify against a proprietor in possession despite having the power to do so precisely because of his innocence and the fact that the land had been his undisturbed home for the previous four years. Indeed, this was despite the fact that the applicant for rectification might have had a difficult task in securing an indemnity, whereas the proprietor in possession would not. See also *Patel v. Freddy's*.

277 Paragraphs 3 (the court) and 6 (the registrar) of Schedule 4 of the LRA 2002.

278 If a property has been converted to take account of the special needs of the registered proprietor, it might be 'exceptional' to refuse to rectify the title against such a person even though the claimant had established his case. If refused rectification, the claimant would turn to a claim for an indemnity.

priority to a lease that was not on the register when the land was transferred to the now owner – this was perfectly proper as it was necessary to correct the mistake. As *Gold Harp* illustrates, once the power to rectify has arisen and is to be exercised, it can have powerful effects.

2.11 Indemnity under the Land Registration Act 2002

The authoritative status of the register means that there will always be cases in which a person suffers loss because of the workings of the land registration system. The power to alter and rectify the register is one response to this. The power of the court to order an indemnity (i.e. compensation) for a person who suffers loss is another response. As originally conceived in the LRA 1925, the entitlement to an indemnity was tied to the power to order rectification and still they remain mutually supportive aspects of the system. However, under the 2002 Act, the payment of an indemnity is more clearly identified as a stand-alone remedy, albeit that most (but not all) cases will 'piggyback' on a claim for rectification.[279] The indemnity provisions are found in Schedule 8 to the Act and triggered by section 103. Note also that all claims for indemnity not settled by 13 October 2003, whether relating to facts occurring before or after the entry into force of the LRA 2002 and whether rectification is ordered because of the application of the old law or the new, are governed by this Schedule.[280]

2.11.1 Indemnity as the consequence of a mistake

A right to claim an indemnity arises in consequence of a mistake that would have, or does, result in a rectification. In other words, for the right to an indemnity to arise, there must both be a mistake on the register and the correction of that mistake must be one which does, or would, prejudicially affect the title of the registered proprietor of the land or a charge over that land, or has already done so. However, that is merely the threshold for claiming an indemnity. In addition, the claimant must also establish any one of three further grounds. First, an indemnity can be paid if the correction of the mistake has caused loss.[281] This implies that a correction has actually been made, and that the correction (not the initial mistake) has caused the loss. An example would be where an innocent person was removed as registered proprietor in order to correct a mistake and thereby loses title to land or who claims title under a disposition that turns out, without their knowledge, to be forged and thereby suffers rectification. This is likely to be the favourite claim (along with the second, which is very similar) because the amount of compensation will be assessed according to the value of the land immediately before

---

279 Paragraph 1, Schedule 8.

280 Paragraph 19(1), Schedule 12 of the LRA 2002.

281 Paragraphs 1(a) and 2, Schedule 8 of the LRA 2002. Rectification arising from an overriding interest does not cause loss, because the overriding interest already binds the land. But, indemnity may still be paid if the overriding interest is a result of fraud, *Swift 1st v. Chief Land Registrar* (2015).

the rectification is ordered.[282] After all, the compensation is because of the correction, not the mistake. Second, an indemnity can be paid where again the register has been corrected because of a mistake in a way that causes loss to the claimant, but the loss was caused by the mistake before the rectification.[283] Third, an indemnity can be paid where there has been a mistake that would justify rectification, but the mistake is not corrected and a person suffers, but in such cases the amount of the indemnity necessarily will be assessed according to the value of the loss when the mistake was made, rather than when the register was rectified.[284] This is because the indemnity in this third type of case reflects loss caused by the mistake itself, not the correction (which, after all, was denied).

However, even after establishing that there was a rectification-type mistake, plus any one of the three factual grounds identified above, the claimant may still not receive an indemnity. This is because there are limits on indemnity claims. First, the claimant loses the right to an indemnity if any part of his loss has been caused by his own fraud – paragraph 5(1)(a), Schedule 8 of the LRA 2002.[285] Second, the claimant loses the right to an indemnity if his own lack of proper care caused his loss – paragraph 5(1)(b), Schedule 8 of the LRA 2002.[286] Third, an indemnity may be reduced if the claimant has partly contributed to his loss by lack of proper care – paragraph 5(2), Schedule 8 of the LRA 2002. Fourth, the right to apply to a court for an indemnity – which will be relevant only in those relatively few cases in which the indemnity issue cannot be settled by negotiation with HM Land Registry – lapses six years after the claimant became aware (or should have become aware) that he had a claim – paragraph 8, Schedule 8 of the LRA 2002.[287] Finally, in respect of the special cases of mines and minerals, it is only possible to claim an indemnity if there is an entry on the register confirming that mines and minerals were included in the title – paragraph 2, Schedule 8 of the LRA 2002.

2.11.2   Indemnity for other reasons

A person may claim an indemnity for losses caused by a range of other circumstances described in paragraph 1, Schedule 8 of the LRA 2002. These are where the loss arises from a mistake in an official search, a mistake in an official copy, a mistake in a document kept by the registrar that is not an original and is referred to in the register, the loss or destruction of a document lodged at the registry for inspection or safe custody, a mistake in the cautions register[288] or failure by the registrar to perform his duty under section 50.[289]

---

282 So, rising land prices mean increasing compensation: see *Pinto v. Lim* (2005).

283 Paragraph 2, Schedule 8 of the LRA 2002.

284 Paragraphs 1(b) and 3, Schedule 8 of the LRA 2002 and *Pinto v. Lim* (2005). Hence, the level of compensation may reflect historic land values, when the mistake was made, not current land values, when the register is rectified.

285 This may include, in appropriate circumstances, fraud by the claimant's predecessors in title unless the claimant took under a disposition for value.

286 This may also include lack of proper care by a predecessor in title unless the claimant took under a disposition for value.

287 But the right to ask HM Land Registry for an indemnity, and to accept its offer, remains after the six-year period has elapsed.

288 Concerning cautions against first registration where the land is unregistered.

289 Concerning specialist interests called 'overriding statutory charges'.

2.12 An Overview of the Land Registration Act 2002

It will be apparent from the detailed analysis above that the 2002 Act represents a fundamental shift in the way we think about registered land. It has been said many times, but the aim is to move to *title by registration* instead of registration of title. The 2002 Act is packed with significant features, but some of the most notable are highlighted below.

- Legal leases of over seven years' duration must be substantively registered with their own title. This trigger is likely to fall further to encompass legal leases of over three years.
- Mortgages of registered land may be created only by the 'charge by deed by way of legal mortgage' (section 23 of the LRA 2002).
- Unregistered interests which override are classified into those overriding a first registration (Schedule 1) and those rights that override a subsequent registered disposition (Schedule 3). Schedule 1 is more extensive than Schedule 3. The role of 'actual occupation' and the impact of easements are redefined and limited for Schedule 3 claims. The aim is to eliminate undiscoverable overriding interests in respect of a disposition falling under section 29 of the LRA 2002.
- The way in which other third-party interests (once called 'minor interests') can be protected is rationalised and simple. All entries by way of Notice confer priority on the right, but the entry may be by way of an Agreed or Unilateral Notice. Restrictions control dealings by the registered proprietor rather than protect rights, but if a registered proprietor cannot deal with the land, he cannot defeat a third-party right.
- Rights arising by proprietary estoppel, 'mere equities' and rights of pre-emption are confirmed as proprietary (sections 115, 116 of the LRA 2002) and so may be protected by the entry of a Notice or a Restriction or may amount to an overriding interest as circumstances permit.
- The circumstances in which the register may be altered have been clarified and the indemnity provisions have been recast. Possession is protected, even in the event of a mistake.
- The Act establishes a comprehensive dispute resolution process, whereby disputes are referred in the first instance to the land registration division of the Property Chamber of the First Tier Tribunal (formerly the Adjudicator to HM Land Registry).
- The Crown will be able to register its land for the first time by granting itself an estate.
- A new system of adverse possession applies to registered land in all cases where the old 12-year period of adverse possession was not completed by 13 October 2003 – the date of the entry into force of the 2002 Act. Under the 2002 Act, rarely will a registered proprietor lose title through adverse possession if he is prepared to take action to evict the adverse possessor. There is no 'limitation period' per se for registered land falling under the 2002 Act.

2.13   Chapter Summary

2.13.1   The nature and purpose of registered land

- To ensure the *free alienability of land* by easing the conveyancing process through the establishment of certainty; by eliminating the vagaries of the old doctrine of notice and thereby protecting the purchaser; by enhancing the role of overreaching and thereby removing some obstacles to the sale of land that is subject to a trust of land.
- To bring certainty to *land ownership* by establishing a register of titles, that is conclusive as to ownership and which is backed by a legislative and financial guarantee; by establishing a defined list of rights that can take priority over the land automatically but which should be discoverable on physical inspection of the land (overriding interests); by establishing a register of rights adverse to the land so that an intending purchaser (including a mortgagee) will be aware of what they are about to buy (registered protected interests).

2.13.2   The three principles of registered land

The mirror principle encapsulates the idea that the register should reflect the totality of rights in and over the land, so as to ease and speed alienability. The mirror is not perfect, due to the existence of overriding interests, but over time it will become considerably more accurate as more rights are registered. The curtain principle encompasses the idea that equitable interests existing behind trusts of land should be kept off the register and dealt with through the mechanism of overreaching. This has been largely achieved, although the cases in which overreaching is not possible has meant that sometimes the purchaser must lift the curtain. The insurance principle encapsulates the idea that the State will guarantee the efficacy of the system by providing statutory compensation (an indemnity) to persons suffering loss by reason of the operation of the system.

2.13.3   An overview of registered land and the various classes of estates and interests

Under the LRA 2002, proprietary rights fall into four broad classes, not necessarily coinciding with their quality as legal or equitable interests.

- *Registrable titles* are the legal freehold absolute in possession and, with minor exceptions, the legal leasehold of over seven years' duration. The grade of title with which the registered proprietor is registered may be absolute, good leasehold, possessory or qualified. The grade of title helps to determine the extent to which the proprietor is bound by pre-existing adverse rights. Registration as registered proprietor confers the relevant estate at law, subject to the rights specified in sections 11 and 12 of the LRA 2002 (first registration) and sections 28 and 29 of the LRA 2002 in respect of dispositions of registered land.
- *Registrable charges*, being legal mortgages.
- *Unregistered interests which override*, being interests that take priority automatically, without registration. They are found in Schedule 1 (first registration) and Schedule 3 (registered dispositions) of the LRA 2002. The most important types are short legal leases, the rights of persons in actual occupation of the land and some legal

easements. There are differences between Schedule 1 and Schedule 3 to reflect their different field of operation.

- *Protected registrable interests*, comprising most third-party rights, are protected by entering either an Agreed or a Unilateral Notice. Unregistered interests generally lose priority in the face of a disposition for value (section 29 of the LRA 2002). The one considerable exception is if the registrable interest qualifies in some way as an overriding interest.

2.13.4   Overreaching

This is a process whereby certain equitable interests are removed from the land and transferred to the cash proceeds of a sale of that land. Overreaching will occur when the equitable right is overreachable *and* a proper overreaching transaction occurs. If these conditions are satisfied, the equitable interest cannot be protected as an overriding interest.

2.13.5   Alteration and indemnity

The register may be altered and a person may claim an indemnity under Schedules 4 and 8 of the LRA 2002. An alteration that amounts to a rectification will generate a potential indemnity claim.

 Further Reading

Cooke, E, 'The Land Registration Bill' [2002] Conv 11.

Cooper, S, 'Regulating fallibility in registered land titles' [2013] CLJ 341.

Cooper, S, 'Resolving title conflicts in registered land' [2015] LQR 108.

Dixon, M, 'The reform of property law and the Land Registration Act 2002: A risk assessment' [2003] 67 Conv 136.

Dixon, M, 'Priorities under the Land Registration Act 2002' [2009] LQR 401.

Dixon, M, 'Rectification and priority: Further skirmishes in the land registration war' [2015] LQR 207.

Goymour, A, 'Mistaken registrations of land: Exploding the myth of "title by registration"' [2013] CLJ 617.

Harpum, C and **Bignall**, J, *Land Registration*, Bristol: Jordans, 2004.

Law Commission, *Updating the Land Registration Act 2002*, Consultation Paper No. 227, London: HMSO, 2002.

Law Commission, *Land Registration for the Twenty-first Century: A Conveyancing Revolution*, Report No. 271, London: HMSO, 2001.

Lees, E, 'Title by registration: Rectification, indemnity and mistake and the Land Registration Act 2002' [2013] 76 MLR 62.

Lees, E, 'Registration make-believe and forgery: Swift 1st Ltd v Chief Land Registrar' [2015] LQR 515.

Nugee, E, 'The feudal system and the Land Registration Acts' [2008] LQR 586.

Now visit the companion website to:

• test your understanding of the key terms using our Flashcard Glossary;

• revise and consolidate your knowledge using our Multiple Choice Question testbank.

www.routledge.com/cw/dixon

Chapter 3
Unregistered Land

3.1 Unregistered Land: An Introduction to the System of Unregistered Conveyancing

As we have seen in Chapters 1 and 2, land law and the conveyancing system in England and Wales underwent radical reform with effect from 1 January 1926. However, it was as obvious then as it is now that the task of transforming a basically feudal system of law into one that could adequately serve the twentieth century and beyond could not be accomplished overnight. Thus, from the very first, it was intended that registration of title and the accompanying provisions of what was then the LRA 1925 would be phased in. Originally, registered conveyancing was restricted geographically to the main urban areas of the country and it was not until 1 December 1990 that all of England and Wales became subject to compulsory first registration of title. This meant that much land remained within the old system of conveyancing for many years, sometimes known as the system of 'private unregistered conveyancing' in order to distinguish it from the State-guaranteed system established by the Land Registration Acts. Although the amount of land that remains unregistered today is relatively small and getting smaller,[1] there is a residual need to understand the basic structure of unregistered land even though it is of diminishing importance.[2]

However, even accepting the unavoidable residual role for unregistered land in modern land law, it was clear a long time before 1926 that the system of 'private unregistered conveyancing' in its original form was unwieldy, complicated and inefficient.[3]

---

[1] Very roughly, in England and Wales, 20 per cent of land by area and 10 per cent by number of titles remain unregistered. This will be either land held by private individuals where there has been no dealing with the land for many years or, more likely, land held by institutions such as universities, churches, local authorities and the Crown as these bodies tend to exist indefinitely and only infrequently transfer or sell their land. It includes large areas of coastal foreshore, waterways and uninhabited countryside held by the Crown that are unlikely ever to change ownership. Note, however under the LRA 2002, the Crown may now grant itself a fee simple estate that it can register (section 79 LRA 2002) and many local authorities are voluntarily registering their titles under special fee arrangements with HM Land Registry. Aside from many other benefits, one advantage for local authorities who have to keep track of large property portfolios is that land registered under the LRA 2002 is protected to a very considerable extent from a claim of adverse possession (squatting) – see Chapter 12.

[2] At one time, it could be said that the registered land system and the unregistered land system were simply different methods of conveying land and that they employed the same basic principles. However, as time marched away from 1925, it became clear that the principles applicable in the unregistered land system and those applicable to registered land were diverging. It is now a basic premise of the LRA 2002 that land of registered title should not be seen simply as a modification of the old law that applied to unregistered title. Rather, it is now clear that different substantive principles may apply in each system, especially in relation to security and transmissibility of title. Thus, the better view now is that land of registered title is of a fundamentally different character from that of unregistered title. For example, section 58 of the LRA 2002 ensures the conclusiveness of the proprietor's registered title irrespective of defects that would destroy the same title if it were unregistered. See e.g. *Walker* v. *Burton* (2013) and *Swift 1st* v. *Chief Land Registrar* (2015). Similarly, the law of adverse possession now operates fundamentally differently in each system.

[3] It was, however, popular with lawyers, but possibly only because it was familiar. Anecdotally, it is said that nearly 40 per cent of solicitors engaged in conveyancing retired before or soon after 1 January 1926 rather than learn the 'new' system of registered title.

The pre-1926 law that operated before the great legislative reforms offered neither certainty to a purchaser nor adequate protection for a person who enjoyed rights over that land. For example, the 'doctrine of notice', and especially the development of constructive notice, could mean that a purchaser was bound by a third-party equitable interest even if that interest seriously devalued the use and enjoyment of his (the purchaser's) land and even though the purchaser 'knew' of the right only in the most vague or technical sense. Conversely, a person seeking to enforce an equitable right over someone else's land (e.g. an equitable easement) might find their interest void (i.e. destroyed) against a purchaser through no fault of their own, and in circumstances in which they could have done little to protect it. Furthermore, the lengths to which a purchaser had to go to investigate the title of a proposed seller in order to ensure that the purchase was safe (e.g. by examining often obscure documents), and the potential number of persons with whom he had to agree a sale in cases of joint ownership, made unregistered conveyancing a burdensome and expensive enterprise.

To meet these problems, and bearing in mind that an immediate move to wholesale adoption of registered title was not feasible, a great part of the 1925 legislative reforms was directed at establishing an intermediate but temporary system of conveyancing built around familiar concepts of unregistered title.[4] This makeshift system was to apply to dealings with land that was not registered at the time of the dealing and was meant to last only 30 years pending the anticipated and widespread registration of title across England and Wales. As we now know, this timescale was overly optimistic and real progress towards widespread title registration was not made until the mid-1950s. Of course, the fact that compulsory first registration of title has been required in England and Wales for nearly 30 years (from 1 December 1990), and that registered titles now comprise the vast majority of all titles, means that the system of unregistered conveyancing is diminishing in practical importance. Unfortunately, the time has not yet come when it can be abandoned completely. That happy day will not be with us for a while, although the entry into force of the LRA 2002 has done much to propel us speedily towards that goal.[5]

3.1.1   What is unregistered land?

To describe a parcel of land as 'unregistered' means one thing only: that the title to the land (the freehold or leasehold estate) is established from old-fashioned title deeds and is not to be found in the register of titles governed by the LRA 2002. Unregistered land is land for which the title must be proved from the conveyancing history of the land as evidenced by the documents of title (i.e. the deeds and related documents such as those creating easements) and not by inspecting a register. It does not mean that there is no provision or opportunity for the registration of other rights and interests affecting the land for, as we shall see, 'unregistered land' has its own system of independent partial registration. It is important that this is appreciated fully. Indeed, it is essential from the outset

---

4 The LPA 1925 applies equally to unregistered land and was supplemented originally by the Land Charges Act 1925. The latter has been replaced by the Land Charges Act 1972.

5 For example, by encouraging voluntary first registration of unregistered titles through reduced fees and emphasising the relative immunity of registered land from claims of adverse possession.

to remember that the system of unregistered land (with its partial system of registration) operates *completely separately* from the system of registered land. Of course, they both deal with the same type of property rights (freeholds, leaseholds, easements, covenants, etc.), and they share the concept of overreaching, but they do so in different and mutually exclusive ways. So, if title to land is not registered under the LRA 2002, it is 'unregistered land' and is to be dealt with according to the principles considered in this chapter. It does not borrow from the system of registered land, or vice versa. As we have seen in Chapter 2, unregistered land will become registered land following a dealing with it, for 'first registration' is now compulsory, but until first registration takes place, the land is 'unregistered' and not subject to the Land Registration Acts.

3.2   An Overview of Unregistered Land

Given that it was intended to be a temporary modification of pre-1926 practice, it should come as no surprise that the system of unregistered land instituted in 1926 relies heavily on many of the old doctrines that characterised dealings with land before the great legislative reforms. Thus, unlike registered land, the distinction between legal and equitable interests is still of crucial importance when considering dealings with unregistered land, although the 'doctrine of notice' has been replaced in all but a few instances by the partial system of registration referred to above (the 'land charge' system). In essence, unregistered land can be viewed in the following way.

3.2.1   Estates in unregistered land

Title to land is not recorded in a register, nor is it guaranteed by the State through legislation. However, the same types of estate may exist at law and in equity in unregistered land as may exist in registered land. As noted in Chapter 1, the substantive law of estates is governed by the LPA 1925 and the 'freehold' and 'leasehold' have the same essential character when found in either registered or unregistered land, albeit that they are proved and transferred in different ways. Thus, any purchaser of an unregistered estate in land must seek out the 'root of title' in order to ensure that the seller has a good and safe title to pass on. Title is proven by an examination of the title deeds and documents relating to previous dealings with the land. In addition, a prudent purchaser will make a thorough physical inspection of the land in order to ascertain whether there are any obvious defects of title *and* whether there are any obvious third-party rights (e.g. frequently used easements) that might prejudice his use of the land.[6]

As title is not registered, the quality of that title is determined according to the old common law rules of title as modified by the LPA 1925.[7] Thus, a legal title, whether freehold or leasehold, encapsulates the essence of ownership for the duration of the estate granted and the owner of a legal estate in unregistered land need not fear that his proper title will be compromised by any extraneous issues affecting the land, other than

---

6 For example, is anyone else in possession of some of the land or are there any boundary issues?

7 Contrast this with registered land, where title is guaranteed by entry on the register and is conclusive (section 58 of the LRA 2002).

those interests binding as proprietary rights according to the rules of unregistered conveyancing. With an equitable estate (e.g. an equitable lease),[8] the estate owner also enjoys full rights over the land subject to the difficulties affecting all equitable interests in unregistered conveyancing: that is, they rank second to any previously created equitable right and are vulnerable if there is a sale of a legal estate in the land to a purchaser for valuable consideration.

3.2.2 Interests in unregistered land: rights over another person's estate

'Interests' in unregistered land are of the same type as interests in registered land. There are easements, mortgages, covenants, profits, co-ownership rights, options and estoppels, as these are creatures of the substantive law.[9] They are examples of proprietary rights that may exist over someone else's land (more accurately, over their estate in it). However, it is the machinery of unregistered land – the way in which these interests affect another person's land particularly on sale or mortgage – that is different from registered title. For the purposes of exposition, and bearing in mind that the picture produced below is necessarily simplified, we may split these proprietary interests into four different groups: legal rights; equitable rights that are registrable under the LCA 1972;[10] equitable rights that are not registrable under the LCA 1972 because they are subject to overreaching; and equitable rights that are neither overreachable nor registrable under the LCA 1972.

3.2.3 Legal interests

Legal interests in another person's unregistered land, such as legal easements, legal mortgages and legal leaseholds, are, in the main, automatically effective against the land over which they exist, even if they were granted by someone other than the landowner.[11] They will bind automatically any person coming into ownership or occupation of the land, be they a purchaser, recipient of a gift, devisee under a will or an adverse possessor. This is the effect of the rule that 'legal rights bind the whole world' and it is a principle of utmost importance in unregistered conveyancing. Necessarily, it requires a clear distinction to be made between legal and equitable estates and interests. As we have seen (Chapter 1), the distinction between legal and equitable rights turns primarily on the scope of section 1 of the LPA 1925, the way in which the estate or interest has been created and the possible existence of a trust. However, once a legal right has been established over the burdened land, there is no need to make further enquiries in order to assess whether the legal right is binding. The 'state of mind' of any transferee of the land, the nature of his title or indeed any other matter is not relevant: legal rights bind

---

8 Which may arise, for example, where the proper formalities for the creation of a legal lease have not been observed.

9 This list is illustrative, not exhaustive.

10 Previously the LCA 1925.

11 If the current landowner is the grantor of the interest, he is, of course, bound by his grant because he gave the right, irrespective of the proprietary quality of the interest.

the whole world. We must not think, however, that this unbending rule causes hardship to purchasers. The manner of creation of legal rights means that generally they are obvious to a transferee either from an inspection of the title documents (i.e. the deed required to create them is likely to be available or referred to in other documents) or from an inspection of the land itself (e.g. a tenant for three years or less with a legal lease may have no deed, but is very likely to be on the land). Consequently, even though a transferee is bound by these legal rights, whether or not he is aware of them, the reality is that in most cases the transferee or bank planning to lend money does in fact discover the existence of these rights before completion of any transfer or mortgage.

The single exception to the rule that legal rights bind the whole world in unregistered conveyancing is provided by the 'puisne' mortgage. A puisne mortgage is a legal mortgage over land for which the documents of title of the mortgaged land have not been deposited with the mortgagee (the lender), usually because an earlier legal mortgage already exists and this earlier lender has the documents. As the puisne mortgagee does not have the documents of title, it does not have the ability to prevent dealings with the land (for which the documents of title are necessary), and so the puisne mortgagee is not protected adequately against further dealings with the burdened land. Consequently, a puisne mortgage is registrable in unregistered land under the special system of Land Charges found in the LCA 1972 as a Class C(i) land charge, and such registration ensures that any subsequent dealings with the land are subject to the mortgage.[12] For example, if A is the unregistered freeholder of a house and granted a legal mortgage to X bank, X bank will retain the title documents to the house and is fully protected because it has the documents and can prevent A from selling the house without paying off the mortgage. If A then grants a second legal mortgage to Y bank, Y bank cannot prevent A from dealing with the land by controlling the documents (because X bank has them) and so Y will register its puisne mortgage as a land charge in order to safeguard it.

3.2.4   Equitable interests that are registrable under the Land Charges Act 1972

The second category of interests in unregistered land comprises those equitable rights[13] requiring registration as Land Charges under the LCA 1972 (replacing the LCA 1925). 'Land charges' are defined in the LCA 1972, and the majority of equitable rights over unregistered land fall into this category, including equitable easements, restrictive covenants, equitable mortgages, equitable leases and estate contracts. The point of being a land charge within the LCA 1972 is that, in order to bind a purchaser of unregistered land, a land charge must be registered in the appropriate way.[14] Failure to register the land charge when required renders the interest void against a purchaser.[15] Importantly, this structure leaves no room at all for the doctrine of notice in respect of interests

---

12 For an example, see *Barclays Bank* v. *Buhr* (2001).

13 Plus the legal *puisne* mortgage.

14 Remembering, of course, that 'registration' does not mean registration under the LRA 2002. This is not registered land.

15 Section 4 LCA 1972. But the interest would remain valid against a non-purchaser of the land, even if unregistered, such as the recipient of a gift, or beneficiary under a will or an adverse possessor.

that qualify as 'land charges', for that doctrine is replaced by the system of land charge registration. Given that the great majority of equitable interests in unregistered land are 'land charges', this means that the doctrine of notice is very nearly redundant as a feature of modern land law.[16] Note also that the registration of land charges has *absolutely nothing* to do with registered land. It refers to an independent, name-based register that operates purely in the field of unregistered conveyancing.

3.2.5 Equitable interests that are not registrable under the Land Charges Act 1972 because they are subject to overreaching

Certain equitable interests in another person's land are not registrable under the LCA 1972 because they are subject to overreaching. These equitable interests are overreachable in the same way as their counterparts in registered land. They comprise equitable co-ownership interests existing behind a trust of land and equitable interests operating behind a settlement established under the SLA 1925.[17] They may also include equitable rights arising from the unconscionability in transactions and equitable estoppels.[18] These interests are overreachable because they are capable of expression in monetary terms (e.g. 50 per cent ownership of a property) and can be quantified as a share of the money received by the seller (and given to the interest holder) when the land is sold. Being overreachable, they will not clog the title of a purchaser, and there is no reason to require them to be entered in the land charges register.

3.2.6 Equitable interests that are neither registrable under the Land Charges Act 1972 nor overreachable

Equitable interests that are neither registrable under the LCA 1972 (because they fall outside the statutory definition) nor overreachable comprise a miscellaneous category of equitable rights that were either deliberately or accidentally left out of the land charges system, or have developed since that system came into operation. As they are neither registrable nor overreachable, the only way in which it is possible to determine whether these rights bind the unregistered title (i.e. are effective against a person purchasing the land) is to utilise the old doctrine of notice. This is the only time that the doctrine of notice remains applicable in modern land law after 31 December 1925. As we shall see, the number of equitable rights that fall into this category is small (and uncertain), and all but one or two arise in very untypical situations. Nevertheless, this category represents a 'hole' in the system of unregistered conveyancing and is one of the main reasons why a brief acquaintance with pre-1926 law and the doctrine of notice is still necessary.

---

16 Of course, it plays no part at all in registered land.

17 As we shall see, SLA settlements are rare, and since January 1997 no new settlements can be created. Thus, the majority of overreachable rights arise under the 'trust of land' governed by the TOLATA 1996. See Chapter 4.

18 *Mortgage Express* v. *Lambert* [2016] EWCA Civ 555. Until this case, only interests behind trusts and behind settlements were thought to be overreachable but *Lambert* suggests that these other rights also qualify because of the precise terms of section 2 LPA 1925.

3.3   Titles in Unregistered Land

The reforms of the LPA 1925 apply in equal measure to estates of unregistered title as they do to estates of registered title. In this respect, broadly speaking, thus, the number of possible legal estates (titles) is limited to two, being the freehold (fee simple absolute in possession) and the leasehold (term of years absolute) (section 1 of the LPA 1925). As noted, 'the title' in unregistered land is not recorded on a register but remains provable from the title deeds and associated documents held by the estate owner.[19] In effect, when a purchaser wishes to buy an estate of unregistered land, there has to be an investigation of the 'root of title' in order to determine whether the seller owns the land and in order to determine the quality of that ownership.[20] This will still be relevant on the occasion of a sale of unregistered land today, save that, after this last sale, the new owner must apply for first registration of title under section 4 of the LRA 2002. This is what is meant by compulsory first registration of title: a sale of an unregistered estate is one of the 'triggers' for compulsory first registration of title and thereafter the land is 'registered land'.[21]

Obviously, then, the search for a root of title in unregistered conveyancing will become less frequent as more land becomes subject to title registration, but it was once a complicated and expensive task. Today, the task is easier because the search for a 'good' root of title has been reduced to an examination of only the last 15 years of dealings with the land, not the 30 years prior to 1970.[22] What this means is that, when the potential purchaser of unregistered land is examining the title deeds for an unbroken chain of ownership to the present seller (in order to prove title), the purchaser need only find a proper conveyance to begin the chain that is at least 15 years prior to the date of the proposed sale. So, if a purchaser wishes to buy unregistered land in 2018, he must seek out a good root of title going back to the first proper conveyance that was executed *before* 2003, and a purchaser is entitled to rely on this proof of ownership even if there is some undisclosed defect in the title beyond the 15-year period. In practice, this search for a good root of title rarely causes hardship to prospective purchasers, especially since most title deeds are kept together or even deposited with a bank that has advanced money by way of mortgage. As we shall see, however, the shortened period for establishing good root of title has caused some difficulties in other areas of the system of unregistered conveyancing, especially in relation to the operation of the land charges system.

The mechanics of a typical sale and purchase of an estate in unregistered land is essentially a matter of conveyancing procedures, and largely falls outside the scope of this text. Briefly, the seller and purchaser will enter into a contract for the sale and purchase of the property ('exchange of contracts') after settling a number of precontractual matters, such as price, general area of land to be sold, existence of planning law obligations and (usually) the existence of any local authority obligations affecting the

---

19   Or held by the lender if there is a mortgage.

20   The same is true if a long lease is granted out of unregistered title.

21   Other triggers include the transfer of a legal lease with more than seven years left to run, the grant of a new legal lease of more than seven years and a mortgage of the title (section 4 of the LRA 2002).

22   Section 23 of the LPA 1969. See also the reforms to the law of co-ownership whereby the maximum number of legal co-owners is limited to four, who must be joint tenants (see Chapter 4).

land.[23] This contract commits each party to the bargain and may be specifically enforced if one party later tries to withdraw. The actual transfer is perfected by 'completion', this being the effective conveyance of the property by deed to the purchaser. In the interval between exchange of contracts and completion, the seller must produce an 'abstract of title' from which the purchaser should be able to deduce a good root of title beyond the 15-year period. Failure by the seller to produce a good root of title permits the purchaser to rescind (withdraw from) the contract. Also in the period between exchange and completion, the purchaser will search the register of land charges to discover whether any are registered under the LCA 1972 and as such binding on the land. The obvious problem with this is that the purchaser is already committed to buying the property *before* he searches the land charges register.[24] This is discussed below.

3.4   Third-party Rights in Unregistered Land

It is inherent in what has been said already about the 1925 reforms that one important aim was to bring certainty and stability to the status of third-party rights in land. There are two reasons for this, whose fundamental importance bears repetition.

1   A potential purchaser of land needs to know with as much certainty as possible whether any other person has enforceable rights over the land, and the extent and nature of those rights.
2   The owner of those rights needs to be sure that his or her rights will be protected (and remain enforceable) if the land over which they operate is sold or otherwise disposed of.

It is, then, in everybody's interest to have a workable conveyancing system wherein there is a balance between potential purchaser and third-party right-holder, and which is so uniform in its operation as to allow accurate predictions of what will happen to third-party rights in the majority of real-life situations. Unfortunately, the system of unregistered conveyancing does not achieve these goals to the extent necessary to pronounce it a success. Of course, it does work – or, rather, it is made to work – but there is no doubt that the system of unregistered conveyancing in place from 1 January 1926 has not stood the test of time. There are few who will be sorry to see it disappear.

Before examining in detail how third-party rights are regulated in unregistered land, three preliminary points should be noted. First, we are about to consider whether a person who obtains title to unregistered land, over which a third-party interest *already* exists, is bound by that interest (e.g. a right of way): in other words, does the third-party interest survive a transfer of the land? This may depend on both the nature of the third-party interest and/or the status of the new owner. Second, in *all* cases, it is vital to know whether the third-party right is 'legal' or 'equitable'. This will, in turn, depend both on the definition of legal interests contained in section 1 of the LPA 1925 and on the way in which the interest originally came into existence. Hence, an easement may

---

23   Known as 'local land charges', and not to be confused with land charges proper under the LCA 1972.

24   It is only after exchange of contracts that the purchaser receives the abstract of title and only then that the names of previous estate owners against whom to search for land charges are revealed.

be legal or equitable (section 1 of the LPA 1925) and everything will depend on how it came into being. Conversely, the burden of a restrictive covenant can only ever be equitable, irrespective of how it is created (section 1 of the LPA 1925). A knowledge of the distinction between legal and equitable rights is vital if the system of unregistered conveyancing is to be understood properly. Third, if it should prove the case that a third-party right is not binding on a new owner of the unregistered land, the right may still be enforceable between the parties that created the right. For example, in *Barclays Bank* v. *Buhr* (2001), the Buhrs had granted a *puisne* mortgage over their land. As noted above, this proprietary right should have been registered as a Class C(i) land charge in order to ensure that it remained enforceable should the land be sold to a purchaser of a legal estate.[25] It was not so registered and hence was not enforceable by the Bank against the new owner of the property – it was in this sense 'void'. Nevertheless, as between the Bank and the Buhrs, the mortgage remained enforceable, as these were the parties that had created the right by a contract between them. Thus, the Bank was able to recover some of its money from the proceeds of sale by suing the Buhrs on this contract when they sold the house.

3.5   The Purchaser of Unregistered Land and the Protection of Legal Rights

With the one exception noted above (the *puisne* mortgage), a fundamental principle of unregistered conveyancing is that 'legal rights bind the whole world'. So, if a person buys, is given, or comes to possess a piece of unregistered land, he will take that land subject to virtually every legal interest over it. Such legal interests may be, for example, a legal lease granted by the previous owner or a legal easement conferring a right of way over the land. Short of obtaining a waiver or release of the right from the person entitled to the benefit of it, there is nothing a transferee can do to avoid being bound. However, lest this be thought to be a harsh and unfair rule, we must always remember that only specified estates and interests may be 'legal', and even then that they must come into being in the proper fashion. Indeed, the most important reason why it is *not* unfair that legal rights should bind the land automatically is that they are usually perfectly apparent to a purchaser who investigates his purchase properly. This is because, first, most legal interests come into being formally, by use of a deed, which is then kept with the title documents; second, the rights may well be obvious to a prudent purchaser making a physical inspection of the land, as is the case where a tenant occupies the land, or the existence of an easement is indicated by a driveway. In other words, a potential purchaser will nearly always know of the existence of these rights and can act accordingly, either by offering a lower price or by walking away from the proposed purchase. However, the correct view is *not* that these rights are obvious and that this is why they bind the land; rather, it is that it is necessary to have some rights that are capable of automatically surviving changes of ownership in land, and one way of avoiding any undue hardship is to ensure so far as possible that only those rights that are apparent or obvious

---

25   It was a *puisne* mortgage (see section 3.6 below), this being the one legal interest that requires registration under the LCA 1972.

have this effect. To recap then, the rule is that legal rights bind a transferee *whether or not* he knew about them, and *whether or not* they were, in fact, obvious from an inspection of the title deeds or land.

3.6 The Purchaser of Unregistered Land and the Protection of Equitable Interests: The Land Charges Act 1972

A major part of the unregistered land system deals with the protection of equitable third-party interests in land. The most important method by which this is attempted is through a system of registration of land charges introduced by the LCA 1925 and now codified in the LCA 1972. To reiterate, this has nothing to do with any of the registration facilities available in registered land under the LRA 2002.

In order to understand the system of registration of land charges, it is important to appreciate that there are three stages in assessing whether an equitable right binds the land when the land passes to a new estate owner.

1   The first issue is whether the equitable interest is *registrable* under the LCA 1972. In other words, does the particular equitable interest fall within any one of the classes of right that are required to be registered as a land charge in order to bind a purchaser of the land? This depends on the statutory definition of 'land charges' in the LCA 1972. If the interest does *not* qualify, and so is *not* registrable, then the equitable interest is either overreachable (see section 3.7 below) or within the exceptional class discussed below in section 3.8.

2   The second question is, assuming that the equitable interest is registrable, has it in fact been registered and what is the effect of the registration?

3   Third, if the right is registrable, but has *not* been registered, what is the effect of the right (if any) on a transferee of the unregistered land?

These three issues will be addressed below, but first the *machinery* of land charge registration needs to be examined. This is of a unique character. Unlike registered land, land charges are not entered against the title to the land – after all, this title is not entered on any register but is provable from the title documents. Consequently, land charges are registered against 'the name of the estate owner whose estate is intended to be affected' as required by section 3(1) of the LCA 1972. For example, if a registrable equitable interest is alleged to bind the land owned by Mr X, having been created during Mr X's ownership, it must be entered on the land charges register against the *name* of Mr X. Indeed, even if the land is then sold to Mrs Y and then to Miss Z, the land charge will remain entered against the name of Mr X. This is known as the 'name-based' system of registration, and it has given rise to a number of practical difficulties for purchasers, as we shall see below in section 3.9.

When a person wishes to purchase unregistered land, he will make a search of the land charges register to determine the existence of any registered land charges. The name-based system means that the purchaser must make an official search against the names of *all* previous estate owners revealed in the root of title in order to discover whether any charges are registered. These names are usually readily discoverable from the documents of title provided by the seller, although the search is usually undertaken *after* the seller and purchaser have entered into an enforceable contract to sell the property, because it is only then that the purchaser has access to the title deeds and is able to discover the relevant names. Of course, this means that a purchaser might discover a registered land charge that would seriously diminish the value of the land they propose to buy, yet he is bound by contract to go through with the sale. To meet the obvious injustice that this situation can create,[26] section 24(1) of the Law of Property Act 1969 provides that a purchaser shall be entitled to escape from the contract if he did not have real notice of the registered land charge at the time he entered the contract. This is a necessary modification to the normal rule that contracts for the sale of land can be specifically enforced and is justifiable because the purchaser's difficulties are generated entirely by the name-based system of registration of land charges, and not because of some act of the parties themselves.

Bearing this in mind, two important consequences flow from the making of an official search of the land charges register. First, if a search is made in the *proper* manner – against the correct name and in respect of the land described in the title deeds – an official search certificate is issued to the purchaser and this is conclusive according to its terms, even if the register itself says something different (section 10(4) of the LCA 1972). Thus, if a registered charge is not revealed through error, the purchaser still takes the land free of that charge (the certificate is conclusive), and the right as a right enforceable against the land is lost.[27] On the other hand, a defective search cannot be relied on, as in *Horrill v. Cooper* (2000), in which the requested search did not adequately follow the description of the land as given in the title deeds and so a 'clear' certificate in the name of the estate owner did not absolve the purchaser from being bound by the correctly registered land charge (a restrictive covenant). Second, the purchaser has a 15-day 'priority period' from the date of the official search in which to complete his purchase, safe in the knowledge that only those charges revealed by the official search will be binding against him. And land charges registered in the interim period (i.e. within the purchaser's priority period) will not be binding on the purchaser if completion of the purchase occurs within that period (section 11(5) of the LCA 1972). However, this presupposes that the purchaser has searched the names correctly, and that all of the relevant names have been searched. In this connection, it must always be remembered that the certificate is conclusive as to the search actually *requested*, and not as to the search that the purchaser should have made. This has caused some difficulties where there are defective searches or defective registrations (see section 3.9 below).

3.6.1   The classes of registrable land charge under the Land Charges Act 1972

Broadly speaking, the interests that are capable of registration as land charges are those equitable rights that have an adverse effect on the value of the land or the enjoyment of it, and which are not suitable for overreaching, being interests that are not easily

---

26 Because the land charge remains binding on the purchaser should he proceed to buy (section 198(1) of the LPA 1925) even though it could not have been discovered until after the contract for sale was made.

27 It may be that the owner of the registered land charge can seek damages from the Land Charges Registrar by suing in negligence, as occurred in respect of the register of local land charges in *Ministry of Housing and Local Government v. Sharp* (1970). However, this is not clear because section 10(6) of the LCA 1972 could be interpreted as preventing such a claim.

translated into a monetary equivalent. With the exception of the *puisne* (legal) mortgage, they are all equitable. Although there are some other matters that can be registered under the LCA 1972 so as to bind transferees (e.g. pending land actions, writs concerning land disputes – see section 3.6.5), we are concerned primarily with the six classes of land charge defined in section 2 of the Act. If an interest falls outside these classes, it is not registrable as a land charge.

A   Class A relates to certain statutory charges that are created on the application of an interested person under an Act of Parliament (section 2(2) of the LCA 1972). These statutory charges usually relate to some work undertaken by a public body in relation to the land (not being a local land charge), the cost of which is chargeable to the owner, or where an Act of Parliament charges land with the payment of money for very specific purposes: for example, certain charges under the Land Drainage Act 1991. In other words, the 'cost' is secured by means of the Class A land charge. Although not rare, rarely do they generate problems, being extinguished by payment of the sum charged.

B   Class B relates to certain statutory charges that arise automatically (section 2(3) of the LCA 1972). These are very similar to Class A land charges, save only that the charge is not created by a person applying to the Registrar of Land Charges but arises automatically as the result of legislation. For example, a charge for the costs (or part thereof) of recovering property with the assistance of legal aid falls within Class B.

C   Class C is one of the most important classes of land charge. It encompasses interests that can have a profound effect on the land over which they exist. Many are genuinely 'adverse' to the estate owner, being rights that control his use and enjoyment of the land, or detract from its capitalised value on sale. Class C is divided into four subclasses.

    C(i)   Being a legal mortgage that is not protected by the deposit of the title deeds of the property with the lender. This is the *puisne* mortgage referred to above, and is the only example of a legal interest being registrable as a land charge (section 2(4)(i) of the LCA 1972). As with all land charges, failure to register a *puisne* mortgage means that it will be void against a purchaser – see *Barclays Bank* v. *Buhr* (2001). As previously noted, this exceptional need to register a legal right is motivated by a desire to offer protection to the *puisne* mortgagee, given that it will not have control of the documents of title. It is interesting, then, that if the mortgagee fails to make use of the registration machinery that exists for its own protection, that mortgagee will suffer the voidness of its charge if the land is transferred to a purchaser.

    C(ii)   Being 'a limited owner's charge': that is, a charge or mortgage that a person such as a life tenant under the SLA 1925 (a 'limited owner') may be entitled to levy against the land because of obligations discharged by him – for example, because of the payment of inheritance tax on death of a previous estate owner (section 2(4)(ii) of the LCA 1972). These special charges are relatively uncommon, but it is important to appreciate that it is the charge or mortgage that is registrable, not the life interest itself.

    C(iii)   Being 'a general equitable charge': a residual category that catches specific charges or mortgages not mentioned elsewhere (section 2(4)(iii) of the LCA 1972). However, this is not a completely open-ended category, for section 2 makes it clear that it does not include an equitable co-ownership interest behind a trust of land or a successive equitable interest under a strict settlement (because both may be overreached) and it does not include any charge that is a charge over the proceeds of sale of land rather than the land itself.[28] Moreover, it appears that it does not include the equity by estoppel (i.e. proprietary estoppel) because, according to *Ives* v. *High* (1967), these interests could not have been in contemplation of the LCA 1925 (as was) given that the doctrine of estoppel had not been developed fully at that time.[29]

C(iv) Being 'estate contracts': that is, enforceable agreements to convey a legal estate (section 2(4)(iv) of the LCA 1972). This class is important as, among other things, it effectively includes all manner of equitable interests that are 'equitable' because of a failure to observe the proper formalities that would have constituted them as legal interests.[30] Thus, equitable leases are registrable as Class C(iv) land charges, as they result from an enforceable contract to grant a legal lease (*Walsh* v. *Lonsdale* (1882), and see Chapter 6), as are equitable mortgages of a legal estate. Also included are simple contracts to purchase a legal estate, such as options to purchase land (*Armstrong* v. *Holmes* (1993)) and certain rights of first refusal to buy land (rights of pre-emption). However, it is clear that only those contracts that are for the grant of a proprietary interest in land fall within this head. Class C(iv) cannot confer any protection for contracts for personal interests in land (*Thomas* v. *Rose* (1968)) or contracts where the seller does not have a proprietary interest at the time of the contract (*Scott* v. *Southern Pacific Mortgages* (2014)). Third, certain special types of claim, not truly contracts, are included in this class by reason of statute because it is desirable that they should be made registrable in order to alert potential purchasers. A good example is a previous tenant's request for an 'overriding lease' made under the LTCA 1995.[31] In practice, then, the 'estate contract' in all of its guises is one of the most frequently registered classes of land charge, both because it can arise in a wide variety of situations and because of the effect an estate contract can have on the value of the land it affects when the time comes to sell it. For example, if A, the freehold owner, has granted B an option to purchase the land, this is an estate contract. If B then registers it against A's name, A's ability to deal subsequently with the land is much reduced; any purchaser from A takes the land subject to B's enforceable right to buy it. Note, however, that in order to be registrable as an estate contract under Class C(iv), the 'contract' must itself be validly created. As discussed in Chapter 1, the majority of contracts for the disposition of an interest in land must be

---

28 See, for example, *Re Rayleigh Weir Stadium* (1954).

29 Consequently, in that case, the equitable estoppel was not a registrable land charge under either Class C(iii) or D(iii) despite having an effect similar to an easement. Note, if *Mortgage Express* v. *Lambert* is correct, such estoppels might now be subject to overreaching.

30 Thus, the Class cannot include those interests that could never be legal under section 1 of the LPA 1925.

31 Section 20(6) of the Landlord and Tenants (Covenants) Act 1995.

made in writing, incorporating all of the terms and signed by both parties within the meaning of section 2 of the LP(MP)A 1989. A contract that does not fulfil these conditions is not registrable as a Class C(iv) land charge because it is not a valid contract at all. Likewise, those proprietary rights that may be created informally (e.g. by proprietary estoppel) are not registrable under this class, as they do not spring from a contract.

D   Class D is divided into three subclasses.

    D(i)   Being a HM Revenue & Customs (formerly Inland Revenue) charge on land in respect of taxes payable on death (inheritance tax) where such liability has not been discharged (section 2(5)(i) of the LCA 1972).

    D(ii)   Being restrictive covenants created after 1925, provided that they are not covenants between a lessor and lessee (i.e. a landlord and tenant, section 2(5)(ii) of the LCA 1972). For example, where one landowner (A) promises his neighbour (B) that he (A) will not carry on any trade or business on his (A's) own land, the neighbour may register the 'restrictive covenant' against A's name. However, if the covenant is made between lessor and lessee and affects the leasehold land (as where a tenant promises not to keep pets on the leasehold premises), special rules apply and these are discussed in detail in the chapter on leases.[32] These special 'leasehold covenant' rules – themselves a mix of common law and statute – provide an adequate system for the enforcement of landlord and tenant covenants outside the registration scheme of the LCA 1972 (and indeed outside that of the LRA 2002 for registered land).

    D(iii)   Being equitable easements, rights or privileges over land created after 1925. Thus, these are easements and similar rights that are equitable because they are created informally or for an estate that is not itself legal[33] (section 2(5)(iii) of the LCA 1972). Importantly, this category does *not* include all equitable easements created over land after 1925, for according to *Ives v. High* (1967), it excludes equitable easements that arise by proprietary estoppel. So, Class D(iii) includes only those rights that could have been 'legal' if properly created, not those rights that are creations of equity alone.[34]

E   Class E relates to annuities created before 1926 (section 2(6) of the LCA 1972), being yearly sums payable to a specific person. Annuities created after 1925, provided that they comply with certain conditions, are registrable as Class C(iii) land charges.

F   Class F relates to a spouse's or civil partner's 'matrimonial home right' arising under section 30 of the Family Law Act 1996 (FLA 1996) and registrable as a land charge by virtue of section 31 of that Act.[35] These rights are essentially personal rights that spouses or civil partners enjoy against their partners to occupy the

---

32   Chapter 6. See *Dartstone v. Cleveland Petroleum* (1969) for problems when such covenants in a lease affect land other than the land that is subject to the lease. Being contained in a lease, they are not registrable under the LCA 1972 but neither do they fall within the special regime applicable to leasehold covenants.

33   For example, an easement attached to an equitable lease.

34   The reasoning was followed in *Shiloh Spinners v. Harding* (1973) in respect of an equitable right of re-entry in a lease.

35   This replaces the former regime of the Matrimonial Homes Act 1983 and in most respects is identical.

matrimonial home. However, despite being personal in nature, and for social and policy reasons, Parliament has determined that these rights should be treated as being equivalent to proprietary rights for certain purposes. This is put into effect by making them registrable as land charges. Consequently, if registered against a spouse or civil partner, that spouse or civil partner[36] and any subsequent purchaser, may be bound by the registered right of occupation. Such registration is relatively uncommon[37] because essentially it is a hostile act against the owning spouse or civil partner, but it can be used as a precautionary step by one of the partners when the relationship starts to deteriorate. However, given that the spouse or civil partner against whom the charge is registered is taken to promise any purchaser that he will give vacant possession (Schedule 4, section 3(1) of the FLA 1996), the effect of registering a Class F land charge is that the partners will have to settle their differences *before* the house is sold. Should the partners fail to resolve matters before a sale, the consequences can be serious, as in *Wroth* v. *Tyler* (1975), in which the husband's inability to complete the contract with the innocent purchaser following the wife's registration of a Class F land charge led to legal action and his bankruptcy.

3.6.2   The effect of registering a land charge

It has been noted already that the machinery of the LCA 1972 requires a registrable charge to be entered on the register against the name of the estate owner who owns the land affected at the time the charge is created. This has three important consequences. First, in order to be sure that a registrable interest will be enforceable against a subsequent purchaser of the land, the land charge must be entered against the correct name of the estate owner that first created the right. Normally, it would be registered by the person who was first given the benefit of the right.[38] For these purposes, the correct name is the full name of the current estate owner as it appears on the title deeds of the land to be affected.[39] If an entry is made against the wrong name (or more likely an incorrect version of the right name), as in *Diligent Finance* v. *Alleyne* (1972), then an official search against the correct name will confer protection on the purchaser for the duration of the priority period, because the charge will not be revealed by the certificate, and the certificate is conclusive. The purchaser will take the land free of the incorrectly registered charge. For example, if the estate owner's name is William Smith, but the land charge is registered against Bill Smith, a purchaser who searches against 'William Smith' will take the land free of the charge, provided also that the search of the name was linked to the relevant land or a reasonable description of it (*Horrill* v. *Cooper* (2000)). However, as illustrated by *Oak Co-operative Society* v. *Blackburn* (1968), if the purchaser also searches against the wrong name, then the registration of the land charge against a version of the correct

---

36 Assuming they own a legal estate in the land (section 31(13) of the FLA 1996).

37 Despite being subject only to a £1 fee for lodging an application.

38 In practice, this would be the solicitor or licensed conveyancer that acted in the transaction that generated the registrable right.

39 *Standard Property Investment plc* v. *British Plastics Federation* (1987).

name (albeit actually incorrect) will protect the land charge.[40] So, if both registration and search are defective as to the correct name, the registration of the charge will be effective to protect the interest, provided that the name against which it was actually registered is a reasonable version of the correct name. For example, assuming that the estate owner's name is William Smith, and the land charge is registered against Bill Smith, if the purchaser searches against Walter Smith, the land charge binds the purchaser. Of course, a defective search will always lose priority to a correctly registered charge. Thus, if the estate owner's name is William Smith and the land charge is registered against William Smith, a purchaser will be bound by the land charge if he searches against the wrong name (e.g. Bill Smith). Also, in cases in which the search was made against the correct name but the affected land is misdescribed (as where a wrong postcode or town is requested in the search), the properly registered charge will prevail because the search certificate is only conclusive as to the actual search made, as in *Horrill v. Cooper*.

Second, the charge must be entered against the name of the person who is the estate owner of the land intended to be bound *at the time the charge is created*. So, for example, if A contracts to sell land to B, B must register this estate contract (a Class C(iv) land charge) against the name of A. This is perfectly straightforward. If B then enters into a subcontract to sell the land to C *before* B actually acquires the unregistered title, C must also register their estate contract against A, because A is the estate owner of the land that is to be bound *at the time the charge is created*.[41] C can only safely register against B if B has acquired title before making the contract with C and failure to register appropriately will mean that the contract is unprotected. This then constitutes a pitfall for purchasers involved in a series of subsales if they do not know the name of the initial estate owner (first seller) or, as is more likely, that they do not realise they are involved in a subsale at all![42]

Third, having taken account of the two points above, a correct registration of a land charge has a powerful effect on the land over which it operates. According to section 198(1) of the LPA 1925, registration of a land charge is 'deemed to constitute actual notice of the fact of such registration, to all persons and for all purposes connected with the land'. Although it is expressed rather elliptically, this means that if the charge is registered, it will bind all future purchasers and transferees of the land. This 'bindingness' is expressed in terms of notice because, from 1 January 1926, this system of registration replaced the old 'doctrine of notice'. However, it is vital to remember that for a registrable land charge, registration alone means that it is binding. It does not matter whether the purchaser actually knew or did not actually know of the existence of the charge. Registration as a land charge is *not* just one form of alerting the purchaser to the existence of the charge; it is the *only* method of alerting the purchaser and therefore making them bound. A potential purchaser who has knowledge of such an adverse right by other means, but where there is no registration of it, will not be bound by the unregistered land charge when they complete the purchase, a point well illustrated by *Midland Bank v.*

---

40 In *Oak*, the correct name was Francis David Blackburn, but the search was made against Francis Davis Blackburn and the purchaser was not protected by the search certificate. This reasoning was approved in *Horrill v. Cooper* (2000).

41 *Barrett v. Hilton Developments* (1975).

42 In registered land, providing the subcontract is registered against the affected title, it is protected, even if the first contract is not so registered, *Rosefair v. Butler* (2014).

Green (1981), in which the House of Lords confirmed that an unregistered option to purchase the land[43] was not binding on a purchaser even though the purchaser had known all about the option (knowing also that it was unregistered) and even though the sole purpose of the sale was to destroy the option.[44]

The powerful effect of properly registering a land charge against the name of the correct estate owner – in that it becomes binding on all future purchasers and other transferees of the land – is further illustrated by the fact that a registered land charge remains binding on a purchaser even if he could not possibly have discovered the names of the estate owners against whom to make a search. So, a purchaser of a leasehold estate will be bound by charges registered against the name of the former owner of the leasehold estate *and* by charges registered against the names of the owners of the freehold estate out of which the lease is carved. This is so even though a leaseholder has no right to investigate their landlord's title,[45] and hence has no way of discovering the names of the freeholders against which to search. According to *White* v. *Bijou Mansions* (1938), this is the clear effect of section 198(1) of the LPA 1925 (even though section 44(5) of the LPA 1925 would seem to say that a tenant in such circumstances is not fixed with notice of the relevant charge). Likewise, a purchaser of unregistered land has no right to view title documents that exist behind the root of title. Yet, root of title is only 15 years, so a purchaser may well be bound by charges registered against names that appear in a conveyance made more than 15 years before the date of the transaction under consideration. These names are potentially undiscoverable – the purchaser having no right of access to them – but the registered land charge is binding (section 198 of the LPA 1925). To meet this particular problem (which was exacerbated when root of title was reduced to 15 years instead of 30, in 1970), section 25(1) of the LPA 1969 provides that a purchaser may obtain compensation for being bound by a registered land charge hidden behind the root of title if:

1   the transaction causing loss takes place on or after 1 January 1970;[46] and
2   the purchaser had no actual (i.e. real) knowledge of the hidden charge; and
3   the charge is registered against the name of an estate owner that is not revealed in any of the documents of title.

Clearly, this provision for statutory compensation is essential, given the possibility that a purchaser might be bound by a land charge hidden behind the root of title. It is, of necessity, a compromise solution and demonstrates clearly the inadequacies of the land charge system of registration.[47]

---

43 It was an estate contract and should have been registered as a Class C(iv) land charge.

44 The seller was the father, the purchaser was the mother and the unregistered option belonged to the son and daughter-in-law.

45 *Patman* v. *Harland* (1881).

46 When a good root of title was reduced to 15 years.

47 That said, claims to compensation are very rare.

3.6.3 The consequences of failing to register a registrable land charge

As the paramount policy of the LCA 1972 is to protect both the purchaser of land and the owners of any third-party rights in that land (by bringing a measure of certainty to dealings with unregistered land), it is not surprising that there is a heavy penalty for failure to register a *registrable* interest. The fundamental point is that, while failure to register a land charge does not affect its validity as between the parties that created it,[48] nevertheless such failure destroys its validity against any future purchasers of the land. In simple terms, if a person purchases land over which there exists a registrable, but unregistered, land charge, that purchaser and all subsequent transferees are not bound by the charge. Lack of registration equals voidness *even if the purchaser actually knew of the charge* – see section 199 of the LPA 1925, as illustrated in the clearest terms by *Midland Bank v. Green* (1981). In that case, the sale and purchase was between husband (the original estate owner) and wife (the purchaser) for a sum considerably less than the true market value and was carried out precisely to defeat an unregistered land charge granted to their son. In a judgment that upholds the integrity of the land charge registration system to the utmost degree, the House of Lords confirmed that it was not fraud to take deliberate advantage of the system by selling the land in order to defeat an unregistered right (there was no obligation of good faith), and that provided that the consideration paid was 'money or money's worth', it did not matter that it was less than the true value of the land.

However, this simple statement of principle hides much detail and, in fact, the precise circumstances in which an unregistered land charge is void depends on the particular class of land charge and the status of the person who takes a transfer of the land burdened by the charge. After all, we should not forget that a central aim of the land charge system is to protect 'purchasers' and so we must consider also whether the 'voidness' rule applies in equal measure to persons who come into possession of the land without being purchasers. Finally, and by way of exception, we should also note there are some special circumstances in which an unregistered land charge may be upheld against a purchaser or other transferee for reasons not connected to the principles of land charge registration. The rules are discussed in detail below.

3.6.4 The voidness rule

In order to determine precisely the consequences of a failure to register a *registrable* land charge, we must consider the precise type of land charge in issue and the nature of the transferee of the burdened land who is seeking to avoid enforcement of the land charge. This is sometimes known as the 'voidness rule', and may be expressed as follows.

1   A purchaser or transferee's knowledge of the existence of a registrable, but unregistered, land charge is generally irrelevant in determining whether it binds him when he becomes the new owner of the burdened land – see section 199 of the LPA 1925 as illustrated by *Midland Bank v. Green* (1981).

---

48 See above, *Barclays Bank v. Buhr* (2001).

2   Class A, B, C(i), C(ii), C(iii) and F land charges, if not registered, *are void against a purchaser of any interest in the land* (i.e. a legal or equitable estate) *who gives valuable consideration* (sections 4 and 17 of the LCA 1972). In other words, a person who buys an equitable or legal freehold or leasehold, or who takes an equitable or legal mortgage, will obtain the land free of these unregistered land charges if they gave 'valuable consideration'. Actual knowledge of the charge is irrelevant. Moreover, as illustrated by *Midland Bank v. Green*, the consideration need only be valuable; it need not be adequate.

3   Class C(iv) and D land charges, if not registered, *are void against a purchaser of a legal estate in the land who gives 'money or money's worth'* – section 4 of the LCA 1972 – as illustrated by *Lloyds Bank v. Carrick* (1996), in which the defendant's estate contract[49] was held void against the purchaser[50] due to lack of registration. That the voidness rule for Class C(iv) and D land charges operates only in favour of a purchaser of a *legal* estate means that its effect is more limited than that applying to the other classes. So, a purchaser of an *equitable* lease, or a bank lending money by means of an *equitable* mortgage, remain bound by an *unregistered* Class C(iv) and D land charge.[51] There is also a difference between 'valuable consideration' and 'money or money's worth', the latter being slightly narrower than the former. So, for example, a transfer of a legal estate in land to a newly married couple 'in consideration of marriage' is valuable consideration, but it is not 'money or money's worth' and the purchasers (the newly married couple) would still be bound by unregistered Class C(iv) or D land charges, but not by those of other classes.[52]

4   All land charges, *even if unregistered, are valid against a transferee of the land who is not a purchaser.* This will include a recipient of the land by way of gift, a devisee under a will (i.e. the beneficiary of a gift of land) and an adverse possessor of unregistered land whether in the process of completing, or having completed, the requisite period of adverse possession. In all of these cases, the new estate owner will be bound by all pre-existing property rights, whether registered or not, precisely because they are not purchasers.

5   All land charges, *even if unregistered, will be valid against a purchaser who has engaged in fraud.* This is another example of the well-established maxim that 'equity will not permit a statute to be an instrument of fraud' (i.e. where the statute is the voidness rule of the LCA 1972). However, the really difficult problem is to identify what constitutes 'fraud' for this purpose. Certainly, the purchaser's mere knowledge or notice of the unregistered charge does not constitute 'fraud' on his part,[53] but neither does such knowledge even if coupled with a deliberate sale to a purchaser at an absurdly low

---

49 It was a contract to purchase the remainder of a long lease.

50 The purchaser was a mortgagee of the premises who had lent money to the owner. This counts as a 'purchase' of a legal estate (the mortgage). See Chapter 11.

51 In fact, although it is possible to purchase only an equitable interest in property, it should be noted that in the great majority of cases concerning the enforceability of Class C(iv) and D land charges, the intending purchaser is indeed a purchaser of a legal interest for money or money's worth.

52 As noted previously, however, the purchaser need not pay adequate 'money or money's worth' to escape unregistered Class C(iv) and D charges: *Midland Bank v. Green* (1981).

53 *Hollington Bros v. Rhodes* (1951).

price for the express purpose of defeating the unregistered interest as in *Midland Bank v. Green* (1981). As already noted, in *Green*, a father granted his son an option to purchase a farm. This was an estate contract and should have been registered as a Class C(iv) land charge. It was not registered. Subsequently, the father sold the farm to the mother for £500[54] deliberately to defeat the unregistered option. Nevertheless, as was made clear by the House of Lords, it is not a fraud to take advantage of one's legitimate rights, even if it seems that there has been some element of 'bad faith'. Consequently, given that the mother was a purchaser of a legal estate for money or money's worth, the unregistered option was not enforceable against the land. In sum then, the courts have taken a strict line with the enforceability of land charges and have not been prepared to permit the 'fraud exception' to make large inroads into the voidness rule. Undoubtedly, this has much to do with the powerful decision of the House of Lords in *Midland Bank* v. *Green* (1981), in which there is a clear preference for the certainty of the register over the apparent 'justice' of the individual case. Indeed, although in *Green* the owner of the option had recourse to other remedies (e.g. suing the solicitor who negligently failed to register the option), the case illustrates that more is needed to trigger the fraud exception than simply that the person who granted the land charge has later attempted to defeat it. Perhaps the result would have been different if, say, the father had assured his son that the option did not require registration and then had sold the land to his wife. This might have generated an 'estoppel' protecting the unregistered charge (below).

6   All land charges, *even if unregistered, will be valid against a purchaser (or other transferee) who is estopped from denying their validity through proprietary estoppel.* Although it is likely to be rare in practice, if a purchaser of an unregistered title has promised to give effect to an unregistered land charge or has led the person seeking to enforce the charge to believe that it is enforceable, and this has been relied upon by the person entitled to the benefit of the land charge to their detriment, the purchaser will not then be able to plead statutory voidness against that person. He will be held to the promise or agreement, although subsequent purchasers from him may not. In such cases, the purchaser making the assurance is 'estopped' from denying the enforceability of the land charge against them[55] and the estoppel allows the otherwise unenforceable property right to be enforced.[56] For example, in the *Green* case, if the mother (the purchaser) had promised that she would give effect to the unregistered option, she may have been bound by an estoppel to give effect to it even though it was unregistered.[57] In fact, the case that many regard as the origin of the modern law of estoppel – *Taylors Fashions* v. *Liverpool Victoria Trustees* (1979) – concerned unregistered Class C(iv) land charges and whether they were enforceable despite lack of

---

54 It being worth nearer £40,000 at the then current values.

55 It is not clear how, if at all, this differs from the 'fraud exception' discussed above.

56 *Taylor Fashions Ltd* v. *Liverpool Victoria Trustees* (1982). Note *Lyus* v. *Prowsa Developments* (1982), where the purchaser is, unusually, required to give effect to the unregistered land charge because he is said to be subject to a constructive trust because of his personal, inequitable conduct. The existence of such a trust is possible, but difficult to prove and rare: *Groveholt Ltd* v. *Hughes* (2012). See the discussion in Chapter 9, section 9.3.7.

57 Assuming there has been detrimental reliance.

registration (see Chapter 10). However, this is a very narrow exception to the voidness rule, and one that will occur only rarely in practice. In *Taylors Fashions* itself, one unregistered land charge was held enforceable through estoppel and the other not.

3.6.5   Other registers under the Land Charges Act 1972

In addition to the land charges register itself, there are four other registers of matters affecting unregistered land regulated by the LCA 1972. These are the register of annuities, the register of deeds of arrangement, the register of writs and orders affecting land and the register of pending actions. These four additional registers contain information relating to rights, remedies and related interests affecting land that are not the typical third-party interests registrable under the LCA 1972. The register of pending actions is used for the registration of disputes pending in court relating to title to land or to the existence of a proprietary interest. For example, a dispute concerning the existence of easement or whether an estate contract was validly made may be registered here, but it does not allow registration of disputes concerning simply the payment of money even if connected with land, rather than disputes about rights in land (*Zeckler* v. *Kylun Ltd* (2015)). Registration ensures that any subsequent purchaser of the land is given notice of the dispute affecting his land. Similarly, the register of writs and orders affecting land contains details of any order or writ issued by a court affecting land, such as a charging order securing a debt on the debtor's land, and, if registered, are binding on all persons. The register of annuities contains details of certain pre-1926 annuities that do not fall within Class E land charges, and the register of deeds of arrangements records deeds executed by a bankrupt in settlement with creditors. Again, registration ensures their validity against future purchasers of the land.

The land charges register and the four other registers operating under the LCA 1972 are administered centrally by the Land Charges Department of HM Land Registry, although this should not be confused with title registration proper. In addition, there are registers of land held by district councils and other local authorities that record 'local land charges'. These have nothing to do with land charges under the LCA 1972. In fact, 'local land charges' are registered against the land itself and concern charges on land or matters affecting land that may have been recorded by a local authority in pursuit of its statutory responsibilities, such as planning matters. They are discussed here because some categories of land charge proper are defined to exclude 'local land charges'. In fact, local land charges operate in unregistered and registered land in exactly the same way: a prospective purchaser of land will make a search of the local land charges register (currently held by the relevant local authority but soon to be administered by HM Land Registry[58]) prior to concluding the contract of sale. This will inform him or her of any matters that may affect adversely the use to which he or she proposes to put the land and may reveal obligations or risks (e.g. of a nearby building development or planned road) affecting the land. As may be imagined, local land charges are very important in practice, and their discovery has ruined many a prospective sale.

---

58 As authorised by the Infrastructure Act 2015.

3.7   Overreachable Rights

The second category of equitable rights operating in unregistered land concerns those that are subject to the process of overreaching. These are those equitable rights that are excluded from the category of land charges (i.e. they *cannot* be registered) because a properly conducted overreaching transaction will sweep the interests off the land and cause them to take effect in the monies paid by a purchaser for that land. Overreaching occurs in unregistered land in precisely the same circumstances as in registered land. To recap briefly, overreaching will occur when:

1   The equitable right is capable of being overreached. These are equitable co-ownership rights existing behind a trust of land[59] or behind a strict settlement (section 2 of the LPA 1925) and probably equities arising from estoppel or from unconscionable transactions.[60]

2   The transaction is a 'conveyance to a purchaser of a legal estate in land' (section 2(1) of the LPA 1925). This clearly includes the sale of a freehold, the grant or assignment of a legal lease and the grant of a mortgage. According to *Baker* v. *Craggs* (2016) it also includes the grant of an easement although the case is subject to an appeal.

3   The conveyance is made by those persons and in those circumstances that are capable of effecting an overreaching transaction (section 2(1) of the LPA 1925). These circumstances are four in number, although the first is the one most frequently encountered:

   (i)   the transaction is made by at least two trustees of land (or a trust corporation) under a trust of land;[61] or

   (ii)   the transaction is made under the provisions of the SLA 1925 relating to the operation of strict settlements; or

   (iii)   the transaction is made by a mortgagee or personal representative in exercise of their paramount powers; or

   (iv)   the transaction is made under order of the court: for example, section 14 of the TOLATA 1996.

As with registered land, it is only if all three requirements are met that overreaching can occur and the equitable right can then be translated into the purchase money paid for the land. However, what is important to understand for present purposes is that these overreachable equitable rights are *not* capable of registration under the LCA 1972 (section 2(4)(iii) of the LCA 1972) and so the 'owner' of such an interest cannot obtain protection through the system of land charge registration just described. The reason for this is clear enough. The protection for these equitable proprietary rights is meant to be found in the fact that, on overreaching, they will take effect in the purchase money paid by the

---

59 For example, as in *City of London Building Society* v. *Flegg* (1988), in which parents of one of a married couple held an equitable interest in the property but the legal title was held by the married couple jointly.

60 *Mortgage Express* v. *Lambert*.

61 As in *City of London Building Society* v. *Flegg*.

purchaser. In theory, they are not lost, but transformed into cash in a sum equivalent to the share that the equitable owner held in the property.[62]

Given then that these equitable rights are not capable of registration as land charges, is it true to say that they are nevertheless 'guaranteed' or vindicated by the overreaching machinery? It would seem not. First, and obviously, it may well be that the equitable owners do not want a cash equivalent for their interest in the land but would prefer to remain in physical possession or otherwise use the land. Overreaching deliberately prevents this. Second, as we have seen in relation to registered land, *State Bank of India* v. *Sood* (1997) decides that in some circumstances no purchase money need actually be paid to the trustees (i.e. the legal owners) to overreach the equitable interests. Thus, in *Sood*, overreaching still occurred even though the legal owners mortgaged the property to secure *future* borrowings and did not receive an immediate payment of a lump sum. Obviously, while this decision may well be convenient for lenders (as purchasers) – because overreaching still operates to protect them – it offers no comfort or protection to the equitable owner because no lump sum of money is in fact paid in which his or her interest could have taken effect. Third, as we have seen, before overreaching can occur, certain conditions must be established: for example, the paramount requirement that there must be a conveyance by at least *two* trustees/legal owners (or a trust corporation). If these formalities are not observed – because there may, in fact, be only one trustee[63] – the equitable rights are not overreached and the purchaser does not take the land *automatically* free of them. In such cases, we must still determine whether the purchaser might otherwise take free of the interest, but we cannot employ the LCA 1972 because such rights are not registrable as land charges. Consequently, in unregistered land we are thrown back on the old doctrine of notice and a purchaser who fails to overreach will be bound by these equitable interests if he has 'notice' of them.[64] This is unsatisfactory for both purchaser and equitable right-holder. To recap then: first, certain equitable rights cannot be registered as land charges because they are susceptible to overreaching and overreaching will occur whenever the statutory formalities are complied with, even if no purchase money is actually paid; and, second, if these equitable rights are not overreached, their effect on a purchaser is determined by the old equitable doctrine of notice.

3.8   A Residual Class of Equitable Interests in Unregistered Conveyancing

So far we have considered three different types of third-party right over unregistered land: legal rights; rights capable of registration as land charges under the LCA 1972; and rights capable of being overreached. In essence, this tripartite scheme was intended to encapsulate the totality of third-party rights in unregistered conveyancing, with only minor exceptions. However, in the same way that land law in this country had developed

---

62 For example, a 40 per cent share of ownership equals a 40 per cent share of net proceeds of sale. Quantification may prove more difficult if equitable estoppels and equities arising from unconscionable bargains are capable of being overreached.

63 See Chapter 4 and *Williams & Glyn's Bank* v. *Boland* (1981).

64 See section 3.8 below.

up to 1926, it has continued to develop since the 1925 legislation, and it is now clear that there is a fourth category of third-party equitable rights that does not fit into this neat scheme. Some of the rights within this category were excluded deliberately from the tripartite pattern just described, being minor exceptions made for policy reasons. Others are new rights, developed since 1 January 1926. However, whatever the reason for their exclusion from the tripartite system, the fundamental rule governing their effect on unregistered land is clear. When a purchaser buys land over which there is alleged to be an equitable right that is neither registrable as a land charge nor overreachable, that equitable right is binding on the purchaser if he has actual, constructive or imputed notice of it. In other words, the ability of these rights (being equitable) to bind a purchaser of unregistered land depends on the historical doctrine of notice, and this is the one significant situation in which the doctrine is still relevant in modern land law. The following are the equitable rights that fall into this residual category.

1   Equitable co-ownership interests behind a trust of land and equitable successive interests under a SLA settlement – section 2(4)(iii) of the LCA 1972 – but only when there is no overreaching.[65] As noted in section 3.7 above, these equitable rights were deliberately omitted from the land charges system because it was believed most would actually be overreached. However, as we now know, it is not always true that they are. When they are not overreached, their effect on a purchaser is to be judged by the doctrine of notice.

2   Pre-1926 restrictive covenants and easements are also deliberately excluded from the LCA (section 2(5)(ii) and (iii) of the LCA 1972). These interests are excluded for the entirely practical reason that it would be very difficult to ensure their registration given that they were created before the entry into force of the land charges legislation.

3   Equitable mortgages protected by deposit of title deeds are excluded because absence of the title deeds will always be notice to an intending purchaser of the land of the existence of such a powerful adverse right. Hence, they do not need protection by reason of registration. Note, however, it is now the case that deposit of title deeds alone cannot actually create an equitable mortgage because such a mortgage does not spring from a *written* contract as required by section 2 of the LP(MP)A 1989.[66] Consequently, no new equitable mortgages of this type can come into existence.

4   Pre-1926 Class B and C land charges (because they pre-date the legislation), until they are conveyed into different ownership when they must be registered (because their conveyance is an opportune time to register) (section 4(7) of the LCA 1972).

5   Restrictive covenants between a lessor and lessee relating to the land held under the lease (section 2(5)(ii) of the LCA 1972). Such covenants have no need to be registered because there is a web of independent rules determining the effect of leasehold covenants on persons who were not the original landlord and tenant. These rules are discussed fully in Chapter 6.

6   Restrictive covenants between a lessor and lessee relating to land that is *not* part of the land leased: that is, where the covenant is found in a lease but relates to other land, such as other land held by the landlord in the vicinity. These covenants are

---

65 Kingsnorth v. Tizard (1986).

66 United Bank of Kuwait v. Sahib (1995).

also outside the land charge registration system (because they are between lessor and lessee – section 2(5)(ii) of the LCA 1972, as above) but, because they do not relate to the land that is the subject matter of the lease, they cannot be enforced under the leasehold covenant rules. Thus, they bind purchasers of the relevant land through the doctrine of notice.[67]

7   A landlord's 'right of re-entry' in an equitable lease, as explained in *Shiloh Spinners* v. *Harding* (1973). This right, which permits a landlord to re-enter the land and terminate (forfeit) the lease when a covenant is broken, will be equitable when it is expressly or impliedly included as a term in an equitable lease. It falls outside all of the classes of land charge because of the plain words of section 2 of the LCA 1972. Consequently, it is enforceable against subsequent purchasers of the equitable lease, or an interest in it (e.g. a subtenancy) through the doctrine of notice.

8   A tenant's right to enter the property and remove 'tenant's fixtures' at the end of an equitable lease, as explained in *Poster* v. *Slough Lane Estates* (1969). Once again, this interest falls outside the strict definition of the LCA 1972 and so its validity against purchasers of the burdened land must depend on the doctrine of notice. It is a right that permits a tenant of an equitable lease to re-enter the leasehold land after the lease has ended in order to remove certain items ('tenant's fixtures') from the land.

9   Interests acquired through proprietary estoppel, as illustrated by *Ives* v. *High* (1967), unless they have been overreached.[68] These powerful interests are generated through the operation of the doctrine of proprietary estoppel and so arise informally by reason of interaction between the landowner and the person claiming the right. They appear to be non-registrable as land charges even if (as in *Ives* itself) the interest created is similar to a class of land charge, such as an equitable easement. The point is, however, that these rights derive from pure equity and their mode of creation is such that their owner may not be aware that they actually have an interest until the land over which they exist is sold to a purchaser. This would, of course, be too late to register and so the *Ives* decision is policy-driven. It is likely that all interests generated by proprietary estoppel are non-registrable as land charges, at least on the occasion of a sale of the land over which they exist to the first purchaser after they have been generated. Subsequent to that, the existence of the interest will be known and the owner of the estoppel interest might be required to register it if it is to be preserved should a further sale take place. However, this has not been settled – and now may never be, given the diminishing frequency of unregistered conveyancing. If such rights are overreachable, and actually overreached, the right holder cannot then use the doctrine of notice to enforce them against a purchaser but instead is satisfied out of the proceeds of sale.

10   A 'charging order'[69] made under the Charging Orders Act 1979 over the interest of an equitable owner of property is apparently not registrable in the register of writs and orders affecting *land*, because such an equitable interest (over which the charge

---

67   *Dartstone Ltd* v. *Cleveland Petroleum Ltd* (1969). The position is not affected by the LTCA 1995 because that Act annexes covenants to 'the premises demised by the tenancy and of the reversion in them', not to land outside the lease (section 3(1)(a) of the LTCA 1995)), a view confirmed by *Oceanic Village* v. *United Attractions* (1999).

68   As suggested is possible by *Mortgage Express* v. *Lambert* (2016).

69   That is, a charge over a debtor's property enforcing a debt arising from a judgment of a court.

is made) is regarded not an interest in land, but merely an interest in the proceeds of sale of land, as explained in *Perry* v. *Phoenix Assurance* (1988). Such an order would, apparently, only bind a subsequent purchaser of a legal estate by reason of the doctrine of notice. This is a consequence of an application (some would say misapplication) of the doctrine of conversion, rather than an inherent problem with the system of land charges. However, the abolition of the doctrine of conversion by TOLATA 1996 appears not to reverse *Perry* because the LCA 1972 is amended by TOLATA to provide that no writ or order 'affecting an interest under a trust of land' may be registered under its provisions (Schedule 3, section 12(3) of TOLATA 1996).

3.9   Inherent Problems in the System of Unregistered Land

Throughout the analysis presented above, reference has been made both to the nature of the system of unregistered land and to the machinery for the registration of land charges. Some of the problems and difficulties that surround the operation of unregistered land are inherent in the system itself, and some have emerged because of legal, social and economic developments in the years after 1925. The more important points are reiterated below.

First, the system of the registration of land charges is incomplete, in that some equitable rights are non-registrable. This means that the old doctrine of notice still has a part to play, albeit of rapidly diminishing importance since first registration of title became compulsory. Nevertheless, it is a serious criticism that a system that was intended to bring certainty to dealings with land was unable to do away with the vagaries of the doctrine of notice.

Second, the land charges register is a name-based register, and this brings several problems, of varying importance.

1   The use of wrong names or incorrect versions of names, both in the registration of a land charge and in a search of the register, causes obvious problems, as charges are not properly protected and a purchaser may obtain a search certificate on which he cannot rely safely.
2   Long-lived land charges may be registered against names which the purchaser cannot discover and cannot, therefore, search against, as where a purchaser of a lease cannot discover the names of previous freeholders and, more importantly, where names are hidden behind the 15-year root of title.
3   Land charges must be registered against the name of the estate owner of the land that is intended to be bound; thus, sub-purchasers in a chain of uncompleted transactions may register against the wrong person.

Third, the official search certificate is conclusive, rather than the register itself. Consequently, in the event that the Registry fails to carry out an accurate search, a properly registered land charge may be lost. The remedy for the person prejudiced by this error may lie in the law of tort against the Registry, but this has not been fully tested.

Fourth, some would question whether the absolute voidness of an unregistered land charge is justifiable, especially where the purchaser has full knowledge of the unregistered charge and acts deliberately to defeat it, as in *Midland Bank* v. *Green* (1981). However, the LCA 1972 is neutral as to 'fault' and is premised on the paramount need for certainty, even at the expense of those who might be thought to have a deserving case. Although the steady demise of unregistered conveyancing makes the matter less pressing, there has been much debate about whether the LCA 1972 should be applied as vigorously as it was in *Green*, or whether the purchaser's 'actual' state of mind should be as important as the registration requirement.

Fifth, the LCA 1972 does not protect the rights of persons in actual occupation of the land; rather, the position is that if a person has a proprietary right over another person's land, that right will be binding if it is either legal or registered as a land charge, or occasionally protected through the doctrine of notice. If, however, a right is registrable, but not registered, then the right is lost and the owner cannot rely on the fact that they are occupying the property. For example, in *Hollington Bros* v. *Rhodes* (1951), equitable tenants had not registered their equitable lease as a Class C(iv) land charge and so it was void against a purchaser, irrespective of their occupation of the land. Again, in *Lloyds Bank* v. *Carrick* (1996), the occupier also was held to have rights under a Class C(iv) land charge that were void through lack of registration. Yet, in both cases, if this had been land of registered title under the LRA 2002, the interests would have been protected as 'unregistered interests which override' within paragraph 2 of Schedules 1 or 3 through the right-holders' 'actual occupation' of the burdened land.[70] This is a serious defect in the system of unregistered conveyancing and means that the continuing validity of a person's rights might actually turn on the chance of whether the land is of registered title or not. Such a disparity in the systems is not justifiable and there is evidence to suggest that it was not intentional, caused possibly by accidental omission of a provision protecting occupiers of unregistered land when the land charges legislation was consolidated in the original LCA 1925.

3.10   A Comparison with Registered Land

The regimes operated by the LCA 1972 and the LRA 2002 are intended to achieve broadly similar objectives, albeit that the latter is far more wide-ranging than the former. In essence, both of these systems are intended to bring stability to the system of conveyancing in England and Wales by protecting purchasers of land and owners of rights over that land. The following points highlight the different methods used to achieve these goals.

1   In registered land, nearly all titles to land are recorded on a register with a searchable, unique title number. The registered title is guaranteed by the State. In unregistered land, a purchaser must rely on the title deeds and has to investigate the title in order to secure a proper root of title. The title is not guaranteed by the State.

2   In registered land, third-party rights are protected through registration against the title by means of a Notice or under the provisions relating to interests which override (Schedules 1 and 3 of the LRA 2002). Of especial importance is the protection given to the rights of persons in actual occupation within paragraph 2 of the Schedules. In unregistered land, 'legal rights bind the whole world' and equitable third-party rights are protected through a flawed 'name-based' system of land charge

---

70   The same result would have been reached under the old LRA 1925, section 70(1)(g), which paragraphs 2 of Schedules 1 and 3 replaced.

registration, or, even worse, by reliance on the old doctrine of notice. In both systems, overreaching is available, but not always possible.

3   In registered land, an owner of an equitable right need not always register his right by means of a Notice (although the LRA 2002 very much encourages such registration) but can sometimes fall back on the protection provided by interests which override, especially through the 'actual occupation' provisions. Although this compromises the integrity of the register, and poses problems for purchasers, it serves an important social purpose. In unregistered land, there is no protection for the rights of people in actual occupation.

4   In registered land, the methods of protecting an interest on the register under the LRA 2002 are relatively straightforward and uncomplicated. Such registration is also very effective in guaranteeing the validity of the right against the burdened land. In unregistered land, the name-based system can cause considerable problems.

5   In registered land, an interest that is not protected through registration (not being an overriding interest) loses its priority in favour of a purchaser of the registered title (sections 29 and 30 of the LRA 2002). The meaning of this is not entirely clear, because the unprotected right is not 'void' for all purposes. The voidness rule in unregistered land is spelt out clearly and has been applied with considerable vigour by the courts.

6   In registered land, it is the register that is conclusive, not any search thereof. In unregistered land, the search certificate is conclusive, even if it contains an error.

7   In registered land governed by the LRA 2002, it will be very rare for an adverse possessor to gain title to another's land, although it is still possible.[71] In unregistered land, it remains very possible for the title owner to lose their estate by reason of a successful claim of adverse possession.

3.11   Chapter Summary

3.11.1   Unregistered land and unregistered conveyancing

'Unregistered land' is land to which title is not recorded in an official register. 'Title' is found in the title deeds and related documents held by the estate owner (or their mortgagee). The purchaser will identify a good 'root of title' by examining the deeds and the land before completing the purchase.

3.11.2   The basic rules of unregistered conveyancing

A purchaser of unregistered land may be subject to another person's proprietary rights over the land, such as another person's lease or a neighbour's easement. In order to determine the precise effect of another person's proprietary rights against a transferee of the land, the following principles apply.

---

71   For example, if the adverse possessor completed 12 years' adverse possession before the entry into force of the LRA 2002, or the registered proprietor does not object to the application by the squatter, or one of the exceptions applies. See Chapter 12.

1   Legal rights bind the whole world, so ensuring that any legal estates or interests affecting the land are binding on all transferees. These legal rights may well have been obvious from inspection of the title deeds or the land itself. The exception is the *puisne* mortgage, a legal interest that is a land charge (see below).

2   Equitable rights fall into three categories.

   (i)   Land charges (being defined in six classes in the LCA 1972) must be regis-tered against the name of the estate owner of the land that is to be bound at the time of the right's creation. If registered, they are binding on a prospec-tive purchaser of the land, even if 'hidden' from that purchaser. If they are not registered, they are void against a purchaser of a legal estate, or a pur-chaser of any interest, depending on the category of land charge. This rule of voidness is strictly applied. The land charges system suffers from many defects, not least that it is name-based. It also fails to protect the rights of those in occupation of the land, even though this protection may be avail-able in registered land. Unregistered land charges remain binding on a person who is not a purchaser, such as a person who inherits the land or receives it as a gift.

   (ii) Overreachable rights, such as co-ownership rights, are not registrable as land charges. The idea is that these will take effect in the money paid by a purchaser: they will be swept off the title by overreaching. The same con-ditions for overreaching apply in unregistered land as in registered land and the same difficulties exist.

   (iii) Equitable interests protected by the doctrine of notice, being a residual cat-egory of rights that were either deliberately or accidentally excluded from the land charges system. The most important are the equitable right of co-ownership when overreaching is not possible and rights generated by proprietary estoppel (also not having been overreached). Whether a trans-feree is bound by any of these rights in the absence of overreaching depends on the doctrine of notice with all its vagaries.

3.11.3   Inherent problems in the system of unregistered land

Some of the problems and difficulties that surround the operation of unregistered land are inherent in the system itself and some have emerged because of legal, social and eco-nomic developments in the years since 1925.

*   The system of the registration of land charges is incomplete, in that some equitable rights are non-registrable. This means that the old doctrine of notice still has a part to play.
*   The land charges register is a name-based register and this brings several problems of varying importance – for example: the use of wrong names or incorrect versions of names both in the registration of a land charge and in a search of the register; land charges may be registered against names that the purchaser cannot discover and cannot search against; and sub-purchasers in a chain of uncompleted transac-tions may register against the wrong person.
*   The official search certificate is conclusive; thus, in the event that the registry fails to carry out an accurate search, a properly registered charge may be lost.

- Some would question whether the absolute voidness of an unregistered charge is justifiable, especially where the purchaser has full knowledge of the charge and acts deliberately to defeat it.
- The LCA 1972 does not protect the rights of persons in actual occupation of the land.

3.11.4 A comparison with registered land

- In registered land, title to land is officially recorded and guaranteed, whereas, in unregistered land, a purchaser must make his own investigation based on the title deeds.
- In registered land, third-party rights are protected through registration or under the provisions relating to overriding interests. In unregistered land, legal rights are safe, but equitable third-party rights are protected through a flawed 'name-based' system of land charge registration or by reliance on the old doctrine of notice. In both systems, overreaching is available.
- In registered land, an owner of an equitable right may be able to fall back on the protection provided by overriding interests, especially through discoverable 'actual occupation' of the relevant land. In unregistered land, there is no protection for the rights of persons in actual occupation.
- In registered land, the LRA 2002 expresses the effect of non-registration in terms of loss of priority, not voidness. It is not entirely clear what consequences this has. In unregistered land, the voidness rule is clear and is applied strictly.
- In registered land, it is the register that is conclusive, not the search certificate. In unregistered land, the search is conclusive.
- In registered land under the LRA 2002, successful adverse possession will be rare. In unregistered land, it remains a viable way of obtaining a title.

 Further Reading

Harpum, C, '*Midland Bank Trust Co Ltd* v. *Green*' [1981] CLJ 213.

Lees, E, 'Title by registration: Rectification, indemnity and mistake and the Land Registration Act 2002' [2013] 76 MLR 62

Wade, HWR, 'Land charge registration revisited' [1956] CLJ 216.

Now visit the companion website to:

- test your understanding of the key terms using our Flashcard Glossary;
- revise and consolidate your knowledge using our Multiple Choice Question testbank.

www.routledge.com/cw/dixon

Chapter 4
Co-ownership

Introduction

The law relating to co-ownership of land[1] forms a major part of most land law syllabuses. More important than that, however, is the fact that this is one area of land law that can have a powerful impact on the lives of everyone in England and Wales. In simple terms, the law of co-ownership operates whenever two or more people enjoy the rights of ownership of land at the same time, whether that be freehold or leasehold land. The co-owners may be married,[2] civil partners, unmarried partners,[3] family members,[4] friends, neighbours or business partners,[5] or stand in any other relationship to each other (or none at all) that we can think of. In other words, 'the law of co-ownership' is a set of rules that governs dealings with property that is owned simultaneously by more than one person. It is not concerned specifically with the property law problems of married or unmarried couples in family relationships. It is not a species of family law. Of course, many of the problems that exist with co-owned property arise precisely because an emotional relationship has broken down, or friends have fallen out, or a mortgage cannot be paid. However, these are the causes of the problem and the law of co-ownership is not designed specifically for these domestic eventualities. It is important to remember the fundamental 'property law' nature of co-ownership when considering the issues discussed below.

The law of co-ownership is a product of statute and the common law. The LPA 1925 and the TOLATA 1996 are particularly important, with the latter amending significantly the original 1925 legislative scheme governing co-ownership. Moreover, social and economic changes also have had a great impact on the frequency with which co-ownership arises and the consequences it brings. It is no longer true that co-ownership is limited to large, country estates or to land held for investment purposes. Neither is it true that co-ownership can arise only on a deliberate conveyance of land to two or more people. The *implied* creation of co-ownership of land – or rather the acquisition of ownership rights by means other than a formal conveyance – is a relatively common phenomenon and an even more common claim. As we shall see, much of the law of co-ownership today concerns the rights and responsibilities of the co-owners of the family home and the way in which they interact with banks, building societies and other purchasers. This change in the role of co-ownership – or, rather, this broadening of the reach of the law on co-ownership away from purely commercial or investment land – has generated significant changes to the original scheme of co-ownership first devised in the 1925 property legislation. These changes have been achieved both by statute (TOLATA 1996) and by judicial development of the common law.

The law of co-ownership can be broken down into its various component parts, at least for the purposes of exposition. There is, first, the nature of co-ownership, and the types of co-ownership of land that may exist since 1 January 1926. Second, there is the

---

1 Sometimes called the law of *concurrent* co-ownership in order to distinguish it from the law of *successive* co-ownership considered in Chapter 5.

2 *Abbott v. Abbott* (2007) on appeal to the Privy Council from Antigua and Barbuda.

3 *Curley v. Parkes* (2004); *Stack v. Dowden* (2007); *Jones v. Kernott* (2011), relationship breakdown of unmarried couples.

4 *McKenzie* v. *McKenzie* (2003), a father and son; *Hapeshi v. Allnatt* (2010), a mother and her children; *Ullah v. Ullah* (2013), a father and his children.

5 *Rodway v. Landy* (2001), in which the co-owned property was a doctors' surgery.

statutory machinery that regulates the use and enjoyment of co-owned land, and the all-important questions of why the 1925 legislation made the radical changes that it did, and why it was felt necessary to amend these further in 1996. Third, there are those statutory and common law rules governing the creation of co-ownership (the acquisition of property rights), both when this is deliberate and where it arises informally from the potential co-owners' dealings with the property and each other. Fourth, there is the impact of co-ownership on third parties, such as banks and building societies (which may have lent money to finance the purchase of the property), and on purchasers and other occupiers. Fifth, there are matters relating to the termination of co-ownership, and the methods by which one form of co-ownership may replace another.

4.1 The Nature and Types of Concurrent Co-ownership

Concurrent co-ownership of property describes the simultaneous enjoyment of land by two or more persons. It is important to remember that we are concerned here with the *simultaneous* enjoyment of property: that is, enjoyment of the rights of ownership by two or more persons at the same time. Successive interests in land, whereby two or more people are entitled to the enjoyment of land in succession to each other, are dealt with in Chapter 5. Before 1 January 1926, concurrent co-ownership of property could take a variety of forms, but co-ownership since 1 January 1926 will either be by way of a *joint tenancy* or a *tenancy in common*. At the outset, it is best to note that 'tenancy' here does not mean a lease or a leasehold interest; rather, it is the description given to the *type* of co-ownership enjoyed by the co-owners, irrespective of whether they own freehold or leasehold land.

4.2 Joint Tenancy

When land is owned by two or more people on the basis of a joint tenancy, each co-owner is treated as being entitled to the whole of that land. There are no distinct 'shares', and no single co-owner can claim any greater right over any part of the land than another. As far as the rest of the world is concerned, the land is treated as if it is owned by one person only and all of the 'joint tenants' participate in that one ownership. In practical terms, this means that when land is subject to a joint tenancy, there is only one formal title to it and that title is owned jointly by all of the joint tenants. So, if four students co-own legal title to a house under a joint tenancy, it is *not* possible to say that they own one-quarter each; they each own the whole. Moreover, if the land is registered, there will be but one title registered at HM Land Registry under one title number, with each co-owner registered as proprietor of that title in the proprietorship section of the register. If the land is unregistered, there will be but one set of title deeds, specifying the four owners. In essence, each joint tenant owns the total interest in the land. This really is 'co-ownership', because there are no shares, no partition of the land, but a right of ownership of the whole of the land enjoyed simultaneously with all of the other owners. The nature of the joint tenancy as a single title owned by more than one person is reflected in its legal attributes. These attributes – discussed immediately below – are regarded as the touchstone of a joint tenancy and the absence of any one is fatal to the existence of this form of co-ownership.

4.2.1   The right of survivorship (the *ius accrescendi*)

By virtue of this principle, if one joint tenant dies during the existence of the joint tenancy,[6] his interest in the joint tenancy (being his right to enjoy the whole of the land and its cash value on sale) *automatically accrues* to the remaining joint tenants. In fact, all that is happening is that the dead joint tenant drops out of the joint tenancy and the remainder continue to enjoy their rights over the whole land. The important practical point is, then, that when a joint tenant dies, no formal conveyance or written document is needed to reflect the new status quo. There is nothing to convey or transfer, so no conveyance or transfer is needed.[7] Indeed, the right of survivorship takes precedence over any attempted transfer on death. So, a person by his will *cannot* pass an interest under a joint tenancy because that interest does not belong to the deceased. The interest of the dead joint tenant accrues to the other joint tenants at the moment of death, so there is nothing to be left to a beneficiary under the will, even if an attempt has been made in the will explicitly to leave the deceased's 'share' in the land to someone else.[8] This means that a joint tenancy can either be very useful, as where it avoids the need for formal documentation when a co-owner dies,[9] or very unfair, as where a co-owner dies and is unable to leave an interest in the property to his family because it has accrued to the remaining joint tenants.

4.2.2   The four unities

Before a joint tenancy can exist, the 'four unities' must be present[10] and it is the presence (or absence) of these unities that enables us to distinguish a joint tenancy from a tenancy in common.

1   The *unity of possession* means that each joint tenant is entitled to physical possession of the whole of the land. Unity of possession means that there can be no physical division of the land and no restriction on any joint tenant's use of each and every part of it. This includes the right to participate fully in the fruits of possession, such as receipt of rents and profits derived from the land. As we shall see, although unity of possession must exist before a joint tenancy can exist, the practical effects of it have been modified by statute so that, in some circumstances, one joint tenant may be excluded from the land on terms and conditions (sections 12 and 13 of TOLATA 1996).[11]

---

6   As we shall see, a joint tenancy may be 'severed' to become a 'tenancy in common' or it may expire naturally on the death of the last-but-one joint tenant, leaving a sole owner.

7   For registered land, the deceased joint tenant's name can be removed from the proprietorship register on application to the registrar but sometimes this is not done until the surviving joint tenants wish to deal with the land in some way.

8   *Gould* v. *Kemp* (1834). Therefore, in order to pass property on death, the joint tenancy must have been brought to an end *before* death – usually by being severed and turned into a tenancy in common.

9   For example, on the death of either the husband and wife who were co-owners of the matrimonial home.

10   *AG Securities* v. *Vaughan* (1988), in which the House of Lords held that a flat-sharing arrangement whereby each sharer signed their own agreement did not amount to a single joint tenancy of the whole premises because of the obviously distinct rights that each occupier had.

11   See *Chun* v. *Ho* (2001).

As a matter of principle, this does not destroy the unity of possession per se; rather, the court's powers under sections 12 and 13 of TOLATA can be used to modify each co-owner's entitlement to occupy. A similar power exists in relation to family disputes under Part IV of the Family Law Act 1996 where the court is given the power to exclude certain persons from the family home.

2   The unity of interest means that each joint tenant's interest in the property must be of the same extent, nature and duration. Thus, all must be joint tenants of the freehold, or of the leasehold, and in remainder or possession (as the case may be). Different qualities of right are inconsistent with the nature of a joint tenancy as a single title, jointly owned.

3   The unity of title means that each joint tenant must derive their title (i.e. ownership) from the same conveyancing documents. Note, however, that in certain circumstances, estate owners may still have a joint tenancy even though as a matter of formality they have each signed different documents. A good example is where leaseholders may be treated as joint tenants because this reflects the true nature of the agreement between all of the parties despite signing separate agreements with their landlord. In *Antoniades* v. *Villiers* (1990), an unmarried couple took a lease of a one-bedroom flat and signed separate documents. In the circumstances, which included the fact that the landlord had provided a double bed and there was only one bedroom, the court took the view that it was absurd to regard these two people as having separate and independent rights to the land. The House of Lords decided that *as a matter of law*, the two joint tenants derived their title from the same document, even though there was more than one piece of paper. Any other conclusion would have been to uphold a pretence. The matter must be one of substance, not of form. Of course, in the normal course of events, the title will have been conveyed to the joint tenants by the same document – as where a man and woman buy a new house as the family home – but the simple fact that different documents may have been signed by the potential co-owners does not automatically mean that there is no unity of title and hence no joint tenancy.

4   The unity of time means that the interest of each joint tenant must arise at the same time, as befitting their ownership of a single title. For example, if a woman purchases a house in 2012 and in 2018, on the occasion of her marriage, grants an equal share in the house to her husband, they cannot be joint tenants: the interests of the co-owners arose at different times.[12] The same is true if, say, the interest of the man arises informally through some act of the parties after the title has been conveyed to his partner. In nearly every case of implied co-ownership, the interest of one co-owner comes later than the other so they are usually not joint tenants.

4.3   Tenancy in Common

When two or more people own land under a tenancy in common, it is often said that they have 'undivided shares in land'. In other words, a tenant in common can point to a precise share of ownership of the land (e.g. one-half, one-fifth, one-quarter, etc.), even

---

12 A joint tenancy could arise, however, if the wife were to reconvey the entire house into the joint names of herself and her husband, rather than simply giving him a share in it.

though the land at present is undivided and treated as a single unit. The distinguishing feature of a tenancy in common is, then, that each co-owner has a distinct and quantifiable share in the land. That does not mean, however, that a particular tenant can physically demarcate a portion of the land and claim it as his own. The land is still 'undivided', and the tenant in common owns a quantifiable share in it, which can be realised if and when the property is sold. To put it another way, there is 'unity of possession' with a tenancy in common despite the fact that such a tenant can legitimately say that they own, say, one-fifth of the land. So, following through the example, if four students co-own the house in which they live under a tenancy in common, it will be possible to say that they each own a defined share. This may be one-quarter each, but it is perfectly possible that A owns one-third, B owns one-third and C and D own one-sixth each. In fact, any combination of proportions of shared ownership is possible with a tenancy in common. If the house were to be sold, then the actual shares would take effect in the money paid by the purchaser, with each tenant in common receiving a sum proportionate to their share in the land. Pending that, however, the land is 'undivided', with each enjoying possession of the whole irrespective of the size of their share.

Although none of the other four unities, apart from possession, must be present for a tenancy in common to exist, it may well be that they are. For example, it is likely that unity of time will exist if the co-ownership came into existence from the moment the property was acquired. Importantly, the right of survivorship does not apply to a tenancy in common, so that a co-owner under a tenancy in common is perfectly able to leave his share on death or may otherwise deal with it during his life. It is for this reason that a tenancy in common is often preferred where the co-owners are not closely connected – the absence of survivorship means that there is no risk that a person's property can accrue in error to his business partner instead of his family. Thus, to summarise, with a tenancy in common:

1   there is an undivided share in land;
2   there is unity of possession;
3   no other unity must be present, although others may be;
4   there is no right of survivorship and so the share may be passed on in the normal way on death or in writing during the co-owner's life.

Finally, we should note that a tenancy in common may come about through the 'severance' of a joint tenancy. This is discussed in more detail below, but it means that the parties to a joint tenancy may choose to terminate that form of co-ownership during their lives and be governed instead by the regime of a tenancy in common. This is often driven by the desire to avoid the right of survivorship, especially after relationship breakdown.

4.4   The Effect of the Law of Property Act 1925 and the Trusts of Land and Appointment of Trustees Act 1996

It goes without saying that it is vital to distinguish in practice between a joint tenancy and a tenancy in common, not least because of the right of survivorship. However, before we can examine in detail how that may be done, it is necessary to consider the regime of co-ownership established by the LPA 1925 and the further changes made by

TOLATA 1996. The 'modern' law of co-ownership begins with the 1925 property legislation and those reforms help us to understand how the law has evolved and why the
current law operates as it does. As will be seen, TOLATA 1996 did not change the basic
principles of the LPA 1925 regarding co-owned land (and so the LPA 1925 must still be
regarded as the source statute), but it does make significant changes to the detail with
effect from 1 January 1997 when it entered into force.[13] To recap then, the changes
made by the LPA 1925 were changes both in substance and procedure and were part of
the wider reforms designed to simplify all dealings with land to meet the economic and
social challenges of the twentieth century. TOLATA 1996 took this further. The reasons
for the 1925 reform are considered below, but essentially they stem from a paramount
policy of ensuring the free marketability of co-owned land.

4.4.1   Before 1 January 1926

Before 1 January 1926, it was possible for a joint tenancy and a tenancy in common to
exist in both a legal and an equitable estate in land. So, if land was conveyed 'to A and B as
tenants in common', they would be tenants in common of the legal title. Similarly, for a
joint tenancy. Again, if land were conveyed 'to X and Y on trust for A and B as tenants in
common', A and B would be tenants in common of the equitable title (in equity), with the
legal title held by X and Y (as either joint tenants or tenants in common as the case may
be). So, if a purchaser wished to buy the legal title of land that was co-owned, he would
have to have investigated either one title (joint tenancy) or all of the individual titles of the
various co-owners (tenancy in common). While this caused no great hardship for a purchaser investigating the one title held by joint tenant legal owners, if the land was co-
owned under a tenancy in common, the complexity of the transaction increased as the
number of tenants in common increased. To purchase from A and B as tenants in common
was only two titles to investigate, but to purchase from A, B, C and D was four, and so on.

4.4.2   From 1 January 1926

We have noted above that one change made by the LPA 1925 was to limit the types of
co-ownership to two: the joint tenancy and tenancy in common. However, the Act also
placed restrictions on the manner in which these forms of co-ownership could come
into existence – see sections 34 and 36 LPA 1925, as amended by TOLATA 1996. The
first and most significant point is that it has been impossible, since 1 January 1926, to
create a tenancy in common at law: a tenancy in common of the legal title to land cannot
exist (section 1(6) of the LPA 1925). In consequence, only joint tenancies of the legal
title are possible and this is true irrespective of the words used when the land is transferred to the co-owners and irrespective of their intentions. For example, no longer is it
possible to convey the legal title to land to A, B, C and D as tenants in common because
this must operate as a conveyance of the legal title to A, B, C and D as joint tenants, even
though the words are plain and the intentions clear. Note, also, that this must mean that
a joint tenancy of a legal title is 'unseverable' – section 36(2) LPA 1925 – because it is
impossible to turn it into a legal tenancy in common.

---

13 TOLATA 1996 implemented the 1989 Law Commission Report, *Transfer of Land: Trusts of Land* (Law Com. No. 181).

Second, however, this joint tenancy of the legal title is of a special kind. The persons to whom the legal title to the land is conveyed – the intended co-owners of the legal estate – are *trustees* of the legal title under a statutorily imposed trust of land (sections 34 and 36 of the LPA 1925). Thus, in *every* case of co-ownership of the legal title of land,[14] that legal title is held by joint tenant trustees on a 'trust of land'.[15] This statutory trust is defined in the LPA 1925 and TOLATA 1996, but essentially imposes on the trustees (the co-owners of the legal estate) a duty to hold the land for the persons beneficially interested in the land (i.e. the equitable owners) and for the purposes for which it was purchased, to which end they are given various powers of management, including the power of sale. So, given that, in the example above, the conveyance to A, B, C and D operated as a conveyance to them as joint tenants of the legal title (irrespective of the words used), A, B, C and D will hold this land as trustees on the statutorily imposed trust of land for the 'real' owners. In this case, the 'real owners' are, in fact, A, B, C and D themselves, also known as the 'equitable owners'. In other words, they are trustees for themselves! The reasons for this apparently complicated machinery are discussed below.

Third, although the legal title to co-owned land must be held under a joint tenancy, the equitable title (the 'beneficial' and valuable interest) may be held *either* as a joint tenancy or as a tenancy in common. Which form of equitable co-ownership exists will depend on the words used to create the co-ownership in the conveyancing documents, the intentions of the parties and the surrounding circumstances. Again, in our case, although A, B, C and D must be joint tenant trustees of the legal title, in equity they may be either equitable joint tenants or equitable tenants in common. In fact, in this example, they will be equitable tenants in common because it is clear from the words used in the conveyance at the time the land was acquired that this was the intended form of co-ownership.

To sum up then, all expressly created co-ownership operates behind a mechanism whereby the formal legal title is held by joint tenant trustees[16] on the statutorily imposed trust of land. The equitable interest takes effect behind this trust and may be either a joint tenancy or a tenancy in common. Furthermore, in many cases, the 'trustees' will be the same people as those who share in the equitable co-ownership. So, if land is conveyed to a man (M) and woman (W), this will operate as a conveyance to them as joint tenant trustees of the legal title, holding on trust *for themselves* as either joint tenants or tenants in common in equity, depending on the circumstances in which the property was purchased. If, for example, the conveyance says 'to M and W as tenants in common', they will still be joint tenants of the legal title, albeit tenants in common of the equitable interest. The same is true irrespective of the gender of the parties or whether they are in any kind of intimate relationship. Indeed, the same result is achieved irrespective of the number of intended co-owners, save that, by statute, the number of *legal* joint tenant trustees is limited to four (section 34(2) of the LPA 1925). The number of co-owners in equity is not limited, be they joint tenants or tenants in common. Consequently, if the

---

14 In cases of implied co-ownership, there may be only one owner of the legal title, although the equitable title may be co-owned: see below.

15 As stipulated by sections 4 and 5 of TOLATA 1996, amending the LPA 1925.

16 As discussed below, in those cases in which there is only one owner of the legal title, but more than one owner of the equitable title, the legal owner will still be a trustee on the statutory trust of land for these equitable owners, but necessarily as a single trustee.

land is purported to be conveyed to more than four people, it is the first four named in the conveyance who become the joint tenant trustees of the land, with all five or six, and so on, owning in equity as either joint tenants or tenants in common as the case may be.[17] The use of the trust is, therefore, a device to ensure that all legal title to co-owned land is held under a joint tenancy, while also ensuring that in equity, where the beneficial interest lies, the co-owners can be either joint tenants or tenants in common. In fact, in those cases – which will be many – in which the trustees are exactly the same people as the beneficiaries, there is no significant consequence to the use of the trust. When, however, the legal owners are different from the equitable owners, the mandatory use of the trust can have important consequences for all the parties.

4.5   The Distinction between Joint Tenancy and Tenancy in Common in Practice: The Equitable Interest

It follows from the fact that legal title to co-owned land must be held under trusteeship, that the important issue is to determine the nature of the co-ownership in equity for herein we find the valuable interest in the sense that it is the equitable owners who may wish to actually use the land and who are entitled to a share in the proceeds of sale if it is sold. The principles applied here are well established, with gradual development to reflect changing social and economic times. Of course, as ever, there are no immutable rules and each case must be decided on its own facts. The following are offered as guidelines only and their influence will vary from case to case. Remember at all times that we are now talking of the equitable interest only. A co-owned legal estate must be held as joint tenancy.

1   If the unities of interest, title or time are absent, a joint tenancy in equity *cannot* exist. In such a case, there must be a tenancy in common. For example, if the interest of one co-owner arises later than the other – as where a woman makes a successful claim by way of constructive or resulting trust to a share in her lover's property – the equitable interest will be held by way of a tenancy in common. The interests arose at different times. This is a very common way for an equitable tenancy in common to come into existence and it is the inevitable outcome of the increased success of claims that a constructive or resulting trust exists.[18]

2   If the original conveyance to the co-owners stipulates expressly that they are 'joint tenants' or 'tenants in common' *of the beneficial or equitable interest*, this is normally conclusive as to the nature of their co-ownership in equity – *Goodman* v. *Gallant* (1986).

---

17 The chances of there being more than four intended owners of the land are not great, at least in connection with residential property.

18 See section 4.10.2 below. Note, it may be unusual for a resulting trust to be used in respect of a residential property because of the comments made (*obiter*) in *Stack* v. *Dowden* (2009) and *Jones* v. *Kernott* (2011). However, it is not out of the question (*Chaudhary* v. *Chaudhary* (2013)) and may be an easier option in mixed family/business situations (*Laskar* v. *Laskar*, *Wodzicki* v. *Wodzicki*). *Marr* v. *Collie* (2017) makes it clear, explaining *Stack*, that a resulting trust may arise in either a domestic or commercial context, if that is the true intentions of the parties.

So, if land is conveyed to 'Rosie and Jim as tenants in common beneficially', they will be tenants in common in equity as the conveyance is conclusive as to the nature of the equitable ownership, irrespective of later events,[19] and there is no room for the use of resulting or constructive trusts – *Pankhania v. Chandegra* (2012), *Re Kone* (2017), *Taylor v. Taylor* (2017). There may be a very limited exception to this where there is clear unconscionability so as to justify a departure from the express declaration on grounds of proprietary estoppel (*Clarke v. Meadus* (2010)).[20] In *Roy v. Roy* (1996), a conveyance to P and D jointly was held conclusive between them as to the existence of a joint tenancy, despite the fact that D had contributed significantly more to the purchase and upkeep of the property over the years, and that P had lived in the property for only a few months just after it was purchased. We should be clear, however, to understand the true scope of this rule. First, a written declaration[21] of the nature of the equitable interest is conclusive only for the parties to that declaration. So, in the *Roy* case, if an imaginary third party (X) had made a claim to an interest in the property, she would not have been bound by the conveyance to accept a joint tenancy unless she had also been a party to the written declaration. Second, the written declaration is conclusive only if valid under the general law: that is, it can be attacked on the basis that it was procured by fraud, misrepresentation, undue influence or any other vitiating factor. Third, such a written declaration may be made at the time the property is acquired, or at a later date. Importantly, the Land Registry now provides an optional form – Form JO – on which to declare expressly the beneficial interests and this may be sent in when a title is submitted for registration.[22] Fourth, as noted, it appears that a valid written declaration may be departed from – and the shares and type of equitable co-ownership varied – if the later conduct of one of the parties amounts to an estoppel, so preventing them relying on the written declaration, as in *Meadus*. However, this must not be viewed as an easy route to undo a written declaration, and *Meadus* is one of the very few cases where this has occurred. Fifth, it is clear from cases such as *Carlton v. Goodman* (2002), *McKenzie v. McKenzie* (2003), *Stack v. Dowden* (2007) and *Jones v. Kernott* (2011) that the parties are bound only when a declaration refers clearly to the *equitable* interest. In these cases, there were two legal owners who necessarily were joint tenant trustees but there was no express declaration as to the *equitable* ownership. Thus, in *Carlton* and *McKenzie*, when one of the legal co-owners claimed to be entitled to the entirety of the equitable interest because effectively they had paid for the property, the other joint tenant of the legal title resisted, claiming an equitable share flowing from their legal ownership. The result, again in

---

19 *Goodman v. Gallant* (1986); *Hembury v. Peachey* (1996).

20 See Chapter 10 for proprietary estoppel.

21 An oral declaration, unsupported by evidence in writing, would not suffice (section 53(1) of the LPA 1925), save only that there is the possibility that it might support a claim in proprietary estoppel.

22 This followed Lady Hale's pertinent criticism in *Stack v. Dowden* that there should be an easy, simple way for the parties to declare the nature of their equitable ownership at the time of purchase so as to avoid later difficulties and litigation. Form JO is a step forward, but many people would argue that its completion should be compulsory when two or more people purchase property and that property professionals should be able and willing to provide the advice to their clients in order for them to make an informed choice about joint tenancy or tenancy in common.

both cases, was that the equitable ownership resided solely in one party – the main provider of the purchase price – thus demonstrating that being a *legal* owner under an expressly declared conveyance does not guarantee a share of the equitable title.[23] Likewise in *Stack*, although Ms Dowden and Mr Stack were joint tenants of the legal title, Ms Dowden successfully claimed a larger share of the equitable interest because the conveyance to them said only that they were joint tenants in law and nothing about the equitable title.[24] *Jones v. Kernott*, in the Supreme Court, confirms this approach. Thus, while in most cases 'equity follows the law', so that the unde-clared equitable title takes the same form as the legal joint tenancy (see below), it is possible to adduce evidence to establish that it was the common intention of the parties that the shares should be different from this.[25]

3   If 'words of severance' are used, then a tenancy in common will exist in equity. Thus, a description of the share of each owner, or the creation of unequal interests in differ-ent co-owners, will mean that a tenancy in common must exist. A conveyance to 'A and B, two-thirds to A' will necessarily create a tenancy in common in equity. The same is true of a conveyance to 'A and B, half each', as this specifies a share. Note, however, that if land is given 'equally' (as in 'to A and B equally'), this can mean either a joint tenancy or a tenancy in common, depending on whether this means 'half each' or 'jointly', although in such cases the next presumption will usually operate.

4   In the absence of an express declaration concerning the equitable interest or words of severance, and if all of the four unities are present, there is a presumption that 'equity follows the law'. Consequently, because the legal title must be a joint tenancy, in the absence of all other evidence, the equitable title 'follows the law' and is deemed to be a joint tenancy also. So, a conveyance 'to A and B' will be taken to be a conveyance to A and B in law as joint tenants (as it must be), and in equity also. However, there are exceptions to this, being situations in which the presumption that 'equity follows the law' can be displaced by a counter-presumption, arising from the facts, that a tenancy in common must have been intended instead. These are cases in which it is recognised that the existence of a joint tenancy may cause hardship to the co-owners, usually because the right of survivorship would be inappropriate or where there is evidence that the parties had a common intention to hold other than as joint tenants (*Jones v. Kernott, Marr v. Collie*). Situations where there is a presumption against a joint tenancy in equity include land held by business partners and in related business arrangements,[26] cases in which the co-owned interest is of a mortgage held by co-mortgagees[27] and

---

23 See also *Abbey National v. Stringer*, where the legal title of one co-owner carried no equitable interest because of their fraud.

24 In *Fowler v. Barron* (2008), in which there was no declaration as to the equitable interest, the interest was held 50/50, not because the legal title was held jointly and equity should follow it, but because this was the appropriate share, taking account of the entirety of the parties' relationship.

25 See further at section 4.10.2 below. *Ullah v. Ullah* (2013) also reminds that 'equity follows the law' in all cases. So, even when there is a sole legal owner, the claimant must prove that they have an interest on one of the grounds discussed below.

26 *Malayan Credit Ltd v. Jack Chia-MPH* (1986).

27 *Re Jackson* (1887). Thus, the death of one mortgagee will not deprive their estate of the security for the loan made because the mortgage will be held under a tenancy in common.

cases in which the purchasers have provided the purchase money in unequal shares, which, in the absence of other evidence[28] establishes lack of a unity of interest.[29] In all three of these examples, where equity will not follow the law, the parties are presumed to have preferred a tenancy in common because of the substantial disadvantage of construing the arrangement as a joint tenancy with a right of survivorship that would have deprived the co-owner's dependants of an interest in the property. A similar possibility arises from the House of Lords' decision in *Stack* v. *Dowden* and the Supreme Court's decision in *Jones* v. *Kernott* (2011) where it was held that equity will *not* follow the law (i.e. the parties will not be joint tenants in equity) if one of the legal co-owners is able to establish a common intention that the equitable interest should be held differently, and this intention may exist at the time of acquisition of the land or later during the time that the parties were using the property.[30] This is because a constructive trust may arise to give effect to that intention, effectively redistributing the equitable shares in accordance with that intention, despite the absence of any written instrument.[31] This is examined in more detail below, and will apply only where there is no express declaration of the equitable interests, but it is a significant development of the law. While it remains true in principle that absent words of severance and any of the four unities, 'equity will follow the law', the ability of the court to quantify the parties' 'real interests' under *Stack* and *Kernott* because of 'exceptional' circumstances necessarily means that it is more difficult to predict whether the parties hold land in equity as joint tenants or tenants in common. It may well encourage litigation as the parties seek to enhance their share.[32]

4.6   The Statutory Machinery Governing Co-ownership

At first glance, the changes made by the LPA 1925, and then by TOLATA 1996, to the pre-1926 law on co-ownership seem complicated and unwieldy. In fact, as we shall see, the statutory framework for co-ownership established by these statutes is designed to

---

28 For example, that one co-owner was making a gift to another.

29 *Lake* v. *Craddock* (1732). Unusually, in *HSBC* v. *Dyche & Collelldevall* (2009), there was no express declaration of the equitable interest in favour of Mr and Mrs Collelldevall (who were not legal owners), but they were held to be joint tenants in equity because both acquired their equitable interests at the same time for the same reason in the same circumstances. Unequal payments may be evidence of a genuine common intention justifying a constructive trust to hold in unequal shares (*Kernott*); or may be evidence to hold in unequal shares because of a resulting trust (*Laskar*). The key is to find the intention (*Marr* v. *Collie*). The difference is in the size of share awarded. A resulting trust generates shares in proportion to what is paid; a constructive trust according to what is fair in all the circumstances.

30 It is clear, therefore, that the equitable ownership might start out as 'following the law' as a joint tenancy, but change to a tenancy in common in non-equal shares over time.

31 Because constructive trusts concerning land are exempt from the need to be in writing – section 53(2) LPA 1925.

32 See also *Ritchie* v. *Ritchie* (2007), where there were 'exceptional circumstances' allowing departure from the principle that equity follows the law in a case involving mother and son.

ensure that dealings with co-owned land can be accomplished effectively and efficiently. Land is, after all, a prime economic asset. Although complicated as a legal mechanism, the law of co-ownership is now much simpler in practice. We can summarise the situation as follows.

1   It is impossible for a tenancy in common of a legal estate to exist. All co-ownership of a legal title (e.g. a registered title) must be by way of joint tenancy.

2   However, the joint tenants are trustees of the legal estate for the equitable owners, holding the property as trustees of land within the LPA 1925 and TOLATA 1996. They hold the property on trust for the equitable owners.

3   The equitable owners are often the same people as the legal owners (the trustees), but there is no necessary reason why this should be so. In equity, the co-owners may be either joint tenants or tenants in common.

4   The number of legal joint tenant trustees is limited to four, usually the first four co-owners named in the transfer to them. The non-legal co-owners remain entitled in equity and the number of potential equitable owners is unlimited.

4.7   The Nature of the Unseverable Legal Joint Tenancy: The Trust of Land

The owners of the legal title hold the property as joint tenant trustees of land, with powers specified in the LPA 1925 and TOLATA 1996. This trust is defined in sections 34 and 36 of the LPA 1925 and Part I of TOLATA 1996.[33] The trustees will hold the land for the persons interested in it and, subject to any express terms of the trust and statute, with the powers of an absolute owner.[34] They may delegate any of their functions to the beneficiaries, save that only the trustees may give a valid receipt to a purchaser if the land is sold.[35] In fact, it is unlikely that the provisions of TOLATA relating to trustees' powers and the ability to delegate will be needed in most cases of domestic concurrent co-ownership, certainly if the trustees and equitable owners are the same people. They will be more relevant in cases concerning successive interests in land (Chapter 5) or where the trust of land is used as an investment vehicle rather than as a statutorily imposed device for jointly owning a home.

Perhaps the most important point to grasp when considering the nature of the trust of land is that the trustees are under no duty to sell the land, as was the case before the entry into force of TOLATA 1996.[36] This important change means that the legal mechanism of co-ownership (the trust of land) now more accurately mirrors how most co-owned land is used in practice – not as land to be sold, but as land to be occupied. As we shall see, if the trustees (or equitable owners, if such power has been delegated to them)

---

33 Section 35 of the LPA 1925 is repealed.

34 Sections 6 and 8 of TOLATA and sections 23 and 26 of the LRA 2002 in respect of registered proprietors.

35 Section 9 of TOLATA.

36 Under the original LPA 1925 scheme, the trustees held the land on a trust *for sale*, with a power to postpone sale, effectively ensuring that the land could be retained if the trustees agreed (the *power* to postpone sale) but would be sold if they disagreed (the *duty* to sell).

cannot agree whether to sell the land at an appropriate time (e.g. on relationship break-down or if one goes bankrupt), any interested person may apply to the court under section 14 of TOLATA 1996[37] for an order for sale or other order concerning the land. However, there is now no duty to sell the land and the trustees have every right to hold the land for the purpose for which it was acquired, or indeed any other lawful purpose that benefits the equitable owners.

TOLATA 1996 came into force on 1 January 1997 and amended the LPA 1925. Most of its provisions are retrospective, in that they apply to co-ownership trusts already in existence on 1 January 1997 and certainly they govern all new instances of co-ownership. We should note, however, that many of the 1996 Act's changes simply brought the legal structure of co-ownership into line with the way in which the courts already had interpreted the 1925 legislation. For example, prior to 1 January 1997, an equitable owner, in theory, did not have an interest in the land itself, but rather had an interest in the proceeds of sale of that land. This arose because of the trustees' duty to sell under the old 'trust for sale' and so the land was treated as having been sold and replaced with money because, in theory, it should have been ('equity treats as done that which ought to be done'). However, for nearly all practical purposes, even before TOLATA 1996, such an equitable owner was treated as having an interest in the land itself[38] and now this has been recognised by section 3 of TOLATA 1996. With these considerations in mind, the following are the specific attributes of the unseverable legal joint tenancy under the trust of land established by TOLATA 1996.

1   The trustees (legal owners) are under a duty to hold the land for the persons interested in it (often themselves). Although the trustees must have regard to the wishes of the beneficiaries, TOLATA 1996 gives them the powers of an absolute owner in relation to the land (section 6) subject to any provision in TOLATA itself or the instrument establishing the trust or entries made against the register of title.[39] However, the trustees may delegate 'any of their functions' to a beneficiary of full age (section 9) and the court may intervene by way of an order under section 14 at the request of a trustee or any other person having an interest in the trust property.[40] As noted, the trustees' powers may be restricted by the instrument (the document) creating the trust, except in the case of public, ecclesiastical or charitable trusts (section 8). Note here, however, that not everything done by a trustee will be a 'function relating to' the trust. So in *Brackley* v. *Notting Hill Housing Trust* (2001), the giving of notice by one joint tenant trustee of a lease (thereby terminating the lease) was not such a function, at least in the case of a periodic tenancy.[41]

2   If the trustees do sell the land,[42] they hold the proceeds of sale on trust for the equitable owners in the same way that they held the land itself. As discussed in

---

37   Replacing section 30 of the LPA 1925.

38   The seminal example being *Williams & Glyn's Bank* v. *Boland* (1981), in which the proprietary nature of Mrs Boland's interest under the (then) trust for sale of land was critical in determining that she had an overriding interest.

39   See sections 23 and 24 of the LRA 2002. The proposed transaction must, of course, be valid under the general law, *Skelwith Leisure Ltd* v. *Armstrong* (2015).

40   For example, an equitable owner of the land or mortgagee of a co-owner's interest.

41   Consequently, the giving of such notice was not a breach of trust.

42   Either of their own choice or as a result of an order made under section 14 of TOLATA.

Chapters 2 and 3, the equitable owners' interests are overreached and take effect in the proceeds of sale, if any.[43]

3   As mentioned above, prior to the 1996 Act, the trust was actually a trust for sale and this had the unfortunate consequence that, for some purposes, the interests of the equitable owners were treated as interests in the proceeds of the sale, not as interests in the land itself, even if the land had not actually been sold.[44] Section 3 of TOLATA 1996 abolishes the 'doctrine of conversion' for all new trusts of land and most old ones and so now it is certain that the interests of the equitable owners behind the statutorily imposed trust of land are interests in that land (i.e. proprietary rights) for all purposes.

4   Although the trustees of land now have no duty to sell the land, they do have a *power* to do so.[45] Given that the trustees are the legal owners of the property, it is their names that will be entered as registered proprietors of the title at HM Land Registry.[46] Consequently, all trustees – as owners of the legal title – must formally join in a conveyance if the land is sold. Not surprisingly, the LPA 1925 foresaw that there might well be disputes between trustees about sale (or the exercise of other powers), so a mechanism was provided for dealing with such disputes. This mechanism is now found in section 14 of TOLATA 1996 and involves an application to the court.[47] It is considered more fully below.

5   A catalogue of the trustees' functions and powers is found in TOLATA 1996 itself. As noted above, most will not be relevant in a 'normal' residential co-ownership situation in which the co-owners are trustees of land holding for themselves in equity. Similarly, the powers of disposal (e.g. to sell, lease or mortgage) will be less effective if there is only *one* trustee of land holding on trust for himself and for others in equity because in such a case overreaching cannot occur.[48] However, in those relatively rare cases of residential co-ownership in which the two or more trustees of land are *not* also the only equitable owners (as in *City of London Building Society* v. *Flegg* (1988), in which a daughter and her husband held on trust for themselves and one set of parents), the powers and functions of the trustees under TOLATA 1996 may become important if the trustees and equitable owners cannot agree on the future use of the land. Of course, the powers and functions of the trustees remain central when the land is non-residential, as where it is held by trustees as an investment for the equitable co-owners.[49]

6   It is intrinsic in everything we have said so far that the ability to deal with the land lies with the legal owners – the trustees. If, as is often the case in a domestic context, these are the same people as the equitable owners, few practical problems arise. However, if the trustees are completely unconnected with the equitable interest (as in an investment situation) or if it is intended that there will be more than four

---

43   This is the balance of funds after paying off any mortgages that had priority to the interests of the co-owners.

44   See, for example, *Perry* v. *Phoenix Assurance* (1988).

45   This may be delegated to the equitable owners.

46   In unregistered land, the trustees would appear as owners under a deed.

47   Replacing section 30 of the LPA 1925.

48   See section 4.9.8 below.

49   See, for example, *Laskar* v. *Laskar* (2008).

co-owners, or if the legal title was conveyed only to certain of the co-owners, or if some of the co-owners acquired their interests at a later date,[50] there will not be this symmetry between legal and equitable owners, and problems can occur. We will examine these more closely below, but for now three points need to be noted.

(i) A sale (including a mortgage) by *all* of the trustees, provided that they are two or more in number, will overreach the interests of the equitable owners (sections 2(1)(ii) and 27 of the LPA 1925).[51] The interests of the equitable owners will take effect in the proceeds of sale, and only a very astute equitable owner has even a chance of stopping this happening.[52]

(ii) If there is only one trustee of the land, as is often the case where the co-ownership has not been created expressly,[53] the interests of the equitable owners cannot be overreached.[54] Consequently, whether the equitable interests can have priority over the interest of a purchaser will depend on the law of registered or unregistered conveyancing (as the case may be).

(iii) If the trust is created by 'a disposition' (which probably means a trust created expressly in writing, and not one arising informally), the exercise of the trustee's power of sale (and other powers) can be made subject to an express requirement that the consent of any (or all) of the beneficiaries be obtained.[55] This is in an attempt to ensure that a sale does not take place contrary to their wishes or at least of forcing a reference to the court under section 14 of TOLATA 1996.[56]

4.8 The Advantages of the 1925 and 1996 Legislative Reforms

In discussing the property legislation of 1925–96 in general, and the law of co-ownership in particular, it is always important to remember that the wholesale reshaping of English property law was prompted by two fundamental objectives:

1 To ensure that the value of land as an economic asset was utilised to the full and, to that end, to promote the free alienability of land. This would entail both simplifying the conveyancing process and providing for the protection of purchasers of land from the myriad rights and interests that might otherwise encumber their use of the land.

2 To ensure, as far as was compatible with this first objective, that no owner or occupier of land and no person with any interest in land was unreasonably prejudiced by the

---

50 As in HSBC v. Dyche (2009).

51 Provided that the sale is genuine, see HSBC v. Dyche (2009), in which two trustees 'sold' to one of them; see [2010] Conv 1.

52 See section 4.9 below.

53 See section 4.10.2 below.

54 *Williams & Glyn's Bank v. Boland* (1981).

55 Section 10 of TOLATA 1996.

56 For the position before TOLATA 1996, *Re Herkelot's Will Trusts* (1964) suggests that it may have been possible to restrict the powers of the trustees in similar fashion.

procedural and substantive changes that were to be made. It was recognised, however, that some people would find that their rights over the land itself had diminished, albeit that such rights could now take effect in its exchange product: that is, money.

These two goals remain, but changes in the way in which land was used and the spread of land ownership among all sections of society meant that the machinery of the 1925 legislation was out of date well before 1996. For example, land is no longer owned by a relatively few wealthy families, nor is co-ownership used primarily for investment purposes. The 'property owning democracy' is a clichéd but accurate description for the widespread land ownership that exists today. In these circumstances, the former statutory mechanism (the old trust for sale of land) was clearly unfit to regulate normal domestic co-ownership given that it was designed to promote the *sale* of land when the purpose of the co-owners was to retain it. Hence, the reforms of 1925 were rightly amended by the 1996 Act in order to reflect the reality of property use and ownership in 1997 and beyond. This should be remembered in the following discussion about the advantages of the 1925 and 1996 legislative reforms.

First, prior to 1 January 1926, any person wishing to purchase co-owned land would have to investigate either the one title of the joint tenants or the individual titles of every single tenant in common. Not only was this time-consuming and expensive, but the objection of just one tenant in common might prevent the land from being sold or mortgaged, even if this would have been for the benefit of every other co-owner. By abolishing tenancies in common at law, the LPA 1925 has ensured that there is but one title to investigate: the legal joint tenancy. Moreover, the number of legal joint tenants is limited to a maximum of four (irrespective of the number of equitable owners), so that a purchaser need only concern himself with obtaining the agreement of, at maximum, four people.[57]

Second, if there are two or more trustees of land (i.e. two or more legal owners), and the purchaser obtains the consent of all[58] to a sale or mortgage, the purchaser safely may ignore all of the equitable owners, subject only to any entries on the register of title restricting the trustees' powers of dealing with the land.[59] This is the magic of statutory overreaching whereby the interests of the equitable owners (whether they be joint tenants or tenants in common in equity) are transferred from the land to the proceeds of sale arising from the money paid by the purchaser. Indeed, such is the power of overreaching that it will operate even if no money is actually paid over in one large sum, provided that a sum is *payable* should the trustees wish to draw on it. Thus, in *State Bank of India* v. *Sood* (1997), overreaching occurred by reason of the fact that the trustees had mortgaged the property in return for an overdraft facility rather than receiving a one-off capital payment.[60]

Third, although a tenancy in common cannot exist at law, in equity both the tenancy in common and the joint tenancy are possible. The equitable owners are secure in the sense that their interests, however held, will take effect in money should the property be sold or mortgaged. Moreover, the existence of a trust means that the equitable owners have powerful proprietary remedies in the event of default by the trustees, as where the

---

57 In most cases of residential co-ownership, there will be only two trustees – usually the same people as the equitable owners.

58 Bearing in mind that there may be a maximum of four only.

59 For example, a requirement to obtain a person's consent before sale by using a Form N Restriction.

60 It would be otherwise if no sum were *payable* at all or if the 'sale' was not genuine: *HSBC* v. *Dyche* (2009).

trustees have spent any money raised by way of mortgage in breach of the terms of the trust. For example, the beneficiaries may establish ownership of any assets purchased by the trustees with the proceeds of sale or, failing that, may sue the trustees personally if they have spent the money on untraceable assets.[61] After all, the trustees are 'trustees' and subject to the normal core obligations of that office.[62]

Fourth, the trustees have a power to sell and this prevents co-owned land becoming inalienable should there be a dispute between the co-owners (or other interested persons). Although all trustees must agree if the power of sale is to be exercised voluntarily, if the trustees disagree about how the land should be used, application can be made to the court under section 14 of TOLATA 1996 for an order for sale (or other order concerning the property). If sale is ordered, the equitable interests will take effect in the proceeds of sale in the normal way. Consequently, co-owned land will not stagnate through the inability to secure the agreement of all of the legal owners. This is consistent with the general aim of the 1925 reforms to ensure the free alienability of co-owned land through simplifying the conveyancing process and of offering protection for the purchaser against any adverse equitable interests (the overreaching machinery). The replacement of the old trust for sale (duty to sell) with the trust for land (power to sell) by TOLATA 1996 reflects the fact that much co-owned land will be retained and the ability to apply under section 14 guarantees that co-owned land never stagnates when there is deadlock.[63] A synopsis of the effect of the 1996 Act is given below.

4.9 The Disadvantages of the Trust of Land as a Device for Regulating Co-ownership

Given what we have just learnt about purchaser protection through the overreaching machinery, it is not surprising that many of the disadvantages of the current mechanism, even after the 1996 amendments, focus on the other half of the equation: the equitable co-owner, particularly the equitable owner who is not also a trustee of the legal estate. However, as we shall see, sometimes even the legal owners of co-owned land find the imposition of a trust unhelpful.

4.9.1 Disputes as to sale

An obvious difficulty of using the trust as a mechanism for co-ownership is that there may well be disputes between the co-owners[64] as to whether the property should be

---

61 See *Arthur v. A-G of the Turks & Caicos Islands* (2012), a decision of the Privy Council which is limited to the particular registered land legislation of the islands. However, it does suggest that there is nothing wrong in principle with a *personal* claim arising in a registered land transaction, and here it was the possibility of a claim against the purchaser rather than the trustees.

62 Of course, in many cases, the trustees will have spent money, the equitable owners will have been overreached and their personal liability will be meaningless: – see e.g. *Flegg*.

63 Although the *express* and deliberate creation of a *trust for sale* is still possible, such trusts will be subject to the strictures of TOLATA 1996 and now carry no advantages.

64 Whether trustees or equitable owners.

sold, retained for occupation by the equitable owners (or one of them) or used to generate income. Admittedly, the difficulty is not as pressing as it was prior to the 1996 Act – the trustees are no longer under a duty to sell – but the potential remains for disputes and litigation. This is, particularly acute in residential situations should the co-owners' relationship break down, or one of the co-owners goes bankrupt and his creditors want to sell the property to realise his assets.

To deal with such disputes, section 14 of TOLATA 1996 provides that any trustee of land, or any person having an interest in land subject to such a trust (e.g. an equitable owner, mortgagee or trustee in bankruptcy[65]) may apply to the court for an order concerning 'the exercise by the trustees of any of their functions' or declaring the nature and extent of a person's equitable interest. In many cases, the application is for an order for sale or sometimes possession and sale. Save in those cases in which the application is made by a trustee in bankruptcy in respect of property in which a bankrupt has an interest,[66] in deciding whether to order a sale (or make some other order), the court is directed to have regard to the matters specified in section 15 of TOLATA 1996. These are: the intentions of the persons who established the trust; the purposes for which the property is held; the welfare of any minor who occupies the land as his home (whether or not as a child of the owner); the interests of any secured creditor; and, in most circumstances, the wishes of any equitable owner. As a matter of law, this list is not exhaustive of the factors the court may consider and consequently other factors can play a part,[67] provided that the factors identified in section 15 are considered.

Clearly, section 15 is designed to ensure that a court does not simply order sale of the property as a quick route to a solution, but instead requires it to consider the matter in its complete context. Thus, under sections 14 and 15, it is perfectly possible for an application for an order for sale to be refused,[68] or for sale to be postponed until some date in the future.[69] It was also the Law Commission's view when commenting on the introduction of sections 14 and 15 of TOLATA that much of the pre-1996 case law developed in respect of the now repealed section 30 LPA 1925 (the forerunner of sections 14 and 15) would remain relevant.[70] The following are examples of factors considered by the court in deciding whether to exercise its discretion as to a sale either under the old section 30 or under the rubric provided by section 15 of TOLATA 1996.

1   Whether the property is still needed as a family home (*Jones* v. *Challenger* (1961)).
2   Whether the property is required to provide accommodation for the duration of the lives of the co-owners, or that of the survivor (*Harris* v. *Harris* (1996)) or until the occurrence of any event. Thus, in *Chun* v. *Ho* (2001), sale was postponed until the completion of the education of one of the co-owners.
3   Whether the property is needed for the provision of a family home for the children of a relationship that has broken down (*Williams* v. *Williams* (1976)). Under section 15 of TOLATA 1996, the welfare of any minor occupying the land as his home is

---

65 Being a person appointed by a court to manage the affairs of a person formally declared bankrupt.
66 See section 4.9.3 below.
67 *Putnam & Sons* v. *Taylor* (2009).
68 For example, *Holman* v. *Howes* (2007).
69 *Chun* v. *Ho* (2001).
70 Law Commission Report No. 181, which led to TOLATA 1996.

made relevant expressly, thus resolving the doubts expressed in *Re Holliday* (1981) and *Re Evers' Trust* (1980). This criterion was decisive in *Edwards v. Lloyds TSB* (2004), in which sale was postponed for five years in order to safeguard a home for the children of the relationship, even though the application for sale was made by a mortgagee whose mortgage took effect over more than 50 per cent of the value of the property.[71]

4 Whether the property is required in order that a business may continue, the land having been purchased for that specific purpose, as in *Bedson v. Bedson* (1965).

5 Where the person seeking a sale is estopped from obtaining an order for sale, having by word or action represented that a sale would not occur, such conduct having been relied on by the other co-owner, or where a sale would be unconscionable in all the circumstances: *Holman v. Howes* (2007).[72]

6 Whether there has been any misconduct by the person applying for sale, or his legal advisers, as in *Halifax Mortgage Services v. Muirhead* (1998), in which sale was refused because the claimant's solicitors had wrongly altered relevant documents.

7 The general circumstances of the beneficiaries of the trust, including their age and health, and the general suitability of the premises – *Edwards v. Royal Bank of Scotland* (2010).

8 The clarity with which the intentions of parties are established, with a written instrument having particular weight – *Cawthorne v. Stephens-Dunn* (2015).

9 Importantly, if the request for a sale comes from a creditor – such as a mortgagee – the courts have taken the general view that a creditor should not be kept out of his money unless there are clear reasons to refuse a sale: *Bank of Ireland v. Bell* (2001). In *Fred Perry v. Genis* (2014), the court noted that although section 15 gave equal weight to all the factors, case law had established that normally a creditor's application for sale would succeed. So, although there are cases where a creditor did not achieve an immediate sale – see *Mortgage Corp v. Shaire* (2001) and *Edwards v. Lloyds TSB* (2004) – there is a clear preference for ordering a sale so as to realise money to repay debts even though this will result in the loss of a home for all the co-owners. See, for example, *First National Bank v. Achampong* (2003), *Pritchard Englefield v. Steinberg* (2004) and *Putnam & Sons v. Taylor* (2009), where a sale was ordered at the request of the mortgagee/chargee even though the interests of the persons in occupation had priority to the mortgagee as a matter of property law.[73] This is considered more fully below.

10 Where one of the co-owners has been formally adjudged bankrupt and his trustee in bankruptcy wants a sale on behalf of general creditors, section 15 TOLATA does not apply. Instead, the court must apply section 335A Insolvency Act 1986. This section provides that a sale must take place unless the circumstances are exceptional – see below.

---

71 The mortgage operated over the former husband's share, but not over the former wife's. But contrast *Edwards v. Royal Bank of Scotland* (2010), where the possibility that a grandchild might visit was not enough to prevent sale.

72 This has echoes of proprietary estoppel. See also *Re Buchanan Wollaston's Conveyance* (1939).

73 This priority would take effect in the proceeds of sale. Thus, the co-owner who is not bound by the mortgage would take their share of the proceeds of sale before any payment to the creditor. Another example is *Edwards v. Royal Bank of Scotland* (2010).

4.9.2   When is a court likely to order sale?

Whether an application under section 14 of TOLATA for a sale will be granted necessarily depends on the particular facts of each case. Furthermore, under TOLATA 1996, there is no duty to sell the land – it is a trust *of land* not a trust *for sale* of land – and pre-1996 statements unequivocally favouring a sale of co-owned property when in cases of dispute must be read with some care and cannot be applied unthinkingly to applications under section 14 of TOLATA.[74] For example, in *Banker's Trust v. Namdar* (1997), a sale was ordered under section 30 of the LPA 1925, but Peter Gibson LJ thought that it was 'unfortunate' that TOLATA 1996 was not applicable (the case arose before TOLATA 1996 came into force) 'as the result might have been different'. What this means in practice is hard to quantify, but much may turn on precisely *who* is requesting a sale under section 14. For example, a court is still likely to order a sale when only the co-owners are in dispute and there are no extrinsic factors (e.g. no children), as this supports the alienability of the co-owned land.[75] Again, a sale is likely to be ordered if the land was purchased as an investment, rather than a home, or if it would be inequitable to deny a co-owner their share of the capital value of land.[76] Conversely, a sale may be resisted if there are children living in the property,[77] if the co-owner wanting a sale is not in desperate financial straits, if all of the co-owners have agreed specifically not to sell unless they all consent (*Finch v. Hall* (2013)), or if one co-owner has special reasons for wishing to remain in occupation. So, in *Chun v. Ho* (2001), a sale was postponed until one co-owner completed her studies because the other co-owner had behaved inequitably, there was no real evidence that the money was needed to pay his debts and the co-owner resisting sale had provided most of the original purchase price. Likewise in *Dear v. Robinson* (2001), in which the wishes of the beneficiaries were critical (even though their consent to a sale was not required formally) and the postponement of sale was in accordance with the original intentions of the creator of the trust.[78] Clearly, then, if the non-trustee equitable owner's consent is *required* before a sale takes place (e.g. where such requirement is imposed in the original instrument creating the trust), a court will be careful before it dispenses with such consent and actually orders a sale against their wishes.

Real difficulty arises in those cases (noted above) in which the rights of creditors are in contest with the rights of the innocent co-owner (assuming no formal bankruptcy).[79] Thus, in *Pritchard Englefield v. Steinberg* (2004), a sale was ordered at the request of a creditor holding a charging order[80] despite the objections of an equitable owner, and this

---

74   *Mortgage Corporation v. Shaire* (2001).

75   But see *Holman v. Howes* (2007), in which a sale was refused in precisely these circumstances.

76   See the discussion in *Barclay v. Barclay* (1970).

77   *Edwards v. Lloyds TSB* (2004).

78   Even if the equitable owners' consent is not a *requirement* of a sale or mortgage by the trustees, their wishes are relevant (see section 11 of TOLATA 1996), although it is unlikely that they will be pivotal.

79   The position if one of the co-owners is bankrupt is discussed separately as a different statutory regime applies.

80   Arising from a court judgment, whereby a debt owed by the landowner is secured by granting a charging order over his land.

followed a pattern established by TSB v. *Marshall* (1998),[81] confirmed by *Bank of Ireland* v. *Bell* (2001). Indeed, in both *First National Bank* v. *Achampong* (2003) and *Fred Perry* v. *Genis* (2015), even the fact that the non-consenting owner had priority over the creditor could not stave off a sale. Likewise, in *Putnam & Sons* v. *Taylor* (2009), a sale was ordered at the request of a claimant with a charging order over H's share of the equitable interest because, generally, a creditor should not be kept out of his money indefinitely, although it may have been relevant in this case that, even after a sale and payment of the debt, there would have been enough money left over to provide a house for H and W.[82] There is, therefore, a clear drift in favour of ordering a sale in such cases, but there are exceptions. In *Mortgage Corporation* v. *Shaire* (2001), it was made clear that the rights of creditors should not prevail automatically, in *Edwards* v. *Lloyds TSB* (2004), a sale was postponed for five years because of the needs of the children and family, even though this would keep the mortgagee out of its security, and in *Amari Lifestyle* v. *Warnes* (2017), a sale was refused at the request of a creditor because it would be futile in the sense of not contributing to the repayment of the debt secured by the charge.[83]

As is obvious then, the court's approach to disputed sales will vary with the circumstances, bearing in mind that there is no longer a default position under section 14 in favour of sale. Sweeping generalisations about how TOLATA 1996 may have affected the court's approach are probably best avoided – for example, in *Shaire* and *Edwards*, much was said about sale under TOLATA no longer being appropriate, and in *Bell* and *Englefield*, there was much talk about TOLATA being used to realise the capital value of the land.

What is clear, however, is that a properly advised co-owner can act to ensure that they are at least consulted before a sale takes place. In registered land, an equitable co-owner may be able to place a Restriction on the title of the co-owned land, which has the effect of limiting the legal owners' (the trustees') powers to act. If an appropriate Restriction has been entered, this will ensure that no dealings can take place unless the conditions specified in the Restriction are fulfilled: for example, that there are indeed two trustees of the land for overreaching, or that the consent of the equitable owners is required and obtained.[84] Any attempt to deal with the land contrary to the Restriction will be discovered and may trigger an application under section 14 of TOLATA 1996 to

---

81 A sale was ordered even though there were children living at the property because there was no realistic prospect of the debt being repaid.

82 This was an explicit reason for ordering sale in favour of a non-priority lender in *Edwards* v. *Royal Bank of Scotland* (2010). Neither was a sale in breach of the ECHR as such an order would be in accordance with the law and in the public interest as permitted under Article 1, Protocol 1 to the Convention. See also *Close Invoice Finance Limited* v. *Pile* (2008).

83 See also *National Westminster Bank* v. *Rushmer* (2010), where sale at the request of a chargee was initially postponed for two years because of the prospect of litigation which might realise enough funds to pay the co-owners' debts. Sale was later ordered when it became clear that the litigation would not be successful.

84 Note, however, that in *Coleman* v. *Bryant* (2007), the court decided that it would not order HM Land Registry (after its refusal) to enter a Restriction requiring the beneficiaries' consent to a disposition as this would destroy overreaching. Indeed it would. It remains unclear whether HM Land Registry would accept the entry of a Restriction requiring the beneficiaries' consent if the requirement for consent was specified expressly in the document establishing the trust. It would be difficult to justify a refusal in such circumstances.

try to prevent sale, or to ensure that it takes place only on certain conditions.[85] Note finally that a court is empowered under section 14 of TOLATA 1996 to revisit a previous application if circumstances change before a sale actually takes place. So, in *Dear v. Robinson* (2001), a previous order for sale was rescinded because circumstances had changed and a majority of the beneficiaries no longer wanted an immediate sale.

4.9.3   The special case of bankruptcy

The list of factors in section 15 of TOLATA 1996 do not apply to disputes concerning sale of co-owned property when an application is made by the trustee in bankruptcy of a person interested in co-owned land. In that case, an application is made under section 14 of TOLATA, but section 335A of the Insolvency Act 1986 provides the list of relevant factors that the court must consider.[86] Note also that, under the Enterprise Act 2002, a trustee in bankruptcy should apply for sale of the property within three years of the bankruptcy, else he risks the property returning to the bankrupt free from the claims of the creditors.[87]

    If one of the persons interested in the co-owned land is made formally bankrupt (whether they are a legal or equitable owner), their assets vest in a 'trustee in bankruptcy'. The 'trustee in bankruptcy' is simply the name given to the person who administers the bankrupt's assets with a view to paying off his creditors. In a co-ownership situation, a trustee in bankruptcy will step into the shoes of the legal or equitable owner who is bankrupt. Naturally, the trustee in bankruptcy will want to sell the co-owned property to realise some of the bankrupt's assets, and, equally naturally, this will be resisted by the other legal or equitable owner, who is often the bankrupt's relationship partner who wishes to stay in the house. If a sale is resisted, the trustee in bankruptcy will apply to the court for an order for sale under section 14 and the court will have to balance the needs of the innocent creditors and the needs of the innocent co-owner within the framework of section 335A of the Insolvency Act 1986. On its face, the section 14/section 335A procedure applies whether or not the co-owners are married, or, indeed, in any personal relationship. However, it is only in the case of spouses or civil partners (not unmarried couples) that spousal/civil partner conduct and the needs of children are expressly mentioned as relevant factors for the court's consideration. However, we should not conclude that this means that the needs of children of non-married couples are irrelevant. Section 335A specifically permits the court to consider 'all the circumstances of the case other than the needs of the bankrupt' and clearly this is wide enough to include the interests of any person residing in the premises or indeed interested in it.[88]

---

85 The legal owner may also apply under section 14 of TOLATA for authorisation to conduct a sale contrary to a Restriction. In addition, any person interested may apply under section 14 for an injunction preventing an anticipated sale, but this is likely to be granted only in the most unusual and exceptional situations – assuming, of course, that the equitable owner knows of a proposed sale or mortgage before it happens.

86 Section 15(4) of TOLATA 1996. Section 335A of the Insolvency Act 1986 replaces the similar, but not identical, section 336(3) of the Insolvency Act 1986.

87 Enterprise Act 2002, section 261, inserting section 283A into the Insolvency Act 1986.

88 Section 335A(2)(c).

Consequently, on hearing an application for sale by a trustee in bankruptcy, the court is directed by section 335A to consider the following matters: the interests of the bankrupt's creditors; the conduct of the bankrupt's spouse as a contributing factor to the bankruptcy; the needs of the spouse and the needs of any children; and all other circumstances – but not the needs of the bankrupt.[89] However, if the application under section 14 of TOLATA 1996 is made more than one year after the bankruptcy, the interests of the creditors are deemed to outweigh the interests of the resisting co-owners unless the circumstances are 'exceptional'. What this means is that, after one year, the court is extremely likely to order a sale of the property in order to satisfy the creditors, but up to then, the court may well delay sale so as to give the 'innocent' occupiers a chance to make alternative arrangements.[90] However, the converse is not also true: it is not the case that the existence of exceptional circumstances *must* mean postponement of a sale. They mean that the interests of the creditors do not *outweigh* other factors, and the court must still exercise a discretion taking all the (now equal) factors into account – *Grant* v. *Baker* (2016), in which a sale was still ordered despite there being exceptional circusmtances.

It is, of course, difficult to identify what my count as 'exceptional' and it is a matter for the trial judge hearing all the evidence (*Grant* v. *Baker*). So, in *Harrington* v. *Bennett* (2000), an application by the trustee in bankruptcy for sale more than one year after the bankruptcy was granted by the court. It was not an 'exceptional' circumstance that the bankrupt appeared to have a purchaser in view who might pay a higher price than that achievable under a sale by the trustee in bankruptcy. Nor is it exceptional that there might be a family who would lose their home – *Begum* v. *Cockerton* (2015), although the medical condition of one of the occupiers can be so serious as to generate an exceptional situation: *Grant* v. *Baker* (daughter of bankrupt), *Claughton* v. *Charalambous* (bankrupt's spouse) and *Re Bremner* (bankrupt was terminally ill, which had to be disregarded, but this led to exceptional circumstances for bankrupt's spouse).[91]

The overall effect of section 335A was considered at some length by Lawrence Collins J in *Dean* v. *Stout* (2004). He summarised the position as follows. First, the presence of exceptional circumstances is a necessary condition to displace the presumption that the interests of the creditors in bankruptcy outweigh all other considerations, but the presence of exceptional circumstances does not debar the court from making an order for sale. Second, typically the exceptional circumstances relate to the personal circumstances of one of the joint owners, such as a medical condition. Third, the categories of exceptional circumstances are not to be categorised or defined and the court should make a value judgment after looking at all of the circumstances. Fourth, the circumstances must be truly exceptional and, as explained in *Re Citro* (1991), this means matters that are outside the usual 'melancholy consequences of debt and improvidence'. Fifth, it is not uncommon for a partner with children to be faced with eviction in circumstances

---

89 See e.g. *Everitt* v. *Budhram* (2009). In this context, and probably for all of section 335A, 'needs' does not mean merely financial need but encompasses (among other things) physical and mental welfare.

90 Note that the trustee is generally required to take action for possession and sale within three years of the bankruptcy (section 383A of the Insolvency Act 1986), else the property revests in the bankrupt to the exclusion of the creditors.

91 See also *Everitt* v. *Budhram* (2009), where the mental state of the bankrupt's spouse was sufficiently 'exceptional' as to justify a further postponement of sale beyond the one-year period of grace.

in which the sale will not produce enough to buy a comparable home in the same neighbourhood or, indeed, elsewhere. Such circumstances cannot be described as exceptional. Sixth, for the purposes of weighing the interests of the creditors of the bankrupt, the creditors have an interest in the order for sale being made, even if the whole of the net proceeds will go towards the expenses of the bankruptcy, and the fact that they will be swallowed up in paying those expenses is not an exceptional circumstance.[92]

To conclude then, it is apparent that section 335A of the Insolvency Act 1986 explicitly favours a sale at the request of the trustee in bankruptcy after one year and there may well be sound commercial and equitable reasons why this should be so. It is up to the person trying to prevent sale to adduce evidence of exceptional circumstances – *Begum* v. *Cockerton*. Nevertheless, while we know from *Dean* v. *Stout* what is *not* 'exceptional', it remains uncertain what actually will qualify so as to justify a postponement of sale beyond the one-year period, although medical conditions carry some weight. Of particular interest in this regard is the case of *Barca* v. *Mears* (2004) in the High Court. In this case, it was argued that a sale should be postponed for longer than one year because of the special educational needs of the son. In the result, and on the particular facts, this was not persuasive, but the Court did make some important observations. First, the Court confirmed that *Re Citro* did assimilate the position of married and unmarried couples and its general approach would apply even if the co-owners stood in no relationship at all. Second, that as the law stood, the pressure for a sale at the request of the trustee in bankruptcy was usually overwhelming. Third, however, the Court held that the protection afforded by Article 8 of the European Convention on Human Rights (ECHR),[93] as implemented by the Human Rights Act 1998, might require a rethink. It was arguable – indeed likely according to the judge – that the near-*automatic* ordering of sale in bankruptcy cases after one year could contravene the ECHR; the point being that a balance had to be struck between the needs of the creditors and the requirements of Article 8. The presumption of a sale after one year, save in exceptional circumstances, as this had been interpreted, might not represent a sufficient balancing exercise. Consequently, what the judge called a 'shift in emphasis' in the interpretation of section 335A might be necessary to ensure compatibility with the ECHR. This could be achieved by recognising that, in the normal case of 'everyday' bankruptcy, the creditors' interests would outweigh all other interests, but also by accepting that what was 'exceptional' should involve a proper consideration of the facts without the presumption of bias in favour of creditors that was evident in the pre-1998 case law. Despite this, subsequent case law has not been as robust in its defence of the rights of innocent co-owners: in *Donohoe* v. *Ingram* (2006), the court paid lip service to the idea that the test within section 335A might have to be reinterpreted to make it Convention-compliant by simply deciding that, even on that basis, there were no exceptional circumstances. Further, in *Nicholls* v. *Lan* (2006) and *Ford* v. *Alexander* (2012), the court found no incompatibility per se between the provisions of the Insolvency Act 1986 and the Convention,[94] thus neutralising the concerns raised in *Barca*. However, we should

---

92 Neither is it an exceptional circumstance that a creditor would *not* suffer by reason of delaying sale: *Donohoe* v. *Ingram* (2006). In this case, a sale at a later date would also have achieved payment of creditors.

93 Respect for private and family life and Article 1 of Protocol 1, respect for property.

94 See above in similar vein *Close Invoice Finance Limited* v. *Pile* (2008). In *Everitt* v. *Budhram* (2009), the human rights point appears not to have been raised at all.

remember two final points. First, *Barca* reminds us that the Convention might have an impact on the interpretation of section 335A and thus 'exceptional' does not mean 'nearly never'. Second, in *Manchester City Council* v. *Pinnock* (2010) and *Hounslow LBC* v. *Powell* (2011), the Supreme Court make it clear that it is possible that the enforcement of a proprietary claim (e.g. a trustee in bankruptcy's claim under section 14) could give way in the face of an Article 8 defence based on the exceptional circumstances of the occupier.[95] The need for proportionality between the claims of the creditors and that of the home owner is recognised in *Ford* v. *Alexander*, but the clear steer from that case is that section 335A almost always ensures a proportionate result. Perhaps then it will be rare for human rights concerns to prevent a sale after the one year's grace, but not impossible.

4.9.4   Summary in relation to sale

It is convenient at this stage to summarise the position in respect of the court's approach when an application for sale is made under section 14 of TOLATA 1996. In most cases, the court must consider the factors listed in section 15 of TOLATA 1996 (the intentions of the creator of the trust; the purposes for which the property is held; the welfare of any child who occupies or might occupy the property as his home; the interests of a secured creditor; the wishes of any beneficiaries), but in cases of formal bankruptcy, they must consider instead those factors listed in section 355A of the Insolvency Act 1986 (the interests of the creditors; for dwelling houses, the interests and conduct of the bankrupt's spouse; the needs and resources of the spouse; the needs of any children; the requirement to sell after one year barring exceptional circumstances).

1   In disputes purely between co-owners, without the intervention of any third party, the court may well be happy to postpone sale and make some other order: for example, that one co-owner pays rent to another (or does not have to – *Chun* v. *Ho* (2001)); or that the land is partitioned (*Rodway* v. *Landy* (2001), *Atkinson* v. *Atkinson* (2010), *Ellison* v. *Cleghorn* (2013)[96]); or that sale is postponed indefinitely to such time as the person in possession does indeed consent (*Holman* v. *Howes* (2007)). Under TOLATA 1996, the trust of land is no longer a trust for sale of land and there is less emphasis on a sale in these circumstances. This is even more so if there are children of the relationship or there is some other pressing reason why a sale should be postponed, bearing in mind that this necessarily keeps one co-owner out of their money.

2   In disputes between a co-owner and a secured creditor (e.g. a mortgagee), where there is no bankruptcy, it is important to assess why the creditor wants a sale. It is worth noting here that a mortgagee does not have to resort to section 14 for a sale if the mortgagee has overreached the beneficial interests by paying capital money to two or more trustees or otherwise takes free of the mortgage (e.g. having obtained relevant consents). In these cases where the mortgagee has priority, like *City of London Building Society* v. *Flegg* (1988) (in which overreaching occurred) and *Le Foe* v. *Le Foe* (2001) (consent), the mortgagee may sell in virtue of its paramount mortgage powers. Consequently, a mortgagee using section 14 of TOLATA 1996 is by

---

95 And note, there appears to be no concerns that this might be 'horizontal effect'.

96 A plot had been purchased jointly in order for the parties to build a house each. Partition was the intended, natural and direct means of achieving the parties' ultimate aims.

definition a mortgagee bound, as a matter of property law, by the prior rights of one of the co-owners. This can be important as the court legitimately may ask why it should deprive a co-owner of possession of the land when the co-owner's right is paramount to that of the creditor. Thus, it can be argued that a creditor should not get an order for sale under section 14 where they simply have failed to protect themselves adequately (as in *Boland*). However, despite this, there are a number of cases in which a sale has been ordered in favour of a non-priority creditor on the simple basis that it is unjust to keep the creditor out of its funds. This is most marked in those cases in which the 'unjustness' is that the mortgagee believed that all of the co-owners had consented to a mortgage but where this turned out to be untrue either because of fraud by one co-owner in forging the consent of the others (*Bank of Ireland v. Bell* (2001); *Bankers Trust v. Namdar* (1997); *Edwards v. Royal Bank of Scotland* (2010)) or because there was a successful claim of undue influence in relation to the consent (*First National Bank v. Achampong* (2003)). Likewise, there are some cases where a sale has been ordered against the wishes of a beneficiary with priority where, on closer analysis of the facts, a sale is actually in their best interests – a good example is *Pritchard Englefield v. Steinberg*.[97] In those cases in which a sale is ordered at the request of a creditor who does not have priority, the equitable owner will have first call on the sale proceeds to the value of her interest and the creditor will be left to take its funds from the balance of the proceeds of sale.[98] The priority in land is thus reflected in priority over the proceeds of sale. Of course, the court may well conclude that no sale should be ordered, at least not without terms and conditions to protect the innocent co-owner (*Mortgage Corp v. Shaire* (2001)) or where there is a greater need to protect the innocent co-owner and any occupying children (*Edwards v. TSB* (2004)).

3   Where one of the co-owners goes bankrupt and his trustee in bankruptcy applies for an order for sale, it will take exceptional circumstances for a sale to be postponed for more than a year. Such a postponement has been rare.

4   It is open to a mortgagee who cannot otherwise obtain a sale under section 14 to make the mortgagor bankrupt. The mortgagor owes a debt that he cannot pay. This will mean the mortgagee giving up its secured status – and becoming an 'ordinary' creditor losing its proprietary right over the property[99] – but it means that the insolvent co-owner's property passes to the trustee in bankruptcy. This trustee can then apply for a sale under section 14 of TOLATA 1966 and this is likely to be ordered under the bankruptcy rules just discussed. Although this appears to be allowing the mortgagee to get by the back door what it cannot get by the front – after all, the mortgagee itself could not get a sale under section 14, otherwise it would not resort to this tactic – it is not an abuse of the process and will not be prevented by the court, as made clear in *Alliance & Leicester v. Slayford* (2001). Of course, as a practical matter, the mortgagee would have to be reasonably certain of getting some money as an unsecured creditor in bankruptcy before giving up its protected status as a secured creditor.

---

97 If sale of the co-owned leasehold had not been ordered, the landlord was likely to forfeit the lease, leaving the innocent co-owner with nothing. At least a sale gave her a cash sum.

98 If there is a shortfall, it might then pursue the mortgagor personally for the outstanding balance.

99 Section 269 of the Insolvency Act 1986.

4.9.4.1   *Other orders under section 14*

Applications under section 14 are not limited to request orders for sale. The court has power to make any order 'relating to the exercise by the trustees of any of their functions' or 'declaring the nature or extent of a person's interest in property subject to the trust'. So, for example, the court may make an order imposing or dispensing with a consent requirement or may order that the co-owned land be partitioned (*Ellison* v. *Cleghorn* (2013)) or that a lease may be extended (*Parkes* v. *Wilkes* (2018)). However, although the court's powers are wide, the order must relate to the 'functions' of the trustees, so the court has no power to order one beneficiary to sell or transfer their share to another, although it does have power to order a sale of the entire land and give one beneficiary the right of first refusal to buy the whole at a price determined by the court (*Begum* v. *Haifz* (2015)). Note also that under section 14, the court has power to declare 'the nature or extent' of a person's equitable interest in the land and this is why so many cases concerning the implied creation and quantification of co-ownership arise under section 14 (e.g. *Barnes* v. *Phillips* (2015) and see section 4.10 below).

4.9.5   The position of a purchaser who buys co-owned land: when overreaching occurs

If a purchaser buys co-owned land from two or more legal owners (i.e. there are two or more trustees of land), then the interests of the equitable owners are overreached. The effect is that their co-ownership interest is transferred from the land and takes effect in the proceeds of sale. The purchaser obtains the land free from their rights, as in City of London Building Society v. Flegg (1988), in which the House of Lords confirmed that a mortgage[100] by the two trustees overreached the interests of Mr and Mrs Flegg so as to give the mortgagee priority when the trustees defaulted on the mortgage payments.[101] This is the same in registered and unregistered land.

Often in a residential context, the two trustees will also be the only equitable owners, having acquired the property as their home and in such cases, overreaching causes no difficulty because any 'equitable owner' can object to a proposed sale or mortgage in his or her capacity as a 'legal owner'. However, in some cases, the equitable owners will be different from the legal owners – as in *Flegg* itself – and if there are two trustees, overreaching will occur. In that situation, the purchaser obtains the land free from the equitable rights, and those equitable rights take effect in the proceeds of sale, even if the equitable owners objected to the sale, knew nothing about it or actually get nothing from the proceeds of sale, as in *Flegg*.[102] In other words, overreaching can occur against the wishes of the equitable owners and they could lose their right to occupy the land and

---

100 Overreaching is triggered by a conveyance of a legal estate, which includes a sale, mortgage and lease. According to *Baker* v. *Craggs* (2016) it also includes the grant of a lease but this is subject to an appeal.

101 Thus the mortgagee could take possession and sell the property. The Fleggs were the parents of one of the trustees (Mrs Maxwell-Brown) and had contributed to the purchase price and thus were co-owners in equity. They were in actual occupation at the time of the mortgage and knew nothing of it. It was their only home. See also *Birmingham Midshires Building Society* v. *Saberhawal* (2000).

102 For example, where the mortgage monies have been spent by the trustees, perhaps on the house or on a business venture, or just dissipated.

must take their interests in the proceeds of sale.[103] This is not affected by section 11 of TOLATA 1996 whereby the trustees must consult the equitable owners and 'in so far as is consistent with the general interest of the trust' give effect to such wishes. This is because section 11 imposes a duty to consult and pay attention to such wishes, not a duty to follow them slavishly, and overreaching will occur even if the trustees have not consulted at all, although, in such cases, the trustees may be liable personally for breach of trust.[104] We should note, however, that overreaching will occur (assuming the requisite number of trustees) only when the sale or mortgage is genuine, in the sense of not being part of a fraudulent design. In HSBC v. Dyche (2009), H & W held on trust for C. H & W 'sold' the land to W alone.[105] As a matter of principle, this could have overreached C, but the judge held that it did not. In the judgment, the judge indicates that overreaching does not work in such circumstances because the purchaser (W) is not in 'good faith' and the sale was not 'authorised' by the equitable owner (C). With respect to the judge, this seems out of place in the law of registered title where the 'good faith' (or otherwise) of a purchaser is largely irrelevant and the trustees have full power to deal with the land and do not need to be 'authorised' by the equitable owners.[106] A better view might be that, on the very particular facts of this case, W was trying to use a statute (section 2 of the LPA 1925 – the overreaching provision) as an instrument of fraud which of course is always a ground to challenge a transaction. It is important, however, that we recognise this as wholly exceptional and do not expand our definition of 'fraud' to include situations in which the trustees merely do something against the interests or wishes of the equitable owners. A wide view of 'fraud' would seriously undermine the integrity of overreaching and would be contrary to the entire philosophy behind the use of a trust in co-ownership.

Clearly, overreaching has a significant effect on equitable owners, depriving them of occupation of the property and causing their proprietary interest in the land to take effect as a share in the proceeds of sale, which may well be illusory (e.g. because all the proceeds have been used to pay off a mortgage). Consequently, we should consider where there are any provisions of TOLATA 1996[107] which impact the effectiveness of overreaching. As we have seen, it is now possible for a settlor (i.e. the person who sets up the trust of co-owned land) to provide that the exercise of the trustees' powers should be subject to the consent of the beneficiaries (section 10 of TOLATA 1996) and further that any interested person (e.g. a non-legal equitable owner) may make an application for an order 'relating to the exercise by the trustees of any of their functions' (section 14). How do these provisions affect the 'trump card' of overreaching when there are two or more trustees of the land?

---

103 Note also that overreaching can occur even if no capital money is actually paid over, provided that it was payable on the sale, as where a mortgage is used to secure a fluctuating overdraft (State Bank of India v. Sood (1997) and see Chapter 2).

104 So, overreaching is not prevented even if the trustees are acting in breach of the terms of the trust, in the sense that it still gives the purchaser priority.

105 W then mortgaged the land and defaulted, hence the claim by HSBC as mortgagee.

106 See section 23 of the LRA 2002 and note how the reference to 'good faith' echoes the discredited decision in Peffer v. Rigg (1978).

107 Section 11 – the duty to consult – is discussed immediately above.

4.9.6   ## If consents are required

If the disposition originally conveying the land to the co-owners makes the trustees' powers (e.g. of sale or mortgage) dependent on obtaining the prior consent of the equitable owners (as envisaged by section 10 of TOLATA 1996), there is a potential conflict with the ability of the trustees to sell the land and overreach the equitable interests. For example, what is the position if the land is sold by the two trustees, but the required consents are not obtained? Is the purchaser bound by the equitable interests, or are they overreached? This is not such an easy question to answer, as the Act is not entirely clear on this point. Although it will be rare for consent requirements to be built into a trust of residential property (because the trustees/equitable owners will usually be the same people), the matter will not be settled conclusively until there has been some case law. Moreover, it should also be remembered that trustees could apply under section 14 of TOLATA 1996 for the removal of a consent requirement in the same way that equitable owners can apply for one to be imposed.

With these qualifications in mind, TOLATA 1996 appears to envisage the following results if land is sold or mortgaged by two or more trustees of land by a proper overreaching transaction yet in violation of a consent requirement. In *registered* land, because the consent requirement is expressed in the 'disposition' establishing the trust (i.e. it will be written in the original conveyance to the two trustees – section 10), the consent requirement is likely to be entered on the register of title in the form of a Restriction against dealings.[108] This means that no dealings with the land should occur until the conditions of the Restriction have been complied with – that is, consent is obtained. If, for some reason, no Restriction is entered or the transaction is carried out contrary to the terms of the Restriction,[109] the better view is that the purchaser obtains a good title to land, the equitable interests are overreached and the equitable owners are left to sue the trustees for breach of trust.[110] This is despite section 8 of TOLATA 1996, which says that the power of sale 'may not be exercised without that consent'. Although there has been some academic criticism of this view, there is no doubt that TOLATA 1996 was *not* intended to restrict the power of overreaching. Case law under the LRA 1925 supported this view,[111] and sections 26, 29 and 30 of the LRA 2002 settle any doubts in favour of the primacy of overreaching in these circumstances. Note finally that a consent requirement imposed by an order of the court following an application made under section 14 of TOLATA 1996 will, of necessity, be registered as a Restriction consequent on the court order.[112]

In unregistered land, there is no mechanism to register a consent requirement under the LCA 1972 even if such is expressly required in the disposition establishing the trust.

---

108 A Form N Restriction.

109 Of course, this should not happen, but it might: e.g. if the Land Registry is informed that the consent has been obtained when it has not, or the consent has been obtained fraudulently.

110 Sections 29 and 30 of the LRA 2002. Or, perhaps, a purchaser if they have dishonestly assisted in a breach of trust or unconscionably received trust property (the land). This is uncertain, and controversial; see *Arthur v. A-G of the Turks and Caicos Islands* (2012) for a discussion.

111 *Birmingham Midshires Building Society v. Saberhawal* (2000).

112 Note, however, that it now seems unlikely that a court will impose such a requirement, unless the circumstances are exceptional (*Coleman v. Bryant* (2007)).

However, section 16 of TOLATA 1996 (which applies only to unregistered land) says that a purchaser is not affected by the trustees' failure to observe a consent requirement included in a disposition provided that the purchaser had no actual knowledge of the consent requirement. In other words, if the purchaser (or his legal adviser) did not actually know that the land was being conveyed in breach of a consent requirement, then overreaching remains effective. By analogy, the same rule should apply if a consent requirement is imposed as a result of an application under section 14 of TOLATA 1996 (although the Act does not address this possibility). This means that the position in registered and unregistered land is broadly similar in effect. Note, however, that the chances of a consent being required in unregistered land are minimal – new trusts will usually take effect in registered land and rare will be the circumstances in which a consent requirement is imposed on an existing trust in unregistered land.

4.9.7   If consents are not initially required

If no consents are required, then clearly the matter is straightforward – overreaching takes its usual course. However, we need to be aware of the possibility that an equitable owner may apply under section 14 of TOLATA 1996 for a court order that the trustees seek his or her consent before a sale or mortgage. This is not precluded by section 14, which says that the court may make any order 'relating to the exercise by the trustees of any of their functions'. It is, however, controversial, for in *Coleman* v. *Bryant* (2007), the court was not prepared to enter a Restriction requiring the consent of the equitable owner before a sale because this would destroy the concept of overreaching. It remains to be seen whether the court will have to develop criteria to determine whether a consent requirement should be imposed, but if such an order is made, the position is as that described immediately above.[113]

4.9.8   When overreaching *does not* occur

Sections 2(1)(ii) and 27 of the LPA 1925 require money to be paid to at least two trustees[114] in order to overreach the equitable interests behind a trust of land. Consequently, the usual reason why overreaching does not occur is that there is only *one trustee* of the property, as in *Williams & Glyn's Bank* v. *Boland* (1981), in which Mr Boland was sole trustee holding for himself and his wife in equity. This situation arises most commonly because of a successful claim to an equitable interest in the property by a non-legal owner utilising the rules of constructive or resulting trusts discussed below.[115] A typical example would be where a single woman buys a house (which is conveyed to her name alone) and then she invites her lover to live with her, and the lover acquires an equitable interest under the principles developed in *Lloyds Bank* v. *Rosset* (1991), *Stack* v. *Dowden* (2007) and *Jones* v. *Kernott* (2011). If that happens, a trust of land arises,[116] but there is only one legal owner. If a purchaser buys the property

---

113 Note, however, that section 8 of TOLATA 1996 talks only of a consent requirement imposed by the disposition
      creating the trust. Perhaps consent requirements imposed under section 14 will be treated differently.

114 Or a trust corporation.

115 Section 4.10.2.

116 *Bull* v. *Bull* (1955).

(or a bank lends money on it), but pays the purchase money to the single trustee only, then the purchaser cannot rely on overreaching to protect him from the rights of the equitable owners. The purchaser may be bound by the rights of the equitable owners and his use of the land severely restricted or completely disrupted. In fact, in the absence of overreaching, the normal rules of registered or unregistered land (as the case may be) take over. Thus, in registered land, if the equitable owner is a person in discoverable actual occupation of the property at the time of the purchase or mortgage,[117] he will have an interest which overrides the interest of the purchaser or mortgagee under paragraph 2, Schedule 3 of the LRA 2002. However, if this is not the situation – that is, the equitable owner is not in discoverable occupation triggering an interest which overrides – the purchaser or mortgagee will take the land free of the equitable interests even if they are not overreached because this is the normal rule in registered conveyancing (section 29 of the LRA 2002).[118]

In unregistered land, these equitable interests *cannot* be registered as a Land Charge (see section 2(4) of the LCA 1972). Consequently, whether they bind a purchaser or mortgagee who has *not* overreached depends on the 'doctrine of notice', this being one of the very few scenarios in which this ancient doctrine is still relevant in modern land law. Usually, if the equitable owner is residing in the property, the purchaser or mortgagee will be deemed to have constructive notice of their interest, and be bound by it, as discussed in *Kingsnorth Trust* v. *Tizard* (1986).

However, in both registered and unregistered land, a purchaser who has failed to overreach, and who is apparently subject to the priority of the equitable interest, nevertheless may be able to plead that the equitable owner has expressly or impliedly consented to the sale or mortgage. In such cases, a court of equity will respect the express or implied consent of the equitable owner with the consequence that the purchaser gains priority over their interest.[119] In order to give the purchaser this relief, the court must be satisfied that the expressed or implied consent is real, although sometimes cases stretch this (see *Wishart* v. *Credit & Mercantile* (2015)). Thus, consent does not exist simply because the equitable owner has *knowledge* of the proposed sale or mortgage – *Skipton Building Society* v. *Clayton* (1993) – but rather this knowledge must be combined with circumstances that indicate an acceptance of the priority of the purchaser or mortgagee. Some examples may help to clarify the situation.

First, if the legal owner attempts to mortgage the land to a bank and his lover (the equitable owner) signs a consent form postponing her interest to that of the bank, we can be sure that (in the absence of undue influence) the consent was real for it has been given expressly. The obtaining of such express consent is the safest course of action for a mortgagee dealing with a single legal owner when it suspects that another person on the land has some equitable interest in it.[120] Second, even in the absence of a signature on a

---

117 *Abbey National Building Society* v. *Cann* (1991); *Cook* v. *The Mortgage Business plc* (2012).

118 As would have been the case in *Thompson* v. *Foy* (2009): see Chapter 2. Note such equitable interests cannot be protected by the entry of a Notice against the title: section 33 of the LRA 2002. See *Haque* v. *Raja* (2016) where there was neither actual occupation or a Form A Restriction.

119 *Paddington Building Society* v. *Mendelson* (1985), registered land; *Bristol and West Building Society* v. *Henning* (1985), unregistered land.

120 The lender failed to do this in *HSBC* v. *Dyche* (2009) even though it knew of C's interest and, when overreaching did not occur, it lost its priority.

consent form, the equitable owner may have so acted in relation to the mortgage (e.g. attending the bank, explaining the need for a mortgage to the bank's employee) that her consent can be implied from her actions. In such cases, the participation of the equitable owner in securing the mortgage undoubtedly implies consent. Third, if the equitable owner is aware that a mortgage is the only way in which the land can be purchased, he or she must be deemed to have consented to that mortgage. Without the mortgage, there can be no property in which the equitable owner can have an interest and so the equitable owner cannot deny the priority of the mortgage. Importantly, this effectively means that it is near impossible for an equitable owner to claim priority over a mortgagee who provides funds for the original purchase of the land – consent will always be deemed to have been given by reason of the necessity of using a mortgage.[121]

Fourth, and controversially, the decision in Wishart v. Credit & Mercantile (2015) suggests that an equitable owner may be taken to have authorised the trustee to complete the transaction (by analogy with the law of agency), simply because the equitable owner knows they are not the legal owner. In Wishart, this was held to be the result even though the equitable owner was completely unaware of the proposed mortgage. This extraordinary decision appears entirely contrary to the Boland principle and, with respect, is very difficult to justify. Fifth, it is established that genuine consent to one mortgage (mortgage X) will operate in favour of a new mortgagee (mortgage Y) if the second mortgagee is providing funds to pay off the first mortgage. This is more properly regarded as a species of subrogation[122] than 'transferred consent' but it is based on the policy that the equitable owner should not benefit (i.e. recover her priority) merely because of a change in the identity of the lender. Consent to one mortgage can be taken to be consent to its replacement.[123] Sixth, by way of contrast, an equitable owner who knows that the legal owner is about to mortgage, but who does not consent expressly or impliedly, should not in principle lose the priority of his or her interest – assuming it amounts to an overriding interest under LRA 2002 through discoverable actual occupation – simply because of that knowledge. Putting aside the complication introduced by Wishart, it is accepted that it is up to the lender to ensure that it has priority by seeking consent; it is not for the equitable owner to offer it or to surrender it accidentally. In practice, of course, as noted above, most lenders will ensure that all possible or potential equitable owners sign a consent form before the lender agrees to advance the money by way of mortgage, thus securing the priority that may not be available through overreaching.

---

121 *Abbey National Building Society* v. *Cann* (1991). It might be otherwise if the equitable owner's interest existed in unmortgaged land that was sold to purchase the new land and the equitable owner knew nothing of the need for a mortgage.

122 Generally, where a person (mortgagee Y) discharges an obligation (e.g. a mortgage) owed by one person (the borrower) to another (mortgagee X), Y can be subrogated to the 'obligation' and be entitled to enforce the mortgage against the borrower. The person discharging the debt effectively steps into the shoes of the former mortgagee.

123 This consent is effective up to the value of the mortgage that is paid off by the replacement mortgage (*Equity and Home Loans* v. *Prestige* (1992); *LeFoe* v. *LeFoe* (2001)).

4.9.9 The position of the equitable owners: problems and proposals

We have noted above that, if a purchaser pays the purchase price to two trustees of the property, the equitable owners' rights are overreached. This means that the equitable rights are automatically transferred to the proceeds of sale – if any – and the trustees hold that money on trust for the equitable owners in the same way as they held the land: that is, as tenants in common or joint tenants. In many cases, of course, the sale will be caused by one or all of the co-owners wishing to realise their investment and the money will be distributed and the trust brought to an end. Alternatively, where the legal and equitable owners are the same people (e.g. a married couple), the money may be used to finance the purchase of a new property that could then become co-owned in the same way as the one sold. These are, indeed, the 'normal' cases and the great majority of dealings with residential co-owned land follow this smooth path. Yet there will always be some legal owners who decide to sell without telling the equitable owners, perhaps in order to abscond with the proceeds, or more frequently those who wish to raise a loan by way of mortgage of the property for their own purposes. What happens then?

The first question is always whether overreaching has occurred and, if not, whether the purchaser or mortgagee is bound by the equitable interests. If overreaching has *not* occurred and the mortgagee/purchaser *is* bound, from the point of view of the equitable owners, the problem may have gone away. The equitable owners remain in possession of the land, save only that a mortgagee could apply for an order under section 14 of TOLATA 1996 forcing a sale of the land in order to realise its security. Whether the court would order a sale in such circumstances has been discussed above.[124] If overreaching has occurred, the fundamental rule is that the equitable owners have no claim against the purchaser or mortgagee to remain in possession of the land (*City of London Building Society v. Flegg* (1988)). They are overreached and their interests now take effect in the proceeds of sale or mortgage money. If the legal owners have absconded or are unable to pay, the equitable owners will have the normal remedies for breach of trust: for example, a personal action against the trustees or a tracing claim to any assets obtained by use of the trust money. Unfortunately, all of this may be of little comfort to an equitable owner who did not want to have the land sold, especially as their share of the proceeds may not be sufficient to pay for alternative accommodation. This is particularly acute in cases in which the property has been used as a family home. Likewise, the rationale for overreaching disappears completely if no purchase money was actually paid on the transaction but overreaching still occurs, as in *Bank of India v. Sood* (1997).

In response to the decision in *Flegg*, and as a way of limiting the effect of overreaching for an 'unwilling equitable owner', the Law Commission once suggested three alternative reforms to the law (Law Commission Report No. 188). They are discussed briefly below to highlight the nature of the issue and to give food for thought, although they are not under active consideration.[125]

---

124 See section 4.9.2.

125 In fact, *Flegg* was an unusual case in a residential context, but it highlights that the general policy of the law is to ensure the alienability of co-owned land rather than to protect occupiers.

1　　Overreaching should not be possible unless one of the trustees is a solicitor or licensed conveyancer. The idea is simply that such a person might offer protection to an equitable owner by looking after their interests and possibly objecting to a sale. However, this is a poor solution, as it would make conveyancing more expensive as well as requiring an 'outsider' to become involved in personal affairs. Moreover, would it work? Would a solicitor have the time or inclination to be the guardian of the equitable owner?

2　　Overreaching should not be possible if the equitable owner has registered their equitable interest. This would require an amendment to the LRA 2002 as such interests currently are *not* capable of protection through a Notice – section 33 of the LRA 2002. This is superficially attractive (for the equitable owner) as the register could be relied on by the purchaser to indicate whether it is safe to proceed and the equitable owner would be protected. Unfortunately, however, this 'solution' presupposed that equitable owners would be *prepared* to register, even if they *knew* they should.[126] It is no accident that, where there is no overreaching, these equitable rights are capable of binding the purchaser *without* the need for registration through their potential as overriding interests.

3　　Overreaching should not be possible without the consent of all of the equitable owners who are of full age and in possession of the property. The first point is that this would certainly work. An equitable owner's rights to the land would be safe from overreaching under this proposal. However, this would also destroy the entire overreaching mechanism of the LPA 1925. The whole point behind the abolition of legal tenancies in common, the institution of the joint tenant trusteeship under a trust of land and the concept of overreaching is precisely that a purchaser should be able to buy co-owned land *without* having to search for every legal and equitable owner and obtain their consent. This proposal would return the law to its pre-1926 state. In fact, it would be much easier to reinstate legal tenancies in common if that is what is wanted. That said, it will be obvious from the above discussion of the effect of TOLATA 1996 that some form of 'consent requirement' can exist. This may not actually prevent a sale by two trustees (see section 4.9.6 above), but it could trigger an application under section 14 of the Act. In essence, then, a partial 'consent bar' may have been created by the 1996 Act, not entirely deliberately, the effect of which is not necessarily to prevent a sale by two trustees, but to trigger the intervention of the court under section 14.

4.9.10　The position of the equitable owners faced with overreaching: the problem in perspective

From the above discussion, we might be left with the impression that the equitable owner is in a poor position. The law appears to favour the purchaser at every turn. However, what is the reality? First, if there is one trustee of the land, overreaching cannot occur. In the very great majority of cases, this will mean that the purchaser is bound by the rights of the equitable owners, both in registered land (as an overriding

---

126　For example, given that many of these equitable interests arise informally without writing or the involvement of solicitors, would a claimant know to register his or her interest 'against' her lover's land? Would she have been prepared to register, especially as this might have been regarded as a hostile act?

interest) and in unregistered land (through the doctrine of notice). Thus, the equitable owner is secure, save for the possibility of a sale against their wishes if the purchaser or mortgagee applies under section 14 of TOLATA 1996. Even then, the equitable owner would be paid the full value of their share before any claim of the mortgagee or creditor.

Second, if there are two trustees of the land, overreaching can occur, but in most residential property cases, the two trustees will also be the *only* two equitable owners: for example, where a couple in a relationship hold the house on trust for themselves. Again, there is no difficulty, because each co-owner can object to a sale in their capacity as legal owner.

Third, it is only where there are two trustees of land and *different* equitable owners that problems really occur. Such was the case in *Flegg*. Yet the question the Law Commission did not ask itself when producing its now-defunct proposals is: how often does this factual matrix occur in the context of residential property? How often, in a domestic context, will there be two legal owners and *different or additional* equitable owners? There is much to suggest that *Flegg* raises an *exceptional* factual scenario, not a normal one.[127] Should the law be changed to meet the 'hard case'? One view is that all that needs to be done is to prevent a *single* trustee from appointing a second trustee (in order to overreach) without the leave of the court or the consent of the equitable owners. Such a move would prevent the artificial creation of a 'two-trustee' situation by a knowledgeable legal owner preparing to sell or mortgage the property. This may be achieved in registered land by the entry of a suitably worded Restriction against the title.[128]

4.9.11   The question of possession and occupation

Prior to TOLATA 1996, the question of who had a *right* to occupy the co-owned land had caused unnecessary difficulty. There was no doubt that the legal owners had a right to occupy the land, subject to the terms of the trust instrument, for they had a legal estate with all of the rights this entailed. If the land was held for investment purposes, the trustees were likely to have relinquished occupation to another (or their right to occupy may have been impliedly or expressly excluded by the original trust instrument), but that would be because of the specific nature of their trust. With residential co-owned land, if all of the co-owners were also legal owners, each could occupy by virtue of their legal estate. Unfortunately, however, problems did arise for non-legal equitable owners. In theory, such persons had only an interest in the proceeds of sale of the land, not the land itself, and consequently could be denied occupation. Obviously, this misrepresented the reality of the situation and cases such as *Bull v. Bull* (1955) and then *Williams & Glyn's Bank v. Boland* (1981) ignored the theory and recognised that the equitable owners had an effective right to occupy, enforceable against the legal owners and (in the absence of overreaching) against a purchaser. This situation has now been regularised by TOLATA 1996. The Act has not altered the trustees' position as legal owners of the land, as they have all of the

---

127 *Flegg* occurred some 70 years after the LPA 1925 came into force. Another example is *Birmingham Midshires BS v. Saberhawal* (2000). The point is not that this scenario never occurs, but rather that it is *relatively* rare. See also *HSBC v. Dyche* (2009).

128 Remember also the *possibility* of using a Restriction to prevent a sale of mortgage by two trustees without the consent of some named person – perhaps the equitable owner.

powers of an absolute owner unless restricted by the trust instrument or an entry on the register of title.[129] However, not only does the Act abolish the doctrine of conversion and effectively declare that the equitable owners shall be regarded as having rights in the land (section 3), but it also provides in section 12 that an equitable owner has a right to occupy the land if this was the purpose for which the trust came into existence.[130] Such a right can be excluded by the trustees in exceptional circumstances, under section 13, but this will be rare in respect of residential property and cannot, in any event, result in the removal by the trustees of a person already occupying land unless they consent (section 13(7)).[131] However, the right to occupy is a right to occupy the physical land itself, not any subsidiary interest. So in *Creasey* v. *Sole* (2013), the complex family history meant that the claimant had an equitable right to some land (which he could occupy provided the purpose criterion in section 12 was satisfied), but also an equitable right to his mother's equitable share in other land. This was not a share in the land itself, so he could not occupy that land and was liable in trespass.[132] Likewise, in *Medlycott* v. *Herbert* (2014) and *Davis* v. *Jackson* (2017), beneficiary did not have a right to occupy under section 12 because this was not a purpose of the trust even though (in *Medlycott*) the trustees did have the power to permit occupation by a beneficiary. That said, TOLATA 1996 has effectively solved any problems that might remain in this regard – as it was intended to do.[133]

4.9.12   The payment of rent

Once again, before TOLATA 1996, there were difficulties in requiring one co-owner to pay rent to the other if only one enjoyed occupation of the property but both were entitled to it.[134] This was because the nature of co-ownership meant that each co-owner was, in theory, entitled to occupy the whole property (not any defined share) and could not be made to 'pay' for enjoying that to which they were already entitled. This is the unity

---

129 See also sections 23 and 26 of the LRA 2002.

130 As in *Chun* v. *Ho* (2001) where the right to occupy was an important consideration in preventing a sale of the house. But see *Davis* v. *Jackson* (2017) where, under the trust, it was never intended that one of the equitable owners should occupy the land and this impacted on their ability to claim an occupation rent from the other (below section 4.9.12).

131 Denial of occupation is possible under order of the court, section 14 TOLATA and Family Law Act (FLA) 1996, Part IV.

132 The mother was the equitable co-owner of the land under a trust of land; the claimant was the equitable owner of that equitable ownership! In other words, there was a sub-trust. This answer might well be accurate on the facts, but there is a counter-argument that, in cases like this (say, where an equitable owner declares themselves trustee of their own equitable interest), the first equitable owner 'drops out of the picture' and the 'sub equitable owner' really does have an interest in the property itself, giving a right of occupation if section 12 is satisfied – for this point, see *Grange* v. *Wilberforce* (1889).

133 Note also the court's power to regulate occupation under the FLA 1996 in respect of 'matrimonial home' rights. Such rights of occupation are a creation of statute and do not depend on the claimant owning any interest in the land. They may be entered on the register of title by means of an Agreed Notice to ensure protection should the land be sold. They may not override.

134 *Davis* v. *Jackson* (2017) makes it clear that where a co-owner has no right to occupy, that co-owner (or their trustee in bankruptcy) is not entitled to rent from the occupying co-owner.

of possession. So, if one co-owner did not occupy when entitled to, the other could not be forced to pay them 'rent' or 'compensation' by way of recompense for sole use. This could have meant hardship for the 'ousted' co-owner, especially if the reason why only one of them was in possession of the property was because of a breakdown in their domestic relationship. Fortunately, even prior to TOLATA 1996, the courts took a pragmatic view and would order the payment of a monetary sum where it was equitable to do so, irrespective of the theoretical niceties.[135] Now, section 13 of TOLATA 1996 provides that compensation may be paid by one co-owner occupying the land to the exclusion of another if certain conditions are met. Of course, the payment of compensation for sole use by way of occupation rent will not be automatic and it was denied to Mr Stack in *Stack v. Dowden* (2007).[136] Likewise, in *Chun v. Ho* (2001), the co-owner was not required to pay rent to the non-occupying co-owner because the latter had had the benefit of the large amount of money that the occupying co-owner had contributed to the purchase price. In this regard, *Davis v. Jackson* (2017) decides that TOLATA does not establish an exclusive regime for considering whether rent should be paid and that the pre-existing rules of 'equitable accounting' can still apply.[137] So, in that case, pre-TOLATA law determined that when a co-owner was not entitled to occupation (under the terms of the trust), his trustee in bankruptcy could not claim an occupation rent on his behalf.

4.9.13 A summary of the Trusts of Land and Appointment of Trustees Act 1996

The effect of TOLATA 1996 has been woven into the preceding text and the picture presented there is of how trusts of land work from 1 January 1997. The following is a short summary of how the Act changed the original 1925 co-ownership scheme.

1   It is not possible to create new strict settlements of land (see Chapter 5) and the entailed interest is abolished (see section 2 and Schedule 1 of TOLATA 1996). Existing strict settlements will remain valid, but most will run their course and eventually disappear.

2   The doctrine of conversion is abolished, effective for all new and nearly all existing trusts of land (section 3).

3   Unless a 'trust for sale' has been created expressly, existing trusts for sale of land become trusts of land (sections 4 and 5) and trusts of land is the model for all trusts henceforth. There is no duty to sell the land. It remains possible deliberately and unequivocally to create a 'trust for sale' of land, but, given that even these deliberate creations are subject to the provisions of TOLATA 1996, there is very little to be gained practically.

---

135   *Re Pavlou (A Bankrupt)* (1993). An equitable co-owner could also be made to account for 'rent' in favour of a trustee in bankruptcy who had succeeded to the interest of the other co-owner: *Re Byford* (2003).

136   Lord Neuberger dissented on this point.

137   Broadly, this is where the court can allocate credit to one co-owner who has contributed more to the enhancement of co-owned land than the other, or can order payments to equalise benefits received by one and not the other. So, even if land is owned 50 per cent each, the actual sum given to each can be adjusted by taking an 'equitable account' of monies paid or owed.

4   The trustees have all of the powers of an absolute owner, but may delegate these to an equitable owner (sections 6–9). They may do this when it is expedient to give the person in possession of the land the power to manage it. However, only the trustees can give a valid receipt for purchase money, hence preserving their role in overreaching.

5   The trustees must consult with the equitable owners and give effect to their wishes in so far as is consistent with the purposes of the trust of land (section 11).

6   The trustees' powers may be made subject to the consent of the beneficiaries or some other person, but only if stated in the instrument creating the trust (section 10), or if imposed by the court after a section 14 application. This may have consequences when a sale is proposed, but the precise effect is unclear as 'consent requirements' are rarely found in standard co-ownership situations.

7   The equitable owners have a right to occupy the property if the terms of section 12 are met, which can be modified subject to safeguards (section 13). Compensation may be ordered for exclusive use of the land by one co-owner.

8   Any person with an interest in the land can make an application to the court under section 14 for a variety of orders, based on the criteria identified in section 15: for example, sale, no sale, override consent requirement, impose consent requirement. The criteria specified in section 15 do not apply in cases of bankruptcy because section 335A of the Insolvency Act 1986 applies instead.

4.10   The Express and Implied Creation of Co-ownership in Practice: Express, Resulting and Constructive Trusts

The sections above have considered the nature of co-ownership in general and the statutory machinery that governs it. Much has been said about the existence of two trustees or one trustee and the rights of the equitable owners. Now it is time to examine the way in which this co-ownership can come about. Put simply, how is it that land becomes 'co-owned' so that the panoply of legal rules just discussed come into play?

4.10.1   Express creation

Any land may be deliberately conveyed to two or more people; a typical example being the purchase of a new house by a couple in a relationship. In such circumstances, the persons to whom legal title is transferred (i.e. by formal conveyance taking effect as a registered disposition under the LRA 2002) will be the legal owners. In the absence of any statement to the contrary, these legal owners will also be taken to be the equitable owners. The result is that land conveyed to A and B as legal owners will be held on trust by them for themselves as either joint tenants or tenants in common. As we shall see, this presumption that the legal owners (or owner) are also the only equitable owners may be challenged by proof of a 'resulting' or 'constructive' trust or under the law of proprietary estoppel.

Before we come to that, however, it is important to note that it is quite possible for a conveyance of land expressly to declare who are the equitable owners, and also the nature of their ownership. Thus, land might be conveyed 'to A and B as legal owners on trust for A and B beneficially as tenants in common' or 'to A and B as legal owners on trust for A, B, C and D as tenants in common' or 'to A and B as legal owners on trust for A and B beneficially as joint tenants'. In these cases, both where the legal and equitable owners are the same people, and when they are not, the trust of land and the equitable ownership is 'expressly declared'. Two points are of importance here.

1   In order for an express trust of land to be valid, it must satisfy section 53(1) of the LPA 1925. This means that an express declaration of the beneficial (equitable) interests of the co-owners can only be relied upon to establish ownership if such declaration is 'manifested and proved by some writing'. Consequently, as a matter of general principle, a purely oral declaration of co-ownership will not be effective.[138] Usually, the 'writing' is the deed of conveyance/registered disposition to the co-owners or it may be found in Form JO which the co-owners may (but not must) submit to the Land Registry when they apply for registration of their title.[139] However, whatever form this written evidence takes, it must amount to a declaration of the *equitable* interest rather than be for some other purpose. Thus, in *Stack v. Dowden* (2007), the House of Lords held that a statement in the conveyance that a surviving trustee could give a valid receipt for any capital monies paid if the land was sold could not be taken as a declaration of the nature of the equitable interest.[140] However, there is an important exception to the requirement of writing: namely, that a person who is *not* a party to any *valid* express declaration of trust may establish a beneficial interest in the property by proving a resulting or constructive trust or (less commonly) under the law of proprietary estoppel. The exception for resulting and constructive trusts is specifically provided for in section 53(2) of the LPA 1925, where they are exempt from the need for writing.[141] Proprietary estoppel is justified as preventing unconscionability – see Chapter 10. Importantly, therefore, as discussed immediately below, it is only if a person is not a party to a written declaration of trust that they can rely on resulting or constructive trusts or estoppel. We should also be aware that, even in the absence of an express declaration of the beneficial interests in the land (i.e. that no trust is declared at all), the very conveyance of the land to two or more people will be very strong evidence of co-ownership in equity (*Stack*; *Jones v. Kernott*, *Marr v. Collie* (2017)) unless it is clear that the conveyance to two persons was merely administrative in order to enable the single 'true' owner to purchase the land in the first place.[142]

2   If the beneficial interests are expressly declared in writing (or evidenced in writing[143]), this is conclusive as to the beneficial ownership for the parties to that express declaration – *Goodman v. Gallant* (1986), *Pankhania v. Chandegra* (2012), *Re Kone* (2017), *Taylor v. Taylor* (2017), unless the written document is fraudulent (*S v. J* (2016)).

---

138 Note, the declaration does not have to be in writing, so long as there is written evidence of it; section 53(1)(b) of the LPA 1925. *Kaki v. Kaki* (2015).

139 Above, section 4.5.

140 The clause was simply to ensure that a surviving joint tenant and so sole trustee could sell when all other trustees had died.

141 See section 4.10.2 below. Consider also the possibility of an interest arising orally through proprietary estoppel, which is not specifically exempted from section 53(1) of the LPA – see section 4.10.7 below.

142 *Goodman v. Carlton* (2001). See also *Abbey National v. Stringer* (2006) and *HSBC v. Dyche* (2009).

143 As in *Kaki v. Kaki* (2015) where a letter constituted written evidence of an earlier declaration of trust.

Thus, persons who are parties to the writing that establishes the trust cannot, thereafter, plead a resulting or constructive trust to establish different interests. There are only very limited exceptions to this principle of conclusiveness: first, as in S v. J (2016), if the express declaration has been procured by fraud or some other vitiating factor such as undue influence; second, in exceptional circumstances, a party can rely on proprietary estoppel to establish that the interests are different from those declared in writing (*Clarke* v. *Meadus* (2010)).[144] Of course, persons not party to the express written declaration of the trust may rely on resulting or constructive trusts or estoppel. A typical example of the latter would be where a claimant to an interest alleges that they have a share by reason of conduct occurring after the legal title was transferred to the registered proprietor – as where X already owns a house and her new lover (Y) claims an equitable share at a later date. Moreover, as noted above, *Stack* and *Kernott* make it clear that any of the parties to a conveyance that does not actually declare the equitable interests, but rather merely records the transfer of legal title to the land to them, may also rely on a constructive trust, resulting trust or estoppel[145] to prove an enlarged share. So, if a conveyance merely records a transfer to A and B without declaring the extent of their equitable ownership, it is possible for either A or B to use a constructive constructive trust (or perhaps resulting trust/estoppel) to claim an enlarged or even total share of the equity. *Stack* and *Kernott* are examples of the constructive trust being used to establish an enlarged share[146] and *McKenzie* v. *McKenzie* (2003) employs a resulting trust.[147]

4.10.2 Creation of co-ownership even though the legal title is in one name only

It often happens that property is bought by one person and conveyed into their sole name. Of course, this has nothing to do with co-ownership for that person owns the land (the estate in it absolutely, be it freehold or leasehold). However, what happens if someone else (e.g. a spouse, a lover, a friend, an adult child, a grandparent) comes to live in that property, or makes some contribution to its purchase price? Is it possible that this new person may acquire an equitable interest in the house that is formally owned by the other? To put the question another way, even though legal title to the land is held by its original owner, in what circumstances may some other person gain a share in that ownership, albeit that such a share must necessarily be in the equitable interest given that the original owner is already holding the legal title? The law of resulting and constructive trusts, and sometimes estoppel, provides the answer. Before considering the

---

144 See Chapter 10 for a discussion of proprietary estoppel.

145 As discussed below, a constructive trust is more likely to be successful, with *Kernott* and later cases indicating that resulting trusts will be less commonly established (but not impossible) in a residential context.

146 Ms Dowden achieved more than a 60 per cent share of the equitable interest via a constructive trust even though she and Mr Stack were joint legal owners, and in *Kernott* where Ms Jones was held to own 90 per cent.

147 The case pre-dated *Stack* and *Kernott*, but in the light of *Marr* v. *Collie* (2017) the resulting trust seems justifiable as this gave effect to the true intentions of the parties.

matter in detail, however, it is vital to understand why it is so important to determine whether such an equitable interest is created.

In cases in which a claim is successful, although there is only one legal owner (A) (the person who originally acquired the property), the fact that another person (B) has established an equitable interest means that in equity the property is co-owned. As made clear by *Bull v. Bull* (1955), this means that a trust of the land comes into existence whereby the original legal owner (A) holds the property on trust for himself and B in equity. In other words, there is *one* trustee of the land, but two co-owners in equity.[148] Because there is only one trustee, a person who wishes to buy the property from the sole legal owner (or a bank that lends money to that owner on the security of the land) cannot rely on overreaching to give them priority over any equitable owner – section 2 of the LPA 1925. Thus, the purchaser/mortgagee may be bound by B's equitable interest according to the rules of registered or unregistered conveyancing.[149] Moreover, because B's equitable interest has arisen *informally* because of a resulting or constructive trust, or estoppel, without writing, the purchaser may be unaware of its existence and may fail to take avoiding action before completing the purchase.[150]

4.10.3 Establishing the equitable interest

The rules considered below are applicable whenever a person seeks to establish a share of ownership in land, legal title to which is held by someone else. This is sometimes called the 'acquisition question' to distinguish it from the 'quantification question', the latter being where we know that co-ownership exists, but not the relative percentage size of the shares of the co-owners.[151] Often, in acquisition cases, legal title will be held by one person and the claimant will be their partner or former partner in a domestic relationship, but there is no need for any romantic relationship between the parties to exist for these rules to apply. There is, for example, a growing number of cases in which the claim is by sibling members of the same family against the legal owner,[152] but the law is the same whatever the factual matrix.[153] Likewise, although the disputed property is most often residential property, it need not be, and in *Lloyd v. Pickering* (2004), the successful claim by Ms Lloyd was to a half-share in a business that was legally in the sole name of Mr Pickering. These rules are also equally applicable when legal title is held by two, three or four people,[154] the only difference being that, where there are two or more trustees, the newly established equitable interest would be capable of being overreached.

Bearing these points in mind, it is possible to categorise the methods by which an equitable interest may be claimed. However, it is to be remembered that, while these

---

148 There is no limit to the number of people who may own the land in equity, whereas legal title is limited to a maximum of four.

149 Overriding interests and the doctrine of notice, respectively.

150 Of course, to be an overriding interest under paragraph 2, Schedule 3 of the LRA 2002, the actual occupation must be discoverable – but that does not mean that the purchaser or mortgagee actually discovered it.

151 Thus, both *Stack* and *Kernott* are technically 'quantification' cases.

152 For example, *Hapeshi v. Allnatt* (2010), *Sandhu v. Sandhu* (2016).

153 For example, *Tinsley v. Milligan* (1993), two women; *Babic v. Thompson* (1999), two businessmen.

154 For example, *Grant v. Edwards* (1986), in which legal title was held by the defendant and his brother.

categories are convenient for the purposes of exposition, in reality, the claimant's and defendant's lives tend to be much more complicated and much less susceptible to objective, forensic analysis than land lawyers would like! The need to rely on possibly half-remembered conversations or disputed facts makes this area of the law a breeding ground for litigation. In this litigation, it is not always possible or desirable to be as 'black and white' as the rules presented below appear to be. This is, in essence, the thrust of the House of Lords' decision in *Stack* v. *Dowden* (2007) and that of the Supreme Court in *Jones* v. *Kernott* (2011), which emphasise the need for a flexible approach in the light of the complex way in which people live their lives.[155]

4.10.4   The express trust

Although it rarely occurs, it is perfectly possible for the legal owner (or owners) deliberately to generate an interest in the land for another person by means of an express trust. In short, the legal owner (A) may declare expressly and in writing (or evidenced in writing as required by section 53(1) of the LPA 1925) that she holds the land on trust for the claimant (B), usually in co-ownership with herself.[156] As an express trust, the equitable co-ownership thereby created is conclusive according to the terms of the declaration, subject only to rectification in the event of fraud or forgery.[157] The parties may also use a written declaration to establish the size of each person's share, as in *Richards* v. *Woods* (2014). It is also possible for the legal owner actually to convey the legal title to himself and another, in which case there will be co-ownership of the legal and equitable title. This is even rarer, for it involves additional expense and the need to re-register the legal title at HM Land Registry, but might occur if the parties need to raise money and use the land as security.[158]

4.10.5   The 'purchase money' resulting trust

A second means by which a person may claim an equitable interest in another's property – thereby triggering co-ownership – is by contributing to the purchase price of the property, despite the fact that their name is not on the legal title. Unless it can be established that the money was given to the legal owner by way of gift or loan,[159] the claimant may have an equitable interest in the land in direct proportion to their contribution to the purchase price – *Wodzicki* v. *Wodzicki* (2017).[160] This is the resulting trust. It is said to arise from an intention to acquire an interest in the property as manifested by the contribution to the acquisition of the property through part-provision of the purchase price.[161] A typical example is where the legal owner has provided some of the purchase price and the balance is provided by a husband, wife or other partner who does not 'go on the title'. In such

---

155 The extent to which the principles found in *Stack* and *Kernott* apply to acquisition cases is discussed below.

156 An example is *Davis* v. *Jackson* (2017) where the wife declared in writing that she held the house on trust for herself and her estranged husband.

157 And possibly a plea in proprietary estoppel – *Clarke* v. *Meadus* (2010).

158 This later happened in *Davis* v. *Jackson*.

159 For example, *Bradbury* v. *Hoolin* (1998).

160 A similar result was reached in *S* v. *J* (2016), although it is not clear if this was because of a resulting trust or a constructive trust.

161 *Tinsley* v. *Milligan* (1993); *Laskar* v. *Laskar* (2008).

cases, legal ownership is in one person and equitable ownership is shared among the contributors, usually as a tenancy in common in proportion to the contribution provided. The principles are the same if all that is provided is the deposit[162] and in certain circumstances may include a notional payment because of a 'right to buy' discount off the purchase price.[163] Note, however, that the contribution must be made to the acquisition of property, not merely to its repair,[164] and it seems that an interest will not arise even if a payment is made if there is positive evidence that no intention to acquire an interest in fact existed.[165]

As a variation on this, there has been some doubt whether an equitable interest may arise if the financial contribution is made to the purchase price over a period of time. The typical scenario would be where the non-legal owner contributes to the repayment or financing of a mortgage that in its turn has been used to purchase the property. Classic theory dictates that a resulting trust can arise only if payments are made at the time of the acquisition of the property and post-acquisition mortgage payments appear to fall outside this. Also, it is factually true that repayment of mortgage monies is not a payment to the seller of the property at all; it is a payment to the lender who has already provided the balance of the purchase price in full and, with an endowment mortgage, is not even repayment of the principal sum borrowed.[166] Thus, in Curley v. Parkes (2004), the Court of Appeal denied Mr Curley an interest in the property because such mortgage repayments as he did make were made after the date of acquisition of the property.[167] This is clearly a narrow view of the role of resulting trusts and it is not immediately apparent why repayment of a mortgage (or the financing of its debt if the mortgage is interest only) that was used to purchase the property cannot be regarded as making a contribution to its acquisition at the relevant time. It takes only a little imagination to regard the mortgagee as the agent of the purchasers, paying at the time of purchase, with the mortgagee being repaid as agent with interest by the contributors. Indeed, cases before Curley had rather assumed that payment of mortgage instalments would suffice. In Carlton v. Goodman (2002) and McKenzie v. McKenzie (2003), both claimants were actually mortgagors, having undertaken mortgage liability in order to secure the relevant finance for the purchase of the property, but because neither had undertaken repayment in order to secure an interest in the house, their claims to an interest failed.[168] Indeed, the other party in both cases was held entitled to the entire equitable interest precisely because they had paid the mortgage instalments. More importantly, in Laskar v. Laskar (2008), the Court of

162 Halifax Building Society v. Brown (1995).
163 Mumford v. Ashe (2000); Laskar v. Laskar (2008). See also Richards v. Woods (2014) where such a discount was used to quantify the share.
164 Bank of India v. Mody (1998). If the couple are married, contributions to repairs might squeeze into section 37 of the Matrimonial Proceedings and Property Act 1970 as an 'improvement' generating an interest: see below.
165 First National Bank v. Wadhwani (1998). This also seems to follow from Marr v. Collie with its emphasis on the paramount need to determine the intentions of parties.
166 Under an endowment mortgage, the monthly repayments are of only the interest on the debt and the capital is repaid by some other means, usually the cashing in of an 'endowment' or savings plan. A repayment mortgage does include repayment of the capital as part of each monthly instalment.
167 He also claimed to have made some lump-sum payments but these also were post-acquisition.
168 Such repayments as they had made were made in order to discharge their contractual liability as mortgagors, not in pursuance of an interest in the property.

Appeal[169] decided that contributions to mortgage repayments could be treated as a contribution to the purchase price and, although in this case the property was purchased for investment purposes – rather than as a home for mother and daughter – there seems no reason to doubt the logic of the decision. A similar approach was taken by the Court of Appeal in *Wodzicki* where financial contributions to its purchase and maintenance over an extended period of time helped establish a resulting trust. This now seems to be the accepted position and *Curley* should be disregarded in so far as it decides otherwise.[170]

However, while the above description reflects an orthodox analysis of resulting trusts, we must consider the impact of three high-profile decisions: *Stack* v. *Dowden* (House of Lords, 2007), *Jones* v. *Kernott* (Supreme Court, 2011) and *Marr* v. *Collie* (Privy Council 2017[171]). All three cases in fact concern the respective shares of persons who were already joint-legal owners of property (sometimes called the *quantification* issue), rather than being about acquiring an interest from a legal owner, but they have much to say about the role of resulting trusts in these types of disputes. In *Stack*, the majority indicated – Lord Neuberger declining to agree with the generality of the majority's reasoning – that resulting trusts should not normally be used as the basis for assessing an interest in property used as a family home. This was because the resulting trust is narrow and focuses on only one aspect of the party's lives – the payment of money. Family relationships are complex and so a better approach – in the sense that it leads to a fairer result – was to use constructive trusts. This approach was confirmed by the Privy Council in the later case of *Abbott* v. *Abbott* (2008)[172] – which was an acquisition case – and by robust dicta in *Jones* v. *Kernott*. In that case, Lord Walker and Lady Hale, with whom Lord Collins agreed in full, stated that:

> in the case of the purchase of a house or flat in joint names for joint occupation by a married or unmarried couple, where both are responsible for any mortgage, there is no presumption of a resulting trust arising from their having contributed to the deposit (or indeed the rest of the purchase) in unequal shares.[173]

However, subsequent cases have seen a reluctance to abandon the resulting trust altogether, both in acquisition and quantification disputes. Thus, a resulting trust seems to have been the reason for the step-mother's interest in *Chaudhary* v. *Chaudhary* (2013) and certainly it was the basis for the decision in *Wodzicki* (2017), having previously been used in *Laskar* v. *Laskar* because of the relative certainty it provides when compared to a constructive trust.[174]

---

169 Lord Neuberger sat in this case prior to his appointment as Master of the Rolls.

170 Note, that many of these types of case can be squeezed into the rubric of constructive trusts, as discussed below, but *Wodzicki* shows that resulting trusts are not redundant.

171 *Marr* is a Privy Council decision in respect of a dispute in the Bahamas, but the judgment by Lord Kerr, on behalf of a panel made up entirely of Supreme Court Justices including the President and Deputy President, applies and interprets principles applicable in this jurisdiction.

172 The two leading protagonists in *Stack* who favoured the rejection of resulting trusts – Baroness Hale and Lord Walker – also sat in *Abbott*. The advice in *Abbott* was delivered by Baroness Hale. Lord Neuberger – who also sat in both – remained silent in *Abbott*, but see *Laskar* v. *Laskar* (2008).

173 Paragraph 25.

174 Lord Neuberger, in *Stack*, did not see why the well-understood and relatively certain law of resulting trusts should be so easily abandoned. In his view, it had a role to play in certain circumstances precisely because it led to certain and predictable results, hence its application by him in the Court of Appeal in *Laskar* v. *Laskar*.

In *Marr v. Collie* (2017), Lord Kerr on behalf of the Privy Council, revisited the relationship between resulting and beneficial (equitable) ownership, albeit not in an acquisition context.[175] He emphasised that *Stack* should not be regarded as being only about 'family' or domestic cases (as opposed to investment or non-intimate relationship cases), but neither should we approach these cases on the basis that there is a clash of legal presumptions – that is, whether equity followed the law or whether there was a resulting trust. Nor were these cases to be seen as a contest between different legal doctrines of resulting or constructive trusts. The key was to understand that context was everything and the role of the court was to search for the parties' intentions, both at the time the land was acquired and as time passed.

What this seems to mean is that if the evidence established that the parties intended to own the land in the proportion they paid for it, a resulting trust would accurately explain how they acquired their interests, but if the common intention of the parties showed a different outcome, the interest would not follow the money, but might follow the legal ownership or require the broad enquiry needed for a constructive trust. Clearly, this means that a court will have to engage in a detailed analysis of the evidence to establish the parties' intentions[176] and should not resort to generalised reasoning based on whether the dispute was 'domestic', 'commercial' or 'investment' while still recognising that the parties might have different intentions in different contexts. We must also recognise that *Stack*, *Kernott* and *Marr* were not 'acquisition' cases as such, and *Marr* especially is influenced by the fact that the parties were already joint-legal owners. Nevertheless, even though one could distinguish the reasoning on this ground, the reminder that we are searching for the parties' intentions and should not resort to generalisations based on categories is powerful. In some cases, the context may readily reveal the parties' intentions to be that of supporting a resulting trust; in others the context may point to an intention to own property on the more flexible basis of a constructive trust or in the same way as the legal title.

Finally, before considering the flexible constructive trust, we must note those cases in which the claimant makes a financial contribution to the cost of running the household, the value of which may have enabled the legal owner to pay the purchase price of the property. An example is where the woman pays all of the regular domestic outgoings and the man pays the mortgage. *Curley*, would suggest that it is unlikely that these can count as an acquisition contribution for the purposes of a resulting trust – even if a resulting trust is the suitable vehicle. *Laskar* did nothing to change this, although *Wodzicki* does suggest that payments towards purchase of the property and its maintenance and general outgoings might be relevant.[177] However, we should remember that such indirect financial contributions can be regarded as evidence of an inferred common intention so as to support a constructive trust (see below).

---

175 The parties were joint-legal owners and the issue was how to determine their beneficial ownership. Did equity follow the law (see below) or should we use resulting or even constructive trusts?

176 This had not been done by the trial court in *Marr*, so the case was sent back for determination.

177 *Lloyds Bank v. Rosset* (1991) is clearly against using general household contributions to establish a resulting trust, although perhaps it is different if they enable the legal owner to purchase the property. This is very difficult to prove. Such a claim failed in *Burns v. Burns* (1984) and appears to be rejected as a matter of principle in the all-important judgment of Lord Bridge in *Rosset*. This is another reason why the courts in *Stack* and *Kernott* favoured the more flexible constructive trust.

4.10.6   The constructive trust

The concept of a 'constructive trust' is used and misused widely in English law. We must be careful when considering the 'constructive trust' in the present context to appreciate that the role it plays in land law does not tell us anything about its function or attributes in other areas of the law. It is a term of 'no fixed abode' and much time has been spent examining whether there is any unifying concept that ties together the various uses of it. That is a debate for another day for it goes well beyond the realms of land law.[178]

In order to claim an equitable interest under the rubric of constructive trust, the essence of the matter is that the legal owner and the claimant must share an express or inferred 'common intention' that the claimant should have some interest in the land, which intention is relied on by the claimant to their detriment.[179] If this is established, a constructive trust arises whereby the land is held on trust by the legal owner (e.g. the registered proprietor) for the legal and equitable owner, usually as tenants in common.[180] The constructive trust does not need to be in, or evidenced in, writing – section 53(2) of the LPA 1925.

The heart of the doctrine is, then, the existence of a common intention, relied on by the claimant to detriment. *Lloyds Bank* v. *Rosset* (1991), a decision of the House of Lords, provided early guidance, but this has now been enhanced by the House of Lords' judgment in *Stack* v. *Dowden* (2007) and the Supreme Court's decision in *Jones* v. *Kernott* (2011). The first of these (*Rosset*) is an acquisition case, and the last two strictly concern quantification where the parties are joint-legal owners and it is not clear how the equitable interest is shared. Although it may well be more difficult to prove a common intention to acquire an interest where none existed before, as opposed to a common intention to quantify (or vary) an equitable interest where the land is clearly already co-owned, the two sorts of case raise the exactly same issue of principle. That is, what factors are relevant in establishing a common intention as to the equitable interest so that it could differ[181] from the legal interest, whether that legal interest be of a sole owner (acquisition case) or joint-owners (quantification case). The analysis below separates out these two types of case in recognition that they generate different practical considerations but that does not mean that they are different in principle.

In *Rosset*, a husband and wife arranged to purchase a derelict farmhouse and legal title was conveyed to the husband alone at the insistence of family trustees who were under a duty under the terms of their trust to ensure that the money for the purchase was given only to the husband. Clearly, however, the renovation was a joint venture, with the wife supervising the work. The property was later mortgaged, the repayments could not be made and the bank sued for possession. The wife resisted on the ground that she had an

---

178 A common view is that the various guises of constructive trust all deal with some kind of unconscionability on the part of a person who holds or acquires property, but this is by no means a watertight analysis. A restitutionary approach might stress the use of the constructive trust as a vehicle for reversing unjust enrichment.

179 In a case involving joint legal owners, this would be a common intention between them as to the relative size of their shares.

180 There is no reason why the claimant should not gain 100 per cent of the equity under a constructive trust. It is more common, however, for the common intention to trigger a share of the equity.

181 If there is detrimental reliance.

equitable interest in the property by way of constructive trust. In the result, her claim was rejected and in the leading opinion, adopted by all of their Lordships, Lord Bridge set out a framework for the law. Taken as a whole, *Rosset* propounds a fairly narrow view of the law and it has therefore aroused some criticism, criticism that led to its refinement in *Stack v. Dowden*, whose rationale is itself adopted in *Kernott*. As decided by *Rosset* – confirming a great deal of earlier case law – there are two fundamental requirements for establishing a constructive trust: a common intention plus detrimental reliance. Neither *Stack* nor *Kernott* dispute this statement of general principle, but rather they have enlarged the circumstances in which a common intention may be established.

4.10.6.1 *Common intention in acquisition cases: three routes to an interest*

In cases where the claimant is seeking to establish that they have an interest for the first time, not being a legal owner, they must establish a 'common intention'. The claimant must adduce evidence of this intention, not merely assert that it exists – *AI v. MKI & Crown Prosecution Service (Intervener)* (2015). According to *Rosset*, this common intention can be established only in two ways, but *Stack* (bolstered by *Abbott v. Abbott*, and developed by *Kernott*) has added a third way (see also *Geary v. Rankine* (2012) and *Ullah v. Ullah* (2013)). However, before we consider these routes to a common intention in detail, we must take note of a reservation. In *Stack v. Dowden* and *Jones v. Kernott*, the parties already jointly owned the legal title and there was no doubt that Mr Stack and Mr Kernott had some equitable interest in the land. The narrow point of both cases was to determine whether Mr Stack and Mr Kernott had 50 per cent of the equity on the basis that 'equity follows the law', or whether either had some other, lesser share (as claimed by Ms Dowden and Ms Jones, respectively). Strictly speaking, therefore, both *Stack* and *Kernott* are quantification cases in which the real issue is 'how much' does each co-owner have, rather than whether the claimant has any interest at all. They are not, therefore, strictly about acquisition like *Rosset* and this was noted (but the consequences not really explored) in *Kernott*. Some critics might argue, therefore, that *Stack* and *Kernott* have no application to acquisition claims and, if this is correct, the third route to a common intention discussed below may not apply. However, it seems clear from reading the majority opinions in *Stack* that there was an intention that at least its reasoning should apply to acquisition claims and it was applied as such by the Privy Council in *Abbott v. Abbott*, by the High Court in *Hapeshi v. Allnatt* (2010), *Crown Prosecution Service v. Piper* (2011) and *Ullah v. Ullah* (2013). The Court of Appeal has adopted the *Stack/Kernott* approach in acquisition cases without hesitation in *Geary v. Rankine* (2012), *Capehorn v. Harris* (2015) and *Sandhu v. Sandhu* (2016).[182] Obviously, it would be open to the Supreme Court to decide that acquisition and quantification cases should be dealt with differently, but that now seems very unlikely.

---

182 See also *Wing v. Eades* (2013), *O'Kelly v. Davies* (2014), *Graham-York v. York* (2015). Sometimes, *Rosset* is still used, *Ambrose v. Ambrose* (2012), but not because *Stack* cannot be.

4.10.6.1.1 *Route 1: Express discussions*

The first route to establishing a common intention (*Rosset*) is to determine whether there has at any time prior to acquisition, or exceptionally at some later date, been any express agreement, arrangement or understanding reached between the parties that the property is to be shared beneficially. The finding of such an agreement or arrangement is based on the words used and discussions held, however imperfectly remembered and however imprecise the terms may have been. Thus, there must have been an overt, express statement or agreement, promise or assurance. In many cases, this agreement will be clear as where A says to B 'Of course half this house is yours', or 'This house is as much yours as mine'. However, promises are also deemed to be made expressly so as to establish a constructive trust when the legal owner makes a statement reassuring the claimant that they have some sort of stake in the property. This can take many forms and is, ultimately, a matter for interpretation in each case. For example, does 'This will always be your home', or 'I would never sell without your agreement', imply a promise as to ownership? If it does, a constructive trust is a possibility. Moreover, it appears that such a promise can be enough to trigger a constructive trust even if it is not genuine on the part of the legal owner. So, in *Eves* v. *Eves* (1975), a promise was held to have been made where the legal owner said, by way of excuse, that the only reason that the property was not conveyed originally to the woman was because she was too young.[183] Likewise, telling the claimant that the property will be conveyed to them in due course can be a relevant assurance, even if it is a lie. The only rule is that an express assurance must be made, in whatever form, and it does not matter that this occurs after the legal owner has acquired the property.[184] However, as shown by *James* v. *Thomas* (2007), assurances given by the legal owner to the claimant when they were living together that were *neither* intended nor understood as a promise of an interest cannot qualify. It would be enough if the landowner did not intend to make such a promise, but it was in fact reasonably understood as such by the claimant.[185]

4.10.6.1.2 *Route 2: Inferred common intention from payments*

If it is not possible to establish the common intention by means of an express assurance, Lord Bridge in *Rosset* notes that, by way of contrast:

> direct contributions to the purchase price by the partner who is not the legal owner, whether initially or by payment of mortgage instalments, will readily justify the inference necessary to the creation of a constructive trust. But, as I read the authorities, it is at least extremely doubtful whether anything else will do.[186]

In other words, according to *Rosset*, the second (and only other) circumstance in which the court may find a common intention is if there have been direct payments towards

---

183 See also *Grant* v. *Edwards* (1986), in which a false excuse was given for not including the claimant as legal owner.

184 *Clough* v. *Killey* (1996).

185 There are parallels here with the law of proprietary estoppel – see Chapter 10.

186 At p. 8.

the purchase price of the property – such as lump-sum payments or mortgage payments. This is enough to infer a common intention. This is critical for it means that, were it not for the *Stack/Kernott* enhancement, 'normal' domestic obligations, childcare responsibilities, indirect contributions,[187] payment of household bills and all manner of other conduct that persons sharing a home might engage in could not lead to the inference of a common intention. Absent an express agreement, only payments towards the purchase price would do[188] and, even then, evidence that no agreement was ever reached – that is, positive proof that the parties *did not* agree – would mean that no common intention could be inferred.[189] This is because an *inferred* common intention is a real intention, and so evidence that no such intention existed must mean that one cannot be inferred from conduct.

Evidently, the *Rosset* approach is relatively narrow: only promises (route 1) or payments (route 2) could lead to a common intention. While promoting relative certainty, it excluded the inference of a common intention even though the parties had engaged in the joint enterprise of family life and for all intents and purposes had treated the land as owned jointly, notwithstanding the fact that title was held by only one of them. The classic example of this type is *Burns* v. *Burns* (1984) – decided before *Rosset* – which is rightly castigated as demonstrating the law's disregard for the way in which people conduct regular family life.[190] In response to mounting criticism of the narrowness of the *Rosset* approach, the Court of Appeal in *Oxley* v. *Hiscock* (2004) (which was an acquisition case) attempted to broaden the circumstances in which a person might prove a common intention by allowing such an intention to be inferred from all of the facts and circumstances of the case. It was essentially an approach seeking to achieve an 'equitable' result bearing in mind the realities of modern life, and proved the catalyst for the House of Lords' analysis in *Stack* v. *Dowden* and its later application in *Jones* v. *Kernott*.

4.10.6.1.3 *Route 3: Inferred common intention from the parties' entire course of conduct*

The majority judgment in *Stack* (Lord Neuberger disagreeing in part as to the reasoning) sets out to make it easier for a claimant to establish a common intention and thereby an equitable interest in land belonging to another. The *Stack* reasoning is adopted and approved in *Kernott* and has since been adopted in acquisition cases as demonstrated

---

187 See *Ivin* v. *Blake* (1993).

188 Necessarily, of course, because the inference comes from payments towards the purchase price, there is an overlap with resulting trusts. See, for example, *Ambrose* v. *Ambrose* (2012), which follows *Rosset* in a contest between the claimant and trustee in bankruptcy.

189 For example, *Lightfoot* v. *Lightfoot Brown* (2004).

190 Mr Burns paid all the mortgage monies and never made any promises. Ms Burns (they were not married) looked after the children and ran the home. She lost her claim. It was never quite clear how typical this case was: was it evidence of widespread unfairness, or merely the one 'hard case'?

above. The essence of the matter is that it is permissible to infer[191] a common intention as to ownership based on the parties' entire relationship with each other. It was not necessary to limit the enquiry to promises or payments. The evidence for this common intention can come from a range of factors because, according to Baroness Hale in *Stack* (who gave the leading judgment and which is approved explicitly in *Kernott*), 'context is everything'.[192] Thus, to establish a common intention it is possible to rely on:

> [m]any more factors than financial contributions.... These include: any advice or discussions at the time of the transfer which cast light upon their intentions then; the reasons why the home was acquired in their joint names;[193] the reasons why (if it be the case) the survivor was authorized to give a receipt for the capital moneys; the purpose for which the home was acquired; the nature of the parties' relationship; whether they had children for whom they both had responsibility to provide a home; how the purchase was financed, both initially and subsequently; how the parties arranged their finances, whether separately or together or a bit of both; how they discharged the outgoings on the property and their other household expenses.[194]

Clearly, these are wide-ranging factors, and the list is not even meant to be exhaustive[195] although some cases do treat it as a checklist (*R v. Taylor* (2017[196])). Of course, this represents a move away from the relative strictness of the *Rosset* approach, but as Lord Walker says in *Stack*, 'in my opinion the law has moved on, and your Lordships should move it a little more in the same direction'.[197] Consequently, there is now a third way in which to establish a common intention in addition to the two routes provided by *Rosset*: it is now possible to *infer* a common intention by examining the whole range of the parties' conduct in relation to the property and, in that context, to each other. As *Kernott* makes clear, and is reiterated by *Piper, Geary* and *Ullah*, this inference must be based on an objective assessment of the parties' conduct – hence it is an intention that they really did have – but it may be deduced from a very wide range of circumstances. Consequently, the claimant must not only prove the facts demonstrating a whole course of conduct, but also that a real common intention can be inferred from it. Necessarily, therefore, positive evidence that there was *not* a common intention is fatal.

---

191   In *Stack*, there is some argument as to whether this intention is inferred or imputed intention. Lord Neuberger is happy to infer an intention, but not to impute one. An inferred intention is a real intention that arises from the facts; an imputed intention is one that the court thinks the parties would have had, had they thought about it, in light of the facts. Inferred common intention has the approval of precedent, but imputed intentions were rejected by the House of Lords in *Gissing v. Gissing* (1971). *Kernott* makes it clear that this is inferred intention. It is now clear that the court cannot impute an intention in either acquisition or quantification (variation) disputes (*Capehorn v. Harris, Barnes v. Phillips* (2015)).

192   *Stack v. Dowden* at [69]. The same point is made in *Marr v. Collie* (2017).

193   This reflects that the case was a quantification dispute.

194   Baroness Hale at [69].

195   Baroness Hale at [70].

196   This was a quantification case but provides a good example of how courts go about applying the flexible criteria to real facts.

197   *Stack v. Dowden*, per Lord Walker at [26].

4.10.6.1.4 *No imputed common intention in acquisition cases*

In *Stack*, there was considerable discussion about whether it was permissible to impute a common intention to the parties and whether this was in fact different from inferring one. Lord Neuberger thought that the difference was clear, and that imputation was not permissible and, indeed, that is an accurate reading of the earlier House of Lords' decision in *Gissing* v. *Gissing* (1971). After *Kernott*, it is now accepted that there is a difference between inferring and imputing a common intention: an inferred common intention is an intention that the parties actually had, albeit evidenced by actions rather than words; whereas an imputed common intention is an intention that the parties would have had, had they thought about it.[198,199] Following *Stack/Kernott*, there were no cases where the claimant's interest arose simply because of an imputed intention and now the Court of Appeal has decided specifically that it is not possible to impute a common intention in an acquisition case – *Capehorn* v. *Harris* (2015).[200]

4.10.6.1.5 *Summary in acquisition cases*

The current position now has been clarified. The relative ease with which a common intention can be established means that a court has considerable freedom in determining the equitable property interests, especially of couples who share a family home. There is already a wide-ranging statutory discretion in relation to separating married couples[201] and the combination of *Rosset*, *Stack* and *Kernott* establish an equivalent jurisdiction in relation to unmarried couples as well as in other contexts.[202] In relationship cases, this is a deliberate response to the lack of legislation dealing with the rights of unmarried couples.[203] In some respects, the use of the constructive trust in these cases is driven by pragmatism rather than principle,[204] but property law has always striven to reflect reality rather than theory.[205]

---

198 In *Kernott*, Lord Walker and Lady Hale noted that 'while the conceptual difference between inferring and imputing is clear, the difference in practice may not be so great', at paragraph 34.

199 See also *Geary* v. *Rankine* (2012).

200 In *S* v. *J* (2016), the trial judge refers to an inferred or imputed intention, but it is clear that he is referring to the judgment in *Stack* which did not clearly distinguish between the two types of intention in the way that later cases insist.

201 See section 24 of the Matrimonial Causes Act 1973.

202 E.g. parents and children, siblings, business partners.

203 Such legislation was proposed by the Law Commission, but has been shelved – see *Cohabitation: The Financial Consequences of Relationship Breakdown* (Law Com. No. 307, 2007).

204 It is difficult to deny that the judgments in both cases are light on analysis in terms of property law. For example, there is no reference to the need for writing to transfer interests in property and why constructive trusts can be an exception to this important rule; no analysis of when or how severance of the equitable joint tenancy arose; no real explanation of why previous binding authority can be departed from; no discussion of detrimental reliance; no clarity about why certain actions can lead to an inference of a common intention, and when they cannot.

205 'The Organic Nature of the Law of Real Property', in *Modern Studies in Property Law* (2017).

4.10.6.2 *Detrimental reliance*

Once a common intention is established, the claimant must then show that they have relied to their detriment on such intention. It is, after all, a tenet of English law that 'equity will not assist a volunteer'[206] and there is no unconscionability if a promise has been made that has had no impact on the behaviour of the claimant. In this regard, 'reliance' – that is, that the claimant would not have behaved as she did without the common intention – is not difficult to establish and may take many forms. In *Greasley* v. *Cooke* (1980), Lord Denning suggests that, if there is evidence of 'detriment', there should be a presumption of reliance. Consequently, in the absence of evidence to the contrary adduced by the legal owner, the court is entitled to assume that the claimant did, indeed, rely on the assurance made. This is so even if there is evidence to suggest that the claimant would have acted as she did for other motives – perhaps out of love for the legal owner. So, in *Chun* v. *Ho* (2001), the claimant was successful even though her actions were motivated in part by her high regard and affection for the legal owner.[207] This is, of course, a generous presumption and it reverses the burden of proof. Nevertheless, it is necessary in order to prevent the legal owner from denying a constructive trust merely because the claimant could not prove her state of mind: that she had relied on the common intention.

Given this generous approach to the question of reliance, it is clear that 'detriment' plays a large part in establishing a constructive trust.[208] In cases where there is an *express* common intention, detriment may take many forms. It can be in the conduct of the claimant, such as doing extraordinary work about the house as in *Eves* v. *Eves* (1975) and *Ungarian* v. *Lesnoff* (1990).[209] The detriment may be financial, such as paying bills or settling other household expenses, provided that the expense is undertaken because an express promise is made. Whatever form it takes, however, the key is that the claimant does something concrete in relation to the express common intention. In this connection, it seems that the 'detriment' does not need to have been 'detrimental' in the sense of harmful. So, giving up existing accommodation in order to move into the legal owner's luxurious property is a 'detriment' (no house to fall back on), as is spending one's life savings on a Porsche in reliance on the legal owner's promise that 'you will never have to find another house' (no money to purchase another property). In addition, giving up other opportunities because the legal owner has assured the claimant that her future is secure can be detriment.[210] As these examples illustrate, it is also true that the

---

206 That is, someone who gives nothing or does nothing in response to the promise or assurance of another.

207 If it were otherwise, the only successful claimants would be those who acted entirely mercenarily simply because they were expressly or impliedly promised something.

208 In *Century UK* v. *Clibbery* (2004), the acts of alleged detriment were so trivial that, even if there had been an assurance, they would not have generated a constructive trust or estoppel.

209 Note the point is that the claimant undertook work of an extraordinary character, such as doing building work in the garden or renovating the property. It is doubtful whether doing 'normal' domestic obligations can count as a response to an express common intention. In *Rosset*, although Mrs Rosset could be thought of as undertaking extensive renovation work amounting to qualifying conduct, there was (as the law then stood) no common intention – no express promise and no payments. Whether Mrs Rosset would succeed under the more relaxed approach of *Stack* is uncertain.

210 *Chun* v. *Ho* (2001).

detriment need not be made in relation to the property in which the claimant acquires an interest. It often is – for example, renovating the kitchen – but it need not be.

Where the common intention is inferred from direct contributions towards the purchase price or from the parties' entire course of dealings, detriment is relatively easy to establish. It is clear from *Rosset* and *Stack* that the actual payments made towards the purchase price or the conduct that gives to the common intention may *also* qualify as the detriment. Thus, the payments or conduct perform a dual role: they are the reason a common intention can be inferred in the first place and they can be the detriment consequent on reliance on that intention.

4.10.7 The nature of the interest generated and identification of the share in acquisition cases

If the claimant establishes a constructive trust or a resulting trust, she will be entitled to a share of the equitable interest. Legal title will continue to be held by the legal owner, but now as a trustee holding for himself and the successful claimant in equity under the statutory trust of land imposed by the LPA 1925 and regulated by TOLATA 1996. The equitable interest will be held by way of a tenancy in common[211] – only the unity of possession is present – and we must ascertain the size of this interest.

4.10.7.1 *The size of the share in resulting trust acquisition cases*

If a claimant establishes a resulting trust, his interest in the property is to be quantified in direct proportion to the amount of the price paid. So, a contribution of 25 per cent made at the time of purchase entitles the claimant to a 25 per cent interest, and so on. This is classical resulting trust theory[212] and cases such as *Midland Bank* v. *Cooke* (1995) and *LeFoe* v. *LeFoe* (2001), which appeared to challenge this by suggesting that an interest established under a resulting trust could be expanded beyond a proportional share by taking a broad view of the entirety of the parties' relationship with each other,[213] are now better regarded as cases of constructive trust.[214]

4.10.7.2 *The size of the share in constructive trust acquisition cases*

If the claimant establishes a constructive trust, identifying the size of the share is more complex. It might be thought appropriate to identify the claimant's share either in the manner that satisfies the expectations generated by the common intention or in the manner that compensates for the value of the detriment suffered. It seems that there are three possibilities. First, *Clough* v. *Killey* (1996) illustrates that, if the terms of the express common intention are clear as to both the existence *and* the size of the equitable interest, then the court should not depart from this as the basis for quantification. So, in that case,

---

211 Note, however, the unusual case of *HSBC* v. *Dyche* (2009), in which two claimants were successful in establishing an equitable interest under a constructive trust and, between themselves, were joint tenants.

212 See, for example, *Springette* v. *Defoe* (1992).

213 Thus Mrs Cooke was awarded 50 per cent of the equity, having only paid just under 7 per cent of the purchase price.

214 Per Chadwick LJ in *Oxley* v. *Hiscock* (2004). See also the criticism in *Kernott* of *Springette* v. *Defoe* as a resulting trust case.

the promise was that Killey should have a 50 per cent share of the equity, and this is what she received, even though there was evidence that the share 'earned' by her detriment would have been only 25 per cent. This has been confirmed by *Oxley* v. *Hiscock* (2004) and presents no difficulty. Second, when the common intention as to acquisition is inferred, it may well be possible also to infer an agreement as to the size of the share. This appears to be Chadwick LJ's reasoning in *Oxley* when he notes that it:

> must now be accepted that (at least in this Court and below) the answer is that each is entitled to that share which the court considers fair having regard to the whole course of dealing between them in relation to the property.[215]

This inference as to the size of the share may be made from all manner of things, including the arrangements the co-owners have made to meet the obligations of normal domestic life, including payments of bills, mortgages, repairs and insurance. This approach has been confirmed in *Stack* v. *Dowden* (2007) and by the Court of Appeal in *Fowler* v. *Barron* (2008) and in *Ritchie* v. *Ritchie* (2007) the analysis was applied to a property dispute between mother and son. Third, it is now clear that if there is no express or inferred common intention as to the size of the share, it is possible to impute an intention to the parties as to the size of their share, being an intention that they would have had, had they thought about it – *Capehorn* v. *Harris* (2015). We need to be clear about this. It is only possible to impute an intention as to the *size* of the share if the existence of the share (the acquisition) has been established by an express or inferred common intention. It is a two-stage process: establish the share by express or inferred common intention; then quantify the size of the share by reference to either the express or inferred intention, or by imputation as a last resort. When such imputation takes place, the point is to award that share that the parties would have agreed – which in most cases will be what the court considers fair in all the circumstances.

4.10.8   When there are two or more legal owners: quantifying the equitable interest and identifying the size of the share

4.10.8.1   *Varying the equitable interest of joint legal owners when there is no written declaration*

Historically, the typical co-ownership dispute has been between a legal owner and a non-legal owner, the latter claiming a share in the property of the former: for example, *Lloyds Bank* v. *Rosset* (1991). However, *Stack* v. *Dowden*, *Jones* v. *Kernott* and *Marr* v. *Collie* are cases in which the parties are *already* joint legal owners and they are disputing the percentage of their share, sometimes alleging that one legal owner has no equitable share at all (*Marr* v. *Collie*). Of course, if the parties have expressly declared in writing the nature or size of their shares (e.g. as 'joint tenants in equity' or '50/50' each), generally they will be held to this agreement (*Goodman* v. *Gallant* (1986), *Re Kone* (2017)) unless there is some fraud or estoppel (*Clarke* v. *Meadus* (2010)). If there is no express written declaration of the beneficial interest, then it is open to one of the legal owners to claim that the

---

215 It is not certain that this is what Chadwick LJ meant. The reference to 'fair' shares may be an indication of an imputed intention – see below.

equitable interest should not be shared equally. In cases where there is no conclusive written agreement the following principles are in play.

First, in the absence of written agreement, *Stack*, *Kernott* and *Marr* determine that we should start from the uncontroversial proposition that 'equity follows the law': that is, because the legal title is held jointly (indeed must be), the equitable title will follow it and also be held jointly and if severed would result in equal shares for the co-owners. In fact, this is a perfectly understandable presumption because, if the equitable co-owners have declined to indicate the nature of their equitable ownership, the law, and third parties, are entitled to assume that they are content with the only formal statement of their co-ownership – as found in the legal title. However, as *Stack*, *Kernott* and *Marr* make clear, this is only a starting point[216] and the court must examine whether the parties intended some other arrangement, utilising the concepts of resulting or constructive trust depending on the nature of that intention. If, however, there is nothing to suggest any contrary intention, equity should follow the law and the co-owners will hold the same way in equity – as in *R v. Taylor* (2017) where the wife failed to displace the principle that joint-legal title usually gave rise to joint-equitable title. Second, if there is evidence that the parties intended that the interests should be commensurate with financial contributions, the shares of the joint legal owners could be determined in accordance with the classic resulting trust, as in *Carlton v. Goodman* (2002), *McKenzie v. McKenzie* (2003). Following *Marr*, this does not depend on whether the case is broadly 'domestic', 'investment' or 'commercial' but whether the relevant intention exists. In this regard, context is important, so a resulting trust intention might be more likely in investment or commercial contexts than a domestic one where the parties' relationship is likely to be more complex. However, the key thing is to search for the parties' intentions. Third, as in *Stack* and *Kernott*, if a common intention can be established, the parties' shares can deviate from the joint legal ownership by reason of a constrictive trust. This may result in them having unequal shares. This must be based on an express or inferred common intention, but *not* an imputed one – *Barnes v. Phillips* (2015). This common intention may arise at the time the property was acquired jointly, or later as the parties' relationship changes. Because of the context, but not as a fixed rule, it is likely to exist more often in domestic cases where the parties' lives are interwoven. In this sense, the nature of the equitable ownership can change over time. It might start out as a joint tenancy in equity (because 'equity follows the law') and finish with each party having distinct and different shares as the common intention develops (as in *Stack* and *Kernott*).[217] As is emphasised in *Stack* and *Kernott*, the departure from equal shares (after severance of the equitable joint tenancy) may only occur if the relevant intention exists, and is an exception to the starting point that equity follows the law. A wide range of factors are relevant in discerning this intention and are discussed in paragraph 69 of Lady Hale's judgment in *Stack* (above section 4.10.6.1.3).

Given the wide-ranging nature of these considerations, clearly it will be difficult to predict when a court will depart from the equal shares indicated by the legal title.

---

216 In *Marr*, Lord Kerr indicates that it is unwise to think in terms of 'presumptions', save perhaps where there is absolutely no evidence of what the parties intended.

217 This also implies that, at some point, the equitable joint tenancy was severed, although neither *Stack* nor *Kernott* discuss this.

In *Fowler v. Barron, Ritchie v. Ritchie* (2007) (a mother and son case),[218] *Kernott* and *Barnes v. Phillips* (2016) the equitable shares differed from the legal title. On the other hand, in *Segal v. Pasram* (2007) and *R v. Taylor* (2017), the court concluded that the equitable interests followed the legal title and were held jointly, and then equally after severance.

Of course, in many instances where land is conveyed to two or more people as joint tenants at law, there is a failure to declare the equitable interest or to discuss it expressly. This is because the parties do not contemplate that their relationship will break down or that it will be necessary to determine who owns what. We would expect a high proportion of these cases not to deviate from the starting point that 'equity follows the law', with the result that the parties will be joint tenants in equity, or tenants in common in equal shares after severance. Where there is evidence of an intention to hold the equity in proportion to the amounts paid, a resulting trust might be used to justify unequal shares (or even 100 per cent ownership for one of the legal co-owners). Where there is evidence of an express or inferred common intention that the equitable ownership should deviate from the legal ownership (which should be regarded as unusual), the constructive trust can be used to justify unequal shares if there was detrimental reliance. The use of the resulting or constructive trust in these cases can, however, generate considerable uncertainty for the parties themselves and any third party (such as a mortgagee) dealing with them, especially as the register of title appears to confirm that they are joint-tenants.[219] Finally, we should note that it is also possible to claim an enlarged share on the basis of proprietary estoppel (*Crossley v. Crossley* (2005)), although this would require proof of the elements of estoppel, including unconscionability, as discussed in Chapter 10.

4.10.8.2 *Identifying the size of the equitable interest for joint legal owners when a resulting or constructive trust has arisen*

Once it has been established that the parties' equitable interests may be different from their jointly held legal title, it is obviously necessary to determine the actual size of those shares. For example, in *Stack* the split was roughly 65/35 per cent and in *Kernott* it was 90/10 per cent. As discussed in acquisition cases, it may be possible to determine the share by reference to the amount paid under a resulting trust, the express common intention supporting a constructive trust, the inferred common intention supporting a constructive trust or the estoppel. Indeed, the court should first attempt to identify the size of the share by reference to the concept used to justify the variation. Failing that, however, it is possible to impute an intention as to the size of the share – *Barnes v. Phillips* (2015). As discussed previously, this is only possible once the variation has been established by resulting trust or constructive trust (using express or inferred intention) and it is a solution of last resort. This imputed intention as to the actual size of the share is an intention that the parties would have had, if they had thought about it. The likely result is a 'fair share' based on all the circumstances.

---

218 See also the pre-*Stack* case, *Abbey National v. Stringer* (2006), in which the mother was awarded 100 per cent of the equity, despite being a legal co-owner with her son. The reasoning in this case is almost non-existent.

219 In *Stringer*, Abbey National's mortgage was effectively destroyed by the finding of 100 per cent equity for Mrs Stringer – a fact that it simply could never have discovered before lending money. It relied – perfectly properly – on the jointly held legal title and was hijacked by the court's decision.

4.10.9 Proprietary estoppel and the overlap with resulting and constructive trusts

Although much academic effort has been expended in seeking to differentiate between the concepts of resulting trust, constructive trust and proprietary estoppel (see Chapter 10), this has not received significant judicial attention. All three concepts have in common the fact that they are a way for a person to obtain a proprietary interest in another's land without the normally required written instrument – they are concerned with the informal creation of property rights. Of course, it is clear from the cases that there are differences between resulting trusts and constructive trusts, but the overlap with proprietary estoppel has not been as extensively explored. Previous case law, such as *Oxley* v. *Hiscock* and *Yaxley* v. *Gotts* made some reference to how constructive trusts and estoppel related and in *Oxley*, Chadwick LJ went so far as to observe that 'the time has come to accept that there is no difference in outcome, in cases of this nature, whether the true analysis lies in constructive trust or in proprietary estoppel'. However, this has proved inaccurate, with Lord Walker in *Stack* denying total assimilation[220] even if there is overlap.[221] In *Southwell* v. *Blackburn* (2014) and *Arif* v. *Anwar* (2015), the court decided that the claimant had not established a common intention sufficient to establish a constructive trust, but nevertheless that there was a sufficient assurance to establish an estoppel. This resulted, in *Southwell*, in the claimant being awarded a monetary payment rather than an equitable interest in the land, but in *Arif* the successful claimant received 25 per cent of the equitable interest (this was less than the 50 per cent claimed under a constructive trust but still a share in the property). It seems that estoppel is, in some way, easier to establish than a constructive trust but that the actual remedy may be less favourable to the claimant or even not be a proprietary interest.[222] A brief assessment of the potential differences between constructive trusts and proprietary estoppel is given at the end of Chapter 10.

4.10.10 Statutory powers

In those cases where the claimant is unable to prove a constructive trust, resulting trust or estoppel, there will be no equitable interest unless he or she can rely on a statutory jurisdiction. If the couple are married or in civil partnership, and then divorce or separate, a 'property adjustment order' can be made in the family court under the Matrimonial Causes Act 1973 and the Civil Partnership Act 2004, but there is no equivalent power if the disputants are unmarried, not civil partners or are just friends or in some other family relationship. The court has a power under section 37 of the Matrimonial Proceedings and Property Act 1970 to award a beneficial interest consequent upon

---

220 In *Stack*, Lord Walker stated, 'I have to say that I am now rather less enthusiastic about the notion that proprietary estoppel and "common interest" constructive trusts can or should be completely assimilated', at paragraph 37.

221 See *Lloyds Bank* v. *Rosset* (1991), *per* Lord Bridge at p. 8: 'Once a finding [of common intention] is made it will only be necessary for the partner asserting the claim to a beneficial interest against the partner entitled to the legal estate to show that he or she acted to his or her detriment or altered his or her position in reliance on the agreement in order to give rise to the constructive trust or proprietary estoppel.'

222 The flexible nature of the remedy for estoppel is explored in Chapter 10.

spousal improvements to property. This is a fairly limited power, restricted by definition to married couples and civil partners. It appears that the value of the interest awarded must be commensurate with (i.e. restricted to) the value added to the property by way of the improvement.

14.10.11   An assessment

The apparently limited circumstances in which a non-owner could claim a proprietary (ownership) interest in another's property under *Rosset* gave rise to much criticism. It seemed unfair that, say, a long-term emotional partner should be unable to claim a share in the family home simply because she could not prove the existence of an express promise or a payment towards the purchase price. Similarly, it appeared as if the law was penalising the couple who made a certain kind of life choice, where they decided that one should work and the other take on childcare responsibilities. Now, after *Stack* and *Kernott*, these concerns have been addressed because it is possible to prove a common intention by relying on a wider range of factors other than a promise or a payment. It is fair to say that the law now reflects more accurately the way that people live their lives, and that cannot be a bad thing. Unsurprisingly, however, this flexibility has generated a different set of criticism. After *Stack* and *Kernott*, is the law too uncertain? How is the identification of an intention, which *Marr* confirms is central, going to be possible without the parties resorting to litigation? How can lawyers advise their clients as to the likely outcome of a claim when so much depends on the context? How can third parties, such as lenders, discover who owns the equitable interest, especially if they cannot even rely on the certainty of a jointly held legal title? Finally, is it appropriate for judges to be developing a discretionary-based jurisdiction to do what is fair under cover of a constructive trust, when some would argue that these types of judgment about society and families should be left to Parliament? Above all, though, it is important to keep things in perspective. First, as mentioned above, if the couple are married or in civil partnership, the court already has discretion to readjust property rights on divorce or judicial separation.[223] There is no need to rely at all on the rules of implied trusts or estoppel unless the claim under the matrimonial legislation fails – as in *AI v. MKI & Crown Prosecution Service (Intervener)* (2015). Second, there were relatively few reported cases in which a claimant in a domestic context actually failed to secure an interest under the strict *Rosset* rules (*Rosset* was one) and this is irrespective of whether the couple were married or unmarried, heterosexual or homosexual. The courts were adept at finding some kind of payment to the purchase price and even keener to identify some kind of express agreement about ownership. In this sense, it is not clear whether *Stack* and *Kernott* really has resulted in more claimants being successful in establishing an interest when they could not have done so before. Perhaps the real impact of *Stack* and *Kernott* will be in joint-legal ownership cases where the argument is as to the size of a share rather than its existence. Third, it is now much more common for persons buying land jointly to expressly record the nature and extent of their equitable interest in the property at the time of purchase. HM Land Registry's introduction of Form JO has encouraged this, even though its use is not

---

223 We should also recognise that joint ownership of the legal and equitable title is now much more common and is
      the usual default position when a couple buy a property as their home.

compulsory. Completion of the form amounts to an express declaration of beneficial entitlement and forestalls any claim of constructive or resulting trust. Fourth, the Law Commission has completed a thorough analysis of the rights of cohabiting couples – *Cohabitation: The Financial Consequences of Relationship Breakdown*[224] – and has recommended the creation of a statutory, structured discretion whereby courts would have the power to alter the property rights of certain types of unmarried persons who had lived together as a couple. Not all unmarried couples would qualify and there would be safeguards to ensure that the scheme did not catch merely casual relationships. At present, the Government has indicated that they do not wish to pursue this proposal, but the development of the law by *Stack* and *Kernott* has gone some way to alleviate the problem. Fifth, although it might be more difficult to establish a common intention constructive trust in relation to investment or commercial property than it is with domestic property, or more likely that a resulting trust will be preferred in non-domestic cases, perhaps this is as it should be. After all, business partners are more likely to have acted deliberately and with some thought about who owns what. Only rarely might there be the kind of emotional pressures and concerns that are present when property is occupied for domestic use. Finally, we should always remember that ownership of family property is often of great concern to third parties – lending institutions, purchasers, creditors and so on. As we have seen in cases like *Williams & Glyn's Bank* v. *Boland* (1981), a simple way to keep a mortgagee out of possession of the family home after non-payment of the mortgage is to prove that the non-legal owner has acquired an equitable interest before the mortgage, which then overrides the bank's interest. So too, an assertion that one co-owner has a larger equitable share in cases of joint legal title can be deployed to defeat creditors if the other co-owner goes bankrupt or their assets are liable to confiscation as the proceeds of crime.[225] Some cases feel as if the claim to an interest, or an enlarged interest, has been manufactured solely for the purpose of defeating a third party. As Fox LJ said in *Midland Bank* v. *Dobson* (1985):

> Assertions made by a husband and wife as to a common intention formed 30 years ago regarding joint ownership, of which there is no contemporary evidence and which happens to accommodate their current need to defeat the claims of a creditor, must be received by the courts with caution.

4.11   Severance

As we saw at the outset of this chapter, co-ownership of the equitable interest in property may be either as a joint tenancy or as a tenancy in common.

A tenancy in common is clearly an 'undivided share' in land, with each co-owner being able to identify their portion of ownership (e.g. one-quarter, one-fifth), even though there is unity of possession of the whole. Conversely, with a joint tenancy, no co-owner has a defined share, but each is the owner of the whole and is subject to the right of survivorship. In practical terms, this means that a joint tenant has no individual

---

224 Report No. 307 of 31 July 2007.

225 This was the reason for the claims in *R* v. *Taylor, R* v. *Kone* and *Liscott* v. *CPS* (2013). See *Premium Jet G* v. *Sutton* (2017) and *Segal* v. *Pasram* for cases involving creditors.

share in the equitable interest in the land that he can sell, give away or leave by will. For some, this may be perfectly acceptable (e.g. married couples) but, for others (e.g. business partners) it means that they or their families are denied the opportunity to liquidate the capital value of the land. In order to meet these difficulties, any joint tenant may 'sever' their equitable joint tenancy and thereby turn it into a tenancy in common. Of course, because of the 1925 reforms, it is only possible to sever an *equitable* joint tenancy (not that of the legal title) because tenancies in common may exist only in equity. That said, there are several methods by which a joint tenant may sever their interest and thereby constitute themselves a tenant in common in equity. One is statutory and the others arise under common law, principally as explained in *Williams v. Hensman* (1861).[226] After severance has occurred, if there were only two joint tenants, necessarily both are now tenants in common, but if there were three or more joint tenants, the others can remain as joint tenants between themselves. So, if land is held by A, B, C and D as legal and equitable joint tenants, and then C and D carry out an act of severance, legal title remains held by A, B, C and D as joint tenants (it is not severable), but the equitable title now exists as a joint tenancy between A and B, with C and D as tenants in common.

4.11.1   Statutory notice: section 36(2) of the Law of Property Act 1925

Under section 36(2) of the LPA 1925, any equitable joint tenant may give notice in writing to the other joint tenants of his intention to sever the joint tenancy. The giving of such notice results in a severance of that co-owner's interest and they become a tenant in common.[227] The severance is entirely unilateral and does not require the agreement or consent of the other joint tenants. Indeed, so long as there is evidence that the written notice was sent (e.g. by registered post), it seems that it does not have to be received by the other joint tenants to be effective to sever.[228] So, in *Kinch* v. *Bullard* (1998), a notice was sent by one joint tenant to the other and arrived at the receiver's address. He never saw it, having suffered a heart attack, and the notice was destroyed by the sender in the hope that she would benefit from the right of survivorship under the alleged joint tenancy that she had sought to end. Not surprisingly, the court held that the written notice was served effectively by delivery[229] – even if it had not been seen – and that it could not be withdrawn after service. Severance had occurred and the wife did not succeed to the entire interest under survivorship. Moreover, it is also clear that the notice may take many forms. For example, in *Re Draper's Conveyance* (1969), a summons claiming sale of the co-owned property was held to constitute written notice of severance under section 36(2) and in *Quigley* v. *Masterson* (2011) an application to the Court of Protection also qualified. Unusually, however, it also seems that a mere oral agreement *not* to sever

---

226 Severance may also result from an unlawful killing of one equitable joint tenant by the other. In such cases, it is a matter of policy that the killer cannot claim the right of survivorship when he is the reason for the death of his co-owner.

227 *Burgess* v. *Rawnsley* (1975).

228 *Re 88 Berkeley Road* (1971).

229 Section 196(4) of the LPA provides that service is effective if sent by registered post. This letter was sent by ordinary first-class post, but the same result was achieved by analogy.

can prevent a later written notice of severance having any effect (although whether this applies also to the *Williams* v. *Hensman* methods is uncertain). In *White* v. *White* (2001), the property had been conveyed expressly to three people as equitable joint tenants and there had been an oral agreement not to sever. In such circumstances, a clear attempted severance by written notice under section 36(2) was held ineffective on the ground that the oral agreement supported the original declaration of the owners as joint tenants. Of course, the whole point of severance is that it can destroy an expressly declared equitable joint tenancy, so perhaps the case is best explained on the basis that the person wishing to sever was estopped from so doing by their conduct (the oral agreement) because it would have been unconscionable in the circumstances to permit that severance.

There is one possible limitation to statutory severance, and this emerges from the words of section 36(2) itself. The section talks of severance by written notice where land 'is vested in joint tenants beneficially'. This seems to encompass only those situations in which the legal and equitable joint tenants are the same people, and not where, for example, A and B hold on trust for A, B, C and D as joint tenants. Fortunately, this limited interpretation of section 36(2) has not been adopted and statutory severance is presumed to be available for all joint tenants, whether they are also legal owners or not.[230]

4.11.2   An act operating on one's own share

In addition to statutory severance, the common law recognises other ways in which it is possible to sever the joint tenancy. These were explained in the case of *Williams* v. *Hensman* (1861), and are sometimes known as the '*Williams* v. *Hensman*' methods of severance. These three methods may still be used, although it will be appreciated that statutory severance by service of a written notice is by far the most reliable and easy way to sever a joint tenancy.

The first *Williams* v. *Hensman* method of severance is 'by an act operating on one's own share'. This occurs when one equitable joint-tenant seeks to deal with 'their share' of the land, so manifesting an intention no longer to be part of the joint tenancy. The very action of dealing with one's own share thereby severs that share. Typical examples are where the equitable owner sells their share to a third party,[231] mortgages it in favour of a bank or becomes bankrupt, so that their property becomes vested in the 'trustee in bankruptcy'.[232] Likewise, attempting to deal with the legal title by forging the consent of the other legal owners to some purported dealing with that title in fact operates to transfer any equitable interest that the fraudster might have, so also effecting a severance. So, an attempted mortgage by one of two legal owners who forges the signature of the other legal owner cannot actually mortgage the legal title, but it can effect a mortgage of the fraudster's equitable interest, thereby also severing any equitable joint tenancy.[233] Importantly, however, leaving one's 'share' in a subsisting joint tenancy by Will can *never*

---

230 But note that this generous interpretation has not been tested judicially. It is rather that there is no case that limits section 36(2) in the way discussed.

231 So the dealing both severs and transfers the share.

232 For example, *Re Dennis* (1992).

233 Section 63 of the LPA 1925 and *Banker's Trust* v. *Namdar* (1997).

constitute severance because the right of survivorship operates immediately on death and takes precedence over testamentary dispositions.[234]

Finally, for this method of severance to be effective, the 'act' operating on the joint tenant's share must be valid and enforceable, unlike the case of 'mutual agreement' considered below. This means that the 'act' that effects the severance must be one that is valid under the general law according to the formality rules for that type of disposition of an interest in land. Therefore, given that nearly all dispositions of an interest in land must be in writing (section 2 of the LP(MP)A 1989), the 'act of severance' by way of mortgage, sale or lease (if over three years) must be in writing and otherwise enforceable if it is to sever. There needs to be a *legally enforceable* 'act' operating on one's own share, not an unenforceable intention to sever.

4.11.3 Where joint tenants sever by 'mutual agreement'

The second *Williams* v. *Hensman* method is that, if all the joint tenants agree among themselves to terminate the joint tenancy, they are taken to have severed the joint tenancy and constituted themselves as tenants in common.[235] Most importantly, this agreement need not take any specific form and it need not be in writing. It need not be enforceable under the general law and may be inferred from the surrounding circumstances. The point is simply that the fact of agreement severs the joint tenancy because it indicates an intention to destroy the joint tenancy. There is no need for the agreement to be acted on to effect a severance.[236] For example, severance by this method may occur when the co-owners agree on the precise distribution of property on the breakdown of their relationship.[237] However, the agreement must contemplate an intention to sever the joint tenancy (i.e. the ownership), and not merely amount to an agreement as to the use of the property.[238] Further, we must take care to distinguish between an agreement among the co-owners to deal with the property together[239] which will not necessarily sever the joint tenancy, and an agreement to deal with it in a way that demonstrates that each co-owner has a distinct share. So, in *Davis* v. *Smith* (2011), an agreement by a separating couple to put their house on the market and share the proceeds was not, of itself, sufficient to sever by mutual agreement.[240] But, when combined with other evidence, the court was able to conclude that there had been a mutual agreement to sever, thus preventing operation of the right of survivorship when one of the co-owners died unexpectedly.[241]

---

234 *Gould* v. *Kemp* (1834).

235 It seems that the agreement must be between them *all*, and an agreement among only some will not sever even for those agreeing – *Wright* v. *Gibbons* (1949), an Australian case but the only clear authority.

236 *Hunter* v. *Babbage* (1994).

237 *Re McKee* (1975).

238 *Nielson-Jones* v. *Fedden* (1975).

239 For example, to sell it.

240 Applying *Marshall* v. *Marshall* (1998).

241 In fact, she died on the day that she was to visit the solicitor to send a written notice of severance. Query: if she thought she needed to send a written notice to sever, is it still possible to conclude that she had *already* severed by mutual agreement?

4.11.4   By mutual conduct

Mutual conduct is a flexible and shifting category that is intended to express the idea that severance may occur because the joint tenants, by their conduct in relation to each other, have demonstrated that the joint tenancy is terminated (*Williams* v. *Hensman* (1861)). Although very similar to mutual agreement, the point here is that the parties have not agreed to sever – formally or informally – but have so acted that it is clear that the continuance of a joint tenancy would be inconsistent with their intentions. There are many possible examples of mutual conduct, but the most common include physical partition of the land so that each co-owner is barred from the other's portion, the writing of mutual wills and negotiations between the joint tenants as to disposal of the property. The last of these is somewhat controversial, for it is difficult to see why a failed severance under mutual agreement (e.g. because the co-owners disagree about the value of the land) can nevertheless amount to a successful severance under mutual conduct because of severance negotiations. This, however, is the clear inference from Lord Denning's judgment in *Burgess* v. *Rawnsley* (1975). Essentially, the matter will turn on the facts of each case and whether the court is prepared, as a matter of policy, to extend the circumstances in which severance is possible. The degree of hardship caused by the operation of the right of survivorship might well be relevant in that calculation, as the courts favour severance if this preserves the 'share' of a deceased co-owner for their family.

4.11.5   By unlawful killing

If one joint tenant unlawfully kills the other, he is unable to benefit from the right of survivorship. The joint tenancy is severed by the killing and the victim's interest is dealt with under their estate (save that the accused cannot benefit under the estate either) – *Dunbar* v. *Plant* (1988). The rule is clearly based on public policy and applies equally to manslaughter – *Chadwick* v. *Collinson* (2014).

4.12   Chapter Summary

4.12.1   The nature and types of concurrent co-ownership

'Concurrent co-ownership' of property describes the simultaneous enjoyment of land by two or more persons. Since 1 January 1926, co-ownership of property will be by way of either a *joint tenancy* or a *tenancy in common*. In a joint tenancy, each co-owner is treated as being entitled to the whole of the land and there are no distinct 'shares'. It is characterised by the right of survivorship and the four unities: unity of possession, interest, title and time (PITT). A tenancy in common exists when two or more people own an 'undivided share in land', giving unity of possession, but where no other unities are necessary and where there is no right of survivorship.

4.12.2   The effect of the Law of Property Act 1925 and the Trusts of Land and Appointment of Trustees Act 1996

Before 1926, it was possible for a joint tenancy and a tenancy in common to exist in both the legal and the equitable estate in the land. However, after 1925, it is now impossible to create a tenancy in common at law. The legal owners of co-owned property must be joint tenants of the legal estate. They will hold the land as 'trustees of land' for the persons entitled in equity (sections 34 and 36 of the LPA 1925; sections 4 and 5 of TOLATA 1996). Co-ownership of the equitable interest may be by way of either a joint tenancy or a tenancy in common.

4.12.3   The equitable interest: joint tenancy or tenancy in common?

First, if the unities of interest, title or time are absent, a joint tenancy in equity cannot exist. Second, if the original conveyance to the co-owners stipulates that they are 'joint tenants' or 'tenants in common' *of the beneficial or equitable interest*, this is normally conclusive as to the nature of their co-ownership in equity. Third, if 'words of severance' are used, then a tenancy in common will exist in equity. Fourth, failing any of the above, 'equity follows the law' and there will be a joint tenancy of the equitable interest (as there must be of the legal) unless the co-owners are business partners, co-mortgagees or (in respect of property that is not the family home) where they as purchasers have provided the purchase money in unequal shares. However, this result (that equity follows the law) can be avoided by reliance on resulting trusts, constructive trusts and possibly proprietary estoppel.

4.12.4   The nature of the trust of land: the effect of the Trusts of Land and Appointment of Trustees Act 1996

The trustees hold the legal title for the benefit of the equitable owners (who may be themselves), but it is the legal owners who have powers equivalent to those of an absolute owner to deal with the land (section 6 of TOLATA 1996). These powers can be restricted by the document establishing the trust or by order of the court (section 14 of TOLATA 1996) and must be exercised in conformity with the TOLATA regime. The trustees may delegate powers to a beneficiary, except the power to conduct an overreaching transaction. The trustees are not under a duty to sell the land. Any person interested in the trust of land may apply to the court under section 14 of TOLATA 1996 for an order affecting the land, including an order for sale. The powers of the trustees, including sale, may be made subject to the consent of a specified person (e.g. a beneficiary), but only in limited circumstances. Provided that the trustees are two or more in number and are in agreement, a sale usually will overreach the equitable interests, sweeping them off the land and into the purchase money so that they do not bind the purchaser.

4.12.5   The advantages of the trust of land as a device for regulating co-owned land

By abolishing tenancies in common at law, the LPA 1925 has ensured that there is but one title to investigate: the legal joint tenancy. The number of potential legal joint tenants is limited to a maximum of four (irrespective of the number of equitable owners). The right of survivorship diminishes the inconvenience and cost if a legal joint tenant dies. If there are two or more trustees of the land, the purchaser may usually ignore all of the equitable owners because of statutory overreaching. The court's powers under section 14 of TOLATA 1996 prevent co-owned land becoming inalienable. TOLATA 1996 gives concrete rights to the equitable owners to possess and enjoy the fruits of the land, subject to overreaching.

4.12.6 The disadvantages of the trust of land as a device for regulating co-owned land

There may be disputes between the legal owners as to whether a sale or mortgage or other dealing should take place or whether the land should be retained for the benefit of the equitable owners. The problem is greater if the trustees' powers are subject to the consent of some other person, although disputes may be resolved by application to the court under section 14 of TOLATA 1996. The powerful effect of overreaching may effectively destroy an equitable owner's valuable rights. The ability to prevent overreaching through the imposition of a consent requirement is of limited value only. The trustees' duty to consult the beneficiaries is likely to offer little practical protection. In cases of bankruptcy, it is very likely that the land will be sold, despite any objections by the equitable owners.

4.12.7 The position of a purchaser who buys co-owned land: overreaching or not?

If a purchaser buys co-owned land from two or more legal owners (i.e. there are two trustees), the equitable interests are transferred to the purchase money and the purchaser obtains the land free from their rights (overreaching). If the purchaser buys the property from a single trustee only, then the purchaser cannot rely on overreaching to protect him from the rights of the equitable owners: he may be bound by them according to the normal rules of registered and unregistered conveyancing.

4.12.8 The position of the equitable owners when overreaching occurs

If overreaching has occurred, the fundamental rule is that the equitable owners have no claim against the purchaser (which includes a mortgagee) to remain in possession of the land (*City of London Building Society v. Flegg* (1988)). However, it is important to see this 'problem' in perspective. Under TOLATA 1996, the trustees' power to sell or mortgage may be made subject to the consent of another person. In registered land, this will prevent overreaching if the consent requirement is registered as a Restriction against the title (assuming consent is not given!), and in unregistered land, a purchaser will not be able to overreach if he has actual notice of the consent requirement.

4.12.9 The question of possession and occupation

All of the legal owners have a right to occupy the property unless there is something specific to the contrary in the document establishing the trust of land. A purely equitable owner has a right to occupy under section 12 of TOLATA 1996, although this may be excluded or made conditional in the limited circumstances specified in section 13 of TOLATA 1996.

4.12.10   The payment of compensation for exclusive use

Under section 13 of TOLATA 1996, a co-owner enjoying exclusive use of the land (i.e. where the other or others are excluded) can be required to pay compensation for such use. This had been the position under the old trust for sale (*Re Pavlou* (1993)).

4.12.11   The express creation of co-ownership

Any land may be deliberately conveyed to two or more people. In such circumstances, the persons to whom legal title is transferred will be the legal owners (joint tenant trustees) and, in the absence of any statement to the contrary, they will also be the equitable owners. This conveyance may also expressly declare who are the equitable owners and the nature of their ownership, and this is conclusive for those parties (*Goodman* v. *Gallant* (1986)), save in exceptional cases where there is fraud or proprietary estoppel.

4.12.12   Creation of co-ownership even though the legal title is in one name only

The legal owner (A) may expressly declare in writing (section 53(1) of the LPA 1925) that he holds the land on trust for the claimant (B) or, more usually, a person may claim an equitable interest through the operation of resulting or constructive trusts or estoppel, as follows:

1   A resulting trust arises where the claimant has contributed to the purchase price of the property. The share of the interest follows the proportion of the purchase price paid.
2   A constructive trust arises either: (i) where the legal owner makes an express oral promise or express oral agreement with the claimant that they 'own' the property or have a share in it, provided that this is relied on by the claimant to their detriment; (ii) a common intention can be inferred from direct contributions to the purchase price, such contributions also providing the required detriment; or (iii) a common intention can be inferred from the whole course of dealings between the parties in respect of their home, such course of dealing also providing the required detriment; but (iv) a common intention cannot be imputed as to acquisition. The actual size of the share may be determined by on the same basis that the share is acquired, but may be based on imputed common intention as a last resort. The same principles apply when there are joint legal owners and one of them seeks to vary the shares.

4.12.13   Severance

Severance is the process of turning an equitable joint tenancy into an equitable tenancy in common, usually in order to avoid the effect of the right of survivorship (a legal joint tenancy cannot be severed). Severance occurs either by statutory written notice under section 36(2) of the LPA 1925, or by the act of a co-owner operating on his own share (e.g. mortgaging it), or where the joint tenants decide to sever by 'mutual agreement', or where an intention to sever is manifested by the 'mutual conduct' of the joint tenants or in cases of unlawful killing.

Further Reading

Dixon, M, 'The never-ending story: Co-ownership after *Stack* v. *Dowden*' [2007] Conv 456.

Dixon, M, 'To sell or not to sell: That is the question' [2011] CLJ 579.

Etherton, T, 'Constructive trusts: A new model for equity and unjust enrichment' [2008] CLJ 265.

Etherton, T, 'Constructive trusts and proprietary estoppel: The search for clarity and principle' [2009] Conv 104.

Ferris, G and **Battersby**, G, 'The impact of the Trusts of Land and Appointment of Trustees Act 1996 on purchasers of registered land' [1998] Conv 168; see also the reply by **Dixon**, M [2000] Conv 267.

Glover, N and **Todd**, P, 'The myth of common intention' (1996) 16 LS 325.

Harding, M, 'Defending *Stack* v. *Dowden*' [2009] Conv 309.

Hopkins, N, 'The Trusts of Land and Appointment of Trustees Act 1996' [1996] Conv 267.

Kenny, P, *The Trusts of Land and Appointment of Trustees Act 1996*, London: Sweet & Maxwell, 1997.

Law Commission, *Cohabitation: The Financial Consequences of Relationship Breakdown*, Report No. 307, London: HMSO, 31 July 2007.

Swadling, W, 'The common intention trust in the House of Lords: An opportunity missed' [2007] 123 LQR 511.

Tee, L, 'Severance revisited' [1995] Conv 105.

Now visit the companion website to:

* test your understanding of the key terms using our Flashcard Glossary;

* revise and consolidate your knowledge using our Multiple Choice Question testbank.

www.routledge.com/cw/Dixon

Chapter 5
Successive Interests in Land

Chapter Contents

Introduction

In the previous chapter, we examined one way in which two or more people could share ownership of land. This was the law of *concurrent* co-ownership, being where all of the co-owners were entitled to the enjoyment of land simultaneously. Typical examples were spouses, civil partners or unmarried couples.[1] However, there is another method by which two or more people can have 'ownership' rights over land at the same time, albeit that only one of them is entitled to the immediate physical possession of the property. This is the law relating to *successive* co-ownership of land, being where one person has an interest in the land for life and another person, or persons, have rights that 'fall into' possession after the 'life interest' has ended.[2] For example, it was once quite common for property to be left by will[3] to one person for their life, then to another, then to another and so on, as where Blackacre is left to A for life, with remainder to B for life, remainder to C in fee simple. In such a case, A has a life interest in possession (and is known, somewhat confusingly, as the 'life tenant'), B has a life interest in remainder (and will be the life tenant when A dies) and C has a fee simple in remainder (and will become the absolute owner on the death of A and B). As is made apparent by this example, the person who established the successive interests[4] was able to control the destination of the land for a considerable period of time.[5] Often, the reason for creating successive interests was 'to keep land in the family' by limiting its ownership to successive generations (e.g. 'my son', 'my grandson', etc.), although it could also be used for business or commercial arrangements. Importantly, even though only one of the co-owners was entitled to the *possession* of the land (being the life tenant), all of the other persons comprised in 'the settlement' also had property interests that could be dealt with in the normal way. That is why it is a form of co-ownership.

5.1 Successive Interests: In General

TOLATA 1996 has had a profound impact on the law relating to successive interests in land. Prior to the Act, there were two methods of creating successive interests: first, under a settlement (or 'strict settlement', as it was known) regulated by the Settled Land Act 1925 (SLA 1925); second, under a 'trust for sale' regulated by the LPA 1925. However, the entry into force of TOLATA 1996 on 1 January 1997 amended the law considerably. The purpose of TOLATA 1996 is to simplify the law, to make dealings with land subject to

---

1 Although, of course, concurrent co-ownership is not confined to persons in family relationships.

2 That is, when the holder of the life interest dies.

3 Or, alternatively, on the occasion of marriage of the eldest son or other child.

4 Usually called 'the settlor'.

5 The length of time for which the settlor could exercise such control was not unlimited. The 'dead hand' of the settlor was only permitted to exert influence over the destination of the land for that period of time that complied with the 'perpetuity rules'. The perpetuity rules have been amended, but still apply to the type of arrangement discussed here: see Perpetuities and Accumulations Act 2009, in force 6 April 2010. One reason to take land out of an existing settlement and to re-organise under different trusts it is to extend the period of time for which the trust might operate by utilising the more generous rules of the 2009 Act, see e.g. *Pemberton v. Pemberton* [2016] EWHC 2345 (Ch.).

successive interests more transparent and to ensure that the rules by which successive interests are regulated reflects the modern use to which this form of co-ownership can be put.

In broad terms, TOLATA 1996 changed the way in which successive interests could in future be created[6] and established a much simpler legal mechanism for regulating successive ownership than that which existed under the SLA 1925. The principal effects of TOLATA 1996 are as follows.

1   Since 1 January 1997, it has not been possible to create any new settlement within the ambit of the SLA 1925. The institution of the 'strict settlement' has been abandoned for all successive interests established after that date (section 2 of TOLATA 1996). The obvious consequence is that no new land can be made subject to the regime of the SLA 1925, and, over time, this creaking statutory regime will be relevant in only rare circumstances.[7]

2   Strict settlements existing immediately before TOLATA came into force remain effective and remain governed by the SLA 1925 – section 2 of TOLATA 1996 – as will resettlements of existing settled land.[8] Inevitably, however, much existing settled land will fall into absolute ownership (i.e. all of the life interests will come to an end on the death of the life tenants), and the land will cease to be 'settled land'. However, as noted, if the 'old' settlement is perpetuated by the creation of new life interests *before* the termination of the existing settlement (a 'resettlement'), then the land continues to be 'settled land' and remains subject to the regime of the SLA 1925. If, by way of contrast, the settlement does indeed terminate, and no land or heirlooms remain subject to it, any subsequent attempt to create a life interest in that land really is a 'new' creation, and will be governed by TOLATA 1996.

3   Successive interests existing on 31 December 1996 but *not* governed by the SLA 1925 – being those taking effect under a 'trust for sale' *prior* to the entry into force of TOLATA 1996 – are now governed by the rubric of TOLATA 1996 and became 'trusts of land'. Technically, if the 'trust for sale' had been created expressly, it will continue to be a 'trust for sale' (rather than a 'trust of land') but this has very few practical consequences. In those rare cases in which successive interests arose by operation of law *and* took effect as a trust for sale prior to TOLATA 1996 (i.e. not expressly), the trust now takes effect as a trust of land within TOLATA 1996.

4   *All* new attempts to create successive interests in land must take effect under the rubric of TOLATA 1996 (sections 4 and 5 of TOLATA 1996). In nearly all cases, this will result in a standard 'trust of land' as instituted by that statute.[9] It will still be possible deliberately to establish successive interests under a 'trust *for sale* of land' on or after 1 January 1997 (but not, of course, a strict settlement), but this will still be governed by TOLATA 1996 and the practical differences between it and the 'trust of land' proper are minimal.[10] It is very doubtful whether many express trusts

---

6   From 1 January 1997, being its entry into force.

7   For a surviving example, see *Howard* v. *Howard-Lawson* (2013).

8   Being where a pre-1997 settlement comes to an end only because it is replaced with a new set of similar arrangements in respect of the same land. It is possible to apply to court to vary an existing settlement and thereby take it out of the ambit of the SLA altogether, *Pemberton* v. *Pemberton*.

9   Replacing the old 'trust for sale of land'.

10 This is because the definition of a 'trust of land' includes a 'trust for sale of land' (section 1 of TOLATA 1996).

for sale will be created after December 1996 because, due to TOLATA 1996, very little would be gained by adopting this approach.

Once again, then, the important practical point irrespective of the precise type of trust involved is that successive interests are now governed by TOLATA 1996, save only for that diminishing category of strict settlements that existed before 1 January 1996 and which remain operational and governed by the SLA 1925.

5.1.1   Successive interests under the Trusts of Land and Appointment of Trustees Act 1996

As we have seen in the previous chapter, TOLATA 1996 effectively abandoned the concept of the trust for sale and replaced it with the trust of land. Furthermore, as noted above, the Act also ensures that all *future* successive interests shall take effect as trusts of land under its rubric.[11] In fact, the great majority of the provisions of TOLATA 1996 were designed specifically with cases of successive ownership of land in mind (rather than the concurrent co-ownership discussed in Chapter 4). This is because, in cases of successive ownership, it is likely (indeed, almost inevitable) that the trustees of the land will be completely different persons from the person who is to occupy the land for life (the life tenant), or the persons who are entitled in remainder should the life tenant die. The trustees may well be a bank or independent professional advisers, and the life tenant will be the person most intimately connected with the land – for example, the eldest child of the settlor. Necessarily, in such typical cases of successive interests, the life tenant will usually wish to occupy the land,[12] and the life tenant is usually the person best placed to manage the land effectively by exercising the various powers open to either him or the trustees.[13] In their turn, the trustees are likely to prefer to hold a 'watching brief' and allow the tenant for life to use the land as befits his limited ownership.

With this in mind, a summary of the provisions of TOLATA 1996 may be given, remembering that these provisions apply to all new successive interests created on or after 1 January 1997 *and* for those previously governed by the rubric of the old 'trust for sale'.

1   Save for pre-1 January 1997 strict settlements,[14] there is to be one set of rules governing the creation and operation of successive interests – the trust of land under TOLATA 1996.
2   The doctrine of conversion is abolished, effective for all new and nearly all existing trusts of land (section 3 of TOLATA 1996). The doctrine of conversion was an ancient doctrine applicable to certain property concepts whereby the interest of the persons entitled under the trust (e.g. in our case, the life tenant) was treated not as an interest in the relevant *land*, but as an interest in the proceeds of sale of that land. Hence, the rights were technically 'personalty' and not 'realty'. Thus, a will leaving 'my personal property' to X would actually have passed the testator's interest under

---

11 As noted, it is possible to create an express trust for sale under TOLATA 1996, but this is within the definition of a 'trust of land' and subject to TOLATA 1996.
12 See section 12 of TOLATA 1996.
13 Hence the trustees' ability to delegate their powers under section 9 of TOLATA 1996.
14 Which will continue to operate under the SLA 1925 until they have run their course.

a trust to X as potentially converted money, even though it looked like an interest in land. The abolition of the doctrine of conversion means, in effect, that the interest of a person under a trust of land[15] is to be regarded as an interest in the land itself, rather than in its monetary equivalent. Clearly, this accords with the perception of the persons having such interests and, in practice, this change in the law will have only limited consequences.[16] The exception under which the doctrine of conversion may still operate is for trusts for sale of land created by the will of a person dying before 1 January 1997 – because such a testator may have ordered his affairs precisely on the basis that the doctrine of conversion was applicable on his death.

3   The legal title to the land will be vested in the trustees of land and they will have all of the powers of an absolute owner (section 6(1) of TOLATA 1996 and section 23 of the LRA 2002). The life tenant and persons entitled in remainder will have equitable interests in the land. However, the trustees' powers are given in virtue of their status as trustees and consequently are subject to the general equitable jurisdiction in relation to the exercise of trustees' powers. In other words, the trustees can be held accountable for the exercise of their powers on normal principles of trustee liability.[17] More specifically, the trustees may delegate certain powers to the life tenant (or other person) and their powers may be restricted by the instrument that establishes the trust.[18] Given that trusts concerning successive interests usually are created deliberately and with considerable formality,[19] it is likely that the trustees will intend from the outset to delegate powers of management of the land to the tenant for life, including the power of sale. However, only the trustees can give a valid receipt for money received on sale ('purchase money') should any of the land be sold, hence preserving their role in overreaching.

4   The trustees must consult with the persons interested in the trust, both the life tenant and the persons entitled in remainder. They should give effect to their wishes in so far as is consistent with the purposes of the trust of land (section 11 of TOLATA 1996). This raises similar issues to those considered in relation to concurrent co-ownership considered in Chapter 4.

5   The trustees' ability to exercise their powers, including the power of sale, may be made subject to the consent of the equitable owners (e.g. the life tenant and persons entitled in remainder), but only if stated in the instrument creating the trusts (sections 8 and 10 TOLATA) or if imposed by the court following an application made under section 14 of TOLATA 1996. Given that the creation of successive interests is not usually undertaken lightly, it is quite likely that a consent requirement will be imposed as part of an overall strategy to deal with the land. In relation to registered land, a

---

15 Including expressly created trusts for sale of land.

16 The courts already treated such interests as 'interests in land' for many purposes irrespective of the doctrine of conversion: see, for example, *Williams & Glyn's Bank* v. *Boland* (1981) in relation to overreaching and the concept of unregistered interests which override – Chapter 2.

17 For a modern example of a settlement, where the question of trustee liability arose, see *Howard* v. *Howard-Lawson* (2013).

18 See generally sections 6–9 of TOLATA 1996.

19 It is quite difficult for successive interest trusts of land to be created accidentally, although this can sometimes be the result of a successful claim of constructive trust or proprietary estoppel, as contemplated by *Ungarian* v. *Lesnoff* (1990) (see Chapter 4, constructive trust) and *Dent* v. *Dent* (1996) (see Chapter 10, proprietary estoppel).

purchaser will be concerned to comply with the consent requirement if it is confirmed by the entry of a Restriction against the title to the land, as otherwise the title cannot be conveyed (section 26 of the LRA 2002). The position in respect of unregistered land is governed by section 16 of TOLATA 1996, on which see immediately below.[20]

6 The trust of land when it governs successive interests is subject to the same overreaching machinery as when it governs concurrent co-ownership interests. This is because the interests of the life tenant and persons entitled in remainder are equitable interests, and the legal title is held by the trustees; for example, where Z Bank plc holds land on trust for A for life, with the remainder to B. Necessarily, on sale of the land, it is the trustees who will have to transfer the legal title and it will be the beneficiaries (e.g. the life tenant) who are susceptible to overreaching in favour of a purchaser. If the overreaching process is successful, the equitable owners will cease to have a right to enjoyment of the land but will instead take their interest in a share of the purchase money. Thus, the tenant for life will receive the income from the capital sum for life, with the balance going to the person entitled in remainder on the death of that life tenant. However, should overreaching not occur (as in a rare case of there being only one trustee of a *successive* interest trust for land),[21] whether these equitable interests bind the purchaser is determined by the application of normal principles of registered or unregistered conveyancing as the case may be. In registered land, the interests of the beneficiaries might override if the beneficiaries are in discoverable actual occupation of the land,[22] but they cannot be protected by an entry of a Notice on the register.[23] Consequently, even in the absence of overreaching, a purchaser will take the land free from the interests of a beneficiary *not* in discoverable actual occupation,[24] and then the only way to ensure protection is by the entry of a Restriction on the register.[25] In unregistered land, such an interest cannot be a land charge,[26] so, in the absence of overreaching, may take effect against a purchaser according to the old equitable doctrine of notice.

7 In addition to the overreaching provisions, the purchaser of land subject to a successive trust of land is given protection should the trustees sell the land in excess of their powers or in breach of the provisions of TOLATA 1996. In respect of land of

---

20 In the unlikely event of a successive trust of land arising informally, there will be no express requirement that the trustees should seek consent, so an application must be made to the court under section 14 of TOLATA 1996 if one is required.

21 A sole trustee who is a trust corporation (e.g. an authorised bank) is sufficient for overreaching (section 2 of the LPA 1925).

22 Or where, being in actual occupation, the beneficiary's rights are known to the purchaser: see Schedule 3, paragraph 2 of the LRA 2002. Interests governed by the SLA 1925 cannot override by reason of actual occupation, LRA 2002, Schedule 3, paragraph 2(a).

23 Section 33(a)(ii) of the LRA 2002.

24 Section 29 of the LRA 2002.

25 Although there is nothing in the LRA 2002 or the Land Registration Rules to prevent the entry of a Restriction requiring consent in order to prevent a sale even if there are two trustees or a trust corporation, it seems that HM Land Registry will refuse to enter such a Restriction at the request of the equitable owners on the ground that overreaching should not be rendered ineffective. This has some backing from the courts: *Coleman* v. *Bryant* (2007).

26 Section 2 of the LCA 1972.

unregistered title, the matter turns on the particular violation committed by the trustees. In some cases (e.g. violation of the duty to consult), it seems that the purchaser will obtain a good title from the trustees, assuming overreaching, and the beneficiaries' remedy lies against the trustees personally. In other cases (e.g. non-compliance with a consent requirement), the purchaser will obtain a clean title, assuming overreaching, provided that he did not have actual notice of the relevant limitation (section 16 of TOLATA 1996). In land of registered title, it is assumed that the limitation on the trustees' powers (if any) will be entered on the register of title by way of Restriction, thus preventing any disposition by the trustees unless the limitation is complied with. Necessarily, this will prevent a purchaser buying the land at all until the Restriction is complied with. If for some very unusual reason (e.g. a solicitor's failure to act properly), the limitation on the trustees' powers is not entered on the register or the Restriction is ignored, it seems likely that a purchaser who can overreach[27] will obtain a clear title free of such interests despite the trustees' non-compliance with the limitation. This is because in registered land, the person entered as proprietor has *all* of the powers of an absolute owner, subject only to entries on the register,[28] and the purchaser's registration as proprietor is conclusive in his favour.[29]

8   The tenant for life 'is entitled by reason of his interest to occupy the land at any time' – section 12 of TOLATA 1996 – provided that this was a purpose of the trust or the trustees make the land so available. However, if occupation of the life tenant was not a purpose of the trust or held out to be so by the trustees, there is no entitlement under section 12 and it seems that the court would not make such an order (*Medlycott v. Herbert* (2014)).[30] The persons entitled in remainder also may have such an entitlement – sections 12(1) (a) and (b) and 12(2) – but in practice this would almost certainly be removed or modified by the trustees under their power to limit the right to occupy, section 12(3) of the Act. Note also that section 13 provides that the trustee may impose reasonable conditions on the person occupying the property, including requiring the payment of expenses or outgoings in respect of the land. Likewise, if the trustees have exercised their powers to exclude or limit other beneficiaries' rights to occupy under section 12(3), they may impose a requirement that the occupying beneficiary pay compensation for exclusive use of the land; for example, the life tenant might be ordered to pay a sum equivalent to

---

27 Failure to overreach opens the purchaser to the possibility of being bound by an overriding interest through the discoverable actual occupation etc. of the equitable interest-holder.

28 Sections 23 and 26 of the LRA 2002.

29 Section 58 of the LRA 2002 and confirmed, in a different context, in *Swift 1ˢᵗ v. Chief Land Registrar* (2015). *HSBC v. Dyche* (2009) might seem to contradict this, but that was a case of a trustee selling to herself in breach of trust and equity will not let a statute (e.g. the overreaching provisions of section 2 LPA 1925) be an instrument of fraud.

30 [2014] EWHC 4177 (Ch). In *Medlycott*, it is not clear whether such a life tenant can never get an order to occupy (e.g. not even under the court's wide discretion to make orders under section 14 TOLATA) or rather whether they are simply not 'entitled' to an order under section 12. There is nothing in section 14 that makes it subject to section 12, so on balance there would be nothing to prevent a court ordering occupation in favour of such a life tenant under section 14 as a matter of discretion even if they were not entitled under section 12. In the case, the judge makes it clear that, in any event, he would not have ordered that the life tenant be given occupation as this was simply not the point of the trust.

the market rent of the land, or some proportion thereof, especially if he is the only person in occupation.[31]

9   Any person with an interest in the land can make an application to the court under section 14 of TOLATA 1996 for a variety of orders in relation to the land, provided the order relates to the functions of the trustees or the size of any beneficiary's interest in the land. For example, an application can be made for sale, to prohibit a proposed sale, to impose or override a consent requirement or for a declaration of the respective values or shares of the beneficial owners. Generally, such orders are made with reference to the criteria specified in section 15 of the Act, save only that section 15 does not apply in case of bankruptcy, for which section 335A of the Insolvency Act 1986 provides a list of the applicable criteria.[32]

5.2   Successive Interests under the Old Regime: The Strict Settlement and the Settled Land Act 1925

As is now clear, the law of strict settlements will apply only to those successive interest trusts created before the entry into force of TOLATA 1996, or any resettlement thereof. Necessarily, this means that the complicated rules of the SLA 1925 have become considerably less important.[33] They are discussed below. Points of comparison with the regime of TOLATA 1996 should be kept in mind during this analysis.

The 'strict settlement' is not a creation of the 1925 property legislation and, indeed, one of the reasons for the SLA 1925 itself was to reform and regulate the pre-1926 rules that had previously governed the creation and operation of successive interests in land. That said, it is to the SLA 1925 that we must look for a comprehensive statement of the pre-TOLATA 1996 law. Unfortunately, the machinery of SLA 1925, and the substantive law, is quite complicated, and it is not an accident that the strict settlement was, for many years, rarely deliberately created or that it has now been abolished for new successive interests. In general terms, a 'strict settlement' exists when land is left on trust (not being a trust for sale) for someone for life, with remainder to another, perhaps also with provision by way of rentcharges for the payment of a regular income to someone else (e.g. the widow of the settlor[34]). However, this is a simplified definition, and sections 1 and 2 of the SLA 1925 define 'settled land' in much more precise terms. Thus, according to the SLA 1925, and bearing in mind that this is not operative for any instrument establishing a new trust on or after 1 January 1997, settled land was either:

1   land 'limited in trust for any persons by way of succession';
2   land 'limited in trust for any person in possession' for an entailed interest (i.e. a fee tail, now abolished by TOLATA 1996) for an infant, for a determinable fee or for a fee simple subject to an executory limitation;

---

31 Section 13(3) of TOLATA 1996.

32 These issues have been discussed at greater length in Chapter 4 in respect of concurrent co-ownership.

33 But not yet redundant; see *Howard* v. *Howard-Lawson* (2013).

34 The person who created the trust.

3   land limited in trust for any person for a legal freehold or leasehold estate that was contingent upon the happening of any event; or

4   land that was charged by way of a family arrangement with the payment of any sums for the benefit of any persons.[35]

There is no denying that this is complicated, but the essential point to remember is that settled land is land where the estate of the owner in possession is 'limited' in some way. Thus, either the owner's interest is limited to his life, or is tied to the happening of an event, or is charged with the payment of money. Importantly, land that is subject to 'an immediate binding trust for sale'[36] is excluded from the definition of settled land and falls outside the SLA 1925. Such land was already governed by the LPA 1925 and of course now takes effect under TOLATA 1996 as a trust of land.

5.2.1   The essential characteristics of settled land

Settled land is land held on trust. Consequently, there will be 'trustees of the settlement', and beneficiaries under the settlement. These beneficiaries may be the owner of a life interest and those persons entitled in remainder – being those entitled when the life interest ends. The settlement will have been created by the settlor, by deed, and this deed will usually identify the trustees. Under the SLA 1925, a range of persons are given statutory powers to deal with the land and it is important to remember that the primary reason why these powers are given is to ensure that the land itself can be freely dealt with: in other words, that the land is alienable and does not get tied up in the settlement. As with concurrent co-ownership, if the land is sold, the rights and interests of the beneficiaries will be transferred to the purchase money.

5.2.2   The specific attributes of settled land

The person under the settlement who is of full age, and entitled to immediate possession of the settled land (or the whole income from it), is generally regarded as the 'tenant for life' (section 19 of the SLA 1925). The tenant for life is holder of the legal estate in the land, and he holds that legal estate on trust for the beneficiaries under the settlement.[37] In the great majority of cases, this tenant for life is also the person entitled to an equitable life interest in the property. Thus, the tenant for life often has two roles: holder of the legal estate in the land and owner of an equitable, but limited, ownership interest, such as a life interest. It is no accident that the person in possession of the land should have the legal title. Before 1925, that legal title could be vested in several trustees, or split up among several beneficiaries, and this made dealing with settled land a laborious and expensive process. Under the SLA 1925, the legal title is vested solely in the tenant for life, for they are the person in immediate possession of the land, and they are the person who may best judge how to deal with it.

The tenant for life exercises most of the important statutory powers to deal with the settled land. These are found in Part II of the SLA 1925 and effectively place the tenant

---

35 For example, *Re Austen* (1929).

36 Section 1(7) of the SLA 1925.

37 Sections 4 and 107 of the SLA 1925.

for life in control of the land. It is in his hands that the power to manage the land for the best interests of all of the beneficiaries is to be found. This is why the strict settlement was ideally suited to 'family' property arrangements, in which the present occupier of the land could have been expected to manage it for the good of the family with, of course, the ability to deal with the land (and sell it) if the need should arise. The settlement will also encompass 'trustees of the settlement', and although they rarely hold the legal title to the land, they exercise general supervisory functions over the settlement.[38] Consequently, it is their responsibility to ensure that the rights and interests of all of the beneficiaries under the settlement are protected, especially if the tenant for life misuses his statutory powers. The identity of the trustees is determined according to section 30 of the SLA 1925, although they will usually be named as such in the trust deeds.

If the person with the statutory powers chooses to sell the settled land, the interests of the beneficiaries are overreached if the purchase money is paid to the trustees of the settlement (who must be two in number, or a trust corporation), or into court. If overreaching occurs, the purchaser need not concern himself with the equitable interests, because these take effect in the purchase money. The purchaser obtains a clean and unencumbered title to the land. If overreaching does not occur, the tenant for life cannot make a good title to the purchaser, and the purchaser may be bound by the equitable interests according to the provisions of the SLA 1925.

5.2.3 The creation of strict settlements under the Settled Land Act 1925

Under the SLA 1925, all strict settlements must be created by two deeds: a 'trust instrument' and a 'principal vesting deed' (sections 4 and 5 of the SLA 1925). The trust instrument declares the details of the settlement, appoints the trustees of it and sets out any powers conferred by the settlement that are in addition to those provided automatically in the Act. The principal vesting deed is less comprehensive and describes the settled land itself, names the trustees, states the nature of any additional powers and, most importantly of all, declares that the settled land is vested in the person to whom the land is conveyed (the tenant for life) on the trusts of the settlement. The principal vesting deed is, in one sense, the statement of ownership of the tenant for life and it is with this that any purchaser will be concerned, not least because the equitable interests detailed in the trust instrument will be swept off the land by overreaching.

5.2.4 The position of the tenant for life and the statutory powers

As indicated above, the tenant for life is given statutory powers to deal with the land. These powers are subject to various controls and the tenant for life is overseen usually by the trustees of the settlement in order to prevent him from taking advantage of his dominant position. Certain controls are specific to certain powers, and these are noted below where appropriate. Furthermore, the tenant for life is trustee of his powers and must have regard to the interests of the other beneficiaries when he exercises them (section 107 of the SLA 1925).

---

38 *Wheelwright v. Walker* (1883).

1   The tenant for life has power to sell the settled land, or to exchange it for other land
     (section 38 of the SLA 1925). However, he must obtain the best price that can be
     reasonably obtained and a court will take action to ensure this.[39] This power is
     subject to the written notice procedure, as outlined below.

2   The tenant for life has power to grant and accept leases of the land, although for
     certain specific types of lease, the duration of the lease which the tenant for life
     may grant is limited (sections 41 and 53 of the SLA 1925). This power is also
     subject to the written notice procedure.

3   The tenant for life may mortgage or charge the land in order to raise money for
     specific purposes, these generally being purposes that would benefit the land per se,
     rather than any individual owner (section 71 of the SLA 1925). This power is also
     subject to the written notice procedure.

4   The tenant for life may grant options over the land, including granting a person an
     option to purchase the land, or an option to purchase a lease (section 51 of the SLA
     1925). This power is also subject to the written notice procedure.

5   The tenant for life has various ancillary powers in relation to the settled land. This
     includes the power to dispose of the principal mansion house (section 65 of the
     SLA 1925), the power to cut and sell timber (section 66 of the SLA 1925), the
     power to compromise claims concerning the settled land (section 58 of the SLA
     1925) and the power to sell and purchase chattels and family heirlooms (section 67
     of the SLA 1925). These powers are subject to the tenant for life obtaining, vari-
     ously, the consent of the trustees of the settlement or the leave of the court.

6   The tenant for life may carry out any other transaction for the benefit of the settled
     land under order of the court (section 64 of the SLA 1925).

7   The trust deeds of the settlement expressly may confer additional powers on the
     tenant for life.

5.2.5   The role of the trustees of the settlement in regulating the powers of the tenant for life

It has been indicated already that a major function of the 'trustees of the settlement' is to act in a general supervisory capacity in order to safeguard the rights of all persons enti-tled to an interest in the land. In addition to this, the most important powers of the tenant for life are subject to the provisions of section 101 of the SLA 1925 – the written notice procedure. Under section 101, a tenant for life who intends to make a sale, exchange, lease, mortgage or charge in respect of the land, or to grant an option over it, must give written notice to each of the trustees by registered post, and to the solicitor for the trustees, of his intention to exercise one of these powers. Each notice must be posted not less than one month before the proposed disposition and, if there are currently no trustees of the settlement, these powers cannot be exercised.[40]

These provisions are designed to ensure that the trustees are aware of all proposed major dealings with the land and are ready to activate the overreaching mechanism where appropriate. However, although at first sight this notice procedure appears

---

39 *Wheelwright v. Walker (No. 2)* (1883).

40 *Wheelwright v. Walker* (1883).

perfectly adequate to protect all beneficiaries, the SLA itself weakens this protection considerably. Thus, a trustee is under no obligation to interfere with a proposed dealing with the settled land of which he has notice[41] and, except for the power to mortgage or charge the land, the tenant for life may give notice of a general intention to exercise these powers rather than specific notice on each occasion (section 101(2) of the SLA 1925). Furthermore, the trustees may, in writing, waive the notice requirement, or accept less than one month's notice[42] and, importantly, a person dealing with the tenant for life in good faith is not required to inquire whether these procedural safeguards have been observed (section 101(5) of the SLA 1925). Clearly then, much depends on the personal determination and interest of the trustees in supervising the tenant for life.

5.2.6 The fiduciary position of the tenant for life

According to section 107 of the SLA 1925, the tenant for life is trustee of his statutory powers for those entitled under the settlement, and 'shall' have regard to their interests when exercising those powers. This is meant to give further protection to those entitled to either the land or its monetary equivalent. It has some practical consequences, albeit of a limited nature. For example, if the tenant for life sells the settled land, he must sell as fairly as a trustee would sell, which effectively means for the best price reasonably obtainable paying due regard to the interests of the people entitled in remainder.[43] Moreover, the tenant for life cannot accept or keep a payment offered to him for exercising the powers because, as a trustee, he is under a duty not to profit from his trust.[44] However, once again, the protection offered by the legislation promises more than it delivers, for it is clear that a court will not invalidate a sale simply because the tenant for life sells the property for a bad motive, or even because he (the tenant for life) is simply uninterested in managing the land.[45]

5.2.7 Attempts to restrict the powers of the tenant for life

It should be apparent from the above that the tenant for life really is in control of the settled land and that the statutory powers he is given are not subject to serious control either by the trustees of the settlement or under the general law of trusts. Consequently, there was a temptation for settlors to attempt to control or restrict the tenant for life in the exercise of his powers by inserting some express limitation in the deeds of the settlement. Unfortunately, this cuts against the philosophy of the SLA 1925 given that the Act was designed to prevent just this sort of control being exercised over the settled land by the 'dead hand' of the settlor. Therefore, according to section 106 of the SLA 1925, any provision inserted in a settlement that purports or attempts to forbid a tenant for life to exercise a statutory power, or any provision that attempts, tends or is intended to induce the tenant for life not to exercise those powers, is void, as in *Re Patten* (1929). Likewise, in *Re Orlebar* (1936), the court discussed a so-called 'residence condition', which

---

41 *England* v. *Public Trustee* (1967).

42 Section 101(4) of the SLA 1925.

43 *Wheelwright* v. *Walker* (1883).

44 *Chandler* v. *Bradley* (1897).

45 *Cardigan* v. *Curzon-Howe* (1885).

stipulated that the tenant for life should lose his interest under the settlement if he ceased to occupy the land, and decided that the tenant for life should not be required to forfeit his interest if he left the land as a result of a proper exercise of a statutory power.[46]

Obviously, section 106 is a very powerful statutory provision and it is largely effective to prevent settlors avoiding the policy of the SLA 1925 by seeking to control the tenant for life through clever drafting of the settlement. However, in Re Aberconway (1953), a majority of the court held that, if that which might be lost to the tenant for life through such a provision controlling his powers was not a benefit to him, section 106 did not apply to make that provision void. Taking a different approach, Lord Denning in his dissenting opinion was of the view that anything that even tended to restrict the tenant for life in the exercise of his powers was void and this does seem more consistent with the overall policy of the Act than does the decision of the majority. Indeed, a simple reading of section 106 appears to confirm Lord Denning's view and it has an echo in section 104 of the same Act, which provides that any contract entered into by the tenant for life himself not to exercise a statutory power is void.

5.2.8   Protection for the beneficiaries

In a very general sense, the beneficiaries under the settlement are protected by the notice procedures discussed above, the general supervisory role of the trustees of the settlement and the overreaching machinery, especially if all they are concerned with is the income that the land may generate rather than the land itself. More importantly, a very powerful provision is found in section 13 of the SLA 1925. As noted above, when expressly created, each settlement should comprise two deeds: the trust instrument and the vesting deed. Under section 13, if no vesting deed has been executed in favour of the tenant for life, any proposed dealing by him during his life with the legal estate operates only as a contract to carry out that transaction; it does not transfer the legal title to the prospective purchaser. In other words, in the absence of a vesting deed, section 13 attempts to paralyse dealings with the legal title except in four specified cases, the most important of which is a sale to a purchaser of a legal estate without notice of the absence of a vesting deed. Simply put, the absence of a vesting deed makes it difficult for the tenant for life to deal with the land. However, if the dealing is a sale in violation of the settlement to an innocent purchaser (as most will be), that purchaser will still obtain good legal title to the land. The protection of section 13 is powerful in principle, but its application can be avoided.

Once a vesting deed has been executed, section 13 no longer applies, and the beneficiaries must look to section 18 of the SLA 1925 for protection in the event of some fraud on the settlement. Under section 18, once a vesting deed has been executed, and until the settlement is discharged, any transaction that is not 'authorised' by the SLA 1925 or other statute is void. Thus, any sale or mortgage, and so on, by the tenant for life that is outside his statutory powers is ineffective to convey legal title to the land. It would operate only in equity to the effect of conveying the tenant's own equitable interest, but no more, to the purchaser.[47] Of course, the existence of a vesting deed normally would inform the purchaser of all material facts in relation to the settlement – or at least indicate areas of concern where

---

46 It would be otherwise if the tenant for life vacated the land for his own private motives.

47 Weston v. Henshaw (1950).

further enquiries might be made – and so a purchaser can have little complaint if he purchases the land as part of what turns out to be an *unauthorised* transaction after inspecting the vesting deed.

5.2.9 Protection for the purchaser of settled land

Once again, in a general sense, the purchaser of settled land is protected by the overreaching machinery. He need be concerned only with the vesting deed and can rely on the interests of the beneficiaries being overreached. However, things can go wrong. To meet this possibility, section 110 of the SLA 1925 makes special reference to the position of a purchaser and provides that a purchaser who deals in good faith with the tenant for life is, as regards the beneficiaries, deemed to have paid the best price and to have complied with all of the requirements of the Act. Although it is sometimes thought that this provision sits uneasily with section 18 (which voids all unauthorised transactions), it seems that section 110 is concerned with matters of detail, not of principle. Thus, section 110 will *not* protect a purchaser if the transaction with the tenant for life is wholly unauthorised (for this falls within section 18), but it will protect him if there are omissions of detail in an otherwise authorised transaction.[48]

5.2.10 The overreaching machinery

Equitable interests under strict settlements are capable of being overreached on a sale of the settled land (section 2 of the LPA 1925). If successful, overreaching will confer legal title on a purchaser free of all equitable interests under the settlement. Of course, no legal rights are capable of being overreached and neither are any equitable interests created *prior* to the settlement (with three minor exceptions: annuities, limited owner's charge, general equitable charge). As with all overreaching, the capital purchase money must be paid to at least two trustees of the settlement or a trust corporation. In unregistered land, failure to overreach may result in the equitable interests binding the purchaser through the doctrine of notice because such interests cannot be registered as a land charge.[49] In land of registered title, when overreaching fails, the position is more complex. Equitable interests under a SLA 1925 settlement cannot be overriding interests,[50] nor may they be protected by the entry of a Notice against the title.[51] In consequence, the beneficiaries must either be content to rely on the protective sections of the SLA itself (sections 13 and 18 above) or have had the foresight to enter a Restriction against the title effectively preventing a sale of the land at all unless the conditions for overreaching are complied with.[52]

---

48 *Re Morgan's Lease* (1972).

49 Section 2 of the LCA 1972.

50 Paragraph 2, Schedules 1 and 3 of the LRA 2002.

51 Section 33(a)(ii) of the LRA 2002.

52 The entry of a Restriction preventing sale unless there are two trustees or a trust corporation would have been normal when the strict settlement was created deliberately. Note that the effect of such a Restriction is to ensure that overreaching occurs – thus forcing the equitable owners to take their interests in money.

5.2.11 The duties of the trustees of the settlement

The supervisory duties of the trustees of the settlement, and their role in regulating the tenant for life in the exercise of his statutory powers, have been mentioned already. In addition to this, the SLA 1925 gives the trustees other responsibilities, not least to take receipt of the capital sum in order to facilitate overreaching. More specifically, the trustees may actually act as 'statutory owner' (with all of the powers of a tenant for life) if there is no tenant for life or if the tenant for life is an infant and, under section 24 of the Act, the court may authorise the trustees to exercise the powers of the tenant for life (in his name) if the tenant has ceased to have a substantial interest in the land, or has refused (but not merely neglected) to exercise those powers.[53]

5.3 The Trust for Sale of Land Before the Trusts of Land and Appointment of Trustees Act 1996

The second method of regulating successive interests in land *before* the entry into force of TOLATA 1996 was the *trust for sale* of land. Although trusts for sale expressly created before or after 1 January 1997 may continue to exist in name, they will take effect under the regime of TOLATA 1996 and there will be little practical difference between these and the more common *trust of land*.[54] Further, any trusts in relation to land that had been, or will be, imposed by statute will take effect as a trust of land subject to TOLATA 1996. This will include any trusts created impliedly by reason of the application of the principles of resulting or constructive trusts (see Chapter 4). Consequently, in terms of pre-1997 law, the other method of creating a trust for successive interests (the old trust for sale) comes under the TOLATA 1996 regime and is, for all practical purposes, equivalent to a trust of land. The principal features of this regime have been discussed above.[55]

5.4 A Comparison between the Strict Settlement under the Settled Land Act 1925 and the Regime of the Trusts of Land and Appointment of Trustees Act 1996

As noted at the outset of this chapter, pre-1997 successive interest trusts for sale, and all new attempts to create successive interests in land, will take effect under TOLATA 1996. This is regardless of whether they take effect as a *trust of land*, or whether they retain their

---

53 As explained in Re 90 Thornhill Road (1970).

54 Above, section 5.2.

55 Section 5.2.1 above.

trust for sale label (having been created as such expressly). Consequently, in order to appreciate more fully the difference that the obligatory application of TOLATA 1996 has made to the law of successive interests, a comparison with the 'old' law of strict settlements of the SLA 1925 is appropriate.

1   Settled land is governed by the complicated provisions of the SLA 1925. The trust of land under TOLATA 1996 (including expressly created trusts for sale) is relatively easy to understand and operate. The abolition of the strict settlement for new successive interests has meant less litigation and less cost.

2   The strict settlement was ideally suited to keeping land 'in the family', especially where the tenant for life may have wished to occupy the land and consequently declined to exercise his power of sale. This was perfectly legitimate, even if those entitled on his death saw the value of their prospective interests dwindle. The machinery of TOLATA 1996 can ensure occupation by interested persons (i.e. the tenant for life), but also has the flexibility to ensure that the land is sold if this is in the best interests of the equitable owners generally (see section 14 of TOLATA 1996).

3   Under a strict settlement, the tenant for life has legal title and is in effective control of the land. Under TOLATA 1996, the trustees have legal title, and have all of the powers of an absolute owner. They will control the land unless they choose to delegate powers to the person with the life interest or other person interested. They will not divest themselves of legal title unless the land subject to the trust is sold.

4   The tenant for life under the SLA 1925 is constrained (albeit lightly) by the fact that his powers and the legal estate are held on trust. Moreover, certain powers are subject to notice procedures or the consent of the trustees of the settlement. The trustees of land under TOLATA 1996 are obliged to consult the beneficiaries (e.g. the person with a life interest), and should consider giving effect to his wishes. However, they are not bound to follow his wishes. Under TOLATA 1996, the trustees may have delegated their powers irrevocably, and the exercise of the powers by the trustees may be made subject to the consent of some other person interested in the land.[56]

5   On the death of a life tenant under a strict settlement, the legal estate can be transferred only by means of the expensive and time-consuming process of obtaining a vesting deed. On the death of a trustee of land under TOLATA 1996, legal title simply accrues to the remaining trustees (being joint tenants of the legal estate) under the right of survivorship. There is no cost, no documents and no fuss.

6   The position of a purchaser of land subject to a strict settlement was not always clear, but was generally quite favourable. Under TOLATA 1996, a purchaser may be bound by equitable interests taking effect as overriding interests, but only if overreaching does not occur. In both the strict settlement and the trust of land, a Restriction may be placed on the register of title controlling the registered proprietor in his dealings with the land, except that overreaching cannot be prevented.

---

56 For example, the life tenant to whom delegated powers have not been given.

5.5   Chapter Summary

5.5.1   What is successive ownership of land?

Successive ownership of land occurs when one person has an interest in the land for life and another (or others) has (have) rights that 'fall into' possession after the 'life interest' has ended. There are two sets of rules concerning the ways in which land can be held subject to successive interests. First, for successive interests created before 1 January 1997, a settlement (or 'strict settlement') may be used. Such land is called *settled land* and falls within the machinery of the SLA 1925. Alternatively, a trust for sale of land could have been used operating under the LPA 1925. Second, all new successive interests created on or after 1 January 1997 fall within the TOLATA 1996 and take effect under that regime. These are trusts of land (or occasionally expressly created trusts for sale of land also subject to the identical TOLATA 1996 regime). No new strict settlements can be created after this date, although resettlements of existing settled land are permitted.

5.5.2   The strict settlement and settled land

A 'strict settlement' will exist in a number of (complicated) circumstances, but the most common are where land is 'limited in trust for any persons by way of succession' or where land is charged by way of a family arrangement with the payment of any sums for the benefit of any persons.

5.5.3   The essential characteristics of settled land

The person under the settlement who is of full age and entitled to immediate possession of the settled land (or the whole income from it) is generally regarded as the 'tenant for life' (section 19 of the SLA 1925). The tenant for life is holder of the legal estate and holds that estate on trust for the beneficiaries under the settlement (sections 4 and 107 of the SLA 1925). The tenant for life exercises most of the important statutory powers to deal with the settled land. These effectively place the tenant for life in control of the land. There are also 'trustees of the settlement' and they exercise general supervisory functions over the settlement. Where the person with the statutory powers chooses to sell the settled land, the interests of the beneficiaries are overreached if the purchase money is paid to the trustees of the settlement (who must be two in number or a trust corporation) or into court.

5.5.4   The position of the tenant for life and the statutory powers

The tenant for life will usually have various powers to deal with the settled land, including the power to sell it, grant a lease of it and mortgage it for specific purposes. These powers are subject to the consent of the trustees of the settlement or the leave of the court, although the tenant for life may carry out any other transaction for the benefit of the settled land under order of the court (section 64 of the SLA 1925). The trusts of the settlement may expressly confer additional powers on the tenant for life. Under section 106 of the SLA 1925, any provision inserted in the settlement that purports or attempts to forbid a tenant for life to exercise a statutory power, or any provision that attempts, tends or is intended to induce the tenant for life not to exercise those powers, is void.

5.5.5 The role of the trustees of the settlement in regulating the powers of the tenant for life

Under section 101 of the SLA 1925, a tenant for life who intends to make a sale, exchange, lease, mortgage or charge in respect of the land, or to grant an option over it, must give written notice to each of the trustees by registered post and to the solicitor for the trustees of his intention to exercise these powers.

5.5.6 The fiduciary position of the tenant for life

Under section 107 of the SLA 1925, the tenant for life is trustee of his statutory powers for those entitled under the settlement and 'shall' have regard to their interests when exercising those powers.

5.5.7 Protection for the beneficiaries

In addition to the notice procedure, the general supervisory role of the trustees of the settlement and the overreaching machinery, the beneficiaries are protected by sections 13 and 18 of the SLA 1925. These sections can paralyse dealings with the land in certain circumstances.

5.5.8 Protection for the purchaser of settled land

Section 110 of the SLA 1925 provides that a purchaser who deals in good faith with the tenant for life is, as regards the beneficiaries, deemed to have paid the best price and to have complied with all of the requirements of the Act. This is concerned with matters of detail and section 110 will not protect a purchaser if the transaction with the tenant for life is wholly unauthorised (section 18).

5.5.9 The overreaching machinery

Equitable interests arising under the strict settlements are capable of being overreached on a sale of the settled land (section 2 of the LPA 1925). No legal rights are capable of being overreached.

5.5.10 The trust for sale of land and Trusts of Land and Appointment of Trustees Act 1996

TOLATA 1996 regulates all new successive interests of land (except resettlements) created on or after 1 January 1997. Legal title is vested in the trustees who have all of the powers to deal with the land. The life tenant and others entitled will have equitable interests. The trustees may delegate their powers (except the power to overreach) to any person and may well give some powers to the person in occupation of the land, usually the tenant for life. The trustees must consult the beneficiaries before dealing with the land, but only in limited circumstances will they have to obtain the consent of the beneficiaries before exercising their powers. The tenant for life (and other beneficiaries) can have an entitlement to occupy the land, although this can be excluded or modified. Usually, only the tenant for life will occupy. A sale (including a mortgage) by the trustees will overreach the equitable owners, provided that the conditions for statutory overreaching are met. Any person interested in the trust of land may apply to the court under section 14 of TOLATA 1996 for an order concerning the land.

Now visit the companion website to:

*   test your understanding of the key terms using our Flashcard Glossary;

*   revise and consolidate your knowledge using our Multiple Choice Question testbank.

www.routledge.com/cw/dixon

Chapter 6
Leases

6.1   The Nature of a Lease

The 'leasehold' is one of the two estates identified in section 1 of the LPA 1925 as capable of existing as either a 'legal' or 'equitable' interest. As we shall see, whether any given lease is legal or equitable will depend primarily on the way in which it has been created. However, irrespective of whether a leasehold is legal or equitable, there is no doubt that it is one of the most versatile concepts known in the law of real property. Even the terminology of leases reflects the many purposes to which they may be put. The 'term of years', 'tenancy', 'sublease' and 'leasehold estate' are all terms in common use, and all of them describe the existence of a 'landlord' and 'tenant' relationship. For example, a 'lease' or 'term of years' is most often used to describe a commercial or long-term letting, whereas the description 'tenancy' is often used for residential or short-term lets. This variety does not mean that different substantive rules apply to different types of lease (although this may be the case where a statute applies only to one kind of lease), but it does indicate the importance that the leasehold plays in the world of commercial and residential property management and investment. In this respect, three fundamental features of the leasehold should be noted at the outset.

First, the leasehold allows two or more people to enjoy the benefits of owning an estate in the same piece of land at the same time: the freeholder will receive the rent and profits, and the leaseholder will enjoy physical possession and occupation of the property. Indeed, if a 'subtenancy' (also known as an 'underlease') is created, being where a shorter lease is carved out of a 'headlease', the number of people enjoying the land or its fruits increases further. For example, if a freeholder (A) grants a 99-year lease to B, and B grants a 50-year subtenancy to C, then A receives rent from B, B receives rent from C and C enjoys physical possession of the land. In theory, there is no limit to the number of leases and underleases that can be created out of a freehold estate, and each intermediate person will be the tenant of their superior landlord and the landlord of their own tenant. It is the ability of the leasehold to facilitate this multiple enjoyment of land that gives it its unique character. It allows the landlord to generate an income through rent (thus employing land as an investment vehicle), while at the same time the tenant is a 'purchaser' of an estate in land through the payment of that rent.[1]

Second, it is inherent in the leasehold estate that both the landlord and the tenant (and all subtenants) have a proprietary right in the land.[2] Thus, the tenant owns the lease, and the landlord owns the 'reversion expectant on the lease' – that is, the right to possession of the property when the lease ends. Importantly, both of these proprietary rights can be sold or transferred while the lease is in existence. The tenant may sell his lease to a person who becomes the new tenant (an 'assignee' of the lease), and the landlord may sell his reversion to a person who becomes the new landlord (an assignee of the reversion). Likewise, the assignees of the lease and reversion may assign (i.e. sell or transfer) their interests further. The result is that the current landlord and current tenant under a lease may be far removed from the original landlord and tenant who actually negotiated its creation. Nevertheless, as explained below, the landlord and tenant

---

1 Sometimes, a long lease will be 'purchased' by a tenant on the payment of an initial capital sum (a 'premium') and
   the rent will consist of a small annual sum (sometimes called a 'ground rent').

2 But note Bruton v. London and Quadrant Housing Trust (1999), below.

currently 'in possession' may well be bound by the terms of the lease as originally agreed. Figure 6.1 represents this diagrammatically.

Third, all leases will contain covenants (promises) whereby the landlord and tenant promise to do, or not to do, certain things in relation to the land. These may be 'express covenants', being obligations agreed deliberately between landlord and tenant and written into the lease, 'implied covenants', being covenants read into the lease as a matter of law (e.g. the repairing covenant implied in certain leases by section 11 of the Landlord and Tenant Act 1985), or 'usual' covenants, being those that are not expressly mentioned but are so common in the landlord and tenant relationship that they are taken to be part of the lease unless clearly excluded: for example, the tenant's obligation to pay rent under an equitable lease (*Shiloh Spinners* v. *Harding* (1973)). Typical examples of express covenants are the landlord's covenant to repair the buildings and the tenant's covenant to pay rent or not to carry on a trade or business on the premises. All these types of covenant are enforceable between the *original* landlord and *original* tenant and, as we shall see, in many circumstances are also enforceable between assignees of the lease or reversion. The particular rules concerning the enforceability of leasehold covenants are discussed below in section 6.4, but the important point is that the ability to make rights and obligations 'run' with the land is a special feature of the landlord and tenant relationship. It is the reason why the leasehold estate is a particularly useful investment vehicle because the freeholder can generate an income while, at the same time, preserving the value of the land through properly drafted covenants (e.g. that the tenant must repair, may not keep pets), which will bind the original tenant *and* any subsequent assignees. Moreover, given that both the benefit of a leasehold covenant (the right to enforce it) and its burden (the obligation to observe it) can run with the land, the use of a leasehold with appropriate covenants can achieve what covenants affecting freehold land cannot: that is, with a landlord and tenant relationship, even positive obligations can be made to run with the burdened estate.[3]

Figure 6.1

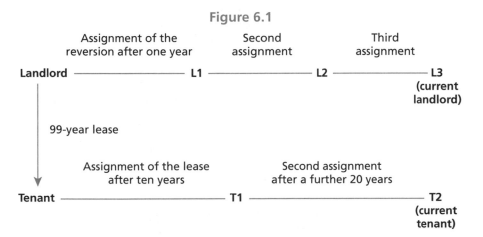

---

3 Contrast the current position in respect of freehold covenants discussed in Chapter 8.

6.2   The Essential Characteristics of a Lease

There are various definitions of a lease, both in statute[4] and in common law, but probably the most commonly cited is that of Lord Templeman in *Street* v. *Mountford* (1985). In his now famous judgment, Lord Templeman identifies the essential qualities of a lease as that arrangement that gives a person the right of exclusive possession of land, for a term, at a rent. These three elements are commonly regarded as the essential elements of a leasehold estate, irrespective of the purpose for which the estate is created.[5] They have been affirmed many times in a residential context,[6] a commercial context,[7] in cases where the landlord is a private individual[8] and where the landlord is a public or semi-public authority.[9] These three components of a lease will be examined in turn.

6.2.1   Exclusive possession

A lease is an estate in the land; it signifies a form of 'ownership' of the land for a defined period of time. However, there are many other ways in which a person may enjoy a limited right to use or occupy land owned by another person and it is sometimes necessary to distinguish these relationships from the leasehold estate. For example, a person may be given a 'licence' to occupy the land of another that, in many ways, might resemble a lease.[10] Yet a licence is a mere personal right, binding only the parties that created it – *Lloyd* v. *Dugdale* (2001). A lease, on the other hand, is properly regarded as a proprietary interest in the land itself and it may be assigned to, and become binding on, any subsequent owner of the reversion. Moreover, 'leases' (but not licences) fall within the statutory regulatory machinery of the Rent Act 1977 and the Housing Act 1988, so restricting the ability of landlords to remove tenants and set rent.[11] There are other differences too. For example: a tenant may sue any person in trespass (including his landlord), but a licensee enjoys only a very narrow right;[12] a tenant may sue in nuisance, but a licensee may do so only in exceptional circumstances;[13] and only a landlord may avail himself of the remedy of forfeiture (and hence only a tenant may claim 'relief'). In fact,

---

4 For example, section 205 of the LPA 1925.

5 However, as discussed below, in fact the absence of an obligation to pay rent does not necessarily mean that there is no lease: see section 6.2.5.

6 *Aslan* v. *Murphy* (1989). See in particular *Berrisford* v. *Mexfield Housing Co-operative* (2011), which does not challenge the need for a 'term certain', albeit that it decides that the requirement may be met more easily. See section 6.2.2 below.

7 *Clear Channel UK* v. *Manchester City Council* (2004); *Vandersteen* v. *Angus* (1992).

8 *Antoniades* v. *Villiers* (1990); *AG Securities* v. *Vaughan* (1988).

9 *Westminster City Council* v. *Clarke* (no lease); *Bruton* v. *London & Quadrant Housing Trust* (lease).

10 The occupier may pay a regular 'licence fee' and treat the land as their home (*Ogwr Borough Council* v. *Dykes* (1989)); *Secretary of State for Defence* v. *Nicholas* (2013)) or use it as a business (*London Development Agency* v. *Nidai* (2009)).

11 Note, however, that the near removal of all statutory regulation of leases in recent years means that the great majority of residential leases no longer fall within the protective ambit of these statutes.

12 *Manchester Airport* v. *Dutton* (1999) suggests that certain licences may give the licensee a right to sue in trespass, but this is controversial and there is no precedent to support it.

13 *Hunter* v. *Canary Wharf* (1996).

in years past, these differences, particularly the absence of statutory protection and rent control for licences, prompted landowners to attempt to draw up agreements with potential occupiers of the land that gave mere licences and not leases. In most cases, this was attempted by seeking to deny the grant of 'exclusive possession' to the occupier, thereby removing a vital element in the creation of a lease. Consequently, a series of cases in the House of Lords and Court of Appeal sought to draw a legal and practical distinction between a 'lease' and a 'licence', and this battle was fought largely over the concept of 'exclusive possession'. Indeed, although legislative changes have made the distinction between a lease and a licence less critical,[14] these important cases still provide the basic tools for identifying whether a right to occupy amounts to a 'lease' or whether instead it amounts to some other arrangement between the parties.

As a basic proposition, a lease will exist when the occupier of land has been granted exclusive possession of the premises. This is a question of fact, to be decided in each case by reference to the surrounding circumstances, the course of any negotiations prior to the grant of the right of occupation, the nature of the property and the actual mode of occupation of the occupier. Further, the landowner cannot avoid granting a lease by merely calling the arrangement between the parties 'a licence', even if this is expressly stated. Labels are not decisive and so, conversely, an agreement called a 'tenancy' may likewise be held to be a licence if that is the substantive effect of its provisions – *Watts* v. *Stewart* (2016). Generally, it is not the parties' intentions (whether expressly stated or not) that are relevant, but the substance of the rights they have created by their agreement (*Street* v. *Mountford* (1985), overruling *Somma* v. *Hazlehurst* (1978)).[15] However, Lord Templeman in *Street* also accepted there are certain exceptional situations in which an occupier of land may have exclusive possession of the property but, for special reasons, no lease will exist. These are cases in which the grant of exclusive possession is referable to some other bona fide relationship between the parties. Examples given in *Street* include a mortgagee going into possession of the property under the terms of a mortgage, usually where the borrower cannot repay the loan,[16] the occupation of the purchaser under an enforceable contract for the sale of the land[17] and where the occupation is based on charity[18] or based in friendship when there is no intention to create a formal legal relationship between the owner and the occupier.[19] In fact, these special cases were explained by Denning LJ in the earlier case of *Facchini* v. *Bryson* (1952) and also include situations in which the occupier is a 'service occupier', being a person who occupies property for the better performance of his duties under a contract of employment with the landowner.[20] Although an occupier in one of these situations may have exclusive

---

14 For example, because of the removal of rent control and security of tenure under various Housing Acts.

15 This remains the key test. See *Camelot Properties* v. *Roynon* (2017) applying *Street* in classic circumstances and finding that the occupier had a lease despite Camelot's intention to give a property guardian's licence. See also *Gilpin* v. *Legg* (2017).

16 See Chapter 11.

17 *Bretherton* v. *Paton* (1986).

18 For example, *Gray* v. *Taylor* (1998). See also *Watts* v. *Stewart* (2016) where an agreement calling itself a 'tenancy' was held to be a charity licence.

19 *Marcroft Wagons* v. *Smith* (1951).

20 *Norris* v. *Checksfield* (1991).

possession of the property,[21] that occupation feeds off his employment contract and does not exist because of a landlord and tenant relationship. Thus, they are a licensee, as in *Carroll* v. *Manek* (1999), in which a hotel manager was held to have a licence of a hotel room (despite being in exclusive possession) because the possession was entirely referable to this employment relationship.[22]

According to Lord Templeman in *Street*, the practical effect of the principle that an occupation agreement is to be assessed according to its substance, not its label, is that a genuine licence can exist in only very limited circumstances. Apart from the *Facchini* exceptions, Lord Templeman's view is that an occupier of premises must be either a 'tenant' or a 'lodger'. This is another way of saying that the only genuine occupation licence that can exist is that held by a lodger. In law, a lodger is someone who receives services and attendance from the landlord, such as room cleaning or meals. Moreover, as *Markou* v. *Da Silvaesa* (1986) illustrates, a mere promise by the landowner to provide such services is *not* sufficient to generate a lodging agreement (i.e. a licence); they must actually be provided. What this means is that it should be a relatively straightforward task to distinguish between a lease and a licence: if the occupier receives 'board and lodging', he holds a mere personal licence; otherwise, he must be a tenant, unless one of the exceptional *Facchini* situations exists. Unfortunately, however, things are never this simple, for if it is true that an occupier is *either* a lodger or a tenant, this implies that no other kind of 'occupation licence' can exist. There can be no intermediate category of licensee who, while not a lodger, is still not a tenant. Obviously, this has far-reaching consequences, for it restricts the options open to a landowner when seeking to make use of his property. It is the triumph of property law over freedom of contract, and it is precisely this legal straitjacket that cases subsequent to *Street* found difficult to accept. Indeed, many of the apparently inconsistent decisions of the Court of Appeal that followed *Street* represent attempts to identify some middle way, some form of occupation that can still give rise to a licence, but where the occupier is not a lodger. *Hadjiloucas* v. *Crean* (1988) and *Brooker Estates* v. *Ayers* (1987), both decisions of the Court of Appeal quite soon after *Street*, are of this type. In fact, although the primacy of the lease/licence distinction based on exclusive possession has been preserved by the House of Lords in cases such as *Antoniades* v. *Villiers* (1990) and *Bruton* v. *London & Quadrant* (1999), and by the Court of Appeal in *Aslan* v. *Murphy* (1989) and *Mikeover* v. *Brady* (1989), there has been an acceptance that property rights, or rights to use property, are not as black and white as the tenant/lodger distinction suggests. Necessarily, this has resulted in a certain refinement of the principles, and some other guidelines have emerged.

First, it is now clear that a licence may exist where two or more people occupy the same property, as in shared houses. It is not that the people occupying the property under a 'multiple occupancy agreement' *cannot* be leaseholders; rather that to be leaseholders of the entire property the 'four unities' must be present so as to support a joint tenancy of the leasehold estate of the entire premises.[23] The matter turns on the nature of the multiple occupancy agreement. For example, if four people occupy a four-bedroom house, but each sign a different agreement, on different days and for different

---

21 Sometimes they will not, but the point is that 'exclusive possession' is not determinative of the occupier's status.

22 In consequence, the occupation will terminate when the employment is terminated.

23 AG *Securities* v. *Vaughan* (1988).

rents, there can be no 'exclusive possession' of the *entire* premises, because there is no unity of interest, title or time. The house, as a whole, cannot be held on a lease because the necessary conditions for a joint tenancy of a leasehold estate do not exist. Of course, each occupier may have a lease of his individual room, with a licence over the common parts, but this is very different from a single, jointly owned leasehold estate of the whole premises. Note, however, that while it is perfectly understandable and indeed practical that no joint leasehold should exist in respect of a property occupied by a shifting population of previously unrelated persons (e.g. house-sharing in London), the same considerations do not apply where the 'multiple' occupancy is that of a romantically linked couple who, for all intents and purposes, are living in the property together, not as separate individuals. In such cases, as explained below, the court might well regard the existence of an alleged multiple occupancy licence as a deliberate and artificial (and hence disallowed) attempt to avoid the grant of a joint leasehold interest.

Second, some cases suggest that there are certain types of public sector landlord who may be able to grant licences in circumstances in which a private landlord could only grant leases. Examples are *Westminster CC v. Basson* (1991), *Ogwr BC v. Dykes* (1989) and *Westminster CC v. Clarke* (1992).[24] In these situations, the landowner may be able to deny exclusive possession to the occupier (and hence deny a lease) because to do otherwise would be to hinder it in the exercise of its statutory housing or other public duties. For example, such landlords may be able to grant personal licences in order to be able to manage their housing stock more effectively without being 'caught' by the greater obligations owed by landlords to their tenants. Seen in this light, the privileged position of public sector landlords is justified by policy rather than principle, but, of course, that does not make it any less sensible. A similar view was taken in *Gray v. Taylor* (1998), in which one ground for denying that the occupier of a charity almshouse was a tenant was that it would be inconsistent with the duty of the particular trustees of the charity to have granted a tenancy and, with it, a measure of residential security. Importantly, however, this view of the *Westminster* cases (i.e. that the identity of the landlord can be a decisive factor in drawing the lease/licence distinction) has been challenged. In *Bruton v. London and Quadrant Housing Trust* (1999), the House of Lords was considering the status of Mr Bruton, who held a property on an express 'licence' from the Trust. The Trust itself held a licence from the freeholder, Lambeth London Borough Council, and was acting in support of Lambeth's housing functions. In deciding that Mr Bruton held a lease (on which, see immediately below), Lord Hoffmann noted (*obiter*) that the law does not accept that the identity or type of landlord is relevant in determining the existence of a lease or licence. This does seem to shut down this line of argument but it is not immediately apparent why, as the earlier Court of Appeal cases demonstrate, the identity of the landlord cannot help to establish whether the giving of a licence to an occupier was a *genuine* response to the unique circumstances of a case rather than an attempt to avoid the grant of a lease per se. So, the fact that Westminster Council has statutory housing functions must impact on the *genuineness* of its attempt to give some of its occupiers 'mere' licences, just as in *Mehta v. Royal Bank of Scotland* (1999), where the Court of Appeal decided

---

24 See also *Ministry of Defence v. Nicholas* (2013), where the occupier was held to be a licensee, although the precise reasons are not clear.

that an occupier of a hotel room had a licence as against the hotel owners (as made clear in his agreement) because this was the only sensible interpretation of the relationship between the particular parties. In fact, as discussed below, *Bruton* is a case that raises other issues about the distinction between a lease and a licence and it is not certain that it is the most reliable authority in this area.

Third, in *Bruton v. London & Quadrant Housing Trust* (1999), Mr Bruton contended that he held a lease from London & Quadrant on the basis that he enjoyed exclusive possession. However, the Trust itself held only a licence from the freeholder, not because of some clever drafting by the freeholder, but because a grant of any lease by Lambeth LBC (the freeholder) would have been *ultra vires* its powers under section 32 of the Housing Act 1985. Naturally (one might think), the Trust resisted the claim that Bruton held a lease on the simple ground that it (the Trust) held no estate in the land and so could not grant such an estate in the land to Mr Bruton: *nemo dat quod non habet*.[25] This was accepted by a majority of the Court of Appeal but, somewhat surprisingly, was rejected by the House of Lords. According to Lord Hoffmann, giving the leading judgment and deciding in favour of the existence of a lease for Mr Bruton, the test of whether an occupier held a lease was simply that of 'exclusive possession' as laid down in *Street*. Bruton, he decided, had exclusive possession, so he had a lease and it did not matter that London & Quadrant held no estate because it was the agreement between the parties that created 'a lease', not the prior existence of an estate in the 'landlord'. Unfortunately, this deceptively simple (and, with respect, simplistic) reasoning has far-reaching consequences. It means, as acknowledged by Lord Hoffmann, that a lease is not always a proprietary right in the land. Apparently, it is a contractual state of affairs between 'landlord' and 'tenant' and whether it is also proprietary in the sense of being capable of binding third parties depends on the circumstances in which the 'lease' arises. To put it another way, apparently there is, in English law, the 'normal' proprietary lease that has been with us for centuries and also the 'non-proprietary lease' or 'contractual tenancy', being a 'lease' between the parties, but not 'a lease' in a proprietary sense. It is an understatement to say that this muddies the waters. The decision in *Street* itself is premised on the assumption that a lease is proprietary and that is why it must be distinguished from a licence! To take the *ratio* of *Street* and apply it to *Bruton* in the manner suggested by Lord Hoffmann does great violence not only to established principles of property law, but also goes against the very purpose of Lord Templeman's judgment in the earlier case. Exclusive *possession* signifies exclusive control in virtue of an estate in land granted by the landlord; exclusive occupation signifies exclusive control in virtue of other arrangements and it might be thought that the occupier in Bruton had the latter, but not the former. No doubt, the decision in Bruton was convenient in that it meant that London & Quadrant were subject to the repairing obligations that are implied into a 'lease' under section 11 of the Landlord and Tenant Act 1985.[26] On the other hand, the 'non-proprietary lease' is a strange creature in English property law and, we might suggest, it already has a name: that is, it is a licence! Subsequent to *Bruton*, the reasoning has been discussed in two cases, *Kay v.*

---

25 In this context, meaning that a person cannot grant what they do not own. The Trust had no lease, so it could not carve one for Mr Bruton.

26 However, it is not clear how London & Quadrant could have performed its obligation. Having only a licence itself, it had no capacity to alter or repair the premises.

London Borough of Lambeth (2006) and London Borough of Islington v. Green (2005), both of which involved 'Bruton tenants' seeking a remedy against the freeholders of the land. However, while in both cases the Court of Appeal adopted the reasoning of the House of Lords (as it had to) that the absence of an estate in the intermediate 'landlord' was not destructive of the occupier's 'non-proprietary lease', in both cases the Court decided that the occupier's 'lease' was purely a contractual arrangement between the intermediate licensor and the occupier – that is, it was without proprietary effect against the freeholder or any other third party. Indeed, when Kay v. Lambeth (2006) was appealed to the House of Lords (partly on other grounds),[27] Lord Scott (with whom all six other Lords agreed), made it clear that the 'Bruton tenancies' had no proprietary character at all and were not governed by any of the principles relevant to leasehold estates.[28] So it is, then, that the 'Bruton tenancy' is 'a lease' but without meaning that it is an estate in the land. In such circumstances, we might ask legitimately why is this a 'lease' at all, as opposed to perhaps a contractual licence.[29] It remains to be seen whether the 'Bruton tenancy' gains any further credibility but it seems likely that the case will come to be regarded as decided 'by reference to its own special facts', as seems inherent in Lord Scott's unsympathetic analysis of it in Kay. In LDC v. Nidai (2009), it was conceded that the occupier held only a licence in the land because the 'landlord' held only a licence. The striking thing is that Bruton was not raised at all by counsel for the occupier in Nidai and it does not feature in the judgment. On the other hand, in Mitchell v. Watkinson (2013), Morgan J noted that the agreement between the parties:

> created a contract of tenancy between Arthur Mitchell as the landlord and the Trustees as the tenants. That contract was valid and effective between the parties to the agreement even though at the date of the agreement, Arthur Mitchell did not have title to the land the subject of the agreement: see Bruton v. London & Quadrant Housing Trust.

On balance, therefore, while it would be a mistake to regard Bruton as authority for the destruction of one of the most fundamental distinctions in property law – that is, the distinction between proprietary leases and personal licences – its use to create 'a contract of tenancy'[30] between the parties where they have some of the attributes of landlord and tenant cannot be discounted.

Fourth, continuing this analysis of cases decided after Street, Lord Oliver in Antoniades v. Villiers (1990) suggests that there may be circumstances in which a landowner can genuinely reserve to himself a right to make use of the premises that they have given over to an occupier and, if such use is made, no exclusive possession will have been granted and

---

27 Questions arose as to the occupiers' right to a home under Article 8 of the ECHR.

28 For example, the agreements were not governed by the leasehold estate principles concerning surrender of the estate by a tenant to his landlord.

29 One reason might be that a 'Bruton tenancy' as between the parties to it (but only those parties) contains some of the obligations of 'landlord and tenant' as regular contractual terms, such as repairing obligations and the like. To the present author, this appears as a sleight of hand, not justifiable as a matter of property law, but to be seen as a device to give certain contractual licensees similar rights as if they were tenants.

30 Whether this is a 'contract' (licence) or a 'tenancy' (lease) is unclear, but even if it were a 'lease' it would not be proprietary. In Gilpin v. Legg (2017), the judge appears to regard Bruton as authority for the creation of a tenancy by estoppel, rather than the more radical solution (non-proprietary tenancy) put forward in the case itself.

a lease will not exist. An example might be where a landowner gives occupation of her house to a student for £100 per week, but reserves a right (subsequently used) to enter at any time and make use of the study. In effect, this is no more than a restatement of the distinction between exclusive *possession* and exclusive *occupation*: the former establishing the legal relationship of landlord and tenant; the latter describing a factual situation, devoid of proprietary effect. However, the ability of a landowner to reserve a right to himself that effectively destroys the grant of exclusive possession is controversial because it appears to offer landowners a way out of the rigours of *Street v. Mountford* (1985). For that reason, it must constitute a rare exception to the *Street ratio*, and the 'pretence' rule (discussed below) may invalidate most attempts by landowners to achieve such an outcome. In any event, this 'exception' would not be applicable if the right reserved by the landowner were consistent with the grant of a lease. For example, a landowner may reserve the right to enter the premises, in order to inspect and carry out repairs, but such a right actually confirms the grant of a tenancy rather than denies it, for this is just the sort of right a landlord would expect to have under a lease.

Finally, the cases also establish that any relaxation of the strictness of the *Street v. Mountford* analysis is possible only where the parties *genuinely* require the occupier not to have exclusive possession. Consequently, attempts by the landlord (or tenant)[31] to deny the grant of exclusive possession are subject to the court's powers to ignore 'pretences' (or 'sham devices'). According to *Antoniades v. Villiers* (1990), a 'pretence' exists where a clause in an agreement for the occupation of land is inserted into that agreement deliberately in order to avoid the creation of the lease that would otherwise arise and where *either* party does not intend to rely in practice on the clause. A pretence may be established from an examination of the surrounding circumstances of the case and may be confirmed by the parties' subsequent practice. For example, in *Antoniades*, an unmarried couple each signed a separate agreement for the occupation of a single-bedroom flat that was clearly going to be their joint home. These agreements gave the landowner certain rights over the property that were unlikely to be enjoyed in practice – for example, the right to nominate another occupier. This was an attempt by the landowner to avoid the grant of a tenancy by artificially destroying the 'four unities' necessary to give the couple a joint tenancy of the leasehold estate and by reserving to himself some power over the property that might be thought to destroy exclusive possession. This was held to be a pretence, as the objectionable clauses had no merit or purpose other than to prevent the occupiers from obtaining a lease. Hence, the clauses were struck out and the agreements given effect without the offending clause – the couple held a joint lease.

6.2.2   A term certain

Although the requirement of 'a term certain' has been the subject of criticism by the Supreme Court – see *Berrisford v. Mexfield* (2011) – it remains an essential ingredient for a lease: the exclusive possession must be granted for a defined and certain period of time. This means not only that the lease must start at a clearly defined moment, but also that the length of the term granted must be certain: for example, one year, one month, one week, one hour. At the commencement of the lease, it must be possible to define exactly the maximum duration of the lease, even if it is possible to end the lease at some time

---

31 For example, where there is a dispute over the rent of property.

before this. So, a lease for 3,000 years is perfectly valid, even if the lease contains 'break clauses' entitling the landlord and tenant to terminate the lease by notice on, say, every tenth anniversary. Any lease, or rather any intended lease, that fails to satisfy this condition is necessarily void, because it does not amount to a 'term certain'. Of course, in the great majority of cases, this condition is easily satisfied because the landlord and tenant will state clearly the duration of the lease. However, problems can arise where the term of the lease is set by reference to some other criteria, such as the happening of an uncertain event. For example, in *Lace* v. *Chantler* (1944), an alleged lease for the duration of the Second World War was held void as being of uncertain maximum duration and in *Prudential Assurance* v. *London Residuary Body* (1992), the House of Lords reaffirmed the rule when deciding that an agreement giving the occupier the land until the land was required for road widening could not amount to a lease in law.

However, stating the principle in these terms reveals only half of the picture. In *Berrisford* v. *Mexfield* (2011), the Supreme Court recognised the validity of criticisms of the 'term certain' rule[32] but decided that it could not be dispensed with in the light of its affirmation in *Prudential*. Leases had to be granted for a term certain. Nevertheless, the Supreme Court did clarify certain aspects of the rule. In particular, the court decided that if the uncertain term was granted to an individual (but not a company), an old common law rule applied which meant that the agreement could be treated as a lease for life, terminable if the uncertain event occurred – *Berrisford* v. *Mexfield*. Further, given that 'leases for life' granted at a rent or for a premium are, by statute (section 149(6) of the LPA 1925), converted to leases for 90 years, terminable by death (if earlier), then the apparently uncertain agreement could be saved. So, by a double step – conversion of an uncertain period to a lease for life by common law and then conversion of the lease for life to a 90-year term by statute – apparently uncertain terms granted to individuals are rendered certain. The resulting lease for 90 years may still be terminated by the earlier death of the tenant (because it is based on a lease for life) or indeed in accordance with the terms of the agreement, for example non-payment of rent.[33] Clearly, this is a subtle piece of reasoning for it maintains the rule in *Prudential*, while at the same time rescuing otherwise uncertain agreements. However, in the later High Court case of *Southward Housing Co-operative* v. *Walker* (2015), Hildyard J decided that the *Mexfield* approach could apply only where the parties originally intended a lease for life, not simply where an uncertain term had been created for an individual. So, in that case, absent such an intention, the uncertain term was not saved and did not amount to a lease. Similarly, in *Gilpin* v. *Legg* (2017), the trial judge questioned whether the cases cited by the Supreme Court in *Mexfield* did indeed justify concluding that an uncertain term could be interpreted as a lease for life. In any event, the *Southward* approach represents an important qualification to the *Mexfield* approach, although it is not entirely clear that this is what the Supreme Court meant. Its effect will be that relatively few uncertain terms will now be saved, and the impact of *Mexfield* will be much reduced, because it will be unusual for the parties to have intended a lease for life. What they intended, one suspects, was a lease for the uncertain term because they could have created a lease for life perfectly deliberately! Finally,

---

32 For example, a lease until the expiry of the war may be void, but a lease for 1,000 years terminable by either party when the war ends would be valid.

33 See *Sterling* v. *Cyron Housing Co-operative* (2013) applying *Berrisford* and requiring the landlord to establish that the lease had been terminated in accordance with its terms, not merely that it was uncertain.

for the avoidance of doubt, we should note that *Mexfield* has done nothing to change the need for proper formalities for the creation of leases – *Hardy v. Haselden* (2011). This is discussed below, but the point is that *Mexfield* deals with the common law rule of certainty of term and does not remove the need for proper formalities such as deeds or written instruments for those agreements which otherwise meet the certainty rule.

6.2.3   Periodic tenancies

In a great many cases concerning residential property, a tenant may occupy premises and pay a regular sum in rent to the landlord, but there may not be an express agreement regulating the occupation. In these circumstances, a tenancy of a certain duration will be implied from the facts. Thus, if money is paid weekly in respect of a week's possession, a *periodic tenancy* of one week will be implied. Likewise, if rent is paid with reference to a monthly or quarterly period, a monthly or quarterly periodic tenancy will result. Obviously, if a further weekly, monthly or quarterly payment is made, a lease will arise for a further period. In this sense, the arrangement can continue indefinitely even though the *total* period of the tenant's possession will not be known in advance. However, although this appears to give rise to a lease of uncertain duration, in fact there is a succession of periodic tenancies, all of which are of a certain term: that is, one week after one week, or one month after one month, and so on.[34] Each new period is, in essence, a new lease. The validity of periodic tenancies was confirmed by *Prudential*, with the court explaining that there is a clear conceptual distinction between a succession of certain periods with simple uncertainty about how many more periods there will be (a periodic tenancy), and a 'term' that, from its outset, is defined by reference to uncertainty (e.g. a tenancy 'until the good weather ends'). As discussed below, because the great majority of periodic tenancies are for individual periods of three years or less (e.g. a month), they will be legal interests.[35]

6.2.4   Statutory provisions concerning certain terms

There are a number of statutory provisions that are related to the principle of 'term certain'. The general effect of these is to convert uncertain periods into certain terms or to invalidate certain types of clearly uncertain arrangements.

1   As noted above, a lease for the duration of the life of any person (whether granted expressly or arising by implication under *Mexfield*), or which is due to end with expiry of any life, or on the marriage of the lessee (all being uncertain terms), which is granted for a rent or a premium, is converted into a lease for 90 years, subject to determination (i.e. ending) if the death or marriage occurs before this (section 149(6) of the LPA 1925). So, a lease of a cottage granted to me by my parents 'until I marry', for £80 per week, or for an initial capital sum of, say, £85,000 (a premium), will take effect as a lease for a certain period of 90 years, determinable when (if) I marry.

---

34 Thus, a monthly periodic tenant who has been in occupation for, say, ten years has had 120 separate monthly tenancies.

35 For example, as a matter of practice, rent is not usually calculated by reference to a period any longer than a quarter, and yearly periodic tenancies are in practice the longest periodic tenancies under this principle.

2   A lease that is perpetually renewable is converted into a lease for 2,000 years (Schedule 15, section 145 of the LPA 1922). So, a lease for 40 years, containing a clause whereby the tenant has the right to renew the lease for a further 40 years at the expiry of *every* period, is perpetually renewable and will take effect as a lease for 2,000 years. This, of course, is tantamount to the grant of a freehold. Note, however, that a lease for 40 years that is renewable only for one further period of 40 years is not perpetually renewable and takes effect in the normal way.

3   A lease that is intended to start more than 21 years after the instrument that creates it is void (section 149(3) of the LPA 1925). So, if Z, by contract with X dated 1 January 2018, attempts to grant a lease of land to start after 1 January 2040, the intended lease is void. The commencement of the lease is postponed for longer than the law allows.

6.2.5   Rent

One of the main motives for the letting of property is the desire to generate income through the payment of rent. Even where the tenant pays a large premium or fine (a capital sum) at the start of the lease, there is usually provision for a 'ground rent' payable annually.[36] Indeed, as noted above, Lord Templeman, in *Street* v. *Mountford* (1985), included 'rent' as part of the definition of a tenancy. However, strictly speaking, the existence of a lease does not depend on a provision for the payment of rent. Section 205(1)(xxvii) of the LPA 1925 provides that a term of years means a 'term of years ... whether or not at a rent'. As it happens, certain types of lease (such as those falling within the Rent Acts and early Housing Acts) must be supported by rent in order to qualify for statutory protection and this is why Lord Templeman in *Street* refers so explicitly to 'rent' as part of the defini-tion of a tenancy.[37] However, it is clear that, as a matter of law, a lease may exist where there is no rent payable.[38] Of course, in reality, the existence of an obligation to pay rent as an adjunct to a lease is so likely that, in the absence of an express promise by the tenant or an express exclusion of rent, a covenant by the tenant to pay rent will be readily implied from the words of a deed. Moreover, although the landlord and tenant can *deliber-ately* exclude the rent obligation and still create a lease, an explicit exclusion of rent (or other clear evidence that rent is not to be paid) may suggest that the parties did not intend to create a lease at all. Necessarily, this will depend on the peculiar facts of each case, but the absence of a rent obligation, if not counteracted by the existence of any of the other hallmarks of a lease (e.g. a repairing obligation), can indicate that no landlord and tenant relationship was intended. In such cases, the occupier may have a mere licence. Note, however, that, as discussed above, the fact that the parties choose to describe the periodic payment as an 'occupation fee', a 'licence fee' or some such similar phrase does not prevent it amounting to 'rent' in law. Again, it is a matter of substance, not form.

---

36 There is likely also to be an annual service charge to meet the cost of running and maintaining any common parts of the building, such as lifts, stairways and shared paths.

37 It was a Rent Act case.

38 See the discussion in *Ashburn Anstalt* v. *Arnold* (1989), overturned on other grounds. Note also that, if rent is payable, its non-payment does *not* mean there is no tenancy. It means, simply, that the tenant is in arrears of rent and may be subject to remedies by the landlord for non-payment.

Finally, it is a common misconception that rent has to be in monetary form. It can be in goods or services, or payable in kind. The only requirement is that the amount of rent must be capable of being rendered certain. Thus, in *Bostock* v. *Bryant* (1990), the obligation to pay fluctuating utility bills (gas, electricity, etc.) could not be regarded as rent, being an ever-changing sum. On the other hand, an annual rent of 'a peppercorn' or 'five tons of flour' is perfectly acceptable.

6.3 The Creation of Legal and Equitable Leases

The existence of a 'term certain', the granting of exclusive possession and (subject to the reservations just discussed) the payment of rent, are the hallmarks of a tenancy. Of course, in most cases, the parties will have agreed a web of other rights and obligations extending beyond acceptance of this bare legal framework: for example, the lease may contain covenants to repair, options to renew the lease, obligations relating to the use of the premises, promises not to part with possession or assign without consent and the like. Generally, the more complicated or extensive these other obligations, the more likely it is that the 'lease' itself will be embodied in a formal document, such as a deed or written instrument. Moreover, while there are very few legal rules concerning the precise words or phrases that must be used to create a valid lease or the obligations therein (although certain 'precedents' or standard wordings have been developed and HM Land Registry requires certain standard clauses for registered leases),[39] there are a number of legal formalities that must be observed before the arrangement agreed by the parties will be enforced as a lease by the courts. These 'formality' requirements are required by statute. They relate to the manner in which a lease may be created, rather than to what a lease must contain. In essence, they are the embodiment of a legislative policy that seeks certainty about dealings with land. So, these statutory rules determine whether an arrangement between owner and occupier that otherwise satisfies the inherent requirements of a lease can nevertheless be enforced as a lease and, if it can, whether the lease so created is legal or equitable.

6.3.1 Introductory points

A lease is a legally binding agreement between landlord and tenant. As such, the creation of a lease may amount to both a contract between them *and* the creation of a proprietary right that exists beyond the mere contract. It can give rise to contractual remedies (such as an action for damages), but it can affect 'third parties' to whom the reversion or lease is assigned.[40] Furthermore, in some cases, the creation of a lease will occur in two stages: the conclusion of a 'contract to grant a lease' between prospective landlord and tenant, and the later execution of the contract by the 'grant' of the lease by deed. This is important in

---

39 The prescribed clauses relate to such matters as identification of the parties, commencement and identification of the land and are mandatory for certain registrable leases. They are designed to aid the process of registration: see *HM Land Registry Practice Guide No. 64*, 24 June 2015.

40 With the exception of '*Bruton* tenancies'.

understanding how equitable leases are created. However, even where a lease is created without first concluding a separate contract to grant it (e.g. the parties simply execute a deed or agree to a written lease),[41] the lease itself will always amount to a contract between them. So, 'the lease as a contract' refers either to an aspect of the landlord and tenant relationship (its contractual aspect) or to the manner in which the lease was created originally.

6.3.2   Legal leases: creation

The creation of legal leases depends on rules laid down by statute and, as with all legal rights, there is an emphasis on formality.

1   Leases for three years or less that give the tenant an immediate right to possession of the land without the payment of an initial capital sum (i.e. a premium), at the best rent, will be legal whether created orally, by written contract or by deed (sections 52(2)(d) and 54(2) of the LPA 1925). Into this category will come many residential or domestic leases, and, significantly, most 'periodic tenancies' created in the way described in section 6.2.3 above. This is simply because the 'period' for which rent is paid and accepted will usually be three years or less (e.g. a week, month, quarter, year).

2   Leases for more than three years, and those of three years or less that do not fall within point 1 above,[42] are required to be made by deed to have any prospect of taking effect as a legal estate (section 52(1) of the LPA 1925). A 'deed' is a more formal written document and, prior to the LP(MP)A 1989, such a document had to be 'signed, sealed and delivered' before it could be regarded as 'a deed'. Now, by virtue of section 1 of the 1989 Act, a document is a deed if it declares itself to be such (e.g. it says 'this is a deed made between X and Y'), it is signed as a deed and is witnessed as a deed by one other person. Clearly, then, the execution of a deed remains a relatively formal process and most leases by deed are drawn up by solicitors or licensed conveyancers.

3   Currently, if the lease is granted by deed out of *registered land* (i.e. where the freehold or superior leasehold is a registered title) and it is for a term *over* seven years, it must also be registered as a title at HM Land Registry (section 27(2) of the LRA 2002). This means it must be entered for registration with its own title number at HM Land Registry and so become substantively registered in its own right. Failure to so register means that the lease takes effect only as an equitable estate (section 27(1) of the LRA 2002).[43] It should be remembered, however, that the very great majority of these long legal leases will have been negotiated and executed with professional advice and so there is every likelihood that they will be appropriately registered. Certain other special shorter-term leases also require registration as titles[44] and it is anticipated that, in due course, this 'registration trigger' will shorten to encompass leases for over

---

41   The creation of leases without first concluding a contract is becoming much more common.

42   For example, where a premium – an initial capital payment – is charged.

43   See *Stodday Land Ltd* v. *Pye* (2016) and *Sackville UK Property* v. *Robertson Taylor* (2018). For an example of how this worked under the LRA 1925, see *Brown and Root* v. *Sun Alliance* (1995).

44   Section 27(2), including timeshare leases, special Housing Act leases and leases where possession is postponed for more than three months after the lease is granted.

three years, thus ensuring that the need for a deed is synonymous with the need for registration.[45] If the legal lease falls outside the registration triggers (i.e. is a normal lease of seven years or less), it takes effect as a legal estate without title registration (assuming a deed where required) and, in fact, qualifies as an unregistered interest which overrides under Schedule 3, paragraph 1 of the LRA 2002.

4   Currently, if the lease is granted by deed out of *unregistered land* (i.e. where the freehold or superior leasehold is not a registered title) and it is for a term of *over* seven years, it must also be registered as a title at HM Land Registry (section 4(1) of the LRA 2002). The grant of such a lease is a trigger for first registration of title of the leasehold.[46] Failure to so register means that the lease takes effect only as an equitable estate (section 7 of the LRA 2002). Certain other special shorter-term leases also require such registration[47] and, once again, it is anticipated that, in due course, this 'registration trigger' will shorten to encompass leases for over three years.

5   If the lease is to take effect in land of unregistered title and the lease is outside the first registration trigger (i.e. when it is for seven years or less), the grant by deed (assuming the period is over three years etc.) is all that is needed to convey the legal leasehold estate to the tenant from the date specified in the deed. Moreover, following the general rule in *unregistered* land that 'legal rights bind the whole world', a legal lease will automatically bind any subsequent purchaser or transferee of the land out of which it is created (i.e. of the landlord's reversion) and, when the purchaser of the reversion applies for compulsory first registration of his title, the lease will override under Schedule 1, paragraph 1 of the LRA 2002.[48]

6   In the future, it is possible that the grant of certain leases will be made subject to compulsory e-conveyancing. This aspect of the LRA 2002 is not yet active, but it would mean that the grant of a qualifying lease (i.e. one specified in the Land Registration Rules) would be required to be made by an electronic entry on the register (section 93 of the LRA 2002). Failure to electronically create and register the lease (for these will be synonymous) will mean that the purported lease is without effect. It is not yet clear when this provision will become active, if at all.

6.3.3   Legal leases and third parties

As far as the effect of legal leases on third parties in *registered* land is concerned (i.e. purchasers and other transferees of the reversion), the current position is governed by the specific provisions of the LRA 2002. First, legal leases that are substantively registered as titles in their own right under the LRA 2002[49] clearly will bind a transferee of the

---

45 As yet, there is no indication of when this will be.

46 But not necessarily of the superior unregistered freehold or leasehold out of which it is granted.

47 See section 4 of the LRA 2002 – timeshare leases, special Housing Act leases and leases where possession is postponed for more than three months after the lease is granted.

48 At first registration of the superior title, the lease may also be entered against that title by means of a notice. This would, of course, supersede its protection as an overriding interest.

49 This includes leases registered as titles in their own right under the LRA 1925 where the registration trigger was for leases granted for more than 21 years, and also existing legal leases that were assigned when there were more than 21 years left to run.

reversion.[50] In the very unlikely event that a registrable lease has not actually been registered, it will take effect as an equitable lease only and its position in respect of third
parties is governed by the principles applicable to equitable leases. Second, legal leases
for seven years or less[51] (with only minor exceptions) are interests which override within
paragraphs 1 of Schedules 1 and 3 of the LRA 2002.[52] Consequently, they bind subsequent purchasers and transferees of the reversion automatically under sections 28 and
29 of the LRA 2002.

In respect of legal leases granted out of *unregistered* land that do not trigger compulsory
first registration of the lease (i.e. generally when the lease is for seven years or less), the
situation is governed by the long-established rules of unregistered conveyancing.[53] Thus,
'legal rights bind the world' and the lease is effective against any transferee of the reversion. Of course, when the reversion is transferred, the reversion will become subject to
first registration and thereafter the legal lease will take effect as an interest which overrides under Schedule 1, paragraph 1 of the LRA 2002.[54]

6.3.4   Equitable leases: creation

While it is true that the LP(MP)A 1989 simplified the requirements for the execution of a
deed, nevertheless some leases are created in the absence of a deed. The majority of these
are for three years or less and qualify as legal interests under the 'short lease exception' discussed above. In practice, it is unusual for a lease of over three years' duration to be created
without the use of a deed – primarily because the parties routinely use lawyers who
proceed to execute the lease by deed in a professional manner. However, there will be situations in which the parties do not use a deed to create a lease longer than three years. For
example, if a written contract is used, the parties may be content to rely on it rather than
execute a deed, or the parties (less commonly) may not use property professionals and so
not realise that a deed is required at all. In such cases – that is, where there is an intended
lease of over three years not executed by deed – if there is a written contract (or a written
record of an agreement that can be treated as if it were a contract), the parties may be taken
to have created an equitable lease. In simple terms, an equitable lease arises from an
enforceable contract between landlord and tenant to grant a lease, but where no grant of a
lease by deed has in fact occurred. There are a number of distinct steps in this process.

1   The contract between prospective landlord and tenant must be enforceable: that is,
     since 27 September 1989, the contract must be in writing, containing all of the
     terms and signed by both parties (section 2 of the LPA 1989, replacing section 40 of
     the LPA 1925).[55] In this connection, 'written contract' means either a written

---

50 Sections 28, 29 and 30 of the LRA 2002.

51 Save those special short-term legal leases that must be registered as titles.

52 For an example under the LRA 1925, see *City Permanent Building Society* v. *Miller* (1952). Such leases, if granted for
    more than three years, may voluntarily be entered on the register by means of a Notice against the registered title
    out of which they are granted, but it is not critical to do so.

53 Such situations will become increasingly rare. Even now, they are not common.

54 Or it may be entered on the register by means of a Notice.

55 Before 27 September 1989, the contract was enforceable even if oral, so long as it could be supported by part
    performance (see the now-repealed section 40 of the LPA 1925).

document clearly expressed to be a contract or a written record of agreement that the law is prepared to treat as a contract. A good example of the latter is where A and B set down in writing (and sign) the terms on which A will let her house to B. A and B may not intend to take any further steps to create the lease, perhaps believing they have done all that is necessary, but their written agreement will be treated as a 'written contract to grant a lease', so as to raise the possibility of an equitable lease.

2   The remedy of specific performance must be available, should either party to the contract actually wish to enforce the contract and compel the grant of a legal lease (*Coatsworth* v. *Johnson* (1886)). Specific performance will be available if the person seeking to enforce the contract has given valuable consideration (e.g. rent), if damages would be an inadequate remedy (as they nearly always are with contracts for land) and if the person seeking to enforce the contract comes to equity with 'clean hands'.[56] If all of these conditions are fulfilled – which will be true in most cases – a court of equity will *treat* the enforceable (but unenforced) contract to grant the legal lease as having created an equitable lease between the parties on the same terms as the potential (but ungranted) legal lease (*Walsh* v. *Lonsdale* (1882)).[57]

The contract/lease analysis discussed above is the usual way in which an equitable lease comes into existence: it arises out of a written, enforceable contract. However, it is also possible for an equitable lease to arise out of the operation of the doctrine of proprietary estoppel. Proprietary estoppel leases will arise where the 'landlord' has promised some right in over land to the 'tenant' orally or by conduct, and this is relied on by the prospective tenant to his detriment. The court may then 'satisfy' the estoppel by giving the promisee a tenancy, albeit an equitable one that has arisen out of the informal dealings between the parties.[58] Such a situation will be rare,[59] and it is discussed in more detail in Chapter 10. For now, the important point is that proprietary estoppel may result in the generation of an equitable lease out of a purely oral or otherwise non-binding agreement. Similarly, if a party to an agreement seeks to use section 2 of the 1989 Act as a vehicle for unconscionable conduct – for example, by pleading that the contract is not in writing and so not valid when that very person had assured the other party that the contract need not be written – the agreed lease might be enforceable under a constructive trust or proprietary estoppel (*Yaxley* v. *Gotts* (1999)).[60]

It will be appreciated from the above that the circumstances in which an equitable tenancy can arise can be distinguished from those concerning the creation of a legal lease by the *relative* informality of the former. However, in one set of circumstances, this is not true: this is the creation of a legal periodic tenancy where the 'period' is three years or less, as these may be 'legal' whether created by deed, in writing or orally. Consequently, it can happen that the same set of facts can presumptively give rise to either an equitable

---

56 Specific performance is an equitable remedy, and so may be denied if the claimant has behaved unconscionably or otherwise inequitably.

57 Of course, there is nothing to stop one of the parties going ahead actually to compel the grant of the legal lease.

58 See generally *Taylor Fashions* v. *Liverpool Victoria Trustees* (1982) and Chapter 10. For an estoppel lease, see *Lloyd* v. *Dugdale* (2001).

59 Usually, if the court is minded to award the claimant a lease as a means of satisfying the estoppel, it will order the landowner formally to grant a lease by deed.

60 The extent to which this is different from a claim in estoppel is a matter of debate: see Chapter 10.

tenancy or a shorter, legal periodic tenancy. For example, in those cases in which the equitable tenancy has sprung from a written contract (or a document taken to be a written contract), the tenant may well have entered the premises and be paying rent to the landlord. It is easy to see that this could be taken to have given rise to the creation of a periodic tenancy in favour of the occupier because of the payment and acceptance of rent. This periodic tenancy will usually be legal, as the period for which rent is paid and accepted will be three years or less. Potentially, then, there is a conflict between the equitable lease arising from the enforceable written contract (which will be of the same duration as the original intended lease), and the implied short-term, legal periodic tenancy. According to *Walsh* v. *Lonsdale* (1882), the equitable lease will prevail, not least because it will contain all of the terms originally found in the contract between the parties and is likely to be of longer certain duration. Of course, if the equitable lease does not arise (e.g. because of a failure to conclude an enforceable contract, or where the contract is not specifically enforceable), the implied legal periodic tenancy can take effect to provide some comfort for the tenant.

6.3.5   Equitable leases and third parties

The above principles concerning the creation of equitable leases apply whether the land is registered or unregistered. However, bearing in mind that one of the main purposes of the 1925 and 2002 reforms was to bring clarity to dealings with equitable interests in land, it is not surprising that the effect of an equitable lease on a third party (i.e. a transferee or purchaser of the reversion from the current landlord) differs according to whether title has been registered or remains unregistered.

6.3.5.1   *In registered land*

Equitable leases are capable of being entered on the register of title of the land over which they take effect. This would be through a Notice.[61] If registered, they are protected by such registration and are effective against later transferees of the reversion (sections 28 and 29 of the LRA 2002). However, even if not registered in this way (and many will not be), most equitable leases will take effect as an interest which overrides a transferee and thus be binding on the new landlord. This is because the equitable tenant will almost certainly be a person in actual occupation within the meaning of Schedule 3, paragraph 2 of the LRA 2002. Here, then, is virtually automatic protection for the equitable tenant in registered land, for the tenant need do nothing – except remain in occupation – to be secure.[62]

6.3.5.2   *In unregistered land*

Equitable leases that arise from enforceable contracts are registrable as Class C(iv) Land Charges ('estate contracts'). Consequently, they must be registered against the appropriate name of the estate owner (i.e. the freeholder or superior leaseholder) in order to

---

61 Usually an Agreed Notice because, after all, the landlord has granted the lease!

62 A lease which overrides may be entered on the register and protected by means of a Notice at a later date, usually
    if it is disclosed when the superior title is transferred, section 71 LRA 2002.

bind a purchaser of a legal estate in the land. Failure to register means that the equitable lease is void against such a purchaser.[63] This can mean the ejection of the equitable tenant if the superior interest is sold (*Hollington Bros* v. *Rhodes* (1951)). However, even an unregistered equitable lease is binding against a non-purchaser (e.g. an adverse possessor, devisee under a will, recipient of a gift), or against someone who purchases only an equitable interest. Importantly, these rules mean that there is no protection for an equitable tenant in unregistered land *merely* because they occupy the land. This should be contrasted with the position in registered land. As a further complication, equitable leases arising from proprietary estoppel (which are rare) may not be registrable as Land Charges at all (see *Ives* v. *High* (1967)) and thus would bind a subsequent transferee of the reversion through the equitable doctrine of notice.[64]

6.3.6   The differences between legal and equitable leases

As noted above, legal and equitable leases are created in different ways, with legal leases generally requiring more formality and many also requiring substantive registration as titles. In a similar vein, the existence of an equitable lease depends on the availability of the remedy of specific performance of the enforceable contract from which it springs.[65] The following further points of difference should also be noted.

First, equitable leases *appear* vulnerable to a sale of the freehold or leasehold estate out of which they are created. So, it *is possible* that a purchaser of the land may not be bound by an existing equitable lease according to the rules of registered and unregistered conveyancing. However, as noted above, the problem is likely to be more acute in unregistered land for which there is no protection per se for the rights of persons in actual occupation. Equitable tenants in registered land need hardly fear this in practice because they are likely to have an interest which overrides.[66] Legal leases do not suffer from this problem and are fully protected in registered and in unregistered land.

Second, as we shall see below, the ability of covenants in leases granted before 1 January 1996 to 'run' to purchasers of the tenant's interest (the lease) depends on the existence of 'privity of estate' between the claimant and defendant. As a general principle, 'privity of estate' exists between the current landlord and the current tenant of a *legal* lease only. Thus, the lack of privity of estate in equitable leases makes it difficult for all leasehold covenants to run to purchasers of the lease. However, the position is different for equitable leases granted on or after 1 January 1996 because of the LTCA 1995.

Third, although most leases contain express covenants – being promises to do or not do certain things by the landlord and tenant – there are situations when the lease is silent and covenants are implied, either as a matter of law or because they are 'usual'. It is arguable that it is possible to imply a 'right of re-entry'[67] into an equitable lease, but not

---

63 LCA 1972, sections 2 and 4.

64 The position of equitable leases arising by estoppel in unregistered land is unclear, as *Ives* v. *High* concerned an estoppel easement. In any event, given the relative scarcity of unregistered land, such a lease will be a rarity.

65 With the exception of the rare estoppel lease.

66 It is, of course, possible that an equitable tenant might not be in discoverable actual occupation under the LRA 2002 and so be denied an overriding interest, but such a situation will be extremely unusual.

67 Which is necessary for the remedy of forfeiture and on which see below, section 6.7.5.

a legal one. However, there is a degree of uncertainty around this as the issues have not been fully tested.[68]

Fourth, as demonstrated in Chapter 7, easements may be created by the operation of section 62 of the LPA 1925 on the occasion of a conveyance by deed of an estate in the land, either freehold or leasehold. In other words, this section applies only to legal leases, so a tenant under an equitable lease cannot claim the benefit of any potential section 62 easements. They may, however, claim the benefit of the rule in *Wheeldon* v. *Burrows* which applies to both legal and equitable leases.

Finally, when the tenant under an equitable lease first enters in to the lease, he is 'only' a purchaser for value of an *equitable* estate in the land. Consequently, the tenant is not a purchaser of a legal estate for the purposes of unregistered land, nor is he treated as having made a registrable disposition for the purposes of section 29 of the LRA 2002 in registered land. This means that the equitable tenant cannot avoid being bound by pre-existing property rights even if those rights do not comply with the relevant protective mechanisms of the LCA 1972 (unregistered land) and the LRA 2002 (registered land), respectively.[69]

6.4   Leasehold Covenants

Nearly all leases contain 'covenants' whereby the landlord and tenant promise each other to do, or not to do, certain things in relation to the land and its environment. For example, the landlord may promise to keep the premises in repair and the tenant may promise not to use the premises for any trade or business. Necessarily, these covenants are binding between the original landlord and the original tenant – being contained in a deed or binding contract to which they are party – and they can be enforced by either of them using a normal contractual or proprietary remedy.[70] However, one of the great advantages of the leasehold estate is that these covenants are *capable* of running both to purchasers of the original landlord's reversion and to purchasers of the original tenant's lease. In other words, both the right to sue on the leasehold covenants and the obligation to perform them can be passed on to successors in title of the original parties (see Figure 6.2).

6.4.1   The separate nature of the 'benefit' of a covenant and the 'burden' of a covenant

In order to understand the law of leasehold covenants, it is first necessary to appreciate that the right to sue on a covenant (the benefit) and the obligation to perform or observe a covenant (the burden) must be treated separately. For example, it may well be true for

---

68 See *Chester* v. *Buckingham Travel* (1981).

69 In unregistered land, the equitable tenant is not a purchaser of the legal estate for the purposes of the doctrine of notice and the enforcement of Class C(iv) and Class D land charges. In registered land, they cannot rely on section 29 of the LRA 2002 and so are bound by all pre-existing property rights under section 28 of the LRA 2002.

70 For example, an action on the contract for damages, or under a right of re-entry leading to forfeiture and the termination of the lease.

Figure 6.2

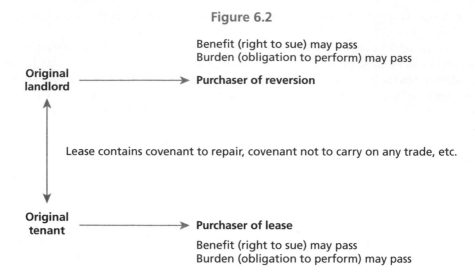

pre-1996 leases (see below for the relevance of the date) that the current tenant under a lease (not being the original tenant) has the benefit of covenants, but is not subject to the burden of them: that is, the tenant has the right to enforce a covenant, but cannot be compelled to observe any obligation the lease imposes. Consequently, in any 'real life' problem, there are always two distinct questions to be answered. First, has the benefit of the particular covenant in issue run to the claimant? Second, is the defendant subject to the burden of it? Only if both of these questions can be answered positively can there be an action 'on the covenant' between claimant and defendant.

6.4.2   Two sets of rules concerning the enforceability of leasehold covenants

The rules relating to the enforceability of leasehold covenants underwent a radical transformation in 1996. As we shall see, the common law/pre-1996 statutory rules were unsatisfactory in many respects and this prompted the Law Commission to propose wholesale reform of the law of leasehold covenants.[71] Although the Law Commission's proposals were not enacted as originally conceived, they did provide the impetus for reform. After much consideration and consultation, a private members' Bill was presented to Parliament and this became the LTCA 1995. This reforming statute applies to all leases – legal and equitable – that are granted on or after 1 January 1996, and it establishes a code for determining the enforceability of leasehold covenants in all such leases. However, for leases granted before 1 January 1996, the old common law/statutory rules still apply, save only that sections 17–20 of the 1995 Act operate retrospectively and apply to them. Consequently, it is necessary to be aware of both the pre-1996 principles and those of the 1995 Act. This is all the more important when we remember that many pre-1996 leases will have been granted for terms in excess of 90 years and will have decades left to run.

---

71 Law Commission Report No. 174.

6.5   Rules for Leases Granted before 1 January 1996

These rules are found in both common law and statute. They are complicated, often inconsistent and may produce injustice. They were ripe for reform.

6.5.1   Liability between the original landlord and original tenant: the general rule

In any action on a leasehold covenant between the *original* landlord and the *original* tenant in a pre-1996 lease, *all* covenants are enforceable.[72] This is simply because the liability of these original parties to the lease is based squarely in contract: that is, the contract between them, which is also the lease. Liability is said to be based on 'privity of contract'. Importantly, as noted, *all* covenants are enforceable, whether or not they relate to the leasehold land or to a personal obligation undertaken by either party. For example, between the original parties, a tenant's covenant to provide the landlord with a free pint of beer (personal) is just as enforceable as a landlord's covenant to repair the premises (proprietary).

6.5.2   The continuing liability of the original tenant throughout the entire term of the lease

The fact that the liability of the original tenant is founded in contract has important consequences. Even though the original tenant may assign (i.e. sell or transfer) his lease to another, he will remain liable on the leasehold covenants in a pre-1996 lease throughout the *entire* term of the lease (*Allied London Investments Ltd v. Hambro Life Assurance Ltd* (1984)). This liability will be enforceable by whosoever has the benefit of the covenants. So, if the current tenant violates any of the covenants (e.g. the covenant to pay rent), the landlord may look to the original tenant to perform the covenant (pay the rent), even though the original tenant may have actually left the land many years ago and had nothing to do with the breach. A typical example is where the original tenant took a 99-year lease in, say, 1950, but the current tenant (say, the fifth assignee) defaults on the rent in 2018. The original tenant remains liable for this rent, despite having parted with possession years before and in ignorance of the identity of all assignees apart from the very first person to whom he assigned. It should come as no surprise that this continuing liability attracted considerable criticism and, as we shall see, it has been abolished by the 1995 Act for leases granted on or after 1 January 1996. For leases granted prior to the Act, the original tenant remains liable throughout the term of the lease, subject only to the following exceptions and mitigating factors.

1   The liability of an original tenant will not continue after an assignment of a perpetually renewable lease.[73] If it were otherwise, the original tenant would forever be liable and there would be no limit or certainty to his obligation.

---

72   'Original' here means the landlord and tenant who were the first parties to the lease, it having been granted between them.

73   Section 145, Schedule 25 of the LPA 1922.

2   The lease between the original landlord and original tenant may stipulate expressly
        that the tenant's liability is to end when the lease is assigned. This is unusual in pre-
        1996 leases, but perfectly possible due to the contractual nature of a lease.[74] It
        depends on the original tenant having a dominant bargaining position. It can occur
        more readily when there is an oversupply of premises for rent, such as during a
        recession in the commercial property market.

3   The original tenant will not be liable for breaches of covenant committed by an
        assignee where the original term of the lease has been statutorily extended under
        the Landlord and Tenant Act 1954 (and, by analogy, under the Housing Act 1988)
        and the breach occurs during the statutory extension (City of London Corp v. Fell
        (1993)). This is because the original tenant's liability is to be construed, as a matter
        of contract, as relating to the period of time as originally agreed, and not to the
        subsequent legislative extension of that term.

4   The original tenant will not be liable if a subsequent assignee of the lease and land-
        lord agree to surrender the old lease and carry out a 'regrant' of the lease on new
        terms. Simply put, the 'original' lease has ended and the original tenant's liability
        with it. In most cases, this surrender and regrant will be explicit, but it can be
        presumed if current landlord and tenant so vary the terms of the 'old' lease that, in
        reality, it ceases to exist. This is a more extreme version of the principle noted
        below, that an original tenant may not be liable if subsequent tenant and landlord
        vary the terms of individual leasehold covenants.[75]

5   If the original tenant is made liable on a covenant through the actual breach of that
        covenant by an assignee, the original tenant under a pre-1996 tenancy may have a
        right to recover any damages or rent paid by them under an indemnity obligation.
        A right to claim an indemnity[76] may be in the form of an express or implied obli-
        gation undertaken by an assignee of the original tenant, and any subsequent
        assignee, to reimburse any monies paid by the original tenant where the actual acts
        of default are attributable to that assignee. An indemnity obligation can take one
        of three forms. First, each assignee in turn may have made an express covenant of
        indemnity with their assignor, promising to indemnify the assignor in respect of
        liabilities arising post-assignment. So, a 'chain' of indemnity covenants may exist,
        stretching from original tenant to current tenant. If, then, the original tenant is
        forced to pay, he may claim an indemnity from his assignee, who may pass that
        liability to their assignee, and so on, until the current (and defaulting) tenant is
        reached. As can be seen, however, a chain of indemnity is only as strong as its
        weakest link and the original tenant may find that the chain is broken before the
        defaulting tenant is reached. Second, in the absence of an express indemnity cove-
        nant, the original tenant may be able to rely on the covenant of indemnity that is
        implied under section 77 of the LPA 1925. However, this covenant may – and often
        is – expressly excluded by the terms of the original lease. Third, the original tenant
        may be able to rely on an action in 'restitution' against the person (i.e. the default-
        ing tenant) whose liability has been discharged by the original tenant but, of

---

74 As explained, in the context of the landlord's position, in London Diocesan Fund v. Avonridge Property Company Ltd (2005).

75 Friends Provident Life Office v. British Railways Board (1996).

76 Effectively, recovery of sums paid.

course, only to the extent that the defaulter was actually liable.[77] This will occur where it can be shown that the defaulting tenant has been unjustly enriched at the expense of the original tenant and so will be required to reverse the unjust enrichment. It has been held that an express exclusion of the section 77 indemnity covenant does not also exclude the implied indemnity available under the rule in *Moule v. Garrett* (1872).[78]

6   The original tenant will not be liable for any *increased* rent resulting from a variation of the terms of the lease. In the case of variations effected on or after 1 January 1996, section 18 of the LTCA 1995 applies retrospectively and it means that the original tenant's liability for rent cannot be increased by any variation to the lease after it (the lease) has been assigned. Note, however, that the original tenant escapes liability only for the *increased* rent attributable to the variation. Liability remains for the originally agreed rent. Further, section 18 does not affect the operation of rent review clauses. So, if a tenant's rent is increased because of the effect of a rent review clause that was itself a term of the original lease (e.g. a clause that says the rent may be adjusted every five years in line with inflation), the original tenant is liable for this increased rent if the current tenant defaults because this increase is contemplated by the lease itself. It does not matter that the increased rent may be far in excess of what the original tenant paid when he actually occupied the premises because the increase has not been caused by a variation to the terms of the lease, but by the lease itself. A 'variation' (i.e. a change in rent for which the original tenant is not liable under section 18) is where the current tenant and current landlord effectively alter the terms of the lease between themselves, and it is quite right that the original tenant should not be liable for any increased rent flowing from this later agreement to which he is not a party. Indeed, such is the common sense embodied in section 18 that the court in *Friends Provident Life Office* v. *British Railways Board* (1996) had already decided, prior to the entry into force of the LTCA 1995, that privity of contract meant privity to the original contract, and not some later variation of it.[79] As it turns out, then, section 18 of the LTCA 1995 was not actually needed. This means that no original tenant will be liable for an increased rent due to a variation, even if that variation occurred before 1 January 1996 and the entry into force of the LTCA 1995.

7   Under section 17 of the 1995 Act, although a pre-1996 original tenant's liability continues throughout the term of the lease, a landlord may enforce a liability against this tenant for a 'fixed charge' – for example, rent, a service charge or liquidated damages for breach of covenant[80] – only by serving a statutory notice (a 'problem notice') within six months of the charge becoming due. This ensures that the original tenant is warned early of the potential liability and, in effect, ensures that only a maximum of six months' charge (i.e. rent, etc.) can be claimed without

---

77 *Moule* v. *Garrett* (1872). The action was formerly said to arise in 'quasi-contract' but English law's recognition of a general principle of restitution has made this fiction unnecessary.

78 *Re Healing Research Trustee Co* (1992).

79 See also *Beegas Nominees Ltd* v. *BHP Petroleum Ltd* (1998).

80 But not for unliquidated damages for breach of covenant or specific performance of other covenants (*RVB Investments* v. *Bibby* (2013)).

the tenant being able to take action to minimise his liability. Failure to serve a notice relieves the original tenant of all liability for that breach of covenant.[81] Moreover, as noted immediately below, the payment by an original tenant of a 'fixed charge' in consequence of receiving a problem notice gives the original tenant certain additional rights in relation to the land that he may utilise in an attempt to recover the sum paid.

8   If an original tenant is served with a problem notice under section 17 of the LTCA 1995 and pays the charge in full (e.g. the rent owed), the original tenant becomes entitled to the grant of a lease of the property (called an 'overriding lease') (section 19 of the LTCA 1995). This effectively inserts the original tenant back into possession of the property as 'tenant' of the current landlord, but as 'landlord' of the defaulting tenant.[82] The advantage of this is that it enables the original tenant – now back in possession – to take action against the current tenant, perhaps by forfeiting (terminating) his lease and thereby to use the land to meet the rental liability. He becomes the tenant of the current landlord but also the landlord of the defaulting tenant. Consequently, the original tenant who takes an overriding lease[83] can then pursue action against the defaulting tenant to recover the monies they have paid: for example, suing for the rent or forfeiting the lease and then assigning it for value to another person. This is the third provision of the 1995 Act that applies to pre-1996 tenancies. The tenant called on to pay the 'fixed charge' may opt for an overriding lease within 12 months of making the payment, and this overriding lease itself is either a pre-1996 or a post-1996 tenancy, depending on the nature of the lease that it overrides.[84] It contains the same covenants as the overridden lease, except covenants 'expressed to be personal'. This right to call for an overriding lease against a landlord who claims payment of the fixed charge is itself an interest capable of protection by means of a Notice against a registered title under the LRA 2002 and as a Class C(iv) land charge in unregistered land.[85] Finally, for completeness, we should remind ourselves that the problem notice/overriding lease system applies only when the original tenant is liable for a 'fixed charge'. So, the original tenant's liability under other covenants, such as the covenant to repair, remains unaltered unless and until that liability is crystallised by a liquidated damages clause.[86]

We should also note, for completeness, that (unlike the position of the original landlord) the original tenant who assigns the lease does not automatically lose the right to sue for breaches of covenant occurring *before* assignment. This tenant may deliberately assign the right to sue for such breaches when he assigns the lease, but it is a matter of choice.

---

81 If, however, the current tenant fails to pay rent in the future, the original tenant's liability arises for that rent and the landlord has six months from that liability arising to serve a problem notice.

82 It is as if the original tenant has created a subtenancy for the defaulting tenant.

83 Despite the similarity of name, this has nothing to do with 'overriding interests' under the LRA 2002.

84 Note, as we shall see, that the same scheme applies where the landlord seeks to enforce a liability for a fixed charge against an 'AGA tenant': see section 6.6.2 below.

85 Sections 19 and 20 of the LTCA 1995.

86 A clause fixing the amount of damages in advance of a breach and triggering the 'fixed charge' procedure.

6.5.3   The continuing rights and obligations of the original landlord throughout the term of the lease

As with the original tenant, as a matter of principle the original landlord remains liable on all of the leasehold covenants throughout the term of the lease, even after assignment of the reversion – *Stuart v. Joy* (1904) – and even to assignees of the tenant if they have the right to enforce the covenants (*Celsteel v. Alton* (No. 2) (1987)).[87] However, the original landlord may well have specified in the lease that his liability is to end on assignment and this contractual limitation is effective to prevent continuing landlord liability.[88] In similar fashion, as a matter of principle, the ability of the original landlord under a pre-1996 lease to sue for breaches of covenant should remain for the full duration of the lease. However, if and when the landlord assigns the reversion, he will, in effect, pass the benefit of covenants (the right to sue) to the assignee. This is the effect of section 141(1) of the LPA 1925 for pre-1996 leases because the section operates to transfer the benefit of all proprietary leasehold covenants to the assignee and, following *Re King* (1963), this means that the original landlord's right to sue passes to the assignee even if that right existed in respect of a breach of covenant occurring before assignment. So, if, in 1989, L has the right to sue T for (say) non-payment of rent, an assignment of the lease by L to L1 in 1990 will pass not only L's right to sue on the benefit of leasehold covenants from thenceforward, but also L's accrued right to sue T for the rent owed in 1989. If L wishes to retain this right, it will have to be reconveyed back explicitly by L1 to L at the time of the assignment.[89]

6.5.4   The assignment of the lease to a new tenant for pre-1996 leases

For the purpose of the following rules, a lease is 'pre-1996' if it was granted before 1 January 1996, even if it is assigned after that date. So, the question here is whether the benefit *and* burden of any of the covenants in the lease made between the original landlord and the original tenant can 'run' with the land automatically when the *lease itself* is assigned. The question is whether the leasehold covenants (benefit and burden) pass automatically to a new tenant on assignment of the lease? This depends on two factors: first, does 'privity of estate' exist between the landlord and tenant so as to allow enforcement of the covenants; and, second, do the covenants 'touch and concern' the land (*Spencer's Case* (1583))?

6.5.5   The claimant and defendant must be in 'privity of estate'

It is intrinsic to the enforcement of leasehold covenants under pre-1996 tenancies by, and against, the assignee of the lease (the new tenant) that he must stand in the relation of 'privity of estate' with a landlord who is also subject to the benefits and burdens of

---

87   This position is modified for tenancies granted on or after 1 January 1996, and is discussed in section 6.6.3 below.

88   For why this remains important under the LTCA 1995, see section 6.6.3 below.

89   *Kataria v. Safeland* (1997).

the covenants. In general terms, privity of estate exists where the claimant and defendant in an action on a leasehold covenant currently stand in the relationship of landlord and tenant under a *legal* lease. This can be broken down into two parts.

1   The claimant and defendant must stand in the relationship of landlord and tenant. Hence, there is the potential for privity of estate between the original landlord and an assignee of the lease, between an assignee of the reversion and the original tenant, and between assignees of the reversion and of the lease while they are sharing the estate in the land. Significantly, however, there is no privity of estate between a land-lord and a subtenant, as they are not *each other's* landlord and tenant. So, in order for the benefit and burden of leasehold covenants to run to an assignee of the original tenant, that assignee must be 'the tenant' of the landlord who is suing or being sued.

2   The claimant and defendant must be landlord and tenant under a *legal* lease. Despite some *dicta* to the contrary,[90] it is clear (if anachronistic) that 'privity of estate' can exist only in respect of a legal lease. This means not only that the original lease must be legal in character,[91] but also that any assignment of the reversion or the lease (as the case may be) must be in the form prescribed for legal interests: that is, by deed in compliance with section 52 of the LPA 1925. In fact, even if the original lease is created as a legal estate without the need for a deed – for example, it is for three years or less – if the 'legal' character of it is to be maintained, any assignment of it must be effected by deed (*Julian v. Crago* (1992)).[92] The insistence that privity of estate can exist only when the assignee tenant and his landlord are tenant and landlord under a legal lease is an historical anomaly generated by the now-defunct distinction between courts of law and courts of equity, but it is a distinction at the heart of the pre-1996 law. Of course, in practice, leasehold covenants are likely to be of importance in long leases where an effective web of transmissible leasehold covenants will be crucial – as in long leases of residential flats. Such leases are very likely to have been granted on legal advice and, as such, will be made by deed and any assignment of them is equally likely to be effected by deed. For leases granted on or after 1 January 1996, the rules concerning the transmissibility of leasehold covenants make no distinction between legal and equitable leases.

6.5.6   The covenant must 'touch and concern' the land

For the benefit and burden of a leasehold covenant to pass to an assignee of the lease, it is not enough that the tenant stands in a relationship of privity of estate with the claim-ant/defendant landlord under a legal lease. In addition, for pre-1996 tenancies, only those covenants that 'touch and concern' the land are capable of being enforced by, and against, the assignee of a lease. The purpose of this requirement is to distinguish 'propri-etary' covenants from merely 'personal' covenants. Proprietary covenants are those that attach to the land and affect its use, while personal covenants are those that were intended to confer an individual benefit on the original tenant alone. Devoid of context,

---

90   Famously, Lord Denning, in *Boyer v. Warby* (1953).

91   See section 6.3.2 above.

92   We should not forget, however, that a legal lease for three years or less is so short that there will be very few practical situations where it will be assigned.

it can be difficult to distinguish between those covenants that do, and those that do not, 'touch and concern' the land, although considerable help has been provided by the guidelines put forward by Lord Oliver in *Swift Investments* v. *Combined English Stores* (1989). Although this test is not to be applied mechanically (i.e. each case depends on its own facts), it is of considerable assistance when determining real life cases. In determining the nature of a covenant, the following points are to be considered. First, could the covenant benefit *any* owner of an estate in the land as opposed to the particular original tenant (indicates a proprietary covenant)? Second, does the covenant affect the nature, quality, mode of use or value of the land (indicates a proprietary covenant)? Third, is the covenant expressed to be personal? Examples of covenants that, by this test, would 'touch and concern the land' are covenants to repair, covenants restrictive of use of the premises,[93] covenants not to assign or sublet without consent and, of course, the tenant's covenant to pay rent. Covenants imposing an obligation to pay money have, in the past, caused some concern, but it is now clear from *Swift* that a 'monetary covenant' that underpins the performance of covenants that touch and concern the land will itself 'touch and concern'. For example, a covenant by a third party promising to underwrite the performance of the covenants (a 'surety covenant') does touch and concern the land – because it underpins proprietary obligations – so that it may be enforced by a person other than the original party to whom it was made.

Note, however, the anomalous position with respect to one particular type of covenant that *should* by any measure 'touch and concern' the land but in fact is treated differently. A landlord's covenant to renew the lease (i.e. to give the tenant a new lease at the tenant's option when the old lease expires through time) clearly fulfils the *Swift* test, but case law has determined that it is not capable of 'running' (i.e. binding a new landlord) under leasehold covenant rules. Following *Phillips* v. *Mobil Oil* (1989), such covenants must be treated as typical third-party interests under the Land Charges and Land Registration Acts, much like one would treat easements or freehold covenants. Hence, in unregistered land, the tenant must ensure that the landlord's covenant to renew is registered against the landlord as a Class C(iv) Land Charge if it is to bind a purchaser of a legal estate in the land (i.e. a new landlord under a legal lease), and, in registered land, the covenant should be registered by means of a Notice against the burdened title, unless it can take effect as an interest which overrides under the 'actual occupation' provisions of Schedule 3, paragraph 2 of the LRA 2002. Albeit illogical, this position is now well established (i.e. property professionals know about it)[94] and has been continued under the system for post-1996 leases.

To sum up then, if the covenants touch and concern the land, they may be enforced by, or against, an assignee of the lease (a new tenant) by or against a landlord with whom the tenant stands in the relationship of privity of estate under a legal lease or legal assignment thereof.

6.5.7   Special rules

As noted above, even if the assignee of the lease is liable under the leasehold covenants, the liability of the original tenant under a pre-1996 tenancy continues throughout the

---

93 For example, not to carry on a trade or business, or not to grow trees over a certain height.

94 It was still novel when it triggered the estoppel claim in *Taylors Fashions* v. *Liverpool Victoria Trustees* – see Chapter 10.

entire term. Given that this is a primary liability, a landlord may resort to the original tenant immediately without resort to the assignee. Hence, it is always in the original tenant's interest to ensure that any assignee of the lease is able and willing to fulfil all covenants. In contrast, the liability of an *assignee* of the lease extends only to breaches committed while the lease is vested in them. Therefore, an assignee is not liable for breaches of covenant committed before assignment of the lease (*Grescot v. Green* (1700)) unless these are of a continuing nature.[95] Likewise, there is no liability for breaches committed after the lease has been assigned (*Paul v. Nurse* (1828)), for that liability must fall on the new tenant. Also, under pre-1996 tenancies, the original tenant is able to sue for breaches of covenants committed while he was in possession of the property, even though the lease may have been assigned subsequently (*City and Metropolitan Properties v. Greycroft* (1987)). The same is probably true for all subsequent assignees. Finally, in contrast with the position of original landlords, we may note that an original tenant who assigns does not lose the right to sue for breaches of covenant occurring before the assignment.

6.5.8   The assignment of the reversion to a new landlord under pre-1996 tenancies

For the purpose of the following rules, a lease and its reversion is 'pre-1996' if the lease was granted before 1 January 1996, even if the reversion is assigned after that date. The question to be considered here is the mirror image of that considered above: that is, whether an assignee of the reversion (the 'new' landlord) is able to enjoy the benefits of the covenants in the original lease and whether he is subject to the burdens they impose. However, although the issue is the same, the relevant conditions are slightly different from those concerning assignment of the lease, primarily because of the intervention of statute.

6.5.9   Section 141 of the Law of Property Act 1925: the benefit of the original landlord's covenants

For pre-1996 tenancies, section 141(1) of the LPA 1925 provides that an assignment of the landlord's reversion carries with it the benefit (the right to sue) of all covenants that 'have reference to the subject matter of the lease'. In essence, this is a statutory transfer of the benefit of all covenants that 'touch and concern' the land (*Hua Chiao Commercial Bank v. Chiaphua Investment Corp* (1987)). It means that the benefit of all 'touching and concerning' covenants are transferred to an assignee of the reversion irrespective of whether privity of estate exists, although, of course, the defendant in an action must still be liable on the covenants and privity of estate may be necessary to establish this. It also means (because of the clear words of the section) that the 'new' landlord acquires the right to sue in respect of breaches of covenant that occurred *before* assignment and that the 'old' landlord loses this right (*London and County (A and D) Ltd v. Wilfred Sportsman Ltd* (1971)). The test of covenants that have 'reference to the subject matter of the lease' (i.e. 'touch and concern') is that specified by Lord Oliver in *Swift*. In practical terms, then, the transfer of

---

95 For example, continuing non-payment of rent after assignment.

the benefit of all proprietary covenants to an assignee of the landlord is a simple matter: statute ensures that they pass automatically with the lease. Note that, under the LTCA 1995, section 141(1) has no application to leases granted on or after 1 January 1996. It is replaced by a provision having wider effect.

6.5.10 Section 142 of the Law of Property Act 1925: the burden of the original landlord's covenants

For pre-1996 leases, section 142(1) of the LPA 1925 provides that an assignment of the landlord's reversion carries with it the burden of (the obligation to perform) all covenants that also 'have reference to the subject matter of the lease'. In essence, this is a statutory transfer of the burden of all covenants that 'touch and concern' the land. Again, this means that the obligation to perform these covenants passes to an assignee of the reversion, irrespective of privity of estate, although the claimant (e.g. the current tenant) may need to plead such privity in order to prove that the benefit of the covenant has run to him. In this respect, the *Swift* test of 'touching and concerning' is again relevant, although, as discussed below, some problems have emerged. Note that, under the LTCA 1995, section 142(1) has no application to leases granted on or after 1 January 1996. Again then, in practical terms, the position for pre-1996 leases is relatively simple: the burden of all proprietary covenants passes to an assignee of the reversion automatically. However, for reasons that are not particularly cogent or convincing, there are some exceptions to this simple rule.

1   It is clear that a landlord's covenant to renew the lease at the tenant's option when the original term expires is proprietary and hence is *capable* of being enforced *against* assignees of the reversion (*Simpson* v. *Clayton* (1838)). However, according to *Beesly* v. *Hallwood Estates* (1960) and *Phillips* v. *Mobil Oil* (1989), the burden of this covenant does *not* pass automatically on assignment of the reversion, despite the clear words of section 142(1) of the LPA 1925. According to the judge in that case (which concerned unregistered land), such a covenant is registrable as a Class C(iv) Land Charge, and must be so registered in order to bind the assignee of the reversion; the burden will not pass automatically. This does seem a strange decision, and has been roundly criticised as being inconsistent with section 142. Indeed, in *Armstrong and Holmes* v. *Holmes* (1993), the judge criticised *Hallwood* and pointed out that it had been disapproved of by the Court of Appeal in *Greene* v. *Church Commissioners* (1974). However, it remains the law and even under the new regime of the LTCA 1995, these covenants will continue to be registrable in both registered and unregistered land (section 3(6)(b) of the LTCA 1995) rather than automatically binding under leasehold covenant rules. Fortunately, however, in respect of registered land, even though the burden of such a covenant cannot pass automatically under 'leasehold covenant rules',[96] it is likely to constitute an interest which overrides under Schedule 3, paragraph 2 of the LRA 2002 and be binding on the assignee of the reversion

---

96 But note the words of section 29(2)(b) of the LRA 2002, that a disposition of a registered leasehold estate is subject to the burden of an interest that is an incident of the estate. Thus, the burden might bind in all cases irrespective of the existence of an overriding interest.

because the tenant who can enforce it will be in actual occupation of the land to which the covenant relates.

2   A covenant by the landlord to repay a deposit given by the tenant does not 'touch and concern' and cannot, therefore, be enforced against an assignee of the landlord who actually received the money under a tenancy granted before 1 January 1996 (*Hua Chiao Commercial Bank* v. *Chiaphua Investment Corp* (1987)). This changes for tenancies subject to the LTCA 1995.

3   A landlord's covenant to sell the freehold to the tenant does not 'touch and concern' the relevant land, and cannot be enforced against an assignee of the reversion (*Woodall* v. *Clifton* (1905)). This is because the covenant does not touch and concern the *leasehold* land, because it relates to the freehold estate. While strictly true, it represents a narrow view of the law and this changes for leases subject to the LTCA 1995.

6.5.11   Special rules

As noted above (and in contrast to the position with the original tenant), the ability of the original landlord to sue for breaches of covenant ceases after assignment of the reversion, even if the breach was committed before that assignment. This is because section 141(1) of the LPA 1925 transfers *all* of the assignor's rights to the assignee whenever they accrue (*Re King* (1963)). Second, the liability of an assignee of the reversion ceases when he assigns the lease to another assignee. However, it is uncertain whether an assignee of the reversion is liable for breaches of covenants committed by the original landlord *before* assignment. As a matter of principle, it would seem that he should not be so liable, but *dicta* in *Celsteel* v. *Alton* (1985) suggest otherwise. Third, the benefit and burden of leasehold covenants under pre-1996 tenancies pass to the assignee of the reversion by statute, not by the doctrine of privity of estate. Therefore, benefits and burdens pass, and may be sued on, in circumstances in which there is no privity of estate, as in the case of equitable leases/equitable assignments, or where the assignee of the reversion sues the original tenant even though the original tenant *had never been* that assignee's tenant (e.g. because the lease was assigned before the reversion was assigned – *Arlesford Trading* v. *Servansingh* (1971)). Fourth, rights of re-entry are special rights reserved by a landlord to 're-enter' the property and terminate the lease as a result of a tenant's breach of covenant. Importantly, every assignee of the reversion under a pre-1996 tenancy obtains the benefit of this right if it was included in the original lease (section 141 of the LPA 1925) and every tenant will be subject to the right of re-entry even if they are not actually liable on the covenants that have been broken (*Shiloh Spinners* v. *Harding* (1973)). This is because the right of re-entry operates against the land, whoever is in possession and irrespective of whether that person was actually the person whose actions breached the covenants. The position is the same for tenancies operating under the LTCA 1996 (see section 4). So, in *Kataria* v. *Safeland plc* (1997), the reversion was assigned together with a right of re-entry, but the 'old' landlord was granted by contract the right to recover rent owed prior to the assignment.[97] The new landlord was not owed rent but, nevertheless, was permitted to enforce his right of re-entry because rent was owing on the land and the right of re-entry stands separately from the covenants that it underpins.

---

97 In effect, the parties contracted out of *Re King* (1963).

6.5.12   Equitable leases and equitable assignments of legal leases

As far as pre-1996 tenancies are concerned, all that has been said above about the running of leasehold covenants to successors in title of the original landlord and original tenant apply when both the original lease was legal and the assignment of it was made in the way appropriate to legal interests: that is, by deed. If, however, the original lease is equitable, or if a legal lease is imperfectly assigned (by written contract, not deed), then for pre-1996 tenancies, different considerations apply because 'privity of estate' does not exist under equitable leases or equitable assignments of legal leases.

6.5.13   The original landlord and tenant

The majority of equitable leases arise from a specifically enforceable written contract between the prospective landlord and prospective tenant.[98] Consequently, the original parties are bound in contract to perform all of the obligations of the lease, even those that are purely personal in nature.

6.5.14   The assignment of the reversion of an equitable lease to a new landlord

The intervention of statute means that, where the reversion of an equitable lease is assigned from landlord to landlord (or a legal reversion is imperfectly assigned),[99] the absence of privity of estate does not seriously prejudice the assignee's position. This is because sections 141 and 142 of the LPA 1925 ensure the transmission of the benefit and burden of leasehold covenants irrespective of the nature of the lease in which they are contained. Therefore, for pre-1996 tenancies, by virtue of section 141(1) of the LPA 1925, the assignee of the reversion of an equitable lease will be entitled to enforce all leasehold covenants (the benefit) that 'have reference to the subject matter of the lease'.[100] Likewise, under section 142(1), the obligation to perform similar covenants (the burden) will pass to the assignee. The position is very similar to that operating for legal leases granted before 1 January 1996.

However, for a pre-1996 tenancy, the position is not quite as straightforward as this first appears. In order for the passing of the 'benefit' or 'burden' to have any practical meaning, the landlord must have someone to sue, or someone who can sue him. If the land is still held by the original tenant, there is no problem, as this will be the original contracting party and he will be subject to the terms of the lease, as to both benefits and burdens. But if the original tenant has also assigned the equitable lease, two further issues must be resolved. First, does the lease itself bind the purchaser of the reversion, so that the new landlord takes the land subject to the equitable tenancy? This falls to be determined by

---

98   *Walsh* v. *Lonsdale* (1882). Or a written instrument that is treated as if it were a contract.

99   That is, where a written instrument is used instead of the required deed.

100   *Rother District Investments Ltd* v. *Corke* (2004), in which the assignee of the landlord was entitled to forfeit prior to his lease being registered and having, in consequence, an equitable title.

the normal rules of registered or unregistered conveyancing.[101] Second, and more importantly for present purposes, before the new landlord can actually rely on the leasehold covenants or be accountable under them, it is also necessary to show that the assignee of the equitable tenant is subject to the burden, or enjoys the benefit of those covenants (as the case may be). For pre-1996 tenancies, this turns on the rules discussed below.

6.5.15   The assignment of the equitable lease to a new tenant

The ability of the benefit or burden of the original tenant's covenants in a pre-1996 tenancy to run with the assignment of an equitable lease (or an imperfect assignment of a legal lease) is complicated. The first point is that traditionally this situation is regarded as lacking the necessary 'privity of estate' and so *Spencer's Case* (1583) does not apply and the covenants cannot pass automatically.[102] However, it is well established that the *benefit* (but not the burden) of any contract can be expressly assigned. Consequently, an equitable tenant is perfectly free to transfer the benefit of every covenant (including personal ones) to the assignee *expressly* when the lease is itself assigned. Indeed, this is normal conveyancing procedure, and has the consequence that most equitable assignees will have the right to enforce the original tenant's covenants against whosoever is subject to their burden. The reason is, quite simply, that the original contracting party has passed the benefits under the contract (the right to sue) to the person to whom he has also assigned the lease.

Unfortunately, however, there are no parallel rules concerning the passing of the burden of the original equitable tenant's leasehold covenants. In fact, as *Purchase* v. *Lichfield Brewery* (1915) illustrates, an equitable assignee of the lease may not be liable to perform *any* of the original tenant's covenants, including the obligation to pay rent. This is the combined effect of the rule that no privity of estate exists between landlord and tenant under an equitable lease (or equitable assignment of a legal lease), so preventing automatic passing of the burden of the covenants, and the rule that burdens of a contract cannot be assigned, so preventing the express *inter partes* transfer of leasehold obligations. So, while benefits may run under an equitable lease (because of express assignment), and the new tenant may sue the landlord, the landlord cannot sue the tenant. Obviously, this can cause considerable hardship to the landlord who may find the value of his reversion substantially diminished through an assignment of the lease and where the land is now possessed by a tenant whom he cannot control. Consequently, a number of alternative, or 'indirect', methods of enforcing the burden of leasehold covenants against equitable assignees of the lease have been developed. These are considered below. For the most part, they will be redundant for tenancies granted on or after 1 January 1996 because of the statutory magic of the LTCA 1995.

First, in *Boyer* v. *Warby* (1953), Denning LJ held that the burden of leasehold covenants that 'touched and concerned' the land *could* pass to the assignee of a lease for three years or less (which is legal without a deed), even though the assignment itself was not by deed. On one view, this could be taken to mean that *Purchase* v. *Lichfield Brewery* (1915) has been

---

101   See Chapters 2 and 3 and the position is noted briefly above.

102   Whether this is a logical position is beside the point. The rule is well established and has governed conveyancing practice for decades.

overruled, and that burdens (and so benefits) can pass automatically for all leases. However, this wide interpretation is very doubtful, and no conclusive reasons were given in *Boyer* other than that 'law' and 'equity' were now fused. Unfortunately, this merely assumes what has to be proven and *Boyer* should be limited to its own facts: that is, because the lease was originally legal, even though not made by deed (being for three years or less), its assignment without deed may be treated as an effective transfer of the legal estate, so preserving the required 'privity of estate' necessary to make leasehold covenants run.

Second, even if the covenants themselves are not binding on the equitable assignee, they can be enforced against that assignee indirectly by means of a right of re-entry (a forfeiture clause) in the original lease. As we shall see, the right of re-entry allows a landlord to recover premises after a breach of covenant and thereby terminate the lease. Such rights of re-entry stand alone, and may be relied on by a landlord if a covenant is broken, even though the covenant itself was not binding on the tenant (*Shiloh Spinners* v. *Harding* (1973)) or, indeed, even if a previous landlord enjoys the personal right to enforce the covenant, as in *Kataria* v. *Safeland plc* (1997). This may seem odd because the right of re-entry is usually seen as a remedy for breach of covenant and thus appears to require that a covenant has been broken by the person subject to the remedy of forfeiture. However, land law is more inventive than this. A proprietary ('touching and concerning') leasehold covenant attaches to the land, even though the current tenant (as an equitable assignee) may not be bound by it. Consequently, if actions take place on the land that contravene the covenant, the covenant has been broken. Admittedly, direct action against the defaulting tenant is not possible (e.g. no action in damages), but action against the land is. So, if the landlord has the benefit of a right of re-entry, the landlord can 're-enter', take possession and bring the lease to an end. Although there are statutory controls on the exercise of the right of re-entry,[103] it will be appreciated that the possibility of re-entry is very persuasive in ensuring that the tenant does, in fact, observe the leasehold covenants. Would the tenant be happy to lose his lease through forfeiture, or instead actually perform the leasehold obligations? We must note, however, that the efficacy of this indirect enforcement method is constrained by the following requirements: that a right of re-entry must exist and its benefit have been passed to the current landlord (this is most likely); that the leasehold covenant is proprietary in nature; and that the tenant is bound by the right of re-entry, even though not bound by the actual covenants. This last restriction operates differently, depending on whether the land is registered or unregistered. In unregistered land, rights of re-entry in an equitable lease are not Land Charges and are binding on a tenant (and any other person in possession) according to the doctrine of notice. A tenant will be deemed to have notice of all terms of the original lease, including the right of re-entry, and hence the condition is satisfied easily. In registered land, the right of re-entry is likely to bind automatically under the express provision in section 29(2)(b) of the LRA 2002.[104]

Third, even though the landlord and equitable assignee do not stand in a relationship of privity of estate, any 'restrictive covenants' (i.e. those preventing the assignee of the lease from doing something on the land) may be enforced by virtue of the principle of

---

103 See section 6.7.5 below.

104 That a disposition of a registered leasehold estate is subject to the burden of an interest that is an incident of the estate.

Tulk v. Moxhay (1848). This is discussed further in Chapter 8 (the law of freehold covenants), but, in essence, the rule in *Tulk v. Moxhay* permits the enforcement of any restrictive proprietary covenant against a person in possession of the land over which the covenant takes effect. This may be an adverse possessor, freeholder or, as here, an equitable tenant. So, if an equitable lease contains a restrictive covenant and the benefit of that covenant has passed to the current landlord (as is most likely – section 141(1) of the LPA 1925), that covenant can be enforced against the equitable tenant by means of an injunction preventing any continuation of the activity that is prohibited.[105] The conditions for this route to enforcement are that the covenant is proprietary ('touches and concerns'), that it has become attached to the land (achieved through section 79 of the LPA 1925)[106] and that it is binding on the tenant. In unregistered land, the restrictive leasehold covenant cannot be a Land Charge, and so will be binding on the tenant according to the doctrine of notice (*Dartstone v. Cleveland Petroleum* (1969)) and the tenant will be deemed to have notice of all covenants contained in the lease. In registered land, the restrictive covenant will be binding because of the effect of section 29(2)(b) of the LRA 2002.

Fourth, it may be possible to argue that a new legal tenancy comes into existence between the landlord and the equitable assignee when the assignee pays rent and this is accepted. Such a periodic tenancy will usually be legal (because it will be for three years or less and no special formality is required) and leasehold covenants will be directly enforceable. However, it is not clear why the covenants implied into the 'new' legal periodic tenancy between landlord and equitable assignee should be the same as those contained in the original equitable lease, and there remains the difficulty that the parties will have intended and believed that their relations are governed by the old equitable lease, not some new artificial creation.

Fifth, it may be possible to imply new contractual obligations on the part of the equitable assignee in favour of the landlord that will then create a direct contractual nexus between those parties. This is similar to the implication of a new periodic tenancy considered above, except that in this case it is simply new obligations that are being implied, not an entirely new lease. The occasions when this implication may be made are a matter of some debate and much will depend on the circumstances under which the assignee has taken the lease. Proprietary estoppel could come to the aid of the landlord, although it will be difficult to prove that there is unconscionability simply because the landlord has been denied the benefit of the covenants.

Finally, if the equitable assignee enters into new *express* covenants directly with the current landlord, then these are enforceable as a matter of contract. In fact, the possibility of new, direct covenants between the intended assignee and the landlord is a real and practical option if the landlord has the right to withhold consent to assignment of the lease. In such a case, the insistence on new direct covenants between assignee and landlord will be the price extracted for the landlord's agreement to the assignment and occurs frequently in practice.[107]

---

105 For example, that the tenant may not carry on a trade or business.

106 See Chapter 8.

107 A landlord will wish to have some control over any new tenant (the assignee) and, while consent to an assignment cannot usually be refused unreasonably, the insistence by the landlord of a direct contractual relationship with the intended assignee reflecting the original covenants is not unreasonable.

The efficacy of these methods of enforcement against the assignee should not be underestimated. The threat of re-entry, the enforcement of restrictive covenants by injunction and the ability of the landlord to extract new direct covenants can prove just as effective in ensuring that the equitable assignee observes the leasehold covenants as would have been the case had the covenants passed automatically. Consequently, the 'new' statutory rules of the LTCA 1995, discussed below in section 6.6, should not be seen as directed primarily at the 'evils' associated with equitable leases.

6.5.16 The position of subtenants

As was indicated at the very outset of this chapter, a tenant may create out of their interest a 'shorter' tenancy for another person. The original tenant under the 'headlease' then becomes the landlord of his own tenant, often called the 'subtenant'. Of course, the subtenancy may contain its own covenants, and often these will be identical to those contained in the headlease. However, it may well happen that it is the subtenant (the actual occupier of the land) who so acts as to cause a breach of the substantive obligation contained in a covenant made between the original landlord and original tenant. An example is where the original tenant has promised not to carry on any trade or business, but then a sublet takes place, and the subtenant does just that. Once again, the 'head landlord' has a problem, as he does not stand in a relationship of privity of estate or privity of contract with the subtenant and cannot enforce leasehold covenants against him directly. There are, however, a number of possibilities that may assist the landlord in this situation, although the landlord will not need them if the *current* tenant is prepared to act against his subtenant under the sublease that exists between them.

1   The head landlord can enforce a right of re-entry against the *current* tenant. This is because, in absolute terms, the acts of the subtenant have caused a violation of the covenant whose performance is owed by the tenant to the landlord. Hence, the landlord has at his disposal the remedy of forfeiture against his own tenant. As is explained below, successful forfeiture of a lease automatically terminates any sub-leases.[108] Necessarily, this is an effective, but drastic, remedy. It results in the landlord having no tenant and hence no income from the land unless a new lease can be arranged. It may not be a remedy of first choice.

2   The head landlord can use the *Tulk v. Moxhay* rules to enforce restrictive covenants directly against the subtenant. The situation is effectively the same as that discussed in relation to the position of equitable assignees and subject to the same limitations, both legal and practical.

3   The subtenant may have entered into direct covenants with the head landlord. These can again be enforced directly as a matter of contract. The head landlord may have been able to insist that these covenants are entered into by the subtenant as a condition of his consent to the grant of the subtenancy in the first place, if that power has been retained in the lease between the landlord and tenant (as it often is).

---

108   *Pennell v. Payne* (1995).

6.5.17   The Law Commission and proposals for reform

Prompted by some of the uncertainties, inconsistencies and perceived injustices of the 'old' law, in 1988 the Law Commission proposed a number of changes to the law of leasehold covenants.[109] The Commission believed that the continuing liability of the original tenant throughout the entire term of the lease both distorted the public perception of the nature of the landlord and tenant relationship,[110] and caused unwarranted and unfair hardship to tenants who found themselves liable to perform rental or other obligations undertaken some time ago and now broken by some tenant over whom they had no control. Consequently, the Commission proposed that when a tenant assigned a leasehold interest, he should be released automatically from all liability in respect of any future breaches of the covenants. The only exception would be where an assignment by the tenant was conditional on the landlord's consent, in which case the landlord could impose a condition whereby the original tenant would guarantee the performance of the covenants by the immediate assignee. However, any continuing liability imposed in this manner could not extend beyond one assignment and it would truly be a guarantee so that the landlord would have to look to the assignee first in the event of any breach.

Somewhat surprisingly, however, the Law Commission did not feel it necessary to protect the landlord from continuing liability under his covenants. Thus, under the scheme drafted by the Law Commission, an original landlord would remain liable for breaches of covenant committed by his successors unless he served a notice on the tenant indicating his desire to be released (see *Reeves* v. *Sandhu* (2015), where failure to comply with the process meant that the original landlord remained liable). Should the tenant disagree with the proposed release, the matter would be resolved in court, with the landlord seeking to establish that it would be reasonable to release him from continuing responsibility.[111] However, as discussed below, the tenant's apparent position of strength in this regard has been mitigated by the House of Lords' decision in *London Diocesan Fund* v. *Avonridge* (2005). The Law Commission also proposed a much more radical reform: the abandonment of the requirement of 'touching and concerning' as the touchstone for the transmissibility of the benefits and burdens of leasehold covenants. As we shall see, this has now been done for leases granted on or after 1 January 1996, even though most of the problems with the 'touching' principle appear to have been generated more by the fact that it is difficult to define in advance what the concept requires, rather than by an analysis of whether the rationale behind the requirement is still compelling.

---

109 *Landlord and Tenant Law: Privity of Contract and Estate*, Report No. 174 (1988).

110 The perception being that the liability of landlord and tenant was co-extensive with their possession.

111 One reason may have been to prevent landlords assigning the lease to a 'shell' company with which they were associated and thereby obtaining release from the covenants for themselves. If the 'shell' were then to prove empty, this would effectively strip the tenant of any remedy. This may now still be possible after *London Diocesan Fund* v. *Avonridge* (2005).

6.6   The New Scheme – The Law Applicable to Tenancies Granted on or after 1 January 1996: The Landlord and Tenant (Covenants) Act 1995

The Law Commission's proposals generated much public interest and resulted eventually in the presentation of a private members' Bill to Parliament. It may seem surprising that such a 'technical' item of legislation should be presented to Parliament under the cumbersome private members' Bill procedure instead of being guided through smoothly as a Government Bill. In fact, opposition to the Law Commission's proposals by landlords' pressure groups and pressure on the legislative timetable, meant that the private members' Bill procedure was, at the time, the only hope of securing any reform of leasehold covenant law. Even then, the strength of this opposition, when combined with the absence of Government protection in the legislature, nearly destroyed the Bill and resulted in the new Act being much more of a compromise between tenants' and landlords' interests than was envisaged originally by the Law Commission. As we shall see, one view of the legislation is that the improvement in the position of tenants secured by the LTCA 1995 is effectively negated by the corresponding advantages secured for landlords, at least in respect of commercial leases.

The LTCA 1995 came into force on 1 January 1996. Save for those sections of the Act mentioned above that apply to all tenancies, the Act regulates the transmission of the benefit and burden of leasehold covenants in all new leases (legal or equitable) granted *on or after* that date. Consequently, for such leases, reference must be made to the Act to determine whether a landlord or tenant is bound by, or may enforce, leasehold covenants relating to the land demised in the lease (*Oceanic Village* v. *United Attractions* (2000)).

6.6.1   General principles of the 1995 Act

This section indicates briefly the general effect of the LTCA 1995 and the principles on which it is based. The sections following will discuss the position in more detail, although the case law on the 1995 Act is still relatively sparse.

First, the Act applies to tenancies granted on or after 1 January 1996, and it applies in the same way to legal and equitable tenancies.[112] The old rules that differentiated between these types of lease are no longer relevant (section 28(1) of the LTCA 1995). Second, the tenant (whether original or an assignee) is released automatically from the burden of leasehold covenants when he assigns the tenancy lawfully (section 5 of the LTCA 1995), subject only to the possibility that he might be required to guarantee performance of the leasehold covenants by the next (but only the next) immediate assignee (section 16 of the LTCA 1995). There is an exception for assignments made in breach of covenant, or assignments made by operation law, when the assigning tenant remains

---

112   The Act applies to the grant of the legal lease or the creation of the equitable tenancy. It does not apply to an option giving a party the right to such a lease (*Ridgewood Property Group* v. *Valero Energy* (2013)). Thus, covenants in an option which might have led to lease could not run to successors in title under the Act.

liable (section 11(2)). Third, the original landlord is not released automatically from the burdens of leasehold covenants,[113] but may serve a notice on the tenant applying for such release (section 6). Release will occur if the notice is not answered within a specified time, or if the landlord's application to the county court in the event of objection by the tenant is successful (section 8). A landlord assigning this reversion in breach of covenant, or by operation of law, cannot serve such a notice (section 11(3)). In any event, a successful notice relieves the original landlord from liability arising only under 'landlord' covenants. It does not relieve the landlord from liability under personal covenants that (being expressed to be personal – see below), have not passed to the assignee (*BHP Petroleum* v. *Chesterfield Properties* (2001)). However, a landlord is able to limit contractually the period of their liability to the period for which they are in possession, thus avoiding the need to give notice at all and contractually securing release from their covenants on assignment (*London Diocesan Fund* v. *Avonridge* (2005)). Fourth, the rule that covenants must 'touch and concern' the land or 'have reference to the subject matter of the lease' in order for the benefits and burdens to pass to assignees of the lease or the reversion is abolished (sections 2 and 3 of the LTCA 1995). Fifth, the benefit and burden of all leasehold covenants pass *automatically* to assignees of the lease and of the reversion so that an assignee may enforce, and will be subject to, any covenant contained in the lease (section 3). This means that there is no need to show 'privity of estate' and that sections 141 and 142 of the LPA 1925 are no longer applicable to tenancies granted on or after 1 January 1996. Only those covenants that are 'expressed to be personal', or that are not actually binding on the assignor, or that do not relate to the premises subject to the lease will not so pass.[114] Note also that, unlike the 'old' law, the transfer of the benefit of a covenant to an assignee of the landlord does not deprive the assignor of the right to sue in respect of breaches occurring before the assignment, so reversing *Re King* (1963) for 'new' leases (section 24(4) of the LTCA 1995). Sixth, in certain circumstances, an assigning tenant can be required to enter into an 'authorised guarantee agreement' (AGA) where they guarantee performance of the covenants by the next immediate assignee, but only that assignee. Seventh, the provisions relating to 'problem notices' and overriding leases, discussed above in relation to pre-Act leases, also apply to tenancies falling under the Act. For example, if an assigning tenant is called on to pay a sum under his AGA for the next immediate assignee, then a 'problem notice' must be served within the proper period (six months from the liability arising)[115] for the guarantee to be enforceable. In such cases, the guarantor has the option of securing an overriding lease. Eighth, the Act generally does not change the law concerning the enforcement of covenants between a head landlord and a subtenant.

6.6.2   The tenant's position in more detail

The 1995 Act has modified considerably the position of tenants under leasehold covenants. The two most important reforms are the statutory release of *all* tenants, including

---

113 Assuming the original landlord would have been liable after assignment under the terms of the lease – see section 6.3.3 above and the effect of *London Diocesan Fund* v. *Avonridge* (2005).

114 Sections 3(1)(a) and 3(2) of the LTCA 1995.

115 And see *Scottish & Newcastle plc* v. *Raguz* (2008) for when liability arises.

the original tenant, from the burden of all covenants when they assign the lease lawfully, and the rule that the benefit and burden of covenants in most cases will pass automatically to an assignee of the lease. Gone are the worries about the continuing liability of an original tenant throughout the entire term of the lease, but no longer does a landlord have to prove 'privity of estate' and 'touching and concerning' before he can enforce leasehold covenants against a tenant in possession. All current tenants under legal or equitable leases granted on or after 1 January 1996 will be bound by the leasehold covenants. For example, an assignee under an equitable lease will be bound to carry out the original tenant's covenant to repair, even though no privity of estate exists with the current landlord. Similarly, the original tenant will be released from this liability, save only that he may have been required to enter an authorised guarantee agreement (AGA) to guarantee performance of the obligation by the tenant to whom he assigns.

Although the 1995 Act has been in force for over 20 years, there is relatively little case law and the statute itself can be difficult to interpret.[116] However, it does apply in equal measure to legal and equitable leases and their assignment. Importantly, however, the statute says very little about the position of subtenants and their legal relationship with head landlords. The Act is concerned with the 'assignment' of a lease or a reversion: a subtenant takes a new lease from his landlord and is not an assignee.[117]

6.6.2.1 *Release of tenants and authorised guarantee agreements*

As noted above, one of the fundamental motives for the legislation was that the original tenant and all subsequent tenants will be released from the obligation to perform the covenants (and lose the right to enforce them) on assignment of the lease, provided that such assignment is not itself in breach of covenant, or otherwise excluded by operation of law (sections 5 and 11 of the LTCA 1995). However, the release of the original tenant from liability on assignment necessarily deprives the landlord of an effective remedy if the tenant currently in possession defaults on the lease. For this reason, a landlord may require the original tenant to enter into an AGA as a condition of the assignment of the lease (section 16). Such an agreement will oblige the assigning tenant to be guarantor of the tenant's leasehold covenants for the next immediate assignee. So, if T wishes to assign to T1, the landlord may be able to require T to guarantee the performance of the covenants by T1. Under the Act, it is only permitted to insist on an AGA in order to guarantee performance by the *next immediate assignee* – *Good Harvest Partnership LLP* v. *Centaur Services Ltd* (2010), confirmed by the Court of Appeal in *K/S Victoria Street* v. *House of Fraser (Stores Management) Ltd* (2011). Thus, T can be required to enter into an AGA to guarantee performance by T1, but on an assignment by T1 to T2, T's AGA is no longer effective and he cannot be asked to guarantee T2. However, T1 can be required to enter into an AGA to guarantee performance by T2 and this entire procedure is regarded as a

---

116 In *First Penthouse* v. *Channel Hotels and Properties* (2003), Lightman J, when construing section 3 of the Act, noted that '[t]he Act is the product of rushed drafting and its provisions create exceptional difficulties'. In *UK Leasing Brighton Ltd* v. *Topland Neptune Ltd* (2015), Morgan J had to assimilate various provisions of the Act that seemed to contradict each other as they applied to the facts before him.

117 Of course, the Act will apply separately to the lease between the tenant and subtenant, but not between landlord and subtenant.

necessary counterbalance to the release of the tenant on assignment and was proposed by the Law Commission in its original report. Somewhat surprisingly, however, it seems that T is permitted to sub-guarantee the AGA that T1 might have to give, thus effectively underwiring T1's AGA.[118]

The circumstances in which a landlord may require a tenant to enter into an AGA are found in section 16(3) of the 1995 Act and their meaning is not altogether free from doubt. The issue is best considered first in relation to the original tenant and then any assignee. It should be noted, however, that any clause in a lease which seeks to exclude, modify or otherwise frustrate the operation of the Act is invalidated – section 25(1)(a) – and so a clause which seeks to impose a liability on an assigning tenant that is greater than the statutory AGA scheme is unenforceable, as in *Tindall Cobham* v. *Adda Hotels* (2014).

6.6.2.1.1 *When may the original tenant be required to enter into an authorised guarantee agreement?*

In considering this issue, it must be remembered that the ability of a landlord to require the original tenant to enter into an AGA is closely connected to the landlord's ability to control assignment by requiring the tenant to seek his (the landlord's) consent before assignment. Clauses requiring a tenant to seek the landlord's consent before assignment are very common in commercial and long-term residential leases.

1   If the lease contains an absolute covenant against assignment, then the landlord is enti-
     tled, without more, to require the tenant to enter into an AGA as a condition to giving
     his consent (section 16(3) of the LTCA 1995). This is as it should be, given that an
     absolute covenant against assignment means that the landlord can simply refuse per-
     mission to assign without reasons. Some commercial leases will contain such a cove-
     nant, but they are unattractive to tenants seeking a long lease of premises because it
     means they (the tenant) may never be able to move on from the original premises.
2   If the lease contains a qualified covenant against assignment – meaning that the
     landlord's consent to assignment may be withheld only in certain circumstances –
     and it is a lease of commercial premises *and* the lease itself stipulates that the giving
     of an AGA can be a condition of the landlord's consent to assign, then the landlord
     may require an AGA. This is so whether or not it is reasonable to impose an AGA
     (section 16(3) of the LTCA 1995 and section 22 of the LTCA 1995).[119] Most leases
     of commercial premises will fall into this category and, in consequence, the impo-
     sition of an AGA will be possible in the majority of cases.[120]

---

118   *K/S Victoria Street* v. *House of Fraser (Stores Management) Ltd* (2011). In practice, there may be little difference between T
      entering into an AGA for T2 (not permitted) and T guaranteeing T1's AGA for T2 (permitted). See also *UK Leasing
      Brighton Ltd* v. *Topland Neptune Ltd* (2015).

119   Section 22 inserts a provision in section 19 of the Landlord and Tenant Act 1927 allowing AGAs in 'unreasonable'
      circumstances. The section also permits other objective conditions to be attached to consent to assign and these also
      may not be attacked on the ground of unreasonableness: for example, the potential assignee company has a certain
      level of capital reserves, or is publicly quoted, or is fully insured, or is backed by appropriate guarantees.

120   That is not to say that one will be insisted on in practice – a landlord may regard an AGA as unnecessary to
      protect its position, given the remedy of forfeiture and there are disadvantages attendant on enforcing AGA
      liability (i.e. that the former tenant liable under an AGA may be entitled to an overriding lease).

3   If the lease contains a qualified covenant against assignment and is of residential or agricultural premises, or of commercial premises where the lease contains no specific obligation to enter into an AGA, then the landlord can require an AGA only if it is reasonable to do so (section 16(3)(b) of the LTCA). It is not yet clear when it will be 'reasonable' to do so, although landlords would argue that it is always reasonable to do so provided that no other conditions are attached to the consent to assign.

4   If the lease (of any kind) contains no covenant against assignment – meaning that the tenant can assign irrespective of the landlord's wishes – then the landlord cannot insist on an AGA. However, it is most unlikely in practice that a lease will omit to give the landlord the right to control assignment either by an absolute or by a qualified covenant.

6.6.2.1.2 *When may an assignee be required to enter into an authorised guarantee agreement?*

This is the situation in which T (the original tenant) has assigned to T1 and T has been required to enter into an AGA guaranteeing T1's performance of the covenants in the lease. If T1 then assigns to T2, it is absolutely clear that T is released from the AGA, for the original tenant can only ever be required to guarantee performance by the next immediate assignee – *K/S Victoria Street v. House of Fraser (Stores Management) Ltd* (2011). But can T1 be required to enter into an AGA to guarantee performance by T2? Although there is some difficulty about this, the position may have been clarified a little by *K/S Victoria Street v. House of Fraser (Stores Management) Ltd* (2011). The difficulty arises because the LTCA 1995 appears to say that an AGA may be required by a landlord only when a tenant is released from liability on covenants by virtue of the Act itself (section 16(1) of the LTCA). This is certainly the original tenant, but an assignee (T1) was never, under the old law, liable after he had assigned to another (T2). The assignee's liability ended when he assigned and did not continue in the same way as that of the original tenant. Hence the assignee (T1) is not released from liability by the Act and so it appears cannot be required to enter into an AGA to guarantee T2.

If this were the final word, it might pose serious difficulty for landlords as they would lose the ability to sue another person as soon as the first assignee assigned to a second assignee.[121] Consequently, there are three arguments countering this reading of the Act. First, if the assignee (T1) enters into direct covenants with the landlord on assignment, these would have continued to bind throughout the entire term of the lease, so T1's release is caused by the Act and so he can be required to enter into an AGA in exactly the same circumstances as the original tenant. This is because, in effect, the assignee has become the original tenant by making direct covenants with the landlord. Given that this will occur in most assignments concerning commercial premises, perhaps there will be few difficulties in practice. Second, if the lease itself contains a covenant requiring a tenant to enter into

---

[121] Where the lease is assigned by the original tenant, ignoring guarantors, the landlord has two potential defendants: the current tenant and the original tenant under an AGA. If the assignee then assigns, the landlord would 'lose' a defendant, now having only the current tenant (T2) and not the original tenant (the AGA lapses) and not the first assignee (T1) as he (on one view) cannot be required to enter into an AGA.

an AGA, this is itself a tenant's covenant that will run to all assignees under the rules of the LTCA providing for the automatic transmission of benefits and burdens. In other words, if the requirement to enter an AGA is treated as a 'normal' covenant, it will run to assignees and is not required by the landlord per se *under the Act* but was freely agreed to in the terms of the lease.[122] This is not discussed directly in *K/S Victoria Street* v. *House of Fraser (Stores Management) Ltd* (2011), but it is implicit in the reasoning because the Court of Appeal accepts that T1 can be required to enter into an agreement to guarantee perform- ance by T2.[123] Third, perhaps controversially, it could be argued that, because the benefit and burden of leasehold covenants now pass to assignees under the Act, their release from those covenants on assignment is, after all, caused by the Act. Hence, the assignee can be required to enter into an AGA after all. This is in effect an argument that the Act has entirely replaced the old law and so any reference to it — by saying that assignees are not released by the Act but by the old law — is inaccurate.

Obviously, these provisions are complicated, not least because of the confusing statu- tory language, but the crucial point is that, if a lease granted on or after 1 January 1996 contains a promise by the original tenant not to assign without the landlord's consent, and the landlord requires an AGA before he will give such consent, the assigning tenant will be required to enter into an AGA in order to assign if that is reasonable or, for leases of commercial premises, simply if the need for an AGA was stated expressly as a con- dition on which consent to assignment could be refused by the landlord: see, e.g. *Tindall Cobham* v. *Adda Hotels* (2014). For assignees, if the assignee has made direct covenants, he will be an 'original' tenant for these purposes. If he has not, then the most sensible inter- pretation of the Act is that he too should be subject to the AGA regime (and so too any further assignees on the same basis) because the AGA covenant (assuming there is one) would 'run' with lease as with other covenants.

Importantly, if a landlord seeks to enforce a (lawful) AGA liability against the last immediate tenant (the 'AGA tenant'), the 'problem notice' procedure of section 17 of the LTCA is applicable.[124] This means that the guaranteeing tenant must be given at least six months' notice of any liability arising under the AGA[125] and, if the liability is met, of claiming an overriding lease under section 18 of the LTCA 1995.[126]

Overall then, although landlords have lost the right to sue the *original* tenant through- out the entire term of the lease, all professionally drafted leases are likely to contain a provision enabling the landlord to impose an AGA on the original tenant (and likely later

---

122 This contractual approach may find favour, given that *Avonridge* makes clear that the LTCA 1995 has not ousted the parties' ability to regulate their own liability.

123 The Court also accepts that T may be required to underwrite T1's guarantee of T2, this not being a direct guarantee of T2 by T and so not void under the Act.

124 The notice needs to be served only in respect of a 'fixed charge', being rent or a liquidated service charge. It does not need to be served if the landlord is seeking to recover damages, or to enforce other covenants, such as a covenant requiring the guarantor to take a new lease (*RVB Investments* v. *Bibby* (2013)).

125 Of course, the actual default is by the tenant to whom he assigned.

126 If the overriding lease is claimed, it will have the effect of propelling the AGA tenant back into possession 'in between' the landlord and the current (defaulting) tenant. It will thus give the AGA tenant the opportunity of forfeiting the lease of the defaulting tenant and either taking beneficial possession himself or assigning the lease for value to a new tenant. This might be worth more money than the liability he has paid.

assignors). It can happen, therefore, that each assignee will have to guarantee performance of the covenants by the tenant to whom they assign (but only that tenant). In effect,
the landlord retains a second defendant as 'compensation' for losing the original tenant
as a second defendant.[127] Seen as such, it seems that the Law Commission's aim of reliev-
ing the original tenant of continuing liability has been achieved at the price of transferring that liability 'down the chain' of assignments to each assigning tenant in turn.
Undoubtedly, this is fairer because it equates liability with physical possession of the
land and places liability for the acts of an assignee on the assignor who chose them.
What the Act does not do, however, is diminish the *overall* number of possible defendants
available to a landlord in the event of tenant default.

6.6.2.2   *Automatic transfer of benefits and burdens*

Second, and as a corollary to the above, the other major effect of the LTCA is that assignees
of the current tenant will acquire the benefit and burden of all leasehold covenants relating
to the demised premises, save only that benefits and burdens of covenants that are
'expressed to be personal to any person' will not pass (section 3(6)(a) of the LTCA
1995).[128] However, this does not deprive the assignor of the right to sue for pre-
assignment breaches, so reversing *Re King* (1963) (section 24(4) of the LTCA 1995). Thus,
for 'new' tenancies, it seems that we need not attempt to differentiate between 'proprietary' and 'personal' covenants, because all pass unless 'expressed to be personal' (*BHP
Petroleum v. Chesterfield Properties* (2001)). It is not at all clear that this was a wise reform. The
distinction between obligations attaching to the land (e.g. 'the tenant must repair') and
obligations attaching only to the person (e.g. 'the tenant must walk the landlord's dog') is
at the heart of property law and the practical difficulties in distinguishing between them
may well have been exaggerated by the Law Commission. At present, it is not certain how
the courts will determine whether a covenant is 'expressed to be personal' so that it will
not run automatically under the LTCA 1995. In *First Penthouse v. Channel Hotels and Properties*
(2003), Lightman J was considering whether a covenant was 'expressed to be personal'
within the meaning of the statute. As well as noting that the statute generally was of low
quality, he decided that a covenant is expressed to be personal 'in whatever terms' if either
it says so in words (e.g. 'this is personal') or if its *substance* is such that its personal character
is expressed through the nature of the obligation it imposes.[129] In other words, that a covenant is expressed to be personal either expressly or impliedly. Clearly, this is but a small
step away from the old 'touching and concerning test' and demonstrates that some judges
are unhappy at abandoning the distinction between personal and proprietary obligations.

---

127 The first defendant is the current tenant whose actions have actually breached the terms of the lease; for example,
     by not paying rent.

128 There is an exception because the anomalous rule in *Phillips v. Mobil Oil* (1989) that covenants to renew a lease
     required separate registration in order to bind an assignee of the reversion remains intact (section 3(6)(b) of the
     LTCA 1995). Consequently, the tenant will not be able to exercise the benefit of the covenant unless its burden
     has been entered on the register of title by means of a Notice; but see also LRA 2002, section 29(2)(b).

129 '[T]he tenancy does not have to spell it out in terms that the covenant is to be personal. The intention may be
     expressed explicitly or implicitly. The intention may be stated in terms or it may be deduced from the language
     used in its proper context' (at [49]).

6.6.3   An assessment of the landlord's position

The landlord may, at first, appear to have lost most by the passing of this new Act. After all, the original landlord is not automatically released from performance of his covenants, but apparently has to serve a notice on the tenant requesting this, and the landlord has lost the right to sue the original tenant throughout the term of the lease. However, as intimated already, all is not as it seems.

First, following the House of Lords' decision in *London Diocesan Fund* v. *Avonridge* (2005), it is clear that a landlord can stipulate in the original lease that his liability ceases when he assigns the reversion. Thus, the lease itself can explicitly provide that when L assigns to L1, that L has no further obligation under the covenants for future breaches and, further, that he does not have to serve a notice on the tenant requesting such release. According to the majority in the House of Lords (Lord Walker dissenting), this is perfectly possible because the LTCA 1995 was not intended to do away with the parties' freedom of contract. However, as pointed out by Lord Walker in his dissent, this effectively makes the notice procedure in sections 5 and 8 entirely redundant and amounts effectively to an avoidance device. As anticipated, most professionally drafted commercial leases now contain an *Avonridge* clause, thus rendering the original landlord immune from liability after he has assigned the reversion and, more importantly, placing the tenant in a position in which he has limited remedies for future breaches of covenant. This is exactly what the LTCA 1995 was intended to avoid.[130]

Second, the benefit and burden of all landlord's covenants will pass automatically to an assignee of the reversion, unless expressed to be personal and with the exception of the landlord's promise to renew the lease at the tenant's option (section 3(6)(b) of the LTCA 1995). With the passing of the benefit and burden of all of the tenant's covenants – even to an equitable tenant and equitable assignee – every landlord can now be certain of having a remedy against the tenant in possession of the land.

Third, the ability to require the original tenant and, with careful attention, all assigning tenants, to enter into an AGA places the landlord in a strong position – the more so in commercial leases, where with careful drafting, there is no requirement of reasonableness. This is even more enhanced because, following *K/S Victoria Street* v. *House of Fraser (Stores Management) Ltd.* (2011), a landlord may be able to ensure not only that T enters into an AGA for T1, but that on a further assignment to T2, T has to underwrite T1's AGA guaranteeing T2. In such a case, T is not entering into an AGA for T2 – this is prohibited – but is guaranteeing T1's AGA for T2.[131]

Fourth, the 'problem notice' procedure for enforcing liability against a person other than the current tenant is tiresome, but will not hinder a careful landlord. The landlord – or, more realistically, his legal advisers – will simply have time limits to observe, and this is

---

130 All that need happen is that the original landlord deliberately assign to L1, under an *Avonridge* clause, thus ensuring its release from liability. If L1 is a mere 'shell' company, then T's remedies are worthless because he cannot sue L, and L1 is a shadow.

131 In practice, the landlord now has two people guaranteeing T2, one directly (T1) and one indirectly (T). Note, should T's liability to guarantee T1's AGA be enforced, T will not be able to claim an overriding lease as this arises on the enforcement of an AGA, not a guarantee of an AGA. T1 would be able to claim the overriding lease.

already a common feature of the landlord and tenant relationship.[132] Moreover, if the tenant called to account under the AGA chooses to take up the option of an overriding lease, this is unlikely to disturb the landlord. After all, the landlord knows that the tenant under the overriding lease is solvent, as they have just paid the sum demanded.[133]

Fifth, the benefit of a landlord's right of re-entry is automatically annexed to the land, thus giving all assignees of the reversion the opportunity to forfeit the lease if the current tenant defaults (section 4 of the LTCA 1995), or, indeed, if there is any default on a covenant affecting the land irrespective of whether the covenant binds the defaulter.[134]

6.6.4   To sum up

It is tempting to shy away from the law of leasehold covenants because of its complexity. This is understandable when dealing with the law applicable to tenancies granted before 1 January 1996 where the old common law/statutory rules still hold sway and where it is vital to distinguish between different types of covenant and different types of landlord and tenant. However, for leases granted on or after 1 January 1996, the position is relatively simple.

1   All leasehold covenants relating to the demised premises bind assignees of the landlord and tenant (including equitable lessees/assignees) unless expressed to be personal (and excluding the landlord's covenant giving the tenant the option to renew the lease). There is no need to worry about 'touching or concerning', privity of estate or sections 141(1) and 142(1) of the LPA 1925. The same is true of the benefit of such covenants.

2   An original tenant is released from liability throughout the term of the lease, but an original landlord must serve a notice requesting such release unless they have the benefit of an *Avonridge* clause.

3   A landlord can require the original tenant to guarantee the next immediate assignee's performance of covenants by means of an AGA (but only directly the next immediate assignee), and can enforce this liability subject to the problem notice/overriding lease procedure. It is possible to ensure that all assigning tenants come under an obligation to enter an AGA for the next tenant if they assign, thus always giving the landlord a guarantor. It is also possible for a prior tenant to guarantee the AGA given by an assigning tenant.

4   The LTCA does not affect significantly the position of subtenants, which continues to be governed by the principles discussed above (see section 6.5.16). Note in particular that restrictive covenants will continue to bind subtenants, subject to registration requirements under the *Tulk v. Moxhay* rules (section 3(5) and (6) of the LTCA 1995).

---

132 And see *Scottish & Newcastle plc v. Raguz* (2008) for a flexible interpretation of when the time limit for serving a notice commences.

133 However, the landlord should stop to consider whether he wishes to forfeit the lease of the tenant in possession and thereby regain control of the land and its capital value. If he sues the AGA tenant, the landlord takes the risk that this tenant will opt for an overriding lease and himself resume possession and thereby have the opportunity of cashing in on the value of the land by selling the lease to a new tenant.

134 As section 6.5.5 above and see *Kataria v. Safeland plc* (1997).

6.7   The Landlord's Remedies for Breach of Covenant

After having established that a particular landlord has the right to sue on a covenant and that the particular defendant tenant is subject to the burden of it, the next matter is to consider the nature of the remedies available to the landlord. These will be considered in turn.

6.7.1   Commercial Rent Arrears Recovery

Prior to 6 April 2014, all landlords were able to use the ancient feudal remedy of 'distress' to recover unpaid rent. This involved entering the land, removing goods and selling them in order to pay the rent. It needed no court authorisation and was a 'self-help' remedy. However, this remedy has been abolished for all leases, and is replaced for *commercial leases only* with a new scheme – the scheme for Commercial Rent Arrears Recovery (or CRAR).[135] There is no scheme for residential leases.

The abolition of distress was first proposed by the Law Commission in 1991,[136] not least because of the potential for abuse and the lack of regulation by the courts. However, landlords' pointed out that it was useful in situations of potential bankruptcy, was quick and efficient and provided a strong incentive for tenants to meet their financial liabilities under the lease. The compromise solution is found in Part 3 of the Tribunals, Courts and Enforcement Act 2007, the relevant part of which entered into force on 6 April 2014. This new statutory scheme still permits recovery of rent without resort to the courts for commercial leases.[137] The CRAR scheme applies only to written leases of commercial premises and never to oral leases of any type of premises. What is 'commercial' is strictly defined and so CRAR is not available if any part of the premises are let for residential purposes unless this is in breach of the lease.[138] Further, recovery is limited to 'pure' rent[139] – so it is not available for service charges or insurance charges. Most significantly of all, at least seven clear days' notice must be given to the debtor before seizure of goods can take place and at least seven days' worth of rent must be owed. As was the case with distress, certain goods are exempt from seizure,[140] but only goods of the debtor may be seized. Seizure is permitted only by a certified agent and usually there must be a further seven clear days after seizure before sale of the goods can take place. In cases where there is a subtenancy, a landlord otherwise entitled to use CRAR may instead serve a notice on the subtenant requiring him to pay the rent directly to the head landlord, and the subtenant may deduct any such payment from the amount it owes its own landlord.

---

135 *The Taking Control of Goods Regulations* 2013, SI 2013 No. 1894, paragraph 1 and see specifically Part 7.

136 Law Commission Report No. 194 (1991).

137 For residential leases, the landlord will have either to sue for the rent or forfeit.

138 So premises with a ground-floor shop and a flat above on a single lease are not subject to CRAR.

139 Including VAT and interest.

140 For example, items necessary for the debtor's work or business, personal and domestic household items, medical items and any 'goods' used as a home (e.g. a houseboat) – see paragraphs 4 and 5 of the Taking Control of Goods Regulations 2013.

The extent to which CRAR will provide an effective remedy remains to be seen. Certainly it is more controlled, and narrower in operation, than the old feudal remedy of distress and it provides protection to a tenant from an over-zealous landlord or his collecting agents. However, the seven-day notice provision must be of concern to landlords, for it might allow a tenant to remove all valuable goods, or abandon the premises altogether, before the landlord can act.

6.7.2   Action for arrears of rent

A landlord can enforce the covenant to pay rent by bringing an action to recover arrears of rent either in the High Court or in the county court, depending on the amount owed. Section 19 of the Limitation Act 1980 provides that a maximum of six years' rent may be recovered in this way and this limitation also applies to guarantors of the tenant's promise to pay rent (*Romain* v. *Scuba* (1996)). It often happens that one reason why a tenant has not paid rent is a real (or perceived) failure by the landlord to perform his covenants, often the landlord's covenant to repair. Usually, leasehold covenants are not linked, so that non-performance by the landlord of his obligations is not an excuse for non-performance by the tenant. For example, the landlord's failure to honour his promise to repair is not usually a lawful reason to withhold rent, and the tenant can be vulnerable to a landlord's remedies for non-payment of rent unless the tenant can show that the withheld rent was actually used to pay for repairs for which the landlord was liable, and which fell due after the disrepair occurred. Note, however, if the landlord does bring in an action for recovery of rent, a tenant may claim to 'set off' a sum representing damages for breach of covenant (e.g. for failure to repair), unless such right is expressly excluded (*Lee-Parker* v. *Izzet* (1971)). Thus, although the tenant has broken his covenant (and importantly opened himself to other remedies), the court can take account of the context of the claim.[141]

6.7.3   Action for damages

The landlord may sue for damages for breach of every covenant other than the covenant to pay rent. Except in the case of covenants to repair, the measure of damages will be that necessary to put the landlord in the same position as if the covenant had not been broken. By virtue of the Landlord and Tenant Act 1927, damages for a tenant's breach of a covenant to repair are limited to the amount by which the landlord's interest (the reversion) has diminished in value through the lack of repair, and although this may be the amount necessary to carry out proper repairs (*Jones* v. *Herxheimer* (1950)), there is a very real likelihood that the amount will be less than this, due to uncertainties about how much the reversion really has declined in value (*Crewe Services and Investment Corp* v. *Silk* (1997)). Note also that, for leases of seven years or more (with at least three years left to run), the procedure relating to 'notices' set down in the Leasehold Property (Repairs) Act 1938 must be followed before a claim in damages can be made.[142]

---

141 See also *Smith* v. *Muscat* (2003), in which set-off against rent arrears for breach of a repairing obligation was permitted when the landlord had assigned his right to sue for the rent to the current claimant.

142 This is relevant in cases of forfeiture, see below.

6.7.4   Injunction and specific performance

At the discretion of the court, a landlord may obtain an injunction to prevent the breach of a restrictive covenant by the tenant, as where the landlord secures an injunction against the keeping of animals on the land contrary to a leasehold covenant. However, the orthodox view is that a landlord cannot obtain specific performance of the majority of tenants' covenants (an exception is a covenant to build[143]), as this would generate problems about how the court could supervise the tenant in execution of the covenant, as well as raise general issues of equity and fairness.[144] So, in *Co-op Insurance Society* v. *Argyll Stores* (1997), the House of Lords refused to order specific performance of a tenant's covenant to keep open retail premises for a specified amount of time each day. However, although *Hill* v. *Barclay* (1811) supports the proposition that a landlord cannot obtain specific performance of a tenant's repairing obligation, Lawrence Collins QC (sitting then as a deputy judge of the High Court) held in *Rainbow Estates* v. *Tokenhold* (1998) that a landlord could obtain specific performance of a tenant's repairing obligation in special and exceptional circumstances, particularly where the landlord had no other remedy and the court's order could be defined with precision and hence was capable of supervision. The approach in *Rainbow Estates* has not been judicially disapproved, but we might wonder why a landlord who has failed to include a right of re-entry in the lease (so as to be able to forfeit the lease – see below), or a right to enter and repair and recover the costs from the tenant, should nevertheless be entitled to an order for specific performance requiring the tenant to carry out the repairs. It might be thought that the 'exceptional' circumstances which mean that the landlord has no other remedy were all of the landlord's own making.

6.7.5   Forfeiture

By far the most powerful weapon in the armoury of the landlord in the event of a breach of covenant is the remedy of forfeiture. In principle, this remedy is available for breaches of all covenants, including the covenant to pay rent, and the effect of a successful forfeiture is to bring the lease to an end. It is a remedy that can result in the tenant's estate in the land being terminated, even if the loss to the landlord because of the breach is small, and even if the ejection of the tenant will give the landlord a windfall gain because he reacquires possession of the unencumbered freehold. The drastic consequences of a successful forfeiture have always attracted the attention of the courts,[145] and it is not surprising that both the opportunity to forfeit and the effect it has on the tenant are now strictly controlled by statute. There is now a powerful jurisdiction to grant 'relief' from forfeiture to a defaulting tenant – *Freifeld* v. *West Kensington Court Ltd* (2015). In fact, the Law Commission has proposed wholesale reform of the law of forfeiture in its numerous reports on

---

143 That is, a tenant's promise to actually build on the land, sometimes known as a 'building lease'.

144 However, a landlord is able to secure specific performance in appropriate circumstances against a tenant's guarantor where this requires the guarantor to take a new lease of the premises (*RVB Investments* v. *Bibby* (2013)).

145 See *Cukurova Finance International Ltd* v. *Alfa Telecom Turkey Ltd* (2013) for an analysis of the court's equitable jurisdiction to relieve a person against seizure of their property following a debt or other liability, whether this be because of a lease, mortgage or other charge.

termination of tenancies,[146] and other changes in procedure have occurred as a result of the entry into force of the Commonhold and Leasehold Reform Act (CLRA) 2002.

6.7.5.1 General considerations

In general terms, for forfeiture to be available at all, the lease must contain a *right of re-entry*. This is a stipulation that the landlord is entitled to re-enter the premises and retake possession should the tenant fail to observe his covenants. All professionally drafted leases will contain such a right, and one will be implied in all equitable leases (*Shiloh Spinners v. Harding* (1973)). By section 4 of the LTCA 1995, the benefit of the landlord's right of re-entry will pass automatically to assignees of the reversion for a legal or equitable lease. Subject to what will be said below about statutory safeguards, which are particularly strong in the context of long residential leases, the existence of a right of re-entry gives the landlord two potential paths to a successful forfeiture. First, the landlord may physically re-enter the property by obtaining actual possession of it, a typical example being the changing of locks, provided that this demonstrates an unequivocal intention to take possession. So, in *Charville Estates Ltd v. Unipart* (1997), the landlord's entry to carry out works that the tenant had covenanted (but failed) to undertake was not a physical re-entry, and the lease remained alive, permitting the landlord to continue to claim rent and, in *Cromwell v. Godfrey* (1998), there was neither evidence of a manifest intention to forfeit, nor the retaking of possession. Second, and more frequently, a landlord may seek to exercise his right of re-entry through an action for possession brought against the tenant in the courts. At one time, a landlord had a free choice about which path to take, but the position is now modified by statute, mainly to protect the tenant from an over-zealous landlord. The limitations on physical retaking of possession in order to forfeit the lease are noted below.

1   The enforcement of a right of re-entry in a residential lease 'while any person is lawfully residing in the premises' must take place through court action (section 2 of the Protection From Eviction Act 1977). Any attempt physically to re-enter such premises without a court order is without legal effect and will result in criminal liability.

2   Even if the lease is non-residential (or otherwise outside the scope of section 2 above), it is only *peaceful* physical re-entry that is permitted and effective, and the landlord must avoid committing offences under the Criminal Law Act 1977. The use or threat of violence for the purpose of gaining entry to premises when there is someone on those premises opposed to the entry, may be a criminal offence and render the forfeiture ineffective.

3   After the decision in *Billson v. Residential Apartments* (1992), even a lawful physical re-entry may be set aside some time later if the tenant applies for 'relief' from forfeiture.[147]

---

146 See, for example, Report No. 142 (1985), Report No. 221 (1994), Report No. 254 (1998), Consultation Paper No. 174 (2004) and the most recent Report No. 303 (2006), *Termination of Tenancies for Tenant Default*. The latest report contains a draft Bill establishing a new scheme for termination of a lease on the grounds of tenant default instead of forfeiture (a 'termination order scheme').

147 See section 6.7.5.3 below.

The net result of these provisions is that physical re-entry is *possible* only when the tenant is holding the premises under a business lease *and* those premises are unoccupied. Further, it may not be *desirable* even then, due to the court's willingness to grant relief from forfeiture after such physical re-entry has occurred.

6.7.5.2　Forfeiture for non-payment of rent

Forfeiture of the lease for the tenant's non-payment of rent stands apart from forfeiture for breaches of other covenants, although both physical re-entry and an action for possession are available (where lawful). In all cases, there must be a right of re-entry (forfeiture clause) in the lease, and the landlord must make a formal demand for rent unless the forfeiture clause dispenses with the need for such a demand (most do), or the rent is six months or more in arrears. In addition, however, as a result of the CLRA 2002, certain additional safeguards exist for tenants under long leases of a dwelling.[148] In such cases, not only is a tenant *not* liable to make a payment of rent (and so is not in arrears so as to trigger forfeiture) unless the landlord has given him a notice concerning payment and the date on which it is to be made,[149] but section 167 of the CLRA 2002 also provides that the landlord may not forfeit *at all* unless the amount owed exceeds a statutory prescribed sum (currently £350) or has been unpaid for more than a prescribed period (currently three years).[150] Of course, in most cases, these are not burdensome conditions but the provisions of the CLRA 2002 in relation to long leases of dwellings are a much overdue measure of tenant protection and they do prevent unexpected forfeiture or forfeiture for trivial debts.

Having surmounted these hurdles, the landlord then may proceed to forfeit the lease either by physical re-entry or by a possession action in the county court. In either case, however, the general rule applies that the 'law leans against forfeiture'. Thus, depending on the circumstances, a tenant will be granted 'relief from forfeiture' if he pays all of the rent due plus all costs within the appropriate time.[151] In the county court, a tenant has a right to stop the possession proceedings on the payment of arrears and costs at any time up to five days before the trial (section 138(2) of the County Courts Act 1984). Further, the county court will postpone execution of a possession order for four weeks (or more if warranted), during which time a tenant has an automatic right to relief on payment of outstanding amounts (section 138(3) of the County Courts Act 1984). Obviously, because the tenant in these circumstances has a right to have the proceedings stayed, it is important to know what sums must be paid to secure relief. Clearly, these include all of the landlord's costs and it is now clear, following *Maryland Estates* v. *Joseph* (1998), that the amount of arrears is calculated up to the date for possession specified in the court order

---

148　Being a lease of over 21 years (section 76 of the CLRA 2002).

149　Section 166 of the CLRA 2002.

150　These provisions also apply to attempts to forfeit for non-payment of a service charge, a much more likely event in these long leases. Moreover, a landlord may not forfeit for non-payment of a disputed service charge until the First-Tier Property Tribunal has determined the amount of the charge – section 81 Housing Act 1996, as amended by the CLRA 2002.

151　The application for relief will be either in the landlord's possession action or by direct application to the court by the tenant.

and not the earlier date on which the tenant was served with the summons for possession. This is perfectly consistent with the concept that a lease remains in existence up until such time as it is actually forfeited, being when the landlord has taken possession and all hopes of relief from forfeiture are gone.[152] In the normal course of events, failure to pay by the date specified in the order will bar the tenant from further relief, and the landlord's possession order becomes enforceable, save only that a tenant may apply for discretionary relief within six months of the landlord taking possession under the court order (section 138(9A) of the County Courts Act 1984).[153]

If the landlord lawfully re-enters physically (i.e. without a court order), the High Court has a discretionary power to grant relief under its inherent equitable jurisdiction (*Howard v. Fanshawe* (1895)), although only in favour of someone entitled to claim possession of the land by virtue of a legal or equitable proprietary right.[154] The county court also has a discretionary jurisdiction to grant relief in the event of physical re-entry, although it is founded on statute. It exists only if the application for relief is made within six months of the re-entry occurring (section 139(2) of the County Courts Act 1984).

6.7.5.3 *Principles for granting discretionary relief for non-payment of rent*

It will be apparent from the above that there are circumstances in which the tenant may claim relief from forfeiture *as of right*. However, in those cases where there is no right to relief, the court has a discretionary jurisdiction to grant relief in the tenant's favour, even in some cases when the landlord has re-let the premises.[155] The underlying rationale for this generosity is the simple point that the purpose of forfeiture in 'rent cases' is to secure the sum owed, and once this has been achieved, forfeiture is no longer appropriate and relief should be granted (*Gill v. Lewis* (1956)). This means that it will be rare for a tenant offering full payment within the period in which relief can be claimed to be denied that relief, even if they are a persistently late or bad payer, even if the breach was wilful, and even if prospects for payment of future rent appear bleak. However, relief will be granted only if the rent is paid or will be paid, so a tenant's claim that related

---

152 For example, see *Ivory Gate Ltd v. Spetale* (1998).

153 Court action for forfeiture for non-payment of rent generally starts and finishes in the county court. In the event that a matter is transferred to the High Court, a tenant has a statutory right under section 212 of the Common Law Procedure Act 1852 to have the possession proceedings stopped if he pays all of the rent due plus costs before the date of the judgment against him, although this right is available only if at least six months' rent is in arrears. Even if the landlord has obtained and executed a possession order, the tenant may apply for relief if he then pays all arrears and costs, provided that the application is made within six months of the possession order being executed (section 210 of the Common Law Procedure Act 1852) and the premises have not been let to a third party. In those cases in which this statutory relief is not available, the tenant may fall back on the High Court's general equitable jurisdiction to grant relief from forfeiture if the tenant pays all outstanding amounts (*Howard v. Fanshawe* (1895)) and this may be useful where the tenant seeks relief more than six months after the landlord has regained possession (*Thatcher v. CH Pearce* (1968)).

154 *Bland v. Ingram's Estate* (2001). See *Cukurova Finance International Ltd v. Alfa Telecom Turkey Ltd* (2013) for a discussion of the court's inherent equitable jurisdiction in forfeiture proceedings.

155 For example, *Bank of Ireland Home Mortgages v. South Lodge* (1996).

legal action will realise enough funds to pay the rent is not sufficient to trigger relief (*Inntrepreneur Pub Co.* v. *Langton* (1999)). On the other hand, it is now clear that the court's generosity can extend to all covenants aimed at securing a liquidated sum from the tenant. So, in *Khar* v. *Delbounty* (1996), the landlord claimed to forfeit for non-payment of a quantified service charge and, although this was a 'section 146 case',[156] the court held that the same principles of generosity should apply as would apply in rent cases and the tenants were granted discretionary relief.

6.7.5.4   *Forfeiture for breach of covenants other than to pay rent*

In all cases in which the landlord is seeking to forfeit the lease because of breach of covenant, other than a breach of the covenant to pay rent (and 'rent' includes a covenant to pay a service charge if the lease declares that the charge is to be treated as rent), the procedure specified in section 146 of the LPA 1925 must be strictly followed, together with additional procedural safeguards introduced for long leases of dwellings by section 168 of the CLRA 2002. Also, of course, the lease must contain a right of re-entry.

In general terms, a landlord may serve 'a section 146 notice' when he believes a breach of covenant has occurred. No doubt, this can itself encourage the tenant to perform his obligations under the lease. Less commendable is the occasional practice of serving section 146 notices to threaten or cajole tenants when there is no real evidence of a breach or where there are only trivial or technical breaches. In order to mitigate this risk, at least for long leaseholds of a dwelling,[157] section 168 of the CLRA 2002 provides that a landlord of such a lease may not serve a section 146 notice for breach of covenant unless the tenant has admitted the breach or a period of 14 days has passed since the First-Tier Tribunal (formerly known as the Leasehold Valuation Tribunal)[158] has decided that a breach has occurred. The aim is once again to prevent unexpected or unjustified forfeitures. Assuming then that a section 146 notice is capable of being served lawfully, the notice must:

1   specify the breach of covenant of which complaint is made;
2   request compensation for breach of covenant if desired and also advise the tenant of their rights under the Leasehold Property (Repairs) Act 1938 if appropriate;[159]
3   request that the breach of covenant be remedied, if that is possible; and
4   if the forfeiture is in respect of a service charge (not being a charge to be treated as rent), the landlord must inform the tenant of the safeguards established by section 81 of the Housing Act 1996 and enhanced by the CLRA 2002.[160]

---

156 See section 6.7.5.4 below.

157 As before, a lease over 21 years.

158 Functions and staff were transferred to the new Property Chamber with effect from 1 July 2013.

159 If three or more years of the lease are unexpired, the section 146 notice must alert the tenant to the protection available under this Act. This is to serve a counternotice on the landlord claiming the benefit of the Act and so ensuring that no forfeiture may proceed without a court order.

160 As above, these are that no forfeiture may occur unless the arrears of a disputed service charge have been established by the Property Tribunal and that they exceed the statutory minimum or have been in arrears longer than the statutory period.

This procedure is designed to give the tenant every opportunity to remedy the alleged breach of covenant and to avoid the serious consequences of forfeiture. Indeed, any attempt to forfeit the lease contrary to the terms of section 146 is void (*Billson v. Residential Apartments* (1992)). After the service of a valid section 146 notice, the landlord may be able to proceed to forfeit the lease, either by a court action for possession or by physical re-entry (if that is available). However, whether the landlord can, in fact, proceed to forfeit, and how long they must wait before doing so after the service of the notice, depends on whether the specified breach of covenant is 'capable of remedy'.

As noted above, the section 146 must request that the breach of covenant be remedied if that is possible. If the covenant is capable of remedy (i.e. it is 'remediable'), then the landlord must give the tenant 'a reasonable time' (e.g. often three months) to effect such remedy, and will not be allowed to forfeit during this period. Of course, if the tenant then remedies the breach of covenant, the question of forfeiture no longer arises, although there may be claims for damages for past breaches. If, however, the covenant is not capable of remedy in the first place, then the landlord may proceed to forfeit relatively quickly, normally after 14 days, again by action or by physical re-entry.[161] Necessarily, therefore, it is vital to know whether the breach of covenant is 'capable of remedy', as this will dictate both the contents of the section 146 notice and the speed with which the landlord may proceed to forfeit, if at all. The basic test of remediability was put forward in *Expert Clothing Service and Sales Ltd v. Hillgate House Ltd* (1986), which in essence recognised that a breach of covenant was 'capable of remedy' if the *damage* the breach had caused could be rectified. Thus, breaches of most positive covenants can be remedied (*Expert Clothing*) because the tenant can do that which they have not done: for example, by carrying out repairs. Conversely, it was commonly thought that breaches of negative covenants were more likely to be incapable of remedy, thus permitting early forfeiture. However, it now seems that breaches of most negative covenants also are to be regarded as capable of remedy, even those where the breach can be regarded as 'once and for all', such as where the prohibited action is irrecoverable (an example is breach of a covenant against subletting)[162] Thus in *Savva and Savva v. Hussein* (1996), the Court of Appeal held that there was nothing in logic to differentiate between positive and negative covenants because the *Expert Clothing* test required that each breach of covenant had to be taken on its own merits. So, in that case, breach of a covenant against alterations was not, in principle, incapable of remedy.[163] It seems that each case must now be considered on its own facts and no assumptions should be made simply because of the type of covenant involved.

Having surmounted the hurdle of remediability, the landlord may proceed to forfeit by an action for possession or by physical re-entry. However, the tenant still has the ability to apply for relief from forfeiture, as stipulated in section 146 of the LPA 1925, either in an action for possession by the landlord or by an independent application to the

---

161 *Scala House and District Property Co Ltd* v. *Forbes* (1974). *Courtney Lodge* v. *Andrew Blake* (2004) decided that four working days is not sufficient time to respond to a section 146 notice.

162 A breach which stigmatises the land might still be irremediable, as in *Dunraven Securities* v. *Holloway* (1982) and *Kelly* v. *Purvis* (1983), concerning the opening of a sex shop and the keeping a brothel. But even a breach of a covenant against immoral user can attract relief in some circumstances, *Patel* v. *K & J Restaurants* (2010).

163 See also *Cooper* v. *Henderson* (1982).

court as one purpose of the section 146 process is to alert the tenant to the possibility of forfeiture and the ability to apply for relief. Generally, then, relief from forfeiture will be granted if the tenant has performed the covenants, or if the court considers that it would be just and reasonable to allow the lease to survive despite the breaches of covenant (*Shiloh Spinners* v. *Harding* (1973)). Several matters will be relevant in determining whether relief should be given: for example, the drastic effect that a successful forfeiture has per se; the value of the lease when compared with the damage caused by the breach; the seriousness or triviality of the breach; whether the landlord has relet the premises to an innocent third party; whether the breach was wilful, negligent or innocent; and the past performance of the tenant in performing the covenants. However, relief can still be granted even if the breach was deliberate and with full knowledge. In *Freifeld* v. *West Kensington Court Ltd* (2015), the Court of Appeal granted relief for a deliberate breach of a subletting covenant. A critical factor in the case was that forfeiture would give the landlord a substantial windfall even though he had suffered no lasting damage. The Court emphasised that forfeiture had to be proportionate to the breach.[164]

Importantly, relief will not be refused just because the tenant breached a negative covenant, or because the breach was itself irremediable, as in *Mount Cook Land* v. *Hartley* (2000) and *Amana Holdings Ltd* v. *Fakhir Shatub al-Darraji* (2003), in which tenants were given relief after breaking a covenant against subletting. In *Patel* v. *K & J Restaurants Ltd* (2010), the court granted relief even though the tenant had breached covenants against parting with possession and immoral user because forfeiture would have been out of all proportion to the breaches and any resulting damage. However, a court is entitled to refuse relief because of the conduct of the tenant or those standing behind it. So, in *Shirayama Shokusan* v. *Danovo Ltd* (2005), the tenant (D) was refused relief after breaking covenants concerning use of the premises because of its own inequitable conduct and that of the people standing behind the company. As the court said, the jurisdiction to grant relief under section 146 was unlimited, but it had to be exercised equitably. Under section 146(4) of the LPA 1925 (and probably the wider section 146(2)),[165] a subtenant or mortgagee[166] of the original tenant may also apply for relief from forfeiture even though the breaches of covenant were committed by the tenant, as in *Bank of Ireland Home Mortgages* v. *South Lodge* (1996), in which relief was granted to the tenant's mortgagee.

6.7.5.5   *Availability of relief when the landlord proceeds to forfeit by an action for possession*

The position here is governed by section 146 of the LPA 1925, as interpreted by the House of Lords in *Billson* v. *Residential Apartments* (1992). As that case makes clear, an action for possession will be the normal method by which the landlord attempts to forfeit the lease. A tenant may apply for relief as soon as the landlord serves a section 146 notice and up to the moment at which the landlord actually recovers possession under an order

---

164 The 'relief' was that the tenant would have an opportunity to sell his lease and bring his relationship with the landlord to an end, thus not losing everything because of forfeiture. See also *Bank of Ireland Home Mortgages* v. *South Lodge* (1996).

165 *Escalus Properties* v. *Robinson* (1995).

166 Including a chargee: *Croydon (Unique) Ltd* v. *Wright* (1999).

of the court. Thus, prompt action to enter into possession under the court order will defeat relief once and for all (*Rogers* v. *Rice* (1892)). However, there will always be cases in which a tenant will wish to apply after the landlord has executed the possession order, and this has generated some discussion as to whether the court's inherent equitable jurisdiction to grant relief has survived the enactment of section 146. The strongest authority is *against* the survival of such a jurisdiction – *Smith* v. *Metropolitan City Properties* (1986) – but it has been asserted *obiter* (*Abbey National Building Society* v. *Maybeech Ltd* (1985)) and it has academic support. Technically, *Billson* leaves the matter open. In *Bland* v. *Ingram's Estate* (2001), the court (uncontroversially) noted the existence of an inherent jurisdiction to grant relief in respect of non-payment of rent but said nothing about such a jurisdiction for breaches of other covenants.

6.7.5.6 *Availability of relief when forfeiture is by physical re-entry*

Prior to *Billson*, forfeiture by re-entry held some attractions for a landlord in that it was thought that the tenant would lose all rights to apply for relief once the landlord had actually entered the premises. So, for example, a landlord who was forfeiting for breach of an irremediable covenant might serve a section 146 notice and physically re-enter and terminate the lease, all within the space of 14 days. In *Billson*, however, the House of Lords adopted a purposive approach to section 146 and held that a landlord was 'proceeding to forfeit' within that section, so giving the tenant a right to apply for relief, even if he (the landlord) had actually physically recovered possession by peaceful re-entry. Consequently, a tenant who suffers physical re-entry may apply for relief against a landlord in possession of the property for a 'reasonable time' after that possession has occurred. Necessarily, this will make the possession of a landlord who has physically re-entered somewhat fragile, and liable to be defeated by a claim for relief, although it is unlikely that relief will be granted if the landlord has since transferred the land to an innocent third party. In other words, the decision in *Billson* encourages landlords to forfeit leases by action in the courts, as no relief is available when the landlord has finally secured possession under a valid court order.

6.7.5.7 *Waiver*

A landlord attempting to forfeit the lease must ensure that he has not waived the right to forfeit the lease. There will be a waiver of forfeiture if there is any act that amounts to an affirmation of the continuing validity of the lease after a breach has occurred, as this is inconsistent with forfeiture. In the typical case, waiver will exist where a landlord has knowledge of a prior breach of covenant and then does an act that manifests an intention to regard the lease as still in existence (*Matthews* v. *Smallwood* (1910)). The most obvious example is where the landlord, or his duly authorised agent, accepts or demands rent after the breach of covenant has occurred, provided that he also knew (or ought to have known) of that breach (*David Blackstone* v. *Burnetts* (1973)). This principle is applied strictly, as the courts are astute to ensure that a landlord does not gain the double advantage of forfeiture and ongoing rent payments.[167] So a 'without prejudice' demand for rent does not preserve the ability to forfeit. Likewise, a landlord is deemed to have the relevant

---

167 *Gill* v. *Lewis* (1956).

degree of knowledge if he is aware that a breach has occurred, even if he did not know the legal consequences of such a breach. However, it remains true that all cases are decided on their own facts, and, for example, in *Yorkshire Metropolitan Properties v. CRS Ltd* (1997), the landlord's demand for payments towards insurance costs did not amount to a waiver. Similarly, a landlord's express or implied waiver relates only to an existing breach of covenant, and not to any future breaches. Thus, a waiver of a breach of a restrictive covenant may be taken as a waiver of only the initial breach and not of any continuing breach.

6.7.5.8   *Breaches of repairing covenants*

All that has been said so far about forfeiture for breach of covenants other than to pay rent applies in equal measure to breaches of the tenant's covenant to repair, save that the tenant is given additional protection because of the propensity of some landlords to use minor breaches of repairing covenants as a means of ending an otherwise valid lease. Under the Leasehold Property (Repairs) Act 1938, the landlord must serve the section 146 notice in the normal way, but this triggers the tenant's right to serve a 'counter-notice' claiming the protection of the 1938 Act. If this counter-notice is served, the landlord may not forfeit the lease without the permission of the court, and such permission may be given only if one of the grounds specified in section 1(5) of the 1938 Act is established. The Leasehold Property (Repairs) Act 1938 applies to leases of seven years or more that have at least three years left to run.

6.7.5.9   *Reform*

There has been pressure for reform of the law of forfeiture for some time.[168] The remedy is seen as disproportionate to the loss to the landlord caused by the breach as well as being capable of misuse in the hands of an unscrupulous landlord who might use the remedy to threaten or cajole a vulnerable tenant. This is particularly true in those cases in which forfeiture by physical re-entry remains possible. Current statutory controls on forfeiture are effective to meet some of the more serious concerns, but in its 2006 report entitled *Termination of Tenancies for Tenant Default*,[169] the Law Commission makes a case for wholesale reform of the law. In that Report, the Commission proposes the abolition of forfeiture and its replacement by a statutory scheme. Under the scheme, a tenancy could be terminated for breach of covenant by a tenant only as a result of the landlord bringing a 'termination action', with only limited exceptions. There would be no need for a lease to contain a right of re-entry. A 'termination action' would be either a 'termination claim' or the swifter 'summary termination procedure', but both would depend on the landlord serving a notice on the tenant. The procedures would be mutually exclusive and the landlord would have to decide which to adopt. Necessarily, the scheme incorporates opportunities for the tenant to remedy any default and to seek what is currently known as relief. The court would have discretion to make such order as it thought appropriate and proportionate, based around a number of specified criteria. The options would

---

168 See for example, Report No. 142 (1985), Report No. 221 (1994), Report No. 254 (1998), Consultation Paper No. 174 (2004) and the most recent Report No. 303 (2006), *Termination of Tenancies for Tenant Default*.

169 Report No. 303.

include a termination order, an order for sale, an order for a new tenancy or an order transferring the tenancy. Likewise, those persons with derivative interests in the land – for example, subtenants and mortgagees – would also have an opportunity to respond to the landlord's termination action. These proposals have not yet been enacted, but they enjoy widespread support. They appear to offer good protection for the tenant while at the same time preserving a landlord's ability to recover the land in the face of a default-ing and carefree tenant. The law would be improved significantly by their enactment.

6.8 The Tenant's Remedies for Breach of Covenant

The tenant's remedies for breach of covenant by the landlord are less extensive than those of the landlord and are based on the normal contractual remedies available to any person who has suffered loss by reason of breach of a binding legal obligation. Impor-tantly, breach by the landlord of his covenants does not generally entitle the tenant to ignore their own obligations under the leasehold covenants (the covenants are *not* inter-dependent), subject only to the limited right to deduct future rent payments as noted below.

6.8.1 Damages for breach of covenant

The tenant may sue the landlord for damages at common law for any breach of covenant that causes loss, and the measure of damages is that which puts the tenant in the same posi-tion as if the breach had not occurred (*Calabar* v. *Stitcher* (1984)). In the context of damages for breach of the landlord's repairing obligations, this means the tenant should be compen-sated for the loss of comfort and convenience that they would have enjoyed had the repairs been undertaken. This can sometimes be reflected in a reduction in rent, having regard to the diminution in the value of the tenancy (*Wallace* v. *Manchester CC* (1998)).

6.8.2 Action for an injunction

The tenant may sue for an injunction to stop a continuing or threatened breach of cove-nant by the landlord. As with all equitable remedies, this lies at the discretion of the court.

6.8.3 Action for specific performance

A tenant may claim specific performance of a landlord's covenant where this is consistent with the supervisory jurisdiction of the court. Such an order has been granted to enforce performance of a landlord's repairing covenant (*Jeune* v. *Queens Cross Properties* (1974)) and other specific covenants such as the landlord's covenant to employ a resident porter (*Posner* v. *Scott-Lewis* (1986)). Under section 17 of the Landlord and Tenant Act 1985, there is a statutory jurisdiction to order specific performance of a landlord's repairing covenant in respect of a dwelling house. This position should be contrasted with that of the landlord where the ability of the landlord to obtain specific performance of a tenant's repairing obligation is uncertain.

6.8.4   Retention of future rent and set off

Following *Lee-Parker* v. *Izzet* (1971), if the landlord is in breach of a covenant to repair, the tenant may carry out the necessary repairs and deduct the cost thereof from future payments of rent. However, the tenant must be careful not to withhold rent already due, as this will trigger liability to the landlord and perhaps the remedy of forfeiture. In a similar vein, if the landlord is in breach of a repairing covenant, and the tenant therefore refuses to pay rent, the tenant may 'set off' any damages they would have received for the landlord's breach if the landlord should bring an action for arrears of rent. It is only in these two limited circumstances that performance of the tenant's covenants (i.e. to pay the full rent) is modified in the face of a breach of covenant by the landlord.

6.9   Termination of Leases

There are several ways by which the landlord and tenant relationship may come to an end. When it does, possession of the land reverts to the freeholder or other person (e.g. headlessee) entitled on expiry of the term.

6.9.1   By effluxion of time

The most obvious way in which a lease will end is when the contractual term has expired. However, some leases may give the tenant the right to extend the lease at the end of the initial period and, of course, this must be honoured. Likewise, the tenant may be able to claim a statutory extension of the tenancy under the Landlord and Tenant Act 1954 (business tenancies), Agricultural Holdings Act 1986, the Rent Act 1977 or the early Housing Acts (residential tenancies).

6.9.2   By forfeiture

This is considered above where it is made clear that a successful forfeiture by the landlord necessarily terminates the lease early.

6.9.3   By notice

Leases sometimes give either or both the landlord and tenant the right to terminate the lease before the end of the contractual period by giving 'notice' to the other party. These 'break clauses' are common in long leases and are intrinsic in periodic tenancies. Importantly, if a *periodic tenancy* is held by two persons as joint tenants, the notice of only one of them is required to terminate the tenancy, irrespective of the other's wishes (*Hammersmith and Fulham LBC* v. *Monk* (1992)), and this is not a breach of the human rights of the tenant who wishes to remain (*Sims* v. *Dacorum BC* (2014)).[170] Further, the giving of such notice

---

170 The allegation was that the *Monk* rule breached Article 8 (right to a home) and Article 1, Protocol 1 (right to property). This was rejected by a seven-strong Supreme Court. Article 8 was not breached because the right to a home was respected under the tenancy agreement and any eviction was controlled by proper judicial process. Article 1, Protocol 1 was not breached because the tenant had lost their property right in the manner envisaged by the agreement they had freely made.

is not a 'function relating to land' within section 11 of TOLATA 1996 and so does not require any tenant who is also a trustee to consult any beneficiary before giving notice (*Brackley v. Notting Hill Housing Trust* (2001)). Although this may seem startling, we should remember that a periodic tenancy is in reality a succession of individual tenancies and each new period is in reality a new tenancy. Thus, any one of the joint tenants can refuse a new tenancy and so break the chain. In addition, in the case of a periodic tenancy, the continued occupation of the remaining tenant and acceptance of rent by the landlord will generate a new periodic tenancy with a sole tenant only (*Burton v. Camden LBC* (1997)). Critically, however, where there is a fixed-term lease (i.e. not a periodic tenancy) containing a break clause, all joint tenants must concur in exercising the break clause for it to be effective.[171]

A notice to quit given by a tenant will automatically terminate any sub-tenancies that that tenant may have carved out of their own interest – *Pennell v. Payne* (1995) – even if the head lease appears to stipulate otherwise.[172] However, sub-tenancies will survive if the head tenancy is terminated by a consensual surrender between landlord and tenant, for a subtenant is not party to this bilateral arrangement (*Barrett v. Morgan* (2000)).

6.9.4 By merger

The tenant may acquire his landlord's interest in the land and thereby 'merge' the lease and reversion, as in *Ivory Gate v. Spetale* (1998).

6.9.5 By surrender

The tenant may surrender his lease to his landlord, and, if accepted, this will terminate the lease. Surrender may be either expressed or implied by operation of law, this being an example of estoppel (*Mattey v. Ervin* (1998)), but in either case, there must be an intention to terminate the lease (*Charville Estates Ltd v. Unipart* (1997)). As noted above, a surrender, being a consensual act between landlord and tenant, will not thereby determine any sub-tenancies.

6.9.6 By enlargement

Under section 153 of the LPA 1925, a tenant of a lease of more than 300 years, of which at least 200 years are left to run, has a right, in some circumstances, to enlarge their leasehold interest into the freehold.

6.9.7 By disclaimer

A lease may come to an end because the tenant denies the landlord's superior title to the land, and thereby disclaims the lease.

---

171 *Crawley LBC v. Ure* (1996).

172 *PW v. Milton Gate Investments*. Note that this is entirely at odds with *Bruton v. London & Quadrant* (1999).

6.9.8   By frustration

Since the decision in *National Carriers Ltd* v. *Panalpina* (1981), it has been accepted that the normal law of frustration of contract applies to leases. Thus, a fundamental change of circumstance after the commencement of the lease may so alter the rights and obligations of the parties that the original lease (contract) between them in no sense represents their original bargain and is frustrated.

6.9.9   By repudiatory breach of contract

Somewhat illogically, although leases could be frustrated, the availability of the other great contractual remedy of repudiation of the lease, because of a fundamental breach of covenant (contract) by the other party, was once not readily accepted in English law. However, in *Hussein* v. *Mehlman* (1992), the High Court took the first steps to recognise this remedy, on the ground that there is no reason in principle why leases should be regarded as different from other types of contract and the availability of repudiatory principles was confirmed in *Chartered Trust* v. *Davies* (1997). This may well prove a valuable 'remedy' for a tenant as it could provide a method by which a tenant can 'terminate' a lease because of a landlord's refusal to perform critical leasehold covenants, especially given that a tenant has no right of forfeiture.

6.10   Chapter Summary

6.10.1   The nature of a lease

The leasehold allows two or more persons to enjoy the benefits of owning an estate in the land at the same time. Both landlord and tenant retain a proprietary right in the land and both of these proprietary rights can be sold or transferred after the lease has been created. All leases will contain covenants (or promises) whereby the landlord and tenant promise to do − or not to do − certain things in relation to the land. These rights and obligations may 'run' with the land on a transfer of the lease or of the landlord's 'reversion'. The essential qualities of a lease are that (a) it gives a person the right of exclusive possession of land (b) for a certain term (c) at a rent (*Street* v. *Mountford* (1985)), although the last of these is not strictly necessary as a matter of law. Leases may be legal or equitable.

6.10.2   The creation of legal and equitable leases

As a general rule, legal leases must be created by deed. Currently, leases for over seven years, even if created by deed, will not take effect as a legal estate until substantively registered with their own title number. Leases for three years or less that take effect immediately in possession where the tenant does not pay an initial capital sum will be legal, however created (orally, in writing or by deed). Most periodic tenancies are legal leases under this exception.

As a general rule, equitable leases must derive from a written contract (or written document equivalent to a contract). This written agreement will create an equitable lease if it is specifically enforceable (as most are). As an exception, an equitable lease can be generated purely orally via the principles of proprietary estoppel.

6.10.3 Leases in registered and unregistered land

In registered land, the majority of legal leases for seven years or less are overriding interests (paragraph 1 of Schedules 1 and 3 of the LRA 2002) and legal leases created for more than seven years are substantively registrable as titles in their own right. (If they are not so registered, they will take effect as equitable leases only.)

Equitable leases can be protected by registration of a Notice, although most equitable leases will be overriding interests and automatically binding against a subsequent purchaser because the equitable tenant will be a person in 'actual occupation' of the land, within paragraph 2 of Schedules 1 and 3 of the LRA 2002.

In unregistered land, a legal lease will bind automatically any subsequent purchaser or transferee of the estate out of which it is created. An equitable lease arising from an enforceable written agreement is registrable as a Class C(iv) Land Charge (and void against a purchaser if not so registered). Estoppel equitable leases probably bind a subsequent transferee of the freehold land through the doctrine of notice.

6.10.4 The differences between legal and equitable leases

Legal and equitable leases are created in different ways. Equitable leases may be vulnerable to a sale of the freehold or leasehold estate out of which they are created, but this is less likely in registered land. For leases granted before 1 January 1996, leasehold covenants will 'run' with the land in a legal lease more easily than in an equitable one. For leases granted on or after 1 January 1996, leasehold covenants will 'run' in legal and equitable leases identically, thanks to the LTCA 1995. Easements may be created by section 62 of the LPA 1925 on the occasion of a grant of a legal lease only, but *Wheeldon* v. *Burrows* applies to legal and equitable leases. There may be some differences in respect of implied covenants. The equitable tenant is a purchaser of an *equitable* estate in the land and therefore cannot be a purchaser of a legal estate so as to avoid being bound by those equitable rights in unregistered land that still depend on the doctrine of notice. An equitable tenant in unregistered land cannot avoid being bound by an unregistered Class C(iv) or Class D Land Charge, both of which are void only against a purchaser of a legal estate.

6.10.5 Leasehold covenants in leases granted before 1 January 1996

In any action on a leasehold covenant between the original landlord and the original tenant, *all* covenants are enforceable: liability of these original parties is based in *contract*. Both original parties will remain liable on the leasehold covenants throughout the entire term of the lease, even after they have assigned their interests. The liability is to any person having the right to enforce the covenant. The position of an assignee of the lease (i.e. the tenant's interest) depends on whether 'privity of estate' exists between the landlord and tenant so as to allow enforcement of those covenants that 'touch and concern' the land. The position of an assignee of the reversion is governed by the application of sections 141 and 142 of the LPA 1925. 'Privity of estate' does not exist in respect of assignees of an equitable lease (although the original parties remain bound in contract). Consequently, although the benefits and burdens of leasehold covenants will be passed to the assignee of the reversion in an equitable lease (because sections 141 and 142 of the LPA 1925 still apply), the benefits and burdens will not pass automatically to an assignee of the tenant.

In addition, first an assignee of an equitable lease may obtain the benefit (but not the burden) of the covenants by express assignment, but the lack of privity of estate means that the burdens cannot run. Second, there may be indirect enforcement of the burdens of leasehold covenants against an equitable assignee: for example, by use of the landlord's right of re-entry and the rules relating to restrictive covenants. Third, sub-tenants do not stand in privity of estate with the head landlord, so are treated vis-à-vis that landlord in the same manner as equitable tenants. A subtenant is in privity with his or her own immediate landlord.

6.10.6   Leasehold covenants in leases granted on or after 1 January 1996: the Landlord and Tenant (Covenants) Act 1995

The LTCA 1995 applies to all leases granted on or after 1 January 1996 whether legal or equitable. The original tenant is released from liability under leasehold covenants on assignment, subject only to the possibility of guaranteeing the next immediate tenant's performance of the covenants under an AGA. The original landlord is not automatically released on assignment, but may apply to the court for such release or may rely on an *Avonridge* clause. The rule that covenants must 'touch and concern' the land in order to run to new landlords and tenants is abolished. All covenants will run unless they 'are expressed to be personal'. By statute, the benefit and burdens of leasehold covenants pass automatically to assignees of the landlord and the tenant without the need to show privity of estate or to rely on sections 141 and 142 of the LPA 1925. A tenant is liable on the leasehold covenants only while in possession of the land, subject only to the possibility that he may be required to guarantee performance of the covenants by the next immediate assignee under an AGA. The rules concerning the imposition of AGAs are favourable to landlords, particularly landlords of commercial premises.

In addition, the provisions of the LTCA 1995 relating to 'problem notices' to enforce liability against a tenant not in possession (e.g. under an AGA) also apply to leases granted *before* 1 January 1996. Hence, the procedure is applicable to the enforcement of original tenant liability in pre-1996 leases. The same is true of the provisions relating to overriding leases.

6.10.7   The landlord's remedies for breach of covenant

The CRAR scheme allows landlords of commercial leases to enter and recover rent without a court order. The landlord can enforce the covenant to pay rent by bringing an action to recover arrears of rent either in the High Court or in the county court, depending on the amount owed. The landlord may sue for damages for breach of every covenant other than the covenant to pay rent. At the discretion of the court, a landlord may obtain an injunction to prevent the breach of a restrictive (negative) covenant by the tenant. It may now be possible to get specific performance of a tenant's repairing obligation.

The most powerful weapon in the armoury of the landlord in the event of a breach of covenant is the remedy of forfeiture. The lease must contain a *right of re-entry*. Re-entry may be by peaceful physical re-entry or through court action, although the former is not possible in all cases. Forfeiture for non-payment of rent depends on the landlord making a formal demand for rent but may be halted if the tenant obtains relief from forfeiture. The matter has been further regulated by the CLRA 2002 in respect of leases of dwellings for over 21 years. Forfeiture of the lease because of a breach of any other covenant is governed by section 146 of the LPA 1925, with additional procedural changes made by CLRA 2002. After the service of a 'section 146 notice', the landlord may be able to proceed to forfeit the lease, either by physical re-entry or by a court action for possession. The tenant may apply for relief from forfeiture, as stipulated in section 146 of the LPA 1925, whether the re-entry is by court order or by physical re-entry. Also, a landlord attempting to forfeit the lease must ensure that they have not waived the breach as this means loss of the right to forfeit for that particular breach.

6.10.8 The tenant's remedies for breach of covenant

The tenant's remedies for breach of covenant are: to sue the landlord for damages at common law; to sue for an injunction to stop a continuing or threatened breach of covenant by the landlord; to sue for specific performance of the landlord's covenants, particularly the landlord's covenant to repair; or to deduct the cost of carrying out the landlord's repairs from future payments of rent. The law of contract may also provide remedies in 'frustration' or repudiatory breach.

6.10.9 Termination of leases

The landlord and tenant relationship may come to an end in several ways: by effluxion of time (the term ends); by forfeiture; by serving notice if the lease contains a break clause; by merger with the superior estate out of which it is carved; by surrender to the landlord; by enlargement into the superior estate; by disclaimer; by frustration; or by repudiatory breach of contract.

 Further Reading

Bridge, S, 'Former tenants, future liabilities and the privity of contract principle: The Landlord and Tenant (Covenants) Act 1995' [1996] 55 CLJ 313.

Bridge, S, 'Putting it right: The Law Commission and the condition of tenanted property' [1996] Conv 342.

Bridge, S, 'Landlord and tenant law', in Tee, L (ed.) *Essays in Land Law*, Cullompton: Willan, 2002.

Dixon, M, 'The rise of the feudal phoenix' [2000] CLJ 22.

Hill, J, 'Intention and the creation of proprietary rights: Are leases different?' (1996) 16 LS 200.

Smith, PF, '*Billson* v. *Residential Apartments Ltd*' [1992] Conv 273.

Sparkes, P, '*Prudential Assurance Co Ltd* v. *London Residuary Body*' [1993] 108 LQR 93.

Thornton, R, 'Enforceability of leasehold covenants: More questions than answers' (1991) 11 LS 47.

Walter, P, 'The Landlord and Tenant (Covenants) Act 1995: A legislative folly' [1996] Conv 432.

Now visit the companion website to:

*   test your understanding of the key terms using our Flashcard Glossary;

*   revise and consolidate your knowledge using our Multiple Choice Question testbank.

www.routledge.com/cw/dixon

Chapter 7
The Law of Easements and Profits

7.1   The Nature of Easements as Interests in Land

Easements are incorporeal hereditaments. They comprise certain limited rights that one landowner may enjoy over the land of a neighbour. Common examples are the right of way and the right of light, but easements are not limited to these two ancient rights. The right to use a neighbour's land in connection with the movement of aircraft,[1] the right to park on land[2] and cross it with shopping trolleys[3] and the right to the enjoyment of lighting and exit signs[4] are more recent examples. As we shall see, the 'definition' of an easement cannot be expressed in simple terms – it is a recipe of many ingredients – but, at the outset, it is vital to realise that every easement will involve two separate pieces of land.[5]

First, an easement confers a benefit on the *dominant tenement* (i.e. the benefited land), enabling the owner for the time being of that land to use the easement: for example, to walk across a neighbour's land, or to receive light or to use a drainage channel. Second, an easement places a burden on the *servient tenement* (i.e. the burdened land), requiring the owner for the time being of that land to suffer the exercise of the easement: for example, to allow a neighbour to walk across it, or not to interfere with the passage of light to a neighbour or to permit the drainage of water.[6] Moreover, as implied by the above analysis, the easement once created confers a benefit and burden *on the land itself*, so that in principle it may be enjoyed or suffered by any *subsequent* owner of the dominant or servient land. In other words, the easement is not merely personal to the persons who originally created it. It is a proprietary interest in land, so that (subject to the rules of registered and unregistered conveyancing) the benefit of it passes with a transfer of the dominant tenement and the burden of it passes with a transfer of the servient tenement.

7.2   The Essential Characteristics of an Easement

The essentially proprietary nature of an easement, which allows its benefit and burden to be passed to whosoever comes to own an estate in the land, means that care must be taken in defining the types of right that may be recognised as an 'easement'. For

---

1   *Dowty Bolton Paul Ltd* v. *Wolverhampton Corp* (No. 2) (1976).

2   *Moncrieff* v. *Jamieson* (2007); *Kettel* v. *Bloomfold* (2012). This may be in a single space: *Virdi* v. *Chana* (2008).

3   *London and Blenheim Estates Ltd* v. *Ladbroke Retail Parks Ltd* (1992).

4   *Bratt's Ltd* v. *Habboush* (1999).

5   This is different from profits, which do not *require* dominant land, although such land may exist (see e.g. *Polo Woods* v. *Shelton-Agar* (2009)). A *profit à prendre* is a right to take something from another's land, such as wood, pasture, turf or fish: see section 7.13 below.

6   Generally, an easement does not require the owner of the burdened land to expend money in order that the easement may be exercised. Thus, the servient owner need not pay the cost of the upkeep of a right of way or drainage channel or take other positive steps to facilitate the easement: *William Old International* v. *Arya* (2009). However, the owner of the dominant land is usually permitted to enter the servient land and maintain the easement and may well be under a positive obligation to pay for its upkeep as a condition of exercising it: *Changeinvest Ltd* v. *Rosendale-Steinhusen* (2004).

example, if too many rights, or rights that are vague and uncertain, can amount to easements, the owner of the servient tenement might find the use and enjoyment of his own land seriously disrupted. Conversely, if the law recognises too few easements, or is stagnant in the face of economic and social change, it would be impossible for the owners of dominant tenements to safeguard the value and amenity of their property.[7] A balance has to be struck. The law of easements must accommodate the needs of the dominant tenement, while at the same time ensuring that the servient tenement does not become overburdened and inalienable, all in the context of a modern society. For this reason, there are established criteria for determining whether an alleged right is capable of amounting to an easement, although it is also clear that these encompass a certain amount of judicial discretion. These four 'essential characteristics' of an easement are taken from the judgment of Evershed MR in *Re Ellenborough Park* (1956),[8] itself an adoption of the criteria put forward by Professor Cheshire in his *Modern Real Property*. They represent the distillation of much case law, but they are not to be treated as if they were a statute. In addition, it must be appreciated that, if these criteria are satisfied, it means that the claimed right is *capable* of being an easement. Satisfaction of the criteria is not enough to ensure that an easement actually exists. As well as being inherently 'easement-like', the right must be *created as an easement* using the appropriate formalities applicable to proprietary rights.[9] Failure to use the appropriate formalities means that the potential easement will not exist and will take effect only as a personal licence.

7.2.1 There must be a dominant and a servient tenement

The first of the traditional conditions necessary for the existence of an easement is that there *must* be a dominant *and* a servient tenement. This criterion lies at the very heart of the nature of an easement. Easements are rights that exist for the benefit of one piece of land and which are exercised over another. This means that there must be land that is benefited (the dominant tenement) and land that is burdened (the servient tenement). In technical terms, an easement cannot exist 'in gross'[10] and both the dominant and the servient land must be identifiable at the time the easement is created. The creation of easements for the benefit of land not yet identified is impossible.[11] Although there are some statutory exceptions to the rule requiring a dominant and servient tenement, as where utility companies are given easement-like rights over land despite not owning any land

---

7 There is an element of public policy in regard to the granting of easements: see *Smith* v. *Muller* (2008), in which it was held that an easement must have been contemplated by the parties, otherwise the claimant's land would have been inalienable.

8 The claimed easement, which was held to exist, was the right to use a private garden for the benefit of certain surrounding houses.

9 Generally, this means using a deed (plus registration in some cases), or prescription (long use) in order to create a legal easement. For equitable easements, it means an enforceable written instrument or a claim of proprietary estoppel.

10 *Hawkins* v. *Rutter* (1892). As noted, this differs from *profits à prendre*, which, while always being a burden on land, may be enjoyed by a person who owns no land himself: see section 7.13 below.

11 *London and Blenheim Estates Ltd* v. *Ladbroke Retail Parks Ltd* (1992).

of their own,[12] the need for a dominant *and* servient tenement limits the impact of easements because not everybody is able to enjoy rights over the servient land.[13] It also confines the ambit of easements to those rights that truly benefit other *land*. Easements are not to be confused with rights which confer merely personal advantages or advantages on particular people.[14]

7.2.2   The separation of the dominant and servient tenement

The second condition is that the creation and continued existence of an easement is dependent on the dominant and servient tenements being owned or occupied by different persons. An easement is essentially a right in another person's land: for example, to walk over it or to enjoy the passage of light or right of drainage across it. For that reason, the dominant and servient tenements must not be both owned *and* occupied by the same person.[15] Moreover, should the dominant and servient tenements come into the ownership and occupation of the same person, any easement over the servient land will thereby be extinguished: a person cannot have an easement against themselves. Note, however, that there is nothing to stop a tenant enjoying an easement over land retained by the landlord, and vice versa, because in that situation the relevant parcels of land are not owned *and* occupied by the same person.[16] Note, however, that if the occupier of land is a mere licensee[17] no easement can be created between this person and the estate owner, since a licensee owns no estate in the land to which either the benefit or the burden of the easement can attach.[18] Finally, if the dominant and servient tenements come into the same *occupation*, but not also the same ownership (as where the freehold owner of the servient tenement takes a lease of the neighbouring dominant tenement in order to enlarge his premises), the easement is suspended for the duration of the common occupation and may be revived thereafter.[19]

---

12 For example, to run water pipes or electricity cables under a person's land, although such companies prefer to obtain the owner's consent: see e.g. *William Old International v. Arya* (2009).

13 Only the owner of the dominant estate, his agents and bona fide guests.

14 In this regard, note *Wall v. Collins* (2007). In that case, an easement was granted for a leasehold estate and the leaseholder subsequently acquired the freehold. The servient landowner alleged that, because the leasehold had become extinguished (it had merged with the freehold), the easement had been extinguished because the dominant estate to which it was attached had ceased to exist. The Court of Appeal wished to avoid this unpalatable result and decided that it was enough if there was a dominant tenement now benefiting from the easement, rather than the original dominant tenement.

15 *Roe v. Siddons* (1888).

16 *Wright v. Macadam* (1949); *Bratt's Ltd v. Habboush* (1999).

17 See Chapter 6 for so-called 'occupation licences'.

18 A 'Bruton tenant' (see Chapter 6) has no estate and so any rights that this occupier might enjoy over the land of their 'landlord' (who may also have no estate – as in *Bruton v. London & Quadrant* (1999) itself) can only be licences effective in contract between the parties.

19 *Canham v. Fisk* (1831).

7.2.3   The alleged easement must accommodate (i.e. benefit) the dominant tenement

The third requirement limits 'easements' to those rights that affect land *as such*. In the language of *Re Ellenborough Park*, the alleged easement must 'accommodate' (i.e. confer a benefit on) the dominant tenement. This is an important requirement because it restricts easements to those rights that attach *to land* and not 'merely' to the person who currently owns or occupies the land. The general idea is that the easement must be concerned with the *user* of the land, the *value* of the land or the *mode of occupation* of the land (like the idea of 'touch and concern' in restrictive covenants), but there are no set criteria for judging whether a use is sufficiently proprietary in nature to qualify as an easement and each case must be decided on its own facts. The following guidelines give a flavour of what is required, but they may give way in the face of peculiar or special circumstances.

1   The servient tenement must be sufficiently proximate (i.e. near) to the dominant tenement to be able to confer a benefit on it.[20] For example, in order for a right of way over the servient land to benefit the dominant land, the plots of land are going to have to be close to each other. Of course, the two tenements need not be adjacent, or share a common boundary to satisfy this requirement, but, in general, the more physically separate the two properties, the less likely it is that a court would regard an alleged easement over one as benefiting the other. For example, it would be difficult to establish a right of way over Blackacre in favour of Whiteacre when the two plots are at opposite ends of the village.

2   The alleged right must not confer a purely personal advantage on the owner of the dominant tenement. This is a necessary but sometimes elusive criterion because, in a very general sense, a benefit to 'the land' necessarily benefits the person currently occupying it. Nevertheless, it is firmly fixed in the case law. For example, in *Hill v. Tupper* (1863), the owner of a canal granted the claimant the right to put pleasure boats on the canal for profit, but this was held to be a personal advantage, not a right attaching to the claimant's land. The right was not sufficiently connected with the claimant's land so as to amount to an easement as he would have benefited from the right whatever land he had owned, or even if he had no land at all. There was no sense in which this particular right conferred a proprietary benefit on the claimant's particular piece of land; there was no connection between the alleged easement and the alleged dominant tenement. However, it is a mistake to think that rights cannot be easements simply because they confer a commercial or business advantage on the alleged dominant tenement. It is not the commercial nature of the right granted that is important, but whether the commercial advantage endures as an aspect of the benefited estate or, in contrast, whether it is given to a person irrespective of whether he owns an estate in the land. So, in *Moody v. Steggles* (1879), it was accepted that there could be an easement to hang a sign advertising a pub on neighbouring land because this benefited a trade or occupation taking place on the dominant tenement as such. Likewise, in *London and Blenheim Estates Ltd* v. *Ladbroke Retail Parks Ltd* (1992), it was accepted that a right to park on adjoining land and to walk

---

20   *Bailey v. Stephens* (1862).

across it with shopping trolleys was capable of existing as an easement for the benefit of the dominant tenement on which there was a supermarket, and in *Platt* v. *Crouch* (2003), the right to moor boats at a riverbank was capable of subsisting as an easement for the benefit of a hotel on the dominant land. In these cases, there was a connection between the substance of the right claimed and the alleged dominant land: the right was *for* that land. Indeed, if it were true that easements could not accommodate a commercial activity on the dominant land, then much of their usefulness would disappear. Consequently, the issue is not whether a commercial use is being facilitated by the easement, but whether the alleged easement is so connected with the land that the 'benefit' accrues to the current owner *because* he owns an estate in the land.

3   It is unlikely that a right that confers a vague and general 'recreational use' on the dominant tenement will be accepted as an easement. For example, a right to wander over open countryside or parkland is unlikely to be accepted as an easement. Given that the law of easements exists to enhance the social and economic value of land, by giving benefits and imposing burdens on the land as such, it is not to be used for the provision of public amenities. However, the point to remember is that only a *pure and undefined* recreational use is suspect. So, in *Re Ellenborough Park* (1956) itself, a defined right to enjoy an enclosed private park was capable of existing as an easement because the park was created for the very purpose of enhancing the utility of the few private houses that had access to it. As was accepted in *Regency Villas* v. *Diamond Resorts* (2015), the law of easements can accommodate recreational use that confers a benefit in clear and defined circumstances, especially if it enhances the value of the dominant land, but it cannot be used to provide benefits for the public at large, or for ill-defined recreational uses. So, in *Regency Villas*, the timeshare owners of 24 properties adjoining a leisure complex could enjoy an easement to use the golf course, tennis and squash courts, putting green and outdoor swimming pool because this was the basis on which the properties had been developed and sold. Once again, however, an easement is a defined use of land, not of equipment on land, so in *Regency Villas* there could not be easements to use a sauna, sunbeds and a gym.

4   In order for an alleged easement to 'accommodate' the dominant tenement, it does not have to be 'needed' by the dominant tenant. The claimant does not have to prove that the alleged right is beneficial in the sense of conferring a distinct advantage that the land would not otherwise enjoy. It is enough if the alleged right has a sufficient connection with the dominant land and enhances its utility even though the dominant owner had other means of achieving the same advantage. This emerges from *Polo Woods* v. *Shelton-Agar* (2009), and although, strictly speaking, this analysis is made in the context of *profits à prendre* (rather than easements),[21] the same test of 'accommodate' applies to both types of incorporeal right.

---

21 The case concerned an alleged profit of pasturage that the alleged dominant tenement did not actually need, but which still 'accommodated' that land.

7.2.4   The alleged easement must 'be capable of forming the subject matter of a grant'

The fourth condition identified in *Re Ellenborough Park* (1956) is that the alleged easement must be *capable* of forming the subject matter of a grant. This is a broad criterion and allows the court to exercise considerable discretion in deciding whether any use is capable of being an easement. Technically, the point is that every easement must be *capable* of being expressly conveyed by deed (even if it is created in some other way) and so must 'lie in grant'. The creation of rights by deed – in other words by grant – was once a laboured process where every detail had to be described with clarity and certainty. After the LPA 1925, this is no longer true but the criterion remains that, to be an easement, a use has to meet the standard of clarity and certainty such that it could have been 'granted'. Today, this criterion has generated a number of sub-rules, and while previous case law is of considerable help in identifying 'easement-type' rights, there is no doubt that the principles are flexible and there is room for judicial inventiveness. The following points arise from the case law.

1   *An easement cannot exist unless there is a capable grantor*: that is, somebody legally competent to create an easement (being the person in possession of an estate in the intended servient tenement). For example, no easement can exist where the purported grantor is a limited company having no power to grant easements under its articles of association.

2   *An easement cannot exist unless there is a capable grantee*: that is, somebody in whose favour an easement may be legally granted (being the person in possession of an estate in the intended dominant tenement).

3   *All rights that are capable of forming the subject matter of a grant must be sufficiently certain*, and this applies just as much to alleged easements as to other types of proprietary right. In the case of an easement, the right must be capable of clear description and precise definition, principally so that the servient owner (and any purchaser from him) may know the extent of the obligation. For example, in *Re Aldred* (1610), a right to 'a good view' could not exist as an easement, as 'a good view' was simply too indefinite to exist as a property right. Likewise, there can be no easement of privacy[22] and no easement to receive light generally as opposed to a right to receive light through a defined window.[23] However, the decision of the Supreme Court in *Coventry v. Lawrence* (No 1) (2014), implies that this criterion should not be applied too rigidly. In this case, in the context of a nuisance claim, Lord Neuberger said that it was perfectly possible (though not in this case) for an easement to exist to create a noise on the dominant tenement, thus burdening the servient land and preventing its owner from taking action to stop the noise. This is something of a departure from conventional wisdom because there appears to be considerable uncertainty in a right to make a noise: how often, how loud etc.? Nevertheless, Lord Neuberger's view was that it would be possible, albeit rare, to define with

---

22   Browne v. Flower (1911).

23   But contrast, *McGrath v. Parkside Hotels* (2011), where an easement to use the servient land as an exit way for fire escape was confirmed, even though no specific route was specified.

precision the amount of noise to be permitted. We must remember, however, that easements may endure through changes in ownership of both the dominant and the servient tenements and so the requirement of exactness is important. Easements affect land both as a benefit and as a burden, and so it is vital to ensure that the scope of the right granted and the burden of the obligation imposed is clear and unambiguous.

4   For a new use to be capable of being an easement, it must be within the general nature of rights that the law recognises as easements. Although 'the general nature' of an easement is not cast in stone and new easements may emerge over time as the uses of land change, nevertheless the law recognises that easements typically follow a pattern. Thus, there is a reluctance to accept as an easement any use which over-burdens the servient land. In particular, it is unlikely that a court will recognise new easements that require the servient tenement owner to spend money.[24] Easements are designed to allow the owner for the time being of the dominant tenement to gain an advantage from the servient land, rather than imposing positive obligations on the servient tenement owner. Such positive obligations are not generally consist-ent with the limited nature of easements.[25] Thus, in *William Old International v. Arya* (2009), the judge held expressly that easements generally could not impose a pos-itive obligation on the servient owner to do something, but rather they operated negatively to prevent the servient owner from interfering with a permitted use.[26] Such exceptions as existed were confined to limited and special circumstances. One recognised exception is the 'easement of fencing', whereby the servient tenement owner is required to maintain a fence, although perhaps only where this is necessary to keep animals secure.[27] That said, we cannot rule out completely the possibility that a court would recognise a new form of 'positive' easement, especially if the denial of the right arises from a partition of land and the seller/alleged servient owner is seeking to 'derogate from his grant'. So, in *Cardwell v. Walker* (2003), Neu-berger J appears to accept that a servient owner can be under an obligation to provide electricity to the dominant land from a private supply[28] because the absence of the easement would make the land unusable for the very purpose for which it was

---

24 *Phipps v. Pears* (1965) – no easement of weatherproofing as the servient owner would have had to maintain the buildings providing the weatherproofing.

25 Thus, in *Moncrieff v. Jamieson* (2007), Lord Scott notes in passing (the case was about an alleged easement to park) that it is unlikely that the right to use a swimming pool could qualify as an easement because it would impose an unacceptable burden of maintenance on the alleged servient owner. However, *Regency Villas* demonstrates that this is possible in particular circumstances.

26 An easement to create a noise fits this pattern. But there can be no easement requiring an owner to maintain their own land for the benefit of a neighbour, *Phipps v. Pears* (1965). The judge in *Old* also made the more general point that English property law rarely allowed positive obligations to run with the land. See also, for example, Chapter 8 on freehold covenants.

27 *Crow v. Wood* (1971).

28 As opposed to merely allowing the transmission of electricity across his land. The dominant owners would pay for the electricity.

sold.[29] As with much in the law of easements, pragmatism is more important than logic.

5   There is also a reluctance to recognise as an easement any right that gives the alleged dominant tenement owner a large measure of occupation or control of the servient land. An easement is a right over the servient tenement for a defined purpose; it is not equivalent to a right of ownership of that land, and if the dominant owner had desired a greater degree of use of the servient land, he should have bargained for a lease. For example, in *Copeland* v. *Greenhalf* (1952), no easement could exist to store tools of the trade on the servient land, in *Grigsby* v. *Melville* (1974), a right of storage in a cellar could not be accepted and in *Hanina* v. *Morland* (2000), the alleged right to use the flat roof of neighbouring land could not be an easement because it was equivalent to ownership. Likewise, in *Batchelor* v. *Marlowe* (2001) and *Central Midlands Estates* v. *Leicester Dyers* (2003), a right to park several cars on the alleged servient land could not be an easement by analogy with *Copeland* as the impact on it was too great and was inconsistent with the limited nature of easements. However, it is a question of degree in each case whether the dominant rights are so extensive as to prevent them being recognised as easements. In *Virdi* v. *Chana* (2008), despite there being space for only one car, an easement to park was accepted because the servient owner already had difficulty accessing the space and in *R Square Properties* v. *Nissan Motors* (2014) the court allowed an easement to park over 80 cars on the servient land because this did not completely deprive the servient owner of the reasonable use of his land. As *R Square Properties* indicates, the key question is whether the alleged easement would leave the servient owner a reasonable use of his own land. This was the issue raised by the House of Lords in *Moncrieff* v. *Jamieson* (2007), a case concerning an alleged easement to park. In *Moncrieff*, Lord Scott suggested (*obiter*) a more radical approach to the problem. In his view, the relevant question is not whether the alleged easement permits the servient owner a reasonable use of their land, but rather whether the alleged easement leaves the servient owner in possession and control of their land. On this view, even very extensive use of the servient land might amount to an easement, provided that the servient owner retained possession and control, and on this basis Lord Scott doubts whether *Batchelor* v. *Marlowe* was rightly decided.[30] However, not all of their Lordships in *Moncrieff* went as far as Lord Scott[31] and certainly *Batchelor* was not overruled and *R Square Properties* shows that it can be distinguished on the facts. The debate is, therefore, whether the relevant test (sometimes known as the 'ouster rule') is 'does the servient owner retain possession and control?' (as suggested by Lord Scott) or 'does the servient owner retain reasonable use?'. The former would allow more extensive easements, the latter less so. Recent authority prefers the 'reasonable use' test, bearing in mind that the law must be flexible in the face of changing patterns

---

29 The seller had sold land on which there were holiday bungalows and kept the land on which the private generator was located. The issue arises as to whether the purchaser could require the generation of the electricity, albeit that it would be paid for. The reasons for finding such an obligation are not clear from the judgment, but it seems that the court felt that the denial of electricity would destroy the purpose for which the land was sold.

30 Lord Scott also has doubts about *Copeland* v. *Greenhalf*, but is prepared to uphold the decision on its facts.

31 Lord Neuberger in particular was not convinced.

of land use.[32] This willingness to seek a pragmatic solution is not new. Thus, in *Wright* v. *Macadam* (1949), the tenant successfully claimed an easement of storage of coal in a small part of the landlord's coal shed and there is perhaps little to distinguish this case from *Copeland* and *Melville*, save only that the court's assessment of the impact of the alleged easement on the servient land in *Wright* revealed that the servient owner would not thereby be deprived of substantial use of his own property.[33]

It is apparent, then, that flexibility is inherent in the *Ellenborough* conditions, especially evident in the fourth criterion, and it would be unfortunate if the development of the law of easements were circumscribed by too exacting and rigorously applied conditions. Fortunately, there is no evidence that this is occurring and new easements can be accepted if this is consistent with precedent and policy. While the title to servient land should not be 'clogged' by haphazard acceptance of new easements, the law of easements must develop in tune with changing social, economic and technological circumstances.[34]

7.2.5   Public policy

Public policy is not mentioned expressly in *Re Ellenborough Park* (1956) as a factor in deciding whether a use may exist as an easement. In any event, as noted above, that case attempted to define the intrinsic characteristics of an easement, rather than laying down comprehensive rules about when the courts would accept that a specific easement actually existed. To put it another way, the *Ellenborough* conditions tell us when a right is *capable* of being an easement; they do not necessarily tell us when that right will be recognised as an easement in a specific case. However, we must proceed with considerable caution when suggesting that considerations of public policy might have an impact on the identification of rights as easements. Rarely are questions of 'public policy' openly discussed in the cases, although one does find references to ensuring that land is freely alienable – either by giving easements that promote this or by denying onerous ones.[35] That said, and despite a natural reluctance to appeal overtly to public policy, the flexible nature of the *Ellenborough* conditions means that there is always scope for a public interest argument. For example, in *Hill* v. *Tupper* (1863), it may well have been against the public interest for a particular individual to have exclusive rights to use a waterway, and the absence of any similar concern in *Moody* v. *Steggles* (1879) might explain the acceptance of a commercial easement in that case. Likewise, was the easement of storage accepted in *Wright* v. *Macadam*

---

32 The Law Commission proposes that this ouster principle should be abolished, so that, provided an expressly created easement does not confer exclusive possession, it could indeed prevent the servient owner from reasonable use of their land – if this was intended. See Law Commission Report No. 327, *Making Land Work: Easements, Covenants and Profits à Prendre*, June 2011, paragraph 3.208. The Commission assumes that *Batchelor* and the 'reasonable use' test are good law.

33 It may be that, in *Wright* v. *Macadam*, the court felt disposed to protect the tenant in the full enjoyment of his rights against an ungenerous landlord.

34 For example, it is clear that it would be possible to create easements to place a television satellite dish on a neighbour's land and to run fibre-optic cables beneath it.

35 *Smith* v. *Muller* (2008).

(1949) to protect a vulnerable tenant against a powerful landlord? And in *Platt v. Crouch* (2003), did the court accept the existence of the easements of mooring and signage because otherwise the claimant's land, which he had purchased from the defendant, would have been rendered commercially unviable?[36]

7.3   Legal and Equitable Easements: Formalities

As noted above, in order actually to exist as an easement, the claimed right must be created with a sufficient degree of formality. An easement may be either legal or equitable[37] depending on the process by which it comes into existence. Importantly, as we have seen in other areas of property law, failure to use the proper formality when required means that no property right – no easement – will exist at all.[38] Further, the distinction between 'legal' and 'equitable' rights retains significance in the law of easements despite the entry into force of the LRA 2002.

7.4   Legal Easements

In order for an easement to be a legal interest, there are a number of essential conditions that must be met. These appear to be quite complicated, but it must be noted that they are satisfied in the great majority of cases. Normal conveyancing practice on the transfer of land usually ensures that the appropriate formalities are completed.

An easement can qualify as a *legal interest* only if it is held as an adjunct to a fee simple absolute in possession or as an adjunct to a term of years (section 1 of the LPA 1925). Quite simply, this means that an easement is only capable of being a legal interest if it is attached to a dominant tenement that is held under a normal freehold or leasehold estate.[39] Of course, most are.[40] Second, and more importantly from a practical point of view, easements are legal only if they are created by statute, by deed or registered disposition, or by the process of prescription (long user). All easements created by other means, even if held for a legal freehold or legal leasehold, must be equitable (if they exist at all).

---

36 The claimant had purchased the land to run a hotel – the same hotel run by the defendant before he sold the land
    to the claimant.

37 Section 1 of the LPA 1925.

38 In such cases, the claimant will be a mere licensee.

39 Note that, in *Wall v. Collins* (2007), there is a suggestion that an easement can attach to the land itself, independent
    of any estate in it. This novel doctrine was important to the result in that case (because the dominant leasehold
    estate had been terminated through enlargement into a freehold), but it is not clear that it is correct outside the
    special facts of that case.

40 Easements held for other periods – for example, with a life interest or a surviving fee tail – must be equitable, but
    they are quite rare.

7.4.1   Easements created by statute

Occasionally, an Act of Parliament may determine that a local authority, a corporation or even a private individual shall be entitled to the benefit of an easement. This is usually for some public purpose such as, for example, to facilitate the completion of a high-speed rail link or the enhancement of an electricity distribution network. Such easements will be legal. Note, however, that creation by statute *does not* refer to the creation of easements under section 62 of the LPA 1925 (on which, see section 7.9.4 below). Here, we are concerned with easements deliberately created by a specific Act of Parliament.

7.4.2   Easements created by prescription

Easements created by the process of prescription are also legal. Prescription signifies the acquisition of a right by long use: for example, where a person has enjoyed a right of way for many years. Prescription is discussed in more detail below, but for now we may note that prescription takes three forms: common law prescription, 'lost modern grant' and prescription under the Prescription Act 1832.

7.4.3   Easements created by deed (unregistered land) or registered disposition (registered land)

The great majority of legal easements are created by deed (in the case of unregistered land) or by registered disposition entered on the register of titles (in the case of registered land). Easements created by this method are necessarily encompassed in a formal document (the deed or registered disposition) and are legal rights. Indeed, the manner of their creation by formal documents ensures that their existence is more readily discoverable by a prospective purchaser of the servient land. As we shall see below, the creation of legal easements by deed or registered disposition may occur in a wide range of circumstances, and may be either express or implied. Note, however, that whether the easement is *expressly* or *impliedly* created by a deed or registered disposition does not affect its quality as a legal interest. Thus, in unregistered land, the mere fact that an easement has been granted (expressly or impliedly) over an unregistered estate by deed is sufficient to constitute it as a legal interest. In registered land, however, the position is more complex.

Under the LRA 2002, an easement *expressly* granted[41] out of a registered estate – that is, where the servient land is a registered title – *must* be entered on the title of the servient land in order to take effect as a legal interest. It must be substantively registered.[42] Failure to do so renders the easement equitable.[43] This is so whenever title to the servient land is

---

41 An easement is not 'expressly' granted by reason of the operation of section 62 of the LPA – see LRA 2002, section 27(7).

42 Sections 25 and 27 of the LRA 2002 and Schedule 2, paragraph 7.

43 Section 27(1) of the LRA 2002.

registered.[44] Moreover, if the dominant land is registered, the benefit of the easement must also be noted against its title.[45] In other words, registration of the burden of an expressly granted easement against the title of the burdened land is a requirement for 'legal' status and, at the same time, ensures that any purchaser of the burdened land both knows about and is burdened by the easement. However, for impliedly granted easements affecting registered land, and easements burdening servient land that is not registered (for example, where the servient estate is a lease for seven years or less), the easement is legal if created by deed in the normal way. Importantly, however, because legal easements arising in these circumstances are by definition not noted on the title of the servient land,[46] they take effect against a purchaser under the complex provisions relating to easements and overriding interests under the LRA 2002.[47]

7.5   Equitable Easements

Easements held for periods less than a fee simple absolute in possession (freehold) or a term of years (leasehold) must be equitable. They are not included in the definition of legal estates and interests found in section 1 of the LPA 1925. However, most easements are created for these two estates, and the equitable quality of easements is more likely to derive from the fact that the parties have failed to use the formalities appropriate for the creation of legal easements. Consequently, an easement will be equitable even if held for a legal freehold or leasehold if it is not created by statute, or by prescription, or by deed/registered disposition provided that either the easement is embodied in a written contract that equity regards as specifically enforceable[48] or the easement is generated by proprietary estoppel.[49] Failure to use a written contract in the absence of proprietary estoppel means that the right cannot be regarded as an easement at all. It may then amount to a licence to use land, but of course this is a mere personal right unenforceable against a purchaser or other transferee of the 'servient' land. Finally, however, we should remember that equitable easements are rare,[50] because in practice most easements arise out of properly completed property transactions and are legal. Where equitable easements do exist, they are vulnerable on a sale of the servient land and must be protected

---

44 Thus, even if the grant took place in the context of a transaction that itself is not registrable – such as the grant of a lease for seven years or less which becomes the dominant title – the easement must still be registered against servient land of registered title even though the lease itself need not.

45 Schedule 2, paragraph 7 of the LRA 2002.

46 Either because they were not expressly created and so no opportunity for registration arises or because there is no registered title to register them against.

47 See below.

48 Section 2 of the LP(MP)A 1989 and *Walsh* v. *Lonsdale* (1882).

49 An easement embodied in a deed which is not substantively registered when it should be, is also equitable, section 27 LRA 2002.

50 For recent examples of an equitable easement arising through estoppel, see *Chaudhary* v. *Yavuz* (2011) and *Hoyl Group* v. *Cromer Town Council* (2015). Note also *Joyce* v. *Epsom & Ewell BC* (2012), where the foundation of the claim was estoppel and the remedy awarded compelled the servient landowner to grant a legal easement of way.

in the appropriate manner in the systems of registered and unregistered conveyancing if they are to remain enforceable after the sale.

1   *Creation of equitable easements by written instrument.* Under section 2 of the 1989 LP(MP)A 1989, a contract for the creation of an interest in land (e.g. an easement) must be in writing, incorporating all of the terms, and be signed by both parties, if it is to be enforceable. So, rather as is the case with equitable leases, if the parties have entered into a written agreement (i.e. instead of a deed or registered disposition) that purports to create an easement, and if this agreement can be regarded as specifically enforceable under the rule in *Walsh* v. *Lonsdale* (1882), a court of equity will treat the contract as having been performed (even though it has not), and an equitable easement will be the result.[51]

2   *Operation of proprietary estoppel.* The above explanation makes it clear that it is no longer possible (since the 1989 Act) for mere oral agreements as such to create equitable easements.[52] However, as discussed in Chapter 10 in detail, an equitable easement may be created through the process of proprietary estoppel. Thus, in *Ives* v. *High* (1967), an oral promise, relied on by the promisee to their detriment, generated an equitable easement against the promisor because it was unconscionable to deny it, in *Chaudhary* v. *Yavuz* (2011), the servient owner was estopped from denying the existence of an easement to use a stairway as a fire escape and in *Hoyl Group* v. *Cromer Town Council* (2015), the local authority was estopped from denying a right of way in respect of a redevelopment project.[53]

7.6   The Significance of the Distinction between Legal and Equitable Easements in Practice: Easements and Purchasers of the Dominant or Servient Tenement

The most important reason for distinguishing between legal and equitable easements is to understand the effect that such easements may have on subsequent purchasers of the dominant and servient tenements. We know that easements are proprietary: thus, the benefit of the easement is *capable* of running with the dominant tenement, and may be enforced by any owner for the time being of an estate in that tenement; and the burden of the easement is *capable* of running with the servient tenement, and may be enforced

---

51 If e-conveyancing is ever implemented, such a paper contract will create nothing at all, save perhaps a personal licence. The easement will be required to be created by an electronic instrument that will both create the right and register it. It would also mean that the distinction between legal and equitable easements will disappear.

52 Prior to the entry into force of the 1989 Act, easements could be created by oral contract if supported by 'acts of part performance' under section 40 of the LPA 1925, as in *Thatcher* v. *Douglas* (1996). Section 40 is now repealed and mere oral contracts (i.e. where no estoppel is involved) cannot create equitable rights.

53 See also *Joyce* v. *Epsom & Ewell BC* (2012) where the local council was estopped from denying the claimant's right of way over a road.

against any owner for the time being of an estate in that tenement.[54] However, whether an easement does in fact run with the land depends on its legal or equitable status and the mechanics of the systems of registered and unregistered title (as the case may be). In practice, it is usually a potential purchaser of the servient tenement who is most concerned with this issue simply because it is they who will have to allow the dominant tenement owner to exercise the easement. After all, the existence of a binding easement may well affect a potential purchaser's willingness to buy the servient land at all.

7.6.1 Registered land

In registered land, the benefit of an easement becomes part of the dominant tenement and automatically passes to a purchaser or transferee of it. This is so whether the easement is legal or equitable. In fact, in practice, the register of title of a dominant tenement often may note the existence of the benefit of a legal easement and, under the LRA 2002, if at the time the easement is expressly created the dominant land comprises a registered estate, the benefit of an expressly created easement must be noted on the register of title of the dominant land.[55] Usually this will occur automatically as a result of the conveyancing transaction in which the easement is expressly created and thus ensures that purchasers of benefited land are aware of the easements that exist for the benefit of the land they are purchasing.[56]

The position in respect of the servient land is more complicated and depends on whether the easement is legal or equitable and whether it was expressly or impliedly granted and when it was created. However, in all cases we must remember that, should the easement fail to be protected in the appropriate manner, then a purchaser of the servient land will take the servient land free from the easement and so could not be required to permit its exercise by the dominant owner.[57]

7.6.1.1 *Legal easements in existence before 13 October 2003 (the date of entry into force of the Land Registration Act 2002)*

The great majority of these legal easements will be registered against the title of the servient land (because of the way in which they were created) and will, therefore, be binding against a subsequent purchaser of it. However, those legal easements created before first registration of title, or which are not registered because they were impliedly created before the entry into force of the LRA 2002 (or which for some other reason were not registered against the servient land), qualified as overriding easements under

---

54 Note also that persons present on the servient land with no estate – such as adverse possessors and licensees – can be compelled to permit enjoyment of the easement (although they cannot create one) precisely because the easement binds the land, not simply the people occupying it.

55 Schedule 2 of the LRA 2002.

56 If the benefit is not noted on the title – perhaps because it was impliedly granted or pre-dated the LRA 2002 – the person entitled to the benefit of the easement in respect of his dominant tenement may apply to have that benefit noted on his title (LRR 2003, Rules 73 and 74).

57 Section 29 of the LRA 2002. If the transferee of the servient land is not a purchaser, the transferee is bound by the easement whether it is appropriately protected or not (section 28 of the LRA 2002).

the LRA 1925.[58] They continue to qualify as interests which override under the LRA 2002 and thus bind the servient land automatically.[59]

7.6.1.2   Legal easements in existence at first registration of title under the Land Registration Act 2002

These legal easements, whenever created and whether arising expressly or impliedly, qualify as interests which override under Schedule 1, paragraph 3 of the LRA 2002. Consequently, they bind the servient land automatically. This is as it should be, because such easements would have bound the applicant for first registration immediately before such an application.[60] However, such easements are likely to be brought on to the register of title in due course when the first registered proprietor disposes of the land because the new owner will come under a duty to disclose such interests by reason of section 71 of the LRA 2002. If registered as a result of this disclosure, they will then bind by reason of their registration.[61]

7.6.1.3   Legal easements expressly created over a registered estate on or after 13 October 2003: those governed entirely by the Land Registration Act 2002

Under sections 25, 27 and Schedule 2 of the LRA 2002, a legal easement expressly created on or after the entry into force of the Act does not actually qualify as a legal interest unless and until it is entered against the title of the servient land. It must be substantively registered.[62] Thus, for these easements, both their status as a legal interest and their ability to bind a purchaser of the servient land depends on their registration. In fact, this will occur as a matter of course if the easement is created during a conveyance of a registered estate, although it will require a deliberate act of registration if the easement is contained in a deed of grant not tied to a sale or transfer of land.[63] Under this provision, the great majority of expressly granted easements will take effect as legal interests binding the servient land. However, failure to register *when required* means that the easement can qualify only as an equitable interest.[64]

---

58 Under the old section 70(1)(a) of the LRA 1925.

59 Schedule 12, paragraph 9 of the LRA 2002. Such easements may be brought on to the register of title by reason of the duty to disclose such interests under section 71 of the LRA 2002 when a person makes an application to register a disposition of a registered estate. They will then bind by reason of their registration.

60 Because 'legal rights bind the whole world' in unregistered conveyancing and the land was transferred as an unregistered title and then first registered.

61 If they are not disclosed and registered, they remain as overriding interests and continue to bind.

62 If the dominant land is also registered, the benefit should be entered against the dominant title also.

63 For example, where two existing neighbours agree to grant mutual easements to each other.

64 Section 27(1) of the LRA 2002.

7.6.1.4 *Legal easements impliedly created over a registered estate or where the servient land is not a registered estate,*[65] *on or after 13 October 2003: those governed entirely by the Land Registration Act 2002*

These legal easements cannot be registered automatically against the servient land either because they are created impliedly and thus the conveyance contains no express mention of them that would trigger their registration, or because the servient land is carved out of a registered estate but is not itself a registered estate and so there is no registered title that can be burdened. For practical purposes, this means legal easements created by reason of prescription, necessity, common intention, the rule in *Wheeldon v. Burrows* (1879), under section 62 of the LPA 1925[66] or where the easement (however created) takes effect against a lease for seven years or less. In all of these cases, because the legal easement cannot be substantively registered, it can be protected as an overriding interest, it will qualify as an overriding interest *only* if it falls within the complex provisions of Schedule 3, paragraph 3 of the LRA 2002. If it does not so fall within Schedule 3, it will not override and will not bind a purchaser of the servient title unless it has otherwise been entered on the register.[67] As discussed in Chapter 2, Schedule 3, paragraph 3 is not the easiest statutory provision to understand, but in essence it stipulates that a legal easement of this type (i.e. impliedly granted or taking effect over a non-registered estate) will take effect as an overriding interest if, but only if:

1   it is registered under the Commons Registration Act 1965; or
2   it would have been obvious on a reasonably careful inspection of the land; or
3   it was known about by the purchaser of the servient land; or
4   it has been used within one year immediately prior to the transfer in question.

Clearly, the point of these provisions is to give the purchaser of the servient land every opportunity of discovering the easement before he buys the land while at the same time seeking to preserve the overriding status of those important easements that are actually used for the benefit of the dominant land. In fact, in practice it is difficult to imagine how any implied legal easement could fail to qualify as an overriding interest under these wide-ranging provisions. At this relatively early stage in the life of the LRA 2002, we might venture the tentative conclusion that virtually all legal easements in principle falling within the Schedule (i.e. impliedly granted or over a non-registered estate) will qualify as overriding despite the obvious intention that at least some should be excluded. Once again, many of these easements are likely to be brought on to the register of title in due course when the registered proprietor disposes of the land because the new owner is under a duty to disclose such interests by reason of section 71 of the LRA 2002. If so registered, they will then bind by reason of their registration.

---

65 For example, where the servient estate is a lease for seven years or less, this is not a registrable estate.

66 These cases of implied grant are considered below.

67 Merely using an easement over the servient land does not qualify as actual occupation of it so as to trigger an overriding interest under Schedule 3, paragraph 2 (*Chaudhary v. Yavuz* (2011)). Note, every easement would, of course, bind a non-purchaser (section 28 of the LRA 2002).

7.6.1.5   Equitable easements that were overriding prior to 13 October 2003

The original scheme of the LRA 1925 envisaged that the great majority of equitable ease-ments would need to be registered if they were to bind a purchaser of the servient tene-ment. However, according to *Celsteel* v. *Alton* (1986), as followed by the Court of Appeal in *Thatcher* v. *Douglas* (1996), equitable easements that were 'openly exercised and enjoyed' within the meaning of the old Rule 258 of the LRR 1925 qualified as overrid-ing interests under section 70(1)(a) of the 1925 Act. If such easements did qualify as overriding because of this provision, they will continue to override under the LRA 2002.[68] Although there is no doubt that this interpretation of the 1925 Act subverted the original registration system, the LRA 2002 does not remove the overriding status of those equitable easements that qualified under this provision and so the anomaly will remain. However, cases are likely to be few and far between, not least because equitable easements are uncommon.

7.6.1.6   Equitable easements at first registration of title under the Land Registration Act 2002

Immediately prior to first registration of title, the land is (of course) unregistered. An equitable easement will be binding on the owner of the unregistered servient land (assuming they were a purchaser of it and not the grantor of the easement)[69] only if it is registered as a Class D(iii) land charge under the LCA 1972. If it is so registered, its reg-istration entry will be transferred to the register of title of the servient land when the ser-vient land is first registered. If it is not so registered as a land charge, it could not have bound the owner of the servient land (assuming he was a purchaser for money of money's worth of a legal estate)[70] and so should not bind at first registration of title. After all, the first registered proprietor was the previous owner of the unregistered estate and the mere act of registration cannot make him bound by something that he was not previously bound by. Thus, equitable easements at first registration are not interests which override and can bind the new registered proprietor only if they are entered on the register of title by reason of a transfer of a previous land charge entry in unregistered conveyancing.[71]

---

68 Schedule 12, paragraph 10 of the LRA 2002.

69 The grantor is bound by the easement as a matter of contract.

70 If the servient owner created the easement himself, he will be bound to respect it in favour of the grantee, irrespective of registration.

71 As noted above, it is most unlikely that an equitable easement would qualify as an overriding interest by reason of 'actual occupation' because, by definition, the dominant owner merely uses the servient land; he is not in actual occupation of it (*Chaudhary* v. *Yavuz*).

7.6.1.7 *New equitable easements and dealings with land already registered*

The rationale of the LRA 2002 is to bring as many rights as possible on to the register. Consistent with this, equitable easements created over registered land after the entry into force of the LRA 2002[72] cannot qualify as interests which override under Schedule 3 of the Act. Paragraph 3 of Schedule 3 is limited to certain types of *legal* easement and it is most unlikely that an equitable easement could qualify as an overriding interest by reason of 'discoverable actual occupation' within paragraph 2 of the Schedule because, by definition, the dominant owner merely uses the servient land; he is not in actual occupation of it – *Chaudhary v. Yavuz* (2011).[73] Consequently, if an equitable easement created after the entry into force of the LRA 2002 is to survive a transfer of the servient land to a purchaser, it must be protected by the entry of either an Agreed or a Unilateral Notice on the register of title of the servient land. Failure to so register would make it unenforceable against a purchaser for valuable consideration of the servient land (section 29 of the LRA 2002), although it would be enforceable against a non-purchaser, such as a recipient of a gift or a devisee under a will (section 28 of the LRA 2002).

At this point, because of the complex nature of the provisions concerning easements under the LRA 2002, a summary may be helpful.

1   *All* easements (legal or equitable) that were overriding before the entry into force of the LRA 2002 continue to be overriding.
2   All legal easements expressly or impliedly granted will override a first registration.
3   Legal easements expressly granted over a registered estate after the entry into force of the LRA 2002 must be substantively registered against the servient land to exist at law and so cannot be overriding. But, they are protected by such entry and are binding for this reason.
4   Impliedly granted legal easements and legal easements over a non-registered estate carved out of registered land created after entry into force of the LRA 2002 will override against a purchaser provided that they are either known to the purchaser, or are patent on a reasonably careful inspection of the servient land, or have been exercised within one year before the sale to the purchaser, or are entered (if permitted) on the special register maintained under the Commons Registration Act 1965. This is the effect of paragraph 2 of Schedule 3 to the LRA 2002.
5   Equitable easements will not override at first registration but will bind only if previously registered as a land charge in unregistered land and such registration is transferred to the register of title of the servient land.
6   New equitable easements will not override a purchaser of an already registered title (provided that they did not override under the old LRA 1925 as being in existence before 13 October 2002) and so must be protected by the entry of a Notice in order to bind a purchaser of the servient land.

---

72 Those that existed prior to entry into force of the LRA 2002, and which overrode under the LRA 1925, continue to do so – see section 7.6.1.5 above.

73 Some commentators argue that use of certain easements may also amount to 'actual occupation': for example, an easement of parking. This is yet to be tested, but it is not clear that this would really be 'occupation' within the current meaning of that term.

7   Non-purchasers of a registered title take the land subject to all pre-existing ease-
     ments (legal or equitable), whether they amount to an overriding interest, or are
     registered or are neither: section 28 of the LRA 2002.

7.6.2   Unregistered land

With regard to unregistered land, the *benefit* of both legal and equitable easements
becomes part of the dominant tenement and automatically passes to a purchaser or other
transferee of it. This is similar to the position in registered land. Once again, questions
concerning the *burden* of the easement are best considered by separating legal and equitable easements. Note, however, that these rules will determine whether the purchaser of
the servient land is bound by the easement *immediately prior* to compulsory first registration
of title following the purchaser's acquisition of the land. At first registration, the effect of
the easement is determined by the LRA 2002, although in reality those provisions effectively ensure that the applicant for first registration is in the same position they were in
immediately prior to such first registration.

7.6.2.1   *Legal easements*

As with all legal rights in unregistered land (except the *puisne* mortgage – see Chapter 3),
legal easements 'bind the whole world'. They are automatically binding on a purchaser
(or other transferee)[74] of the servient land, who must allow the owner of the dominant
tenement to exercise the easement.

7.6.2.2   *Equitable easements*

Most equitable easements are Class D(iii) land charges under the LCA 1972. As such,
they must be registered in order to bind a subsequent purchaser for money or money's
worth of a legal estate in the land. If an equitable easement is not registered as a Class
D(iii) land charge, it will be void against such a purchaser, but will remain enforceable
against others; for example, a squatter, recipient of a gift or person inheriting under a
will.[75] The single exception to this need to register may be equitable easements created
by proprietary estoppel. According to Lord Denning in *Ives* v. *High* (1967), equitable
easements created by estoppel are not within the statutory definition of Class D(iii)
land charges, apparently because that category includes only those equitable easements
that could once have been legal but are rendered equitable by the 1925 legislation.
Estoppel easements are, of course, purely equitable, and always will be. Therefore,
equitable estoppel easements will be binding against a purchaser of the servient land
according to the old 'doctrine of notice'. This means that an equitable estoppel easement will be valid against everyone except a bona fide purchaser for value of a legal
estate in the servient land who has no notice (actual or constructive) of the
easement.[76]

---

74 For example, a person inheriting under a will.

75 See generally *Midland Bank* v. *Green* (1981).

76 But it would not bind at first registration without an entry being made against the title by means of a Notice.

7.7   The Creation of Easements

We have noted above that there are various ways in which a legal or equitable easement may come into existence.[77] To sum up, they are: by statute (legal easement); by prescription (legal easement); by deed or registered disposition (legal easement); by a specifically enforceable written contract, not amounting to a deed or registered disposition (equitable easement); and by estoppel (equitable easement). The creation of easements by statute for particular and special circumstances need not be considered in any detail, and prescription is considered in section 7.10 below. The operation of the doctrine of proprietary estoppel is considered in Chapter 10, where it will be seen that it is a general doctrine under which the emergence of an easement is only one way in which a court might choose to 'satisfy' the estoppel. It is best considered separately. The following section therefore considers the creation of easements by deed or registered disposition, or by written contract. However, although the use of one of these three methods of creating an easement may give rise to a different quality of easement (i.e. a legal or equitable easement), it should be appreciated that all three 'methods' will operate against the same factual background. Whether the parties to a transaction choose, or are required to use, a deed, a registered disposition or a written contract to carry out their intentions, will depend on the nature of the land (unregistered or registered) and their own appreciation of the needs of the situation at the time. What is important, therefore, is to analyse the *factual* scenarios in which easements may be created, and only after that ascribe a legal or equitable status to the easement thereby created according to the actual formalities used by the parties. To put it another way, what is important is the different factual situations (excluding statute, prescription and estoppel) in which easements may be created. These are described immediately below.

7.8   Express Creation

Easements may be created expressly, either by express *grant* or by express *reservation*.

7.8.1   Express grant

An easement is expressly granted when the owner of the potential servient tenement grants (i.e. gives) an easement over that land to the owner of what will become the dominant tenement. This may occur in two principal scenarios.

1   Where the servient and dominant tenements are already in separate ownership, the servient tenement owner may grant an easement over his land to his neighbour: for example, A grants B (a neighbouring landowner) a right of way over A's land in return for a one-off payment, or simply to be neighbourly. This is relatively uncommon,[78] but might occur when a landowner proposes to change the use of

---

77 Deeds, registered dispositions, written instruments and estoppel.
78 See *CP Holdings* v. *Dugdale* (1998) for an example.

his or her land and requires an easement over a neighbour's land in order to accomplish it.[79] If the grant is by deed or registered disposition[80] (as the case may be for unregistered or registered land), the easement will be legal, and if it is by enforceable written contract, the easement will be equitable.

2   Where land is owned by a potential servient owner and he then sells or leases a piece of that land to another, the potential servient owner (and seller) may include in that sale/lease a grant of an easement to the purchaser. The land remaining in the seller's possession becomes the servient tenement and the piece sold/leased becomes the dominant tenement. The seller has granted an easement over his own land along with the sale/lease of the dominant part and the easement is mentioned expressly in the conveyance of the dominant part to the purchaser. If that conveyance is by deed or registered disposition (as the case may be), the easement is legal;[81] if the transfer is by written contract, the easement is equitable. An example is where a person sells part of his land and includes in that sale the right to lay water pipes under his retained land for the benefit of the part sold: an easement has been expressly granted. This is a very common way to create easements, an example being *Hillman* v. *Rogers* (1998), which concerned an easement to cross a road at a defined point.

7.8.2   Express reservation

An easement is expressly reserved when the owner of the potential dominant tenement keeps (i.e. reserves) an easement for the benefit of the land kept, operating over other land. In practice, this is the opposite of express grant by sale or lease, considered above. For example, where land is owned by the potential dominant owner, and he then sells or leases a piece of that land to another, the potential dominant owner may include in that sale/lease a reservation of an easement for himself. The land remaining with the seller becomes the dominant tenement, and the piece sold/leased becomes the servient tenement. The seller has reserved an easement for the benefit of his own land in the sale/lease and the easement is expressly reserved in the transfer of the servient part to the purchaser. If that conveyance is by deed or registered disposition (as the case may be), the easement is legal; if the transfer is by written contract, the easement is equitable. An example is where a person sells part of his land to a builder, but reserves a right of way over the land sold: an easement of way has been expressly reserved. Note, however, there is a general rule that a conveyance carries with it full rights to the land sold (i.e. a seller 'may not derogate from his grant').[82] Consequently, the reservation of an easement for the benefit of land retained, to take effect over land just sold, must be clearly and unequivocally expressed.

---

79 For example, the building of an extension might require an easement of drainage through pipes under a
    neighbour's land.

80 And substantive registration of it where required in registered land.

81 And substantive registration of it where required in registered land.

82 For an example, see *Donnington Park Leisure* v. *Wheatcroft* (2006).

7.9   Implied Creation

The above section dealt with the express creation of easements, either by grant from the owner of land on a sale/lease of part of it or by reservation of an easement by that person for the benefit of his retained land. In either case, the point is that the easement is expressly mentioned in the transfer of the dominant tenement (grant) or servient tenement (reservation). Furthermore, the easement will be legal or equitable depending on whether the transfer of the land is by deed/registered disposition, or a specifically enforceable written contract. Of course, given that a transfer of an estate in land is involved, the use of a deed/registered disposition is very probable and thus most easements are in fact legal. It may happen, however, that a transfer of land does not expressly mention an easement, even though this would have been expected or desirable in the circumstances. What if, for example, a seller of part of his land meant to grant an easement of way to a purchaser or to keep an easement of drainage for himself but the conveyance was silent on the matter? In some of these situations, an easement can be implied into a transfer of the relevant land, so creating an easement in a similar manner as if it had been expressly created. These situations are discussed below, and encompass cases of *implied grant* and *implied reservation*. In each case, however, if the easement is implied into a deed/registered disposition, the easement will be legal, and if it is implied into a specifically enforceable written contract, it will be equitable. The easement takes the character of the document into which it is implied.[83]

7.9.1   Implied by necessity: grant and reservation

An easement may be impliedly granted, and occasionally impliedly reserved, because of necessity. The most common example is where the land sold (grant) or land retained (reservation) would be useless without the existence of an easement in its favour. Although the implication of an easement by necessity can be prevented by clear words in the relevant conveyance, the courts will not readily reach such a conclusion, especially if this would render the land unusable.[84]

7.9.1.1   *Grant*

Although it is perfectly possible for any type of easement to be implied into a conveyance for reasons of necessity, easements of necessity arise most frequently in connection with easements of way or light. So, if A sells part of his land to B, but it is impossible for B to gain access to his new land without walking over the land retained by A, an easement of way by necessity will be impliedly granted in favour of B's land over A's retained land: that is, the grant of an easement will be implied into the transfer of the dominant part to B. Another example is provided by *Wong v. Beaumont* (1965), in which an easement of ventilation by necessity was held to exist when land sold to a purchaser was intended to be used as a restaurant, but could not be so used without an easement

---

83 Note, however, that expressly created legal easements and impliedly created legal easements are dealt with
   differently by the LRA 2002. See above in respect of registration requirements and overriding status.

84 *Hillman v. Rogers* (1998).

permitting a ventilation shaft to be constructed over the land retained by the seller.[85] Generally, it is easier to claim an implied *grant* of an easement of necessity than it is an implied reservation but, in all cases, as *Re MRA Engineering* (1988) shows, a real necessity must exist. We are considering easements of necessity, not of convenience. So, in *Manjang* v. *Drammeh* (1990), an easement of way by necessity could not exist over the alleged servient land, because the owner of the alleged dominant tenement could access his land by boat along a navigable river. This is similar to *Re MRA Engineering* itself in which access to land by foot was possible, and so this prevented the implication of an alleged easement of way by reason of necessity for vehicles. Likewise, in *Walby* v. *Walby* (2012), the court has emphasised that it is not enough if the easement is necessary for the *reasonable* enjoyment of the dominant land: the test is a strict one and the claimant must show that, without the easement, the land could not be used at all.

7.9.1.2   *Reservation*

Again, using an easement of way as an example, if A sells part of his land to B, but it is impossible for A to gain access to the land he has *retained* without walking over the land sold to B, an easement of way by necessity can be said to be impliedly reserved in A's favour: that is, the reservation of the easement will be implied on the occasion of the transfer of the servient part to B.[86] Note, however, that the reservation of easements by necessity is rare because not only is it required to establish that the land retained by the seller would be unusable without the easement claimed, it is also the case that the seller had it entirely within his power to expressly reserve an easement as a condition of the sale. Thus, the court looks closely at such claims of implied reservation because the seller could have achieved the same result expressly.[87] Consequently, the law 'leans against' the seller,[88] and he will have to discharge a heavy burden of proof before the court will agree that an easement of necessity should be impliedly reserved in his favour. For example, no easement of way will be implied where it is merely inconvenient to use another route, as in *Re Dodd* (1843), although in *Sweet* v. *Sommer* (2004), an easement of way was impliedly reserved because the alternative access could be achieved only by the destruction of a physical barrier that both seller and purchaser agreed had to remain in place. *Sommer* is, perhaps, one of the more generous applications of the doctrine of implied reservation.

---

85 It is arguable that, if *Wong* were decided today, it would be on the basis of implication by reason of 'common intention'; on which, see below. The land could still have been used without the ventilation easement, though not for the purpose for which it was leased.

86 *Pinnington* v. *Galland* (1853).

87 In cases of express *grant*, the purchaser is not usually in such a strong position and so implied grant can be easier to establish.

88 Often expressed in the idea that a person 'may not derogate from their grant', meaning that the seller cannot easily claim to have retained some right over land when granting it to another.

7.9.2   Implied by common intention: grant and reservation

Easements may be impliedly incorporated into sales of land, either in favour of the purchaser (grant) or in favour of the seller (reservation), if this is required to give effect to
the common intention of the parties. The result of such a doctrine is identical to the
implied grant and reservation of easements by necessity, considered above, except that
the easement does not have to be *necessary* for the use of the land. The point is, rather:

> whether there was a common intention of the parties that the land granted [or
> reserved] should be used in some definite or particular manner and, secondly,
> whether the grant [or reservation] of the easement is necessary to give effect to that
> intention.[89]

Clearly, the acceptance of such a doctrine facilitates the implied creation of easements in
a much wider range of circumstances than that of 'necessity', and what is required is
proof that the parties shared an intention as to a definite use of the land and that the
easement is required in order to facilitate that use. A clear example is provided by *Stafford*
v. *Lee* (1993) in the Court of Appeal, in which Nourse LJ makes it clear that 'common
intention' is distinct from necessity per se. So, in *Stafford*, the claimant (the purchaser)
wished to build a house on his own land, when the only practical access for construction
purposes was over the defendant's land. As the land had been sold to the claimant by the
defendant with a view to the construction of a house, an easement of way for the
purpose of construction was held to have been granted. Likewise in *Donovan* v. *Rana*
(2014), an easement was impliedly granted to achieve the common intention of the
parties that the building of a dwelling-house on the dominant land would be able to
connect to the normal utilities running under the servient land. Indeed, it seems that the
relevant 'common intention' which is to be achieved by the implied easement does not
itself have to be something intrinsic to the land. So, in *Linvale Investments* v. *Walker* (2016),
an easement of way was implied in favour of the purchaser Linvale in order to facilitate
the common intention that the land be fully utilised so as to maximise profit for the
owners. The defendants were not allowed to derogate from their grant by compromising
the purpose behind the purchase.

It is also clear that easements can be reserved by reason of 'common intention'. In
Peckham v. *Ellison* (1998), an easement of way was held to be impliedly reserved in favour
of the seller, although, like all cases of *reservation*, this is not lightly to be presumed. So in
Chaffe v. *Kingsley* (1999), the Court of Appeal refused to impliedly reserve an easement by
way of common intention, distinguishing *Peckham* on the ground that the alleged easement in its case was too unspecific and imprecise to justify such a step. To conclude
then, the implied creation of easements by reason of common intention is possible, but
not always permissible. After all, we must not forget that, if the alleged easement was so
crucial to the parties' common intention, why was it not expressly inserted in the relevant conveyance?

---

89 *Davies* v. *Bramwell* (2007), applying *Pwllbach Colliery* v. *Woodman* (1915). On this basis, *Wong* properly may be regarded
   as an easement by reason of common intention.

7.9.3   Easements implied by reason of section 62 of the Law of Property Act 1925: grant only

The third method by which easements may be impliedly created arises because of the effect of section 62 of the LPA 1925. The factual matrix for the application of section 62 is where an owner of land sells or leases part of it to another, and that sale or lease impliedly carries with it certain easements for the benefit of the part sold, burdening the part retained. In this respect, the operation of section 62 is similar to *Wheeldon v. Burrows* (1879) – considered below. Importantly, easements may only be *granted* to the purchaser by reason of section 62 LPA 1925 and they may not be reserved for the seller. Further, as we shall see, although there are some differences in the application of section 62 and *Wheeldon v Burrows*, the two rules do overlap to a considerable extent.

At first glance, section 62 appears to have little to do with easements, and especially little to do with the creation of *new* rights over land where none existed before. The material part says that:

> a conveyance of land shall be deemed to include and shall by virtue of this Act operate to convey, with the land, all buildings, erections, fixtures ... liberties, privileges, easements, rights, and advantages whatsoever, appertaining or reputed to appertain to the land, or any part thereof.

So, in simple terms, if a landowner has two or more plots of land and then conveys a legal estate[90] in one of those plots to a purchaser, the purchaser will be granted, by the automatic action of section 62 of the LPA 1925, all those rights that were previously enjoyed with the land. This is straightforward enough, but section 62 is a powerful statutory provision. Its importance lies in the fact that it will convert into easements (for the benefit of the land sold, to the burden of the land retained) all of those rights that were previously enjoyed for the benefit of the land sold (or leased),[91] even though, prior to sale, they were merely 'precarious': that is, they were exercised over the land now retained by the seller only by virtue of his permission, and not as of right as easements. An example will be given shortly, but first we must note the conditions that must be fulfilled before section 62 can create new easements in favour of the purchaser.

1   Section 62 LPA 1925 applies only to sales or leases that are made by 'conveyance', and a conveyance means the grant or transfer of a legal estate. In all cases, save for leases for three years or less, this means that a deed or a registered disposition must be used. Consequently, section 62 will create easements only when the sale or lease to the purchaser is made by a deed or registered disposition (as the case may be) not when it is made by written contract. Consequently, section 62 creates only legal easements, because the easement will be implied into the transfer of a legal estate.

---

90 A 'conveyance of land' within the section means the grant of a legal estate and includes a legal freehold and legal leasehold. Thus, the section is triggered by the use of a deed (except for leases of three years or less, etc.) and not a 'mere' written instrument. A 'registered disposition' is a deed and therefore a 'conveyance' in registered conveyancing and within the section.

91 It is essential that the right was *previously* enjoyed, not enjoyed after the sale, *Campbell v. Banks* (2011).

2   The operation of section 62 can be excluded by the conveyance to the purchaser, either expressly by clear words or where the circumstances existing at the time of the conveyance show that the parties intended to exclude the section.[92] In fact, most professionally drafted conveyances will exclude section 62, as this prevents the seller of land creating new easements burdening any land that they might retain. Consequently, the cases in which section 62 operates today usually are the result of some conveyancing blunder or result from some other entanglement between the parties where they were uncertain about the need for easements (and hence implied creation was not excluded). P & S Platt v. Crouch (2003), considered below, is of this type.

3   Like the rule in Wheeldon (see below), only those rights that are intrinsically capable of being easements may be impliedly created by virtue of section 62. So, even though the 'right' over the land that is then turned into an easement by a convey-ance under section 62 is not (prior to that conveyance) an easement (because, for example, the landowner gave merely a limited, verbal and temporary permission), it must fall within the general nature of rights recognised by easements under the law. A mere permission to park a car can turn into an easement of way by section 62 (as in Hair v. Gillman (2000)), but a mere permission to play football somewhere on the land never can. Section 62 can impliedly create only that which could be expressly created.

4   The use which it is alleged is turned into an easement and must be taking place prior to the conveyance of the alleged dominant part to the purchaser. Section 62 cannot create easements when the use occurred only after the dominant part was sold (Campbell v. Banks (2011)), because at that time there was no 'use' to imply into the sale.

5   A common circumstance in which section 62 will operate is where the plots of land owned by the seller were in separate occupation (but not ownership) before the sale or lease. This is what is called 'prior diversity of occupation' and is explained more fully below and was once a point of difference with the rule in Wheeldon. This application of section 62 – where there is prior diversity of occupation – is found in the important cases of Long v. Gowlett (1923) and Sovmots v. Secretary of State for the Environment (1979) and it was once thought to be absolutely essential for the opera-tion of the section, save perhaps in respect of easements of light.[93] However, it is now clear that it is not essential for the land to have been in 'prior diversity' before section 62 can operate. If, instead, the alleged use was 'continuous and apparent' (in the sense discussed below in connection with Wheeldon), then prior diversity is not needed – P & S Platt v. Crouch (2003), Alford v. Hannaford (2011), Wood v. Waddington (2015).

6   In those cases where the alleged easement is not continuous and apparent, 'prior diversity' is needed. This means that, before the potential dominant tenement is

---

92   Birmingham, Dudley and District Banking Co. v. Ross (1888); Hair v. Gillman (2000), confirmed in Platt v. Crouch (2003). Implied exclusion will be difficult to prove when the alleged rights are so obviously for the benefit of the land conveyed, as in Platt. Consequently, a well-drafted conveyance will expressly exclude the operation of section 62 and, indeed, Wheeldon v. Burrows.

93   Broomfield v. Williams (1897).

sold, different persons must have been occupying that land and the land retained by
the seller (the potential servient tenement). Effectively, this means that the seller
will have been occupying the potential servient land and the potential dominant
tenement will have been occupied by his tenant or licensee. It is this classic 'landlord and tenant' scenario that gives rise to many cases concerning section 62.
Indeed, usually this tenant or licensee will be the person who then purchases or
leases the property by conveyance and thereby obtains the easement under section
62, but it is not essential that this be so, provided that such diversity did exist prior
to the conveyance of the dominant plot to the purchaser.[94]

7   To sum up: first, if the alleged easement is 'continuous and apparent', section 62
may generate an easement in favour of the purchaser;[95] second, if the alleged easement is not 'continuous and apparent', there must be 'prior diversity of occupation'; third, if there is an alleged easement of light, prior diversity is not needed but
it is not clear whether this is because such a use is always 'continuous and apparent'
or because of a special rule for easements of light.[96]

If the above conditions are fulfilled and a conveyance of the potential dominant tenement is made (e.g. a sale, a lease, a renewal of a lease), then the purchaser will be
impliedly granted as legal easements those rights that were previously enjoyed for the
benefit of the land sold. Clearly, however, it will be apparent from the above explanation
that the operation of section 62 is dependent on the existence of the proper factual background and the fulfilment of appropriate legal formalities for a 'conveyance'. It is also
important to remember that this is the creation of an easement where none existed
before; it is not the purchase of already burdened land by the purchaser and so questions
of priority and third parties are not relevant. The following example demonstrates how
section 62 might operate in practice.

7.9.4   An example of the creation of easements by section 62 of the Law of Property Act 1925 in cases of prior diversity

The following is an example of the operation of section 62 in a 'prior diversity' case
because this often causes the most difficulty. Remember that section 62 will also operate
when there is no 'prior diversity' and where the alleged easement is 'continuous and
apparent' or if there is an alleged easement of light.

Smith owns two houses, one of which she occupies herself and one of which she lets
by lease or licence to Jones (therefore the land is in 'prior diversity of occupation').
Smith allows Jones to walk over the garden of the house that Smith occupies as a short
cut to the road. This is a mere licence, being an informal personal permission, but there
is no path and the use is irregular (not continuous and apparent). Smith then grants a
new lease by deed to Jones (or sells him the house). The effect of section 62 of the LPA

94 Hence the purchaser may be some unconnected person, or be the original occupier whose prior lease or licence
has come to an end. See Hillman v. Rogers (1998).
95 It seems that section 62 does not also require that the use was 'necessary for the reasonable enjoyment' of the land
and so is different in this respect from Wheeldon.
96 Broomfield v. Williams (1897).

1925 is to turn the mere permission to walk over the garden into an easement of way. An easement has been implied into the conveyance of part of the land from Smith to Jones. Note, also, the result would be the same if Jones had vacated the property and Smith had conveyed it by deed to Xavier; Xavier would then have been impliedly granted the same easement with and for the benefit of the land he had purchased. The crucial elements in this example are as follows:

1 The alleged easement was not continuous and apparent, nor an easement of light.
2 Both plots of land were owned by the seller originally (Smith), but there was prior diversity of occupation (Smith and Jones on separate plots). The status of Jones (tenant or licensee) prior to the 'easement creating' conveyance is immaterial.
3 The use – the right of access over Smith's land – was taking place before the conveyance of the plot to Jones.
4 Smith then sold the part of the land that enjoyed the benefit of the right by a conveyance (transfer of a legal estate) without excluding section 62. The sale in this example was to Jones (the person previously on the land), but could have been to a completely new person.
5 The 'precarious' right is inherently capable of being an easement. Section 62 may only generate easements where the prior use is capable of being an easement according to the criteria explained in *Re Ellenborough Park*.[97]

Section 62 of the LPA 1925 has many uses, but the creation of easements by implied grant is one of its most startling. Obviously, a seller of land that has been occupied in part by some other person prior to the sale (or where some use has been continuous and apparent) must be very careful not to impliedly grant new easements in favour of a purchaser. For example, in *Goldberg v. Edwards* (1950), a licensee enjoyed a limited access by permission over her 'landlord's' land, and when a new tenancy by deed was granted to her, that permissive right was transformed into an easement,[98] and in *Hair v. Gillman* (2000), the seller inadvertently granted a legal parking easement to a former tenant when the tenant purchased the freehold of what became the dominant land.

7.9.5 Easements implied under the rule in *Wheeldon* v. *Burrows*: grant only

The rule in *Wheeldon v. Burrows* (1879) may appear complicated at first, but it is only a variant of the situation considered above where a person sells/leases part of his land and thereby grants to the purchaser an easement for the benefit of the part sold, burdening the part retained. As with section 62, the easement is not *expressly* created, but is deemed to be implied into the sale of the land because of the circumstances surrounding that sale. Again, like section 62, easements may only be *granted* by this method and the rule in *Wheeldon* may not be used impliedly to reserve an easement for the benefit of the land retained.[99]

---

97 Note *Wheeldon* would produce the same result in this circumstance, if the use was also 'reasonably necessary'.
98 See also *Wright v. Macadam* (1949).
99 Confirmed in *Peckham v. Ellison* (1998).

The rule in *Wheeldon* provides that, where a person transfers part of his land to another, that transfer impliedly includes the grant of all rights in the nature of easements (sometimes called 'quasi-easements') that the seller enjoyed and used prior to the transfer for the benefit of the part transferred, provided that those rights are 'continuous and apparent' and 'reasonably necessary' for the enjoyment of the part transferred. As we know, no easement can exist where the dominant and the servient tenement are owned and occupied by the same person. However, it often happens that a landowner will use one part of his land for the benefit of another, as where a landowner walks across his own field to get to his house. These are so-called 'quasi-easements', because they would have been easements had the plots been in different ownership or possession. Thus, under the rule in *Wheeldon*, if the owner of the entire plot of land sells or leases the 'quasi-dominant' part of his land to another (being the land benefited by the right – in our example, the house), the purchaser is taken to have been impliedly granted the right previously used for the benefit of that part (in our case, a right of way over the retained field). The purchaser's land then truly becomes the dominant tenement, and the land retained by the seller (in our example, the field) is truly now the servient tenement. Clearly, this is a remarkable rule for it might operate unexpectedly to impose a proprietary burden on the land retained by a seller simply because he made use of that land for the everyday benefit of the part he has just sold or leased. It is no surprise, therefore, that this rule is subject to a number of conditions.

1   The rule can be expressly excluded, as where a seller stipulates that the only easements granted to the purchaser are *those expressly* provided for in the sale or lease. This is a most important point and it is standard conveyancing practice to exclude the implied grant of easements when an owner sells or leases part of their land. However, as *Millman* v. *Ellis* (1996) shows, the exclusion of the rule in *Wheeldon* must be clear and the express grant of a lesser (but similar) easement is not to be taken as equivalent to the exclusion of the implied grant of a wider easement. So, in that case, the express grant of an easement of way over a road did not exclude the implied grant, under *Wheeldon*, of an associated easement of way over an adjoining lay-by. Likewise, in *Hillman* v. *Rogers* (1998), the express grant of an easement to cross a road did not exclude the implied grant of a right of way over the road under *Wheeldon*. So, the clearest words should be used to exclude the rule for there is no certainty that a court will agree that it has been excluded simply because the conveyance contains complementary express easements.

2   Only those rights that are *capable* of being easements within the *Re Ellenborough* criteria may become easements by operation of the *Wheeldon* rule. An easement cannot be impliedly created if it could not be expressly created. Such a non-proprietary use would be a licence.

3   Clearly, the alleged right must have been being used prior to the sale or lease. Failure to establish that the right was being used is fatal, even if it is obvious that it *could* have been used to benefit the quasi-dominant plot. So, in *Alford* v. *Hannaford* (2011), the claimant failed under *Wheeldon* as she adduced no evidence of the degree of use of the track over which she claimed a right of way.[100]

---

100 This is clearly connected to whether the use was 'reasonably necessary' or 'continuous and apparent', below.

4   The rule applies to those quasi-easements that are used by the *owner* of the whole
land for the benefit of the part sold *before* the lease or sale of the alleged dominant
part. It does not appear to be enough that some other person used the quasi-
easement, save only if this other person can be regarded as the original owner's
agent or *alter ego*. So, if the owner of land always flew by helicopter to his house, but
all visitors approached the house by walking across his adjoining field, it is debatable whether sale of the house to a third party would carry with it an easement of
way over the field; the right alleged to be an easement was not used by the owner
of the common part for the benefit of the land sold. It would be otherwise if any of
those using the field could be regarded as the owner's agent, *alter ego* or as acting at
his direction and with his permission, as in *Hillman* v. *Rogers* (1998), in which the
owner of the whole land had given permission for others to use the right of way
that was subsequently impliedly created when he sold the dominant part.

5   The quasi-easement must have been 'continuous and apparent' *and* 'necessary for the
reasonable enjoyment' of the part granted. Despite some earlier doubts, and some
uncertainty in *Wheeldon* itself, the Court of Appeal decision in *Wood* v. *Waddington*
(2015) assumes that both these conditions need to be satisfied (see also *Millman* and
note the contrary view in *Rogers*). Of course, it remains open to the Supreme Court to
take a different view, although given the paucity of cases applying *Wheeldon*[101] this is
not likely. A quasi-easement is 'continuous and apparent' if it is used regularly
(*Wood*) and visible on inspection of the servient land over which it exists, or so
obvious that its use for the benefit of the part sold is beyond doubt. In *Millman*, the
fact that the lay-by was covered in tarmac was evidence that it was used as part of a
right of way and was proof that it was 'continuous and apparent'. Similarly, the
passage of light through a defined window would be continuous and apparent, even
though the window itself is the only outward sign of the right. Moreover, 'continuous' does not mean 'in continuous use', in the sense that the owner continuously used the right now alleged to be an easement (e.g. there is no need to walk
over the field every day); rather, it is that the use must occur regularly in an uninterrupted manner (*Wood*).[102] The rule in *Wheeldon* converts real use into an easement,
not the infrequent enjoyment of another's land. The requirement that the quasi-
easement must be 'necessary for the reasonable enjoyment' of the dominant part can
cause greater difficulties. Strictly speaking, the requirement is *not* that the easement is
'necessary' for the enjoyment of the land – these are not easements of necessity.
Rather, it is that the easement is necessary for the 'reasonable enjoyment' of the land.
The emphasis is on reasonable enjoyment, not necessity. In *Millman*, therefore, the
fact that use of the lay-by as part of the easement of way made access to the property
considerably safer was enough to establish its contribution to the reasonable enjoyment of the land. By no stretch of the imagination was this lay-by actually 'necessary' in order to access the land; it merely facilitated its reasonable use. However, in

---

101 Because the rule is usually expressly excluded.

102 It may be that the rule in *Wheeldon* can be displaced by the common owner ceasing the activity at some time
     before selling the alleged dominant part. The owner would not then have been using the land before the sale.
     Indeed, this might be done deliberately to prevent any chance of *Wheeldon* applying, although what amount of
     time would have to elapse before a subsequent sale cannot be identified with certainty.

Wheeler v. *JJ Saunders* (1995), decided before *Millman*, and also in the Court of Appeal, it was held that a proposed easement of way was not 'necessary for the reasonable enjoyment' of land because other access to the property existed. While, on a simple view, this could be correct – that is, the existence of another access can mean that the proposed easement of way adds nothing to the reasonable enjoyment of the land and is not, therefore, 'necessary' for its reasonable enjoyment – the judgment in *Wheeler* comes close to equating this criterion with the much stricter test for easements of necessity. This is unfortunate, as the rationale for the two methods of easement creation are different. Easements of necessity do not depend ultimately on the express or implied intentions of the parties but are 'granted' in order to ensure that use of land can be maximised: it is almost policy based.[103] Easements created by *Wheeldon* are much more clearly rooted in the parties' intentions, as demonstrated by their actions prior to sale of the dominant part. The decision in *Wheeler* was subjected to close analysis in *Hillman* v. *Rogers* (1998), and this later case makes it clear that 'necessary for reasonable enjoyment' should not be equated with 'necessity'.

6   Although the most common example of the application of *Wheeldon* is where the common owner keeps the potential servient land, having sold the potentially dominant land, it seems that the rule also operates where the original landowner grants the quasi-dominant part to X and, at the same time, grants the quasi-servient part to Y. According to *Swansborough* v. *Coventry* (1832) and *Hillman* v. *Rogers* (1998), this double conveyance would operate to give X an easement over Y's land. In other words, the rule will operate for simultaneous transfers of the prospective dominant and servient parts even though (in our example) X and Y had not been dealing with each other and were in neither privity of contract nor privity of estate. So, if A (original landowner) walks across a field to get to his house, and then sells the house to X and the field to Y, X enjoys the right of way across Y's land. In respect of Y, this is *not* a case in which the burden of an *existing* easement is passing to Y. This is a case of a new easement being created over Y's land, so Y is, in fact, the first owner of the servient tenement. For the purposes of this principle, transactions will be regarded as 'simultaneous' if clearly part of a design to deal with all of the land.[104]

As in the case of easements of necessity and common intention, the character of the easement implied by *Wheeldon* v. *Burrows* follows the character of the document into which it is implied. So, a sale or lease of the dominant part by a deed (or registered disposition plus registration in registered land) means that the easement will be legal, and a sale or lease of the dominant part by an enforceable written contract (as in *Borman* v. *Griffiths* (1930)) means that the easement will be equitable.

Finally, although the rule in *Wheeldon* does appear complicated, its operation is well established and well known. It is a trap for the unwary conveyancer and should be excluded by clear words in the conveyance to the purchaser. Its justification is that a person (the seller) cannot 'derogate from their grant' when transferring land unless there are clear words to the contrary. So, unless specific provision is made, a seller must transfer his land with all of the rights attaching to it, even if this means that 'new' easements are created over his retained land.

---

103 Hence, the court will not readily agree that implied grant by reason of necessity has been excluded.
104 *Hillman* v. *Rogers* (1998).

7.9.6   A comparison between section 62 of the Law of
        Property Act 1925 and the rule in *Wheeldon* v.
        Burrows

The circumstances in which section 62 and *Wheeldon* v. *Burrows* (1879) operate are so similar – even more so after *Platt* v. *Crouch* (2003) – that they are often regarded as interchangeable, as in *Hillman* v. *Rogers* (1998) and *Platt* itself. This may be true, and there is no doubt that they have the same origin in the rule that a person must not derogate from their grant on the conveyance of land. However, their assimilation is not complete and while section 62 and the rule in *Wheeldon* operate against the same factual background, the conditions on which they depend are different in detail.

1   *Wheeldon* operates where the common seller was in occupation of all of the land before the sale of the dominant part and he (or his *alter ego*) used the potential easement. Section 62 can operate in the same circumstance if the easement is continuous and apparent, but it has a wider application to cases of 'prior diversity' which are not within *Wheeldon*.
2   *Wheeldon* creates easements only where the right is 'continuous and apparent' *and* 'necessary for the reasonable enjoyment of the land'. Section 62 does not depend on necessity of reasonable enjoyment. However, in cases where there is no 'prior diversity of occupation', section 62 then requires that the alleged easement be continuous and apparent.
3   *Wheeldon* can imply easements into a legal or equitable sale or lease and may, therefore, create legal or equitable easements. Section 62 operates only where the sale or lease is a conveyance and can create only legal easements.
4   Both *Wheeldon* and section 62 of the LPA 1925 can be excluded by clear words in the conveyance of the alleged dominant tenement. Section 62 can be impliedly excluded by circumstances existing at the date of the conveyance and it would be surprising if this were not also the case for *Wheeldon*.

7.10   Easements Resulting from Prescription

Another method of creating easements is by 'prescription'. To be more precise, we should say easements are 'generated' by prescription, rather than 'created' because 'prescription' is more a process than a deliberate act. In general terms, 'prescription' occurs when the owner of what will be the dominant tenement establishes *long use* over what will be the servient land. If the use is capable of being an easement (i.e. if the *Re Ellenborough* conditions are satisfied), the long use can mature into an easement proper. All easements created in this fashion will be legal. As we shall see, the period for which the use must be established may vary from case to case (depending on which of the three 'methods' of prescription is used), but the essential point is that easements generated by prescription are easements created through the actual use of the potential servient land for the 'right' that is later claimed. So, if the owner of Pinkacre has walked across Blueacre for the required period of time in the appropriate circumstances, an easement of way by prescription (long use) may be established in favour of Pinkacre over Blueacre.

Before going on to consider the conditions for the acquisition of an easement through prescription, it is important to appreciate the basis of this doctrine. After all, it seems strange that one person can acquire a powerful right over their neighbour's land in the absence of any written document or express grant of the right. In fact, the rationale for prescription is a subtle one. The essential point is that the fact of long use of the 'right' by the owner for the time being of the dominant tenement gives rise to a *presumption* that a grant of the right was actually made.[105] This is so even though there clearly is no grant at all! In this sense, prescription is not 'adverse' to the owner of the servient tenement, for the fact of long use is taken to be conclusive evidence of the servient owner's grant of the right.[106] Unlike the law of adverse possession (Chapter 12), the owner of the dominant tenement is taken to have acquired the easement through the acquiescence of the servient owner. Also, again unlike the law of adverse possession, the effect of a successful prescriptive claim is to create a new right for the dominant tenement owner, not merely to extinguish the rights of the owner on whose land the long use occurs.[107] Consequently, the law of prescription is sometimes known as the law of 'presumed grant': the grant of the easement is presumed in favour of the dominant tenement owner from the fact of long use. Of course, there is also policy at play here, and in *R v. Oxfordshire County Council, ex p Sunningwell Parish Council* (2000), Lord Hoffmann made the point with the utmost clarity by noting that 'any legal system must have rules of prescription which prevent the disturbance of long-established de facto enjoyment'.

7.10.1 General conditions for obtaining an easement by prescription

As mentioned already, there are three 'methods' or 'routes' to a successful claim of prescription. They are common law prescription, common law prescription under the rules of 'lost modern grant' and prescription under the Prescription Act 1832. However, these methods are not inherently different, but simply describe the three different ways by which the person claiming the prescriptive right may establish that the long use was, indeed, *long enough* to mature into an easement. All three take the same common thread, that long use presumes a grant of the easement in favour of the dominant tenement. Therefore, the following sections discuss the general conditions for establishing an easement by prescription and, where the different methods have different requirements, this will be noted.

7.10.2 Easements of prescription lie in fee simple only

Although it may now appear to be somewhat anomalous, the origin of prescriptive easements is that they are presumed to 'lie in grant', meaning that they are presumed to have arisen by a grant from the fee simple owner of the servient tenement absolute in possession to the fee simple owner of the dominant tenement absolute in possession.

---

105 See also *Welford v. Graham* (2016) where it was held that the simple fact of the long use gives rise to a presumption that the use was 'as of right'. It would be up to the alleged servient owner to rebut this presumption.

106 *Neaverson v. Peterborough Rural District Council* (1902).

107 We might note, however, that, where an adverse possessor is registered as the new proprietor of title to the land, this looks very much like the creation of a new title in his favour.

Consequently, easements of prescription are always legal, and always attach to the fee estate (the freehold): they are 'permanent' in the same sense that a fee simple is permanent. There can be no easement by prescription in favour of, or against, a leaseholder or an estate that exists in equity only, such as a life interest.[108] This has certain consequences that limit the circumstances in which a prescriptive easement can arise.

1   The long use must be by a fee simple owner of the alleged dominant tenement. This is not necessarily a serious problem, because if the dominant land is possessed by a tenant, the tenant's use of the alleged easement (i.e. by walking across a neighbour's land) can be held to be on behalf of his landlord: that is, on behalf of the fee simple owner. So, provided that the tenant is not asserting that the alleged easement should endure only for so long as the tenancy, this requirement can be met, as explained in *Hyman v. Van den Bergh* (1907).

2   The long use must be *against* a fee simple owner of the servient tenement. This is the converse of the above and means that easements by prescription cannot exist against tenants (however long their lease) or any equitable estate-holder. Moreover, there are further difficulties here, because if the long use occurs at a time when a tenant is on the alleged servient land, it might be difficult to prove that the long use was against the fee simple (freehold) owner – after all, at the time of the long use, a tenant was on the land. This was the case in *Llewellyn v. Lorey* (2011), where the freeholder of the alleged servient tenement had no knowledge of the use on his land, it being in the possession of his tenant, who had not informed him. On the other hand, as *Williams v. Sandy Lane (Chester) Ltd* (2006) makes clear, there is no rule of law that prevents an easement from arising simply because the servient land was in the possession of a tenant *at some time* during the long use. Prescriptive easements rest on acquiescence, not on the fact of whether there was, or was not, a lease. Two different situations need to be distinguished. First, there is no objection to the presumption of an easement from long use if the fee simple owner was in possession of the servient land at the commencement of the long use, but then subsequently leased the land to a tenant.[109] This is because, at the time the long use started, it is possible to presume that the grant was made by the fee simple owner – the fee simple owner had the power to terminate the use before the tenancy took effect. Second, where a tenant is in possession of the alleged servient land *before* the long use commenced, it remains possible to presume a prescriptive easement against a freeholder, albeit that it might be difficult to establish on the facts, and this was the problem for the claimant in *Lorey*. This is because the generation of an easement by prescription rests on the acquiescence of the freeholder and it is perfectly possible for a freeholder to acquiesce in the long use (so as to burden the freehold) even though the land was in the possession of his tenant when the use commenced. If, however, the long use commenced while a tenant was on the land *and* the freeholder had no power to exclude the long use while his tenant was in possession,[110] it would be almost impossible to establish a prescriptive easement against the

---

108 *Kilgour v. Gaddes* (1904).

109 *Pugh v. Savage* (1970).

110 For example, because the right to control the land had been given to the tenant exclusively for the duration of the lease.

freeholder because a person (the freeholder) cannot be taken to acquiesce in something that they cannot prevent.

3   The above rules have additional practical implications. It is impossible for a tenant to claim a prescriptive easement against his own landlord and vice versa. If L (landlord) occupies Plot 1, and leases Plot 2 to T (tenant), T can never claim an easement by prescription against L, and L can never claim an easement by prescription against T. In both cases, the fee simple owner cannot be presumed to have granted an easement against himself. Likewise, if L leases both plots to different tenants, the tenants cannot claim an easement by prescription against each other, since neither is a fee simple owner.

4   It has been confirmed, in *Simmons* v. *Dobson* (1991), that the above limitations apply to both common law prescription proper and common law prescription under 'lost modern grant'. In principle, they should apply in the same measure to prescription under the Prescription Act 1932. However, it seems that the words of this statute may have modified the position. Thus, if the 40-year period of the Act is applicable (see section 7.11.3 below), it may well be that objections based on the lack of a fee simple owner fall away. This is because, under section 2 of the Act, a claim to an easement based on 40 years' use (without consent) is said to become 'absolute and indefeasible' and, according to *Wright* v. *Williams* (2001), this is enough to oust objections based on (at least) the lack of a fee simple servient owner.[111] Likewise, under section 3 of the Act, it is clear that claims to easements of light do not have to fulfil all of the common law conditions. One of the consequences is that, when relying on the Prescription Act 1832 to prescriptive easements of light (but only light), it is possible for them to run in favour of, or against, land held for the leasehold or life interests. In other words, under the Prescription Act 1832, a tenant may acquire an easement of light by prescription against his landlord (and vice versa), and two tenants of the same landlord may acquire such easements for and against each other.

7.10.3   Use must be 'as of right', so as to presume the grant

A second general requirement for the acquisition of an easement by prescription is that the long use must be 'as of right'. To some extent, this is circular. An easement is only truly 'a right' after it has been acquired, but in order to be generated by prescription, the requirement is that the long use must already be 'as of right'! What is meant, then, is that the dominant tenement owner's use of the servient tenement owner's land must be in the character of a use as of right, and not be explicable for any other reason. As is sometimes said, the use must be *nec clam* (without secrecy), *nec vi* (without force) and *nec precario* (without permission).[112] Thus, in *Odey* v. *Barber* (2007), a claim to a prescriptive right of way failed because use of the track had been with the permission of the alleged servient owner. Indeed, it does not matter whether that permission is express, implied, solicited or unsolicited. In *Odey*, the claimants had never sought permission, but it had been given and they were aware of it; hence, their use was not 'as of right'. *Odey* is,

---

111   *Davies* v. *Du Paver* (1953) appears to doubt this proposition.

112   *Solomon* v. *Mystery and Vintners* (1859). See now *R (on the application of Kevin Lewis)* v. *Redcar and Cleveland BC* (2010).

perhaps, generous to the alleged servient owner and is explicable only on the ground that the claimants had effectively accepted the unsolicited permission. In most cases, an unsolicited permission will not suffice to defeat a prescriptive claim because the claimant's assertion of use as of right cannot be defeated unilaterally by the acts of the landowner offering a licence. Thus, *Odey* can be contrasted with *London Tara Hotel Ltd* v. *Kensington Close Hotel Ltd* (2010). In *Tara*, a prescriptive easement was established even though the servient owner believed that a previous licence was still in force. In fact, the previous licence had ended and, looked at objectively, the servient owner appeared to be acquiescing in the use – hence it was 'as of right'. Similarly, a claim 'as of right' cannot be denied simply because the person alleging an easement was solicitous in allowing others to use the same easement – if anything, this is consistent with their claim of right as it re-enforces the sense that power to control the use lay with the alleged dominant owner and not the owner of the servient land (*R* v. *Redcar and Cleveland Borough Council* (2010)). In *R (on the application of Barkas)* v. *North Yorkshire CC* (2014), the Supreme Court considered the meaning of 'as of right' in the different context of an application to register a town or village green. In that case, the Court emphasised that 'as of right' meant without actual permission and was not the same as 'by right': the latter meant with permission and was fatal to a claim to register a town or village green. The same analysis would apply to prescriptive easements: user 'by right' is permissive and cannot establish an easement by prescription, whereas user 'as of right' signifies that the user is asserting their own right and is prescriptive. Of course, user as of right must be established on the facts, but as *Welford* v. *Graham* (2016) makes clear, the simple fact of long use raises a rebuttable presumption that it was 'as of right', and then it is for the alleged servient owner to establish that the use was in fact permissive. This fits well with the idea that prescription is about regularising long use (Lord Hoffmann in *Sunningwell* above) and recognises that it would be difficult for a claimant to an easement to prove a negative – that is, the absence of permission.

7.10.3.1 *Use without secrecy*

No easement can be acquired by prescription unless it arises in circumstances in which a grant can be presumed. Consequently, a secret, hidden use by the owner of the alleged dominant tenement is not sufficient because it demonstrates that no grant can be presumed: a grant presumes a degree of awareness on the part of the servient owner, albeit not positive permission. In practice, this now means that prescriptive easements can be generated only if the use has been 'open' – that is, 'of such character that an ordinary owner of land, diligent in the protection of his interests, would have, or must be taken to have, a reasonable opportunity of becoming aware' of the use (*per* Romer LJ in *Union Lighterage Co* v. *London Graving Dock Co* (1902)). For example, the wearing of a path on the servient land, or the open use of an existing path, is not secret, but the hidden discharge of water on to a neighbour's land would be.

7.10.3.2 *Use without force*

No easement can be acquired by prescription if the owner of the alleged dominant tenement must use 'force' to accomplish the use. Again, the need to use force shows that no grant can be presumed. 'Force' in this situation means either forcible assertion of the use (e.g. breaking down a fence), or continued use in the face of protests by the alleged servient owner. The latter is a forcible assertion of a use, even though no violence is used. A typical example of use 'with force' (and hence no prescription) is where the alleged dominant owner continues with the use after the alleged servient owner has threatened to take, or has taken, legal proceedings (provided, of course, that this does not occur *after* the completion of the period of use sufficient to establish the prescriptive claim).

7.10.3.3   *Use without permission*

As we have seen, the acquisition of an easement by prescription assumes the grant of a right to the dominant tenement. The crucial matter, then, is the servient tenement owner's acknowledgment of the dominant tenement owner's 'right' to the use (as of right), not the servient owner's consent to it (by right). The servient owner must acquiesce in the right, not give his permission for the use, because 'consent' implies that the alleged dominant owner has no right. Consequently, evidence that the alleged servient owner has consented to the use, perhaps by giving a licence, will bar a prescriptive claim, as in Hill v. *Rosser* (1997), and this may be effective even where the permission is unsolicited – *Odey* v. *Barber* (2007). Necessarily, however, the line between acquiescence (the claim to an easement succeeds) and consent (the claim fails) is a thin one. Generally speaking, the servient owner cannot argue that their mere knowledge of the use amounts to implied consent so as to defeat the claim[113] and the dominant and/or servient owner's belief that consent has been given, when it has not, does not necessarily defeat prescription, as in *Tara* above.[114] Neither is if for the claimant to prove an absence of permission: there is a rebuttable presumption that long use was 'as of right' unless the alleged servient owner can establish otherwise (*Welford* v. *Graham* (2016). A good checklist for determining whether the use has been without consent (but with acquiescence), and, therefore, may generate a prescriptive easement, is provided by Fry J in *Dalton* v. *Angus and Co* (1881).

1   Is there a use of the servient owner's land?
2   Is there an absence of a strict right to carry on the use?
3   Does the servient owner have knowledge (actual or constructive) of the use?
4   Does the servient owner have the ability to stop the use, either practically or legally?
5   Has the servient owner abstained from stopping the use for the period required for a successful prescriptive claim?

If these can be answered positively, the prescriptive claim is likely to succeed, although one must be wary of dismissing claims simply because they fail to meet these criteria in some insignificant respect. Finally, it is in the nature of many prescriptive easements that they start out as being exercised with the servient owner's consent and then cease to be consented to at a later date: for example, where a neighbour is given permission to walk across land for one month, but continues after that time. If it can be established that the use became without consent, the prescriptive claim can succeed, with the period of use

---

113 Mills v. *Silver* (1991), and see R v. *Redcar*, above.
114 See also Bridle v. *Ruby* (1989).

being calculated by reference to the moment the consent ended – *London Tara Hotel Ltd* v. *Kensington Close Hotel Ltd* (2010).

7.10.3.4   *A limited exception*

As we have seen above, claims to easements of light under section 3 of the Prescription Act 1832 do not have to fulfil all of the common law conditions. A further consequence is that the long user does not have to be 'as of right', in the sense just discussed. There-fore, under the Act (but only the Act), easements of light may be established even if it is clear that the servient owner was consenting to the right of light.

7.10.4   Use must be in the character of an easement

This is an obvious condition because, after all, we are discussing the generation of a proprietary right that will affect the dominant and servient tenements, irrespective of who later owns the land. Thus, no 'easement' by prescription can arise unless the 'use' itself satisfies the inherent characteristics of an easement explained in *Re Ellenborough Park*. Something cannot be presumed to be granted if it could not be expressly granted. For example, no easement to wander over land can arise by prescription, because such a right can never be an easement; and no prescriptive easement of drainage for the benefit of 'higher' over 'lower' land can exist, because the drainage is natural and not in the way of a right that the owner of the lower land could ever have prevented – *Palmer* v. *Bowman* (1999). However, as *Coventry* v. *Lawrence* (No 1) (2014) shows, this does not mean that new types of easement cannot arise by prescription and in that case Lord Neuberger saw no difficulty in the possibility of a prescriptive easement to make a noise (though not established on the actual facts). However, if both the dominant and the servient tene-ments have come into common ownership at some time during the period of long use, there may be difficulties in establishing a prescriptive claim. In such cases, there is a union of the two tenements, and a landowner cannot have a true easement against himself. The period of long use would, therefore, be terminated and would have to recommence if the tenements later separated.

7.10.5   Use must be lawful

It is also the case that long use may mature into an easement by prescription only if the use itself is lawful. In general terms, easements may not exist for unlawful purposes and no servient owner can be presumed to grant one. However, it is clear from more recent authority that this is not an insurmountable obstacle to the prescriptive grant of an ease-ment, or rather that we must be clear what 'unlawful' means. In *Bakewell Management Ltd* v. *Brandwood* (2004), the question arose whether the defendants had acquired prescriptive vehicular rights of way over common land. If they had not, Bakewell Management, as owner of the common, could charge a large fee. Under statute,[115] a person who drives a vehicle on common land without lawful authority commits a criminal offence and Bakewell argued that no vehicular prescriptive right could have arisen because the alleged

---

115 See section 14(1) of the Road Traffic Act 1930 and section 193(4) of the LPA 1925.

use was unlawful as contrary to the criminal law.[116] The issue, being one of national as well as individual importance, found its way to the House of Lords. In the result, their Lordships overruled prior authority and found that there was an easement by prescription. While it was true that no easement could be acquired by prescription that involved a *substantively* unlawful purpose, that did not prevent the acquisition of easements the substance of which would be lawful *but for* the lack of lawful authority in the first place. Thus, a vehicular easement of way was, in itself, a perfectly lawful purpose, and it was only the lack of 'lawful authority' that rendered it unlawful, but this was the very reason why the easement was being claimed. So, the alleged easement was not inherently unlawful, but was made unlawful by reason of the very facts that required an easement to be granted. While this distinction between a purpose that is substantively unlawful (no prescription) and one that would be lawful but for the denial of right by the landowner (prescription possible) may seem a fine one, it is submitted that it is perfectly in keeping with the rationale of prescription to preserve the quiet enjoyment of those who have exercised otherwise perfectly rights undisturbed for many years. Thus, mere 'unlawfulness' will not always prevent a successful claim of prescription. A similar approach has been taken in relation to a claim of adverse possession, even where that adverse possession amounts to a criminal offence, *Best v. Chief Land Registrar* (2015) (see Chapter 12).

7.11   Methods of Establishing an Easement by Prescription

As indicated previously, there are three recognised varieties of prescription: prescription at common law; prescription at common law utilising the doctrine of 'lost modern grant'; and prescription under the Prescription Act 1832. We have seen, also, that the inherent nature of a prescriptive claim is the same under all three methods, save that prescription under the Prescription Act 1832 has less rigid requirements in matters of detail, due to the wording of that statute. In fact, when it comes to making a prescriptive claim, the owner of the potential dominant tenement may rely on any or all three methods.[117] This illustrates their common origin because the methods differ essentially only in the way in which the claimant must establish the long use and the length of time for which he must have undertaken the use. However, in all three methods, even though the period of long use required for a successful claim can vary, the claimant must establish that the use has been 'continuous' throughout the relevant period.

'Continuous user' (sometimes referred to as 'continuity of user') does not mean that the claimant must use the 'right' incessantly, never stopping. It denotes, rather, that there is a regular, consistent use of the alleged right for the relevant period, commensurate with the nature of the right. 'Regular' use will be a question of fact. The exercise of a right of way might be 'continuous' in one case if it is exploited only two or three times a year but, in another set of circumstances, monthly use might be required. Again, some easements are, by nature, more obviously exercised 'continuously' – such as an easement

---

116 See *Hanning v. Top Deck Travel Group Ltd* (1993), overruled by *Brandwood*.

117 In *Brandwood*, the claim rested on either the Act or lost modern grant.

of way – while others (an easement to enter and cut obstructing trees) are not. The continuity of some easements is often completely hidden – as with the easement of support offered by a wall on the servient owner's land. Likewise, unimportant inconsistencies in the long use cannot defeat a claim, as where the route of a path deviates over time, or a replacement sign is hung in a slightly different position on the servient owner's land. Thus, in *Propertypoint Ltd* v. *Kirri* (2009), an easement of way by prescription was established even though the exact manner in which the servient land had been used (in respect of turning vehicles) had varied over the years. Assuming, then, that the claimant can establish that he is a continuous user, what period of time is necessary to propel this into an easement proper?

7.11.1 Prescription at common law

At common law, long use could mature into an easement if it could be shown to have occurred since before 'legal memory'. According to the Statute of Westminster 1275, 'legal memory' is fixed at the year 1189, so a claim of prescription may succeed at common law only if it can be shown that the use existed before then. Obviously, this was well-nigh impossible, so it became accepted that use for 20 years raised a presumption that use commenced before 1189.[118] Unfortunately, however, this did not mean that 20 years' use generated a prescriptive easement. It remained the case that the claim could be defeated by any evidence that the use could not, in fact, have started before 1189. So, for example, a claim to a right of light, even if used for 150 years, could be defeated by showing that the building so benefited was built 'only' in the year 1190. The ease with which an alleged servient owner can defeat the 20-year presumption effectively ensures that this form of common law prescription is hardly ever successful.

7.11.2 Prescription at common law: lost modern grant

The doctrine of lost modern grant developed as an antidote to the manifest deficiencies of 'pure' common law prescription. In fact, this doctrine is really no more than a fictional gloss on the old common law rules. As we know, the rationale for prescription is a presumed grant of the right by the servient owner. Under 'lost modern grant', the law assumes that 20 years' use of the right is conclusive evidence of such a grant being made by the servient owner. The grant is 'modern', because it is assumed to have been made at some time after 1189, and it is 'lost', because it cannot now be produced – of course, it does not actually exist, but this is the convenient fiction. Stripped of its trappings, the doctrine means that 20 years' continuous use by the owner of the dominant tenement is sufficient to establish an easement by prescription (*Dalton* v. *Angus* (1881)). This is so even if the servient owner produces evidence that no grant had been made – which, of course, is true. Indeed, it seems that the one way in which the servient owner can defeat the claim (apart from the absence of other requirements mentioned above) is if he shows that the servient owner who is assumed to have made the grant (i.e. the owner at the commencement of 20 years' use) was legally incompetent at the time, being a minor or

---

118 *Dalton* v. *Angus* (1881).

lunatic. Even then, although there is authority to support this limitation,[119] it seems strange to deny a prescriptive claim on the ground that the person supposed to have made the fictitious grant was unable to do so, when everybody knows that he never made the grant at all! Why is legal incapacity a bar, when actual non-existence of the grant is not? Be that as it may, the doctrine of lost modern grant is sufficient in most cases to ensure that long use for 20 years, as of right, matures into an easement.

7.11.3   The Prescription Act 1832

The Prescription Act 1832 is not a replacement for the common law (especially lost modern grant) and, considering some of its mystifying language, this is just as well. It is intended to bolster the common law, supplementing it where necessary, with the general aim of making it easier to establish easements by prescription. It is doubtful whether it does this, but that is its purpose. The Act divides easements into two classes: easements of light and all other easements.

7.11.3.1   *All easements except easements of light*

Under section 2 of the Act, a period of 20 years' use is sufficient to establish a prescriptive claim, provided that the 'right' was enjoyed 'without interruption' for that period (see, for example, the successful claim of way in *Denby v. Hussein* (1999)). Evidence that the 'right' was not enjoyed, or lacked some other quality, in the period *before* commencement of the 20 years cannot defeat the claim. Moreover, an interruption by the servient owner during the 20 years is sufficient to defeat the claim only if the alleged dominant owner tolerated the interruption for one year or more. However, the Act does not remove the need to satisfy the conditions for prescription *during* the 20-year period. Thus, any inability to meet the common law conditions during the 20 years' use is fatal to the claim. Finally, there is a further practical limitation in that the alleged dominant owner cannot pick *any* 20 years' use: the 20 years' use must be calculated by reference to the 20 years immediately prior to 'some suit or action'. This has the unfortunate consequence that no easement of prescription can arise if, say, the use has been enjoyed for 100 years, but no 'suit or action' is brought, or if the easement was enjoyed for 200 years in conformity with the common law conditions, but at some time in the last 20 years before a suit one of the common law conditions was not met.

In contrast to this, section 2 provides as an alternative that 40 years' use without interruption ensures that the right is 'absolute and indefeasible' unless exercised with the consent of the servient owner. This effectively eases the conditions imposed by section 2 for 20 years' use. It remains the case (with the same problems) that the 40 years' use must be that which is immediately prior to a 'suit or action', and the same principles of 'interruption' apply. However, because 40 years' use makes the right 'absolute and indefeasible', it seems that it does not matter that someone other than the fee simple owner (e.g. a tenant) was in possession of the land at the start of the period, provided that the period is completed. On the other hand, the remaining common law conditions appear to apply, save only that, if the servient tenement's consent is given at the start of the use

---

119   *Oakley v. Boston* (1976).

(or possibly the start of the 40-year period – the Act is unclear), it must be in writing or by deed to negate the prescriptive claim. The issue of 'consent' occurring at any other time during the 40 years is determined by reference to the common law.

7.11.3.2   *Easements of light*

Under section 3 of the Act, use of light for a period of 20 years (probably that period prior to any 'suit or action' – again, the Act is unclear) 'without interruption' becomes 'absolute and indefeasible' unless the servient owner consents in writing or by deed. In particular, there is no provision in section 3 that preserves the conditions of the common law, so uninterrupted use for 20 years without written consent will mature into an easement even if there is some defect that would have defeated a common law claim. However, written consent of the alleged servient owner does prevent an easement of light from arising. Whether there has been written consent is, furthermore, a matter of construction of any agreement, and so, in *Salvage Wharf Ltd v. G & S Brough Ltd* (2009), an agreement concerning aspects of a building project and *existing* rights to lights did not amount to an agreement giving consent within section 3. On the other hand, a written agreement need not specifically refer to 'light' in order to qualify under section 3, provided that its effect necessarily implies exclusion of a right to a light, as in *RHJ v. F T Patten* (2007). Likewise, in *CGIS City Plaza Shares 1 Ltd v. Britel Fund Trustees Ltd* (2012), a clause in a conveyance authorising the alleged servient owner to build on his land was taken to amount to consent to the claimant's use of light if such building did not occur, thereby preventing an easement. Note, also, that there can be 'an interruption' of light for the purposes of section 3 by the alleged servient owner without that owner actually physically blocking the light. The servient owner can take steps to register a notice in the local land charges register as provided by the Rights of Light Act 1959. This notice acts in law as an interruption and may prevent the acquisition of a right of light under section 3. Its purpose is to remove the need for the erection of numerous anti-light structures by potential servient owners as the end of a 20-year period approaches.[120]

7.12   The Extinguishment of Easements

Given that an easement is essentially a right enjoyed by one landowner over the land of another, it is vital to its existence that the dominant and servient tenements are in separate ownership or occupation. Thus, the most common reason why easements cease to exist is that the dominant and servient land comes into the ownership *and* possession of the same person. Note that there must be unification of both ownership and possession, for it is perfectly possible for a tenant to enjoy an easement against their landlord and vice versa,[121] although, as just noted, an easement between landlord and tenant cannot be generated through prescription. Importantly, there is no statutory mechanism by which a person may apply for the judicial termination of an easement, unlike the

---

120 See *CGIS City Plaza Shares 1 Ltd v. Britel Fund Trustees Ltd* (2012) for a discussion of the operation of section 3 in relation to rights to light.

121 For example, *Wright v. Macadam* (1949).

position with restrictive covenants. Consequently, failing extinguishment through unification of the tenements, easements may only be terminated by a release of the easement by the current owner of the dominant tenement (express or implied through conduct), by abandonment (mere non-use, even for extended periods, is not abandonment – *Benn v. Hardinge* (1992), *Dwyer v. City of Westminster* (2014) – non-use of a right of way for 40 years was not abandonment), or by a specific Act of Parliament. Equitable easements may also become void and unenforceable against subsequent purchasers of the servient tenement by reason of a failure to register (if required) in registered or unregistered land.

7.13   A Note on *Profits à Prendre*

Profits à prendre are often considered alongside easements, not least because they also give rights over land belonging to another. The essential nature of a profit is that it is a proprietary right to enter upon another's land and take for oneself the profits of the land. For example, the profit of piscary entitles a person to enter another's land and take fish, likewise with the profits of turbary (turf) and estovers (wood).[122] Profits may also be legal or equitable and fall within the regime of the LRA 2002 in similar fashion to easements. Again, with the possible exception of the rule in *Wheeldon v. Burrows* (1879), profits may be created in the same ways as easements. However, there is one important difference that is worthy of note: whereas an easement can exist only if there is a dominant and a servient tenement, a profit may exist to confer a benefit on a dominant tenement or may exist 'in gross'. A profit 'in gross' exists over servient land, but the person entitled to the benefit of it does not have to own land of their own. The burden of a profit attaches to land (hence its proprietary status), but the benefit may be held by any person or indeed any number of persons.[123] Profits can be commercially important, as with profits of piscary in salmon-rich waters. For this reason, the LRA 2002 enables legal profits to be registered with their own title.[124]

7.14   Reform

In June 2011, the Law Commission published its final report on *Making Land Work: Easements, Covenants and Profits à Prendre*.[125] Much of the report is taken up with proposed reform to the law of covenants, as this presents more pressing problems.[126] In respect of easements and profits, the proposals are modest and sensible and are directed more to ironing out the wrinkles in the law rather than to wholesale reform. The main proposals in respect of easements are: the abolition of the existing methods of prescription and their replacement with a single, statutory method; the rationalisation of the law on extinguishment of easements (including clarifying the effect of *Wall v. Collins*) and including

---

122 See also *Polo-Woods Foundation v. Shelton-Agar* (2009) for the profit of grazing.

123 Of course, many profits are attached to dominant land – see the discussion in *Polo Woods v. Shelton-Agar* (2009).

124 Section 3 of the LRA 2002.

125 Law Com. No. 327. See also Consultation Paper No. 186, March 2008.

126 See Chapter 8.

the creation of a statutory jurisdiction to discharge or modify easements and profits in similar fashion to that existing for covenants; the acceptance that an easement could still exist where the dominant and servient land was owned by the same person provided that benefit and burden of the easement were registered against the respective titles; abolishing the existing rules on implied creation and replacing them with a single statutory rule based on what is necessary for the reasonable use of the land. This would entail disapplying the current operation of section 62 LPA (and would prevent profits from arising by implication); and removing the 'ouster principle' in easements so that easements could exist even if they deprived the servient owner of much of the use of their land, provided that such an easement is granted expressly and does not confer exclusive possession. There are no other proposals to change the essential definition of an easement.

7.15   Chapter Summary

7.15.1   The essential characteristics of an easement

The traditional criteria for determining whether a use amounts to an easement are found in *Re Ellenborough Park* (1956).

1 There must be a dominant and a servient tenement (easements cannot exist in gross).
2 The dominant and servient tenements must be owned or occupied by different persons.
3 The alleged easement must accommodate (i.e. benefit) the dominant tenement, meaning that the servient tenement must be sufficiently proximate (i.e. near) to the dominant tenement, the alleged easement must not confer a purely personal advantage on the owner of the dominant tenement and the alleged easement must not confer an undefined 'recreational use' on the dominant tenement or a recreational use which relates only to equipment.
4 The alleged easement must 'be capable of forming the subject matter of a grant', meaning that an easement cannot exist unless there is a capable grantor, an easement cannot exist unless there is a capable grantee, an easement cannot exist unless the right is sufficiently definite and the right must be within the general nature of rights recognised as easements.
5 Public policy may also be relevant, although it is not mentioned in *Re Ellenborough Park* (1956).

7.15.2   Legal and equitable easements: formalities

An easement can qualify as a legal interest only if it is held as an adjunct to a freehold or leasehold estate and if it is created by statute, by prescription, or by deed (unregistered land) or registered disposition (registered land). Easements held for less than a freehold or leasehold must be equitable. Even easements held for the freehold or leasehold estate will be equitable if not created properly (or not registered appropriately under the LRA 2002 on express creation). In that event, the easement may be equitable, provided that it is embodied in a written contract or instrument that equity regards as specifically enforceable or it arises through proprietary estoppel.

7.15.3 The significance of the distinction between legal and equitable easements in practice: third parties

In *registered land*, the benefit of an easement becomes part of the dominant tenement and automatically passes to a purchaser, whether legal or equitable. The burden of a legal easement in registered land currently will either be substantively registered against the title of the servient land or be an overriding interest under Schedules 1 and 3 of the LRA 2002, depending on when the easement came into existence and whether it was expressly or impliedly created. In order for new equitable easements (those arising after the entry into force of the LRA 2002) to bind a purchaser of the servient land, the easement must be registered by means of a Notice.

In *unregistered land*, the benefit of an easement becomes part of the dominant tenement and automatically passes to a purchaser, whether legal or equitable. The burden of a legal easement in unregistered land will 'bind the whole world'. The burden of an equitable easement in unregistered land must be registered as a Class D(iii) land charge under the LCA 1972 in order to bind a purchaser, save that estoppel easements bind according to the doctrine of notice.

7.15.4 The express creation of easements

An easement may be expressly granted by the potential servient owner to the potential dominant owner: for example, where the servient and dominant tenements are already in separate ownership and a grant is made, or where land is owned by a potential servient owner, and he then sells or leases a piece of that land to another and includes an express grant in the sale.

An easement may be expressly reserved by the potential dominant owner when that owner sells or leases a piece of that land to another and includes in that sale a reservation of an easement for themselves.

7.15.4.1 *Note*

The easement is legal or equitable depending on the character of the document in which it is contained. A legal conveyance creates a legal easement and transfer of an equitable estate creates an equitable easement.

7.15.5 The implied creation of easements

7.15.5.1 *Necessity*

An easement may be impliedly granted, and occasionally impliedly reserved, because of necessity, as where the land sold (grant) or land retained (reservation) would be useless *without* the existence of an easement in its favour.

7.15.5.2 *Common intention*

An easement may be impliedly incorporated in a sale of land either in favour of the purchaser (grant) or exceptionally in favour of the seller (reservation) if this is required to give effect to the common intention of the parties as to the use of the land.

7.15.5.3   *Implied under section 62 of the Law of Property Act 1925 (grant only)*

If a landowner has two or more plots of land and then conveys, by deed, one of those plots to a purchaser, the purchaser will be granted, by section 62 of the LPA 1925, all of those rights that were previously enjoyed with the land. This is so even if before the sale the 'rights' were enjoyed purely by permission and not as of right. Section 62 applies only to conveyance of a legal estate.

7.15.5.4   *Wheeldon v. Burrows (grant only)*

Where a person transfers part of their land to another, that transfer impliedly includes the grant of all rights in the nature of easements (called 'quasi-easements') that the seller enjoyed and used prior to the transfer for the benefit of the part transferred, provided that those rights are either 'continuous and apparent' or 'reasonably necessary for the enjoyment of' the part transferred.

7.15.5.5   *Note*

In cases of implied creation, the easement is legal or equitable depending on the character of the document into which it is implied.

7.15.6   Easements by prescription

Prescription occurs when the owner of what will be the dominant tenement establishes long use 'as of right' over what will be the servient land. If the 'right' so used is inherently capable of being an easement, the long use can mature into an easement proper. All easements created in this fashion will be legal. The period for which the use must be established will vary from case to case, depending on which of the three 'methods' of prescription is used.

7.15.6.1   *General conditions for obtaining an easement by prescription*

- Easements of prescription lie in fee simple only. There can be no easement by prescription in favour of, or against, a leaseholder or an estate that exists in equity only, such as a life interest. So, the long use must be by a fee simple (freehold) owner of the dominant tenement and it must be against a fee simple owner of the servient tenement. It is impossible for a tenant to claim a prescriptive easement against his own landlord and vice versa (or against another tenant). These rules have been modified for claims made under the Prescription Act 1832.
- The use must be 'as of right'. The long use must be *nec clam* (without secrecy), *nec vi* (without force) and *nec precario* (without permission).
- The use must be in the character of an easement, as satisfying the criteria of *Re Ellenborough Park* (1956).

7.15.6.2   *Methods of establishing an easement by prescription*

For all 'methods' of establishing an easement by prescription, the claimant must establish first that the use has been 'continuous' throughout the relevant period. The length of the required period varies with each method.

- *Prescription at common law.* The use must have occurred since before 'legal memory', that being before 1189. Use for 20 years raises a presumption that use commenced before 1189, but the claim can be defeated by any evidence that the use could not, in fact, have started before then. Such claims hardly ever succeed.
- *Prescription at common law – lost modern grant.* The law assumes that 20 years' use of the right is conclusive evidence of a grant of the easement being made by the servient owner. This means that 20 years' continuous use by the owner of the dominant tenement is sufficient to establish an easement by prescription, even if the servient owner produces evidence that no grant had ever been made – which of course is true.
- *Prescription Act 1832.* For all easements, except easements of light, a period of 20 years' use is sufficient to establish a prescriptive claim, provided that the 'right' was enjoyed 'without interruption' for that period. Alternatively, 40 years' use without interruption ensures that the right is 'absolute and indefeasible', unless exercised with the consent of the servient owner. For easements of light, a period of 20 years' use 'without interruption' becomes 'absolute and indefeasible', unless the servient owner consents in writing or by deed.

7.15.7   The extinguishment of easements

This can occur in a variety of ways. For example: the dominant and servient land may come into the ownership and possession of the same person; the dominant owner may 'release' the easement, expressly or impliedly through conduct; or the easement may be terminated by Act of Parliament.

7.15.8   *Profits à prendre*

A 'profit' is a proprietary right to enter upon another's land and take for oneself one of the 'profits' of the land. Profits may be legal or equitable. With the possible exception of the rule in *Wheeldon* v. *Burrows* (1879), profits may be created in the same ways as easements. Note, however, that profits may exist 'in gross': that is, they may exist over servient land even if the person entitled to the benefit owns no land himself. Examples are the profit of piscary (to take fish), the profit of turbary (to cut turf) and the profit of estovers (to cut wood). Under the LRA 2002, legal profits are capable of being registered with their own title.

Further Reading

Barnsley, DG, 'Equitable easements 60 years on' [1999] 115 LQR 89.

Dixon, M, 'Easements and contradictions' [2011] Conv 167.

Dixon, M, 'Editorial' [2012] Conv 1.

Douglas, S, 'Reforming implied easements' [2015] LQR 251.

Luther, P, 'Easements and exclusive possession' (1996) 16 LS 51.

Tee, L, 'Metamorphoses and s 62 of the Law of Property Act 1925' [1998] Conv 115.

Now visit the companion website to:

- test your understanding of the key terms using our Flashcard Glossary;
- revise and consolidate your knowledge using our Multiple Choice Question testbank.

www.routledge.com/cw/dixon

Chapter 8
Freehold Covenants

Introduction

The law concerning covenants made between freeholders ('freehold covenants') represents yet another way by which one landowner may control or affect the use of neighbouring land.[1] In some respects, the principles discussed below are similar to those seen in respect of leasehold covenants (Chapter 6) and easements (Chapter 7), in that a binding freehold covenant entails both a benefit and a burden in respect of two estates in land held by different people. Similarly, covenants represent another species of proprietary obligation, albeit one that owes its origin to the remedial jurisdiction of the courts of equity.[2]

In simple terms, 'freehold covenants' are, as their name implies, promises made by deed ('covenants') between freeholders,[3] whereby one party promises to do or not to do certain things on their own land for the benefit of neighbouring land. Thus, the owner of house No. 1 may promise the owner of house No. 2 not to carry on any trade or business on his (No. 1's) land, or the owner of house No. 3 may promise the owner of house No. 4 not to build above a certain height or without first obtaining the agreement of the owner of house No. 4.[4] Consequently, the landowner making the promise on behalf of his land is the covenantor (where the burden lies), and the landowner to whom the promise is made is the covenantee and his land is where the benefit lies. As in these examples, the great majority of covenants between freeholders are 'restrictive' (negative) in nature, in that they prevent a landowner from doing something on his own land, as opposed to requiring him to take positive action. Of course, that is not to say that 'positive' covenants cannot exist (e.g. a covenant to erect and maintain a boundary fence),[5] but, as we shall see, the enforcement of a positive covenant between persons other than the original covenantor and original covenantee is difficult to achieve.[6] Consequently, much of the law in this area has concentrated on restrictive covenants, and many textbooks refer to this topic as 'the law of restrictive covenants'. Similarly, 'freehold covenants' may be contrasted with 'leasehold covenants', the latter being promises made between landlord and tenant in a lease and usually (but not necessarily) referring to the land that is the subject matter of the lease (see Chapter 6).

---

1 Technically, this is the law concerning covenants made between persons who are not in privity of estate. In the main, this means covenants affecting freehold land, but it also includes the enforcement of covenants between head landlords and subtenants. In addition, for reasons that will become clear, sometimes these rules are described as the law relating to restrictive covenants, a convenient but inaccurate description.

2 Covenants as proprietary obligations – as opposed to mere personal contractual obligations – developed because courts of equity were prepared to grant a remedy against a landowner who acquired land in the knowledge that it was affected by a covenant. The court of equity could not, in conscience, allow a landowner to escape an obligation affecting the land of which he was aware, even though it had been created by some other person – see *Tulk* v. *Moxhay* (1848).

3 Or other persons who do not stand in relationship of privity of estate: above footnote 1.

4 For example, *Margerison* v. *Bates* (2008).

5 For example, *Norwich City College of Further & Higher Education* v. *McQuillin* (2009).

6 The Law Commission has completed consideration of the law of covenants and, among other things, has made recommendations concerning the enforcement of positive covenants between persons other than the original parties to it – *Making Land Work: Easements, Covenants and Profits à Prendre* (Law Com. No. 327, June 2011). See section 8.9 below.

8.1   The Nature of Freehold Covenants

A covenant is a promise made in a deed[7] and, as such, is enforceable between the covenantor (promisor) and covenantee (promisee) irrespective of whether contractual consideration is given. The covenant may be given in a stand-alone transaction by one neighbour to another, but is more likely to arise when a person sells part of their land to another and either gives (or extracts) covenants as part of the bargain. Thus, a landowner might agree to sell part of his land to X, but X will covenant as part of the transaction that he (X) will not build more than one dwelling on the land, or will not carry on a trade or business or undertake some other obligation of importance to the seller. In this sense, covenants can be an important source of private planning law because they may be used to preserve the character of a neighbourhood by preventing activity contrary to the *status quo* (e.g. 'no trade') or by limiting the impact of development ('not more than one dwelling'). This is particularly important in large-scale developments where a web of interlocking covenants and easements can be used for the benefit of all future purchasers of land within the development.[8] Moreover, if covenants are able to 'run' with the land in the sense of conferring proprietary benefits on one plot of land and proprietary burdens on another, these obligations may assume a permanence that endures irrespective of who comes to own the benefited and burdened plots in the future. With this in mind, the nature of freehold covenants can be analysed in the following way.

8.1.1   Positive and negative covenants

Covenants between freeholders may be either positive or negative in nature. Positive covenants require the owner of the burdened land to take some action on their own or adjoining property, usually requiring the expenditure of money. An example is a covenant to keep one's own buildings in good external repair in order to maintain the character of a neighbourhood. Negative or restrictive covenants require the owner of the burdened land to refrain from some activity on his own land. An example is a covenant not to carry on any trade or business on the land perhaps because it is intended to preserve the residential character of a neighbourhood.[9]

8.1.2   Covenants as contracts

Covenants are promises made by deed by one person to another to do, or more usually not to do, something on their own or adjoining land. The covenant is made between the *covenantor* and the *covenantee*. Covenants are binding and enforceable between the parties to it, irrespective of the presence or absence of consideration. Consequently, the original

---

7 Consequently, it must comply with the formalities required for the execution of deeds found in section 1 of the LP(MP)A 1989.

8 Commercial, as well as residential, developments may benefit. Thus, restrictive covenants may be used to limit the type of products that are sold on individual premises, thereby preserving a diversity of local shops in a high street and protecting income. In some cases, however, such covenants can amount to a restraint of trade or be anti-competitive.

9 For example, *Gafford v. Graham* (1998).

covenantor must do, or refrain from doing, that which he promised (and, therefore, is subject to a burden), and the original covenantee has the right to sue for performance of the covenant (and therefore enjoys a benefit).

8.1.3 Covenants as interests in land

Most importantly, covenants are now clearly regarded as proprietary interests in land, albeit equitable in nature.[10] This means that they have the following attributes.

8.1.3.1 *The covenantor's land: the burden of the covenant*

The contractual nature of a covenant means that the original covenantor (he who made the promise) is under the burden of the covenant. He must refrain from doing something on his own land if the covenant is restrictive (negative), or he must carry out the terms of the promise if the covenant is positive. As we shall see, however, performance of this burden may not be limited to the original covenantor, but may (if certain conditions are fulfilled) pass or 'run' with the land itself. In other words, any person who subsequently comes into possession of the original covenantor's land may be subject to the burden of the covenant and be required to observe its terms. So, if Mr Smith, the owner of Pinkacre, covenants with Mr Jones, the owner of Blackacre, that he (Smith) will not carry on a trade or business on Pinkacre, it is perfectly possible for any future owner (or, indeed, a mere occupier) of Pinkacre to be bound to observe the covenant, whether or not that new owner specifically agrees to the covenant. As we shall see, however, the burden of a covenant may 'run' with the land only when the covenant is restrictive.

8.1.3.2 *The covenantee's land: the benefit of the covenant*

The original covenantee (the person to whom the promise was made) has the 'benefit' of the covenant and may enforce it as a matter of contract. He has the right to sue for performance of the covenant and may be awarded damages (for past breaches of covenant), an injunction (to prevent impending breaches of covenant) or a decree of specific performance (to compel performance of a positive covenant). Once again, however, in certain circumstances, the ability to enforce the covenant may 'run' with the land benefited by the covenant and pass to any subsequent owner of it, giving that person the ability to obtain the appropriate remedy. So, adopting the above example, if Mr Jones, the owner of Blackacre (the land having the benefit of the covenant) sells that land to another person, the new owner may obtain the benefit of the covenant because it (the benefit) may have been attached to the land he acquires. He may sue the person now

---

10 They may subsist only as equitable interests – section 1 of the LPA 1925. The Law Commission has proposed that certain types of covenant should become enforceable as legal proprietary interests affecting the land and this would require section 1 of the LPA 1925 to be amended – see section 8.9 below. Note, however, as a 'mere' contract enforceable between the original parties, the covenant may create obligations enforceable at law, such as founding a claim in damages. As proprietary interests, covenants may only be equitable, but as personal contractual obligations, they may be enforced at law or in equity like any other contract.

subject to the burden of it. As can be seen, this means that the landowners who are parties to 'an action on the covenant' may, or may not, be the original covenantor and original covenantee. Assuming the requisite conditions are satisfied (on which see below), the parties to an action can be the *current* owners of the burdened and benefited land, rather than the original parties to the covenant.

8.1.3.3   *The duality of benefit and burden*

In practice, what we have just discussed is the proprietary nature of covenants: that is, their ability to impose benefits and burdens on land so that any owner or occupier of the land may be affected by the covenant, either as to the burden or as to the benefit. In short, the covenant has been attached to the land itself. Obviously, in practice, the person claiming the benefit of a covenant usually will be the owner for the time being of the benefited land, and the person allegedly subject to the burden usually will be the owner for the time being of the burdened land. Indeed, it is important to realise that in all cases in which a person is seeking to enforce a freehold covenant, it is necessary to show that *both* the benefit of the covenant has run to the claimant *and* that the burden has run to the defendant. In the following sections, we shall see that the conditions for the transmission of the benefit and then of the burden of a freehold covenant are different. However, the essential fact remains that, before any covenant can be enforced, it must be shown separately that the benefit has passed to the claimant (under the appropriate rules) and that the burden has passed to the defendant (under the appropriate rules). Without this duality, there can be no action 'on the covenant'.[11]

8.2   The Relevance of *Law* and *Equity* and the Enforcement of Covenants

The history of land law is replete with references to the differences between 'common law' and 'equity' and the law of freehold covenants is one area in which the old distinctions still have some relevance today. Historically, this distinction resulted from the different types of remedy available in a court of law or in a court of equity and particularly because of the latter's willingness to allow the covenant to 'run' with the land more easily. It was, in essence, the willingness of courts of equity to give a remedy against a person other than the original covenantor that caused the evolution of the covenant from a purely contractual animal (giving a remedy 'at law') to a proprietary animal (giving a remedy at first in equity and now also occasionally at law). This duality – that a covenant is both a contract and a proprietary obligation – persists to this day and the distinction between enforcement *at law* (whether contractual or proprietary) and enforcement *in equity* can still have consequences, although there is a tendency to downplay these in practice.[12]

---

11 *Thamesmead Town* v. *Allotey* (1998).

12 For example, in *Gafford* v. *Graham* (1998), the court observed that the defence of acquiescence (usually an equitable defence) should operate identically whether the claimant was claiming suit at law or in equity.

8.2.1   Suing at law

If a person sues on a covenant at law, he will be claiming that the defendant is subject to the burden of the covenant at law and should pay damages. If successful, the claimant has a right to those damages, which the court cannot refuse. As we shall see, the circumstances in which a remedy lies at law (i.e. for damages) are narrower than the situations in which a remedy lies in equity.

8.2.2   Suing in equity

The story of the courts of equity is that they would always act to mitigate the harshness of the common law and this is reflected in the modern rules concerning the enforcement of freehold covenants. Consequently, not only is it easier to enforce a covenant in equity, but the range of potential defendants is much greater because the burden of a covenant may run with the land in equity in a way that is impossible at law. Moreover, because enforcement of the covenant is in equity, equitable remedies are available, although unlike remedies at law they are subject to the discretion of the court and may be withheld in an appropriate case. These remedies are the injunction (for restrictive covenants) and the decree of specific performance (for positive covenants).[13] Finally, and perhaps most importantly of all, if the claimant sues in equity, either because they are required to (as where the defendant is not the original covenantor) or out of choice (because they do not want 'mere' damages), then the normal principles of registered and unregistered conveyancing come into operation. These will be considered below, but for now, the point is that a restrictive covenant[14] may need to be registered in the manner appropriate to either registered or unregistered land (as the case may be) in order to be enforceable against certain kinds of defendant.

   To sum up then, in any concrete case involving the enforcement of freehold covenants, there are always two issues of primary importance: first, has the benefit of the covenant run to the claimant in law or equity; and, second, has the burden of the covenant also passed to the defendant in law or in equity? Importantly, it also seems that there must be symmetry about the running of the benefit and burden. So, if the claimant is suing at law, he must establish that the defendant is subject to the burden at law and if the claimant is suing in equity, he must establish that the burden has passed to the defendant in equity.

8.3   The Factual Context for the Enforcement of Freehold Covenants

As the title of this chapter makes clear, the rules about to be discussed operate when one freeholder has the right to enforce a covenant against another freeholder. This may be when the claimant and defendant are the original parties to the covenant, or where the

---

13 In appropriate cases, damages may be awarded in lieu of an injunction (see e.g. *Small v. Oliver & Saunders* (2006)), but usually the claimant wants to compel the defendant to perform the covenant or to desist from some activity that breaches it.

14 As we shall see, the burden of positive covenants cannot pass at all, either at law or in equity.

claimant or defendant have acquired the benefited or burdened land from the original parties and the covenant has 'run' with the land. However, it is not only in actions between freeholders that these rules may be relevant. In fact, they may be applicable between any claimant and defendant who do not stand in a relationship of 'privity of contract' or 'privity of estate'. Consequently, as well as regulating actions on the covenant between freeholders, these rules also will be relevant when a landlord seeks to enforce a covenant contained in a lease against a subtenant and where a landlord seeks to enforce a leasehold covenant against a person who has taken only an equitable lease or an equitable assignment of a lease under an assignment taking effect before 1 January 1996.[15] Finally, the rules may also be relevant where the claimant is seeking to enforce a restrictive covenant (but not a positive one) against someone whose claim to an estate in the burdened land is merely possessory: for example, an adverse possessor.

8.4 Principle 1: Enforcing the Covenant in an Action between the Original Covenantor and the Original Covenantee

A covenant is equivalent to a legally binding contract between the covenantor and the covenantee. As such, the covenantee may sue the covenantor for damages at law for breach of covenant or, in appropriate circumstances, obtain one of the equitable remedies of injunction or specific performance. This is straightforward, and is a reflection of the 'privity of contract' that exists between the original covenantee and original covenantor. However, because the benefits and burdens of certain types of covenant are transmissible to *subsequent* owners of both the original covenantor's and the original covenantee's land, a number of different situations must be identified.

8.4.1 Both original parties to the covenant in possession of their respective land

If the original covenantor and original covenantee are still in possession of their respective land, the matter is relatively straightforward. *All* covenants between them are enforceable and the covenantee may obtain damages, an injunction (to prevent breach of a restrictive covenant) or specific performance (to ensure compliance with a positive covenant) against the covenantor. This is a matter of contract. For example, in an action between original covenantor and original covenantee, the claimant can enforce a covenant to maintain a boundary fence and a covenant prohibiting the carrying on of a trade or business on the land. Both positive and negative covenants are enforceable between the original parties who remain in possession of their lands.

---

15 For equitable leases/assignments taking effect on or after 1 January 1996, the LTCA 1995 generally ensures the enforcement of a restrictive covenant against the owner or occupier of land (sections 3(5) and 3(6) of the Act and see Chapter 6). In respect of actions against a subtenant or other occupier of leasehold land, it is not clear whether section 3(5) of the LTCA 1995 means that restrictive covenants contained in a lease always will be enforceable against subtenants, or whether the conditions about to be discussed must continue to be fulfilled. The second view is more likely, given the focus of the Act.

8.4.2 After the original *covenantor* has parted with the burdened land

If the original covenantor has parted with the land that was subject to the covenant, he remains liable on all of the covenants to whosoever has the benefit of the covenant. This is because of the contractual nature of the covenant: the original covenantor has promised that the covenant will be performed. However, in most cases, a claimant will want to enforce the substance of the obligation (i.e. to make sure the covenant is actually performed) and so will take action against the person *currently* in possession of the burdened land. Consequently, a remedy against the original covenantor who is no longer in possession of the land is of little practical use unless this is the only person against whom there is a realistic chance of a remedy and where damages are acceptable to the claimant.

8.4.3 After the original *covenantee* has parted with the benefited land

If the original covenantee has parted with the land that had the benefit of the covenant, he may still be able to enforce a covenant against whosoever has the burden of it. However, the right to sue at both law and in equity may have been expressly assigned to the new owners of the land when the land was transferred to them, so preventing the original covenantee from taking action.[16] In any event, if claiming damages at law, any damages are likely to be only nominal because the real loss has fallen on the person who is actually in possession of the land rather than the original covenantee who is no longer in possession. If suing for an equitable remedy (i.e. for an injunction or specific performance), the court is likely in its discretion to refuse to grant an equitable remedy to an original covenantee who no longer is in possession of the benefited land because, in reality, such a person suffers no loss.[17]

8.4.4 Original *covenantor* having had no land *at all* at the time the covenant was given

It has always been the case that a covenantor, even if he never had any land burdened by the covenant, is liable on a covenant at law (but *not* in equity). This is because the contractual nature of the obligation is not dependent on the original covenantor holding any estate in land. Therefore, in *Smith and Snipes Hall Farm Ltd* v. *River Douglas Catchment Board* (1949), the defendant was liable on its positive covenant to repair and maintain river banks even though it had no land itself. A covenant is, after all, a contractual promise, breach of which entails liability at law.

8.4.5 Defining the original covenantee and covenantor

It goes without saying that it is vital to be able to determine exactly who is an 'original' covenantor or covenantee, particularly if either is still in possession of the land. Usually, of course, this is quite simple, they being the parties to the deed of covenant and

---

16 See section 8.6.2 below.

17 *Chambers* v. *Randall* (1923).

identified as such, having signed the deed in the presence of a witness: as where the deed recites that 'Mr Smith, freehold owner of Pinkacre, hereby covenants with Mr Jones, freehold owner of Blackacre', and both sign the deed in the presence of a witness. However, it is possible under section 56 of the LPA 1925 to extend the range of original covenantees (but not covenantors) beyond those persons who are actually parties to the deed in the sense just described. By virtue of section 56, a person may enforce a covenant (i.e. be regarded as an *original* covenantee), even if they are not actually a party to it (i.e. have not signed it under witness), provided that the covenant was intended to confer this benefit on the person *as a party* and the person is in existence and identifiable at the date of the covenant.[18] What this means in practice is that more people may have the right to the benefit of a covenant as an *original* covenantee (which may then be transmitted on a sale of *their* land) than simply the person who signs their name to the deed, provided only that the deed does not purport to confer these benefits on 'future' owners of land or persons who cannot be identified. A good example is where A covenants with B 'and with the present owners of Plots 1, 2 and 3' not to carry on any trade or business on his (A's) land. Here, A is the original covenantor, B is an original covenantee and party to the deed, and the existing owners of Plots 1, 2 and 3 are also original covenantees by virtue of section 56, provided that they are intended to be treated as parties. Thus the 'benefit' of the covenant is enjoyed originally by four persons, each of whom may pass that benefit with their land if the conditions discussed below are satisfied. Note, however, that it now seems established that section 56 only has this effect when the persons identified in the covenant as being entitled to its benefit are intended to be treated as *parties*, not simply additional persons to whom the benefit has been given. The covenant must be made 'with' them, not merely 'for' them.[19] This is a fine distinction, and although it can be crucial (as in *Amsprop Trading Ltd* v. *Harris Distribution* (1996)), the difficulty can be avoided by careful drafting. Simply put, the point is that section 56 is intended to ensure that specific, identifiable persons are treated as parties to the covenant and is not intended to confer the benefit of the covenant on many landowners simply because they fall within the literal ambit of a particularly widely drafted covenant.

8.5　Principle 2: Enforcing the Covenant against Successors in Title to the Original Covenantor – *Passing the Burden*

One of the great steps forward in real property law in England and Wales was the transformation of freehold covenants from purely personal obligations governed by the law of contract to proprietary obligations governed by the law of real property. This is generally regarded as having been achieved by the landmark case of *Tulk* v. *Moxhay* (1848), in which a covenant not to build on open land in Leicester Square, London, was enforced against the defendant when the defendant was not the original covenantor but a purchaser from

---

18　*White* v. *Bijou Mansions* (1938).

19　*Amsprop Trading Ltd* v. *Harris Distribution* (1996). The point is that it is not enough that the persons are intended to take a benefit; they must be intended to be parties.

him. What this means in simple terms is that if the various conditions discussed below are satisfied, a covenant can be enforced not only against the original covenantor, but also against anyone who comes into possession or occupation of the land burdened by the covenant (i.e. the land over which the covenant operates). Obviously, this might be a severe limitation on the uses to which the burdened land can be put by a successor in title to the original covenantor (e.g. if the land is subject to a covenant against business use, as in *Re Bromor Properties* (1995), or against building, as in *Tulk* itself), and so it is not surprising that there are strict limitations defining the precise circumstances in which the burden of a covenant may 'run' with the land under the *Tulk* principle.

First, it is not possible for the burden of a covenant between freeholders to run *at law* in any circumstances.[20] There can be no claim at law against a successor to the original covenantor. This is simply not possible.[21] However, as noted above, equity is not as strict as the common law and it *is* possible for the burden of *some* (but not all) covenants to run with the land in equity. In short, if a burden is to run at all, it must be in equity. This has its own consequences – in particular, that a claimant relying on the equitable claim takes the risks associated with the enforcement of all equitable rights over land. These are dealt with below, but importantly encompass the rule that the award of a remedy is discretionary (even if the burden has actually run to the defendant) and that the covenant must have been registered appropriately in the systems of registered and unregistered land to be enforceable against purchasers of the burdened land.

Second, even in equity, it is not the burden of every covenant that is capable of passing on transfer of the covenantor's land. The rule is simple – some would say simplistic – and is that only the burdens of restrictive covenants are capable of passing.[22] This means that it is not possible for the burden of a positive covenant to be enforced against a successor to the original covenantor, and so only the original covenantor can be liable on positive covenants. For example, if the original covenantor and owner of Plot X has made a covenant with the owner of Plot Y (the original covenantee) not to carry on a trade or business and a covenant to maintain a fence, and then Plot X is sold to a third party, the new owner *could* be liable on the covenant restricting use but *cannot* be liable on the covenant to maintain the fence. Positive burdens cannot pass. This is vitally important. What it means in practice is that, as soon as the land has passed out of the hands of the original covenantor, only restrictive covenants can be enforced against the land, and then only in equity. Indeed, although the claimant (i.e. he entitled to enforce the covenants) may well have the benefit of both positive and restrictive covenants, the defendant can only be liable for breaches of the restrictive ones. Despite some criticism of this rule, there is no doubt that it remains the law. It has been reiterated by the House of Lords in *Rhone v. Stephens* (1994) and applied (albeit with considerable reluctance) by the Court of Appeal in *Thamesmead Town v. Allotey* (1998).[23] In both cases, there was distinct judicial criticism of the rule, but the fact that conveyancing practice has developed around it (and because of it!), and the reluctance of the House of Lords to

---

20 As we have seen, however, the burdens of positive and negative *leasehold* covenants can run with the lease and the reversion in law and in equity – Chapter 6.

21 *Rhone v. Stephens* (1994).

22 *Hayward v. Brunswick Building Society* (1881); *Thamesmead Town v. Allotey* (1998).

23 See also *Cantrell v. Wycombe DC* (2009).

intervene, means that it can be changed only by Act of Parliament. This course of action was urged strongly by the Court of Appeal in *Thamesmead Town*, and even though the Law Commission has recommended a change in the law, this is still under consideration.[24] For now then, it remains vital to be able to distinguish between those freehold covenants that impose on the covenantor an obligation to act (positive), and those that impose an obligation to refrain from acting (negative). The precise conditions for the passing of the burdens of restrictive covenants are discussed below.

8.5.1   The covenant must be restrictive or negative in nature

As noted immediately above, and mentioned here for the sake of completeness, it is vital that the covenant be restrictive (or negative) in nature. Importantly, this is a question of substance, not of form, and it is irrelevant how the covenant is actually worded – as in *Tulk* v. *Moxhay* itself, in which the covenant was expressed as an obligation to positively keep land as an open space and this was held rightly to be negative in substance. It was actually a covenant not to build. The essence is that a covenant is negative if it prevents the landowner from doing something on his own land, irrespective of how it is worded. So, in *Holland Park* v. *Hicks* (2013), a covenant requiring a neighbour's agreement to a planning application was held to be restrictive in substance because it operated to prevent development. More typical examples include a covenant not to carry on any trade or business, a covenant not to build and a covenant not to sell certain types of product. Conversely, a covenant that compels the owner of land to spend money on his property will usually be regarded as positive, and hence unenforceable against successors to the original covenantor. A covenant to maintain a boundary fence is a good example,[25] as is the covenant to repair a roof, considered by the House of Lords in *Rhone* v. *Stephens* (1994).

8.5.2   The covenant must touch and concern the burdened land

It is axiomatic that only a covenant that relates to the use or value of the land should be capable of passing with a transfer of it. The law of property is generally concerned with proprietary obligations, not personal ones. Consequently, only the burdens of restrictive covenants that 'touch and concern' the land are capable of being enforced against successors in title to the original covenantor.[26] There is one possible exception to this rule, being the case in which a head landlord attempts to enforce a leasehold restrictive covenant against a subtenant. Such parties do not stand in either privity of contract or privity of estate, so, as noted above, the 'freehold covenant rules' are applicable. However, according to section 3(5) of the LTCA 1995, 'any' landlord or tenant's restrictive covenant contained in a lease to which the Act applies[27] 'shall' be capable of being enforced

---

24 See section 8.7.7 below. Note that positive covenants may run under the rules concerning leasehold covenants and this explains why some new building developments are sold as leaseholds rather than freeholds. See Chapter 6.

25 For example, *Norwich City College of Further & Higher Education* v. *McQuillin* (2009).

26 The original covenantor is, of course, liable on all covenants. Thus, as explained above, it is not even necessary for the original covenantor to have land in order to be liable on the covenant at law.

27 Leases granted on or after 1 January 1996.

against any owner or occupier of the land.[28] There is nothing in this section that requires a leasehold restrictive covenant concerning the demised land to 'touch and concern', and it may be that this requirement has been abolished (possibly accidentally?) in those cases in which the burden of a *leasehold* restrictive covenant is being enforced under the 'freehold covenants' rules. The above point aside then, there is no doubt that, for restrictive covenants between freeholders,[29] the requirement of 'touching and concerning' still applies.[30] This is reflected in the fact – discussed below – that the burden of these covenants must also be registered to bind purchasers of the affected land, and the registration systems of the LCA 1972 and LRA 2002 only apply to proprietary obligations.

In essence, whether any particular restrictive covenant does 'touch and concern' will depend on the facts of each case, but a general test has been laid down by Lord Oliver in *Swift Investments* v. *Combined English Stores* (1989).[31] This test, which is not rigid in its application, but is a valuable guide, requires us to ask a number of questions. First, could the covenant impose a burden on *any* owner of an estate in the land as opposed to the particular original owner? If it could, it may 'touch and concern' as this shows that the covenant has purpose and meaning even though the original covenantor is no longer in possession of the estate. Second, does the covenant affect the nature, quality, mode of user or value of the burdened land?[32] Again, if the covenant affects how the land may be utilised or affects its value irrespective of the identity of the current owner, it is likely to touch and concern. So, in *Holland Parks* v. *Hicks* (2013), a covenant to seek a neighbour's approval of the detail of planning permission was held to touch and concern, despite the absence of previous authority, because it allowed the neighbour to control the development of the property. Third, is the covenant actually expressed to be personal so that, irrespective of its substance, it is meant to operate only as a promise binding the original covenantor?[33] It has always been possible for the parties, by clear words or necessary implication, to ensure that a covenant obligation is not proprietary, and this perhaps reflects their origin pre-*Tulk* as only operating personally.[34]

Consideration of these issues should be enough to determine whether the restrictive covenant 'touches and concerns' the land and they will be applied in the context of the large amount of case law on this point. Perhaps the safest route for a conveyancer when

---

28 See sections 8.5.5–8.5.6 below.

29 And in other situations in which the 'freehold rules' are relevant, except (as immediately above) possibly in a lease granted on or after 1 January 1996.

30 See, for example, *Robins* v. *Berkeley Homes* (1996).

31 Although developed in the context of leasehold covenants, this test applies with equal force to freehold covenants. See recently its use in *Bryant Homes* v. *Stein Management* (2016).

32 For example, the classic user covenants, such as that not to carry on a trade or business, or a certain trade, not to build and not to keep any animals.

33 An example is *Margerison* v. *Bates* (2009). Express words may be used, as where a covenant is expressed 'to be enforceable only against the person hereinafter named as the original covenantor' or this may arise from construction of the covenant, as in *Margerison*, in which the covenant was limited to 'the vendor', thus indicating that it was not intended to operate as a proprietary obligation.

34 It seems then that, unlike issues surrounding the creation of a lease (*Street* v. *Mountford* (1985) – Chapter 6), the intention of the parties can be decisive in settling that nature of the obligation undertaken. See also *Sugarman* v. *Porter* (2006).

attempting to ensure that a covenant 'touches and concerns' is to follow the advice of Wilberforce J in *Marten v. Flight Refuelling* (1962) that a covenant that *expressly* states that it is imposed for the purpose of affecting land will normally be taken by the court as being capable of doing so. Assuming, then, that this hurdle has been cleared, the remaining conditions must be met.

8.5.3 The covenant must have been imposed to benefit land of the original covenantee

This condition is one that expresses most clearly the nature of a covenant as affecting both benefited and burdened land. It means that the burden cannot pass at all unless the *covenantee* had land at the time the covenant was made *and* that that land was capable of benefiting from the covenant *and* that the burden was imposed in order to benefit that land.[35] In other words, the covenant must have been made to benefit *land* and if there is no benefit or no such land, the covenant is unenforceable other than against the original covenantor. In the language of easements, there must be a 'dominant tenement' that could benefit from this restrictive covenant,[36] although the condition is satisfied if the covenant was made to benefit the proprietary interest of the covenantee, such as that held by a lessor or a mortgagee.[37]

A common reason why there may have been no land owned by the covenantee at the time it was given is the simple one that the original covenantee may not have retained any such land at that time. For example, if Smith sells Blackacre to Jones, and in the sale Jones (as original covenantor) covenants with Smith (as original covenantee) not to build on Blackacre, the burden may run to Jones' successors in title only if Smith retained some land at the time the covenant was executed.[38] If Smith sold everything at that time (i.e. he kept no portion of Blackacre), he remains the original covenantee, but has no benefited land, and so the burden cannot pass to successors of the original covenantor. Likewise, the covenant must have been undertaken in order to benefit the land and the land must be capable of so benefiting. Thus the substance of the covenant must be such that it confers a proprietary advantage on the covenantee's land[39] and the relationship between the plots of land

---

35 *Whitgift Homes Ltd v. Stocks* (2001).

36 *London and South Western Railway v. Gomm* (1882).

37 There is no separate physical land in these cases, but there is a separate benefiting estate. There are also statutory exceptions in favour of local authorities under the Town and Country Planning Acts and Housing Acts, and in favour of certain other bodies such as the National Trust. So, contrary to the general rule, certain restrictive covenants may be enforced against a landowner by a local authority, even if it (the authority) did not own land at the time of the covenant – see *Cantrell v. Wycombe DC* (2009), applying section 609 of the Housing Act 1985, but where it is made clear that all of the other conditions must still be met. See also the last sale by a developer under a 'building scheme' – the developer retains no land, but the covenant is still effective – below.

38 *Formby v. Barker* (1903).

39 This appears to be equivalent to the touching and concerning requirement. 'Land' here means the estate of the covenantee, so a covenant *specifically* imposed to benefit a tenant's leasehold interest may be enforced only by the tenant and not the freehold owner (*Golden Lion Hotel v. Carter* (1965)). Note, absent a specific limitation to a particular estate, the benefit may then be enforced by the holder of any estate in the land and, in the case of restrictive covenants, by an adverse possessor (section 78 of the LPA 1925).

must be such that a benefit does indeed accrue.[40] So, like easements, it would be unusual for a covenant to be transmissible if it were to impose a burden on one plot of land for the alleged benefit of land that was not reasonably geographically close.

8.5.4 The burden of the restrictive covenant must be intended to run with the land

A further condition is that the burden of the restrictive covenant must have been intended to run with the land of the original covenantor: that is, there must be evidence to establish that the 'burden' was intended to be enforceable whosoever came into possession of the burdened land. However, this is not difficult to establish because, in the absence of a contrary intention, the burden of a restrictive covenant is deemed to be attached to the land (i.e. intended to run) by virtue of section 79 of the LPA 1925. According to section 79(1):

> A covenant relating to any land of the covenantor ... shall, unless a contrary intention is expressed, be deemed to be made by the covenantor on behalf of himself, his successors in title and the persons deriving title under him.

By virtue of this section, the burden of a covenant is deemed to be made by the original covenantor on behalf of himself and all future owners of the land, thereby annexing the burden of the covenant to that land because of a statutory presumption of an intention that it shall run.[41] The burden may then become enforceable against such successors. A 'successor' is someone with a legal or equitable estate in the land[42] and, for restrictive covenants only, includes any person in occupation of the land without an estate, such as an adverse possessor (section 79(2) of the LPA 1925). Of course, this statutorily assisted annexation of the burden occurs 'unless a contrary intention appears', and it is clear that the covenant does not have to recite specifically that section 79 is inapplicable to exclude its effect.[43] A 'contrary intention' will 'appear' from the instrument creating the covenant if there is anything in it indicating that successors in title or assigns of the original covenantor would not be bound, as in *Morrells v. Oxford United FC* (2000), in which section 79 was found to be excluded by the whole tenor of the arrangement between the parties. Clearly, whether section 79 of the LPA 1925 is so excluded is a matter of construction, and so the safest course for someone wishing to exclude statutory annexation of the burden would be to say so in clear terms in the deed of covenant itself.

8.5.5 Registration

The fifth and final condition that must be satisfied before the burden can be enforced against a successor to the original covenantor arises because such burdens may be enforced only in equity. Restrictive covenants are equitable interests in another's land, and in consequence must comply with the rules of registered and unregistered conveyancing relating to such interests.

---

40 A covenant that is conventionally worded – i.e. similar to many others used in other cases – will be taken to confer such a benefit unless there are clear reasons for holding otherwise, *Bryant Homes* (2016).

41 *Tophams Ltd v. Earl of Sefton* (1967).

42 *Mellon v. Sinclair* (1996).

43 *Re Royal Victoria Pavilion, Ramsgate* (1961).

8.5.5.1   *Registered land*

If the person against whom the restrictive covenant is being enforced is a purchaser of a registered title for valuable consideration under a properly registered disposition (which includes a mortgage), the covenant must have been protected by the registration of a Notice against the burdened title in order to be enforceable.[44] Should it not be so registered, it loses its priority and cannot be enforced against the purchaser (section 29 of the LRA 2002).[45] Of course, in practice most transferees of the burdened land will be purchasers and will be properly registered as the new estate owner[46] and most restrictive covenants will have been protected by registration of a Notice at the time they were created. However, even if not protected by the entry of a Notice, a restrictive covenant will nevertheless remain enforceable against a transferee in two cases (section 28 of the LRA 2002). First, it will remain enforceable (whether registered by Notice or not) against a new registered proprietor who is not a purchaser of the burdened land for valuable consideration: for example, the recipient of a gift, a devisee under a will or an adverse possessor. Second, it will remain enforceable (whether registered by Notice or not) against someone who purchases only an equitable interest in the land: for example, an equitable tenant or a purchaser who fails to register his or her disposition.[47]

8.5.5.2   *Unregistered land*

If the person against whom the restrictive covenant is being enforced is a purchaser of a legal estate in the burdened land for money or money's worth, the covenant must be registered against the name of the original covenantor as a Class D(ii) land charge under sections 2(5) and 4(6) of the LCA 1972 in order to be so enforceable. Of course, most transferees will be purchasers of this type and most covenants will have been registered in this way. If the restrictive covenant is not registered in this way, it will be void and unenforceable forever if the land is sold to a purchaser[48] and cannot be revived by

---

44 Given that registration will occur normally when the covenant is made, registration is likely to be with the agreement of the registered proprietor of the burdened plot (the original covenantor) and thus an Agreed Notice may be used. However, a Unilateral Notice may be used if such agreement is not forthcoming or indeed if it is desired to keep specific details of the covenant away from public inspection.

45 The rule was the same prior to the LRA 2002, with such a covenant being registrable as a minor interest under the LRA 1925 and void against a purchaser (section 20 of the LRA 1925).

46 Or treated as such, as with a legal lease that cannot be substantively registered being for seven years or less, which is treated as if it were a registered disposition (section 29(4) of the LRA 2002).

47 Such a purchaser does not take the title under a registered disposition because it has not been registered. In addition, it is plausible that a purchaser under a registered disposition might agree expressly to give effect to an unregistered covenant in return for paying a lower price for the land. In such a case, the purchaser may be required in equity to give effect to the unprotected covenant by means of a personal constructive trust (*Lyus* v. *Prowsa Developments* (1982); *Binions* v. *Evans* (1972); but see *Chaudhary* v. *Yavuz* (2011), where *Lyus* is described as 'a very unusual case'). See also *Groveholt* v. *Hughes*.

48 Such a purchaser will purchase under the rubric of unregistered conveyancing and will apply for first registration of title. If the covenant was registered as a Class D(ii) land charge, it will be transferred to the new registered title and a Notice will be entered against the newly registered title. If it is not so registered, it would have become void on the sale and remains void at first registration (section 11 of the LRA 2002).

subsequent registration when the land becomes land of registered title. Note, however, that even an unregistered restrictive covenant can be binding in unregistered conveyancing in some circumstances: first, against someone who is not a purchaser – for example, the recipient of a gift, the devisee under a will or an adverse possessor; second, against someone who does not give 'money or money's worth' – for example, the recipient of land under marriage consideration; and, third, against someone who purchases only an equitable estate – for example, an equitable tenant.[49]

8.5.6   The equitable nature of the remedy

To conclude, then, the burden of a restrictive covenant may run in equity to successors of the original covenantor if certain conditions are met. In the great majority of cases, the conditions will be met, and the only real issue is likely to be whether the covenant was appropriately registered. Assuming that it was – and the other conditions are satisfied – the burden runs and the defendant is liable. Even then, however, the award of equitable remedies is discretionary, and the claimant may not get what he asked for. For example, in *Thamesmead Town v. Allotey* (1998), damages were awarded instead of the desired injunction.[50] In the worst possible scenario for the claimant, the court might decide that he has behaved so inequitably that neither an injunction nor damages should be awarded, despite the fact that the burden of the covenant has run to the defendant. This might occur in cases in which there has been unreasonable delay on the part of the person seeking to enforce the covenant or where the claimant has stood by while the defendant has breached the covenant. So, in *Gafford v. Graham* (1998), the claimant was denied both an injunction and damages in respect of the breach of one covenant because he had acquiesced in the conduct that was in breach and was granted only damages in respect of another breach. Importantly, however, it is now clear that the denial of a remedy depends on the claimant having behaved unconscionably (*Harris v. Williams-Wynne* (2006)). For example, in *Williams-Wynne*, the defendant had never believed that he was bound by the covenant against building and thus the claimant's acquiescence in the breach was not the reason why the defendant had gone ahead. Consequently, the claimant was not denied a remedy given that his actions had produced no effect on the defendant, and so it was not unconscionable to seek to enforce the covenant. Damages were awarded.[51] Although one can see the logic of this position – that if a defendant would have behaved as they did in any event, then the claimant's acquiescence is not the reason for the breach of covenant – the decision here might well be as far as we can go. We might argue that the relevant point is not whether the claimant's acquiescence *caused* the defendant's breach of covenant, but whether the claimant should have done something to stop the defendant breaching the covenant. Thus, if the *claimant* knew that the covenant was binding, and knew that the defendant incorrectly believed that it was not,

---

49 Note also the possibility of a personal constructive trust, noted at footnote 46 above.

50 See also *Small v. Oliver & Saunders* (2006). After *Coventry v. Lawrence* (2015) which is not about covenants as such but involves a discussion of the remedy of injunction as opposed to damages, it is possible that the award of damages will become more frequent.

51 There was no claim to an injunction or order of specific performance, possibly because on the facts it was unlikely that these remedies would have been awarded.

then perhaps the claimant is behaving unconscionably by allowing the defendant to continue in his mistaken belief, such unconscionability becoming operative as an estoppel when detriment is incurred.[52]

8.6 Principle 3: Passing the Benefit to Successors in Title to the Original Covenantee

As indicated at the beginning of this chapter, in all cases in which it is proposed to enforce a covenant, it must be possible to show both that the defendant has the burden and that the claimant has the benefit of the covenant. There must be correlative rights and obligations. Before dealing with the matter in detail, a number of preliminary points relating to the passing of the benefit should be noted.

First, the benefit of a covenant may be passed at law or in equity (unlike the burden, which passes only in equity). The conditions for the transmission of the benefit in equity are slightly easier to satisfy than those needed to pass the benefit at law. Second, the benefit of both positive *and* restrictive covenants may pass at law and in equity, although the fact that only the burdens of restrictive covenants may pass means that, if the *original covenantor* has parted with the land, only restrictive covenants are likely to be in issue in a real case. Third, given again that only the burden of restrictive covenants may pass, and then only in equity, in practice the claimant usually pleads that the benefit has also passed in equity (as explained in *Gafford v. Graham* (1998)). This will give us our claimant (benefit) and defendant (burden) both acting in equity. In effect, then, this means that the passing of the benefit of covenants *at law* and the passing of the benefit of *positive* covenants are relevant in practice only when the claimant is suing the *original covenantor* as this is the only person liable in such circumstances.

8.6.1 Passing the benefit of positive and negative covenants at law

To reiterate, passing the benefit of positive and negative covenants at law will be relevant only when the claimant – the successor to the original covenantee – is claiming the benefit of such covenants in order to sue the *original* covenantor. If any other person is the defendant, the claimant must sue in equity, and on a restrictive covenant, as it is only the burdens of these that are capable of passing. With that practical limitation in mind, the conditions for the passing of the benefit of a freehold covenant at law are as follows.

1   The covenant must 'touch and concern' the land of the original covenantee (*Rogers v. Hosegood* (1900)). In other words, as before, the covenant must relate to use of the land and not be merely personal in nature. The test of 'touching and concerning' is the same as that discussed above. In essence, we are searching for a covenant that could benefit *any* estate owner as opposed to the particular original covenantee,

---

52 See Chapter 10 on proprietary estoppel.

or for a covenant that affects the nature, quality, mode of user or value of the land, not being one that is expressed to be personal to the original covenantee.[53]

2   The claimant must have a legal estate in the land, although, by virtue of section 78 of the LPA 1925, the claimant does not have to have the *same* legal estate as the original covenantee. Thus, the original covenantee may have been the freeholder, but the claimant will succeed even if they have 'only' a legal lease. Importantly, however, *any* occupier (including an adverse possessor) may enforce the benefit of a *restrictive* covenant. This is because section 78 of the LPA 1925 deems 'the owners and occupiers for the time being' to be successors in title for the purpose of enforcing restrictive (but *not* positive) covenants.[54]

3   The benefit of the covenant must have been annexed to a legal estate in the land, either expressly or by implication. A covenant may be annexed expressly by words that make it clear that the covenant is for the benefit of certain land, or by words that make it clear that the covenant is intended to endure for successive owners of the land; for example, where a covenant is with the 'heirs and successors of X, the owner for the time being' of Plot 2. In either case, however, the land must be readily identifiable, and capable of benefiting from the covenant (*Re Gadd's Transfer* (1966)) and this must be possible at the time the covenant is executed, rather than the (later) time when the title to which it relates (i.e. on which the benefit is conferred) is presented for registration.[55] This has the side-effect that the benefit of a freehold covenant still annexes to the estate in the land even if the first owner of the benefited land (i.e. the original covenantee) delays or forgets to apply for registration as proprietor. This is to be contrasted with the result produced by *Brown and Root* v. *Sun Alliance* (1996) in the law of *leasehold covenants* in pre-1996 leases, where lack of registration of the lease seriously disrupts the passing of the leasehold covenant.[56] A covenant will be assumed to benefit land where it affects the value, method of enjoyment or mode of use of the land to which it is annexed. Importantly, however, as well as annexation by the act of the parties, the benefit of a covenant[57] may be annexed by virtue of section 78 of the LPA 1925, as discussed in *Federated Homes* v. *Mill Lodge Properties* (1980), *Whitgift Homes* v. *Stocks* (2001) and *Crest Nicholson Residential* v. *McAllister* (2004). According to the Court of Appeal in *Federated Homes*, section 78 of the LPA 1925 has the effect of statutorily annexing the benefit of every covenant – both positive and negative – to each and every part of the benefited land. The only conditions are that the land is capable of benefiting from the covenant and that the land can be easily identified from the deed of covenant itself. This second condition – that the land to be benefited must be easily identified from the covenant and not *only* by extrinsic evidence – was confirmed by *Crest Nicholson* after some uncertainty. In that case, McAllister was seeking to enforce covenants

---

53 *Swift Investments* v. *Combined English Stores* (1989) and see *Sugarman* v. *Porter* (2006), *Holland Park* v. *Hicks* (2013).

54 For implications in relation to the burden of restrictive covenants, see section 79(2) of the LPA 1925 and section 8.5.4 above.

55 *Mellon* v. *Sinclair* (1996).

56 See further Chapter 6.

57 That is, covenants entered into, on or after 1 January 1926. For pre-1926 covenants, express or implied annexation by act of the parties is required.

that had not been expressly annexed and Chadwick LJ was faced with the puzzle posed by *Federated Homes*. In essence, his Lordship applied the test put forward in the earlier case of *Marquess of Zetland* v. *Driver* (1939) and decided that, in order for statutory annexation to apply, the deed must describe the land in such a way that it is easily ascertainable from the covenant, albeit with the assistance of some extrinsic evidence. This accords with the principle that the benefit is being attached to land by the covenant and so the covenant itself must identify the land, albeit that extrinsic evidence may be used to clarify the words used in the covenant.[58]

In practice, the outcome of *Federated Homes* is that, unless a contrary intention is clearly shown,[59] the benefit of most covenants will now be annexed to the covenantee's land and be available to a purchaser of it, or even just part of it,[60] provided that the covenant itself identifies the land in such a way that the benefited land is easily ascertainable.[61] The overall effect is to ensure that the benefit of covenants (created after 1925) will in most cases run to successors in title of the original covenantee, even if the original benefited land is subsequently sold off in parts. So, if X (original covenantor) covenants with Y (original covenantee) that no trade or business is permitted on X's land, the benefit of that covenant will attach to each and every part of Y's land, and subsequent purchasers of the whole, or part of it, will obtain the benefit of the covenant.[62] If we then imagine that Y is a property developer, selling off individual plots on a housing estate to numerous purchasers, the wide impact of section 78 is obvious, as apparent from very similar facts in *Whitgift Homes* (2001). However, although much has been written about *Federated Homes* – for example, whether section 78 of the LPA 1925 was ever intended to have this wide effect – it is not at all clear that the interpretation has had a significant impact on how freehold covenant disputes are decided in practice. In most cases, the covenant will have been drafted with annexation in mind – either expressly to provide for it, or to exclude it.[63] This means that the practical impact of *Federated Homes* will be felt most readily in those less frequent cases in which the covenant is silent or ambivalent about its intended effect on purchasers of the benefited land (usually as a result of inattentive drafting), in which case statutory annexation to each and every part may follow. *Whitgift Homes* v. *Stocks* (2001) is just such a case, concerning a dispute over a housing development completed in the 1920s and 1930s and in which statutory annexation was central to the question of whether certain covenants were enforceable some 70 years later.

4   As an alternative to annexation, it is possible for the benefit of a covenant at law – the right to sue – to be assigned expressly to another person. This is in essence the assignment of a 'chose in action' within section 136 of the LPA 1925 and must be

---

58 This was effectively the position adopted earlier in *Whitgift Homes* v. *Stocks* (2001) and is now applied routinely. See for example *Holland Parks* v. *Hicks* (2013).

59 *Roake* v. *Chadha* (1984), confirmed in *Crest Nicholson*. See also *Holland Park* v. *Hicks* (2013).

60 See *Bryant Homes* (2016) where it was crucial that the benefit was annexed to each and every part of the land, so that owners of just part could enforce the covenant.

61 *Holland Park* v. *Hicks*; careful drafting of covenants should eliminate most difficulties.

62 For example, *Robins* v. *Berkeley Homes* (1996) and *Bryant Homes* (2016).

63 And possibly to provide for express assignment of the benefit instead – see section 8.6.2 below.

in writing, with written notice being given to the covenantor. It is of course unnecessary if there has been express annexation.[64]

So, to conclude this analysis, if the above conditions are satisfied, the claimant, being a successor to the original covenantee, may sue any person *at law* who is subject to the burden of the covenant. However, in practice, because of the limited ability of burdens to pass (not positive ones) and then only in equity, the defendant to an action on the covenant *at law* is going to be the original covenantor. No other person can be liable at law.

8.6.2   Passing the benefit of covenants in equity

This brings us to consideration of the principles concerning the passing of the benefit in equity. The rules about to be discussed apply equally to positive and negative covenants, but (once again) because the burden of a positive covenant cannot run, the principles have developed primarily in the context of restrictive covenants and their enforcement against successors of the original covenantor. With that significant point in mind, there are a number of conditions to be satisfied in order to establish that the benefit of a covenant has passed in equity.

1   The covenant must 'touch and concern' the land of the original covenantee (*Rogers v. Hosegood* (1900)). This is identical to the position 'at law' discussed above. We might note, however, that if the claimant is trying to use the 'freehold' rules to enforce a leasehold restrictive covenant against, say, a subtenant or adverse possessor (i.e. *not an assignee* of the original tenant), it is arguable that the LTCA 1995 has removed the 'touching and concerning' requirement for a restrictive covenant contained in a lease granted on or after 1 January 1996. So, for example, if the head landlord is attempting to enforce a restrictive covenant prohibiting 'any occupier wearing brown shoes' – which clearly does not touch and concern – it is arguable that the benefit of this covenant runs to a new landlord because of the 1995 Act. We shall probably never know whether this is correct because, in practice, it is unlikely that a landlord would ever wish to enforce such a clearly personal leasehold restrictive covenant against an occupier.

2   The claimant must have a legal or equitable estate in the land of the original covenantee. Again, this is similar to the position 'at law' and, by virtue of section 78 of the LPA 1925, the claimant does not have to have the same estate as the original covenantee. For example, the claimant may be the equitable tenant of the original covenantee. Moreover, it remains true that *any* occupier (including an adverse possessor) may enforce the benefit of a *restrictive* covenant because section 78 deems 'the owners and occupiers for the time being' to be successors in title for the purpose of enforcing restrictive (but *not* positive) covenants. It will be appreciated that this is particularly important given that a claim in equity usually will be to enforce a restrictive covenant against a successor of the original covenantor who may well be surprised that the benefit is enforceable even by a person adversely possessing the land.

---

64 And, of course, *Federated Homes* would save many poorly drafted covenants if there was no assignment.

3   The benefit of the covenant must have been transmitted to the claimant in one of
     three ways.

     (i)   *Annexation: express and statutory.* The benefit of a covenant can be expressly
            annexed to the land in equity in exactly the same way as at law. Indeed, the
            same words will annex the benefit of the covenant at law and in equity
            simultaneously. Again, it is important that the words establish that the cove-
            nant is for the benefit of the land itself, or make it clear that the covenant is
            intended to endure for successive owners of the land. This was not the result
            in the marginal decision in *Lamb* v. *Midas Equipment* (1999), in which the Privy
            Council held, on appeal from Jamaica, that a covenant to X and 'his heirs,
            executors, administrators, transferees and assigns' (surprisingly) did not
            result in express annexation to the land but was meant to describe the cove-
            nantee personally. Further, the land must be readily identifiable at the time
            the covenant is executed – *Mellon* v. *Sinclair* (1996) – and be capable of bene-
            fiting from the covenant, according to the general test laid down in *Re Gadd's
            Transfer* (1996). Once again, however, it is the effect of section 78 of the LPA
            1925, as discussed in *Federated Homes* and clarified by *Crest Nicholson*, that is also
            relevant here. As already explained in the context of covenants running at
            law, according to section 78: '[a] covenant relating to any land of the cove-
            nantee shall be deemed to be made with the covenantee and his successors in
            title and the persons deriving title under him or them, and shall have effect
            as if such successors and other persons were expressed'. Although this was
            thought to be a 'word-saving' provision that simply ensured that 'succes-
            sors', and so on, were deemed to be included in the deed, but without doing
            away with the necessity of finding the relevant express intention to annex,
            Brightman LJ, in *Federated Homes*, makes it clear that the effect of section 78
            (by deeming these words to be included in the deed) is to annex automati-
            cally the benefit of the covenantee's land and each and every part of it. Again,
            of course, the land has to be readily identifiable from the deed itself as
            explained in *Crest Nicholson* and capable of benefiting from the covenant, but if
            these conditions are satisfied, the benefit of the covenant is annexed to each
            and every part of the land.[65] It will, therefore, be available to a purchaser of
            the whole or any part of it. Again, as noted, this 'automatic statutory annexa-
            tion' can be avoided by an express contrary intention (*Roake* v. *Chadha*
            (1984)).[66] All in all, however, the effect of *Federated Homes*, is to ensure that
            the benefit of a covenant passes where the parties have failed to draft the
            covenant clearly to ensure express annexation, unless this failure is thought
            to be a deliberate measure to prevent annexation.

     (ii)   *Assignment: express or implied.* As an alternative to annexation, the claimant may
            rely on the general rule that the benefit of a contract may be assigned
            expressly to another person. This means that it is perfectly possible for the

---

65 If the benefit is claimed by a purchaser of part, it must be possible for that part to actually be benefited by the
    covenant.

66 See also *Sugarman* v. *Porter* (2006), in which there was an intention to benefit only the original covenantee, thus
    providing a sufficient contrary intention to prevent the operation of section 78 of the LPA 1925.

original covenantee expressly to assign (that is, transfer) the benefit of a covenant to another person at the same time as he transfers the land.[67] Again, the
land must be capable of benefiting from the covenant, and must be readily
identifiable and, if the claimant is suing someone other than the original covenantor, the assignment must be made together with a transfer of the benefited land.[68] It is important to note here that this is an assignment of the
benefit of the covenant *inter partes* (i.e. between people); it is not an annexation
of the covenant *to the land* (*Marten* v. *Flight Refuelling* (1962)). Theoretically, therefore, if the purchaser of the land, who has had the benefit of the covenant
assigned to them, transfers the land again, there should be another assignment
of the benefit to the second purchaser and so on. So, if the benefit is to be
transmitted with the land in perpetuity, a 'chain of assignments' appears to be
necessary, as held in *Re Pinewood Estates* (1958). However, some earlier cases
suggest that, once the benefit has been assigned personally alongside the land
initially, it thereafter becomes annexed to the land,[69] although this does
appear an illogical conclusion if one has chosen the express assignment
method precisely because the benefit was not annexed! Thus, although some
doubt remains, the better view is that put forward in *Re Pinewood Estates* that a
chain of covenants is needed.[70] Note, however, that there is a further untested
argument that, if there has been an initial express assignment of the benefit,
future transfers of the land will include an *implied* assignment of the benefit of
the covenant to the purchaser under section 62 of the LPA 1925,[71] although
obiter dicta in *Kumar* v. *Dunning* (1989) that restrictive covenants are outside the
scope of section 62 would seem to tell against this.[72]

(iii)   *A scheme of development: a 'building scheme'*. A third alternative is to establish that the
benefit of the covenant has passed in equity under a 'scheme of develop-
ment' (sometimes known as a 'building scheme'). The ability of the benefit
of covenants to pass under a 'scheme of development' derives from a rule
based on 'common intention' and practicality. In simple terms, it allows a
common vendor of land (such as a property developer or builder) to transfer
the benefit of any covenants received by him from the purchasers of a plot of
the land to every other purchaser of a plot of that land. Thus, it represents an
attempt to create mutually enforceable obligations by giving the benefit of
every covenant, made by every purchaser, to every other purchaser.
(The burdens pass in the normal way, if the conditions are met.) In itself,
there is nothing unusual about a scheme of development, as it is perfectly
possible for a common vendor of land to transfer the benefit of covenants
already made by previous purchasers (and, therefore, attaching to his

---

67 The assignment would normally be clearly expressed, but it is sufficient if there were a clear intention to assign.

68 *Chambers* v. *Randall* (1923). The original covenantor is, of course, liable on the covenant and so the claimant under
    an assignment need not establish that he (the claimant) has land.

69 *Renals* v. *Colishaw* (1878).

70 In *Sugarman* v. *Porter* (2006), Peter Smith J declined to decide the point as it was no longer relevant on the facts.

71 This section, relevant also in the law of easements, transfers the benefits of all rights *relating to the land* to a transferee of it.

72 In *Sugarman* v. *Porter* (2006), Peter Smith J tends to support the doubts expressed in *Kumar*.

remaining land) to subsequent purchasers of parts of it under the rules of annexation or assignment considered above. However, the advantage of a scheme of development is that it allows the benefit of later purchasers' covenants to be annexed to the land *already* sold (i.e. to that now owned by previous purchasers), notwithstanding that this should not be possible because the covenantee (the builder) no longer owns *that* land. It means that, despite the fact that previous purchasers bought their land before later purchasers had made their covenants, the benefit of those later covenants still pass; the benefit of every covenant is available to *all* purchasers within the scheme of development, *irrespective* of the time of their purchase of a plot. For example, if Bloggs & Bloggs own 20 plots of land on which they have built houses, they may extract a covenant preventing use for a trade or business from any person who buys a house – say, Mr A. The burden will follow the plot purchased by Mr A in the normal way, and the benefit will pass to all land then owned by Bloggs & Bloggs. When Bloggs & Bloggs sell a second plot to Mr B on the same terms, Mr B is buying part of the land benefited by Mr A's covenant and can enforce it against Mr A's land. Mr B is also an original covenantor and burdens his own land in the normal way, for the benefit of the (now smaller) land remaining with Bloggs & Bloggs. Alas, however, under the normal rules, Mr A cannot get the benefit of Mr B's covenant, because Mr A already owns his land. Mr B made the covenant *after* Mr A had purchased a plot. A 'scheme of development' ignores this problem of timing and permits the passing of the benefit of every purchaser's covenant to every other purchaser, irrespective of the order of purchase. It also permits benefits to pass even though, on the occasion of a sale of the last plot, the covenantee (e.g. Bloggs & Bloggs) no longer owns any land capable of being benefited. In order to generate these effects, it must be clear that the entire parcel of land (before being sold in plots) was intended to fall within a common scheme of covenants, and be governed by similar rules. The necessary factual conditions for a building scheme were laid down in *Elliston* v. *Reacher* (1908), as explained by the Court of Appeal more recently in *Birdlip* v. *Hunter* (2016). These are that there must be a common vendor, that the land must be laid out in identifiable plots, that the benefit of every purchaser's covenants must be intended to be mutually enforceable (i.e. to pass to every other purchaser), that the purchasers must have bought the land on condition that this was intended and that the area subject to the scheme must be well defined. In addition, in *Birdlip*, the Court of Appeal indicated that a scheme of development usually required the fact of its existence to be reasonably clear from the original conveyancing documents, for it was necessary that all future purchasers should understand that a scheme was intended. This was one of the reasons why there was no scheme in this case. Of course, as one might expect with a rule of equity, these conditions are not inflexible and, on one view, the *Elliston* conditions are not conclusive or mandatory but merely evidence of a more general rule stemming from common intention. So, a 'scheme' has been accepted where there was no plan identifying discrete plots (*Baxter* v. *Four Oaks Properties* (1965), approved in *Whitgift Homes* v. *Stocks* (2001)), where there was no common vendor (*Re Dolphin's Conveyance* (1970)), where the property was laid out in subplots (*Brunner* v. *Greenslade*

(1971)) and even following the demerger of separate plots that had been 'joined' after the scheme had come into existence. However, recognition of a building scheme has been rightly refused when it was clear that each purchaser's covenants were different in substance, and therefore lacking the element of mutuality of purpose (*Emile Elias v. Pine Groves* (1993)) and where there was no evidence to support the conclusion that a scheme was originally intended (*Birdlip v. Hunter* (2016)). Importantly, it is clear from *Whitgift Homes* that it is crucial for the existence of a scheme of development, and the generous rules it brings, that the area subject to the scheme be defined with sufficient certainty – that is, sufficient certainty to ensure that *all* purchasers of plots know the extent both legally and physically of their mutual obligations. The extent of the development to be within the scheme must be defined when the scheme crystallises (*Birdlip v. Hunter* (2016)). In *Whitgift*, a housing development had been completed in the 1920s and 1930s and there was no doubt that a mutually enforceable scheme had been contemplated at the time the site was developed. However, there was real uncertainty as to the physical reach of the alleged scheme, and although one could say that certain plots in the development may have been within a scheme, there were a number of areas of the estate about which one could not be certain whether they were included or excluded. Consequently, a scheme could not operate even for those areas that appeared to have mutually enforceable obligations because there was fatal uncertainty as to the physical (and hence legal) reach of the alleged mutual obligations. No purchaser could be certain of the extent of his benefits and burdens.

Finally, we should note, for the avoidance of doubt, that a successful scheme of development does not affect the running of the burden of covenants and if the obligations are to be truly mutually enforceable, the normal steps for transmitting the burden of restrictive covenants must be followed. Usually, this will mean registration of the covenants against the title of all purchasers as they make their purchase. That said, however, it is also clear that the courts are very reluctant to disturb the 'local law' established by a scheme of development, and once one has been validly created, the courts will not readily refuse a remedy to a claimant seeking to enforce the benefit that he has been given. Neither will the Upper Tribunal (Lands Chamber) (formerly the Lands Tribunal) easily agree to the discharge or modification of building scheme covenants under the procedure for the modification or discharge of covenants laid down in section 84 of the LPA 1925.[73]

8.7   Escaping the Confines of the Rules: Can the Burden of Positive Covenants be Enforced by Other Means?

The position, as it stands so far, can be summarised quite easily. First, the benefit of positive and negative covenants can run with the land at law or in equity. Second, only the

---

73 See *Re Bromor Properties' Application* (1995); *Re Lee's Application* (1996).

burden of negative covenants may run, and then only in equity. Third, therefore, the great majority of disputes involve a triple claim that the benefit has passed in equity, that the covenant is negative and that the burden has passed in equity. However, in the practical world of property management, this is not an entirely satisfactory position, as both *Rhone* v. *Stephens* (1994) and *Thamesmead Town* v. *Allotey* (1998) illustrate, because in both cases the claimant was denied the enforcement of a *positive* covenant against a successor to the original covenantor when it was clear both that the successor knew of the obligation and that it was of real benefit to the original covenantee's land. Indeed, there seems no reason why, in principle, the burden of positive covenants should not be able to run with the land and it is difficult to find such a restriction in *Tulk* v. *Moxhay* (1848) itself, even though it appears clearly in later cases.[74] Moreover, it is not unknown for the law to allow positive obligations, including those requiring expenditure of money, to pass as proprietary obligations in other contexts – see, for example, the law of leasehold covenants, the easement of fencing[75] and the feudal chancel repair liability.[76] Given also that any positive burden would need to be registered to be binding (as currently with negative burdens), all prospective purchasers of affected land would be well warned that they were accepting such a liability and could act accordingly – they could walk away from the purchase, offer a lower price or take out insurance. This is, in essence, the substance of the Law Commission's criticism of the current law and the reason why it has proposed that the law be amended to allow positive obligations to run with freehold land, subject to registration requirements.[77] Nevertheless, be that as it may, the current rule is that the burden of positive covenants cannot run and any claimant under a positive covenant is limited to suing the *original* covenantor in damages. This has led to the development of a number of indirect methods of enforcing positive covenants, none of which is entirely satisfactory.

8.7.1   A chain of covenants

A chain of covenants is common in practice, although it only gives a remedy in damages. In essence, each purchaser of the burdened land covenants separately with their immediate predecessor in title (their seller) to carry out the positive covenant. Thus, if the original covenantor is sued on the covenant, he (the original covenantor) will be able to recover any damages he has had to pay out from the person to whom he sold the land (and who covenanted with him directly to perform the positive covenant), and so on down the chain. The well-known defect is that the chain is 'only as strong as its weakest link', so that (for example) the death, insolvency or other circumstance affecting any person in the chain may render the device useless. After all, personal liabilities such as these are not as robust as proprietary obligations. A variation on this is to ensure that each successive purchaser of the burdened land covenants directly, at the time they purchase the land, with the person entitled to the benefit of the covenant. In *Thamesmead*

---

74   *Austerberry* v. *Oldham Corporation* (1885).

75   *Crow* v. *Wood* (1977). Note also the seemingly positive easement actually to supply electricity in *Cardwell* v. *Walker* (2003).

76   *Aston Cantlow* v. *Wallbank* (2003).

77   See section 8.7.7 below.

Town, for example, the original covenantor had covenanted with the claimant (the person entitled to the benefit) to pay certain charges relating to the maintenance of the common parts of a housing estate. When the defendant purchased the land from the original covenantor, it was intended that he should then make a covenant with the claimant to like effect; in fact, the original covenantor had promised the claimant that, when they sold the land, they would *require* their purchaser to make such a covenant. This was, therefore, an attempt to create a series of covenants, with each new owner of the burdened land promising separately to pay the charge. It failed because when the defendant purchased the land, he was not asked to make this new covenant! Here, the chain broke the first time it was tested. Note, however, that if the land burdened is of registered title, it is possible to register a Restriction against that title requiring the purchaser of the burdened land to enter into the positive covenant as a condition of the purchase. This would have been effective in *Thamesmead Town* to ensure that the positive obligation was undertaken when the land was sold to a new purchaser. The entry of such a Restriction is the most effective way of ensuring that positive burdens are undertaken by purchasers of the original covenantor's land.[78]

8.7.2   The artificial long lease

As seen in Chapter 6, positive covenants in leases are quite capable of binding successive owners of the reversion or the lease. Thus, by artificially creating a long lease containing the desired positive covenants, and then 'enlarging' the lease into a freehold under section 153 of the LPA 1925, the original positive covenants will bind successive owners of land, because the 'leasehold rules' remain applicable even though the land is now freehold. The process of enlargement to a freehold does not destroy what were originally perfectly valid leasehold covenants. It is, however, cumbersome and expensive.

8.7.3   Mutual benefit and burden

It is a general principle of equity that a person who takes the benefit of a deed of covenant must also share any burden inherent in it. Thus, if a landowner enjoys the benefit of a covenant to use a private road or sewer, they must also take the burden of the upkeep of the road or sewer. They may take the benefit of the covenant only if they share its burden (*Halsall* v. *Brizell* (1957)). Consequently, any later owner of the land will also be subject to the burden of the positive covenant, if they wish to enjoy the benefits it offers. The proper ambit of the 'benefit and burden' principle has been the subject of judicial consideration, and a number of uncertainties about its scope have now been resolved. In *Davies* v. *Jones* (2009), followed in *Goodman* v. *Elwood* (2013), the Court of Appeal summarised the three broad conditions necessary for the principle to operate. First, the benefit and burden must be conferred in the same transaction, which usually will be the original deeds of covenant; second, the enjoyment of the benefit must be relevant to the imposition of the burden in the sense that the former must be connected to the latter; and, third, the person on whom the burden is alleged to have been imposed

---

78 This depends, of course, on HM Land Registry checking that the Restriction is complied with before registering the purchaser of the allegedly burdened land as its new registered proprietor.

by these rules must have or have had the opportunity of disclaiming the enjoyment of the benefit in practice. A good example of these conditions in operation is found in *Thamesmead Town* v. *Allotey*.

In *Thamesmead Town*, the claimant alleged that the defendant was liable to pay maintenance charges (i.e. liable to observe a positive covenant), because those charges related to facilities from which the defendant took a benefit. In fact, the charges related to two distinct 'benefits': a charge for the upkeep of roads and sewers, and a charge for the maintenance of common parts, such as walkways, open spaces and so on. The Court of Appeal decided that the benefit and burden rule allowed recovery of the charges in respect of roads and sewers, but not in respect of the 'general facilities'. This was because a person could be liable on the burden of a positive covenant only if the burden was intrinsically related to the benefit gained.[79] It was not enough that the documents of title said that a person could take a benefit from the land provided they accepted an attached burden: the mere linking of a benefit with a burden was insufficient. What was required was that the burden be the 'flip side' of the benefit: the burden had to be inherent in the benefit obtained and the benefit needed to be enjoyed.[80] There was no need for the covenant to expressly link the benefit and burden, but this had to be the clear effect of the substance of the obligations – *Wilkinson* v. *Kerdene* (2013). So, if a landowner wanted to use sewers and a private road, he had to pay for those sewers and that road. This was mutual benefit and burden, the mutuality being that the benefit and burden were simply two halves of the same coin.[81] However, if a landowner was required to pay a sum towards the upkeep of open spaces, and this was linked on paper to the benefit of not having his neighbours carry on a trade or business, this was not mutual benefit and burden. The benefit would run, but the burden would not, because the burden was not inherently connected to the benefit: it was not mutual. The benefit and burden rule allows the enforcement of a positive covenant if it conforms to 'if you want to use X, you must pay for it'; it does not allow the enforcement of a positive covenant in terms that 'I will give you X, if you will give me Y'. This must be correct. Otherwise, careful drafting of covenants could utilise the 'benefit and burden' principle to circumvent almost entirely the rule against the transmission of the burden of positive covenants. The decision in *Thamesmead Town* also illustrates the third of the *Davies* conditions because the court held that a person could be liable on the burden of a truly mutual positive covenant only if they chose to exercise the corresponding benefit. It was not enough that they had a right to the benefit, they had to use the right: 'the person on whom the burden is alleged to have been imposed must have or have had the opportunity of rejecting or disclaiming the benefit, not merely the right to receive the benefit' – *Davies*.

---

79 See also *Wilkinson* v. *Kerdene* (2013). In *Kerdene*, the defendants could only avoid the burden – the financial charge – if they could show that it had no relation to the rights they continued to enjoy.

80 Thus, if the benefit was not utilised, even if the covenant gave the right, the mutual burden could not be imposed; see immediately below.

81 See also *Changeinvest Ltd* v. *Rosendale-Steinhusen* (2004), in which the owner of dominant land was required to pay for the cost of upkeep of the road by which he exercised his easement over the servient land.

8.7.4 Construing section 79 of the Law of Property Act 1925

It has been noted that section 79(1) of the LPA 1925 is taken to annex the burden of restrictive covenants to land so that, other things being equal (e.g. registration), the burden passes to a successor in title in equity. In fact, a careful reading of section 79(1) reveals that it is not in terms limited to restrictive covenants, and there is nothing in the statute itself that prevents it being interpreted as annexing the burden of positive covenants as well. Indeed, the fact that it was felt necessary deliberately to confine the effect of section 79(2) to restrictive covenants[82] surely implies that the general principle of section 79(1) is not so limited. Be that as it may, the argument is all but over. Section 79(1) has been interpreted narrowly for reasons of policy rather than necessity: that is, that section 79(1) does not change substantive principles of law, but merely facilitates the passing of that which could already pass, being burdens of restrictive covenants in equity.

8.7.5 Rentcharges and rights of re-entry

A rentcharge is a periodic payment charged on land[83] and it may be annexed to a right of re-entry − that is, a right to enter the burdened land and forcibly terminate the landowner's estate unless the sum is paid. It is possible to use the combination of a rentcharge (to secure a sum of money, a positive burden) and the right of re-entry (to force payment) to support a positive covenant. The right of re-entry is itself an interest in land that can bind purchasers of the burdened land even though it supports a positive obligation. Consequently, careful drafting of these 'estate rentcharges', as they are known, can indirectly ensure performance of a positive obligation because non-payment of the charge underlying the positive obligation means loss of the defendant's estate in the land!

8.7.6 Commonhold

The CLRA 2002 represents an attempt to create an alternative method of owning land other than the freehold and leasehold. It is designed to give parties to the commonhold the security of a freehold title but with the flexibility of a lease. An essential element was the idea that positive obligations could run with the commonhold titles. Thus, a commonhold development could comprise a block of flats, a housing development, a retail or industrial development or a mixed use development. Had it been a success, it would have enabled positive burdens to run − for example, the obligation to pay for common parts, facilities − without the owners of a 'commonhold unit' having to be tenants under leases. However, the commonhold system has been a complete failure. The entire structure is complex and unwieldy and very expensive to instigate and run. It did not attract the support of property developers, investors or potential purchasers of commonhold units. The legislation is largely defunct in practical terms, although it still remains in force and could be used if the parties so desired. Had it been a success, the Law Commission would not have needed to propose reform of the law of covenants (see section 8.9

---

82 That is, when adverse possessors are in possession.

83 By way of contrast, 'rent' in a landlord-and-tenant context − technically 'rentservice' to distinguish it from a *rentcharge* − is a periodic payment in respect of a lease.

below). That said, the Law Commission's proposals are a much simpler, efficient and direct. Were they to be adopted – and that is uncertain – they would work.

8.8   Discharge and Modification of Restrictive Covenants

As noted briefly above, section 84 of the LPA 1925 contains a jurisdiction to discharge or modify restrictive covenants affecting freehold land. In fact, section 84(2) gives the court a useful power to declare whether any land is subject to the burden of a restrictive covenant – thus providing a simple method of determining whether a burden has 'run' – and section 84(1) gives the Upper Tribunal (Lands Chamber)[84] power to discharge or modify restrictive covenants. The power contained in section 84(1) is critical, for the enduring nature of restrictive covenants means that they can impose restrictions on the use of land that may become outdated or even positively detrimental. For example, a restrictive covenant against building may impede the development of land for social housing or may obstruct the economic regeneration of a depressed industrial area. Conversely, one landowner may seek the discharge of a covenant against building in order to build a second house in his capacious garden that he wants to sell for a large capital gain. The Upper Tribunal will exercise its jurisdiction in all of these cases, but no discharge or modification will occur unless the claimant can make out one of four general grounds: first, that the covenant is obsolete by reason of changes in the property or the neighbourhood; second, that the continuance of the covenant would obstruct the reasonable use of the land for private or public purposes; third, that the person entitled to the benefit has agreed to the discharge or modification; or, fourth, that the discharge or modification would cause no loss to the person entitled to the benefit.

8.9   Reform

In 2008, the Law Commission published a Consultation Paper on *Easements, Covenants and Profits à Prendre* (No. 186) in which it asked for views on reform of the law of covenants.[85] In June 2011, the Commission published its full report and made a number of firm proposals for the reform of easements, covenants and *profits à prendre*.[86] A draft Bill was attached to the Report. In this Report, No. 327 *Making Land Work: Easements, Covenants and Profits à Prendre*, the Commission proposes a new scheme to replace the current law of freehold covenants. This would involve the introduction of a 'land obligation', which could be either positive or negative in substance, and whose benefit and burden would be registered against the title of the covenantee's and covenantor's titles respectively. If so

---

84 Formerly the Lands Tribunal, whose jurisdiction was transferred to the Upper Tribunal in 2009 by the Transfer of Tribunal Functions (Lands Tribunal and Miscellaneous Amendments) Order 2009.

85 Consultation Paper No. 186, March 2008. This builds on its earlier 1984 report, *Transfer of Land: The Law of Positive and Restrictive Covenants* (Report No. 127). The 2008 paper also proposed some changes to the law of easements and profits (see Chapter 7).

86 See also Chapter 7.

registered, the land obligation would be enforceable by successors in title to the covenantee's land against successors in title to the covenantor's land, irrespective of whether it was positive or negative. Moreover, the original parties to the land obligation would cease to be able to enforce it, or be liable on it, once they had parted with their land. In this sense, land obligations would resemble easements more closely and, of course, the current position whereby only negative covenants can run with the land would be amended. Further, the fact that it is intended that the land obligation should be registered substantively on the title of the respective plots of land (like easements now) necessarily means that a land obligation would be a legal interest in land – only legal interests can be substantively registered in this way.[87] Consequently, an amendment to section 1 of the LPA 1925 would be needed in order to create a new type of legal property interest. Existing covenants would remain unaffected and would not be converted into new land obligations and the position in unregistered land would be unaffected. Thus, there would be two sets of rules operating in this general area: the law of covenants, being as it is now, for pre-reform covenants in registered land and for unregistered land; and the law of land obligations under the new scheme in relation to land of registered title.[88] Covenants and land obligations would have many characteristics in common – for example, land obligations would still have to 'touch and concern' the land and the remedies for breach of each would be similar – but the new scheme would be free of the technicalities of the current law. The simple idea would be that a positive or negative land obligation could run if registered. As yet, there is no news about when, or if, this very sensible proposal for reform will be implemented.

8.10 Chapter Summary

8.10.1 Positive and negative freehold covenants

Covenants between freeholders may be either positive or negative (restrictive). Positive covenants require the owner of the burdened land to take some action on his own property or property related to it, usually requiring the expenditure of money. An example is a covenant to pay for the upkeep of a private road. Negative (or 'restrictive') covenants require the owner of the burdened land to refrain from some activity on his own land. An example is the covenant against carrying on any trade or business on the land.

8.10.2 Covenants as contracts

Covenants are promises by one person to another contained in a deed to do, or more usually not to do, something on their own or related land. The covenant is made between the *covenantor* and the *covenantee* and is enforceable like any other contractual obligation between these original parties.

---

87 The idea is not to protect the land obligation by a Notice – for then it could be equitable – but that the act of substantive registration would both create and protect the legal land obligation, as is the position now with expressly created easements.

88 It would not be possible to create new covenants governed by the 'old' rules in registered land.

8.10.3 Covenants as interests in land

Covenants comprise both a benefit (the right to sue) and a burden (the obligation to perform). If the proper conditions are fulfilled, both the benefit and the burden may be 'attached' to the benefited and burdened land respectively, so that they pass to later purchasers or transferees of it. Although the benefit and burden of each covenant may pass independently, in practice a covenant can be enforced only if it can be shown that the claimant has the benefit of the covenant and that the defendant has the burden.

8.10.4 The relevance of 'law' and 'equity' in the enforcement of covenants

If a person sues on a covenant *at law*, he will be claiming that the defendant is subject to the burden of the covenant under the common law and should pay damages. The remedy is as of right. If a person sues on a covenant *in equity*, he will be claiming that the defendant is subject to the burden of the covenant under the rules of equity and susceptible to the discretionary equitable remedies of injunction and specific performance and to rules of registration. Note that if the burden has passed to the defendant in equity, so must the benefit have passed to the claimant in equity.

8.10.5 Principle 1: enforcement between the original covenantor and the original covenantee

If the covenantor and covenantee are still in possession of their respective land, all covenants are enforceable and the covenantee may obtain damages, an injunction or specific performance (i.e. they may sue at law or in equity). If the original *covenantor* has parted with the land (or never had land) that was subject to the covenant, he remains liable on all of the covenants to whomsoever has the benefit of them, although damages are available only because the covenantor has no land on which to perform the covenant. If the original *covenantee* has parted with the land that had the benefit of the covenant, he may still be able to enforce a covenant against whosoever has the burden of it. However, in practice such a claim is unlikely to achieve anything other than merely nominal damages even if the right to sue has not been assigned away. Note that it is important to identify exactly who are the original parties to the covenant, especially as for covenantees this may go beyond the actual signatories to a deed (section 56 of the LPA 1925).

8.10.6 Principle 2: enforcement against successors to the original covenantor (passing the burden)

It is not possible for the burden of *any* covenant to run at law. In equity, the burden of restrictive covenants *only* may pass, provided that:

1   The covenant is restrictive in nature.
2   The covenant touches and concerns the land (except possibly where the LTCA 1995 applies to a leasehold covenant not enforceable under 'leasehold rules').
3   At the date of the covenant, the covenant actually did confer a benefit on land owned by the original covenantee.

4   The burden of the restrictive covenant must have been intended to have run with the land of the original covenantor (section 79 of the LPA 1925).

5   In registered land, the covenant must be registered by means of a Notice against the burdened land in order to bind a purchaser for value who becomes the registered proprietor (section 29 of the LRA 2002).

6   In unregistered land, the covenant must be registered as a Class D(ii) land charge to bind a purchaser of a legal estate who gives money or money's worth.

7   The claimant is granted a remedy by virtue of the court's discretion.

8.10.7   Principle 3: enforcement by successors to the original covenantee (passing the benefit)

The benefit of both a positive and a restrictive covenant may be passed at law or in equity. However, given that only the burden of a restrictive covenant may pass, and then only in equity, most practical examples concern the passing of the benefit of a restrictive covenant in equity. This will give us our claimant (benefit) and defendant (burden) in suit in equity.

If it is necessary to consider passing the benefit of a covenant *at law* (e.g. the original covenantor may be the defendant), then:

1   The covenant must 'touch and concern' the land of the original covenantee.

2   The claimant must have a legal estate in the land, although not necessarily the same legal estate as the original covenantee: for restrictive covenants only, this may include an 'occupier' – for example, an adverse possessor (section 78 of the LPA 1925).

3   The benefit of the covenant must have been annexed to a legal estate in the land either expressly or by implication, or by statute – that is, by express words or necessary implication from express words or by statute under section 78 of the LPA 1925.

In order to pass the benefit of a covenant *in equity*, then the following must be true:

1   The covenant must 'touch and concern' the land of the original covenantee.

2   The claimant must have a legal or equitable estate in the land of the original covenantee, although not necessarily the same estate as the original covenantee. For restrictive covenants only, this may include an 'occupier': for example, an adverse possessor (section 78 of the LPA 1925).

3   The benefit of the covenant must have been transmitted to the claimant in one of three ways:

(i)   By annexation: express, implied or by statute. The benefit of a covenant can be expressly annexed to the land in equity in exactly the same way as in law: that is, by express words or by statute under section 78 of the LPA 1925.

(ii)   By assignment: express or implied. Following the general rule that the benefit of a contract may be assigned to another, the original covenantee may expressly assign the benefit of a covenant at the same time as he transfers the land. For future sales of the land, an assignment of the benefit of the covenant may be implied by section 62 of the LPA 1925, subject to criticism in *Kumar v. Dunning* (1989).

(iii)   By a scheme of development (building scheme). This allows the benefit of later purchasers' covenants to be passed to the land already sold by a common vendor (i.e. to previous purchasers), notwithstanding that this should not be possible because the original covenantee (the common vendor) has already parted with the land. The conditions are flexible, because reciprocity of obligation is the key, but at the very least it must be the case that the obligations were intended to be mutually enforceable (i.e. to pass to every purchaser and be similar in substance) and the physical area of the scheme must be clearly defined.

8.10.8   Devices that may allow the passing of the burdens of positive covenants in practice

These include: a chain of covenants; the artificial long lease; mutual benefit and burden; reinterpreting section 79 of the LPA 1925; Restrictions on the title of registered land; and the use of rentcharges, coupled with a right of re-entry and the defunct commonhold scheme.

 Further Reading

Law Commission, *Making Land Work: Easements, Covenants and Profits à Prendre,* Report No. 327, 2011.

Martin, J, 'Remedies for breach of restrictive covenants' [1996] Conv 329.

O'Connor, P, 'Careful what you wish for: Positive freehold covenants' [2011] Conv 191.

Scamell, EH, *Land Covenants,* London: Butterworths, 1996.

Sutton, T, 'On the brink of land obligations again' [2013] Conv 17.

Walsh, E and **Morris,** C, 'Enforcing positive covenants: A practical perspective' [2015] Conv 316.

Now visit the companion website to:

•   test your understanding of the key terms using our Flashcard Glossary;

•   revise and consolidate your knowledge using our Multiple Choice Question testbank.

www.routledge.com/cw/dixon

Chapter 9
Licences to Use Land

9.1   Licences

In Chapters 7 and 8, we examined in some detail two important ways in which one person might enjoy limited rights over the land of another. In many respects, these easements (Chapter 7) and freehold covenants (Chapter 8) were seen to be similar, especially where the effect on the 'servient' or 'burdened' land was 'restrictive', in that it prevented the current owner from engaging in some activity on their own land. Of course, both easements and restrictive covenants are proprietary in nature: both are interests in land that may 'run' with the benefited and burdened land and are not personal to the parties that created them. However, a moment's thought will reveal that easements and freehold covenants can cover only a small fraction of the situations in which one person may wish to use the land of another. For example, what is the position where I ask my neighbour if I can park my car on his land, or my children play football there? Again, what are my rights if I pay an entrance charge to go to a play or a film on someone else's land, or use a neighbour's garden for the day for a party, or wish to store something on his land or in his outbuildings? All of these are activities undertaken on another person's land, but they may not fall within the realm of easements or freehold covenants.

This is where the 'licence' to use land comes into play. 'Licences' are a third way in which a person may enjoy some right or privilege over the land of another person and very often they are created deliberately as a way of regularising one-person use of another's land. However, as we shall see, they are fundamentally different in nature and effect from both easements and freehold covenants. In essence, they are personal rather than proprietary and the difference is critical.[1] However, even though the conceptual difference between a proprietary right and a licence is clear and unambiguous, it can be more difficult to tell them apart in practice, especially where the substance of the proprietary right and licence appears to be the same. For example, the same type of activity may qualify as either a licence or an easement depending on the manner and circumstances in which it arises. In *Batchelor* v. *Marlowe* (2001), a right to park a number of cars was held to be a licence, even though a similar right may in the appropriate circumstances be an easement – *Moncrieff* v. *Jamieson* (2007). Likewise, absence of the proper legal formalities for the creation of an alleged easement will mean that the claimant obtains only a licence even if the right could have been an easement, as where no deed or written instrument is used. So, while it is important to understand the conceptual difference between a proprietary right and a licence, it is equally important to understand the practical ways in which that distinction might arise.

9.2   The Essential Nature of a Licence

Licences are permission given by the owner of land to another person, who may or may not own land themselves, to use the owner's land for some specific purpose. The permission (or 'licence') can be to do anything at all: for example, attending a cinema (*Hurst* v. *Picture Theatres Ltd* (1915)), parking a car (*Colchester & East Sussex Co-op* v. *Kelvedon Labour Club*

---

1 For example, proprietary rights can usually be registered by means of a Notice under the LRA 2002, whereas licences cannot.

(2003)),[2] erecting an advertising hoarding (*Kewall Investments* v. *Arthur Maiden* (1990)), running a school (*Re Hampstead Garden Suburb Institute* (1995)), using buildings as a social club (*Onyx* v. *Beard* (1998)) or allowing children to play in your garden. Licences can even give a limited right of residential occupation as with those 'occupation licences' considered in Chapter 6 that can be difficult to distinguish from leases.[3] Indeed, the range of activities that can be covered by the giving of 'a licence' is virtually limitless simply because it is impossible to foresee all of the circumstances in which one person may wish to use the land of another! With this in mind, the following points about licences should be noted.

1   A licence is given by the owner of land (the licensor) to some other person (the licensee), permitting him to do something on the owner's land. The licensee need not own any land themselves, and usually does not.[4] They are classically defined in *Thomas* v. *Sorrell* (1673) as a *personal* permission to use land belonging to another such that, without the permission, the use would amount to a trespass. Necessarily, therefore, licences may cover any activity – long or short term – that may be undertaken on land. This versatility means that licences can arise in all manner of situations and may easily be confused with proprietary rights such as leases, easements and freehold covenants, all of which also allow one person to use another's land but which have the essentially different quality of being 'real property'.[5]

2   There are no formal requirements for the creation of a 'licence' as such, although occasionally a licence may depend on the fulfilment of conditions imposed by some other branch of the law; for example, with contractual licences, an 'offer and acceptance' and consideration is as essential as for any other type of contract. Licences are often created deliberately in order to give the licensee some limited use of the licensor's land. Consequently, licences may be created orally or in writing, or even be found in a deed or registered disposition, especially if they are ancillary to the grant of some proprietary right or interest in land. A good example of a licence found in a registered disposition is on a conveyance of a house from A to B, wherein B is given a personal right to park his car on adjoining land retained by A. As is obvious, however, where licences are found in formal documents (and sometimes where they are not!), there is always the danger that they will be confused

---

2 In this case, the ability to park was a licence rather than an easement because this was the express intention of the parties. As noted above, it is possible for a right to park to be an easement if it is created in the appropriate way (e.g. by registered deed or written contract) and so long as it does not oust the landowner from their own land, *Moncrieff* v. *Jamieson* (2007).

3 See *Street* v. *Mountford* (1985) and *Ogwr BC* v. *Dykes* (1989). See also the distinction between licences and life interests in Chapter 5, as in *Dent* v. *Dent* (1996). Note also the decision in *Bruton* v. *London & Quadrant Housing Trust* (1999), discussed in Chapter 6, which suggests that 'a lease' is not always proprietary, but may instead give rise to a merely contractual (and personal) landlord and tenant relationship. Whether this legal creature – the non-proprietary lease – really exists or is in fact just a licence by another name is a matter of considerable controversy: see Dixon [2000] 59 CLJ 25.

4 As seen in Chapters 7 and 8, both easements and covenants require there to be both benefited and burdened land.

5 Some people describe this by saying that property rights exist in *rem*, whereas licences exist in *personam*. This is not an entirely helpful way of putting it because many rights unrelated to land may exist in *rem* (e.g. in relation to ships) whereas some land rights (e.g. leases) may exist in *personam*. It is better to stick to 'proprietary' or 'personal'.

with true proprietary rights, especially if the substantive right granted (e.g. to park a car) is, in fact, capable of being either a licence or a proprietary right. Importantly, if the formalities required by statute for the creation of a proprietary right are not satisfied – for example, if the required written instrument or deed is not used – the right thereby given to the claimant cannot amount to a proprietary right at all but it may still result in the claimant having a licence. For example, if A were verbally to permit B a right of passage across A's land, this *could have been* a legal easement had it been properly granted by deed and correctly registered against the burdened title, but, failing this, it amounts to a licence such that B does not commit a trespass when he uses the right of way.[6]

3   It follows from the above that a licence to use land is either: (a) a permission to use land that could *never* have amounted to proprietary right because it does not fall into a recognised category of such right (e.g. a permission given to wander anywhere on farmland). Consequently, it is irrelevant how the licence is created.[7] Or (b) a permission that might have amounted to a proprietary right had it been created with proper formality, but where that formality is missing (e.g. an oral permission to park a single car on neighbour's land).[8] Furthermore, the creation of a licence as opposed to a proprietary right (where both were possible) might be accidental (as where the parties forget to use a written instrument), but equally it could have been deliberate, as in *Colchester Co-op* v. *Kelvedon* (2003), where the parties' express written intention was to create a parking licence even though that right could have existed as an easement. In this regard, it is interesting to note that the parties' intentions are permitted to play a pivotal role when distinguishing between an easement and a licence, but not (as we have seen in Chapter 6) when distinguishing between a lease and a licence.[9]

4   To reiterate the point made briefly above, a licence may be given to any person for any lawful purpose, not only to someone who also owns land. In this respect, licences are different from easements and most freehold covenants. Thus, there is no *need* for a 'dominant tenement' (as in easements) or 'benefited land' (as in covenants) although there is no rule saying that the licensee may not own adjoining or other land. So, when A conveys land to B, he may grant a parking licence over his adjoining retained land to B (who is a landowner). But A may also decide to give or sell a parking licence to X, a person with no land at all, who simply wants somewhere to park his car.

5   If the relationship between the licensor and the licensee is based in contract – a permission given in return for a counter-benefit, such as payment of money – then the parties are subject to normal principles of contract law concerning remedies and damages for breach of the contractual licence. The fact that the subject matter of the contract is land does not elevate the status of the licence to anything more than a personal relationship between licensor and licensee. However, given that the licensor and licensee are likely to have been in close contact over the use of the land,

---

6   Of course, being now only a licence, it cannot bind a successor to A's land.

7   So, it might be oral, in writing or even in a deed.

8   The relevant formality rules for the creation of proprietary rights are discussed in Chapter 1.

9   *Street* v. *Mountford* (1985).

it is possible that their relations with each other may have generated a *separate and independent* claim in proprietary estoppel. The existence of such an estoppel – considered in Chapter 10 in fact is not dependent on any prior relationship of licensor and licensee, but many successful claims of estoppel have arisen out of such a relationship precisely because the parties are already dealing with each other over the use of land. An example is *Parker (9th Earl of Macclesfield)* v. *Parker* (2006), in which, according to the court, the claimant's confirmed entitlement to use land arose *either* under a licence or out of estoppel, depending on how one viewed the facts.[10] Given that the nature of proprietary estoppel as a property right has now been settled[11] and that a licence is clearly personal, it is important not to confuse these two concepts. If the parties were bound together under a contractual licence, and then there was an estoppel, the proper way to look at this is that first there was a personal right between the parties (the contractual licence) and then there was a new proprietary right between them, generated by estoppel. When the estoppel started (or 'crystallised' – see Chapter 10), the licence ended. There is no sense in which the estoppel somehow 'made the licence proprietary'; the estoppel is a new thing and the licence has ceased to exist.[12] As discussed in *West End Commercial* v. *London Trocadero* (2017), an estoppel arises in relation to an assurance or promise about a property right; an assurance or promise about a licence must be personal.

6   Putting all this together, it being so important that it bears repetition, the orthodox (and correct) view of licences is that they are *not* proprietary in nature. As Vaughan CJ makes clear in *Thomas* v. *Sorrell* (1673), the traditional analysis of licences is that they 'properly passeth no interest nor alter or transfer property in any thing'. A licence is not an interest *in* land, but rather a right *over* land, and one that is personal to the parties who created it (the licensor and licensee). This is so whatever the circumstances in which the licence arises: for example, the substance of the right might be inherently personal (e.g. to play on land) or the permitted use might be something which could have been proprietary had it been created properly. As a consequence of being personal, the right conferred by a licence can be enforced only against the person who created it, sometimes using contractual remedies. But, it does not 'run' with the land (unlike easements and freehold covenants) and cannot be enforced against a purchaser or transferee of the land over which it exists. The licence is not within the realm of 'real property' and is incapable of binding third parties when the licensor transfers the 'burdened' land. So, a licence cannot be protected by a Notice against a registered title, and it cannot amount to an overriding interest through 'actual occupation' under paragraph 2 of Schedule 1 or Schedule 3 LRA 2002. Nor can it be a 'Land Charge' under the Land Charges Act 1972 in relation to unregistered land. For example, assuming A has indeed granted a parking licence over his retained land to B, if A then transfers (by sale or gift) the 'burdened' land to P, P is under no obligation whatsoever to continue to allow B to park his car and there is nothing that B can do to achieve this. The point is, simply,

---

10 As it transpired, it was not necessary to determine which was correct as the defendant – he who gave the licence or generated the estoppel – was not proposing to deal with the land while the claimant resided there.

11 Section 116 of the LRA 2002, and see Chapter 10.

12 This makes it clear that the phrase 'estoppel licence' has no meaning and is best avoided.

that a licence is incapable of binding land: it is personal to licensor and licensee. Although many attempts have been made to challenge this fundamental and critical distinction between 'interests in land' and 'licences', it remains a core concept in modern land law. We shall consider the matter in more detail when examining 'contractual licences' and so-called 'estoppel licences'.

9.3   Types of Licence

Although a licence to use land may be given for any lawful purpose, it is possible to classify licences according to the functions they serve, the circumstances in which they arise or the way in which they are created. The following classification draws the traditional distinctions between different types of licence. However, it is important to remember two things. First, whatever 'type' of licence we are discussing, the essence of all licences is the same. They are at their core personal rights to use land. Second, the real discussion points about licences revolve around practical matters concerning their enforcement, and not what particular label we give them. Thus, although the following analysis will proceed on the basis that there are different types of licence, the important matter is to determine how each 'type' deals with the following four practical matters.

1   What are the general attributes of the licence and how might it be created?
2   What are the obligations of the licensor to the licensee, and vice versa?
3   Considering that there has been considerable academic debate about the matter, is the licence *in any sense* an 'interest in land' or does it ever behave like one?
4   Are there any circumstances in which the licence can take effect against a third party: that is, can a person who purchases land over which the licence already exists *ever* be required to give effect to that licence?

9.3.1   Bare licences

A bare licence is probably the most common form of permission that a landowner gives to another person to use his land. It comprises permission to enter upon the land and carry out some activity there, given voluntarily by the owner, who receives nothing in return. The giving of the licence is 'gratuitous' in that it is not supported by 'consideration' moving from the licensee. There is no contract between the parties, merely a bare permission to do that which the landowner has allowed and which otherwise would be a trespass. Typically, such licences allow the licensee to carry on some limited activity on the licensor's land, as where permission is given to use a garden, to deliver some previously ordered goods or to enjoy a limited and revocable right of access. These bare licences can be given in any manner and require no particular form. Many are given verbally or simply implied from the landowner's lack of objection to the activity taking place. It is also inherent in a bare licence that it lasts only for so long as the licensor wishes. Thus, the licensor may terminate the licence by giving reasonable notice to the licensee (*Robson* v. *Hallet* (1967); *Re Hampstead Garden Suburb Institute* (1995)), and the licensee has no claim in damages or specific performance should this happen. The licence exists at the will of the landowner and the landowner incurs no liability by withdrawing his permission. There is no doubt that a bare licence is *not* an interest in land; it is personal only to the original licensor and licensee. As such, it is incapable of binding a third party and any person who subsequently acquires the licensor's land may disregard the bare licence and require the licensee to stop using the land. In reality, of course, the often temporary and transient nature of bare licences means that the licensee is hardly likely to contemplate continuing the activity when the land changes hands. Of course, the new owner might themselves decide to allow the activity to continue and this amounts to the giving of a new bare licence.

9.3.2 Licences coupled with an interest (or 'grant')

This is a rather loose category of licences covering a range of activities that are grouped together because the licences are said to be 'coupled' with an interest in land or with the grant of an interest in land. For example, as discussed in Chapter 7, a landowner may grant another person a *profit à prendre* over their land: that is, a right to take from the land some natural resource, such as fish, pasture, wood or turf. Necessarily, in order to exercise this 'profit', the grantee must be able to enter upon the land and remain there for an appropriate time. This is achieved by means of a licence attached to (or 'coupled' with) the profit, as in *James Jones and Son v. Earl of Tankerville* (1909). To some extent however, to identify this permission as a separate 'licence' at all is misleading, for the permission is practically necessary for the exercise of the right that has actually been granted over the land (the profit). The licence merely facilitates the achievement of the primary purpose; it is not a purpose in itself. So where, as is the case with profits a prendre, the primary right granted is proprietary in nature (i.e. it is an interest in land), the licence that attaches to it *appears* also to be proprietary, because it lives or dies with the proprietary grant. The licence will last for as long as the profit exists and will be enforceable against whomsoever the profit is enforceable against because it is an inherent component of the greater right. Likewise, should the grantee of the profit be unlawfully denied the proprietary right granted, the normal remedies will be available to prevent interference with it or to compensate for its denial. Obviously, the licence only has these characteristics because it facilitates the exercise of a real property interest; it has no proprietary status of its own and it might even be said that it has no independent existence. For example, the holder of the proprietary right is only able to use 'the licence' when seeking to exercise the proprietary grant. In our example, the right holder cannot wander on the land for any purpose: only to exercise the *profit à prendre*.

9.3.3 Contractual licences

Contractual licences are similar to bare licences with the important difference that contractual licences are granted to the licensee in return for consideration. Two examples are the purchase of a cinema ticket and the 'occupation licence' discussed in Chapter 6. Simply put, there is a contract between the licensor and licensee, the subject matter of which is the giving of a licence to use land for a stated purpose. Crucially, therefore, contractual licences are governed by the ordinary rules of the law of contract. They do not need to be created with any particular formality and may arise orally, be implied through conduct, or under a written document or may be evidenced by a written document (e.g. the terms and conditions on the back of a car park ticket or cinema ticket). Importantly, although these contractual licences are contracts concerning the use of land, they are not contracts for the *disposition of an interest in land*. They are not contracts for the creation or transfer of an interest in land. Consequently, they do not need to meet the requirements of section 2 of the LP(MP)A 1989 and are not *required* to be in writing, signed by both parties etc. within the meaning of that statute.[13] The characteristics of contractual licences are discussed below.

9.3.4   Remedies and contractual licences

As these licences are founded in contract, normal contractual rules apply. Both licensor and licensee may enforce the terms of the contract and can utilise the normal remedies for breach of contract in the event that either fails to carry out the terms of the licence. Thus, either party may sue for damages for breach of contract, although it is usually the licensee that needs such a remedy when the licensor fails to allow him to use the land for the purpose for which the licence was purchased. More importantly in practice, it is now clear that, as with other contracts, an injunction or order of specific performance may be obtained by the licensee in appropriate circumstances. An injunction can be obtained to prevent the licensor from revoking the licence before its contractual date of expiry,[14] or an order of specific performance may be obtained requiring the licensor to permit the activity authorised by the licence to take place.[15] Given that both of these remedies support the contractual licensee's actual use of the land, their effect can be to make the licence in practice irrevocable between the *original* parties throughout the contractual period of the licence. In this respect, a contractual licence is very different from a bare licence which can be terminated on reasonable notice. A contractual licence can amount to an unbreakable arrangement between the *original* parties lasting for the agreed duration of the licence.[16] So, if A, the operator of a car park, gives B a licence to park on A's land for three years, at £100 per year, this is a contractual licence of three years' duration. If A should then seek to deny the right, A may be liable in damages for breach of contract or held to the licence for the three years by injunction or specific performance (depending on how the dispute arose). Critically, however, these remedies operate between the original parties to the contract only, they do not extend to any other person – this is privity of contract. Consequently, if A breaks the contract because he has sold the land to P within the three years and therefore has no land on which B can now park, A will remain liable in damages, but, of course, P cannot be subject to an injunction or specific performance because the licence does not affect the land: it affects the people who created it. It is personal, not proprietary and cannot 'bind' a third party. The position of P in these circumstances and his liability (if any) is discussed in sections 9.3.6 and 9.3.7 below.

---

13 Of course, the parties may decide to encapsulate their agreement in a written document that they both sign, but this is not necessary for the contractual licence to exist, as it would be if the contract was concerned with a proprietary right.

14 *Winter Garden Theatre* v. *Millennium Productions Ltd* (1948).

15 *Verrall* v. *Great Yarmouth BC* (1981).

16 Of course, not every contractual licensee will be able to obtain an injunction or order for specific performance. Sometimes, damages will be the appropriate remedy.

9.3.5 Can contractual licences amount to interests in land? Can they affect purchasers of the licensor's land?

There is nothing surprising in parties being held to their contract throughout the life of the contract. So, we should not be surprised that a contractual licence can be held to be irrevocable between the *original* parties for the duration of the licence. If you pay me in order to park on my land for three years, the law can hold you that bargain. However, because contractual licences involve immoveable land, and because land can change hands, there have been concerns in the past that the purely personal nature of licences was causing hardship. For example, if A grants a contractual licence to B allowing B to park her caravan in his garden for five years, a court may well enforce this by injunction for five years *against* A. Yet, what if, after three years, A sells his land to P? Why can P ignore the licence when A could have been held to give effect to it for two more years? To put it another way, if a contractual licence is irrevocable between the original licensor and licensee, should a purchaser from the licensor also be required to give effect to it for the remainder of the contractual term? Would that not be appropriate, especially if the purchaser knew of the existence of the contractual licence before he purchased? In essence, this boils down to two important questions: first, are contractual licences 'interests in land' in some circumstances so that they may bind a purchaser of land in the normal way according to established principles of registered or unregistered conveyancing? Second, even if contractual licences cannot be interests in land, can they take effect against a purchaser of the licensor's land for any other reason?

9.3.6 Can contractual licences be interests in land? Can they be proprietary?

The starting point for a discussion of this question is the famous *dictum* in *Thomas* v. *Sorrell* (1673) that we have seen already: that a licence 'properly passeth no interest nor alters or transfers property in any thing'. This states that, as a matter of principle, a licence operates merely personally between the parties and creates no interest in land that might be enforceable against a third person. Indeed, this has been confirmed by the House of Lords in *King* v. *David Allen and Sons, Billposting* (1916), which decided expressly that contractual licences were not proprietary and thus could not bind third parties. Nevertheless, despite this clear and principled position, the many uses to which licences could be put generated academic and judicial discussion as to whether this orthodox view should prevail in all circumstances. Were there, perhaps, circumstances in which a 'contractual licence' could be regarded as a new species of property right in much the same way that restrictive covenants became proprietary after *Tulk* v. *Moxhay* (1848)? In particular, the widespread use of 'occupation licences' as a deliberate alternative to leases[17] meant that some licensees were occupying their homes under a 'mere' licence that could be defeated simply by a sale of the land from licensor to a new owner. For example, could it be 'equitable' that a landowner might allow a person to occupy their property under a licence for an agreed period of (say) five years, but, just one month after completing the deal, sell their land to P and thereby defeat the licence, with the result that the occupier

---

17 See Chapter 6.

would be turned out on to the street? Of course, in these circumstances, the licensee might well be able to claim damages for breach of contract from the licensor, but this is not the same as enjoying the benefits of occupation. Likewise, an injunction or decree of specific performance as a remedy for breach of a contractual licence against the licensor is not much use once the land has been sold.[18]

This was the issue facing the courts and for some judges and commentators it was a problem that needed a solution, especially in the case of occupation licences before *Street v. Mountford* (1985) revealed their true character as leases. In typical fashion, it was addressed head on by Lord Denning in *Errington v. Errington* (1952). In that case, Lord Denning regarded the claimant's contractual licence as binding on a wife who had received land under a will from her husband, he being the original licensor. His reasoning was that, as the licensee could have prevented revocation of the licence by the licensor for its agreed duration (i.e. by injunction), there was no reason why the licence could not continue against a third party in appropriate circumstances. The 'appropriate circumstances' seemed to be when the contractual licence was 'supported by an equity' (for this gave it proprietary status), and an 'equity' would exist where it would be unjust to deny the continued existence of the licence. Unfortunately, however, all of this simply assumes that which must be established. It assumes without reasons that contractual licences are *already* interests in land that are *capable* of binding third parties. The supporting 'equity' is just another way of saying that we would like contractual licences to bind third parties and the 'reason' why they cannot, which Lord Denning thought was lacking, is that they are inherently personal. In reality, then, the real question is not *when* can a contractual licence bind a third party? It is, rather, whether it is *possible* that a contractual licence can do this? If it is *possible* in principle, then the circumstances *when* it may happen in practice can be identified. If it is not possible, then the 'when' becomes irrelevant. Lord Denning in *Errington* never got to the heart of this problem, preferring (no doubt deliberately) to concentrate on the result rather than the reasoning. Moreover, Lord Denning did not attempt to explain why the House of Lords' binding decision in *King* could be ignored by his Court of Appeal – or perhaps he knew that in truth it should not be? Neither is Lord Denning's appeal to 'justice' very persuasive, because it may always be 'unjust' in one sense to deny the continuing validity of a licence against a purchaser of the licensor's land. Similarly, it can be very 'unjust' for a landowner to be able to ignore an unregistered option to purchase the land, even though such options really are proprietary interests, but as we have seen in *Midland Bank v. Green* (1981), this is the principled answer. The House of Lords in that case did not contemplate the judicial repeal of the Land Charges Acts simply because, on a populist view, the result appeared 'unjust'. Further, even if we put aside the powerful arguments of principle and policy that should have led Lord Denning to the opposite conclusion in *Errington*, it is not necessarily 'unjust' to allow a purchaser of land to escape from a valid licence granted previously by the seller, even if he knew of its existence, because this possibility may have been the very reason why the seller gave 'a licence' to the claimant in the first place. Perhaps the seller deliberately chose to limit the claimant's rights to those of a merely personal character to enable him to sell the land quickly and unburdened at a moment of

---

18 Of course, neither order would in fact be obtained in practice because they are discretionary and the court will not order pointless remedies.

his choosing. Put another way, the whole purpose behind the identification of a group of rights to use land as 'licences' instead of 'property rights' is *precisely* to ensure that they are not interests in land and cannot bind the land in the hands of a third party. In terms of a general theory of land law then, the very definition of, and the role for, 'licences' is that they are not proprietary.

Despite these powerful arguments, and despite the existence of the House of Lords' decision in *King*, initially *Errington* was followed by a number of decisions involving the Court of Appeal and the High Court and these appeared to be generating a head of steam that could have resulted in recognition of the proprietary status of contractual licences. Even then, however, the matter was not clear, for many of these apparently rogue decisions – albeit purportedly following *Errington* – can be explained on the simple grounds that the claimant never really had a contractual licence at all, but that on a true analysis they had proprietary rights within the accepted categories of such right (e.g. a lease, life interest, easement or equitable co-ownership right). Naturally, such substantive rights, although mis-labelled by the courts as 'contractual licences', could be binding on third parties in the normal way and the error lay in calling them 'licences' in the first place.

Finally, on the question of principle, the Court of Appeal in *Ashburn Anstalt* v. *Arnold* (1989) re-examined the matter afresh and reasserted the orthodox view. In that case, Fox LJ relied on the House of Lords' decisions in *King* and in *National Provincial Bank* v. *Ainsworth* (1965) to confirm unequivocally that licences, including contractual licences, were not, and could not be, interests in land. They were personal rights between licensor and licensee, and nothing more. Furthermore, in so far as *Errington* decided otherwise, it was *per incuriam* (being decided without reference to *King*) and could in any event be explained on other grounds. For example, perhaps the claimant in *Errington* did not have a contractual licence at all but an estate contract (an accepted interest in land) binding a non-purchaser in the normal way, or perhaps there was a *Lloyds Bank* v. *Rosset* (1991) type of equitable ownership, or perhaps the third party was bound by an estoppel. However, whatever spin we place on *Errington* to justify its actual result, Fox LJ's judgment in *Ashburn* makes it clear that, *as a matter of principle*, licences are not interests in land and for that reason cannot bind third parties. This view has been confirmed now on many occasions, but none with more force than Mummery LJ in *Lloyd* v. *Dugdale* (2001), who noted that '[n]otwithstanding some previous authority suggesting the contrary, a contractual licence is not to be treated as creating a proprietary interest in land so as to bind third parties who acquire the land with notice of it'. This is, of course, a thoroughly orthodox and convincing approach to the problem and it serves to highlight the fundamental distinction between interests in land and purely personal interests, even those that just happen to relate to property. It is submitted that the contrary view now is unarguable.[19] Indeed, if one takes Lord Wilberforce's definition of an interest in land, in *National Provincial Bank* v. *Ainsworth* (1965), that

> before a right or interest can be admitted into the category of property, or of a right affecting property, it must be definable, identifiable by third parties, capable in its nature of assumption by third parties and have some degree of permanence or stability,

---

19 Now that the House of Lords has asserted in *Street* v. *Mountford* (1985) that residential occupation usually gives rise to a lease and not a licence, many of the practical concerns about the non-binding status of contractual licences have been removed. It was, after all, these 'licences' that appeared to deserve protection against third parties. In fact, they did deserve protection, but that was because they were really leases.

it is obvious that licences per se have no claim to proprietary status. Of course, this does mean, as noted above, that courts must be very careful to categorise rights correctly: is the claimant's right really a licence, or is it really something else? This is not always easy, but it is easier than floundering in the chaos created by dissolving the distinction between personal and proprietary rights.[20]

9.3.7 Can the contractual licence take effect against a purchaser from the licensor despite not being an interest in land?

Following the decision in Errington, a second, related attempt was made by Lord Denning's Court of Appeal to explain why a contractual licence could affect a purchaser of the licensor's land. In Binions v. Evans (1972), a purchaser of land subject to what looked like a contractual licence expressly agreed to purchase the land subject to that licence. The purchaser then sought to evict the licensee and he was prevented from doing so. In fact, two judges in the Court of Appeal actually decided that no licence was involved at all; rather, the occupier had a life interest under a strict settlement (a true proprietary right) that was protected under the SLA 1925.[21] Lord Denning, however, took a different view and decided that the purchaser was bound to give effect to the contractual licence because he had purchased the land expressly subject to it. In Lord Denning's view, the licensee was protected against eviction by the purchaser because equity would impose a constructive trust on the purchaser behind which the licence could take effect. Subsequent decisions, such as Re Sharpe (1980), have followed this reasoning. The net result is that the contractual licence is said to take effect against a purchaser because that particular purchaser is bound by a constructive trust because of that particular purchaser's conduct. It will be apparent from this explanation that the words and actions of the particular purchaser are crucial here. Importantly, the licence takes effect only against the particular purchaser, and then only because of his conduct. The licence is not, in fact, an interest in land but is merely protected against being revoked by that particular purchaser. It still remains incapable of binding the land as such, even though it may take effect personally against one particular purchaser of it.

The 'constructive trust' idea was also re-examined by Fox LJ in Ashburn Anstalt v. Arnold (1989) and he accepted that, in appropriate cases, a contractual licence may take effect behind a constructive trust and be enforceable against a purchaser. However, it was not enough that the purchaser simply agreed to buy the land subject to the licence for that would be to repeat the heresy of Errington; rather, the purchaser must have so conducted himself that it would be inequitable and unconscionable for the licence to be denied. An example would be where the purchaser promised to give effect to the licence, obtained the land from the licensor for a lower price in consequence of that promise and then

---

20 Occasionally, the confusion re-emerges. In K Sultana Saeed v. Plustrade (2001), the Court of Appeal, following a concession from counsel, expressed the view that it did not matter whether the claimant had a licence to park or an easement to park as either was enforceable against a third party as an overriding interest if actual occupation existed. This is entirely incorrect. Like Lord Denning in Errington, this begs the question because whether a right to use land can amount to an overriding interest depends, in the first place, on it being an interest in land.

21 See Chapter 5.

refused to honour the licence.[22] Moreover, as Fox LJ makes absolutely clear, the licence is only protected behind a *personal* constructive trust binding on this particular purchaser because of his particular conduct: the licence has not thereby assumed the status of an interest in land.[23] It 'takes effect' against a particular purchaser and, in strict terms, is not 'binding' on the land. So, if the first purchaser is bound to give effect to the licence by means of a personal constructive trust because of his conduct, but then sells the land to a second purchaser, the second purchaser takes free of the licence (it is only a personal right) unless he also becomes personally affected through his own unconscionable conduct.

The limits of this special intervention by equity have been examined subsequently by the Court of Appeal in *Lloyd v. Dugdale* (2001), and the conditions it establishes for its exercise have been approved by the same court in *Chaudhary v. Yavuz* (2011) and then applied in *Groveholt v. Hughes* (2012).[24] In *Dugdale*, it was claimed (among other things) that a purchaser of land was obliged to give effect to the claimant's otherwise unenforceable interest because of a personal constructive trust. On the facts of the case, it was clear that Mr Dugdale had some kind of interest in the property (possibly a proprietary one), but equally clear that he had neither registered it nor was he in actual occupation of the property so as to gain an overriding interest under the then applicable law of the LRA 1925.[25] In such circumstances, his interest could not bind Lloyd (the purchaser) in the normal manner for one of two alternative reasons: either the interest was merely personal or, even if it was proprietary, it had no protection in the system of registered land. Lloyd had, however, purchased the property apparently subject to such rights that Dugdale could claim. In rejecting the submission that Lloyd was bound by a personal constructive trust, Mummery LJ summarised the relevant principles. First, a contractual licence is not to be treated as creating a proprietary interest in land. Second, that even where a seller has stipulated that the purchaser shall take the land subject to potential adverse rights that are not otherwise binding (including a contractual licence), there is no general rule that a constructive trust is to be imposed on the purchaser to give effect to those rights. Thus, a standard clause in a contract of sale does not suffice, as was made clear in *Chaudhary v. Yavuz* (2011). Third, a constructive trust will not be imposed unless the court is satisfied that the purchaser's conscience is so affected that it would be inequitable to allow him to deny the rights of the claimant. A claimant's conscience is not affected merely because he knows about the right. Fourth, the critical question in deciding whether the purchaser's conscience is bound is to assess whether the purchaser has undertaken some new obligation in favour of the claimant, not merely offered to

---

22 Note there is no estoppel in favour of the licensee directly because the purchaser makes his promise to the seller, not the claimant.

23 As an aside, this looks rather like a remedial constructive trust, imposed simply to effect a remedy, despite the denial that such trusts exist in English law.

24 In *Groveholt* the court acknowledged that, as a matter of principle, the personal constructive trust could protect a proprietary right that was unprotected because it had failed to be registered. But, as with *Dugdale* and *Yavuz*, the claim was not made out on the facts.

25 The now repealed section 70(1)(g) of the LRA 1925 which protects persons in actual occupation and is re-enacted with some modifications in paragraph 2 of Schedule 1 and 3 LRA 2002.

give effect to a pre-existing obligation.[26] Fifth, evidence that the purchaser has paid a lower price can indicate the acceptance of a new obligation so as to trigger the constructive trust. Sixth, and perhaps most importantly, 'it is not desirable that constructive trusts of land should be imposed on inferences from slender materials'. Clearly, this is an orthodox and, it is submitted, entirely cogent explanation of the relevant principles. It highlights the need to protect a claimant where appropriate but also reminds us that the courts will not sidestep 'normal' property law principles by unwarranted use of the constructive trust. As *Chaudhary v. Yavuz* and *Groveholt v. Hughes* (2012) remind us, this is even more important now that the LRA 2002 has provided us with a comprehensive code for the enforcement of property rights.

9.3.8 A summary

To summarise the above position regarding contractual licences. First, given that they arise through a binding contract, the availability of normal contractual remedies may make them irrevocable between the licensor and licensee for the agreed duration of the licence. Second, however, licences are not, as a matter of principle, interests in land. They are not proprietary and cannot be registered within the system of registered or unregistered land. If they are so registered by mistake (which would mean getting past the scrutiny of the Registrar), the registration is of no effect, for it cannot confer a status that the right does not have.[27] As licences, they cannot bind third parties who purchase the licensor's land. Third, licences can 'take effect' against a particular purchaser if it is possible to impose a constructive trust on that purchaser. This can occur in limited and exceptional circumstances, and is personal to the individual whose conscience is bound. It would not affect a second or third purchaser unless that purchaser was also personally affected. Finally, we should note, that, following the general rule that the 'benefits' of a contract may be assigned (i.e. transferred) to another person, the right to *enjoy* a contractual licence may be expressly transferred by the original licensee to another. This is purely a matter of contract and has nothing to do with property law. So, if B enjoys a licence to park his car on A's land, B may transfer ('assign') that benefit to P expressly, *provided* that the licence does not expressly, or by implication, prohibit such assignment. In practice, however, the benefit of many licences (i.e. the right to use the land for the stated purpose) is indeed declared to be available only to the original licensee and this is why many contractual licences, such as theatre, sporting and car park tickets, are declared in the terms and conditions to be 'non-transferable'.

---

26 In *Groveholt*, there was no new obligation.

27 See section 32(3) of the LRA 2002 (registration does not validate an otherwise invalid interest) and note *Nationwide v. Ahmed* (1995), in which it was held that a contractual licence could not be an overriding interest under the then operative section 70(1)(g) of the LRA 1925, even if the licensee were in actual occupation, precisely because a licence is not proprietary. The same is true under Schedules 1 and 3 of the LRA 2002. Likewise, a licence cannot magically become a genuine land charge in unregistered conveyancing under the Land Charges Act 1972 if it somehow became registered against the name of a previous land owner.

9.3.9 The operation of proprietary estoppel: so-called estoppel licences

As we shall see in the next chapter, proprietary estoppel may be pleaded by a person claiming that they have an interest in land or a right to use land for some specific purpose.[28] This claim arises from an assurance made to them, upon which they have relied to their detriment. If a claimant is successful, a court may 'satisfy' the estoppel in any way it chooses, at least up to the maximum extent of the right assured to the claimant[29] and, as a minimum, in such a way as to do justice between the parties.[30] The court has a wide discretion about what precise remedy to give. This may, in fact, result in the award of a 'licence' to the successful claimant, as may have occurred in *Binions* v. *Evans* (1972) and *Bibby* v. *Stirling* (1998). This is sometimes called an 'estoppel licence' or a 'licence coupled with an equity' and has generated the same issues as contractual licences. In particular, given that the licence arises only because the landowner has engaged in unconscionable conduct, is it appropriate that it (the estoppel licence) can be defeated by a sale of the land to a purchaser? Or is an 'estoppel licence' an interest in land that can bind third parties?

These are not simple questions and they cannot be answered without an analysis of the nature of proprietary estoppel itself. For that reason, full consideration of the nature of so-called estoppel licences (and every other right created through the process of proprietary estoppel) must be deferred to Chapter 10. Bearing that in mind, however, it is important to realise that the term 'estoppel licence' has been misused to describe rights arising in a number of different situations and that these situations may not share common attributes. The term has been used loosely and to call something an 'estoppel licence' is not helpful or meaningful in modern land law. The different circumstances in which something has been described as an 'estoppel licence' are considered below. However, in general, the term is best avoided.

The first, and most usual, scenario where the term 'estoppel licence' has been used where a person is already enjoying some access to another's land by means of a genuine licence and then the owner makes some assurance (e.g. that the right shall continue or be enlarged) that is relied upon in such a way as to generate an estoppel in favour of the promisee. An example is where B enjoys a right to park his car on A's land for two years, and A then encourages B to believe that B can always park his car on the land, in reliance on which B at his own cost improves A's land to make parking easier. It is obvious why this has been called an estoppel licence – because it arose in the context of a pre-existing licence. However, this label is misleading. Clearly, as between the landowner (A) and the promisee (B), the effect of the estoppel is to prevent the former from going back on his promise: A is estopped from denying his assurance; in our example, the assurance of a permanent right to park. However, if A then sells the land to a purchaser, it is by no means clear that the purchaser will be bound to give effect to the estoppel. This depends crucially on the nature of proprietary estoppel itself, particularly whether it gives rise to,

---

28 Some cases, e.g. *West End Commercial* v. *London Trocadero* (2017) decide that the claimant must have been promised an interest in land before proprietary estoppel can arise, rather being assured of a general right to use land. This is discussed more fully in Chapter 10.

29 *Orgee* v. *Orgee* (1997).

30 *Crabb* v. *Arun DC* (1976); *Jennings* v. *Rice* (2002).

or is itself, an interest in land. Moreover, just because the estoppel arose out of a situation in which a licence already existed, that does not mean that the 'right' generated by the estoppel is actually a licence. It could be a lease, or an easement, or some other proprietary right. In other words, what we really have is an estoppel – it merely arose out of a licence situation. Its proprietary status and its ability to affect third parties has nothing to do with the prior licence relationship between the parties but depends instead on the wider question about the nature of proprietary estoppel itself.

Second, 'estoppel licence' has been used when a landowner and the promisee had no previous arrangement concerning the land in question. Thus, it is perfectly possible for a landowner (A) to make an assurance to any person (B) that they shall enjoy some right over A's land, which is relied on in such a way as to give rise to an estoppel. It does not matter that they did not stand in any prior legal relationship. If then the court chooses to 'satisfy' the estoppel by awarding the claimant (B) a licence, it is tempting (but mistaken) to say that an 'estoppel licence' has been created. It is, of course, simply a mere licence that has been created entirely informally – that is, by the oral promise or conduct of A – and the landowner will be compelled to give effect to the licence for so long as the court orders (which may be the period that A originally had promised). An example is where A orally promises B that B can use A's land as a short cut, and, in reliance, B spends money improving access to A's land but the court decides to satisfy the estoppel by means of a licence. This is explained more fully in Chapter 10. In these situations, there is no sense in which the new licence binds the land just because it is the result of an estoppel. The estoppel has been satisfied, and is extinguished, and the result is that the claimant has a licence. Just because the licence arose out of an estoppel, does not make it anything other than a licence and it is still a merely personal right over land.

The third scenario in which the term 'estoppel licence' has been misused is where a landowner (A) grants a licence over her land to another person (B), but then sells the land to a purchaser (P), and P then assures B that he may continue to enjoy the licence. An example is where A has granted B a licence permitting B's children to play on A's land, A sells to P, P assures B that the children can continue to play, in reliance on which B purchases a new climbing frame to build on P's land. Crucially, there is not an estoppel between A and B (merely the licence they had previously created), nor a licence between P and B but there is an estoppel directly between P and B due to the former's assurance to the latter. In consequence, it is important to realise that this is not an example of an existing licence (between A and B) becoming binding on a third party (P). It is the creation of a new estoppel between two new parties (P and B). If the court then decides to satisfy this estoppel by requiring P to give a new licence to B, this is still a licence. It may well be, in fact, that this licence is irrevocable between P and B (this will depend on its terms), but it cannot bind the land if P then decides to sell the land to Z. It is still a licence, and the fact that it arose out of an estoppel does not change its character.

9.4 Chapter Summary

9.4.1 The essential nature of a licence

There are no formal requirements for the creation of a 'licence' as such. A licence is given by the owner of land (the licensor) to some other person (the licensee), permitting them to do something on the owner's land. Without such permission, the activity would amount to a trespass. A licence may be given for any lawful purpose and not only to someone who also owns land. The orthodox view of licences is that they are not proprietary in nature: they do not create interests in land and they cannot bind third parties. They are not registrable under the Land Registration Act 2002 and cannot amount to overriding interests. Neither are they capable of being a Land Charge in unregistered land under the Land Charges Act 1972.

9.4.2   Types of licence

A bare licence is a permission to enter upon and use the land given voluntarily by the owner, who receives nothing in return. A bare licence lasts only for so long as the licensor wishes, terminable on reasonable notice.

A 'licence coupled with a grant' is a permission that enables a person to exercise some other right connected with the land, usually a *profit à prendre*. It has no existence outside the grant that it facilitates. A contractual licence is granted to the licensee in return for contractual consideration. It is founded in contract and the normal remedies for breach of contract are available in the event of a failure by licensor or licensee to carry out its terms. The effect of these remedies can be to make the licence irrevocable between the parties throughout the contractual period of the licence. Contractual licences are not interests in land, even if they are irrevocable between the original parties. Notwithstanding this, a contractual licence can take effect against a purchaser of land by means of a *personal* constructive trust.

A so-called 'estoppel licence' has been said to exist in a number of situations, but the term is best avoided.

Further Reading

Battersby, G, 'Contractual and estoppel licences as proprietary interests in land' [1991] Conv 36.

Bright, S, 'Bright: The third party's conscience in land law' [2000] Conv 388.

Howard, M and **Hill**, J, 'The informal creation of interests in land' (1995) 15 LS 356.

Now visit the companion website to:

•   test your understanding of the key terms using our Flashcard Glossary;

•   revise and consolidate your knowledge using our Multiple Choice Question testbank.

www.routledge.com/cw/dixon

Chapter 10
Proprietary Estoppel

Chapter Contents

10.1 Proprietary Estoppel

Land law is the study of proprietary rights, being estates or interests in land. When discussing the creation, operation or transfer of these rights, we have seen that generally a certain amount of formality is required. Usually, 'interests in land' can be created only by deed, registered disposition or a specifically enforceable written contract (or, perhaps in the future by electronic versions of the same). Similarly, a will is needed to transfer land on death and the absence of a valid will is usually fatal to a person's claim to own land that they allege has been promised orally during the deceased's life. Of course, there are exceptions to this, such as certain leases for three years or less (Chapter 6), rights in unregistered land acquired through adverse possession (Chapter 12) or easements acquired by prescription (Chapter 7), but the overall picture is clear enough. Further, the reason why formality is required is also obvious. Proprietary rights become bolted to the land itself and may endure through successive changes in ownership of it, so it is imperative that their existence and scope is certain and well defined both for the immediate parties and for any intending purchasers or mortgagees. Necessarily, there is a price to pay for this certainty, especially if it is secured through the use of mandatory formality requirements. In land law, that price is flexibility, and occasionally fairness. A person may claim that they have a right in land, and it may be 'fair' or 'just' that this be recognised but, nevertheless, their right could be denied because it was not created with due regard to the formality requirements laid down by statute.

Importantly, the LP(MP)A 1989 was passed in order to bring more clarity and more certainty to the creation and disposition of interests in land. It requires more formality for dealings with land than was the case under the old section 40 of the LPA 1925 by which a purely oral contract could generate an interest in land if the contract was 'partly performed'.[1] A direct and intended consequence is that informal arrangements that once would have generated an interest in land for the claimant are now invalid.[2] This emphasis on the need for formality in dealings with land continues today under the LRA 2002.[3]

Fortunately, the difficulties that can flow from an over-rigorous reliance on formality are mitigated by the doctrine of proprietary estoppel. Proprietary estoppel is the name given to a set of principles whereby an owner of land may be held to have conferred some right or privilege connected with the land on another person, despite the absence of a deed, registered disposition, written contract or valid will.[4] Typically, the right or privilege conferred will arise out of the conduct of the parties, usually because of some assurance made by the landowner, which is relied upon by the person claiming the right. In this sense, proprietary estoppel is to be understood as a mechanism whereby rights in, or over, land can be created informally. This is important in two principal ways.

---

1 In effect, section 2 means that oral contracts for the disposition of an interest in land are invalid and it abolishes the doctrine of part-performance: *Singh* v. *Beggs* (1996).

2 For example, a mortgage can no longer be created simply by the deposit of title deeds, because even if the deposit is evidence of a contract to grant a mortgage, that contract is not in writing as required by section 2 of the LP(MP) A 1989: *United Bank of Kuwait* v. *Sahib* (1995).

3 More rights need to be substantively registered, such as the lease of over seven years.

4 It would also be applicable in cases of failure to comply with the electronic formalities of e-conveyancing if these are introduced under the LRA 2002.

First, proprietary estoppel can provide a defence to an action by a landowner who seeks to enforce his strict rights against someone who has been informally promised some right or liberty over the land. For example, an action in trespass by the landlord can be met by a plea of estoppel, in that the landowner had assured the 'trespasser' that they could enjoy the right now being denied. In *Lester* v. *Hardy* (2010), estoppel operated as a defence to an allegation of nuisance by the landowner and in *Wormall* v. *Wormall* (2004), the defendant successfully pleaded estoppel in defence to an action in trespass brought against her by her father. In short, the landowner is not permitted to plead that the defendant has no right or privilege to use the land if this would be inequitable, where such inequity is generated by the landowner's own conduct. This is proprietary estoppel as a defence or shield. Second, as indicated already in this chapter, proprietary estoppel can have a much more dramatic effect. There is no doubt that, if successfully established, it can generate a new property interest in favour of a claimant. As is commonly stated, proprietary estoppel can be a sword in the hands of a claimant who has relied on an assurance by a landowner that they will be given some right or privilege over the land.[5] A court of equity will 'satisfy' the estoppel by awarding the claimant that right or interest (or other remedy[6]) that it deems appropriate, although the actual remedy must be proportionate to the detriment suffered and so cannot go beyond the maximum the claimant was informally promised or expected[7] and will seek to do that which remedies the unconscionability suffered by the claimant.[8] This means that proprietary estoppel can result in an appropriate case in the creation of an interest in land without any formal dealings between landowner and claimant. It represents the creation of rights by reason of equity acting on an individual's conscience and is the antidote to unconscionable reliance on formality rules.

10.2   Conditions for the Operation of Proprietary Estoppel

Proprietary estoppel has had a role in property law for many decades, being another example of the intervention of equity to mitigate the consequences of lack of compliance with the formality requirements of the common law or statute. At one time, the conditions for the operation of proprietary estoppel were fairly strictly drawn and these were codified by Fry J in *Willmott* v. *Barber* (1880). He identified the so-called 'five probanda' of proprietary estoppel and, as can be seen, they required the claimant to jump a high hurdle to be successful. As Fry J specified, the following had to be established.

1   The claimant must have made a mistake as to their legal rights over some land belonging to another.
2   The true landowner must know of the claimant's mistaken belief.
3   The claimant must have expended money or carried out some action on the faith of that mistaken belief.

---

5 *Crabb* v. *Arun DC* (1976).

6 E.g. a cash sum, *Southwell* v. *Blackburn* (2015).

7 *Orgee* v. *Orgee* (1997), *Davies* v. *Davies* (2016).

8 *Jennings* v. *Rice* (2002).

4   The landowner must have encouraged the expenditure by the claimant, either directly, or by abstaining from enforcing their legal rights.
5   The owner of the land over which the right is claimed must know of the existence of their own rights, and that these are inconsistent with the alleged rights of the claimant.

Perhaps we should not be surprised that these conditions were onerous because a successful claim of proprietary estoppel could result in the creation of an interest in land that would not only affect the immediate estate owner in his current or planned use of the land, but also future purchasers or transferees of the land. Indeed, the informal way in which the estoppel can arise means that it is not certain that any intending purchaser or mortgagee would or could be aware of the existence of the estoppel-generated adverse right. After all, the right would have been created without a deed or written instrument or registration. However, since these early days of estoppel, there have been many social and economic changes in the use of land and in the structure of land ownership,[9] and when combined with a tightening of the formality rules themselves (e.g. section 2 of the LP(MP)A 1989), it was perhaps inevitable that proprietary estoppel would grow in importance and its defining features would change.

In the result, and as a reflection of modern conditions, the original criteria for establishing an estoppel have been largely abandoned and the modern approach is to be much more flexible about the way in which an estoppel can arise.[10] According to Oliver J in *Taylor Fashions* v. *Liverpool Victoria Trustees* (1982), a claimant will be able to establish an estoppel if they can prove an assurance, reliance and detriment in circumstances in which it would be unconscionable to deny a remedy to the claimant. This has confirmed that the emphasis in cases of proprietary estoppel has shifted away from an examination of the actions and beliefs of the landowner and has become more focused on the position of the claimant. For example, in *Hoyl Group Ltd* v. *Cromer Town Council* (2015), an estoppel was established even though the landowner (the Council) was unaware that the claimant believed they had a right of way because the landowner's encouragement was entirely consistent with such a right existing – the absence of the *Willmott* second condition did not prevent an estoppel arising. Moreover, as we shall see, *Gillett* v. *Holt* (2001) and *Jennings* v. *Rice* (2002) make it clear that these four features of estoppel – assurance, reliance, detriment and unconscionability – are not to be seen as isolated features, but that each case must be looked at 'in the round'[11] in order to determine whether the landowner should be able to go back on his assurance to the claimant about the use of land. The proper approach is to adopt a holistic approach to establishing proprietary estoppel, a point reiterated by a majority of the House of Lords in *Thorner* v. *Major* (2009) and now firmly established in the case law.[12]

Before examining in more detail the conditions necessary to establish an estoppel in modern land law, it is important to appreciate that it is not a universal remedy that can

---

9   For example, shared family ownership of property and occupation by extended family groups.
10 That said, the modern approach is to be seen as an organic development of the *Willmott* criteria, rather than a wholly new way of thinking, *Hoyl Group Ltd* v. *Cromer Town Council* (2015).
11 See also *Ottey* v. *Grundy* (2003) for a successful claim on this basis and *Murphy* v. *Burrows* (2004) for an unsuccessful claim on this basis.
12 E.g. *Davies* v. *Davies* (2016), *Hoyl* v. *Cromer Town Council* (2015).

cure every defect in the creation of property rights. If it were, there would be little point in having formality rules at all. As the court of first instance emphasised in *Prudential Assurance* v. *Waterloo Real Estate* (1998), estoppel is a drastic remedy and it is a major step for a court to award a claimant a proprietary right over another's land in the absence of due formality, even more so if the effect of the estoppel is to compel a transfer of ownership of the land itself. So, in *Taylor* v. *Dickens* (1997) and *Uglow* v. *Uglow* (2004), the claimant had been promised property in a will, but when the promise was not honoured, the court rejected the claim that the property should be transferred under proprietary estoppel; in *Evans* v. *James* (2000), proprietary estoppel did not cure the absence of a valid contract between the parties relating to the transfer of land; in *Canty* v. *Broad* (1995), the claimants, having failed to conclude a contract for the sale of land in accordance with section 2 of the LP(MP)A 1989, were unable to claim the land by estoppel; in *Cobbe* v. *Yeoman's Row Management* (2008), the House of Lords refused to allow estoppel to enforce effectively an oral agreement that both parties knew was only 'binding in honour' until it was reduced to writing;[13] in *Shirt* v. *Shirt* (2012) a son could not use estoppel to claim possession of the family farm because his father's oral assurances were vague and unspecific;[14] and in *Secretary of State for Communities & Local Government* v. *Praxis* (2015), a case from Northern Ireland, there was no estoppel because the landowner had never encouraged the claimant in its belief that it had a lease, even though the claimant had spent money refurbishing the land. By way of contrast, the claimant was partially successful in *Matharu* v. *Matharu* (1994), using estoppel as a means to live in a property for the rest of her life; in *Wayling* v. *Jones* (1993), *Gillett* v. *Holt* (2001), *Jennings* v. *Rice* (2002), *Ottey* v. *Grundy* (2003), *Thorner* v. *Majors* (2009), *Suggitt* v. *Suggitt* (2012), *Lothian* v. *Dixon* (2014), *Lloyd Davies* v. *Lloyd Davies* (2015) and *Davies* v. *Davies* (2016) the claimants established an estoppel because particular land had been promised, but not left to them (or was not going to be left) by will; in *Sleebush* v. *Gordon* (2004), the claimant had succeeded to half the interest in a property on the death of her husband but was successful in recovering the other half by way of estoppel even though it had been left by will to another; in *Bibby* v. *Stirling* (1998), the claimant used estoppel to establish a right to use a greenhouse erected on the defendant's land; in *Flowermix* v. *Site Developments* (2000), a contract that was void for uncertainty (as to the extent of land concerned) was nevertheless effectively enforced by reliance on the estoppel rules; in *Kinane* v. *Alimamy Mackie-Conteh* (2005), the Court of Appeal used proprietary estoppel and constructive trust[15] to validate a mortgage that failed completely to meet any of the formality requirements usually required for the creation of either legal or equitable mortgages; in *Bradbury* v. *Taylor* (2012), the claimants succeeded to the property promised them by their uncle in which they had lived for many years, even though relations had then soured; and in *Ghazaani* v. *Rowshan* (2015) estoppel operated to transfer land to the claimant even though there was no written contract as required by section 2 of the LP(MP)A 1989.

These are just a sample of the numerous cases in which estoppel is pleaded. Of course, many of the cases in which the plea was unsuccessful can be explained on the basis that, say, the assurance was never made (e.g. *Williams* v. *Walmsley* (2011)), or not

---

13 Applying *AG for Hong Kong* v. *Humphreys* (1987).

14 See too *Creasey* v. *Sole* (2013).

15 On which, see below.

made clearly enough (e.g. *McDonald v. Frost*; *Creasey v. Sole*), or the alleged detriment was never suffered or too minimal (e.g. *Century UK v. Clibbery* (2004); *Creasey*), or there was no unconscionability (e.g. *Cobbe*; *Murphy v. Rayner* (2011)). However, to apply the *Taylor Fashions* criteria mechanically is to miss the point: *Hoyl v. Cromer Town Council* (2015). Estoppel is available to cure absence of formality when, but only when, it would be unconscionable for the defendant to rely on the lack of formality to defeat the claimant – see, for example, *Hopper v. Hopper* (2008). Unconscionability is at the heart of the doctrine and the existence of unconscionability is the reason why the lack of formality can be excused. This is examined in more detail but it is mentioned at the outset to reinforce the link between formality and the plea of estoppel.

10.2.1   The assurance

Proprietary estoppel is a flexible doctrine that acts on the conscience of a landowner. Accordingly, the landowner must have made some kind of assurance to the claimant that either he would refrain from exercising his strict legal rights over his own land or, more commonly, that the claimant might have some present or future right or use over that land. While, in many cases, the assurance will be as to some specific property right over the land (e.g. 'you can have a lease'), it is clear from the House of Lords' decision in *Thorner v. Major* (2009) that this is not necessary in order for proprietary estoppel to be established. In that case, the landowner had never promised the claimant any specific right, or even made any express promises (the assurance was implied), but the claim of estoppel was upheld. According to Lord Walker, the assurance had to be 'clear enough' and this would depend hugely on context. In the context of a family arrangement concerning a farm (*Thorner*), it might be enough for some general assurance to have been made concerning the future ownership of the land.[16] In the context of a commercial arrangement, however, it was likely that a much more specific assurance would be needed (*Cobbe*) and the more specific the right claimed, the more specific the assurance needs to be (*Secretary of State for Communities & Local Government v. Praxis*). Thus, according to *Thorner*, the House of Lords' earlier decision in *Cobbe* was not to be taken as always requiring an assurance of a specific property right, but as the later *West End Commercial v. Trocadero Ltd* (2017) decides, this must be an assurance of a right relating to property and not merely that the claimant can have a licence or other contractual right.[17]

Importantly, these cases should not be taken as requiring us to distinguish between 'family' and 'commercial' cases as a *matter of principle*, for everything depends on context. Thus, in *McDonald v. Frost* (2009) and *Shirt v. Shirt* (2012), typical family disputes, the court found that no adequate assurance had been made in the context of the parties' complex relationships, but in *Hoyl v. Cromer Town Council*, an estoppel was found to exist

---

16 But, even in a 'family' context, vague and ill-defined words cannot amount to an assurance (*Creasey v. Sole*).

17 *West End* suggests that the assertion must be as to a *proprietary* right. It is not clear that this is justified on the earlier authorities, which can be read as requiring that the assurance simply must be of a right to use property, but not a mere contractual liberty (as was the case in *West End* where the assurance was only ever that the claimant could have a licence.

in a case recognised by the court as clearly commercial.[18] The point is that we should be aware that 'family' disputes and 'commercial' disputes have a different factual background, rather than require different legal principles (*Whittaker* v. *Kinnear* (2011)). Consequently, the important point is that the House of Lords in *Thorner* did not adopt the strict approach put forward earlier in *Cobbe*, essentially because this would have unjustifiably reduced successful estoppel cases to a mere trickle.[19] Instead, the majority in *Thorner*[20] maintained the flexible, holistic approach that had developed in the Court of Appeal, particularly in *Gillett*, and accepted that estoppel responds to a 'certain enough' assurance that must depend on the context in which it is given. In addition, and to be clear, there is no doubt that the assurance must be about, or relate to, some reasonably identifiable land and be about a right to use land – *Thorner*, *Praxis*, *West End*. However, it does not matter if the exact scope of the land is uncertain, or even if over time some land is sold and other purchased, provided that it is reasonably clear which land the assurance relates to at the time the claim of estoppel falls to be considered. In *Thorner* v. *Major* (2009), the land was reasonably well identified,[21] in *Secretary of State for Communities & Local Government* v. *Praxis* it was not.

This analysis of estoppel necessarily means that the form that the assurance takes is irrelevant and it may be given orally, arise from conduct or even be in the form of a written instrument that is not itself enforceable as a contract to transfer an interest in land (as apparently in *Flowermix* v. *Site Developments* (2000)). The assurance may be 'unilateral' in that it was offered freely by the landowner, but it might also arise from a mutual understanding between the parties about the use of the land. The assurance may be express[22] or implied, as where a landowner refrains from preventing the claimant using his land in a particular way,[23] or the landowner by actions rather than words effectively assures the claimant about use or ownership of the land (e.g. *Thorner* v. *Major*). Similarly, the landowner can 'assure' the claimant by acquiescence, that is 'standing by' while the claimant acts detrimentally in relation to the land, although it is clear that the landowner must in some sense be responsible for allowing the claimant to incur the detriment. The key in the acquiescence cases is to distinguish those cases where the landowner has done nothing by silent inaction to encourage the claimant (no estoppel) and those cases where silent inaction is equivalent to encouragement to continue (estoppel). This is not always easy and is fact dependent, with perhaps 'commercial' cases requiring more evidence of

---

18 Counsel for the defendant had argued specifically that an estoppel could not exist because of the commercial context, and this was addressed and rejected by the Court of Appeal.

19 That, of course, may have been the point behind Lord Scott's analysis in *Cobbe*, and it seems to have been a position that his colleagues in *Thorner* were not prepared to endorse.

20 Lord Scott did not recant from the view of estoppel he put forward in *Cobbe*, but instead chose to regard *Thorner* as an example of a remedial constructive trust.

21 'The owl of Minerva spreads its wings only with the falling of the dusk' – *per* Lord Hoffmann in *Thorner*. 'It would represent a regrettable and substantial emasculation of the beneficial principle of proprietary estoppel if it were artificially fettered so as to require the precise extent of the property the subject of the alleged estoppel to be strictly defined in every case', *per* Lord Neuberger in the same case.

22 For example, in *Ottey* v. *Grundy* (2003), there was a letter of intent, and in *Gillett* v. *Holt* (2001), there were repeated public statements about the claimant's future on the farm. See also *Salvation Army Trustees* v. *West Yorkshire CC* (1981).

23 *Ramsden* v. *Dyson* (1866).

silent encouragement than non-commercial cases, but even in commercial cases a successful claim is possible (*Hoyl*).

Importantly, irrespective of how the assurance is established, it must be such as to generate unconscionability if withdrawn. For example, in *Murphy v. Burrows* (2004), the fluid and uncertain nature of the parties' relationship meant that the assurances did not give rise to estoppel as it was unclear whether the assurances were given, or reasonably understood, as assurances about property. By way of contrast, and perhaps surprisingly, it seems from *JT Developments* v. *Quinn* (1991) that an estoppel can arise even though the assurance was given in circumstances in which there was clearly no intention to create binding obligations between the parties at all, as where the parties had attempted to negotiate a contract governing use of the land, but had failed.[24] Again, in *Lim Teng Huan* v. *Ang Swee Chuan* (1992) and in *Flowermix*, a written, although unenforceable, agreement was held to constitute the requisite assurance, with the consequence that the unenforceable agreement was indirectly given effect through the intervention of proprietary estoppel, even though this appears to be enforcing a contract that the parties have not put into effect properly through their own fault. Similarly, in *Kinane* v. *Alimamy Mackie-Conteh* (2005), the borrower had agreed by letter to charge his land as security for a loan, but the written instrument did not meet with the formality requirements of section 2 of the 1989 Act as both borrower and lender did not sign it. Therefore, it did not amount to an equitable mortgage, but the Court of Appeal was prepared to use estoppel to support the creation of the mortgage and so give the lender his proprietary remedies when the loan was not repaid.

The *Kinane* case is, perhaps, the most liberal approach to proprietary estoppel that developed in the years following the tightening of the formality rules by the LP(MP)A 1989. In it, and in *Lim Teng Huan*, it is difficult to see why the formality rules could be ignored *just because* the claimant had partly performed the unenforceable contract. In both cases, there is a need to demonstrate why it would be unconscionable to apply the formality rules that apply to other transactions and this is not clear from the judgments. As a contrast, in *Ghazaani v. Rowshan* (2015), an estoppel also arose resulting in the transfer of land to the claimant despite the absence of a written contract within section 2, but the judge was clear that this was exceptional because it was the only way to remedy the unconscionability caused by the defendant. The important point to remember then is the one emphasised in *Cobbe* v. *Yeomans Row* (2008) that it is not permissible to use proprietary estoppel to circumvent the formal requirements of section 2 of the 1989 Act,[25] but, as other cases show, estoppel may be available even when there is a failed or missing contract if it is necessary to prevent unconscionability. Circumvention of formality is not permissible. But remedying of unconscionability is desirable and it is perfectly possible for the estoppel to exist independently of the failed or missing contract (see section 9.5.4

---

24 The real question is whether the person to whom the assurance was made reasonably believed that this was an assurance about a current right to use property. If they knew that the assurance was part of tentative negotiation, it is difficult to see how it could generate an estoppel.

25 Consequently, in *Cobbe*, the claim of estoppel failed because both the parties knew that they should have entered into an enforceable written contract if they wanted to create a binding legal agreement and they had chosen not to. The same point is made in *Herbert* v. *Doyle* (2010), where estoppel did not save the failed contract because in that case both parties clearly intended that further formalities would follow. This analysis is not challenged by *Thorner* because there was no attempted contract in *Thorner* and hence section 2 of the LPA 1989 was not in play.

below). In this sense, the law of estoppel has survived the enactment of section 2 of the 1989 Act as expressly decided in *Whittaker* v. *Kinnear* (2011) and applied in *Ghazaani* v. *Rowshan* (2015). The point is to identify the appropriate cases where estoppel can operate – in general terms, being those where it would be unconscionable to deny the assurance, bearing in mind that it is difficult (but not impossible) to establish unconscionability where the parties have intended and failed to conclude a written contract. In this regard, it seems that the law of constructive trusts is developing to explain how some otherwise unenforceable contracts can be enforced, and this is discussed further below.[26]

Finally, it is clear that an estoppel can succeed provided that the claimant reasonably believes that an assurance has been made, even if the landowner did not intend to make an assurance by words or deeds – *Thorner, Creasey* v. *Sole*. The landowner cannot defeat the estoppel merely by claiming that he did not intend an assurance if any reasonable claimant would have believed that one had been made. However, we must be careful here. If the landowner knows nothing (and could not reasonably be expected to know) of the claimant's belief that he (the claimant) has been promised some right in or over the land, and the landowner has done nothing to encourage, by action or silence, the claimant's belief, then it is going to be difficult to establish an estoppel. For example, if A promises B the right to park a car on A's land, but B takes this as a promise to give him the land, which belief is neither encouraged nor acquiesced in by A or reasonably held by B, no estoppel involving transfer of the land can arise (although a right to park the car might). In the same vein, in *Creasey* v. *Sole* (2013), the court emphasised that it must approach a claim of estoppel with scepticism when the only evidence of an assurance is the uncorroborated evidence of the claimant.[27]

What we need to remember is that we should adopt a holistic approach to estoppel and should not be tied to a mechanical application of the requirement for an assurance. A forensic dissection (and limitation) of the 'assurance' requirement is unlikely to be in keeping with the inherently equitable nature of the doctrine. All depends on context. Thus, it will be rare for the court to find that an assurance has been made in the context of negotiations between parties intending to complete a fully binding contract, especially if the negotiations are expressly 'subject to contract'.[28] But even general words, or a general understanding implied from the parties' behaviour, may well be enough in other cases, especially if the litigants acted without the benefit of legal advice. The cases tell us that the assurance must be in the way of an understanding or unilateral promise between claimant and defendant, but not necessarily amounting to the promise of some specific right in property. The assurance must be clear enough in context. It should be given to the claimant personally and must relate to land that is readily identifiable at the time the estoppel is crystallised. It is sufficient, save for exceptional circumstances,[29] if the claimant reasonably believes that an assurance has been made.

---

26 Section 10.5 – see *Matchmove* v. *Dowding* (2016) and *Saunders* v. *Al Himaly* (2017).

27 Contrast *Creasey*, where the assurance was said to have taken place in private conversations between the landowner and his son concerning the family farm, and *Gillett* where the landowner broadcast his intention to benefit the claimant in public and repeatedly. In *Creasey*, the claim failed.

28 *Edwin Shirley Productions* v. *Workspace Mana Ltd* (2001); *Haq* v. *Island Homes Housing Association* (2011). But see *Matchmove* v. *Dowding* (2016) where an agreement 'subject to contract' was effectively enforced vis-à-vis a constructive trust, below section 10.5.

29 Regarded by Lord Neuberger as a possibility in *Thorner*, but not elaborated.

10.2.2   The reliance

As we have seen, the 'assurance' may be entirely informal, but whatever form it takes, it is essential that it produces an effect on the claimant. The claimant must 'rely' on the assurance, in that it must be possible to show that he was induced to behave differently because the assurance had been given. It is sufficient if the claimant reasonably relies on the assurance, even if the landowner did not intend that he should so rely – *Thorner*.

Of course, in practice, reliance can be very difficult to prove and a court may well be prepared to infer reliance if that is a plausible explanation of the claimant's conduct. Thus, in *Greasley* v. *Cooke* (1980), the Court of Appeal held that, if clear assurances have been made and detriment has been suffered, it is permissible to assume that reliance has occurred. Likewise, in *Wayling* v. *Jones* (1993), the Court of Appeal looked only for a 'sufficient link' between the assurance made and the detriment incurred by the plaintiff, the existence of which would throw the burden of proof on to the defendant to show that there had, in fact, been no reliance. The crucial point seems to be that there will be no reliance only when it can be shown that the claimant would have incurred detriment completely irrespective of the defendant's conduct. In *Orgee* v. *Orgee* (1997), for example, it was clear that much of the plaintiff's alleged detriment was ordinary expenses that would have been incurred normally and in any event. However, even this must not be taken too far. In *Campbell* v. *Griffin* (2001), the claimant had been a lodger in the landowner's house and over time had taken on the responsibility of caring for his 'landlords', an elderly couple. There was clear evidence of relevant assurances about the property. At trial, the claimant admitted that he would have assisted his landlords out of ordinary human compassion rather than in clear reliance on their promises. Nevertheless, the Court of Appeal upheld the estoppel claim, noting that a dual motive for action (the assurance plus normal human compassion) does not thereby diminish the fact that reliance has occurred. This might seem overly generous, but it would be harsh indeed to dismiss a claim simply because the claimant was not, after all, a thoroughly selfish individual who was prepared to help only because of what was on offer. A further example of this is provided by *Chun* v. *Ho* (2001), in which Miss Chun successfully established a claim in estoppel[30] to a share in a business and its property because her actions in giving up her career and establishing a life with the landowner to the disgust of her family[31] could not be explained solely on the basis of her love for him. There must have been some reliance on his clear assurances about the business. Evidently, then, the existence of reliance is critically dependent on the peculiar facts of each case and is not to be discounted merely because of family or emotional ties between claimant and landowner that might otherwise explain a course of action. So, in *Bradbury* v. *Taylor* (2012), the parties' failed attempts to regulate formally the claimant's use of the land, which came to nothing, did not mean that the claimant had ceased to rely on the informal assurances.[32]

---

30 She also claimed constructive trust and the court drew no distinction between the claims.

31 He was serving a prison sentence in Hong Kong.

32 The landowner suggested that, because the claimants knew that their use of land should be formally regulated, this meant that they could not have relied on the assurances. The court rejects this, making the point that knowledge that there was another way to regulate their use of the land, did not mean that they could not rely on the landowner's promises that their use would be safe.

Equally clear is the point made by the Court of Appeal when upholding the estoppel claims in *Gillett* and *Jennings*: assurance, reliance and detriment are necessarily interwoven and the court should not approach them forensically as if they were entirely separate requirements. The case must be viewed in the round.

10.2.3   The detriment

Equity has always been wary of 'volunteers': that is, claimants who seek to enforce a promise even though they have given nothing in return. Similarly, proprietary estoppel cannot be established unless the claimant can prove that he has suffered some detriment in reliance on the assurance. Not surprisingly, so long as the detriment is not minimal or trivial, it may take any form because it is not a narrow or technical concept (*Lothian* v. *Dixon* (2014)). For example, it may be that the claimant has spent money on the land or advanced money to the landowner in reliance on the assurance,[33] or has physically improved the land in some way, or has devoted time and care to the needs of the landowner,[34] or has forsaken some other opportunity,[35] or has positioned his entire life on the faith that the land might be his one day.[36] Indeed, as *Campbell* v. *Griffin* and *Jennings* v. *Rice* show, it is not necessary that the detriment be related to land at all, or the land in dispute.[37] It may be, for example, that the claimant has spent their money in other ways, on the faith of an assurance that they would have somewhere to live or an inheritance to enjoy. It is even true that detriment in this technical sense can exist even though the claimant has derived some benefit from his association with the landowner. In *Gillett* v. *Holt* (2001), Mr Gillett might be thought to have done rather well out of his relationship with Mr Holt as the former now owned valuable shares in the farm company and held property in his own right. Nevertheless, he still incurred the detriment of lost opportunities.[38] The point is simply that an estoppel cannot be established unless there has been some detrimental reliance, for that is what makes a retraction of the assurance potentially unconscionable,[39] and one way to demonstrate it is to show that the other options available to the claimant were more advantageous than remaining linked with the landowner.[40]

Sufficient detriment is always a question of fact and many claims fail because there was neither an assurance nor detriment, as in *Creasey* v. *Sole*. This should be no surprise as people do not usually act to their detriment unless they are certain that they have been

---

33 *Kinane* v. *Alimamy Mackie-Conteh* (2005).

34 *Campbell* v. *Griffin* (2001).

35 *Ottey* v. *Grundy* (2003); *Lloyd* v. *Dugdale* (2001); *Thorner*.

36 *Suggitt* v. *Suggitt* (2011). See also *Lothian* v. *Dixon* (2014), where the claimants put their life on hold in helping the landowner run a hotel and *Moore* v. *Moore* (2016) where the claimant had sacrificed much to run the family farm.

37 In *Ottey*, one disputed property was in Jamaica, and see *Wayling* v. *Jones* (1993).

38 See also *Bradbury* v. *Taylor*, where the court recognised that the claimants had benefited from the occupation of the land, but that this did not outweigh their detrimental reliance. So too in *Lothian* v. *Dixon* where the claimants derived benefits from their occupation of the hotel, but not enough to nullify their detriment.

39 *Gillett* v. *Holt* (2001).

40 Morgan J notes in *Creasey* v. *Sole* that the claimant could not establish that the other options available to him were more advantageous than continuing to work on the family farm – hence no detriment.

promised something concrete. Consequently, detriment itself, however extensive, is not enough. In *Taylor v. Dickens* (1997), the plaintiff worked for a number of years without pay in the expectation that he would inherit from the deceased. The deceased changed her will in favour of other beneficiaries. Detriment was clear enough but, according to the trial judge, there was no assurance that the deceased would *never* change her will and so the claim failed for lack of an enforceable assurance. This case was settled before an appeal but now looks harsh in the light of the decisions in *Gillett, Grundy, Jennings* and *Thorner*. Even so, it remains the case that unencouraged detriment is not sufficient to establish an estoppel, as in *Praxis*. Finally, in case there is doubt, *Lloyd v. Dugdale* (2001) makes it clear that the detriment must be incurred by the person to whom the assurance is made. There is no concept of 'derivative detriment' and so Mr Dugdale had to prove (as he did successfully) that the detriment was incurred by him personally and not on behalf of his company (a separate legal entity).

10.2.4   Unconscionability

It is clear that Oliver J in *Taylor Fashions* regarded unconscionability as the very essence of a claim of proprietary estoppel. Indeed, in the great majority of cases, the simple fact that the landowner is seeking to retract an assurance given and relied upon will be unconscionable. In *Gillett*, at first instance, Carnwath J put the matter succinctly by noting that '[n]ormally it is the promisor's knowledge of the detriment being suffered in reliance on his promise which makes it "unconscionable" for him to go back on it', and this was reiterated by the Court of Appeal in the same case. As noted above, it is this unconscionability that frees the court from the strictures of the formality requirements imposed by statute and allows the claimant to succeed. So, an oral agreement deliberately made 'subject to contract', as in *Canty v. Broad* (1995),[41] or a void executory contract (i.e. one that might never be binding as to substance),[42] or a conditional assurance, the conditions of which are not fulfilled,[43] cannot be enforced via estoppel, because there is no unconscionability in relying on the absence of formality in these circumstances, even if there has been reliance and detriment.[44] This may be a better explanation of why the claim failed in *Cobbe* because both parties knew that an enforceable contact was required and the landowner had never suggested that she would honour the claimant's 'rights' without one. So, also, the common understanding that a person is free to change their will makes it difficult to plead unconscionability when a will is changed or property left to another in a new will,[45] although unconscionability may exist if the assurance is withdrawn after it is repeated so often and so loudly that no one could doubt that the landowners meant what they said about the destination of their property on their death, as in *Gillett v. Holt* and *Ottey v. Grundy*. In *Gillett* itself, Mr Holt had promised Mr Gillett over a

41 Also *AG for Hong Kong v. Humphreys* (1987); *Secretary of State for Transport v. Christos* (2003). See also *Yeoman's v. Cobbe* (2008), which confirms that void oral contracts cannot be enforced by estoppel.

42 *Ravenocean v. Gardner* (2001).

43 *Uglow v. Uglow* (2004).

44 But note the trend to use constructive trusts to support these otherwise unenforceable contracts: *Matchmove v. Dowding* (2016), *Saunders v. Al Himaly* (2017).

45 *Taylor v. Dickens* (1997); *Murphy v. Burrows* (2004); *Driver v. Yorke* (2003).

40-year period that he (Gillett) would be the beneficiary of Holt's will. When Holt changed his will to exclude Gillett, a claim based on estoppel was successful, the Court of Appeal noting that the mere withdrawal of the assurance after such detriment (that is, 40 years of work at less than the market wage) was sufficient to establish unconscionability. A similar result is reached in *Thorner*, although the period of detriment in that case was shorter.

The analysis in *Gillett* is driven by the understanding that estoppel claims should not be dissected too closely by analysis of the 'ingredients' of a claim but should be looked at in total to see if the denial of the claimant's alleged right to the land is unconscionable. Of itself, this formula presents certain difficulties for it appears to define unconscionability purely in terms of assurance, reliance and detriment (i.e. unconscionability exists when the assurance is withdrawn after detrimental reliance) and so the 'all-important' criterion of unconscionability, the *raison d'être* of estoppel,[46] becomes a mere shadow of the other three components. *Gillett* itself can be justified on the ground that (as noted above) the repeated assurances implied that Mr Holt would not exclude Mr Gillett from the will and hence the unconscionability lay in the attempt to plead the formality of the new will after years of repeated assurances. This might also be the reason why the claimant succeeded in *Thorner*, even though the period of detriment was shorter than that in *Gillett*. Clearly, the law must be astute to protect a claimant when there is genuine estoppel, but should not permit estoppel to be an easy way of avoiding the formalities normally required for conducting dealings with land. Thus, the common understanding that there is no contract for the sale of a house until formalised in writing explains why a house owner may accept and reject offers for the house at any point up to exchange of (written) contracts without behaving unconscionably. In the final analysis, unconscionability is, by its nature, a fluid concept and much depends on the facts of each case. It does not mean that the claimant must prove 'fraud' by the defendant, although there are elements of fraud in the concept.[47] It means, simply (and unhelpfully!), whether, in all of the circumstances, the landowner can resile from the assurance he has given and on which the claimant has relied to detriment (*Hopper v. Hopper* (2008)). As an illustration of the difficulty of defining the concept, the courts have suggested at least three approaches to identifying when unconscionability exists and they are not necessarily compatible with each other! First, it can arise when the assurance is withdrawn after detriment (*Gillett*; *Lloyd Davies v. Lloyd Davies* (2015)); second, it can arise if the claimant has promised not to rely on the otherwise required formality (and so denied in *Attorney-General of Hong Kong v. Humphreys Estate (Queen's Gardens) Ltd.* (1987)); third, it can arise from all of the facts, taken together (*Yeo v. Wilson*; *Ghazaani v. Rowshan* (2015)). Crucially, even if the claimant has relied to detriment on an assurance, there can be no proprietary estoppel without unconscionability.

Conversely, however, it is clear from the House of Lords' decisions in *Cobbe* and *Thorner* that it is not the purpose of estoppel to remedy unconscionable conduct per se. Estoppel is a response to an assurance about land, relied on to detriment, where it would be unconscionable for the assurance to be withdrawn. Unconscionability is necessary, but it operates within the parameters proved by the assurance, reliance and detriment.

---

46 *Taylor Fashions* (1982).

47 *Orgee v. Orgee* (1997).

In *Cobbe*, many observers might well regard the behaviour of the defendant as being 'sharp', unfair or even unconscionable in a general sense. But lacking the factual basis of a claim – that is, a clear enough assurance in context – there could be no estoppel. *Thorner* does nothing to depart from this, save only to remind us 'that focusing on technicalities can lead to a degree of strictness inconsistent with the fundamental aims of equity'.[48] One final point: if the *claimant* himself has behaved unconscionably, no amount of assurance, reliance and detriment is going to be enough to establish estoppel – *Yeo v. Wilson* (bullying by the claimant); *Murphy v. Rayner* (undue influence by the claimant); *Gonthier v. Orange Contract Scaffolding Ltd* (2003) (fabricated documents). Estoppel is an equitable remedy, and he who wants equity must behave equitably.

10.3 What is the Result of a Successful Plea of Proprietary Estoppel?

The myriad circumstances in which proprietary estoppel can be established necessarily means that the remedy will vary from case to case. Broadly speaking, however, two possibilities are available. First, if the proprietary estoppel is established by a defendant in an action by the landowner for recovery of the land or exclusion of the defendant or denial of some right alleged by the defendant, the landowner's claim will be dismissed and the defendant will be left to enjoy the right that the landowner was seeking to deny. This is estoppel as a shield, and is illustrated by *Gafford v. Graham* (1998), in which the landowner entitled to the benefit of a restrictive covenant was estopped from enforcing it due to his acquiescence in conduct contrary to the covenant by his neighbour.[49] Second, and more importantly for our purposes, if the estoppel is established by a claimant seeking to enforce a claim against a landowner in consequence of an assurance, the court can award the claimant such remedy as it deems appropriate, save only that *Orgee v. Orgee* (1997) suggests that the court cannot award more than the claimant was ever assured. In fact, as is made clear by *Jennings v. Rice* (2002), the precise reach of the remedy awarded should be tailored to remove the unconscionability suffered by the claimant.

As explained in *Crabb v. Arun DC* (1976), on a practical level, this means that the court can 'satisfy' the equity in any manner that is appropriate to the case before it, provided that at least it does the minimum to achieve justice between the parties.[50] The remedy may be 'expectation-based' (the claimant gets that which was promised), 'reliance-based' (the claimant gets a remedy commensurate with the extent of their detrimental reliance) or a mixture of the two, provided that the unconscionability is remedied.[51] Crucially, therefore, a court can award the claimant any proprietary *or* personal right over the defendant's land, or no substantive remedy at all. For example, in *Dillwyn v. Llewellyn*

---

48 Lord Neuberger, in *Thorner*.

49 See also *Lester v. Hardy*, where estoppel was a defence to a claim for an injunction to prevent a nuisance.

50 In *Wormall v. Wormall* (2004), the successful claimant was granted a right to occupy the land for a stated period, but on appeal to the Court of Appeal, her claim to additional monetary compensation was dismissed. The time-limited right to occupy was the minimum necessary to do justice between the parties.

51 It is sometimes said that the actual remedy must be 'proportionate', as in *Bradbury v. Taylor*, where the claimants were awarded the entirety of the property.

(1862) and *Pascoe* v. *Turner* (1979), the claimant was actually awarded the fee simple in the land; in *Celsteel* v. *Alton* (1987), *Bibby* v. *Stirling* (1998), *Joyce* v. *Epsom & Ewell* (2012) and *Hoyl* v. *Cromer Town Council* (2015) an easement was the result; and in *Voyce* v. *Voyce* (1991), there was a complete readjustment of the parties' rights over the property. Yet although in all of these cases the successful claimant was awarded a proprietary right in the land, it is possible that he will be given only a personal right (a licence) to use the land. On one view, this occurred in *Inwards* v. *Baker* (1965), in which a father had encouraged his son to build a bungalow on his (the father's) land, and when the son went ahead, the court appeared to grant the son a licence to use the land for life. Likewise, in *Matharu* v. *Matharu* (1994), the claimant's claim for a share of beneficial ownership was rejected, but she was awarded a licence to occupy for life, and in *Parker* v. *Parker* (2004), a licence appears to have been awarded as a result of estoppel. Again, there is no reason why any right *over land* – proprietary or personal – should be awarded at all. For example, in *Wayling* v. *Jones* (1993), the claimant was awarded compensation in lieu of a proprietary interest because the relevant land had been disposed of previously, in *Campbell* v. *Griffin* (2001), the claimant was given a charge to the value of £35,000 over the property and was not permitted to remain in possession,[52] in *Lothian* v. *Dixon* (2014) the claimants were awarded the residuary estate of a will and in *Davies* v. *Davies* (2016) the parties agreed (after the finding that an estoppel existed) that the most appropriate remedy was a cash sum and not either sale or transfer of the land.[53] Similar results were achieved in *Jennings* and in *Ottey* and this would have been the judge's solution in *Murphy* v. *Burrows* (2004) had he believed that the estoppel was made out in the first place. Interestingly, in *Murphy*, the judge regards the monetary award as a *lesser* form of relief – justified in that case by the weak acts of detriment. Certainly, in both *Jennings* and *Campbell*, it seems clear that the claimant would have preferred a proprietary stake in the property.

The question of remedy is perhaps the most open-ended and fluid issue in the law of estoppel. The decision as to the appropriate remedy is necessarily retrospective, with the court looking back at all that has occurred. No doubt, a judge's perception of the appropriate remedy will be influenced by his or her findings as to the extent of the expectation generated, the degree of detriment suffered and the magnitude of the consequential unconscionability. *Davies* v. *Davies* (2017) suggests that the clearer the expectation, and the longer the detriment is incurred, the more likely it is that the claimant will get what they were promised. There is, according to *Davies*, a sliding scale where giving a remedy based on the expectation generated becomes less likely as the assurances become less certain or the detriment less meaningful. Moreover, Lewison LJ in *Davies* argues that '[p]roportionality lies at the heart of the doctrine of proprietary estoppel and permeates its every application'. It is not entirely clear, however, if this is the same as the *Jennings* approach which places the alleviation of unconscionability at the heart of estoppel, and it begs the question of what the remedy should be 'proportional' to: the expectation, the detriment, the claimant or defendant's conduct? There is a sense in *Davies* – no more than that – that the court is trying to rein in estoppel remedies through the medium of proportionality

---

52 The house was to be sold and the claimant paid out of the proceeds.

53 They did, however, have different views about how large the sum should be. The Court of Appeal reduced the trial judge's award from £1.3 million to £500,000.

and certainly the reduction of the trial judge's award from £1.3 million to £500,000 by the Court of Appeal has that flavour to it.

As we can see, the range of remedies available to the court in estoppel cases is open-ended, and, importantly, does not necessarily have to result in the grant of a traditional proprietary interest at all, as where a licence is granted or a money award made. Of course, this flexibility does produce a measure of uncertainty, both for the claimant and for any potential purchaser of the land over which the estoppel is asserted. In fact, the most difficult problems in practice occur when the 'burdened' land is sold to a purchaser *before* the estoppel has been crystallised by decision of the court, as in *Bibby v. Stirling* (1998) and *Lloyd v. Dugdale* (2001). Naturally, the purchaser is likely to deny that the claimant has any right over the land – after all, there is no written evidence of the right and the purchaser is not responsible for generating the estoppel. In these circumstances, the court is faced with the classic property law issue: whose right to the land should have priority, that of the person alleging the estoppel, who by definition has been treated unconscionably, or that of the purchaser, who has paid value for land that now might be burdened by an adverse right? In fact, this dilemma hides layers of further questions. First, does the claimant benefit from an estoppel; and, second, does that estoppel bind the purchaser? In turn, this second question will depend on both the nature of propri-etary estoppel itself *and* (assuming estoppel is 'proprietary' in character) whether the appropriate rules of registered and unregistered land have been observed.

10.4 The Nature of Proprietary Estoppel and its Effect on Third Parties

Prior to the LRA 2002, the nature of proprietary estoppel was not easy to determine and there were two major strands of thought. On one view, proprietary estoppel (or an 'equity by estoppel') was itself an interest in land, although necessarily an equitable interest because of the informal way it arose. In other words, it was irrelevant how the court satisfied the equity (e.g. by easement, fee simple or licence) because the *estoppel* was proprietary in nature and itself capable of binding a purchaser of the land. Thus, a pur-chaser buying land over which there was a potential estoppel could find the land subject to an adverse right if the claimant could prove that the *former* owner had 'created' an estoppel in his favour. Support for this view was derived from the argument that 'estop-pel licences' were interests in land and from cases such as *Ives v. High* (1967) and *Inwards v. Baker* (1965), in which the 'bindingness' of estoppel appears to be accepted. In the latter case, the court indicated that the claimant should be awarded a licence to occupy the land as a result of an estoppel, which could then bind a third party, and the same solution was adopted in *Greasley v. Cooke* (1980) and in *Re Sharpe* (1980).[54] Likewise, in *Habermann v. Koehler* (1997) and *Birmingham Midshires v. Saberhawal* (1999), the Court of Appeal intimated, without deciding, that if the claimant could establish an estoppel, it might amount to an overriding interest under the then applicable section 70(1) of the LRA 1925, thus indicating its proprietary status.[55] However, it is also true that both

---

54 In *Re Sharpe*, the court accepted that the estoppel (the 'equity') could bind a trustee in bankruptcy.

55 The argument would be equally applicable to paragraph 2 of Schedules 1 and 3 of the LRA 2002.

Inwards and *Cooke* could have been justified on other grounds (i.e. that the claimant should have had a life interest under a settlement)[56] and *Bibby* v. *Stirling* (1998) is probably an example of an *existing* easement binding the burdened land. So also in *Williams* v. *Staite* (1979), another case often cited in support of this view, the matter was assumed, rather than argued. Significantly, however, in *Lloyd* v. *Dugdale* (2001), the Court of Appeal took the view that, if the claimant had been in actual occupation of the property, his right arising by estoppel would have bound the purchaser (Lloyd) as an overriding interest under the then applicable section 70(1)(g) of the LRA 1925.[57] This was, prior to the LRA 2002, the clearest evidence that estoppels were themselves proprietary.

The second view did not see proprietary estoppel as a right in itself, but rather as a method of creating rights: a means to an end, not the end itself. On such a view, the estoppel was regarded as a process whereby rights in, or over, land were created, rather like a contract or a deed but much less formal. Consequently, it was not the fact of estoppel that was relevant, but the right that was created by the court when it satisfied the estoppel. So, for example, if the estoppel gave rise to a lease, a freehold, an easement or any other proprietary right, then there was no doubt that a third person buying the land over which the right took effect might be bound by it, being bound in the same way that any lease, freehold or easement would bind. The essence of the matter was that the estoppel had generated a proprietary right and it was the *right* that was binding, not the estoppel. The obvious consequence of this was, however, that if the estoppel generated a personal right (i.e. a licence or a money award) that licence or award was incapable of binding a purchaser, simply because it was personal and the method of its creation (estoppel) was irrelevant. For some commentators, this alternative view of proprietary estoppel had much to commend it, not least that it maintained a clear distinction between proprietary and personal rights and did not fetter a court in its discretion. If, for example, the court wished to ensure that a future purchaser of the 'burdened' land was bound by an estoppel, it could have awarded the claimant a proprietary right arising from it. If the court wished to ensure that the estoppel was effective *only* against the maker of the assurance, it could have awarded a personal remedy. However, it is true that there was little judicial support for this theory, and not only because the effect of an estoppel on a third-party purchaser was rarely a live issue in the courts. It had the great disadvantage that a right so painstakingly established by the claimant, stemming from the landowner's unconscionability, could be defeated by the simple device of conveying the land to another.

10.4.1   Estoppels after the Land Registration Act 2002

While there may have been doubts and arguments about the nature of proprietary estoppel before the entry into force of the LRA 2002, these doubts have been resolved by express provision in the Act itself. Section 116 provides that:

---

56 *Dodsworth* v. *Dodsworth* (1973).

57 Consequently, were it not for the unfortunate circumstance that Mr Dugdale's company was in actual occupation rather than he personally, he would have succeeded in his claim against the purchaser because his estoppel would have bound as an overriding interest.

[F]or the avoidance of doubt that, in relation to registered land ... an equity by estoppel ... has effect from the time the equity arises as an interest capable of binding successors in title (subject to the rules about the effect of dispositions on priority).

This import of this section is clear enough and is spelled out in the Law Commission report on which the LRA 2002 is based. It means that an *uncrystallised* estoppel (the 'equity by estoppel') has proprietary character, with the consequence that if the normal priority rules of registered conveyancing are satisfied ('rules about the effect of dispositions on priority'), the uncrystallised estoppel will bind a third party. An uncrystallised estoppel exists where the claimant establishes that an estoppel existed but the land over which it existed was transferred before the court determined the precise remedy. In practice, this means that we must examine the precise circumstances in which it is alleged that an estoppel is alleged to bind a third party. There are three possibilities.

1   The landowner (A) generates an estoppel in favour of B. Before B can sue A to determine the precise remedy he will receive, A sells the land to P. The uncrystallised estoppel − the equity by estoppel − is declared by section 116 to be proprietary and so it has the potential to bind P. Whether *in fact* it binds P depends on the normal rules of registered conveyancing. Thus, B would either have to have entered the estoppel against A's registered title by means of a Notice[58] or, as is more likely, claim an overriding interest by reason of actual occupation. If neither are true − as of Mr Dugdale in *Lloyd* v. *Dugdale* (2001) − the purchaser takes the land free of the uncrystallised estoppel, as provided by section 29 of the LRA 2002, even though it is proprietary. Of course, if the transferee is not a purchaser − perhaps A gifts the land to his daughter or leaves it by will − then the transferee is bound by the estoppel because it is a proprietary right and has priority (section 28 of the LRA 2002). This is simply the application of normal rules of registered conveyancing to a property right − the uncrystallised estoppel.

2   The landowner (A) generates an estoppel in favour of B. B sues A and the court awards an estoppel remedy in the nature of an orthodox proprietary right, such as a lease, easement or the like. This is not uncrystallised, because an actual remedy has been awarded. It is highly likely in such a case that the order of the court will be carried out by the formal grant of the right so awarded: for example, A grants a formal lease or easement to B or conveys the freehold and the register of title of the burdened land will be amended accordingly.[59] In such cases, the formal grant of the right will be registered and so the claimant will be protected against any future transferee of the land. If by some rare chance the land is transferred by A to a purchaser (P) before the court order is carried out, B nevertheless has a proprietary right that might bind P. This is because B has a specific proprietary right arising

---

58 *Nugent* v. *Nugent* (2013), registration of a Unilateral Notice. A well-advised claimant might try to register their estoppel as a means of crystallising their claim. The entry of the Notice is likely to be challenged by the landowner, with an application that it be removed ('vacated'), thus requiring the estoppel claim to be judicially determined, as in *Nugent*. See also *Henry* v. *Henry* (2010), where the bindingness of an estoppel was confirmed by the Privy Council in the context of an appeal from St Lucia.

59 See *Joyce* v. *Epsom & Ewell*, where the successful estoppel was crystallised by the court ordering the defendant to grant an easement, i.e. to execute a deed in favour of the claimant, thereby creating a legal easement.

from the claim in estoppel (e.g. a lease), and if this is to bind P, the right must be protected in the manner appropriate to registered title as specified by the LRA 2002.[60] Note, however, that the fact that a court has ordered that B should be given a specific property right makes it highly unlikely that a transfer would take place before this right is formally granted.

3   The landowner (A) generates an estoppel in favour of B. B sues A and the court awards an estoppel remedy in the nature of a personal remedy against A, such as a money award or a licence. Again, the estoppel has been crystallised and A is under an obligation to ensure that B receives that which the court has ordered. If A then sells to P, a strict reading of section 116 means that P cannot be bound by 'the equity by estoppel' because the 'equity by estoppel' no longer exists. It has been satisfied by the court order. This is, indeed, perfectly understandable if the award against A was a money award; after all, why should P have to pay out the award when it was ordered against A? The issue appears more troublesome if B is given a licence over A's land, for on this reasoning the licence will be defeated by a transfer to P – the estoppel is satisfied and a licence is personal. In fact, however, this is not a surprising result and should not cause eyebrows to be raised. If the court has seen fit to crystallise the estoppel by means of a licence – after all, it had free choice as to the specific remedy – it may well be because B's claim was not regarded as of sufficient merit to justify the potential carry-over of that remedy against P. The licence or money award might have been chosen deliberately to ensure that no purchaser could be bound. Of course, if this is a true interpretation of section 116,[61] then what is most needed is for a court to consider carefully the precise remedy it gives to a successful claimant.[62]

10.4.2   Estoppel and e-conveyancing

As discussed in Chapter 2, an important element in the original scheme of e-conveyancing was to ensure that the creation of rights in registered land occurred simultaneously with their entry on the register – see section 93 of the LRA 2002. The necessary consequence could have been that paper deeds and written contracts would have become redundant, although the precise way in which the system of e-conveyancing would have worked was unclear. Had e-conveyancing been implemented in its purest form – i.e. encompassing mandatory and exclusive electronic formality – the parties' reliance on paper transactions would have had no legal effect, thus creating many and various opportunities for estoppel to operate in much the same way as it does now when the parties use it to support purely oral arrangements. Presently, it is not clear how e-conveyancing will develop given that the Law Commission has indicated that the original conception

---

60   Again, usually this will be because the right qualifies as an overriding interest by reason of actual occupation.

61   Currently, there are no cases that raise this issue.

62   An example of this is *Parker (9th Earl of Macclesfield)* v. *Parker* (2004), in which it is not clear whether the claimant is awarded a licence or some other estoppel-based right. Consequently, in the unlikely event (on the facts) that the property would be sold, it would not have been clear whether the purchaser would have been bound by the claimant's interest.

should be abandoned.[63] The point to note is, then, that proprietary estoppel could become as much as an antidote to the failure to use mandatory e-formalities as it is to a failure to use mandatory written formalities.

10.4.3 Estoppel in unregistered land

Although section 116 of the LRA 2002 formally applies only to registered land, the balance of the case law before the 2002 Act was in favour of the proprietary status of the 'equity by estoppel'. It is certain, therefore, that uncrystallised estoppels are now to be regarded as proprietary in unregistered land. Again, this means that they would be capable of binding a third party on a transfer of an unregistered title.[64] Equitable interests in unregistered land usually must be registered as Land Charges under the LCA 1972. However, the 'equity by estoppel' is not within any of the statutorily defined classes of Land Charge. Consequently, whether an estoppel binds a purchaser of the 'burdened' unregistered land will depend on the old 'doctrine of notice'. For example, in Ives v. High (1967), the Court of Appeal held that an estoppel easement was binding on a third party through the doctrine of notice. Necessarily, this will now be a rare event given that the overwhelming majority of transferable titles are already registered.

10.4.4 An apparently similar, but very different, situation

In the above sections, we have been considering the situation in which A's actions are such that they generate an estoppel interest in favour of B over A's land, and then A sells that land to a purchaser, P. The issue then is, clearly, whether the right existing between A and B can be binding on P, a third party. However, another possibility exists that appears to be very similar, but which is logically and legally different. Thus, A may act so as to generate an estoppel in favour of B over A's land, and A again may sell the land to P. Yet this time, after the sale, P may confirm by words or conduct the continuance of B's right and so a new estoppel between P and B comes into existence. This is not a case of a pre-existing right binding P, but the generation of a new right by P's own conduct in favour of B. Indeed, one explanation of Ives v. High (1967) is that A and B had, by their action, created an easement binding on A's land, and, when the land was sold to P, P so acted as to be estopped from denying the continuance of the right. In effect, this has nothing to do with the transfer of existing rights against a third party, because the alleged 'third party' transferee is bound by estoppel due to their own actions: P is bound by his own estoppel, not that which existed between A and B.

---

63 Perhaps 'modified' would be kinder. But the reality is 'abandoned'. See Law Commission Consultation Paper, *Updating the LRA* 2002.

64 That transfer will, of course, trigger compulsory registration of the title, but the position of the new owner (and potential first registrant) will be judged according to the principles of unregistered conveyancing and then, on first registration, by the LRA 2002.

10.5   Proprietary Estoppel and Constructive Trusts

It will be apparent from the above analysis of the principles of proprietary estoppel that the doctrine has much in common with that branch of constructive trusts considered in Chapter 4 – that is, constructive trusts concerning the acquisition of an equitable interest in another person's land. As we know, an estoppel is triggered by an assurance, relied on to detriment where it would be unconscionable for the assurance to be withdrawn, and a 'common intention' constructive trust is triggered by an express promise or assurance as to ownership that is relied on to detriment. The similarities are obvious and in a number of cases, such as *Ottey* v. *Grundy* (2003), *Oxley* v. *Hiscock* (2004) and *Kinane* v. *Alimamy Mackie-Conteh* (2005), the court was content to rely on either (or both) doctrines in pursuit of a just outcome. This tendency was always latent in constructive trust cases,[65] but it was given prominence by the Court of Appeal in *Yaxley* v. *Gotts* (1999).

In *Yaxley*, the claimant originally alleged an estoppel against Mr Gotts because of an agreement between them concerning ownership of land and its redevelopment. The Court of Appeal allowed the claim, but on the basis that Mr Yaxley was the beneficiary under a common intention constructive trust that was in some way linked to the estoppel. The case clearly raised questions concerning the relationship between the doctrines – questions that the judgments themselves do not answer. However, in *Stack* v. *Dowden* (2007), the House of Lords reconsidered the role of constructive trusts in co-ownership cases[66] and Lord Walker – who had given the leading judgment in *Yaxley* v. *Gotts* – noted that he was 'now rather less enthusiastic about the notion that proprietary estoppel and "common interest" constructive trusts can or should be completely assimilated'. Furthermore, recent cases have tended to expand the role of constructive trusts into places that estoppel might fear to tread. In *Matchmove* v. *Dowding* (2016) and *Saunders* v. *Himaly* (2017), the Court of Appeal and High Court respectively had to consider whether oral agreements for the disposition of interests in land were enforceable, despite a failure to comply with section 2 of the LP(MP)A 1989 which generally requires such contracts to be in writing. In both cases, the court upheld the oral agreement on the basis that the parties had agreed to undertake a 'joint venture', which agreement had been detrimentally relied on by the claimants. This was said to give rise to a constructive trust[67] which of course is exempt from writing under section 2(5) of the 1989 Act. A very similar argument, but based around proprietary estoppel, had been rejected by the House of Lords in *Cobbe* on the grounds that the requirement for section 2 formality could not be sidestepped, at least where the parties were fully aware that the agreement should have been concluded in writing. In fact, *Cobbe* had not decided that estoppel could never be used to cure an absence of section 2 formality, rather that, on the facts of the case, it was not unconscionable for the defendant to rely on section 2 as a reason not to carry out the agreement. Nevertheless, *Cobbe* and the earlier *Herbert* v. *Doyle's* insistence that section 2 cannot be sidestepped seems to have caused a switch in these cases to a rationale based

---

65 See the remarks in *Grant* v. *Edwards* (1986), *Re Basham* (1986) and *Lloyds Bank* v. *Rosset* (1991).

66 See Chapter 4.

67 This is sometimes known as a *Pallant* v. *Morgan* equity, from the case of that name.

on constructive trust – probably because constructive trusts are specifically exempt from the need for writing under section 2 whereas claims based on estoppel have to be otherwise justified.[68] This switch seems to be bearing fruit as the courts seem happy to uphold an oral agreement on the ground that it generates a constructive trust in circumstances where an estoppel claim might fail.

Bearing these general points in mind, the following is a very tentative attempt to compare and contrast constructive trusts and proprietary estoppel. However, it should be noted that this is not meant to be a definitive analysis and not all of the points are strong ones. It is a template for discussion.

1 Both constructive trusts and proprietary estoppel are triggered by an assurance (including an express promise), reliance and detriment. In consequence, there are many cases in which a claimant could plead either doctrine and in many cases they do. It is generally thought, however, that estoppel is available in a wider range of circumstances because the 'assurance' in constructive trusts appears to have a higher evidential threshold – perhaps because it is thought of as a 'common' intention. As an example, in *Arif* v. *Anwar* (2015), the court determined that the dealings were too vague and uncertain to establish a constructive trust, but were enough to establish proprietary estoppel. A similar view was taken in *Southwell* v. *Blackburn* (2014).[69]

2 The constructive trust is said to arise from a 'common intention' between the parties, whereas an estoppel can arise from a 'unilateral' assurance. This is the basis of Arden LJ's distinction between the doctrines in *Kinane*, in which she emphasised the mutually shared nature of the common intention constructive trust. *Cook* v. *Thomas* (2011) takes a similar view. However, it is not at all clear that constructive trusts really do result from a shared intention relating to the land – in what sense did Mr Stack and Ms Dowden ever have a shared intention?[70] Conversely, there are cases in which an estoppel arose from a common intention that once existed – see, for example, *Gillett* v. *Holt* (2001). We can only conclude, therefore, that the theory that constructive trusts are 'mutual', whereas estoppel is 'unilateral', is not proven, albeit that it is superficially attractive.

3 The constructive trust tends to be relied on in matrimonial or quasi-matrimonial disputes concerning the family home. Proprietary estoppel tends to be used for all other cases, both as between strangers and between persons in other family or friendship arrangements. This may be merely historical or traditional and without any logical base. Alternatively, it may not. In *Oxley* v. *Hiscock* (2004), Chadwick LJ came close to stating that proprietary estoppel was a better ground for deciding the shared home cases, but this has been overtaken by the clear view of the House of Lords in *Stack* that a broad-based concept of constructive trust is more appropriate.

4 Both the constructive trust and proprietary estoppel are a means of enforcing an 'informal' promise by a landowner made in favour of a claimant. They are methods by which a person may acquire an interest in land without having been granted

---

68 The justification does exist – that estoppel claims are outside section 2 LPA 1989 because they prevent unconscionability rather than act to enforce an otherwise unenforceable contract.

69 But see *Yaxley* v. *Gotts* where the concepts appear to be interchangeable, subject to the same evidentiary requirements.

70 See Chapter 4.

that interest in writing or by deed and hence are exceptions to the need for 'formality' in land transactions. There is, however, a reluctance to use estoppel in cases where the parties have clearly tried, but failed, to conclude a binding contract. Recent cases suggest that courts are prepared to use 'joint venture' constructive trusts to uphold such agreements.

5   The constructive trust is statutorily exempt from the normal formality requirements for transactions involving land – section 53(2) exempts it from the requirements of section 53(1) of the LPA 1925 and section 2(5) exempts it from the requirements of section 2 of the LP(MP)A 1989. There is no statutory exemption for proprietary estoppel. In consequence, courts may feel on safer ground when relying on constructive trust, as, for example, in *Yaxley* and *Brightlingsea Haven* v. *Morris* (2008). Likewise, there is a need to explain why claims of proprietary estoppel are exempt from these formality requirements (there is no statutory approval) and this is usually done by reference to the criterion of 'unconscionability'. This may explain why 'unconscionability' is more overtly central in estoppel claims. For example, in *Ghazaani* v. *Rowshan* (2015), the failure of the parties to conclude a written contract within section 2 did not prevent a finding of estoppel (without reference to a constructive trust) because that was necessary to prevent unconscionability.

6   The lack of statutory approval for proprietary estoppel has led some courts to suggest that, when an estoppel is made out, it is supported by or protected behind a constructive trust. This was suggested in *Yaxley* and appears also in *Ottey, Jiggins* v. *Brisely* (2003) and *Brightlingsea Haven*. However, it appears an unnecessary and confusing addition to an already confused debate and may have been rejected by Lord Walker in *Stack*. If proprietary estoppel can generate property rights without formality – as is patently and historically obvious – then it has no need of the shelter of a constructive trust to explain its validity. Its validity is justified because it prevents unconscionability. It is a creature of equity and needs no statute or constructive trust to validate it – *Ghazaani* v. *Rowshan* (2015).

7   A successful plea of common intention constructive trust results in an equitable share of ownership for the claimant with the legal owner holding the land under a 'trust of land' governed by the TOLATA 1996. A successful plea of a joint venture constructive trust seems to result in the oral agreement being enforced. A successful proprietary estoppel may be 'satisfied' by the award of any proprietary right, any personal right (including a money award) or no right at all. In this sense, proprietary estoppel is more flexible and this understandably holds attraction for some judges (see *Southwell* v. *Blackburn*). This difference in the outcome of each claim seems to have been at the heart of Lord Walker's acceptance in *Stack* that they should not be assimilated.

8   A constructive trust is certainly proprietary (it gives an equitable interest behind a trust of land), and now, following *Lloyd* v. *Dugdale* (2001) and section 116 of the LRA 2002, so is the *uncrystallised* estoppel.

9   It is sometimes said that a successful claim to a constructive trust is akin to a claim of right (i.e. an interest *will be* awarded), whereas a successful claim of estoppel is more discretionary (i.e. an interest *may be* awarded). However, such a distinction may be more apparent than real. Both are equitable doctrines and a court may refuse to grant relief) where it is not 'deserved'. It may be simply that courts are more open about their discretion in estoppel cases. Indeed, the decision in *Oxley* that the court should strive to reach a fair and reasonable quantification of a

beneficial interest under a constructive trust, now confirmed by *Stack, Jones* v. *Kernott* (2011) and *Capehorn* v. *Harris* (2015), illustrates clearly that constructive trusts also contain a large element of discretion.

Clearly, it is dangerous to draw firm conclusions from these arguments. Many academics see the concepts as virtually indistinguishable as *concepts* while recognising that, in practice, they are used in different types of cases. Other academics maintain that the concepts are inherently different, albeit that in some cases they overlap. The latter view appears to have been adopted by Lord Walker in *Stack* v. *Dowden*, but that was a change of mind from his earlier view in *Yaxley* v. *Gotts*.

10.6   Chapter Summary

10.6.1   The role of proprietary estoppel

Proprietary estoppel can provide a defence to an action by a landowner who seeks to enforce his strict rights against someone who has been informally promised some right or liberty over the land. Proprietary estoppel can also generate new property interests in favour of a claimant. It can be a shield or a sword.

10.6.2   Conditions for the operation of proprietary estoppel

The modern doctrine of *Taylor Fashions* v. *Liverpool Victoria Trustees* (1982) is that there must be the following.

1   *An assurance*. The form of the assurance is irrelevant and it may be implied from conduct, or be based in acquiescence, so long as the landowner is aware, or ought to have been aware, that the claimant is relying on the assurance. It need not amount to the promise of a specific property right, so long as the assurance is 'certain enough' and is not an assurance about a mere personal right. Everything depends on the context in which the assurance is given. Contrast *Thorner* v. *Majors* (2009) with *Cobbe* v. *Yeoman's Row* (2005).

2   *Reliance on the assurance*. This can be assumed from the fact that the claimant acted to his detriment. The assumption can be rebutted by evidence that the claimant would have behaved the same way irrespective of the landowner's assurance.

3   *Detriment*. This may take many forms, provided that it is not minimal. It may involve expenditure on the land, work undertaken in connection with the land or work undertaken for the landowner without pay or at less than market pay, or lost opportunities.

4   *Such circumstances that it would be unconscionable to allow the landowner to escape from his promise.* Unconscionability is the reason why oral assurances can be enforced despite non-compliance with normal formality requirements. If the facts do not reveal unconscionability, then a simple assurance, reliance and detriment on their own cannot generate an estoppel. Similarly, estoppel is not available to remedy unconscionability per se if the factual prerequisites are not established.

10.6.3 What is the result of a successful plea of proprietary estoppel?

If a defendant establishes the proprietary estoppel in an action by the landowner, the landowner's claim will be dismissed and the defendant will be left to enjoy the right that the landowner was seeking to deny. If the estoppel is established by a claimant seeking to enforce a right against a landowner in consequence of an assurance, the court can award the claimant any remedy it deems appropriate, although probably not in excess of that which was actually promised. The aim of the award is to remedy the unconscionability and to do the minimum necessary to satisfy the equity, with recent cases deciding that the remedy must be proportional.

10.6.4 The nature of proprietary estoppel and its effect on third parties

This has now been settled by section 116 of the LRA 2002. If the estoppel is uncrystallised before the transfer of the burdened land, then it is a property right capable (subject to registration principles) of binding a third party. If the right is crystallised in a proprietary way before such transfer, the same is true. If the right is crystallised in a personal way before transfer, it remains a personal right.

Further Reading

Baughen, S, 'Estoppels over land and third parties: An open question?' (1994) 14 LS 147.

Bright, S, 'Bright: The third party's conscience in land law' [2000] Conv 388.

Cooke, E, 'Estoppel and the protection of expectations' (1997) 17 LS 258.

Dixon, M, 'Proprietary estoppel and formalities in land law and the Land Registration Act 2002: A theory of unconscionability', in Cooke, E (ed.) *Modern Studies in Property Law*, Vol. 2, Oxford: Hart, 2003.

Dixon, M, 'Defining and confining estoppel' (2010) 30 LS 408.

Howard, M and **Hill**, J, 'The informal creation of interests in land' (1995) 15 LS 356.

McFarlane, B and **Robertson**, A, 'Apocalypse averted: Proprietary estoppel in the House of Lords' [2009] LQR 535.

Milne, P, 'Proprietary estoppel in a procrustean bed' [2011] MLR 412.

Samet, I, 'Proprietary estoppel and responsibility for omissions' [2015] 78 MLR 85.

Now visit the companion website to:

*   test your understanding of the key terms using our Flashcard Glossary;

*   revise and consolidate your knowledge using our Multiple Choice Question testbank.

www.routledge.com/cw/dixon

Chapter 11
The Law of Mortgages

Introduction

A mortgage is an extremely versatile concept in the law of real property. For most people, a mortgage signifies the method by which they may raise enough capital to purchase a house or other land. However, the use of a mortgage to finance the purchase of property is a relatively recent phenomenon, and mortgages have been used as security for the repayment of a loan, or for the performance of some other obligation, for much longer.

11.1 The Essential Nature of a Mortgage

A mortgage has a number of different attributes, the most important of which are discussed below. As we shall see, a mortgage is a concept that partakes both of the law of contract and of the law of real property. This duality provides the basis for the versatility of the mortgage in the modern world of property ownership, property investment and capital finance. It gives the mortgagee – the lender – a proprietary right that it can shape to its own use depending on its particular requirements, and it provides the mortgagor – the borrower – with a relatively economic and efficient way of turning an immoveable asset (their land) into a liquid one (its cash value). Mortgagee/lender and mortgagor/borrower are used interchangeably throughout this chapter and no significance attaches to the choice. Judges may use either in their judgments.

11.1.1 A contract between borrower and lender

Like many other concepts in the law of real property, a mortgage is also a contract, this time between the borrower and the lender. Usually, this contract is express – as where the parties negotiate and execute a mortgage by deed based on the standard terms and conditions of the lender – but sometimes it is implied, as where the court decides that the conduct of the parties in relation to an asset (i.e. land) amounts to a mortgage (or 'charge'), whether or not this was the intention of the parties or spelt out in their agreement. In the typical mortgage of land, with which this chapter is concerned,[1] the borrower of money (the mortgagor) will enter into a binding contract with the mortgagee (the lender – for example, a merchant bank, high street bank or building society), whereby a capital sum will be lent on the security of property owned by the mortgagor. As a matter of contract, the mortgagor and mortgagee are free to stipulate whatever terms they wish for repayment of the loan, the rate of interest and so forth. Consequently, one of the remedies available to a mortgagee, when faced with a mortgagor who will not or cannot repay the loan, is to sue the mortgagor personally on the contract for repayment of the sum borrowed, plus interest and costs.[2] On the other hand, and as we shall see, the contractual nature of a mortgage is not always consistent with its status as a proprietary interest in land under the control of the court exercising its equitable

---

1 Mortgages of ships and aircraft, which are common, are outside the scope of this chapter, although many of the same rules apply, especially when the lender seeks to exercise its remedies; see *Alpstream AG* v. *PK Airfinance* (2013).

2 *Vedalease Ltd* v. *Cascabel Investments Ltd* (2009). See also the discussion in *Alliance & Leicester* v. *Slayford* (2001).

jurisdiction. Of course, these two aspects of a mortgage often complement each other,[3] but it is possible for the contractual obligations freely undertaken by the parties to be in conflict with the essential nature of a mortgage as a proprietary concept. It is then for the court to assess which has precedence – the contractual terms of the mortgage or the proprietary aspects of the mortgage security.[4]

11.1.2   An interest in land in its own right

Although a mortgage is a contract, and the parties to it are subject to contractual rights and obligations, a mortgage is also a proprietary interest in the land over which it takes effect. Thus, under a mortgage, the lender is regarded as having a proprietary interest in the land of the borrower with all that this entails, and the borrower retains an 'equity of redemption' – itself a proprietary right – which encapsulates his residual rights in the property.[5] In fact, both mortgagee and mortgagor may transfer their respective property interests under the mortgage to third parties and this often occurs when a bank transfers its 'mortgage book' to another lender. In addition, the proprietary nature of a mortgage brings with it the intervention and attention of equity and, as noted above, this can result in a conflict between the mortgage as an interest in land and the mortgage as the subject matter of a contract.

11.1.3   The classic definition of a mortgage

At its root, a mortgage is security for a loan. The inherent attribute of a mortgage of real property is that it comprises a transfer (a 'conveyance') of a legal or equitable interest in the mortgagor's land to the mortgagee, with a provision that the mortgagee's interest shall end upon repayment of the loan plus interest and costs. The lender's contractual rights (including the right to sue for the debt) are thus supported by a proprietary interest in the land.[6] However, it is a fundamental principle of the law of mortgages that 'once a mortgage, always a mortgage', even if this contradicts the terms of the contract between the parties. In other words, the borrower has the right to have their land returned unencumbered once the loan secured on it has been repaid and any clause of the mortgage that destroys that right will be struck out as inconsistent with the essential nature of a mortgage.[7] Conversely, the proprietary nature of the mortgage lasts only for so long as the debt remains outstanding, and the lender's remedies (which can be proprietary or contractual in nature) endure only so long as the borrower owes money or the mortgage still exists.

---

3 For example, in *Alliance & Leicester* v. *Slayford* (2001), the mortgagee pursued its contractual remedies against the mortgagor after its proprietary remedies proved ineffective.

4 See, for example, *Jones* v. *Morgan* (2001), section 11.9.3.1 below.

5 Today, the modern method of creating mortgages – the use of 'a charge' – does not actually transfer an interest in the land to the mortgagee. However, the legal mortgagee (the lender) under 'a charge by deed by way of legal mortgage' is treated as having such a right for all purposes (section 87(1) of the LPA 1925) and such charges are of course registrable under the LRA 2002.

6 *Santley* v. *Wilde* (1899). In addition, the mortgagee gets 'the same protection, powers and remedies' as if they had taken a conveyance of an estate – section 87(1) of the LPA 1925.

7 *Jones* v. *Morgan* (2001).

11.1.4   The mortgage as a device for the purchase of property

In recent years, the mortgage has come to the fore as the major device by which individuals may finance the purchase of property. Of course, the mortgage is still security for a loan, but now the purpose of the loan is to purchase the very property over which the security is to take effect. Necessarily, this has given rise to some conceptual problems, not least that the purchaser must actually own the property before he can create a mortgage over it, but, of course, he cannot own it until he has the money to pay for it and this is what the mortgage will provide! In formal terms, this problem is dealt with by the transfer (i.e. the completed sale) of the estate in the land to the new owner, followed immediately thereafter by the execution of a mortgage over that property and a transfer of the purchase price to the vendor.[8] This is simple enough, but it does mean that *logically* there is a 'time gap' between the purchaser acquiring the property and the execution of the mortgage over it. This is known as a *scintilla temporis* – a sliver of time. In practice, this *scintilla temporis* may only be a matter of a few minutes or moments, but it has the potential to create problems. For example, if the new owner holds the land on trust for another person (e.g. their spouse or partner),[9] the moment that the new owner acquires title is also the moment when the equitable owner's interest springs into life. Such an equitable interest would, logically, come into existence a few moments before the mortgage is created and thus apparently have the potential to take priority over the mortgage.[10] Figure 11.1 will make this clear.

Fortunately, this logical problem has now been solved in a practical way. According to the House of Lords in *Abbey National Building Society v. Cann* (1991), and accepted by the Supreme Court in *Scott v. Southern Pacific Mortgages* (2014), as a matter of *law*, there is no *scintilla*

Figure 11.1

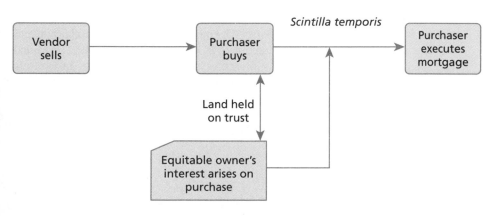

---

8   The monies are usually held by a conveyancer or solicitor until all these steps are complete.

9   For example, because the equitable owner has contributed to the purchase price, or contributed to the purchase price of a previous property the proceeds of the sale of which are being used to buy this one, or has in some other way contributed to the acquisition of the property – see generally *Stack v. Dowden* (2007), *Jones v. Kernott* (2011) and Chapter 4.

10   For example, as an interest that was in existence before the mortgage it might override through discoverable actual occupation: see Chapter 2.

temporis between a purchaser's acquisition of title to a property on completion of the purchase and the subsequent creation of a mortgage over that property if the mortgage has enabled the purchase to take place. This pragmatic solution, which recognises the reality of the bargain between the parties, applies with equal force to unregistered land and registered land governed by the LRA 2002.[11] Consequently, any potential equitable interest held by another person must always rank second in time to the mortgage, and therefore cannot take priority over the lender.[12] For all practical purposes, this must be correct, for not only does it reflect the reality of conveyancing practice, but it also reflects the fact that the property could not have been purchased at all without the mortgage. It is entirely appropriate in such a case that the interests of all of the owners of the property (legal and equitable) should give way to the rights of the mortgagee.[13] However, it is important to note that the lender only obtains priority over those equitable interests whose very existence depended on the acquisition of the land that is financed by the mortgage – as in Figure 11.1. If the property is *already* held on trust for a claimant before any thought of a mortgage, so that the mortgage is *not* the reason why the claimant has an interest in the first place, then a mortgagee cannot rely on the *Cann* principle, and priority is determined by the application of the normal rules of registered or unregistered conveyancing.[14]

11.1.5 Types of mortgage

The contractual nature of a mortgage means that each mortgage is potentially unique depending on the needs of the particular mortgagor and mortgagee. The following is a non-exhaustive list of the different types of mortgage in general use, although it must be remembered that all are 'mortgages' within the LPA 1925 and are governed by that Act and the principles of registration found in the LRA 2002.

1   The 'repayment mortgage' is used frequently for the purchase of residential property and to finance commercial activities. The mortgagor borrows a capital sum and agrees to pay back that sum plus interest over a fixed period of time. The capital and interest are paid back in instalments, with (usually) the early instalments representing pure interest, and the later instalments comprising a greater and greater capital element. At the end of the period, the mortgage has been redeemed (paid off), the registered mortgage (known as a registered charge) is discharged and the mortgagor owns the property absolutely.

---

11 *Abbey National* v. *Cann* was a case decided under the LRA 1925, but *Scott* applied the same principle to the LRA 2002. There is one remaining uncertainty. *Cann* and *Scott* decide that there is no *scintilla temporis* between completion of the purchaser and a mortgage. This is sufficient for our purposes. What is not clear is whether there is a *scintilla temporis* between the earlier *contract for purchase*, then completion of that purchase and then the mortgage. There was disagreement in the Supreme Court in *Scott* about whether *Cann* applied to this tripartite event, but it was *obiter* and very unlikely to be an issue in practice.

12 See also *Leeds Permanent Building Society* v. *Famini* (1998) in relation to a mortgagee having priority over a tenant of the property.

13 Even if there was a *scintilla temporis* in law, it is arguable that the equitable owner had in any event impliedly consented to the mortgage, this being necessary for the very acquisition of 'their' interest in land (*Abbey National* v. *Cann*).

14 That is, whether there has been overreaching or whether the claimant's interest binds the mortgagee as an overriding interest (in registered land) or through the doctrine of notice (in unregistered land) – see Chapters 2 and 4.

2   The 'endowment mortgage' is also used for the purchase of residential property, though less frequently in commercial transactions. The mortgagor borrows a capital sum for a fixed period (usually 25 years). This accumulates interest and the mortgagor repays that interest in regular monthly instalments. No part of the instalments goes towards repaying the capital sum. However, the mortgagor also enters into an 'endowment policy' (i.e. a savings plan), whereby he pays a regular sum towards the purchase of an 'endowment', which will mature (become payable) at the same time as the mortgage period ends. The endowment should generate a large enough capital sum to pay off the capital mortgage debt at the end of the period and, possibly, leave a sum of 'spare' money for the mortgagor. However, if, when the endowment policy matures, it does not realise enough money to pay off the capital debt, the mortgagor must provide the balance from other funds or remortgage and continue to pay instalments.

3   The 'current account mortgage' may be advantageous to borrowers whose only or principal debt is a mortgage. The lender will agree an overdraft facility on a bank current account to the value of the mortgage. The lender will provide these monies for the purchase of property in the normal way (or for any other agreed purpose) and interest will be charged at the agreed rate. The borrower will pay funds into the mortgage current account (e.g. a monthly salary) and some of these funds will pay the interest and/or capital repayments and will be taken by the lender. Any surplus funds in the current account will go towards paying off the debt. This has the advantage that the mortgage debt decreases the more that surplus funds are paid into the account. Further, given that interest will be payable only on the actual mortgage debt, the borrower pays less interest over the period of the mortgage (assuming the capital debt is decreasing) than with a conventional repayment or endowment mortgage. This is even more the outcome if the borrower overpays the agreed instalments, as this further reduces the capital debt and the interest. Moreover, as the lender has promised an overdraft facility to the level of the original mortgage, the borrower can draw on the current account up to this limit (in effect recover any surplus paid) should the need arise or circumstances change.

4   The secured overdraft is common where funds are required for commercial purposes, as where an entrepreneur uses the family home to raise finance for his company. In essence, the lender promises to make an overdraft facility available and the borrower may draw monies up to this agreed overdraft limit as and when they are needed. No lump sum is paid, interest is charged on the amount of the actual debt and the total amount owed varies according to the level of actual indebtedness. Hence the value of the mortgage secured over the land fluctuates (or 'floats') in line with the indebtedness, as in *State Bank of India v. Sood* (1997).

5   The 'charge': as we shall see, generally mortgages are created by the use of a charge.[15] A 'charge' does not refer to a specific type of mortgage, but rather to the manner in which any type of mortgage may be created. It is mentioned here because many judicial decisions refer to a mortgage of land as a 'charge over property' or 'a charge by deed by way of legal mortgage', irrespective of whether the actual mortgage is a repayment, endowment or other type of mortgage.

---

15 This method is now mandatory for legal mortgages of registered titles: see section 23(1) of the LRA 2002 and below.

11.2   The Creation of Mortgages before 1925

Although it will be rare for a mortgage created before the LPA 1925 still to be in existence today, a brief discussion of how these mortgages were created will help understand why modern mortgage law is constructed as it is. Before 1 January 1926, if an owner of a legal or equitable estate in land wished to raise money on the security of that land, the borrower's entire interest in the property was usually conveyed in full to the lender. In other words, the borrower divested themselves entirely of their interest in return for the loan. Of course, the mortgagee promised to reconvey the land (or the borrower's interest in it) on repayment of the principal (i.e. the capital sum), interest and costs but, importantly, the mortgage contract allowed the mortgagee to keep the borrower's land if he failed to repay the loan on the date stipulated in the mortgage contract. This date, known as the 'legal date of redemption', was crucial, and the consequences for the borrower of missing payment on that date were theoretically severe. To a large extent, however, the position was mitigated by the intervention of equity. Applying the policy that 'once a mortgage, always a mortgage', an 'equity of redemption' was held to exist, whereby the borrower was entitled to a reconveyance of his property if he paid the full sums due under the mortgage, even though the 'legal date' for redemption had passed. This was simply an aspect of the rule that a mortgage really was security for a loan and did not represent an opportunity for the mortgagee to obtain the property of a mortgagor if the debt could be repaid. Importantly, however, because the mortgagor conveyed everything to the mortgagee, there was no estate remaining with the borrower that could be used to create second or subsequent mortgages and the mortgagor had to take positive steps to recover their estate if it were not reconveyed when the debt was repaid.

11.3   The Creation of Legal Mortgages on or after 1 January 1926

The LPA 1925 made significant changes to the ways in which mortgages could be created. The overall intent was to ensure that a mortgagor retained the fullest interest possible in their own property, even when seeking a mortgage of it, provided that the mortgagee had suitable remedies in the event of failure to repay the loan. In general terms, as a consequence of the reforms of the LPA 1925, today a mortgage of a legal estate does not occur through the transfer of the mortgagor's entire interest in the land to the mortgagee. Instead, the mortgagee is given some lesser proprietary right in the mortgagor's land appropriate to the type of mortgage created. Furthermore, since 13 October 2003 – the date of entry into force of the LRA 2002 – legal mortgages of registered titles may be created only by the use of a 'charge' and thus the long leasehold method described below is now available only for land of unregistered title.[16]

---

16 In fact, mortgages of unregistered titles will almost invariably take the form of a charge and, of course, trigger compulsory first registration of title. Even for registered land mortgaged before the entry into force of the 2002 Act, the 'long lease' method would rarely have been employed.

11.4 Legal Mortgages of Freehold Estates before 13 October 2003

Under section 85(1) of the LPA 1925,[17] there are two methods of creating a legal mortgage of an unregistered freehold estate and these two methods also could have been used to create a mortgage of a registered title *before* the entry into force of the LRA 2002. For the avoidance of doubt, section 85(2) also provides that these two methods cannot be circumvented (where they are still available) and thus it is impossible to create a mortgage by a conveyance (i.e. transfer) of the mortgagor's entire interest to the mortgagee.

11.4.1 The long lease method

The first method is where the mortgagor grants the mortgagee a long lease over the land with a provision for the termination of the lease on repayment of all sums due under the loan. In technical terms, the mortgagor will 'demise a term of years absolute' to the mortgagee 'subject to a provision for cesser on redemption'. In the typical case, the mortgagee's lease is usually for 3,000 years, although the mortgage contract will fix an earlier contractual date for repayment and redemption. This earlier date comprises the legal right to redeem and may be a mere six months after the date of execution of the mortgage. However, as was the case before 1926, the mortgagor has an equitable right to redeem the mortgage, and thereby to terminate the long lease, on the payment of all sums due at any time after this legal date has passed. Indeed, this may be recognised explicitly by the inclusion of a right to pay by instalments that necessarily postpones the legal date for redemption. Of course, the grant of the exceptionally long lease to the mortgagee is something of a fiction, but it does have a number of important consequences.

First, the mortgagor retains the legal fee simple (the freehold) throughout the term of the mortgage. The borrower always retains an estate in their own land and the mortgage is more accurately shown to be what it really is – the security for a loan. Second, the mortgagee acquires a proprietary interest in the land, being the leasehold granted to them. This preserves the efficacy of their remedies in the event of non-payment of the mortgage debt. In particular it means that, as a leaseholder, the mortgagee has a right to possession of the property although, in most cases, this will not be exercised and the mortgagor will be allowed to remain in occupation. Third, it means that the mortgagor may create further legal mortgages of his land in order to raise further sums. For example, because the mortgagor retains his legal fee simple, it is perfectly possible to obtain another mortgage from a different lender by granting a second leasehold over the property for a period longer than the first lease, say, 3,001 years. The term granted to the second mortgagee will necessarily always be longer than that granted to the first, as this gives the second mortgagee a notional legal interest in the property distinct from that of the first mortgagee – in our example, one year more. Of course, the actual sum lent on the second mortgage will be calculated by reference to the value of the land taking account of the debt owed under the first mortgage, but again the mortgagor

---

17 This does not apply to mortgages of registered land executed on or after 13 October 2003.

retains the ultimate fee simple and the second mortgagee also receives a proprietary interest in the land. For example, if land is worth £100,000, the freehold owner (A) may seek a mortgage from XYZ Bank in the sum of £45,000. XYZ Bank will be granted a mortgage by way of a 3,000-year lease (with provisions for termination on repayment), and A retains the freehold. A may then seek a second mortgage from PQR Bank, which may be willing to lend anything up to £55,000, taking a 3,001-year lease by way of mortgage (with provisions for termination on repayment), A still retaining the freehold. As noted above, however, the long lease method is not available for mortgages of registered titles granted after the entry into force of the LRA 2002.

11.4.2　The charge

The second method of mortgaging registered titles (and this still applies after the entry into force of the LRA 2002) and unregistered titles is the *charge by deed*. Instead of the relative complexity involved in granting the mortgagee by a long lease over the land, the mortgagor could create a mortgage by executing 'a charge by deed' (sections 85(1) and 87 of the LPA 1925). This is a much simpler method of creating a mortgage. It was (and remains) the common form of mortgaging land and most mortgages now are created in this way. More importantly, since the entry into force of the LRA 2002, it is the only method of mortgaging registered titles. Consequently, it is dealt with more fully below.[18]

11.5　Legal Mortgages of Leasehold Estates: Unregistered Leases and Registered Leasehold Titles Mortgaged before 13 October 2003

For unregistered leasehold land and pre-LRA 2002 registered leasehold titles, there are also two methods of creating legal mortgages, and these are substantially similar to those used for the freehold.[19]

11.5.1　Long subleases

As with freeholds, the first method of creating a legal mortgage of an unregistered leasehold, and a mortgage of a registered leasehold taking effect before the LRA 2002, is to grant the mortgagee a lease over the property. Of course, given that the mortgagor himself is a leaseholder, the 'mortgage-lease' will actually be a sublease (a 'sub-demise'). This sublease necessarily will be shorter than the lease that the leaseholder has, simply because the mortgagor cannot grant a greater term than they have. In practice, the mortgagee's term will be ten days shorter than that of the original leaseholder. For example,

---

18　Section 11.6 below.

19　Once again, before 1 January 1926, the leaseholder (the tenant) would assign his entire lease to the mortgagee but, once again, this is not now possible (section 86 of the LPA 1925).

if the mortgagor has a lease of 100 years, a first mortgage will operate by the grant of a legal lease to the mortgagee of 99 years and 354 days. In turn, this will ensure that the leaseholder can grant second and subsequent legal mortgages of the leasehold property by creating further subleases. These additional subleases will be longer than the first mortgagee's lease (so as to give the second mortgagee a separate interest in the property), but shorter than the mortgagor's own lease. Using the above example, the second mortgagee will be granted a legal lease of 99 years and 355 days. Any attempt to avoid these provisions by providing that the leaseholder's entire term is assigned to the mortgagee will operate only as a sublease for a term shorter than that of the mortgagor.[20]

11.5.2   The charge

The second method of creating a legal mortgage of an unregistered leasehold, and pre-2002 Act registered leaseholds, is to use the 'legal charge by deed' under section 87 of the LPA 1925 and referred to above. This is substantially the same as for freeholds, and is the common form. It is discussed immediately below because, once again, it is the only permissible form of mortgaging registered leasehold titles under the LRA 2002.

11.6   Legal Mortgages of Registered Titles under the Land Registration Act 2002

Although before the entry into force of the LRA 2002, it was possible to create legal mortgages by the long lease method, almost invariably the common form was the legal charge. Now, by virtue of section 23(1) of the LRA 2002, the legal charge is the only permissible method of creating a legal mortgage of a registered freehold or leasehold estate. In fact, section 23(1) contemplates two ways in which a registered title may be 'charged' so as to create a legal mortgage: the first is the usual 'charge by deed expressed to be by way of legal mortgage'; and the second is the less common method of simply charging the land with the payment of money.[21] However, in practice, it makes little difference which version of the charge is used because, under section 51 of the LRA 2002, a charge on the land (the second version) is to take effect as a 'charge by deed by way of legal mortgage'.

As noted above, the charge by deed by way of legal mortgage is the standard and widespread method of mortgaging legal estates. Under section 87 of the LPA 1925, the charge must be made by deed, and it must be expressed to be by way of legal mortgage: that is, it must declare itself to be a 'legal mortgage made by charge'. Technically, the charge[22] does not confer any proprietary interest on the mortgagee (the 'chargee') but section 87 of the LPA 1925 also makes it clear that a chargee obtains 'the same protection, powers and remedies' as if the mortgage had been created by a long lease of 3,000 years in the old way.[23] This means that, for all practical purposes, the legal charge is as

---

20 *Grangeside Properties v. Collingwood Securities Ltd* (1964).

21 Section 23(1)(b) of the LRA 2002; *Cityland and Property (Holdings) Ltd v. Dabrah* (1968).

22 In either version contemplated by section 23 LRA 2002.

23 *Regent Oil Co v. Gregory* (1966).

effective as if a proprietary right had actually been conferred on the mortgagee and charges are treated as such. In fact, the charge is a quick, economical and simple way of mortgaging land and it is no surprise that the LRA 2002 provided that it should be the only method of creating mortgages of registered estates on or after 13 October 2003.

11.7 Registration of Legal Mortgages under the Land Registration Act 2002

After the charge is executed by the mortgagor, it must be substantively registered as a 'registered charge' against the registered title if it is to take effect as a legal mortgage.[24] The registration is done by the mortgagee and the entry will show the mortgagee as the proprietor of the charge. As well as being necessary to actually create the *legal* mortgage, registration ensures that the mortgage qualifies as a 'registered disposition' for the purpose of obtaining priority for the mortgagee over prior rights – except previously registered interests and overriding interests (section 29 of the LRA 2002). Registration also guarantees the mortgage's validity as a charge on the title even if there might have been some problem leading to the execution of the mortgage – *Swift 1st v. Chief Land Registrar* (2015).[25] In the absence of such registration, the mortgagee only has an equitable interest[26] and may lose its right to priority over the land in the event that the mortgagor disposes of the legal title by a registered disposition.[27] This is the natural consequence of the registration system: properly created legal mortgages need registration to ensure their existence and priority as a legal interest,[28] and those that are not properly registered default to an equitable interest.[29]

Of course, in the normal course of events, the mortgagee will ensure that the mortgage is registered and such registration is no more than an administrative act

---

24 Sections 25 and 27 of the LRA 2002.

25 Thus a charge is valid once properly registered even if, for example, the borrower's signature was forged. Of course, there may well be a good claim to rectify the register.

26 Section 27 of the LRA 2002.

27 This might be a registered sale of the land or a properly registered legal mortgage under section 29 of the LRA 2002. See *Halifax plc* v. *Popeck* (2009), in which, in the result, the disputed transaction by the registered proprietor did not amount to a transfer for valuable consideration within section 29 of the LRA 2002, but instead fell within section 28 of the LRA 2002, and thus Halifax's unprotected equitable charge did not lose its priority.

28 See, for example, *Barclays Bank* v. *Zaroovabli* (1997), in which failure to register the mortgage meant that it lost its priority to a subsequently created legal lease of the land. In *Leeds Permanent Building Society* v. *Famini* (1998), the mortgagee was more fortunate in that, although it had failed to register its mortgage, the later lease was itself equitable and so the rule that 'the first in time prevails' became operative and the prior equitable mortgage prevailed. A similar result to *Famini* is found in *Popeck*.

29 If the mortgage is made by deed, and not registered, it becomes an equitable mortgage, but given that it was made 'by deed', the lender may still be able to rely on those remedies available to a lender under a mortgage made by deed – such as the power of sale, *Swift 1st* v. *Colin* (2011). However, the now equitable mortgage remains vulnerable to a later registered disposition of the registered title as explained above.

for institutional lenders.[30] The Land Registry is developing a Digital Mortgage Service that will allow conveyancers to complete, sign and deliver a charge to the Land Registry electronically. This is not full e-conveyancing as the Registry itself would still make the entry on the register rather than this be done directly by the lender electronically. Note, however, at present registered charges can be discharged – that is removed from the register after the loan is fully repaid – directly by the lender using the Land Registry's Electronic Discharge (ED) service without any involvement of the Registry.[31]

11.8   Equitable Mortgages

The above sections have discussed the creation of mortgages where the borrower owns a legal estate in the land and mortgages it in return for a loan. The result is a legal mortgage. By way of contrast, it is perfectly possible to create equitable mortgages of land and these may arise in a variety of circumstances. In simple terms, a mortgage may be 'equitable' either because the borrower originally has only an equitable interest in the land or because the borrower has a legal interest and the mortgage is not executed with the formality required by statute for the creation of a 'legal' interest.

11.8.1   Mortgages of equitable interests

It may well be that the potential mortgagor only has an equitable interest in the land, as where they are an equitable owner behind a trust of land,[32] or have only an equitable lease.[33] Necessarily, it follows that any mortgage of that equitable interest will itself be equitable. The mortgagor can mortgage only that which they own. The LPA 1925 and the LRA 2002 have not affected this matter to any great extent and mortgages of equitable interests are still carried into effect by a conveyance of the whole of the mortgagor's equitable interest to the mortgagee. This will, of course, be accompanied by a provision for retransfer of the equitable interest when the loan is repaid (*William Brandt* v. *Dunlop Rubber* (1905)). Importantly, however, given that a mortgage of an equitable interest is achieved through a full transfer to the mortgagee (a 'disposition'), there are still certain formalities to be met. There is no need to use a deed,[34] but because the mortgage will be a 'disposition of a subsisting equitable interest' (i.e. the equitable interest of the

---

30 In *Popeck*, failure to register Halifax's mortgage over the primary land was due either to the incompetence of a solicitor's conveyancing clerk or to his willing participation in the borrower's fraud. In *Swift 1st* v. *Colin*, failure to register arose because the lender did not obtain the consent of a prior mortgagee in time.

31 This is genuine e-conveyancing, computer to computer at the instigation of the lender.

32 For example, *Banker's Trust* v. *Namdar* (1997) and see Chapter 4.

33 A lease of sufficient length to be a good security is likely to have been created with professional advice and thus likely to be legal. Consequently, equitable mortgages of equitable leases will be very rare.

34 However, a deed will often be used so as to import the power of sale for the mortgagee in the event of default by the mortgagor: section 101(1) of the LPA 1925.

mortgagor), it must comply with section 53(1)(c) of the LPA 1925. This requires the mortgage of the equitable interest to be in signed writing, on penalty of voidness.[35]

11.8.2   'Informal' mortgages of legal interests

As we have noted above, a legal mortgage of a freehold or leasehold estate is usually accomplished by the execution of a legal charge by deed that must then be registered. It is perfectly possible, however, for the mortgagor and mortgagee to create a mortgage of a legal interest by 'informal' means: in other words, either by not using a deed or by failing to register the deed that they do use. In the former case, the parties might choose deliberately (but usually unwisely) not to use a deed, and in the second example, registration may be omitted by error, negligence or fraud. However, whatever the reason for failure to comply with the formalities for the creation of a legal mortgage, these 'informal' mortgages can, in appropriate circumstances, take effect as an equitable mortgage of the legal estate.

Where the 'informality' arises because of a failure to register the mortgage as required, the mortgage is equitable by force of statute (section 27 of the LRA 2002).[36] Where no deed has been used at all, the mortgage will be equitable only if it complies with the less stringent requirements for the creation of equitable interests – that is, there must be a written instrument within section 2 of the LP(MP)A 1989. This is because the written instrument is treated as a valid contract for the creation of a mortgage within section 2, which, if specifically enforceable, can take effect as an equitable mortgage under Walsh v. Lonsdale (1882).[37] Of course, if there is no written contract, or such a contract is not specifically enforceable, the mortgage will be void at both law and in equity, unless it can be saved by the doctrine of proprietary estoppel.[38]

11.8.3   Mortgages by deposit of title deeds

Before the LP(MP)A 1989, it was also possible to create an equitable mortgage by depositing the title deeds of the property with the mortgagee. The deposit of the mortgagor's title deeds was treated as both evidence of a contract and 'part-performance' of that

---

35 In Murray v. Guinness (1998), the court appears to have held that the creation of an equitable charge (as distinct from an equitable mortgage proper) did not have to be in writing under section 53(1)(c) of the LPA 1925, because technically no interest in land is actually transferred to the chargee under a charge. However, even if this is accurate, it may well be that an equitable charge will be caught by section 2 of the LPA 1989 as equivalent to a contract for the disposition of an interest in land – a security interest – and will require writing for that reason: see Kinane v. Alimamy Mackie-Conteh (2004).

36 In Cheltenham & Gloucester plc v. Appleyard (2004), the mortgagee was unable to register its mortgage because of difficulties with a prior lender and so was effectively forced to take an equitable mortgage. Note, as Swift 1st v. Colin (2011) makes clear, the equitable mortgagee still enjoys the power of sale because 'a deed' has been used. See also Skelwith Leisure v. Armstrong (2015) where failure to register a transfer of an existing registered mortgage to a new lender rendered the mortgage equitable in the hands of the transferee.

37 For example, Parker v. Housefield (1834).

38 See section 11.8.4 below and then Chapter 10 generally.

contract under the then operative section 40 of the LPA 1925.[39] This was, of course, a very informal but relatively efficient way of creating a mortgage, and the lender was protected because it held the documents of title, so preventing the borrower from further dealing with the land. After 1989, however, contracts for the disposition of any interest in land (including therefore a contract to create a mortgage) must be made by signed writing and this cannot be presumed to exist from the mere fact of the deposit of title deeds. Consequently, although some commentators once argued that the enactment of section 2 of the 1989 Act was not intended to do away with this informal method of creating equitable mortgages, the Court of Appeal in *United Bank of Kuwait* v. *Sahib* (1996) has confirmed that deposit of title deeds is an attempt to create a mortgage by unwritten contract and therefore is void. No such mortgage can be created. This might be thought to be unfortunate in the sense that it makes matters much less convenient for both borrower and lender – especially for short-term loans – but it is consistent with the policy of the 1989 Act to bring more formality to dealings with interests in land. If the mortgage was created by deposit of title deeds before 27 September 1989,[40] it remains a valid equitable mortgage.

11.8.4   Mortgages by estoppel

As we have seen in Chapter 10, proprietary estoppel may operate to give a claimant an interest in land even though the claimant cannot produce the deed or written instrument that is normally required to establish a proprietary right. Moreover, we also know from *Jennings* v. *Rice* (2002) and cases before it, that the court has an equitable jurisdiction to award the remedy that is appropriate to negate the unconscionability that triggered the estoppel – sometimes described as 'the minimum equity to do justice between the parties'.[41] There is no reason why this remedy should not be an equitable mortgage over the defendant's land, even despite the absence of formality. This is unlikely to be the case where the defendant landowner has made some unspecific or vague promise to the claimant,[42] but what if the defendant has done some act that leads the claimant to believe they actually have a mortgage and the claimant acts on that belief?

As we know from *Taylor Fashions* v. *Liverpool Victoria Trustees* (1982), if one person promises an interest in land to another, and that is relied on to their detriment, equity will take account of the promise and give effect to the claim of the promisee. So, if a lender has actually advanced money on the basis of a promise (either given orally or perhaps by conduct), it is possible that the 'mortgage' will be enforced despite the absence of any formality. The difficulty is, of course, that to use estoppel in these circumstances appears to be sidestepping the statutory imposed requirement of formality – after all, the lender will have an action in debt for recovery of the money and why should estoppel be used to create a proprietary claim simply because the parties failed to use the proper formalities? The answer is that estoppel can operate in these circumstances not *simply* because formalities were not used, but because it would be unconscionable in the circumstances

---

39 *Re Wallis* (1974).

40 The date on which the LPA 1989 entered force.

41 *Wormall* v. *Wormall* (2004).

42 Such an assurance might still generate an estoppel, but the award of an equitable mortgage is unlikely.

to deny the mortgage. Thus, in *Kinane* v. *Alimamy Mackie-Conteh* (2005), the Court of Appeal accepted that the claimant had a mortgage by estoppel because he had lent money to the claimant on the faith of an assurance that a valid mortgage would be forthcoming. When that mortgage did not materialise – the written agreement attempted by the parties did not comply with section 2 of the 1989 Act[43] – estoppel stepped in. In particular, the Court of Appeal specifically decided that a failed contract could indeed form the basis of the assurance necessary to support an estoppel. Critically, this was not to be regarded as the avoidance of statutory formalities, because a failed contract could form the assurance necessary to generate an estoppel if there was unconscionability.[44] In the words of the Court, '[t]he cause of action in proprietary estoppel is thus not founded on the unenforceable agreement but on the defendant's conduct which, when viewed in all relevant aspects, is unconscionable'. In this case, then, a mortgage was generated by estoppel because of the unconscionability of the borrower in leading the lender to believe that a valid mortgage did indeed exist.[45] Another example is provided by *Halifax plc* v. *Popeck* (2008), in which Halifax's charge appears to have arisen by estoppel because it lent money on the faith of an assurance by the borrowers that it would be granted a legal mortgage over the whole of the borrower's land. When it transpired that Halifax only had a registered legal charge over a narrow strip of land – because of fraud perpetrated by the borrowers – it was awarded an equitable mortgage over the entire property because of estoppel. In the result, this equitable mortgage prevailed over the other claimants to the proceeds of sale of the land.

11.8.5   Equitable charges

Finally, mention must also be made of the equitable charge, a completely informal way of securing a loan over property. This requires no special form of words, only an intention to charge property with a debt.[46] Such a method is extremely precarious for lenders, and is not often used deliberately for either commercial or residential mortgages. There is some doubt as to what type of formality is required for such a mortgage. *Murray* v. *Guinness* (1998) suggests that, because such a charge does not technically involve a disposition of an interest in land, it need not comply with section 53(1)(c) of the LPA 1925. However, whether this means that no written formalities are required at all has been questioned – without any conclusive answer – in *Kinane* v. *Alimamy Mackie-Conteh* (2005), in which Arden LJ ponders whether such a charge might nevertheless fall within section 2 of the LPA 1989 and thus require a written instrument under this statute.

---

43 It was signed by the mortgagor, but not by the mortgagee.

44 Thus the court was able to distinguish the House of Lords' decision in *Actionstrength Ltd* v. *International Glass Engineering SpA* (2003). See also *Ghazaani* v. *Rowshan* (2015) – estoppel perfecting a full transfer of land despite no written contract.

45 If the mortgagee had made a general claim based on the estoppel, rather than a specific claim that there was an equitable mortgage, the court might have ordered the borrower to grant a formal mortgage by deed to the lender. Thus, the estoppel would have been crystallised by the grant of a legal mortgage.

46 *National Provincial and Union Bank of England* v. *Charnley* (1924).

11.8.6 A problem with equitable mortgages and equitable charges over land

An equitable mortgage suffers from the same vulnerability that affects all equitable rights in land: that is, the equitable mortgagee could lose his priority over the land because of a subsequent sale of the mortgaged estate, either by a deed in unregistered conveyancing or by a properly registered disposition for valuable consideration within section 29 of the LRA 2002.[47] Therefore, the equitable mortgagee must act to protect his interest.

1   If the equitable mortgage exists over unregistered land, it is registrable as a Class C(iii) land charge under the LCA 1972. If then so registered against the name of the estate owner who granted it (i.e. the mortgagor), it is binding on all subsequent transferees of the land over which the mortgage exists. This means, of course, that the mortgagee will be able to exercise his rights against the land in priority to the new owner. However, if not so registered, the mortgage will be void against any purchaser for valuable consideration of a legal or equitable interest in the land.[48] It will remain valid against someone who does not 'purchase' the land, such as the recipient of a gift, devisee under a will or a squatter.

2   In registered land under the LRA 2002, the equitable mortgagee should seek to protect his mortgage by means of the entry of a Notice against the mortgaged registered title.[49] This will ensure its protection against any later registered disposition for valuable consideration, including a later legal mortgage (sections 29 and 30 of the LRA 2002). Failure to enter a Notice will result in the equitable mortgagee losing priority in favour of a properly registered purchaser of the land (including a later legal mortgagee) unless the equitable mortgagee happens to be able to claim an overriding interest under paragraph 2, Schedule 3 to the Act as being in actual occupation of the land.[50] Although not impossible, this last is unlikely (for example, why would the lender be on the land?) and it is unwise for an equitable mortgagee to rely on being able to claim an overriding interest.

3   In registered land, even an unregistered equitable mortgage will retain priority over a transferee who does not give valuable consideration, such as the recipient of a gift or person who inherits under a will or on intestacy, or against later equitable mortgages – section 28 of the LRA 2002. An example is provided by Halifax v. Popeck (2008), in which the transferee was held not to be a 'purchaser' and thus Halifax's equitable charge retained its priority.

---

47 Before the LP(MP)A 1989, an equitable mortgagee by deposit of title deeds was in practice protected because no other dealings with the legal title could be carried out while the deeds were in the mortgagee's possession.

48 LCA 1972, sections 2 and 4.

49 Given that the mortgage will usually have been granted by the mortgagor deliberately, an Agreed Notice may be used. A restriction may also be entered and this serves to alert the mortgagee to any proposed dealings with the legal title by the mortgagor.

50 For example, where the equitable mortgagee is a family member living in the property who lent money to the registered proprietor.

4   We should also note that the remedies available to an equitable mortgagee differ in some respects from those available to a legal mortgagee – see below.[51] These differences are not so significant as to be critical in most cases, but they should be appreciated. If the equitable mortgage is made by deed, the mortgagee benefits from all the powers implied into a mortgage made by deed under section 101 LPA 1925, even though it be equitable.[52]

11.9   The Rights of the Mortgagor: The Equity of Redemption

The fact that a mortgage is both a contract between lender and borrower and that it is equivalent to the grant of a proprietary right, means that both parties may have rights in contract and rights in property. For example, the lender may sue the borrower for a normal contractual debt and a court of equity is always willing to protect the mortgagor's property rights in the face of unconscionable dealing by the mortgagee. However, one important point should not be forgotten: whatever the contract says, a borrower under a legal mortgage always retains paramount legal title to the estate they are mortgaging. The owner of a legal freehold or leasehold never conveys all that they have to the lender when the mortgage is created.[53]

11.9.1   The contractual right to redeem

As a matter of contract, the mortgagor has a contractual right to redeem (i.e. pay off) the mortgage on the date specified in the mortgage contract. This is the legal date for redemption. Where it is still employed,[54] this is usually six months from the date of execution of the mortgage, although it may be any date specified by the parties, subject to the 'clogs and fetters' rules discussed below.[55] Obviously, it is rare for a mortgagor to redeem on the legal date for redemption: after all, the parties expect the mortgage to endure for some time and for interest to be paid on the unpaid capital debt. In any event, due to the intervention of equity, the mortgagor has the right to redeem the mortgage at any time *after* the legal date for redemption has passed simply by paying the principal debt, interest and costs. This right to redeem beyond the date fixed by the contract is known as the 'equitable right to redeem'. Nevertheless, the relevance of the passing of the contractual date for redemption – whether fixed or determined by reference to the

---

51 Section 11.11.

52 For example, the power of sale, *Swift 1st v. Colin* (2011). Note, in *Skelworth v. Armstrong* (2015) the High Court held that an equitable mortgagee (arising by reason of a failure to register) did not have the power to convey the legal estate to the mortgaged property, despite having the power of sale and having 'owner's powers' under section 24 of the LRA 2002. This is a surprising decision that seems to conflict with *Swift 1st v. Colin*.

53 However, as we shall see, default by the borrower may well result in him losing his paramount legal title if the property is sold.

54 Many modern mortgages no longer employ the device, being content to contract for repayment by instalments whereby one missed instalment makes the borrower liable to repay the entire loan.

55 Section 11.9.3 below.

payment of instalments – is that its passing can trigger the availability of the mortgagee's remedies under the mortgage. As we shall see when considering the remedies of the mortgagee, the actual date on which the monies become owed under the contract is important for setting the limitation period within which the mortgagee can sue on this contract for recovery of the debt.[56]

11.9.2 The equitable right to redeem

At one time, if the mortgagor did not redeem on the legal date for redemption, the property was lost. A few days or even hours late entitled the mortgagee to keep the property even if its value was far greater than the loan secured on it. Obviously, here was great opportunity for abuse and unfairness. In consequence, the court of equity, acting under the maxim 'once a mortgage, always a mortgage', would allow redemption of the mortgage after this date – *Thornborough* v. *Baker* (1675). This became known as the 'equitable right to redeem'. The equitable right to redeem is the epitome of the property lawyer's approach to a mortgage – the mortgage is a security for a loan, not an opportunity for the mortgagee to obtain the mortgagor's property or impose any other burden upon him. It meant, in effect, that payment of principal, interest and costs even after the contractual date for redemption would free the land from the mortgage.

11.9.3 The equity of redemption

The equitable right to redeem the property at any time after the legal date for redemption has passed is certainly one of the most valuable rights that a mortgagor has. If it were otherwise, mortgage lending in England and Wales would be wholly different from that which now exists. In fact, however, the intervention of equity goes further than this because the equitable right to redeem is just part of the wider rights that a mortgagor enjoys under the mortgage. These wider rights are collectively known as 'the equity of redemption'. The equity of redemption represents the sum total of the mortgagor's rights in the land that is subject to the mortgage. In essence, it comprises the residual rights of ownership that the mortgagor has, both in virtue of their paramount legal estate in the land and in the protection that equity affords them.[57] Indeed, the equity of redemption is itself valuable, and is a proprietary right, which may be sold or transferred in the normal way. It represents the mortgagor's right to the property (or its monetary equivalent) when the mortgage is discharged (redeemed) or the property sold, and its existence is the reason why second and third lenders are willing to grant further loans. Fundamentally, a mortgage is not seen as an opportunity for the lender to acquire the mortgagor's property: it is security for a debt. For this reason, a court of equity will intervene to protect the mortgagor and their equity of redemption against encroachment by the mortgagee and will ensure that the mortgage ends when the debt is repaid. This protection manifests itself in various ways.

---

56 *Wilkinson* v. *West Bromwich Building Society* (2004).

57 See, for example, *Re Sir Thomas Spencer Wells* (1933).

11.9.3.1   The rule against irredeemability

It is a general principle that a mortgage cannot be made irredeemable: that is, it is impossible for a mortgage to be so constructed that it is legally impossible to pay back the loan. It is a security for a loan, not a conveyance, and the right to redeem cannot be limited to certain people or certain periods of time (*Re Wells* (1933)). Thus, any provision whereby the mortgagor is said to forfeit his property on the expiry of the legal right to redeem is void, and any undue postponement or limitation on the mortgagor's right to redeem thereafter will not be enforceable (*Jones* v. *Morgan* (2001)). However, this does not mean that the parties' hands are always tied, especially in cases of mortgages negotiated between commercial parties at arm's length. Consequently, a provision postponing the date of redemption may be valid where the mortgage is not otherwise harsh and unconscionable, so long as the right to redeem is not made illusory. In such cases, the mortgagor might be held to his bargain by being compelled to pay all of the interest that would accrue up to the lawfully postponed date of redemption if he wishes to redeem early.[58] For example, a provision in a mortgage of residential property that the borrowers cannot redeem for 20 years unless they pay an additional percentage (say 15 per cent) as a 'redemption fee' is likely to be void as tending towards irredeemability. It might also be caught, and disallowed, under the new regulatory regime found in the Mortgage Credit Directive Order 2015 (MCD), which makes changes to the regulatory regime for mortgages on land with effect from March 2016 (see 11.9.5 below). A similar provision in a mortgage between Powerful Industries plc and MegaBank plc might be permitted and would not be caught by the MCD.

11.9.3.2   The mortgagee and attempts to purchase the mortgaged property

A provision in a mortgage contract that provides that the property shall become the mortgagee's or which gives the mortgagee an option to purchase the property is void. It is not necessary to show in addition that either the mortgage itself or the offending term is unconscionable (*Samuel* v. *Jarrah Timber* (1904)). Such a term is repugnant to the very nature of a mortgage and is offensive to both the legal and equitable right to redeem and is void both at law and in equity (*Jones* v. *Morgan* (2001)). The rationale is thus part contractual (it offends against the essence of a mortgage) and part equitable (that the vulnerable mortgagor should not be forced into a conveyance when he requires only a loan). Importantly, however, it is clear that it is necessary to determine, first, that the transaction really is a mortgage, and, second, that the offending term is part of that mortgage transaction. In *Warnborough Ltd* v. *Garmite Ltd* (2003), the court made it clear that the true nature of the agreement between the parties must be determined by reference to its substance rather than the label given to it. Thus, in that case, what appeared at first to be a mortgage with a provision permitting the mortgagee to purchase the property (which would have been void) was in fact a complex sale and repurchase transaction that did not attract the intervention of the court. Second, an option to purchase the property given to the mortgagee in a *separate and independent transaction* can be valid, provided that it does not in fact form part of the mortgage itself (*Reeve* v. *Lisle* (1902)). A mortgage is a mortgage, but

---

58 Knightsbridge Estates v. Byrne (1940); Fairclough v. Swan Breweries (1912).

separate agreements will be enforced in the normal way. Of course, there may be some doubt as to whether the option to purchase is truly a separate transaction, and its artificial separation from the mortgage is not enough. So, in *Jones* v. *Morgan* (2001), a clause in a document executed in 1997 whereby the lender became entitled to a 50 per cent share of the borrower's land after the borrower had redeemed the mortgage was held void and this was so even though the document was executed some three years later than the mortgage. The 1997 document was treated as a variation of the original mortgage and as part of it, and so the clause was unenforceable as being repugnant to the very nature of a mortgage. Finally, for the sake of clarity, it should be noted that the rule prohibiting the mortgagee from having a right to purchase the land as a term of the mortgage, does not prevent the mortgagee exercising its normal rights over the land in the event of the mortgagor's default on the loan: for example, its power of sale. Purchase by the mortgagee is repugnant to the very nature of the mortgage; sale by the mortgagee in the event of default is the enforcement of the security that they have been given.

11.9.3.3 *Unfettered redemption: collateral advantages*

As a matter of principle, the borrower should be able to redeem the mortgage and have the lender's rights extinguished simply on the payment of the principal debt, interest and costs. There should be no other conditions attached to the right of redemption because a mortgage is merely the security for a loan that ends when its reason – the money – has been repaid. Consequently, courts can strike down 'collateral advantages' made in favour of a lender, as where the mortgage contract stipulates that the borrower should fulfil some other obligation as a condition of the redemption or continuation of the mortgage. An example is where, in addition to repayment of the loan, the borrower promises to buy all of his supplies from the lender, or to give the lender some other preferential treatment. Typical cases would be a brewery/lender requiring a pub landlord/borrower to buy only the brewery's beer, or similar arrangements between oil companies and the owners of petrol stations. At one time, such collateral advantages were uniformly struck down as being a 'clog' or 'fetter' on the equity of redemption (*Bradley* v. *Carrit* (1903)). They were seen as striking at the essence of the mortgage as security for a loan. However, it is now clear that there is no objection to a collateral advantage that ceases when the mortgage is redeemed. This is a matter of contract between the parties, and provided that the terms of the collateral advantage are not unconscionable, or do not in fact restrict the right to redeem,[59] they will be valid.[60] This is a fair outcome given the reality of many commercial mortgage transactions which are more in the nature of a comprehensive tie between borrower and lender than simply about a loan. Indeed, with commercial mortgages made between equal parties at arm's length, *Kreglinger* v. *New Patagonia Meat Co* (1914) suggests that a collateral advantage that *does* continue after redemption (e.g. a continuing obligation to take supplies from the lender even though the mortgage has ended) may be acceptable, so long as the borrower's land returns to them in the same form that it was mortgaged. It seems that such commercial arrangements are acceptable because they

---

59 For example, a contractual clause that provided that the mortgagor had to buy so great an amount of oil before he could redeem that in fact redemption was practically impossible would be void.

60 See the earlier cases of *Santley* v. *Wilde* (1899) and *Biggs* v. *Hoddinot* (1898).

neither restrict the borrower's use of the land as such, nor hinder the redemption of the mortgage. They are truly 'collateral' and, therefore, not objectionable.

It is apparent that this is one area in which the 'contractual' nature of a mortgage may be in conflict with its 'proprietary' nature. As we have been discussing, the extent to which the parties to a mortgage should be able to modify the essential nature of a mortgage and provide additional benefits to the lender is a matter for argument. For example, does it matter if the parties are commercial organisations, and should the same considerations apply to residential mortgages? How far may the parties to a mortgage – especially those with whole armies of legal advisers and accountants – be permitted to change the essential nature of a mortgage from a security for a loan to something outside the realm of property law altogether?

11.9.3.4 *Unconscionable terms, unconscionable use of remedies and unreasonable interest rates*

It is also clear that a court has the power to strike down any term of a mortgage – or indeed the whole mortgage – where it is the result of an unconscionable bargain and irrespective of whether it also amounts to a clog or fetter on the equity of redemption. The basic proposition is that found in the judgment of Browne-Wilkinson J in *Multiservice Bookbinding Ltd* v. *Marden* (1979) to the effect that a term will be unconscionable (and hence unenforceable) where it is in substance objectionable and has been imposed by one party on the other in a morally reprehensible manner.[61] This means, in essence, that there must be some impropriety both in the substantive term and in the conduct of the party imposing the term that, taken together, 'shocks the conscience of the court'. An example is an interest rate at such a high level that it renders the equity of redemption valueless, as explained in *Cityland Properties* v. *Dabrah* (1968).[62] However, in exercising this jurisdiction, the court is not concerned with excusing a mortgagor from the consequences of a bad bargain, especially if they have had the benefit of legal advice. Such a deal is the mortgagor's own affair and a bad bargain, or hard terms, do not necessarily make an unconscionable mortgage. Thus, in *Jones* v. *Morgan* (2001), the mortgagor had the benefit of legal advice and was able to evaluate the options presented to him and so, even though aspects of the mortgage were struck down on other grounds, the mortgage itself was not unconscionable.

It also appears to be the case that a court of equity has an inherent equitable jurisdiction to interfere with a mortgagee's use of its remedies, even if the mortgage itself is not tainted by unconscionability. In the Privy Council case of *Cukurova Finance International* v. *Alfa Telecom* (2013), it was held that there was a residual discretion to interfere with a chargee's exercise of its remedies if the use of those remedies was to achieve a purpose unconnected with the recovery of the debt or was otherwise unconscionable. The power to ensure that remedies are used for a proper purpose in good faith is well established (*Downsview Ltd* v. *First City Corporation Ltd* (1993); *Co-operative Bank* v. *Phillips* (2014)) but the wider jurisdiction to interfere on general grounds of unconscionability has been little used. Indeed, the Privy Council make it clear that this inherent equitable jurisdiction should be exercised very sparingly and was not to be regarded as a 'new' way to

---

61 Confirmed in *Jones* v. *Morgan* (2001).

62 In this case, the interest rate amounted to the equivalent of 57 per cent and was held unconscionable.

interfere with the vast majority of debts secured on property. In fact, *Cukurova* involved a charge over company shares – not land – and being a decision of the Privy Council (on appeal from the British Virgin Islands) is not formally binding. Nevertheless, the advice of the Privy Council makes much reference to mortgage cases (e.g. *Quennell* v. *Maltby* (1979)), and there is no suggestion that the equitable jurisdiction is different in England and Wales from in the British Virgin Islands. It may well be that the exercise of this wider jurisdiction – that is, wider than the established power to interfere when a remedy is used for an improper purpose – is very unlikely in the highly regulated world of mortgages of land, but it remains a weapon in the armoury of the court.

In similar vein, it also seems from *Nash* v. *Paragon Finance* (2001) that a mortgagee – at least a commercial mortgagee – could be under an implied contractual obligation (a 'limited duty') not to set interest rates dishonestly, for an improper purpose, capriciously or arbitrarily and not in a manner that no reasonable mortgage lender would countenance (so-called '*Wednesbury* unreasonableness'). However, with due respect to the Court of Appeal in *Nash*, it is not immediately clear where such a wide principle comes from. A commercial mortgagee is not in any sense a public authority (such as to trigger *Wednesbury* unreasonableness) and the Court gives little authority for the proposition that these implied terms can be imported into the parties' mortgage contract. In *Paragon Finance* v. *Pender* (2005), a later Court of Appeal accepted the *Nash* argument in principle, but noted that it did not prevent a lender, for good commercial reasons, from raising interest rates to such a level that borrowers, or a class of borrowers, might be forced to seek refinancing elsewhere. Consequently, it remains to be seen how far the *Nash* argument can run.

11.9.4   Undue influence

There have been many cases in which a mortgagor has claimed that the mortgage is void (i.e. unenforceable against them in whole or in part) because of undue influence, misrepresentation or duress. In general terms, a mortgage may be struck down on the ground that it was obtained by the undue influence of the mortgagee directly, or by the undue influence of a third party that is attributable to the mortgagee: for example, a husband inducing his wife to sign a mortgage over the jointly owned matrimonial home.[63] In either case, if the plea is successful, the person (joint mortgagor or guarantor of the mortgagor)[64] who is released from the mortgage because of the undue influence might nevertheless be required to repay part of the sums lent if she derived some material benefit from it, but the mortgage itself may be unenforceable.[65] However, the law in this area has undergone several transformations in recent years, not all of which are consistent with each other or earlier authority. Consequently, the following is an attempt to highlight the basic principles of undue influence *after* the House of Lords' decisions in *Barclays Bank* v. *O'Brien* (1992), *CIBC Mortgages plc* v. *Pitt* (1993) and *Royal Bank of Scotland* v. *Etridge* (No. 2) (2001).

---

63 For example, *Castle Phillips Finance* v. *Pinnington* (1995).

64 This is the person who promises the lender to meet the obligations under the mortgage should the mortgagor default.

65 *Allied Irish Bank* v. *Byrne* (1995). In such a circumstance, the mortgagee would lose its proprietary claim to the land in preference to the victim of the undue influence. Such a mortgagee may have to resort to other means of recovery, e.g. suing on the contract, as in *Alliance & Leicester* v. *Slayford* (2001).

A mortgage will be set aside for undue influence in so far as it binds the 'victim' when either there is 'actual undue influence' or 'presumed undue influence'. Actual undue influence arises where the claimant (i.e. the mortgagor or guarantor) proves affirmatively that undue influence has been exerted. This will be established from the facts of the case, ranging from a husband standing over his wife with a shotgun threatening her unless she consents to the mortgage, to a woman threatening to leave her lover unless he signs. The possibilities are endless. However, the influence must be both 'actual' and 'undue'. Persuasion after full explanation of what was involved is not undue, even though the influence may have been actual (in the sense of causative of the consent). Walking, eyes wide open, into a bad bargain, having made an informed choice, is unfortunate, but it is not the result of undue influence.[66] However, as *Steeples* v. *Lea* (1998) illustrates, it is the *consent* of the claimant that must be given freely. So, being aware of the nature of a mortgage, after having received advice as to its effect, does not mean an absence of undue influence if the claimant can prove that she was not making a 'free' choice at the time. As the Court of Appeal emphasised in *Stevens* v. *Leeder* (2005), the critical point is not only that the claimant knew what she was doing, but also why she was doing it, for only then could she genuinely consent. A similar approach is evident in *Burbank Securities* v. *Wong* (2008), in which the victim understood generally that she was borrowing money but had no conception as to the import of a mortgage transaction in the light of the actual undue influence exercised over her. Importantly, if 'actual' undue influence is proved, it is not necessary for the 'victim' to establish that the transaction was to their 'manifest disadvantage', meaning a transaction obviously not to their benefit. It is enough in such cases that the victim was persuaded to enter into a transaction that they would not otherwise have entered into.[67]

By way of contrast, 'presumed undue influence' arises where the relationship between the person who is alleged to have exercised undue influence (e.g. the claimant's spouse or partner) and the victim is one of trust and confidence, so making it likely that unacceptable influence has been exerted. After the House of Lords' decision in *Barclays Bank* v. *O'Brien* (1992), presumed undue influence cases were subdivided into class 2A and class 2B type cases. Class 2A cases were where the relationship between persons was of such a nature that the presumption existed independently of the facts of the case. Typical examples are the relationships of doctor/patient, solicitor/client and parent/child,[68] but do not include the bank/customer and husband/wife relationship. These class 2A cases are rare in mortgage transactions, not least because patients and clients do not normally lend money to doctors or solicitors and rarely go into business with them. On the other hand, class 2B cases of presumed undue influence were where, although the relationship was not one of the 'special' cases, nevertheless the substance of the relationship between the parties was such that one person placed so much confidence in the other that the presumption of undue influence should arise. Clearly, husband/wife or lover/lover could fall within this class, as might employer/employee.[69]

---

66 See the forceful judgment of Scott VC, in the context of presumed undue influence, in *Banco Exterior Internacional* v. *Thomas* (1997) and note also *Bank of Scotland* v. *Bennett* (1998).

67 *Barclays Bank* v. *O'Brien* (1992).

68 For example, *Langton* v. *Langton* (1995).

69 *Steeples* v. *Lea* (1997).

In fact, the difference between class 2A 'presumed' cases and class 2B 'presumed' cases has been explored again by the House of Lords in *Royal Bank of Scotland* v. *Etridge (No. 2)* (1998) and this long and impressive judgment sheds much light on the issue. As is made clear in *Etridge*, if the case is not one of actual undue influence, it is indeed possible that undue influence may be 'presumed'. However, this presumption is properly to be regarded as an evidentiary presumption that simply shifts the burden of proof from the victim to the alleged wrongdoer (the influencer).[70] In other words, for presumed undue influence to exist, it is necessary for the claimant to show a relationship of trust and confidence that, if established, requires the alleged wrongdoer to explain the impugned transaction. So, in *Turkey* v. *Awadh* (2005), there was no presumed undue influence because, although there was a relationship of trust and confidence, the transaction was easily explicable; in *Popowski* v. *Popowski* (2004), the relationship of trust and confidence did not lead to a transaction that was manifestly disadvantageous to the claimant, thus displacing the presumption of undue influence; and in both *De Wind* v. *Wedge* (2008) and *Thompson* v. *Foy* (2009), the impugned transactions were explicable as exactly the sort of transactions family members might enter into, even if they were unwise.[71] In other words, the alleged wrongdoer may dispel any suggestion of undue influence by producing evidence as to the propriety of the transaction, based in part on producing a credible reason for it. Importantly, when viewed in this light, *Etridge* makes it clear that there is no real merit in adopting the *O'Brien* categories of 'class 2A' and 'class 2B' presumed undue influence. There are some relationships, such as parent/child and doctor/patient (the old 'class 2A' cases), which necessarily and irrebuttably establish a relationship of trust and confidence and, if the transaction called for an explanation (i.e. it was 'manifestly disadvantageous'), this shifts the burden of proof to the alleged wrongdoer to explain the transaction. Failure to do so necessarily leads to a finding of undue influence. There are other cases in which the claimant can demonstrate on the evidence that a relationship was one of trust and confidence (the old 'class 2B' cases) and, if the transaction called for an explanation (i.e. it was 'manifestly disadvantageous'), this then shifts the burden of proof to the alleged wrongdoer to explain the transaction.[72]

Consequently, two things are now clear. First, the 'presumption' of undue influence is no more than a tool to explain the shift of the evidentiary burden from the claimant and so 'manifest disadvantage' is necessary to establish liability as it explains why the burden should shift. The 'presumption' is not that undue influence exists, but that it will exist if the wrongdoer cannot explain the transaction (i.e. discharge the burden of proof). Thus, as noted above, manifest disadvantage (meaning a transaction that needs explaining) is not needed in 'actual undue influence' cases, because the claimant has already established undue influence on the facts. Second, the difference between the now defunct class 2A and class 2B cases is simply that, in the former, the fact of trust and confidence could not be disputed by the wrongdoer, whereas in the latter, it could. So, in the second type of case (class 2B), the wrongdoer could adduce evidence to show that no such

---

70 *Turkey* v. *Awadh* (2005).

71 See also *Evans* v. *Lloyd* (2013), where, in a non-mortgage context, the court emphasised that we should not forget that some acts of generosity are entirely explicable by normal family relationships.

72 If there is no 'manifest disadvantage', the burden of proof does not shift and the alleged victim must then adduce evidence of undue influence; *Governor & Co of the Bank of Ireland* v. *Zone* (2012).

relationship existed and hence avoid even having to explain the transaction. In the former case, a disadvantageous transaction always needs an explanation. Although this seems complicated, *Etridge* has made the matter rather straightforward, and certainly more straightforward than was the case under *O'Brien*. In cases of actual undue influence, any transaction (disadvantageous or not) can be attacked if the victim has shown by positive proof that they have been unfairly persuaded to enter a mortgage. In cases of a successful plea of presumed undue influence, only transactions that are 'manifestly disadvantageous' to the victim can be impugned (being transactions that on their face appear not to be for the benefit of the victim), because it is the existence of this disadvantage that, if not explained away, permits the court to infer that undue influence has occurred.

With this matter now clarified by *Etridge*, we must consider the circumstances in which a mortgage actually can be voided as a result of proven actual or presumed undue influence. Of course, in reality, there are few cases in which the mortgagee itself exerts the undue influence over the victim, and the usual scenario (considered below) is that the victim claims, first, that they were unfairly induced (actual or presumed) to enter the mortgage by another person (usually the victim's domestic or business partner who co-owns the property and who is pressing for the mortgage), and, second, that this undue influence taints the mortgagee. According to *O'Brien*, there are two sets of circumstances in which a mortgagee will not be able to enforce the mortgage against the victim, even though the mortgagee itself has not exercised undue influence: first, where the real inducer (the husband/wife, lover, etc.) was acting, in a real sense, as agent of the mortgagee (this is quite unlikely in the majority of cases); or, second, where the mortgagee has actual or constructive notice of the inducer's unfair conduct and has *not* taken steps to ensure that the claimant has been independently advised. Moreover, a mortgagee will be deemed to have notice of the unfair conduct (and therefore risk losing the security unless they have offered independent advice) when the transaction is *prima facie* not to the advantage of the mortgagor, and the transaction itself is of such a kind that there is a substantial risk that undue influence may have been exerted. Such a risk, and therefore notice to the mortgagee, will be present when a person signs a mortgage as guarantor (surety) for the debts of their domestic partner (*O'Brien*), although such a risk may not be present, and therefore no notice to the mortgagee, when a person signs a mortgage as joint mortgagor for a loan made to the mortgagors jointly for their joint benefit (*Pitt*). In the end, however, as explained in *O'Brien*, the existence or absence of such notice very greatly depended on the particular facts and, following *Barclays Bank v. Boulter* (1997), it is clear that the burden is on the mortgagee to prove that it is not tainted by the undue influence (or misrepresentation or duress) of the actual inducer. So, the claimant may raise undue influence as a defence to an action on the mortgage instigated by the mortgagee, and the burden of proof then shifts to the lender.[73]

As expected after *O'Brien* and *Pitt*, there was a wave of claims of 'undue influence' by mortgagors/guarantors/sureties facing repossession of their homes or a demand for payment of monies owed. Unfortunately, a consistent approach did not emerge and two difficulties became apparent. First, if the mortgagee was to avoid being fixed with notice of another person's undue influence (e.g. that of the husband/wife, lover), the mortgagee had to ensure that the mortgagor was 'independently advised'. But did this mean advised independently from their partner (the undue influencer), independently of the

---

73 See, for example, *Burbank Securities v. Wong* (2008).

mortgagee, or both? Some cases suggested that the mortgagee escaped liability by ensuring that the claimant was advised by someone other than its own staff,[74] and conversely did not escape when the adviser was closely linked with the mortgagee (*Allied Irish Bank v. Byrne* (1995)), save only that a mortgagee did not seem to incur liability simply because the same solicitor acted for both wrongdoer and victim.[75] Other cases suggested that such advice must also be given independently from that given to the wrongdoer.[76] Second, given that the mortgagee had to take steps to see that the claimant had been independently advised, what steps were sufficient? Could the mortgagee avoid its potential liability by merely recommending the mortgagor to take independent advice? The decision in *Crédit Lyonnais Bank v. Burch* (1997) (*contra* to the tenor of *Albany Home Loans v. Massey* (1997)) suggested that merely advising the claimant to seek advice might not be sufficient if the claimant did not then seek or receive such advice. So did this mean that the claimant had to be led like a horse to water to a solicitor's office and be 'made' to listen? Again, *Parker-Tweedale v. Dunbar* (1991) and *Midland Bank v. Kidwai* (1995) made it clear that, having received advice, the mortgagee was not tainted by wrongdoing if the claimant then chose to ignore it. So why could a claimant not legitimately choose to ignore the advice to seek advice? Similarly, could the mortgagee avoid liability by relying on a solicitor's certificate (a formal letter) that the claimant had been given advice – even if this was not true? *Banco Exterior Internacional v. Mann* (1995) suggested that reliance could be placed on a solicitor's certificate that independent advice had been given, even if this was not the case. *TSB v. Camfield* (1995) suggested, however, that the mortgagee would not avoid liability if, in fact, no proper advice had been given, even if the mortgagee had been misled by a solicitor's certificate into believing that it had been.[77]

Clearly, this was an unsatisfactory state of affairs and it became apparent that O'Brien had failed in its aim to clarify the law. In fact, there was a litigation industry and the result of O'Brien appeared to be that mortgagors merely had to raise the plea of undue influence to propel the mortgagee into a (usually unsuccessful) attempt to explain why undue influence had not in fact been incurred.[78] Indeed, after O'Brien, there were still many cases going to the Court of Appeal, not all taking a consistent approach to the problem and, in consequence, there was considerable uncertainty among lenders and borrowers alike. It was thus no real surprise when the House of Lords reconsidered the issue in *Royal Bank of Scotland v. Etridge* (and seven other co-joined appeals). In that case, Lord Bingham put the matter succinctly and his words bear repetition and need no elaboration:

> The transactions which give rise to these appeals are commonplace but of great social and economic importance. It is important that a wife (or anyone in a like position)

---

74 *Midland Bank v. Massey* (1995), *Banco Exterior Internacional v. Mann* (1995) and *Scottish Equitable Life v. Virdee* (1998).

75 *Bank of Scotland v. Bennett* (1998).

76 *TSB v. Camfield* (1995).

77 See also *HSBC Bank Plc v. Brown* (2015) where the mortgagee could not rely on the advisor's certificate because the mortgagee had not followed the proper procedure in advising the victim of undue influence to seek advice in the first place.

78 One wonders how many of these O'Brien cases really involved undue influence or were rather the clever tactical deployment of the undue influence plea by mortgagors who saw the O'Brien defence as the way out of an onerous mortgage.

should not charge her interest in the matrimonial home to secure the borrowing of her husband (or anyone in a like position) without fully understanding the nature and effect of the proposed transaction and that the decision is hers, to agree or not to agree. It is important that lenders should feel able to advance money ... on the security of the wife's interest in the matrimonial home in reasonable confidence that, if appropriate procedures have been followed in obtaining the security, it will be enforceable if the need for enforcement arises. The law must afford both parties a measure of protection.... The paramount need in this important field is that these minimum requirements should be clear, simple and practically operable.[79]

This concern, echoed by Lord Nicholls in the leading judgment,[80] led the House of Lords to lay down a set of procedures that, while not being cast in stone, would bring certainty and stability to this sector of the mortgage market. Sometimes known as 'the *Etridge* protocol', these steps (or a tailored version to the same effect) are now followed as a matter of routine by most institutional lenders.

First, for a claim of undue influence to succeed, it is necessary to prove actual or presumed undue influence by the 'wrongdoer' over the claimant. This has been discussed above and the impact of *Etridge* on the law of presumed undue influence should be noted here. In particular, the House of Lords explains the role of 'manifest disadvantage' and how the mortgagee can dispel the presumption of undue influence by producing an explanation for the impugned transaction.

Second, we must determine whether the mortgagee is put on inquiry as to the existence of the undue influence: in other words, assuming no agency,[81] does the lender have notice of the undue influence so as to put its mortgage at risk? In this connection, the first point is that the House of Lords makes it clear that 'notice' does not mean that the lender is in some way being bound by a proprietary right of the claimant. This is not property law 'notice' of some equitable interest; rather, it is a loose description of the idea that the lender can be affected by undue influence in certain circumstances and that, if so affected, it must take steps to prevent its mortgage being tainted.[82] More importantly perhaps, the House then adopts a robust and blunt approach to the question of when such 'notice' exists. Recognising that there are difficulties, and that its approach is 'broad-brush' rather than precisely analytical, the solution is that a lender will always be put on inquiry if a person is standing surety (guarantor) for another's debts,[83] provided that such surety is not offered as a commercial service.[84] This is clear and means that there is always 'notice' when one person is a non-commercial surety for another. This has the great merit of ensuring that lenders do not have to probe the relationship of the

---

79 At paragraph 2.

80 Lord Nicholls noted that couples should not be restricted in using the matrimonial home to raise finance for small businesses or any other purposes and that: '[t]hese businesses comprise about 95 per cent of all businesses in the country, responsible for nearly one-third of all employment. Finance raised by second mortgages on the principal's home is a significant source of capital for the start-up of small businesses.'

81 As noted above, it will be rare for a mortgagee to have formally appointed one borrower to act as its agent in securing the consent of the other.

82 This confirms *Barclays Bank* v. *Boulter* (1997).

83 That is, mortgaging their own property, or share of property, to guarantee a loan that benefits the other party.

84 For example, a bank might stand as guarantor for a fee.

parties in order to assess whether they notice, because it is not the relationship between the parties that triggers the 'notice', but rather the very nature of the transaction irrespective of the relationship. If, however, the loan is made to the parties jointly for their joint purposes (i.e. the claimant is not merely guaranteeing the wrongdoer's borrowing but is also taking a benefit from the mortgage),[85] then the lender is not put on inquiry unless it is aware (or possibly 'ought to be aware') that in reality the money is for the wrongdoer's purposes alone. An example is provided by *Chater* v. *Mortgage Agency Services* (2003), in which a joint loan to mother and son did not, on the facts, put the lender on notice of the undue influence that had occurred. However, as one would expect, the court will examine carefully whether the victim really obtains a benefit from the mortgage or whether the transaction is simply cast that way in order to mask the fact that the real benefit is being taken by the wrongdoer – as in *Burbank Securities* v. *Wong* (2008).

Third, there remains the question of what the mortgagee must do in order to avoid being tainted by the undue influence of which it has notice, for failure to take appropriate steps could result in the loss of its security. It is this aspect of the *Etridge* decision that is of the greatest practical importance. Lenders are not in the business of taking chances so, undue influence or not, they adjusted their lending practices just in case there was the possibility of the transaction being attacked. In fact, it seems that the judgment in *Etridge* is not principally concerned with preventing the occurrence of undue influence over a claimant at all, but rather with identifying what a lender must do to avoid being tainted by it if such influence occurs. Fortunately, the steps that a lender must now take are such that the chances of undue influence occurring will be much reduced, but it is important to appreciate that the primary purpose of these steps is to protect the bank, not to stop the undue influence. Thus, for past cases – that is, mortgages executed prior to the *Etridge* decision – the lender must have taken steps to ensure that the wife understood the risk she was running and should have advised her to seek independent advice. For current cases – that is, mortgages executed post-*Etridge* – the lender must insist that the wife attend a private meeting with the lender at which she is told of the extent of her liability, warned of the risk she is running and urged to take independent legal advice.

The clear import of these decisions is that if the lender follows the practical steps indicated in *Etridge*, the lender will have the security they have bargained for and mortgages will be set aside for undue influence only in a minority of cases – cases where the lender has failed to follow the simple guidelines. First, the lender should check directly with the potentially vulnerable party for the name of the solicitor who is acting for her or him, advising that it will seek written confirmation that advice about the proposed transaction has been given. The potentially vulnerable party should be told that this is because the lender does not intend that he or she should be able to dispute the mortgage later. The potentially vulnerable party should also be told that he or she may (but not must) use a different solicitor from that which his or her partner uses. The lender must await a response from the potentially vulnerable party before it proceeds. Second, the lender should provide the advising solicitor with all of the necessary financial information required for the solicitor to give proper advice: for example, level of total indebtedness of the husband and a copy of the application form. This usually will require the

---

85 See, for example, *Governor and Co of the Bank of Ireland* v. *Zone* (2012), where the claimant had been actively involved in the business funded by the mortgage.

consent of the other proposed mortgagor, failing which the mortgage is unlikely to go ahead and of itself will give a pause for thought as to the wisdom of the mortgage. Third, the lender must inform the solicitor of any concerns it has over the genuineness of the potentially vulnerable party's consent or understanding and, of course, this will vary from case to case and often be non-existent. Fourth, the lender should obtain written confirmation from the solicitor that all of these steps have been complied with and that appropriate advice has been given. If, after taking such steps, the lender is provided with a written certificate from the advising solicitor, the lender will be protected against a claim of undue influence[86] even if it transpires that such influence did in fact occur. Consequently, the lender's mortgage will be secure unless it knew, or ought to have known, of some defect in the advice or some material untruth in the solicitor's certificate of compliance.[87] In this sense, the purpose of the *Etridge* guidelines is to provide a firm base for institutional lending that might also prevent undue influence being practised on the unwary.[88] It is, however, the first of these results that is the avowed aim of the *Etridge* protocol.

In conclusion then we should remember that it is not the lender's responsibility to see that no undue influence has been exerted and nor is it necessary that the lender seeks confirmation from a solicitor that no such influence exists, although the advisor must confirm that advice was given. This is because the solicitor will be acting for the claimant and the lender can expect the solicitor to act properly for his or her client. Consequently, if a solicitor gives inadequate advice, the lender is not affected, provided that the lender does not know (or ought to have known) that no advice was received or that it was inadequate. After all, the claimant can sue the solicitor.[89] In reality, then, the practice of relying on solicitor's certificates will suffice in most cases, unless the lender knows or ought to have known that the claimant was not thereby properly warned of the nature of the transaction or of the risks it posed.[90] In this sense, *National Westminster Bank* v. *Breeds* (2001) is rightly decided as the lender should have known that the advice given to the claimant was defective despite receiving a certificate from the advising solicitor, and in *National Westminster Bank* v. *Amin* (2002), the House of Lords sent a case back for retrial on the basis that the bank might have known that the solicitor had not given appropriate advice (e.g. the bank knew that the mortgagors could not speak English and the solicitor could not speak Urdu) and that it was not clear in any event whether the solicitor was acting for the mortgagors or for the bank when giving advice. A similar result was reached in *HSBC Bank* v. *Brown* (2015) where, despite the existence of a solicitor's certificate, the lender could not enforce the mortgage after undue influence because the lender had failed to inform the surety of the purpose of seeking independent advice and had failed to provide the solicitor with the details of the mortgage sufficient for them to give advice.

---

86 As in *Kapoor* v. *National Westminster Bank* (2010).

87 As in *National Westminster Bank* v. *Amin* (2002).

88 The risk of litigation, therefore, passes to the advising solicitor.

89 *See Padden* v. *Bevon Ashford Solicitors* (2013) where the solicitor's advice was wholly inadequate in the circumstances and they had just followed their 'usual practice'.

90 *Bank of Scotland* v. *Hill* (2002).

Finally, and for the sake of those cases in which, despite *Etridge*, undue influence can be established,[91] we must consider the effect of a successful plea on the mortgagee. For example, is the mortgagee's entire security voided completely (*Camfield; Castle Phillips Finance v. Pinnington* (1995)), or is it voided only to the extent that the undue influence was operative, as where the claimant genuinely agreed to a mortgage of £X, but in fact signed a mortgage for £X + Y?[92] In *Barclays Bank v. Caplan* (1998), the court held that, if a claimant could establish that only part of the mortgage transaction was void for undue influence, that void part could be severed, with the balance of the mortgage remaining valid. This might arise, for example, where the original mortgage was validly consented to, but a 'top-up' sum was secured from the mortgagee only after undue influence. It is submitted that this is, indeed, the correct approach. The purpose of the undue influence principles is to ensure that mortgagors enter mortgages freely; it is not to give them a windfall by voiding an entire mortgage if only part is tainted by undue influence.[93] Another way of apparently achieving the same result is to void the entire mortgage on condition that the claimant gives credit to the mortgagee (i.e. pays them) for any sums advanced that resulted in a benefit to that claimant (*Allied Irish Bank v. Byrne* (1995)). However, although this seems attractive, in fact there is no necessary correlation between the extent of the undue influence and the benefit received by the victim. To put it differently, should the victim be made to account for a benefit they may not have wanted, and which was given in a transaction already held to have been procured by undue influence? Seen in this light, whether the claimant secured a benefit or not is *not* the real issue. A better view might be that either the entire mortgage is void for undue influence or it remains valid in part to the extent of the borrowing to which the claimant really did consent.[94]

11.9.5 Restraint of trade

A mortgage that attempts to tie a mortgagor to a particular company or mortgagee may well fall foul of the contractual rules prohibiting contracts in restraint of trade. Typical examples include brewery mortgagees using the mortgage to tie the pub landlord to the brewery as sole supplier of beer, and oil company mortgagees using the mortgage to tie in the owner of a petrol station.[95] However, once again, the unwillingness of the courts to interfere unduly with contractual relationships must be remembered, and in the same way that the courts have become more relaxed about collateral advantages, so these 'solus' agreements are less likely to be disturbed.

---

91 Which, as noted above, may well involve transactions other than mortgages, because mortgagees learn quickly.

92 Of course, the undue influence may be operative to void the entirety of a charge, or number of charges – see *Burbank Securities v. Wong* (2008).

93 In the same vein, if an initial mortgage is void for undue influence, a replacement mortgage that paid off that mortgage is also void: *Yorkshire Bank v. Tinsley* (2004).

94 This is a property-based approach. A restitutionary analysis would require the victim to account for benefits received, save to the extent that she could claim to have changed her position in reliance on such receipt.

95 See, for example, *Esso Petroleum v. Harpers Garage* (1968).

11.9.6   Regulating mortgages as financial products: Financial Services and Markets Act 2000 – Financial Conduct Authority Mortgage Conduct of Business regime

Previously, a relatively small number of mortgages were governed by the Consumer Credit Act (CCA) 1974 (as amended by the CCA 2006) as regulated credit agreements. These were primarily second mortgages and buy-to-let mortgages offered to consumers. However, most mortgages of land were 'exempt agreements' with the effect that the provisions of the consumer credit regime did not apply. Instead, these were regulated by the Financial Conduct Authority's (FCA) MCOB regime (Mortgage Conduct of Business) under the Financial Services and Markets Act (FSMA) 2000.[96] In addition, previously, some mortgages (but not a first legal mortgage over residential land that was otherwise regulated by the FCA under the FSMA 2000) were subject to a consumer credit test of whether they were the result of an 'unfair relationship' between creditor and debtor.[97] However, with effect from 21 March 2016, all mortgages of land offered to consumers are regulated under the FSMA regime by the FCA. This is the result of the implementation in the UK of the Mortgage Credit Directive, a European-wide drive to harmonise mortgage protection. Those few mortgages that were governed by the CCA regime transferred over to the FCA regime. The FCA regime is considered below.

Mortgages offered to consumers entered into on or after 31 October 2004 will usually fall within the consumer protection regime of the FSMA 2000 as amended. This umbrella statute, which seeks to regulate many aspects of financial services, requires providers of 'regulated mortgage contracts' to ensure that the 'consumer' is treated fairly and is not open to excessive or hidden charges. The detail is found in MCOB rules. It is, essentially, an early warning system that is designed to alert the borrower as to the full extent of their liability in the worst possible case. The provision of mortgage business must thus conform to the good practices of the FSMA 2000, as overseen (since 1 April 2013) by the FCA.[98] It has led primarily to the adoption of pre-mortgage administrative practices by lenders whereby warnings about the nature and extent of liability follow a ritualised pattern. With effect from 21 March 2016, this protection was enhanced by the entry into force of the Mortgage Credit Directive, a European-wide initiative to standardise mortgage protection for consumers.[99] These enhanced arrangements also apply for the first time to second mortgages over land and buy-to-let mortgages, which are taken out of the consumer credit regime noted above. Whether this enhanced regulatory framework will actually ensure that borrowers are treated fairly – or whether borrowers in need of finance will simply carry on regardless – remains to be seen.

11.9.7   Powers of the mortgagor

As well as benefiting from the protective mechanisms outlined above, the mortgagor also has certain powers and rights under the mortgage or by statute. In outline, these are: the

---

96 See below 11.9.7.

97 CCA 2006, sections 19–22.

98 The FCA replaced the Financial Services Agency under the Financial Services Act 2012.

99 Implemented by the Mortgage Credit Directive Order 2015, SI 2015 No. 910.

power to redeem the mortgage, which may be enforced by action in the courts (section 91 of the LPA 1925); the power to lease the property for certain limited purposes and the power to accept surrenders of existing leases (section 99 of the LPA 1925), but not if this is contrary to the terms of the mortgage;[100] the power to claim possession where this is not claimed by the mortgagee (section 98 of the LPA 1925); and the ability to apply for an order for sale of the property under section 91 of the LPA 1925 (*National Westminster Bank v. Hunter* (2011)), even in the teeth of objections by the mortgagee. On this last point, the court's discretion to order sale on an application by the mortgagor is now thought to comprise a power to order sale even if the proceeds of sale will not pay off the mortgage debt – *Palk v. Mortgage Services* (1993)[101] – and possibly even if the mortgagee is seeking possession of the property because of the mortgagor's inability to pay any sums due.[102] Indeed, the right to ask the court for sale under section 91, and to have it granted against the wishes of the mortgagee, is particularly valuable to a mortgagor whose debt is increasing because of his inability to meet interest payments. Sale in such circumstances slows the increase in the debt because the mortgagor remains liable only for outstanding sums after partial redemption. If this jurisdiction exists in the wide form advocated by *Palk*, it will be used sparingly because of the adverse effect on mortgagees and the value of their security.[103]

11.10 The Rights of the Mortgagee under a Legal Mortgage: Remedies for Default

A mortgage is as valuable to a mortgagee as it is to a mortgagor. Obviously, the main benefit is that a rate of interest can be charged for the money lent and an income is generated for the mortgagee on the security of what is, in all but the most severe economic conditions, an asset that is not going to depreciate significantly in value. However, just as the property owner uses the mortgage to liquidate his assets, the mortgagee uses the mortgage to capitalise his income. As is apparent from all that has gone before, the essential characteristic of a mortgage is that it is security for money lent, and the ultimate goal of any mortgagee will be to recover payment of the principal debt, plus interest and related costs. As we shall see, this can be achieved in a number of ways, some of which spring from the nature of a mortgage as a contract, and some of which spring from the fact that the mortgagee has a proprietary interest in the land. In this respect, a lender under a mortgage created by 'a charge by deed expressed to be by way of legal mortgage' – the only way now to create legal mortgages of registered estates – obtains the

---

100 *Leeds Permanent Building Society* v. *Famini* (1998).

101 See also *Lloyds Bank* v. *Polonski* (1999).

102 *Palk*, but see contrary to this view *Cheltenham and Gloucester plc* v. *Krausz* (1997) and *Scottish & Newcastle* v. *Billy Row Working Men's Club* (2000). See also section 11.10.3 below and *State Bank of New South Wales* v. *A Carey Harrison III* (2002).

103 *Cheltenham and Gloucester* v. *Pearn* (1998). See also *National Westminster Bank* v. *Hunter* (2011), which confirms the existence of the jurisdiction, but where Morgan J declined to act on the ground that a sale by the mortgagor personally would upset the arrangements already made for the disposal of the property.

same powers and remedies as if the mortgage actually had involved the grant of a proprietary right to the mortgagee.[104]

The particular remedy employed by the mortgagee will depend on the precise
nature of the default of the mortgagor and the particular requirements of the mortgagee. So, some remedies are more suitable for the recovery of unpaid interest, while
others are more suitable for recovery of the entire loan and the termination of the mortgage, or even the termination of the mortgagor's rights over the property. Moreover,
whereas the mortgagee can never recover more than the principal debt plus interest and
costs,[105] it is clear that the mortgagee's remedies are cumulative and the mortgagee may
deploy them in combination or successively until the debt is repaid. Where one fails,
another might be employed until the mortgagee is successful in recovering in full or all
remedies are exhausted.[106]

11.10.1   An action on the contract for recovery of the debt

It is in the very nature of a mortgage as a contract of loan between the parties that the
mortgagee has an action on the mortgagor's express contractual promise to repay the
money owed. Such a contractual term forms part of every mortgage. In short, the mortgagor will promise to repay the sum due on a certain date plus accrued interest. This is
the legal date of redemption (encapsulating the mortgagor's legal right to redeem), and
as soon as this date has passed, the mortgagee has a personal action on the contract for
repayment of the sum owed, unless the mortgagee has also promised to defer the
remedy pending the payment of instalments.[107] If the mortgagor fails to repay (or fails to
pay a due instalment), the mortgagee can have the personal judgment debt satisfied
in the normal way, including execution against the property of the mortgagor or by
making the mortgagor bankrupt: *Alliance & Leicester* v. *Slayford* (2001). It may seem surprising that the mortgagee has a remedy as soon as the legal date for redemption has passed
(or an instalment is missed), but this flows naturally from the mortgage as a contract,
wherein each party has promised to fulfil certain obligations. Of course, in the normal
course of events, the mortgagee will not sue for the money owed immediately the date
for redemption has passed (or indeed until instalments are significantly in arrears), but
instead will be happy to collect the outstanding interest and continuing repayments.
However, an action on the contract always remains a possibility, and may be used whenever the mortgagee wishes to recover the full amount of the debt, often in conjunction
with other remedies.

It is particularly useful if, after default by the mortgagor, a sale of the mortgaged
property fails to realise enough money to pay off the debt and the mortgagor has sufficient additional assets to meet their mortgage liability. The mortgagee can use this action

---

104 Section 87(1) of the LPA 1925 and *Regent Oil Co* v. *Gregory* (1966). The assumption is that the mortgagee is treated
     as if they had been given a long lease by deed – importantly, this ensures that the right of possession still exists.

105 Or the secured property itself (by foreclosing) where its value is less than the entirety of the debt. Foreclosure is
     rare.

106 For an exceptional example, see *Alliance & Leicester* v. *Slayford* (2001).

107 *Wilkinson* v. *West Bromwich BS* (2004). The date of default is usually the date on which the first instalment is missed
     as this is when the mortgagee's right to receive the money accrues.

to recover any shortfall. Of course, being a personal remedy against the mortgagor (that is, not against the land itself), it may be valueless if the mortgagor is bankrupt.[108] On the other hand, being an action in debt for a specific sum (rather than for damages for breach of contract), the mortgagee is under no duty to mitigate its loss, and, therefore, cannot be compelled to exercise any of its other remedies (*Lloyds Bank* v. *Bryant* (1996)). Moreover, it is clear that, in most cases, the mortgagee has 12 years from the date of default in which to sue the mortgagor for the principal sum owed under the mortgage, rather than the usual six years on a 'normal' contract. This is because the right usually arises under a 'speciality' (i.e. a deed) and so benefits from a longer limitation period than other contractual debts.[109] However, should the mortgagee fail to commence proceedings during this period, the debt will be unrecoverable (*Wilkinson* v. *West Bromwich BS* (2004)), although any acknowledgment of the debt due by the borrower during this time will restart the 12-year period (*Bradford & Bingley plc* v. *Rashid* (2006)). Although most lenders have voluntarily agreed (via the Council of Mortgage Lenders)[110] that they will not enforce a claim to the principal debt beyond six years from the date of default, it remains a valuable weapon and allows a mortgagee to return to a defaulting mortgagor many years after the property has been sold if that sale did not pay off the entire debt. If money is owed, therefore, a mortgage does not end with the disposal of the mortgaged property by the mortgagee under its power of sale.[111]

11.10.2 The power of sale

Another remedy that is designed to recover the whole sum owed, and also thereby to terminate the mortgage if the loan is fully repaid, is the mortgagee's power of sale of the mortgaged property. In most cases, a mortgage will contain an express power of sale, but, if not, a power of sale will be implied into every mortgage made by deed by virtue of section 101(1)(i) of the LPA 1925,[112] unless a contrary intention appears.[113] This means that, subject to any express provision in the mortgage itself, a mortgagee will be able to sell the mortgaged property and use the funds to satisfy the mortgage debt if two conditions are fulfilled. First, the power of sale must have *arisen*. A mortgagee's power of sale will *arise* as soon as the legal (contractual) date for redemption has passed or, in the case of instalment mortgages, usually when one instalment is in arrears (*Twentieth Century Banking* v. *Wilkinson* (1977)). Once again, this reflects the contractual nature of a mortgage and the liability of the mortgagor in debt when the stipulated date for redemption has passed. Second, the power of sale must have become *exercisable*. The mortgagee's power of

---

108 In such a case, the lender would share *pro rata* in the bankrupt's assets along with other unsecured creditors.

109 Sections 8 and 20 of the Limitation Act 1980. The mortgagee has the normal six years to recover any unpaid interest.

110 The representative body to which most institutional lenders belong.

111 If a mortgagee were to 'foreclose' in the proper sense of this word, the mortgage would come to an end and the mortgagee would not be able to sue on the personal covenant – because it would no longer be operative. However, as noted below, foreclosure is rare to the point of extinction and always needs permission of the court.

112 Including an equitable mortgage by deed, *Swift 1st* v. *Colin*.

113 This is why it is good practice to execute equitable mortgages by deed, even though a deed is not required for their validity.

sale becomes *exercisable* when the conditions specified in section 103 of the LPA 1925 are satisfied. These require either that notice requiring payment of the whole of the mortgage money has been served by the mortgagee, and the mortgagor is three months in arrears with such payments since the notice was served, or the interest under the mortgage is in arrears and unpaid for two months after becoming due, or that the mortgagor has breached some provision of the mortgage deed (other than the covenant to pay the sum due), or a relevant provision of the LPA 1925.[114]

11.10.2.1 The consequences of a sale

The point of the above provisions is that they give the mortgagee an effective power of sale of the mortgaged property should the mortgagor be in serious default because of either a breach of the promise to repay the debt with interest or a breach of any other obligation in the mortgage.[115] The consequences of a sale are that the proceeds of sale are applied to meet the mortgage debt and associated liabilities in the order specified in section 105 of the LPA 1925: that is, first, in payment of the costs and charges incurred by the sale; second, in satisfaction of the principal debt, interest and costs, with the aim of discharging the mortgage; and, third, if there is any surplus, to the person entitled under the mortgage, usually being the mortgagor, as in *Halifax Building Society v. Thomas* (1995). The mortgagee does not make a profit from the sale if the land sells for more than the debt.

Necessarily, a successful sale by a priority mortgagee extinguishes the mortgagor's equity of redemption and transfers the land to the *purchaser* free of any claim of the mortgagor. The mortgagee has this right to transfer legal title to the purchaser by the proper exercise of the power of sale – the borrower's legal title is technically overreached[116] – because the mortgagee has the right to the economic value of the land that has been used as security for his loan. If it were otherwise, the mortgage as a *secured* debt would be meaningless. In addition, the purchaser takes the land free of any *subsequent mortgages*: that is, those granted later than the mortgage under which the sale has taken place,[117] but subject to any previous mortgages. All subsequent mortgagees will be entitled to the balance of any money left after discharge of the mortgage under which sale has occurred in the order in which those mortgages were made, but before payment of any balance to the mortgagor. In other words, subsequent mortgagees are 'persons entitled' to the proceeds of sale of the mortgaged property under section 105 of the LPA 1925, as noted above. What this means in practice is that, provided that property values have not fallen too far, and that subsequent mortgagees operated a sensible lending policy, there should be enough money to pay off the debt of the selling mortgagee and the money owed under the later mortgages. For example, if a property worth £100,000 were subject to a first mortgage of £85,000, a second mortgage of £5,000 and a third mortgage of £7,000, a sale at £100,000 by the first mortgagee would enable payment of all three mortgagees plus some balance (if any, after costs) to the mortgagor. Similarly, if the

---

114 For example, the mortgagor may have let the premises without permission, or failed to insure the property.
115 For example, to insure the property.
116 Section 2(1)(iii) of the LPA 1925.
117 Sections 88 and 113 of the LPA 1925.

second mortgagee were to exercise its power of sale, a purchaser would buy the land subject to the first mortgage, probably paying less than £15,000 (£100,000 minus the £85,000 of the first mortgage), and the second and third mortgagees would be paid.

11.10.2.2 *Regulating the power of sale*

It is clear that a sale of the mortgaged property is a calamitous event for the mortgagor. Essentially, it means forced loss of the land – often the home – with only the balance of the purchase price (if any) as a comfort. Not surprisingly, therefore, in addition to the limitations on the circumstances in which a sale by the mortgagee may be undertaken at all, the mortgagee is placed under common law and statutory obligations with respect to the conduct of the sale.

First, if a mortgagee sells the property *before* the power of sale has arisen, the purchaser obtains only the mortgagee's interest, and the mortgagor remains unaffected. It is as if the mortgagee had transferred only the mortgagee's rights to the purchaser. Second, if a mortgagee sells after the power has arisen, but before it has become exercisable, the purchaser takes the land free of the mortgage, save that the mortgagor may be able to set the sale aside if the purchaser had notice of the mortgagee's fault – section 104 of the LPA 1925 and see *Cuckmere Brick Co v. Mutual Finance* (1971).

Third, and most importantly in practice, in cases in which the power of sale has both arisen and become exercisable,[118] the mortgagor must rely on the intervention of equity to protect his position. This intervention is premised once again on the fundamental point that a mortgage is security for a debt and that a mortgagee is entitled to his remedies in such a way that ensures fair payment of the debt and nothing more. In essence, a 'selling mortgagee' is under a duty of care to the mortgagor to obtain the best price reasonably obtainable (*Standard Chartered Bank v. Walker* (1982)). This has a number of different facets. The primary duty is, of course, to get the best price *reasonably* obtainable, so a sale by open public auction, even when prices are low, satisfies this duty (*Cuckmere Brick Co v. Mutual Finance* (1971); *Wilson v. Halifax plc* (2002)). Where this course is not pursued and a number of offers are made for the property, the court will consider the steps the mortgagee took to sell the property and then consider whether, in accepting the offer to contract at a price, this was within an acceptable bracket for the property.[119] However, the mortgagee is not obliged to take those steps that an owner might take in selling the property, so there is no obligation on the mortgagee to pursue planning applications or the grant of leases that might make the property more valuable (*Silven Properties v. Royal Bank of Scotland* (2003)) or to sell certain fixtures separately in the hope of raising more money.[120] Further, there is no liability even if the proper steps to sell are not taken if this does not, in fact, result in a lower price than that which is reasonably obtainable.[121] Neither is the duty owed to any person other than the mortgagor – particularly, it is not

---

118 Of course, this is nearly always the case.

119 *Michael v. Miller* (2004), in which the initial offer was perfectly acceptable, being within the values specified by professional valuers, but the failure to fulfil the duty was caused by the last-minute reduction in the price of some £25,000.

120 *Michael v. Miller* (2004) – no obligation to sell commercially grown lavender plants separately.

121 *Meah v. GE Money Home Finance* (2013).

owed to a person with an equitable interest in the property[122] – and so the mortgagor may agree specifically to a sale by a mortgagee at a price lower than the market price and, in that way, become estopped from relying on any breach of the duty of care.[123] Similarly, the mortgagee is not a trustee of the power of sale – he is exercising it for himself, not for the mortgagor – and therefore his motives in choosing to exercise the power of sale are generally irrelevant, although it would be a breach of duty if *no* part of his motive in selling was to recover the debt (*Meretz Investments* v. *ACP Ltd* (2006); *Co-operative Bank* v. *Phillips* (2014)).

It should not be thought, however, that the general duty to obtain the best price reasonably obtainable is without substance. In particular, the mortgagee may not sell the property to himself or his agent or his employee[124] (*Williams* v. *Wellingborough Council* (1975)) and if a mortgagee sells to a company in which he has an interest, or is even associated with, the burden of proof of establishing that the sale was at the best price reasonably obtainable lies with the mortgagee, and if he cannot discharge it, he is liable.[125] Likewise, the mortgagee fails to discharge this duty if he chooses a method of achieving a sale that is not likely to achieve the best price reasonably obtainable. In *Bishop* v. *Blake* (2006), the mortgagee failed to put the property up for auction and failed to advertise it sufficiently and then sold the property to a tenant of the mortgagor with whom the mortgagee was developing a commercial relationship, leaving the conduct of the sale in the hands of the purchaser's solicitors. The mortgagor was able to recover some £115,000, being the difference between the price actually paid and the best price reasonably obtainable. In general, failure to discharge this duty will result in the award of compensation – being the difference between the price obtained and the true price reasonably obtainable[126] – but if the sale was to a connected person, it may be set aside completely,[127] and may even be set aside against an unconnected purchaser, but only if the purchaser had actual knowledge of the impropriety surrounding the sale at an undervalue.[128]

---

122 *Parker-Tweedale* v. *Dunbar* (1991). But see *Alpstream AG* v. *PK Airfinance* (2013), where it was held that a mortgagee's duties (in respect of an aircraft mortgage) were owed to the residual beneficiary of the proceeds of sale. This would include an equitable owner, but *Parker-Tweedale* was not cited.

123 This appears to be the *ratio* of *Mercantile Credit Co* v. *Clarke* (1997), although it does assume that the mortgagor's agreement to sale at a lower price was not tainted by undue influence or unconscionable action on the part of the mortgagee.

124 In *Halifax* v. *Corbett* (2002), the mortgagee was held liable in damages for sale at an undervalue. In fact, it had been purchased by an employee of the mortgagee acting deceitfully, but this was unknown to the mortgagee.

125 *Mortgage Express* v. *Mardner* (2004); *Bradford & Bingley* v. *Ross* (2005); *Alpstream* v. *PK Airfinance* (2013). If he so desires the property, the mortgagee may apply to the court under section 91 of the LPA 1925 for authority to sell to himself, in which case the propriety of the transaction will be assessed by the court. The fact the borrower also could have applied under section 91, thus taking the sale out of the hands of the mortgagee, and thereby avoiding a wrongful sale, does not reduce the mortgagee's liability for such a wrongful sale, *Alpstream*.

126 *Blake, Corbett* v. *Halifax* (2002); *Alpstream* v. *PK Airfinance* (2013).

127 When the sale is to a connected person, the mortgagee's duty to obtain the best price reasonably obtainable is paramount and any mixed motives may tend to prove that the duty has not been fulfilled, *Alpstream* v. *Airfinance* (2013).

128 *Corbett* v. *Halifax* (2002).

11.10.2.3 *Judicial sales*

Although generally it is the mortgagee who will choose to sell the mortgaged property, a *mortgagor* may apply to the court under section 91 of the LPA 1925 for an order requiring a sale. As noted above, this is particularly beneficial to a mortgagor whose outstanding mortgage is greater than the value of the property because a sale in these circumstances will crystallise the mortgagor's immediate liability.[129] Of course, in such circumstances, the mortgagor will still be liable on their personal contractual promise to repay the whole sum borrowed, although insurance can be obtained for this eventuality.

11.10.2.4 *Sale before possession*

A selling mortgagee will normally seek possession prior to sale.[130] This minimises the risk of the mortgagor sabotaging the sale and usually will lead to a higher price, especially as purchasers tend to want vacant possession. However, it is clear that a mortgagee is not required to take possession before sale because a selling mortgagee has the power to convey the legal estate to the purchaser even if the mortgagor remains in possession.[131] The effect of such a sale is illustrated clearly by *Horsham Properties v. Clarke and Beech* (2009), in which the mortgagee sold the property to Horsham, which became the registered proprietor, and effectively rendered the mortgagors trespassers in their 'own' home. As such, Horsham was entitled to possession of the property as of right as against the mortgagors/trespassers. This had the further unhappy consequence that the mortgagors could not rely on the statutory protection given to mortgagors of dwelling houses when facing an action for possession by a mortgagee (being section 36 of the Administration of Justice Act (AJA) 1970)[132] because such protection is available only when a *mortgagee* seeks a possession order. It is not clear in *Horsham* whether the sale by the mortgagee without first taking possession was undertaken deliberately to sidestep the protection given to mortgagors of dwelling houses, but it certainly had that effect. Further, Briggs J in *Horsham* held that such a manoeuvre did not entail an infringement of the mortgagors' human rights under the ECHR[133] and there appears to have been no suggestion that a mortgagee selling in such circumstances might not have obtained the best price reasonably obtainable.[134] Indeed, such was the alarm caused by this case – given that it highlights an easier path for a mortgagee seeking to realise its security – that there was a proposal in Parliament to amend section 36 of the AJA 1970 but this was withdrawn.[135] Instead, a private members' Bill – the Home Repossession (Protection) Bill – was introduced in February 2009 to remedy the situation,[136] but this was later dropped

---

129 *Mortgage Services Funding* v. *Palk* (1993).

130 This is easy to achieve: see section 11.10.3 below.

131 Section 2(1)(iii) of the LPA 1925; section 101(1)(i) of the LPA 1925.

132 Considered in detail below.

133 As he was bound to do, given *Doherty* v. *Birmingham City Council* (2008).

134 While a selling mortgagee is under no obligation to take steps to improve the value of the property – *Silven Properties* v. *Royal Bank of Scotland* (2004) – have they obtained the best price 'reasonably' obtainable if not selling with the benefit of vacant possession, given that such possession is not difficult to achieve?

135 I am grateful to Gary Webber of Property Law UK (www.propertylawuk.net) for this information.

136 By requiring mortgagees to obtain a possession order from the court in all cases involving dwelling houses.

due to lack of parliamentary time and support. However, as a response to these initiatives – and because of the furore caused by *Beech* – the Ministry of Justice published a Consultation Paper that contained the tentative proposal that the law should be amended so as to provide that a mortgagee of a dwelling house should not be able to exercise its power of sale without either the consent of the borrower or an order of the court. Under these proposals, the court's discretion would be exercisable on the same basis as that found in section 36 of the AJA 1970 in relation to orders for possession.[137] However, at present, nothing has come of these initiatives and it remains the case that exercise by a mortgagee of their power of sale does not, as a matter of law, first require possession to be obtained from the mortgagor.[138]

11.10.3   The right to possession

The most effective way for the mortgagee to realise its security, in the event of default by the mortgagor, is to sell the property in the manner explained above. In most cases, in order for sale to maximise the chances of the mortgagee recovering its loan in full, the mortgagee will want the property to be put on the market with vacant possession: that is, after having ejected the mortgagor from the premises. In practice, therefore, it is still usual for the mortgagee to exercise his right to possession of the mortgaged property before attempting to sell. Moreover, although possession is often a prelude to sale, it can also be used as a method of securing recovery of the outstanding interest on a loan. For example, the mortgagee may take possession of the premises and manage them in such a way so as to generate income that can then be used to satisfy the mortgagor's obligations. Possession, then, does not necessarily mean the end of the mortgage, although realisation of the security through a sale may follow.

The mortgagee's right to possession is *exactly* what it says. By virtue of the way in which legal mortgages are created, the mortgagee is regarded as having an estate in the land and this gives the mortgagee an immediate right to possession the moment the ink is dry on the mortgage.[139] It is important to realise, then, that the mortgagee may take possession of the property at any time, *even if the mortgagor is not in default*, subject only to any provision to the contrary in the mortgage itself or in statute. Of course, in the normal course of events, the mortgagee will not exercise this right, and will be content to allow the mortgagor to remain in possession so long as the terms of the mortgage are observed and agreed payments are made. Indeed, the mortgagee may have contractually promised not to seek possession unless the mortgagor defaults on the repayments or breaches some other obligation but, if such default occurs, possession may then be obtained in virtue of the *right* of the mortgagee, not in virtue of a remedy to be asked for from the court.[140] For this reason, an order of the court is *not* required before a mortgagee may take

---

137 Ministry of Justice, *Mortgages: Power of Sale and Residential Property*, Consultation Paper, 29 December 2009. See also the Mortgage Repossessions (Protection of Tenants etc.) Act 2010, giving limited protection to tenants occupying land likely to be repossessed.

138 The Council of Mortgage Lenders has indicated that its members would normally seek possession before sale, usually by court order, thereby triggering the section 36 AJA 1970 jurisdiction.

139 *Four Maids* v. *Dudley Marshall* (1957); *Ropaigealach* v. *Barclays Bank* (1999).

140 See section 98 of the LPA 1925.

possession, not even of a dwelling house (*Ropaigealach* v. *Barclays Bank* (2000)). A lender may take peaceful possession in virtue of its right, although it may not use or threaten force. In fact, in most cases concerning residential property, a lender will go to court to obtain an order for possession (for which the borrower pays the costs) as this obviates any difficulties that might arise and is a quick and effective process.

11.10.3.1 *The consequences of the mortgagee taking possession*

Although the mortgagee has a right to possession, subject only to self-limitation as expressed in the mortgage contract, it is not always productive to exercise this right. A mortgagee in possession of the mortgaged premises will be called to account strictly for any income generated by their possession (*White* v. *City of London Brewery* (1889)). This means that the mortgagee will be taken to have received not only the actual income generated by their management of the property (which can go towards repayments), but also any income that *should* have been received assuming the property had been managed to the high standard required. Any shortfall between the actual income and the reasonably expected income will have to be made up by the mortgagee, who may find that he actually owes money to the mortgagor if the income that should have been received is greater than the money owed. This is why most commercial mortgagees desist from seeking possession, and why most residential mortgagees seek possession only as a prelude to sale.[141]

11.10.3.2 *Statutory restrictions on the right of possession*

In the residential context, where the mortgage may well have been used to finance the purchase of the property in the first place, it is rare for the mortgagee to seek possession other than as a prelude to sale. The mortgagor will occupy the property unless there is a problem with mortgage repayments and the mortgagee is likely to have contractually bound themselves not to seek possession unless this occurs. Moreover, if a mortgagee[142] brings an action to recover possession of land 'which consists of, or includes, a dwelling house', whether as a prelude to sale or not, the mortgagor may avail themselves of the protection afforded by section 36 of the AJA 1970 (as amended by section 8 of the AJA 1973). Under section 36 (as amended), an application by a mortgagee for possession of a dwelling house may be suspended, adjourned or postponed by the court, in its discretion, if it appears that the mortgagor would be likely to be able to pay within a reasonable period any sums due under the mortgage. Whether a property is a 'dwelling house' for the purpose of section 36 is to be determined by reference to the state of the premises at the time the order for possession was sought, not by reference to their use at the time

---

141 A notable exception was *Mortgage Services Funding* v. *Palk* (1993), in which the mortgagee wished to take possession in order to keep the mortgage alive in the hope that property prices would rise and wipe out some of the escalating debt. In effect, this was the mortgagee gambling at the mortgagor's expense, for while the mortgagee was in possession, the interest would accumulate faster than any reasonably expected income from the property. This explains why the mortgagor was successful in obtaining an order for sale under section 91 of the LPA 1925.

142 But only a mortgagee – see *Horsham Properties* v. *Clarke* (2009), section 11.10.2.4 above.

the mortgage was executed.[143] By virtue of the section 8 amendment,[144] 'any sums due' may be treated only as those instalments that have not been paid by the mortgagor as they fell due and not, as most mortgages provide when one mortgage payment is missed, the whole mortgage debt.[145] Likewise, the statutory relief is available for endowment mortgages, despite the elliptical wording of the statute,[146] although there is some doubt whether the statutory discretion is available if the mortgagor is not actually in default under the mortgage.[147] The statutory discretion is not available once a warrant for possession has been executed: that is, if the mortgagee has actually recovered possession (*Mortgage Agency Services* v. *Ball* (1998)).

It is important to realise the precise limitations and effect of section 36 of the AJA 1970 (as amended), for although it clearly benefits mortgagors in general, in reality it comprises a fairly limited power. First, as noted above, it is available only in respect of dwellings and does not apply to commercial premises. Second, the court's discretion is triggered by an application for *an order* for possession. If the mortgagee, in exercise of its right to possession, takes possession without a court order – as it is perfectly entitled to do – then the court has no jurisdiction to control or suspend the possession (*Ropaigealach* v. *Barclays Bank* (2000)). Third, as noted above, the jurisdiction is available when a mortgagee seeks a possession order, not a purchaser from the mortgagee – *Horsham Properties* v. *Clarke* (2009). Fourth, the mortgagor must be likely to be able to pay any sums due within a reasonable period. While it is clear that a 'reasonable period' in which to repay the arrears might actually be the rest of the mortgage term,[148] the court has no discretion to make an order if there is no prospect of the mortgagor making a reasonable attempt actually to repay the accumulated arrears, let alone meet future repayments.[149] Thus, the court must embark on a fairly detailed analysis of the mortgagor's overall income and outgoings in order to see if even the rescheduled arrears can be paid back alongside future obligations. Of course, an intended sale of the property by the mortgagor is a factor that could justify suspension of a possession order under section 36, as this might mean that the mortgagor is likely to be able to pay *all* monies due within a reasonable period (*National and Provincial Bank* v. *Lloyd* (1996)), but it is clear that there must be firm

---

143 *Royal Bank of Scotland* v. *Miller* (2001).

144 Effectively reversing *Halifax Building Society* v. *Clark* (1973).

145 It is not clear, however, whether additional costs, such as fees, administrative charges and interest on the arrears (as opposed to interest on the capital debt) count as 'any sums due' for the purpose of section 36. If they do, the jurisdiction is less helpful than it might be as the hurdle facing the borrower is higher. In *Santander (UK) Plc* v. *McAtamney* (2013), a case of only persuasive authority in this jurisdiction, the Master determined that the only relevant sum due for the purpose of section 36 was the arrears on the current debt, and not any additional charges.

146 *Bank of Scotland* v. *Grimes* (1985).

147 *Western Bank* v. *Schindler* (1977). Section 36 does not say in terms that it applies only when the mortgagor is in default, so it is arguable that it is applicable whenever the mortgagee seeks possession by court order. However, if the mortgagor is not in default, it will be a rare mortgage that has not curtailed the right to possession in this circumstance.

148 *Middlesbrough Mortgage Corp* v. *Cunningham* (1974); *Cheltenham and Gloucester Building Society* v. *Norgan* (1996). Thus, the arrears effectively may be rescheduled to be repaid alongside future scheduled repayments.

149 *First National Bank* v. *Syed* (1991); *Bristol & West Building Society* v. *Dace* (1998); *Barclays Bank* v. *Alcorn* (2002).

evidence that a sale is likely, not merely that it might occur or that the mortgagor will now take steps to secure a sale. In order to suspend possession because of an impending sale under section 36, the court must be satisfied that the sale will pay off the mortgage in full (*Cheltenham & Gloucester v. Krausz* (1997)) or else the borrower pays a sum into court to cover any possible shortfall (*LBI HF v. Stanford* (2015)). Mortgagees are rightly worried that mortgagors will attempt to use the section 36 jurisdiction to stay in their homes while the debt mounts up, without any real prospect of the payment of arrears or of future installments.

Prior to the important Court of Appeal decision in *Cheltenham & Gloucester Building Society v. Norgan* (1996), the courts had become rigid with their practice relating to a mortgagor's request to suspend or dismiss a possession application under section 36, with the courts generally suspending possession for an 'automatic' two years, so that the mortgagor had to make up the arrears in that time. As noted above, however, section 36 itself lays down no such time limit and *Norgan* establishes that a 'reasonable period' depends on the facts of each case and may even be the whole of the remaining mortgage term. Clearly, the thrust of *Norgan* is that section 36 should be used more effectively to protect mortgagors of residential property, and, to that end, the case established that a court should address a number of issues before deciding whether to exercise its discretion. These considerations are designed to ensure that the particular circumstances of each mortgagor are given due weight. They include consideration of: how much the mortgagor can afford to pay given his other commitments; whether the mortgagor is in temporary difficulty, or whether his problems are more enduring; what the reasons are for the arrears; how much of the original mortgage period is left; the nature of the contractual terms relating to repayment of the capital sum – in particular, whether this is an instalment mortgage; how long the particular mortgagee could reasonably be expected to wait for repayment of the arrears, bearing in mind that the mortgagee could be asked to wait even longer than the original mortgage term; and, finally, how the value of the land relates to the amount borrowed and now owed.

Obviously, these considerations cover virtually all eventualities and the Court of Appeal is essentially advising county courts to take more care to assess individual circumstances rather than adopt an institutional, unthinking approach to its discretion. Even then, however, we must recognise section 36 for what it is. It is an extremely useful response for borrowers in short-term difficulty who are likely to be able to cope after an unexpected disaster or whose fortunes are likely to improve. For these homeowners, a temporary setback will not mean loss of the family home. However, for those borrowers who are simply overcommitted, section 36 offers no comfort. It is a temporary fix for a temporary problem; it does not allow the borrower to escape from an unwise bargain. Indeed, let us not think that mortgagees find section 36 necessarily troublesome: mortgagees do not want possession, or the expense of a sale; they want the mortgage repaid according to its terms. A suspended possession order under section 36 gives the mortgagee all it could ask for: an order for possession, albeit suspended, *and* an order requiring the borrower to repay the arrears and to stick to a schedule for future payments. This might explain why so many section 36 applications are not resisted by mortgagees.

We should also note in this connection that there is some control on a mortgagee's ability to commence possession proceedings in the first place. Where a court order for possession of a dwelling house is sought (but not in respect of other land), a lender should first comply with the procedures established by the Pre-action Protocol for Possession Claims based on Mortgage or Home Purchase Plan Arrears in Respect of

Residential Property.[150] The central thrust of the Protocol is to ensure that lenders follow a uniform, clear and structured approach to dealing with mortgage arrears leading to possession claims of residential properties. It provides a series of steps that are designed both to keep the borrower fully informed of their indebtedness and to ensure that lenders give borrowers every opportunity to avoid repossession by rescheduling the debt, utilising State support or selling the property. The emphasis is on transparent communication between borrower and lender – within defined time limits – and is designed to reduce the circumstances in which a mortgagee is driven to take possession. In fact, where the borrower intends to deal with the debt by selling the property himself, the Protocol provides:

> If a borrower can demonstrate that reasonable steps have been or will be taken to market the property at an appropriate price in accordance with reasonable professional advice, the lender should consider postponing starting a possession claim. The borrower must continue to take all reasonable steps actively to market the property where the lender has agreed to postpone starting a possession claim.[151]

In this respect at least, the Protocol goes a little further in the borrower's favour than section 36 of the AJA 1970, which usually requires the borrower to be able to demonstrate a very real likelihood of a sale before the mortgagee can be kept out of possession.[152] The Protocol is enforced through a Practice Direction issued by the Head of Civil Justice, and non-compliance by a mortgagee can be penalised by case management orders and in costs. Significantly, however, non-compliance does not result in the loss of the right of possession[153] but, that said, most major lenders will adhere to its very modest requirements.[154] Indeed, most responsible lenders will already have a similar mechanism in place as part of their own internal enforcement processes.

Finally, to return to a matter touched on briefly above, it is important to appreciate that a mortgagee does not actually need a court order to secure possession. The mortgagee's ability to possess arises *as of right* by virtue of the interest they have in the land. Possession may then be taken peacefully through self-help without any application to the court. In most cases, of course, a lender will not pursue this option, not least because there is a real risk of committing criminal offences in the act of taking possession if there should be any person lawfully residing on the premises at the time. Moreover, the lender may well want the security that a court order brings and the assurance that the mortgagor is not trying to defeat the mortgage (and hence the right to possession) on other grounds (e.g. undue influence). Importantly, however, as just discussed, if a lender does take possession of a property without a court order, the court then has no power to

---

150　See www.justice.gov.uk/courts/procedure-rules/civil/protocol/prot_mha. See also the Mortgage Repossessions (Protection of Tenants etc.) Act 2010, which came into force on 1 October 2010, and gives a court the power to postpone possession for up to two months where possession of a dwelling house is sought against a landlord who has let the property to an unauthorised tenant.

151　Protocol, paragraph 6.2.

152　Often the real issue in section 36 proceedings is whether the borrower or lender should have charge of the sale; the Protocol clearly favours the former.

153　'This Protocol does not alter the parties' rights and obligations' – paragraph 1.2.

154　Notice that the Protocol talks of what the lender 'should' do, not what it 'must' do.

suspend the possession under section 36 of the AJA 1970. Clearly, this may represent an advantage for a lender, as exemplified by *Ropaigealach* v. *Barclays Bank* (2000), in which the lender took peaceful possession without a court order while the habitually defaulting mortgagor was elsewhere. Although this is perhaps not the first option for an institutional lender operating under the Council of Mortgage Lenders Code of Practice and the FSMA 2000, it is an effective and inexpensive way of realising the security of those mortgagors who appear to have no real intention or ability to repay the debt.[155]

11.10.3.3 *Other possible limitations on the right to possession*

The fact that possession is a right, rather than as a remedy, means that the court only has such powers to keep a determined mortgagee out of possession as are given to it by statute or which arise out of the conscience of equity. Of course, many would argue that this is just as it should be: after all, what use is a security if the creditor cannot realise it easily? Nevertheless, the widespread use of the mortgage not only as a means of raising capital on the security of land but also as a means of buying that land in the first place means that the taking of possession has a disruptive influence on more than simply the finances of the borrower. It can render a family homeless or require them to live apart. Consequently, much attention has been paid, judicially and academically, to assessing whether there are other grounds for keeping a mortgagee out of his right. Most of the possible 'solutions' to this 'problem'[156] are either narrow in scope or arise in very special circumstances. They are outlined below.

1   In *Quennell* v. *Maltby* (1979), Lord Denning suggested that a court of equity could restrain a mortgagee from taking possession whenever there was no justifiable reason for that possession. His view was that possession could be sought only for the genuine realisation of the mortgagee's security. Obviously, this directly contradicts the mortgagee's pure right of possession springing from their status as a deemed holder of estate in the land. Consequently, it is doubtful whether the *dicta* in *Quennell* are correct and they have found little support in subsequent cases.[157]

2   Following on from *Mortgage Services Funding* v. *Palk* (1993) in the Court of Appeal, it appears that a court may suspend a mortgagee's possession application if it concurrently orders sale of the property at the request of the *mortgagor* under section 91 of the LPA 1925. This presents no difficulty if the proceeds of sale would pay off the entire sum owed – anyway, section 36 of the AJA 1970 could have been used to like effect. However, if the sale proceeds would not pay off the whole debt – as in *Palk* itself – section 36 is inapplicable and so the suspension of the mortgagee's possession in *Palk* seems to have derived from the wide discretionary power found in section 91 itself. This is a novel use of section 91, and in *Cheltenham & Gloucester BS* v. *Krausz* (1997), the Court of Appeal appears to have held that there is no power to

---

155 Note also that many borrowers voluntarily surrender possession without any court intervention when they realise they cannot pay the sums due.

156 Not everyone would agree that there is a 'problem'. After all, the existence of an effective and inexpensive means of realising the security might encourage easy and inexpensive lending by mortgagees.

157 Note, however, a similar argument found favour in *Meretz Investments* v. *ACP Ltd* (2006) in relation to a mortgagee exercising its power of sale: section 11.10.2.2 above.

suspend a mortgagee's possession outside of section 36. Yet, *Krausz* does not over-rule *Palk* (itself followed in *Lloyds Bank* v. *Polonski* (1999)) because *Palk* was said to be limited to its 'special facts'. However, criticism of *Palk* made in *Krausz* is not convincing, and while the balance of authority favours the narrow *Krausz* view, the matter is not yet finally determined. Therefore, for the present, if the mortgagor applies for sale under section 91 of the LPA 1925, there may be an opportunity for the court to utilise an ancillary power to suspend a mortgagee's possession order while the sale takes place, whether or not the sale would pay off the entire debt.

3   *Albany Home Loans* v. *Massey* (1997) establishes that a mortgagee cannot be granted possession of land mortgaged by joint mortgagors where, in fact, the mortgage turns out to be binding on only one of them. In that case, the mortgage of the house had been executed by the man and woman jointly and they were in default. However, the mortgage was held void as against the woman on the grounds of undue influence. In consequence, possession of the land could not be ordered, even though the man would remain living on the land with his partner.[158] In other words, if the mortgagee does not have priority for any reason – for example because a co-owner has an overriding interest – then the lender cannot obtain possession, *William & Glyn's Bank* v. *Boland* (1980).

4   There are other statutory restrictions on the mortgagee's right to possession, which arise in very particular circumstances. These concern attempts by the mortgagee to gain possession outside the time limit set by the Limitation Act 1980 (*National Westminster Bank* v. *Ashe* (2008)),[159] possession claims under the Rent Act 1977 and the Housing Acts 1985–96, or possession contrary to the insolvency legislation.

5   The mortgagee is given rights and powers under the mortgage for the purpose of enforcing payment. Consequently, it is an abuse of the process if the mortgagee uses the rights and powers – such as the right to possession – for a purpose other than enforcing payment, *Downsview Ltd* v. *First City Corporation Ltd* (1993). If this is the case, the court can prevent exercise of any right or remedy under its inherent equitable jurisdiction. However, this is not any easy claim to make because the mortgagee may use its rights and powers even if they have no prospect of success, providing that the purpose is to put pressure on the mortgagor to pay. So, in *Co-operative Bank* v. *Phillips* (2014), a lender brought possession proceedings in order to pressurise the borrower (and his family) to repay the loan even though possession and sale had no chance of paying off the debt. This was permissible, if unpleasant, because it was part of the lender's enforcement strategy.

6   It remains to be seen whether a mortgagor can claim that the *mortgagee*'s exercise of the right of possession contravenes the borrower's right to peaceful enjoyment of their property[160] or their right to family life[161] guaranteed by the ECHR, as

---

158 Note, however, that the mortgagee may still apply for a forced sale of the land under section 14 of TOLATA 1996, which, if successful, will result in the land being sold and the innocent mortgagor receiving their equity as a first call on the proceeds of sale – see, for example, *First National Bank* v. *Achampong* (2003).

159 The borrower remained in possession for more than 12 years after the bank's right to possession had arisen. Consequently, the mortgage was extinguished under sections 15 and 17 of the Limitation Act 1980.

160 Protocol 1, Article 1.

161 Article 8.

implemented in the United Kingdom by the Human Rights Act 1998. Such an argument is tenable, but faces difficulties.[162] For example, a mortgagee's claim to possession is in pursuit of their legitimate rights under the mortgage, especially if such possessory rights are a proportionate response to the mortgagor's default. At present, the tenor of decisions in related issues surrounding possession is against the success of the human rights argument,[163] and this view has been strengthened by the decision in *Horsham Properties* v. *Clark*.[164] Of course, the law of human rights is dynamic and *McDonald* v. *McDonald* (2016) does not completely rule out human rights impact in cases between private individuals.[165]

11.10.4   Appointment of a receiver

The ability of a mortgagee to appoint a receiver to manage and administer the mortgaged property is another method by which it can recover the interest owed, and possibly sell the mortgaged property as a 'going concern'.[166] The right to appoint a receiver is often expressly included in the mortgage contract, but, in any event, such a power will be implied into every mortgage by deed (section 101 of the LPA 1925). The implied power becomes exercisable only in those circumstances in which the power of sale becomes exercisable, and it is often an alternative to that remedy (or used in conjunction with it)[167] and the duties of a receiver may generally be regarded as similar to those imposed on a selling mortgagee.[168] The great advantage of the appointment of a receiver is, however, that it avoids the dangers of the mortgagee taking possession of the property themselves. This is because the receiver is deemed to be the agent of the mortgagor, not of the mortgagee[169] with the consequence that any negligence in the administration of the property is not attributable to the mortgagee and neither is the mortgagee liable to account for any income generated (or not generated) by the receiver. However, the receiver owes an equitable duty to the mortgagor (and any person with an interest in the equity of redemption) to manage the property properly and will be liable to pay compensation if they breach this duty – *Medforth* v. *Blake* (2000).

---

162 See *Barca* v. *Mears* (2004) in the context of a sale of family property after bankruptcy.

163 See *Manchester City Council* v. *Pinnock* (No. 2) (2011) and *Hounslow LBC* v. *Powell* (2011), which accept the possibility of a human rights defence in possession proceedings (in a landlord and tenant case) but which also emphasise the importance of enforcing proprietary rights. Given the importance of lending to the domestic economy, the public interest in enforcing a mortgage security usually will outweigh the potential compromise of the borrower's human rights – to say nothing of the fact that the borrower has contracted to use the land as security for a debt.

164 Above section 11.10.2.4.

165 *McDonald* v. *McDonald* involved a private landlord and tenant and the human rights argument was ultimately unsuccessful, but not ruled out as a matter of principle. In *Santander (UK) Plc* v. *McAtamney*, a case in Northern Ireland not binding in England and Wales, it appears to have just been accepted that human rights could be in play in a case between mortgagee and mortgagor.

166 See, for example, the *Billy Row* case (2000).

167 As in *Horsham Properties* v. *Clark* (2009).

168 *Silven Properties* v. *Royal Bank of Scotland* (2003). See, generally, *Medforth* v. *Blake* (2000).

169 *Chatsworth Properties* v. *Effiom* (1971); *Lloyds Bank* v. *Bryant* (1996).

11.10.5   Foreclosure

The remedy of foreclosure was once the most powerful remedy in the armoury of the mortgagee, although it is now used very infrequently and perhaps may never be used again. For all practical purposes, the remedy is redundant and any attempt to utilise it would almost certainly be met by the court ordering sale instead.

Were it to occur, successful foreclosure would extinguish the equity of redemption and result in the transfer of the mortgaged property to the mortgagee, free of any rights of the mortgagor. In other words, the effect of a foreclosure is to vest the mortgagor's estate in the mortgagee and to extinguish the mortgage and its terms (section 88 of the LPA 1925).[170] So, if the property is freehold, the mortgagee will acquire that freehold, and similarly for a leasehold. The mortgagee's right of foreclosure arises as soon as the legal date for redemption is passed, although it is common for the mortgagee to promise not to foreclose without notice, and only in respect of specified breaches of covenant. Essentially, should the need arise, the mortgagee will begin an action in court asking for foreclosure unless the mortgagor repays the mortgage within a specified time. If repayment does not occur, the mortgagee will be given a foreclosure nisi, which, in effect, gives the mortgagor a further period (usually six months) in which to raise the money to pay off the loan. Failing that, the order of foreclosure will be made 'absolute', and the mortgagor's interest in the property will be extinguished. This is usually the end of the matter, save that, in exceptional circumstances, the court may open a foreclosure absolute and allow the mortgagor to redeem the mortgage at a later date. This would be very unlikely if the mortgagee had already sold the property to a purchaser who had no notice of the mortgage (Campbell v. Holyland (1877)).[171]

11.10.5.1   Statutory control of foreclosure

In view of the powerful nature of foreclosure, the court has power, under section 91(2) of the LPA 1925, to order sale in lieu of a foreclosure. If such a sale occurs, the proceeds will be distributed according to section 105 of the LPA 1925 (as above in the context of a mortgagee's power of sale), and this means that the mortgagor will receive surplus funds (if any) after the mortgage is paid off. Obviously, such a solution is desirable from the mortgagor's point of view, especially where the value of the property is greater than the mortgage debt. In fact, the ability of the court to order sale in lieu of foreclosure has meant the disappearance of successful foreclosure actions. After all, it is a remedy that can destroy the mortgagor's entire interest in the property and for that reason alone should be viewed with considerable suspicion.

---

170 The mortgage is extinguished completely, and so the mortgagee may not sue the mortgagor personally for any shortfall debt.

171 In *Cukurova Finance* v. *Alfa Telecom* (2013), the Privy Council held, when considering the enforcement of a security which resulted in the transfer of ownership of property to the creditor, that there was a residual equitable discretion to grant relief from such forfeiture in exceptional cases. This would apply to foreclosure under a mortgage in the unlikely event that it was sought by a mortgagee.

11.10.5.2   *Effect of foreclosure on other mortgagees*

If there were to be a case where a mortgagee foreclosed successfully, this would inevitably have consequences for any other mortgagee who had also lent money to the mortgagor. First, the rights of mortgagees in respect of mortgages that were created *before* the mortgage that triggered the foreclosure are unaffected. Whoever obtains the land after the foreclosure takes it subject to all prior mortgages. Second, the rights of mortgagees in respect of mortgages that were created *after* the mortgage that triggered the foreclosure will be destroyed. This is because the foreclosure would vest the mortgagor's estate in the 'foreclosing mortgagee' free of any subsequent interests. However, the subsequent mortgagees are given an opportunity to redeem any previous mortgages if foreclosure is likely. In effect, they are given the opportunity to take the place of previous mortgagees by paying them off.

11.11   The Rights of a Mortgagee under an Equitable Mortgage

The rights and remedies of a mortgagee under an equitable mortgage or charge are similar to that of a legal mortgagee, although modified, because the mortgagee cannot be regarded as having a legal estate in the land. Briefly, first, the equitable mortgagee or chargee has the right to sue for the money due in the same way as the legal mortgagee. This right is founded in the contract between the parties. Second, where the equitable mortgage is made by deed, the mortgagee has the power of sale,[172] although no power to convey the legal estate to a purchaser. This defect can be overcome by conveyancing devices in appropriate cases.[173] Where the power of sale does not exist, the equitable mortgagee may apply for sale at the court's discretion under section 91(2) of the LPA 1925. Third, an equitable mortgagee under a mortgage created by an equitable lease/sublease probably has the right to possess the property (i.e. as an equitable tenant), or may be given this expressly in the mortgage contract. An equitable chargee does not have a right of possession, as they have no estate in the land, unless possession is specifically given in the mortgage contract. Fourth, the position in respect of the appointment of a receiver is the same as with the power of sale. Finally, an equitable mortgagee has a right of foreclosure in the same way as a legal mortgagee. An equitable chargee has no power to foreclose as they have no estate in the land.

11.12   Chapter Summary

11.12.1   The essential nature of a mortgage

A mortgage is a contract and the mortgagor and mortgagee are free to stipulate whatever terms they wish for repayment of the loan, the rate of interest and so forth. However, a mortgage also generates a proprietary interest in the land for both parties: both mortgagee and mortgagor have (or are treated as having) an estate in the land.

---

172 For example, *Swift 1st v. Colin* (2011).

173 This explains why even equitable mortgages are often made by deed.

11.12.2   The classic definition of a mortgage

A mortgage is security for a loan. A mortgage of land comprises a transfer (conveyance) of a legal or equitable interest in the borrower's land to the mortgagee, with a provision that the mortgagee's interest shall lapse upon repayment of the loan plus interest and costs.

11.12.3   The creation of mortgages

For a legal mortgage, the mortgagor (having a legal estate) may grant a legal mortgage of a registered title by means of a charge by deed expressed to be by way of legal mortgage: sections 23 of the LRA 2002, and sections 85(1) and 87 of the LPA 1925. Legal mortgages of unregistered land may be created by a charge (and usually are) but also by the 'long lease' method. Equitable mortgages may exist when there is a mortgage of an equitable interest, when there is an informal mortgage of a legal interest (i.e. when writing but not a deed is used, or where registration of a deed does not take place), under the rules for equitable charges, and via the operation of proprietary estoppel.

11.12.4   The rights of the mortgagor: the equity of redemption

The mortgagor has a contractual right to redeem the mortgage on the date specified in the mortgage contract. Under the maxim 'once a mortgage, always a mortgage', a court of equity would allow redemption after the legal date for redemption had passed. A mortgagor also enjoys the equity of redemption, which represents the sum total of the mortgagor's rights in the property, including his paramount title out of which the mortgage is granted. The mortgagor's rights within the equity of redemption include: the rule against irredeemability; the invalidity of a mortgagee's option to purchase the property; the insistence on unfettered redemption and the scrutiny of collateral advantages; and the objection to unconscionable terms.

11.12.5   Undue influence

A mortgage (or a severable part of it) may be struck down if it was obtained by the undue influence of the mortgagee or a third party acting on behalf of the mortgagee. Undue influence may be 'actual' or 'presumed'. In cases of actual undue influence, it is not necessary to prove that the mortgage was to the 'manifest disadvantage' of the claimant. In cases of 'presumed' undue influence, it is necessary. In cases in which the mortgagor or guarantor is claiming that they were unfairly induced to enter the mortgage *not* by the mortgagee directly, but by another person, then the mortgagee will not be able to enforce the mortgage if either:

1   the real inducer was acting as agent of the mortgagee (rare); or
2   the mortgagee had actual or constructive notice of the inducer's unfair conduct and had not taken the steps specified in *Royal Bank of Scotland* v. *Etridge* (No. 2) (2001) to ensure that the claimant was independently advised and thereby itself protected.

11.12.6   Restraint of trade

A mortgage that attempts to 'tie' a mortgagor to a particular company or mortgagee may fall foul of the contractual rules prohibiting contracts in restraint of trade.

11.12.7   Regulation of Mortgages

From March 2016, all mortgages of land to consumers are regulated under the FSMA 2000, by the FCA applying the MCOB rules, as enhanced by the Mortgage Credit Directive.

11.12.8   The rights of the mortgagee under a legal mortgage: remedies for default

1   *An action on the contract for recovery of the debt.* The mortgagee may sue specifically for the mortgage debt and need not mitigate his loss by using other remedies.
2   *The power of sale.* If the power of sale has both arisen and become exercisable, the mortgagee may sell the property and apply the proceeds of sale to meet the mortgage debt and associated liabilities according to the provisions of section 105 of the LPA 1925. It is not dependent on the mortgagee first taking possession.
3   *The right to possession.* By virtue of the way in which legal mortgages are created, the mortgagee will have the equivalent of an estate in the land and an immediate right to possession, even if the mortgagor is not in default, subject only to any provision to the contrary in the mortgage itself or in statute. The consequences of taking possession are that the mortgagee will be called to account strictly for any income generated by their possession. If a mortgagee brings an action to recover possession of land 'which consists of or includes a dwelling house', the mortgagor may plead the protection of section 36 of the AJA 1970 (as amended by section 8 of the AJA 1973). Certain other limitations on the mortgagee's right to possession may exist.
4   *Appointment of a receiver.* The right to appoint a receiver is often expressly included in the mortgage and such a power will be implied into every mortgage by deed: section 101 of the LPA 1925. The receiver is deemed to be the agent of the mortgagor, not of the mortgagee, and so the mortgagee can avoid the dangers of taking possession.
5   *Foreclosure.* If successful, foreclosure would extinguish the equity of redemption and result in the transfer of the mortgaged property to the mortgagee, free of any rights of the mortgagor: section 88 of the LPA 1925. The court has power, under section 91(2) of the LPA, to order sale in lieu of a foreclosure and the proceeds will be distributed according to section 105 of the LPA 1925. Foreclosure is effectively redundant as a remedy in modern land law.

11.12.9   The rights of a mortgagee under an equitable mortgage

The rights and remedies of a mortgagee under an equitable mortgage or charge are similar to those of a legal mortgagee, although modified because the equitable mortgagee is not treated as having a legal estate in the land. The equitable mortgagee has the right to sue for the money due on the contract; where the equitable mortgage is made by deed, the mortgagee has the power of sale, although no power to convey the legal estate to a purchaser. Where the power of sale does not exist, the equitable mortgagee may apply for sale at the court's discretion under section 91(2) of the LPA 1925. An equitable mortgagee under a mortgage created by an equitable lease/sublease probably has the right to possess the property or may be given this expressly in the mortgage contract. An equitable chargee does not have a right of possession as he has no estate in the land, unless possession is given specifically in the mortgage contract; the appointment of a receiver is as the power of sale; an equitable mortgagee has a right of foreclosure in the same way as a legal mortgagee. An equitable chargee does not, as he has no estate in the land.

 Further Reading

Bamforth, N, 'Lord Macnaughten's puzzle: The mortgage of real property in English law' [1996] CLP 207.

Capper, D, 'Undue influence and unconscionability' [1998] 114 LQR 479.

Conaglen, M, 'Mortgagee powers rhetoric' [2006] 69 MLR 583.

Dixon, M, 'Combating the mortgagee's right to possession: New hope for the mortgager in chains?' (1998) 18 LS 279.

Dixon, M and **Harpum**, C, 'Fraud, undue influence and mortgages of registered land' [1994] Conv 421.

Haley, M, 'Mortgage default: Possession, relief and judicial discretion' (1997) 16 LS 483

Law Commission, *Land Mortgages*, Report No. 204, London: HMSO, 1991.

O'Neill, C, 'The Mortgage Repossessions (Protection of Tenants etc.) Act 2010: Sufficient protection for tenants?' [2011] Conv 380.

Whitehouse, L, 'The mortgage arrears pre-action protocol: An opportunity lost' [2009] 72 MLR 793.

Cases

Horsham Properties Group Ltd v. *Clark* [2009] Conv 283.

Ropaigealach v. *Barclays Bank* [1999] 3 WLR 17; [1999] CLJ 281.

Now visit the companion website to:

*   test your understanding of the key terms using our Flashcard Glossary;

*   revise and consolidate your knowledge using our Multiple Choice Question testbank.

www.routledge.com/cw/dixon

Chapter 12
Adverse Possession

Introduction

The law of adverse possession is one of the more remarkable features of English law. It is, in effect, a set of rules that offers an opportunity[1] to a mere trespasser actually to acquire a better title to land than the person who 'legally' owns it and to whom it was once formally conveyed with all of the solemnity of a deed or registered disposition. In fact, adverse possession is rooted in the feudal origins of English land law and it is the most obvious modern example of the 'relativity of title' that once lay at the heart of how we conceived of land ownership. Given that in English law no person may own land itself – only an 'estate' in it – it is in theory perfectly possible for someone other than the 'paper' or 'real' owner to gain a better title without any formal transfer of 'ownership'. A person's title to land, including the paper owner's, is, as a matter of theory, only as good as the absence of a person with a better title. Title is thus relative – it is either relatively better or relatively worse than that of another person. However, as we shall see, this explanation of adverse possession is fast becoming out of date. Although it remains the case under the LRA 2002 that a person is still registered with an estate – not with the land itself[2] – registration as proprietor under the 2002 Act is a much more robust guarantee of ownership than anything that has gone before. As we have seen in Chapter 2, there is still room for alteration of the register, and adverse possession of a registered title is not impossible, but registration of a person as proprietor under the LRA 2002 is the closest thing in over 900 years to absolute ownership of land.[3] This has led to a radical overhaul of the law of adverse possession as it applies to registered land and this must be remembered in the ensuing discussion. Similarly, the introduction of a general criminal offence in relation to squatting in a residential building may have an impact on the 'squatter's' ability to claim title as it may result in fewer 'squatters'[4] possessing the land for the requisite period of time.[5] Both of these matters are considered more fully below.

---

1 As we shall see, the LRA 2002 has diminished substantially the chance of a successful claim to adverse possession of a registered title. Just how much of an 'opportunity' now exists remains a matter of debate. By contrast, if the land is unregistered at the time of the adverse possession, the adverse possessor has a good chance of success.

2 Hence the Crown is authorised to grant itself an estate in order to register its own land – it cannot just 'register it'.

3 See, for example, sections 23 and 58 of the LRA 2002. See section 2.5, Chapter 2.

4 There is no legal distinction between 'adverse possessors' and 'squatters', unless we reserve the former term only for those people who have actually acquired, or are intending to acquire, title from the paper owner as opposed to mere transient trespassers. 'Squatters' and 'squatting' are often used in a derogative sense and conjure up an image that is not a true reflection of the usual people who succeed in claims of adverse possession: see, for example, the successful claimants in *Pye v. Graham*.

5 Squatting in a residential building was made a criminal offence with effect from 1 September 2012 under section 144 of the Legal Aid, Sentencing and Punishment of Offenders Act 2012. There is also an older offence under section 7 of the Criminal Law Act 1977 for a trespasser to fail to leave residential premises when requested by a 'displaced residential occupier' or 'an individual who is a protected intending occupier'. The Land Registry's *Landnet* publication, No. 32, October 2012, contains a helpful summary of the impact of the criminal offence and some of the text is used in this chapter with due gratitude to the Land Registry.

The fact that the common law should have developed a set of principles that might operate to deprive a 'paper' owner of his title to land is not a surprise.[6] Historically, the common law always has been more concerned with the development of remedies for concrete situations rather than the formulation of abstract rights, and what appears to be a lack of regard for the 'rights' of the paper owner is actually a reflection of a practical concern about how (and when) landowners can take action against those compromising use of their own land. So, even allowing for the radical approach of the LRA 2002, the doctrine of adverse possession can be justified on substantive grounds. In terms of the legal process, adverse possession is an expression of a policy that denies legal assistance to those who sleep on their rights, as well as ensuring that there is an end to disputes concerning ownership of land.[7] Similarly, land is a finite and scarce resource, and the principles of adverse possession can help to ensure its full economic and/or social utilisation, as in *Hounslow v. Minchinton* (1997), in which the adverse possessor brought neglected land back into use. All this said, however, it would be a mistake to accept unquestioningly the relevance of adverse possession in our modern system of land law. This is especially so in the context of land of registered title where registration of the 'paper owner' in an open, public register, with a title guaranteed by the State, suggests that we should be very slow to accept that an interloper might acquire that ownership by mere possession of the land. Indeed, there is a point of principle here, and in so far as adverse possession had developed as a response to difficulties of proving title to land (e.g. where deeds were lost or no good 'root of title' could be shown), compulsory and widespread registration of title has removed much of its *raison d'être*. If being registered as proprietor of an estate in the land is supposed to be a guarantee of the validity of that title to the whole world (subject only to the limited power to alter the register under the LRA 2002), should the registered owner *ever* be susceptible to the claim of a mere trespasser?[8] Finally, we should not ignore the public perception that 'squatters' are to be equated with 'land thieves', getting something for nothing. Even if this is a false comparison, it has proved influential politically and helped persuade Parliament to introduce the general criminal offence of squatting in a residential building referred to above.

On the whole, this reassessment of the role of adverse possession has proved persuasive, at least in respect of land of registered title and registered title comprises over 85 per cent of all titles. The new scheme of the LRA 2002 has been in force for nearly 15 years and successful new claims to adverse possession of registered land[9] have slowed to a thin trickle. That said, for so long as there remain substantial areas of unregistered

---

6 Limitation of actions is a feature of all legal systems, whether based on common law or civil law. The impact in relation to land varies considerably between different jurisdictions.

7 *RB Policies v. Butler* (1950).

8 These questions would be even more pertinent should we move to a system of e-conveyancing, because then it would be paramount that the e-register and e-transactions should take priority over the claims of a 'mere' factual possessor. The anticipated introduction of e-conveyancing was part of the motivation for the LRA 2002 and its approach to adverse possession. However, given that e-conveyancing in its original form is now unlikely, does this mean that adverse possession retains its relevance?

9 That is, claims in which the adverse possessor had not completed 12 years' adverse possession of the registered title prior to 13 October 2003 – the date of entry into force of the LRA 2002. See *Baxter v. Mannion*.

land,[10] and while it is at least *possible* to claim title by adverse possession under the LRA 2002, we need to understand the substantive law. In simple terms then, in modern land law, there remains one common set of rules concerning how adverse possession might be established, but two sets of divergent rules about the effect of such a claim on the paper owner's title. The rules common to both registered and unregistered land are the substantive principles developed through case law over many decades and now largely set out by the House of Lords in J A Pye Ltd v. *Graham* (2002). These rules establish when a claim of adverse possession might succeed factually and apply equally to registered and unregistered title. Beyond this, however, there is divergence, with the 'traditional principles' of limitation applying to land of unregistered title and the statutory scheme of the LRA 2002 (with a modification in respect of adverse possession under the LRA 1925) applying to land of registered title. In fact, it is difficult to imagine a contrast so marked as now exists: adverse possession of unregistered land remains a real possibility, but successful[11] adverse possession of registered land is improbable in those cases governed wholly by the LRA 2002.[12] In fact, so safe is land of registered title from new claims of adverse possession, that owners of unregistered estates – particularly local authorities and public bodies with scattered and unmonitored holdings of land – are applying for voluntary first registration of title primarily to bring themselves within the protective umbrella of the new legislation.[13]

12.1 How is Adverse Possession Established? The Rules Common to Unregistered and Registered Land

Whether the claim for adverse possession is made in respect of unregistered land, or registered land subject to the old regime of the LRA 1925[14] or registered land subject to the new regime of the LRA 2002, the crucial question still remains: when will a trespasser be able to establish 'adverse possession' such that he might be able to stake a claim to the land? Or, to put it another way, how is 'adverse possession' established factually? The rules about this are the same, irrespective of whether the land is of unregistered or registered title.[15]

---

10 Although less than 15 per cent of titles are now unregistered, this comprises very roughly some 20 per cent of land by area. In other words, unregistered titles comprise large parcels of land, often owned by the Crown, the Church, ancient institutions and local authorities. Some of these bodies have a reputation for neglecting to care for their land, thus opening up the possibility that their title might be challenged by adverse possessors.

11 'Successful' in the sense of the adverse possessor actually acquiring title.

12 The position in respect of registered land governed by the LRA 1925 – because 'time' was complete before the LRA 2002 came into force – is considered below, but generally favours an adverse possessor.

13 The Land Registry offers a 'one off' fee for such a service irrespective of the number of titles being registered, thus also encouraging greater title registration.

14 Being land where the adverse possession was completed before 13 October 2003, the date of entry into force of the LRA 2002.

15 See Schedule 6, paragraph 11 of the LRA 2002.

The relevant principles are not found in statute, not even in the Limitation Act 1980 itself,[16] but have been developed through case law over generations. As judge-made law, these are flexible, changeable and malleable and have not always been uniform in approach. Apparently inconsistent decisions are not difficult to find. This has the advantage that the substantive principles may respond to changing times, but the disadvantage of making it less easy to predict a court's decision. There is no doubt, for example, that some modern decisions have been 'adverse-possessor-friendly', in the sense that the courts no longer manifest an inbuilt hostility to the adverse possessor (e.g. *Chambers v. Havering LBC* (2011))[17] but the picture is not uniform and sometimes the paper owner is vindicated even though the adverse possessor appears to have a strong claim (*Smith v. Molyneaux* (2016)[18]).[19] It is also clear that the acquisition of title by adverse possession does not violate the human rights of the paper owner – see *Ofulue v. Bossert* (2008), which accepts the authority of the ECHR decision in *Pye v. UK* (2008) on this point.[20]

A claim of adverse possession raises both questions of law and fact and therefore the circumstances which may trigger a claim are virtually unlimited. However, in *J A Pye Ltd v. Graham* (2002), the House of Lords sought to bring stability to the law by providing a framework within which cases could be considered. Together with the earlier decision of the Court of Appeal in *Buckinghamshire CC v. Moran* (1990),[21] the judgment in *Pye* provides a definitive statement of the fundamentals of the modern law, without inhibiting its application to unique circumstances. The reasoning of the House in *Pye* forms the basis of the following discussion. In simple terms, adverse possession may be established by demonstrating the required degree of exclusive physical possession of the land, coupled with an intention to possess the land to the exclusion of all others, including the paper owner. It is, therefore, the conjunction of acts of possession with an *animus possidendi* (intention to possess) that establishes adverse possession.

16　This governs the situation in unregistered land and, prior to the LRA 2002, the position in registered land also. It is considered more fully below.

17　See also *Port of London Authority v. Ashmore* (2009) (adverse possession of a river bed by a floating moored vessel), settled prior to an appeal with the claimant accepting a licence for life.

18　Although a decision of the Privy Council in respect of a claim in the British Virgin Islands, the substantive law of adverse possession is identical to that in England and Wales.

19　Note also that, as a matter of law, adverse possession cannot operate in respect of land over which a public right of way exists, *Bromley LBC v. Morritt* (2000); *R (on the application of Smith) v. Land Registry (Peterborough Office)* (2009).

20　In which the Grand Chamber of the European Court of Human Rights decided that the law of adverse possession under the LRA 1925 (i.e. the law applicable to registered titles before the 2002 Act entered into force) was compatible with the ECHR. Therefore, so must be the law under the LRA 2002, given that it is less generous to adverse possessors. Contrast this with the earlier High Court decision in *Beaulane Properties v. Palmer* (2005), which attacked the essence of the law of adverse possession on human rights grounds. *Beaulane* must now be regarded as unreliable, especially in the light of the decision in *Ofulue*. HM Land Registry no longer relies on *Beaulane* – see Land Registry Practice Guide No. 5, September 2015.

21　In turn, this decision owed much to the earlier remarkable judgment of Slade J in *Powell v. McFarlane* (1977), which was explicitly approved in *Moran* and in *Graham*. According to Lord Browne-Wilkinson in *Graham*, 'the principles set out by Slade J as subsequently approved by the Court of Appeal in *Buckinghamshire County Council v. Moran* [1990] Ch 623 cannot be improved upon'.

12.1.1   An intention to possess

As recognised by Slade J in *Powell* v. *McFarlane* (1979), the requirement that the adverse possessor must 'intend' to possess the land to the exclusion of all others to some extent is artificial. For example, some adverse possessors may appreciate entirely that the land is not theirs and act deliberately to exclude the world; others may believe honestly that the land is theirs already, and so do not for one moment think they are excluding the 'true' owner; others still may have formulated no intention at all, but simply treat the land as their own because it is there. In other words, we are not looking here for 'intention' in the traditional legal sense of *mens rea*, either objectively or subjectively established. What is required is evidence that the adverse possessor, for whatever reason, had an intention to possess the land and put it to his own use, whether or not he also knew that some other person had a claim or right to the land.[22]

Most importantly, as *Pye* makes clear, this means that the 'necessary intent is an intent to possess not to own and an intention to exclude the paper owner only so far as is reasonably possible'.[23] In other words, the claimant is not required to prove that he believed that the land was his, or wanted to acquire it, but, more simply, that he meant to exclude all others if he could.[24] This is crucial. It means that the focus is on the intentions of the claimant, not the landowner. Consequently, it is immaterial whether the claimant was aware that the landowner had an intention to use the land in the future that was consistent with the actual present use by the claimant – the landowner's state of mind is irrelevant. This makes clear, if it were needed, that the 'implied licence' theory (wherein the claimant is automatically deemed to have been given a licence to use the land simply because his actions were not contrary to an intended use by the landowner) is invalid and incorrect in law.[25] It is, in the language of Lord Browne-Wilkinson, 'heretical and wrong'.[26] As much was settled by *Moran*, and although there may be occasions for the *genuine* implication of such licence, Lord Bowne-Wilkinson in *Pye* also makes it clear that this will be exceptional. As he says, if the claimant:

> is aware of a special purpose for which the paper owner uses or intends to use the land and the use made by the adverse possessor does not conflict with that use, that may provide some support for a finding as a question of fact that the adverse possessor had no intention to possess the land in the ordinary sense but only an intention to occupy it until needed by the paper owner. For myself I think there will be few occasions in which such inference could be properly drawn in cases where the true

---

22 See *Mitchell* v. *Watkinson* (2013) for an example of how a possessor may believe that they have a right to land for many reasons, but still succeed through adverse possession.

23 Lord Browne-Wilkinson at [46]. Or, in the words of Slade J in *Powell*: 'an intention, in one's own name and on one's own behalf, to exclude the world at large, including the owner with the paper title if he be not himself the possessor, so far as is reasonably practicable and so far as the processes of the law will allow'.

24 *Williams* v. *Jones* (2003).

25 See also Limitation Act 1980, Schedule 1, paragraph 8(4).

26 A point made again in *Chambers* v. *Havering LBC* (2011), where the Court of Appeal sent the case back for retrial because, among other things, the trial judge appears to have used the implied licence theory to defeat the claim of the possessor.

owner has been physically excluded from the land. But it remains a possible, if improbable, inference in some cases.[27]

Likewise, the intention to possess can still exist even if the claimant would have been prepared to accept permission to use the land had it been offered,[28] or even if he would have quitted possession if required.[29] Such willingness is not inconsistent with a current intention to possess even if any subsequent actual acceptance of permission (e.g. acceptance of a lease or licence) would destroy the intention. A later admission of the landowner's title by the claimant is not inconsistent with the claimant having an intention to possess in the meantime. This was, in fact, the situation in Pye itself, in which Graham had made it clear that he would have accepted a grazing licence from Pye, but as one was not offered, Graham's current intention to possess the land until a licence was offered (and accepted) was enough to secure title by adverse possession. So also, Mitchell v. Watkinson (2013), where the claimants had no right to the land between 1974 and 1990, but accepted a licence in 1990. By then, however, they had possessed the land long enough (1974–90) to gain title through adverse possession. Conversely, however, although the adverse possessor's mere knowledge of another's claim to the land is no bar to adverse possession,[30] a belief that the land is *currently* possessed with the permission of the paper owner is fatal. This was the case in Clowes Developments v. Walters (2005), in which the claimant's belief – even if mistaken – that the land was held under a licence meant that they simply could not have the relevant intention to possess. Awareness that the land belongs to another cannot prevent the existence of a current intention to possess (Blackburn), but an acknowledgment that the land belongs to another will do so.[31] Put simply, you cannot intend to treat the land as within your ultimate control if you believe that you are permitted to be there by the owner.

In this respect, unilateral permission given by the paper owner to the adverse possessor can be fatal for the possessor's claim even if the possessor does not acknowledge or accept the permission. This was the case in BP Properties Ltd v. Buckler (1987) where the paper owner unilaterally and unexpectedly gave permission to a possessor shortly before the expiry of the limitation period. There was no evidence that this had been accepted by the adverse possessor, and certainly it had never been requested. The point seems to be that the giving of such permission, even if unwanted, *can* be evidence that the adverse possessor no longer has an intention to possess, even if there is no evidence that the permission was accepted. This was confirmed by the Privy Council in Smith v. Molyneaux (2016), but it was made clear that this should not be taken as the re-emergence of the 'implied licence' theory referred to above. Rather, the giving of unilateral permission, unacknowledged or unaccepted, can lead to a genuine factual inference that the adverse possessor

---

27 A case that comes close is Stadium Capital v. St. Marylebone Property Company plc (2009) – adverse possession denied. However, there may have been an express licence in this case.

28 So, in Lambeth LBC v. Blackburn (2001), Blackburn was able to demonstrate an intention to possess the land – through clear acts of possession – even though he knew that the land was another's and would have accepted a permission (a lease) if one had been offered.

29 J Alston & Sons Ltd v. BOCM Pauls Ltd (2008).

30 The contrary view in Batt v. Adams (2001) cannot be good law after Graham.

31 BRB (Residuary) v. Cully (2001). See also Smart v. Lambeth LBC (2013), where an occupier failed in his claim because he had by his conduct accepted a licence from the owner.

no longer had the requisite intention. Presumably, therefore, in order to maintain their adverse possession, the possessor should make it clear that such unwanted permission is rejected.

Finally, as also demonstrated by *Pye* and *Mitchell*, if the alleged adverse possessor once occupied the land with the permission of the paper owner, but continued in possession after that permission has ended (e.g. the lease or licence has ended[32]), this can be sufficient to support a claim of adverse possession if the *animus possidendi* is shown as arising when the permissive use ends.

It will be appreciated immediately that this intention to possess might be difficult to prove. There are few difficulties if the alleged adverse possessor has acknowledged the true owner's title in some way[33] or, conversely, if the adverse possessor has placed a sign at the entrance to the land saying 'Keep Out: Private Property'. Most cases are, however, somewhere in between and can be complicated if the paper owner seeks to give permission despite this being unwanted by the paper owner. *Moran* itself establishes that the actions of the adverse possessor in seeking to assert physical possession of the land may give a strong indication as to whether the necessary intention exists. This must be correct, for it is wrong to regard the question of intention and of physical possession as being entirely separate and disconnected. They are part and parcel of the same inquiry: that is, has the claimant established adverse possession? So, enclosing land by a fence may both constitute the act of possession and demonstrate the intention to possess (*Moran*), as might changing locks to a flat (*Blackburn*) or grazing animals within an enclosed field (*Pye*), and the burden of proving the intention may be lighter in cases in which the true owner has, to the knowledge of the adverse possessor, abandoned the land (*Minchinton*). It is clear, then, that unequivocal conduct in relation to acts of possession on the land is the best evidence of an intention to possess. Such acts may need to be more overt where the land was once occupied with permission (*Mitchell*) or where the paper attempts to give permission, but it will be a question of degree in each case.

12.1.2   Physical possession of the land

As well as demonstrating an intention to possess the land, the adverse possessor must also demonstrate the physical taking of possession. Before the decision in *Pye*, much academic and judicial ink had been spilt in trying to determine in what circumstances possession could be deemed to have been taken and when it also was 'adverse' to the paper owner. So, there was much discussion of the apparent differences between *discontinuance* of possession by the paper owner followed by possession by the claimant, and *dispossession* of the paper owner caused by the taking of possession by the claimant. However, in *Pye*, Lord Browne-Wilkinson explained why too much analysis was a bad thing. In his view:

---

32 Or is *treated* as ended, because of the intervention of statute; *Mitchell*, noting the effect of paragraph 5(1) of Schedule 1 to the Limitation Act 1980.

33 For example, in *Archangel* v. *Lambeth LBC* (2000), the alleged adverse possessor had acknowledged the landowner's title in written correspondence. See also *Rehman* v. *Benfield* (2006).

much confusion and complication would be avoided if reference to adverse possession were to be avoided so far as possible.... The question is simply whether the
defendant squatter has dispossessed the paper owner by going into ordinary possession of the land for the requisite period without the consent of the owner.

In other words, we should not seek to over-conceptualise what is 'adverse' and what is
not, but ask ourselves the simple ordinary question: is the claimant in possession of the
land without the permission of the landowner?

Seen in this light, factual possession means a sufficient degree of physical custody
and control for one's own use. It is, in essence, a matter that must depend on the circumstances of each case, the particular nature of the land and the manner in which that
land is commonly used.[34] The ultimate touchstone is, in the words of Slade J in *Powell*,
whether 'the alleged possessor has been dealing with the land in question as an occupying owner might have been expected to deal with it and that no-one else has done so'.
Thus, the taking of possession might reside in a series of events,[35] or some one-off activity that is maintained thereafter.[36] It is not necessary for the paper owner to be aware that
they have lost possession,[37] or for the paper owner to be inconvenienced by the acts of
possession.[38] Moreover, whereas possession will not be presumed lightly from acts that
are equivocal in nature or temporary in purpose, such as growing vegetables or clearing
land to enable one's children to play,[39] even small acts of custody and control might
suffice if the land has been abandoned, is inaccessible by the paper owner or is of such
quality that it does not readily admit of significant possessory acts.[40] Thus, in *Dyer v. Terry*
(2013), basic cultivation was enough in respect of land unusable by anyone else, but
mowing the grass and picking up litter in a different, larger area was not. Neither does it
matter that the acts of possession serve a dual purpose, so long as they give custody and
control to the claimant for his own benefit. For example, in *Minchinton*, the successful
adverse possessor had fenced off part of the claimant's land, apparently to prevent the
escape of her dogs, which she exercised on the land. Not surprisingly, counsel for the
paper owner submitted that the enclosure was not designed to exclude the world, but to
confine the animals, and should not, therefore, be regarded as possession. The court,
however, took the view that it was the effect of the adverse possessor's actions that was

---

34 This essentially is the test put forward in *Powell* and adopted in *Graham*. See *Dyer v. Terry* (2013) for an example of
how fine the line is between 'possession' and 'mere use'. In *Dyer*, the adverse possessor succeeded in respect of
some but not all of the land because their acts of possession varied on the different parcels of land.

35 The last of which crystallises the moment of possession.

36 For example, enclosing the land and gating it.

37 *Powell v. Mcfarlane* (1979).

38 *Treloar v. Nute* (1976).

39 *Techbild v. Chamberlain* (1969). In *Central Midlands Estates v. Leicester Dyers* (2003), the parking of an unlimited number of
cars on the land was not sufficient as it did not amount to enough control of the land to establish factual
possession.

40 See also *Red House Farms v. Catchpole* (1977), where simple acts of possession on marshland, accessible only by boat,
were sufficient and *Williams v. Jones* (2003), where grazing sheep on quarry land was sufficient.

important, not the motive with which they were done.[41] So, if the effect of the fence was to keep out the world as well as keep in the dogs, it amounted to physical possession.[42] So, in answering the question 'has the adverse possessor demonstrated physical possession of the land?', in the sense of acquiring custody and control for his own use, it is the whole of his activity on the land that is relevant. The individual activities may seem equivocal or trivial, but if taken together they paint a picture of a person in control of land, they will amount to possession.

Assuming that the claimant has established both an intention to possess and factual possession of the land under the *Pye* rules, what does this mean? The answer is that it may mean much, particularly in unregistered land, or it may in the end mean very little, particularly in registered land governed by the LRA 2002. Of course, failure to establish the evidential base for adverse possession is fatal, and many cases fall at this hurdle before consideration is ever given to what happens next. In fact, 'what happens next' depends on whether the adverse possession has been evidentially established against an unregistered or registered title and the impact (if any) of human rights principles and criminal offences.

12.1.3 The impact of human rights on adverse possession

The clear and uncompromising approach to possession affirmed by the House of Lords in *Pye*, lays to rest old ghosts and places the substantive principles of adverse possession on a firm footing. But, *Pye* was decided without reference to the impact of the Human Rights Act 1998[43] and the question remained whether the principles of the ECHR could, or should, modify our approach to the law of adverse possession. In this respect, it is important to appreciate that there are always two parties in these disputes, both of whom may be claiming a violation of their human rights, albeit different rights under the Convention: the landowner who may lose their title, and the adverse possessor who may lose their home.

First, in respect of a potential violation of the paper owner's rights, in *Beaulane Properties* v. *Palmer* (2005), Deputy Judge Strauss QC, sitting in the Chancery Division of the High Court, had sought to reintroduce a version of the 'heresy' rejected by the House of Lords in *Pye* as a means of dealing with an *apparent* inconsistency between the principles of adverse possession and human rights guaranteed by the Human Rights Act 1998.[44] It is now clear, following the decision of the Grand Chamber of the European Court of

---

41 Of course, the adverse possessor was still required to demonstrate an intention to possess, although, in *Wreatham* v. *Ross* (2005), the court notes that the search for factual possession is more important than the question of whether the adverse possessor intended to exclude the paper owner.

42 This was confirmed in *Chambers* v. *Havering LBC* (2011), where it was made clear that the impact of fencing was very much dependent on the facts of each case.

43 All the relevant events took place before the Human Rights Act 1998 entered into force and it was accepted that it did not have retrospective effect, a view confirmed by the House of Lords in *Wilson* v. *First County Trust Ltd* (2003).

44 The issue turned on adverse possession under the old law of the LRA 1925. The judge in *Beaulane* took the view that the new mechanisms of the LRA 2002 whereby the registered proprietor did not automatically lose title (in fact, he is very likely to retain it) meant that the LRA 2002 was consistent with human rights principles. This must be correct – see *Pye* v. *UK* (2007).

Human Rights in *Pye* v. *UK* (2007), that the law of adverse possession as it applies in favour of the adverse possessor under the LRA 1925[45] (and therefore also to claims to unregistered title and to title under the LRA 2002)[46] is consistent with human rights law, in particular with Article 1 of Protocol 1 to the Convention. The law of adverse possession is a proportionate and legitimate response to a public interest concerning the need to limit claims in relation to land and a landowner cannot plead (say) a violation of their right to property under Article 1 Protocol 1 of the Convention if they 'lose' their title to an adverse possessor. Consequently, there is no need to 'reinterpret' principles of adverse possession in order to make them human rights compliant (because they already are), and the gloss placed on the *Pye* principle by *Beaulane* is no longer good law. In *Ofulue* v. *Bossert* (2008), the Court of Appeal confirmed that principles of adverse possession are, *as a matter of principle*, compliant with human rights law and thus a landowner could not seek to challenge a loss of title on human rights grounds because of his own particular circumstances unless (perhaps), following *Manchester City Council* v. *Pinnock* (2010) and *Hounslow LBC* v. *Powell* (2011), the particular circumstances of the paper owner are truly extraordinary.[47] The decision of the Supreme Court in *McDonald* v. *McDonald* (2016), recognising that matters of human rights might be relevant in a dispute between private landowners (because a court is a 'public authority') does not change this outcome because, it having been determined in *Pye* v. *UK* that the concept and implementation of adverse possession is human rights compliant, there is no basis to challenge individual applications of the law unless perhaps the circumstances are truly exceptional as recognised in *Pinnock*.

Second, while the above analysis seeks to demonstrate that a *paper owner* whose paper title is extinguished by adverse possession cannot challenge that result on human rights grounds (save perhaps where circumstances are exceptional), there is also a converse question. What happens when an adverse possessor who has not acquired title (because 'time' has not run in his favour or, perhaps, because of the application of the LRA 2002), alleges that his human rights are violated when the landowner recovers possession? The argument might be that the recovery of possession from an adverse possessor without title, even in virtue of the owner's paramount title, contravenes the adverse possessor's right to a 'home' under Article 8 ECHR. This argument was tested in *Malik* v. *Fassenfelt* (2013), where Sir Alan Ward (but not the other members of the Court) noted that Article 8 of the ECHR could apply where squatters had trespassed on to private land and established a home there, but that it would be rare for their removal to be so disproportional as to be contrary to Article 8. In most cases, the granting of possession in favour of the paper owner would be a proportionate way of enforcing the owner's property rights.

---

45   Being where the adverse possession was completed before the entry into force of the LRA 2002. This means, almost certainly, that the law applicable under the LRA 2002 is also human rights compliant.

46   It follows in relation to unregistered land because the public interest in bringing certainty to title by allowing adverse possession is even greater than in registered title; and it follows in relation to land governed by the LRA 2002 because the effect of adverse possession is much less severe on the landowner.

47   Both cases concerned possession applications in a landlord and tenant situation and recognised that the landlord's property rights could, as a matter of principle and in exceptional cases, be subservient to the human rights of the possessor, but not often. It must therefore be conceivable that a paper owner could mount such an argument successfully, even though the context is very different.

Three things are worthy of note. First, it is not controversial – but often a surprise – that a person without any right to the land may nevertheless claim it is their 'home', protected by Article 8. This is long established in the jurisprudence of the ECHR and the UK.[48] Second, Sir Alan Ward accepts that it is possible to enforce human rights obligations in disputes about land between *private* citizens, on the basis that the court itself is a public authority.[49] This recognition of so-called 'horizontal effect' was contentious at the time, albeit that now McDonald recognises it as a possibility, even if a remote one. Previous cases had approached the issue with more hesitation than Sir Alan Ward in Malik, recognising the serious (and unwarranted) impact that widespread reliance on human rights could have in property disputes (e.g. between private landlords and tenants, lending banks and mortgagors). For example, in the earlier case of *Family Housing Association* v. *Donellan* (not cited in Malik), Park J adopted the then conventional view that the Human Rights Act and the ECHR were not relevant in disputes between private citizens.[50] As noted, the Supreme Court in McDonald did not see the matter as a choice between so-called 'horizontal' and 'vertical' effect, but rather whether the substantive law effectively balanced the human rights of the parties to a dispute. This was much more likely in private party disputes where the existing statutory and common law framework for the resolution of disputes would normally be taken to have achieved human rights compliance. Consequently, it would be a rare case where an adverse possession dispute would be determined by reliance on the Human Rights Act. Third, Sir Alan Ward agrees – consistently with Pinnock and McDonald – that, even if Article 8 were engaged, normally the paper owner would be entitled to possession as this would be a proportionate way of enforcing their own property rights. Clearly, there is the possibility that exceptional circumstances might exist which would protect the adverse possessor's home against the re-taking of possession by the paper owner, but usually, as made clear in Pinnock, the proprietary claim of the owner will prevail.

Thus, as things stand – and bearing in mind how swiftly the law of human rights can develop – the normal result is that an adverse possessor who achieves title is unlikely to be disturbed because of a violation of the human rights of the paper owner (their Article 1, Protocol 1 rights are not violated). But, conversely, an adverse possessor who is evicted before they achieve title cannot usually complain that this compromises their human rights to a home (their Article 8 rights).

12.1.4 The impact of criminal offences on claims to adverse possession

It has been noted above that squatting in a residential building was made a criminal offence with effect from 1 September 2012 under section 144 of the Legal Aid, Sentencing and Punishment of Offenders Act 2012. This is not, as commonly believed, the first time that squatting could trigger a criminal offence because under section 7 of the Criminal Law Act 1977 a trespasser commits an offence if they fail to leave residential

---

48 McCann v. UK (2008).

49 See sections 3 and 6, Human Rights Act 1988.

50 Donellan involved an issue under Article 1, Protocol 1 and so was an example of a landowner seeking to use human rights to protect itself against an adverse possessor.

premises when requested by a 'displaced residential occupier' or 'an individual who is a protected intending occupier'.[51]

The merits of the 'criminalisation' of squatting are hotly contested, and there is a debate over the proper scope of the new offence (largely driven by those antagonistic to it), as well as proposals that it should be extended to commercial premises. Importantly, it is not every squatter of any premises who commits an offence. The new offence is not committed by a person who was a licensee or tenant when they entered the premises and 'holds over' when the lease/licence ends, and not all adverse occupations will qualify. Hence, the defendant must be a trespasser in a residential building (so not just land) having entered as a trespasser, they must know or ought to have known they were a trespasser and must live in the building or intend to live there. The offence is not retroactive – in that past squatting per se cannot be an offence – but clearly a person who stays in a residential building after 1 September 2012 may then commit an offence on that day and going forward if the other conditions are met.

While the new offence raises a range of social, economic and public interest questions, the present issue is to consider how the commission of a criminal offence[52] by an adverse possessor affects their assertion to title. In short, can a person build a claim to a title based on what might be an unlawful act?

The Land Registry's original view[53] was that, if the applicant based his 'possession' on acts which would amount to a criminal offence, then the application for title by adverse possession had to be rejected outright. However, this was challenged by a claimant to adverse possession whose application had been rejected by the Land Registry because he appeared to have been committing the new criminal offence. In *Best v. Chief Land Registrar* (2015), the Court of Appeal, confirming the High Court, held that the commission of the criminal offence was not itself a bar to achieving title by adverse possession. The legislation establishing the offence was silent on the matter[54] and it was well established that not all unlawful acts concerning land were fatal to a claim over the land. So, in *Bakewell Management Limited* v. *Brandwood*, the House of Lords had made a distinction between acts that always would be unlawful (and hence could not be the basis of a claim to land) and acts which were unlawful only because the claimant did not have the right he was now claiming.[55] Consequently, if the criminal offence arose only because the claimant did not have a title to the land, trying to get that title through the established law of adverse possession remained possible. In short, the criminalisation of squatting per se does not prevent a squatter who commits the offence from obtaining title by

---

51　A 'displaced residential occupier' is the person who was using the premises as their home immediately before the trespass, and a 'protected intending occupier' is a person designated by a local authority or housing association as the person to occupy, or a purchaser who has just bought the premises and then finds them occupied by a trespasser.

52　The offence will usually be the new offence, although the same considerations apply to the offence under section 7 of the Criminal Law Act 1977.

53　*Landnet* publication, No. 32, October 2012.

54　The reality is that the offence was rushed through Parliament and no one gave any serious thought to the consequences.

55　In *Bakewell*, it was an easement; see Chapter 7.

adverse possession. This will be the case whether the land is registered or unregistered, although because of the LRA 2002 successful claims are much less likely when title is registered.

12.2 Adverse Possession and Unregistered Land

The ability of an adverse possessor to acquire a better title to unregistered land than the paper owner is based on the principle of limitation of actions. In simple terms, 'limitation of actions' expresses the idea that a person must sue for an alleged wrong within a specified period of time from the moment the alleged wrong took place.[56] In the context of adverse possession of unregistered land, this means that a person (i.e. the paper owner of the land) may be 'statute-barred' from bringing a claim against the adverse possessor to recover possession of their land after the period of limitation has passed. Thus, as against the adverse possessor, the paper owner has no means of recovering the land, and so the adverse possessor has 'acquired' a better title to the land. Title is relative. To look at it slightly differently, if an unregistered estate owner sleeps on his rights, those rights will be extinguished in the sense that a court will not enforce them against the person actually in possession of the land. In this sense, therefore, adverse possession operates negatively: it prevents an estate owner from suing on his rights and operates to extinguish his title. Conventionally, this is taken to mean that adverse possession does not actually give a title to the adverse possessor but, by virtue of the doctrine of relativity of title, the person now in actual possession has the best claim to the land, and may thereby become 'owner' of it to all intents and purposes. Importantly, the idea of limitation of actions has no application to land of registered title governed by the LRA 2002[57] where it has been replaced by a statutory mechanism that protects the registered proprietor in all but a limited number of situations.[58]

12.2.1 The limitation period for unregistered land

If the essence of adverse possession of unregistered land is that a paper owner will be prevented from bringing an action to recover land against the person in actual possession of it, it is crucial to know exactly when this 'bar' will come into effect. In other words, how long must an adverse possessor be in adverse possession before the paper owner is statute-barred from bringing an action to recover that possession? How long is the limitation period for unregistered land? It should come as no surprise to learn that the limitation period for actions concerning land depends on the type of claim and the type of paper owner, although there are some general rules.

First, in the great majority of cases, the limitation period will be 12 years from the moment of adverse possession of the unregistered title by the adverse possessor (section

---

56 See currently the Limitation Act 1980.
57 It does apply to registered land where the adverse possession was completed prior to the entry into force of the LRA 2002.
58 See section 12.4 below.

15 of the Limitation Act 1980). This is the normal period of limitation for actions concerning land, although now it has no application to land of registered title governed by the LRA 2002. Second, where the paper owner of the land is a 'sole' charitable corporation (such as a bishop), the period of limitation is 30 years from the moment of adverse possession (Schedule 1, paragraph 10 of the Limitation Act 1980). Third, where the paper owner of the land is the Crown, the period of limitation is 30 years from the moment of adverse possession (Schedule 1, paragraph 11 of the Limitation Act 1980). Fourth, if land is owned by someone for life, with remainder in fee simple to another person (for example, to A for life, remainder in fee simple to B), then the limitation period is either adverse possession of six years from the date at which the interest in remainder falls into possession (i.e. the death of the life tenant), if 12 years or more already have been completed against the life tenant; or adverse possession of 12 years from the time the life tenant was dispossessed, whichever is the longer (section 15 of the Limitation Act 1980). So, assuming land is held by A for life, remainder to B, adverse possession of 12 years or more against A will extinguish A's interest, and a further six years will be necessary on the death of A also to extinguish B's interest. Fifth, if the current paper owner is a tenant of the land under a lease, the period of limitation against the tenant is 12 years.[59] Expiry of the period will, therefore, extinguish the tenant's title in respect of a claim by the adverse possessor. Importantly, however, extinguishment of the tenant's title has no immediate effect on the title of the reversioner (i.e. usually the freehold landlord), simply because, until the end of the lease, the landlord has no right to possess the land at all. Therefore, time does not begin to run against the landlord until the original term of the lease expires (or, possibly, is otherwise brought to an end: see section 12.2.3.3 below). When the original term of the lease expires, and assuming 12 years' adverse possession against the tenant, the landlord will have a further 12 years to recover the land (section 15 and Schedule 1, paragraph 4 of the Limitation Act 1980). Obviously, it is crucial for the application of these rules to know when the lease has ended. This will usually be the expiry of the stated term (or statutory extension thereof), although for an oral periodic tenancy, this is treated as the end of the first period or on receipt of the last payment of rent, whichever is the later.[60] Note, however, that, although the normal rule is that the landlord's right of action against the adverse possessor arises when the original term of the lease ends, there is an exception to this. So, if the lease itself gives the tenant an option to renew the lease when it expires, the adverse possessor who has evicted that tenant also may rely on the right to renew to defeat the landlord's claim to possession.[61] The landlord (and any person claiming through the landlord, such as an alleged new tenant) must, it seems, wait until the period given under the right to renew also has expired. The rationale is that, as the landlord could not have evicted the original tenant (because of the option to renew), so the landlord cannot evict the adverse possessor who has displaced that tenant. This is logical, but it does give the lie to the idea that the adverse possessor's title is completely unconnected to that of the paper owner he dispossesses (i.e. the former tenant).

---

59 Chung Ping Kwan v. Lam Island Development Co (1996).

60 Paragraphs 5(1), Schedule 1 to the Limitation Act 1980. This was critical in *Mitchell v. Watkinson* (2013) for it determined when the period of adverse possession started, and hence was complete.

61 Chung v. Lam (1996).

Whatever period of limitation is applicable, it starts to run against the relevant paper owner of the unregistered title from the first moment of adverse possession. Consequently, if the alleged adverse possessor never, in fact, has been in adverse possession, time cannot start against the owner at all, and he cannot lose title. For example, in *Smith v. Lawson* (1997), the defendant had been given an occupation licence of the disputed land for life, and so her possession was always with the consent of the paper owner. Although this meant that the claimant had no right to recover the land during the defendant's life, it also meant that the defendant had no claim in adverse possession. Of course, once time *has* started, it is sufficient to establish that the full period has been completed at any time before the paper owner seeks to enforce his title to the land. It is not necessary to establish that the adverse possessor is in adverse possession at the moment the action for recovery is commenced, provided that the period has by then been completed.[62] For example, if S, the adverse possessor, has adversely possessed A's land for 12 years, but has left possession before A commences an action to recover the land, A's title will be barred and A will be unable to recover the land from whomever now is in possession. A's title to the unregistered land has been extinguished. Of course, if S has left the land and nobody is in possession, then A may retake possession, but will himself have to wait a further 12 years before being confident of defeating a returning S. Note, however, that the issue is complicated if the *paper owner* applies for first registration of title *after* the adverse possessor has completed 12 years' adverse possession. In that case, at first registration of title, the registered proprietor (against whom adverse possession has run for the limitation period) is bound only by adverse possession of which he has notice, or by the rights of an adverse possession as an overriding interest if (but only if) the adverse possessor is in actual occupation – section 11 of the LRA 2002.[63] This means that, absent notice, an adverse possessor going out of possession before first registration, even after completing the relevant period of adverse possession against an unregistered title, would have no rights against the first registered proprietor, although it is arguable that the adverse possessor could apply for rectification of the register on the ground that the paper owner's first registration was a 'mistake'.[64]

12.2.2   Stopping the clock of limitation for unregistered land

In unregistered land, if the claimant is in adverse possession of the land, this means that the paper owner has the limitation period (usually 12 years) to assert his paramount title and recover possession. It is thus important to determine what action may 'stop the clock' of limitation and so prevent the adverse possessor from completing the required

---

62 *Hounslow v. Minchinton* (1997). Note, however, different considerations apply in relation to adverse possession under the LRA 2002 – see below.

63 See Schedule 1, paragraph 2 of the LRA 2002 for interests which override at first registration.

64 It is uncertain whether the adverse possessor who has completed the 12-year period prior to first registration but whose interest does not override under Schedule 1 could apply successfully for rectification of the register in order to secure title for himself. Section 11 LRA would seem to suggest not, but it is certainly arguable that there has been a mistake which should be rectified. We should not forget, however, that the occasions on which the first registered proprietor does *not* have notice of the adverse possession *and* where the adverse possessor is *not* in actual occupation will be rare indeed.

period. If the clock is stopped successfully, then the paper owner's title is secure unless, of course, the adverse possessor begins to possess afresh – in which case the clock of limitation starts afresh.

1   A *successful* action for possession or an action seeking a declaration of title by the paper owner before expiry of the period will necessarily 'stop the clock' and any claim of adverse possession will have to begin again.[65] In this respect, a letter sent by the paper owner merely asserting title is not sufficient to stop the clock,[66] nor in most cases is the mere issuing of a claim for possession.[67]

2   Sections 29 and 30 of the Limitation Act 1980 provide that an adverse possessor cannot succeed if they have 'acknowledged' the paper owner's title before[68] the expiry of the limitation period. This may be by the payment of rent or by a written acknowledgment of title. What amounts to a written acknowledgment of title is, however, not always clear, and it seems that every case falls to be determined on its own facts. Obviously, a signed document will be sufficient. In *Ofulue* v. *Bossert* (2009), the House of Lords determined that a statement in court pleadings could amount to an acknowledgment of title for the purpose of section 29 of the Limitation Act 1980, but also that any written acknowledgment usually operated only at the time it was given and did not amount to a continuing acknowledgment. Thus, if the adverse possessor continued to assert adverse possession after giving a written acknowledgment of title, time would begin to run afresh from the date of the acknowledgment and the adverse possessor would acquire title if a 'new' period of limitation was completed – as in *Ofulue* itself. Further, as also made clear in *Ofulue*, if what appears to be a written acknowledgment of title is made in correspondence between the paper owner and the adverse possessor that is formally 'without prejudice' (that is, usually when the parties negotiate without meaning to affect or compromise their strict legal position), then it does not operate as an acknowledgment in law and may be discounted.

3   It *may* be sufficient for the paper owner to retake physical possession of the land himself before the expiry of the limitation period. However, such self-help is not always successful and may attract the attention of the criminal law. As *Smith* v. *Waterman* (2003) illustrates, the claimant's adverse possession cannot be interrupted *merely* by the paper owner going on to the land and doing some symbolic act – otherwise, mere entry on the land at some time by the paper owner would always stop the limitation clock (*Zarb* v. *Parry* (2011)).[69] Indeed, as the judge said in *Waterman*, factual possession (by the person claiming adverse possession) does not require continuous physical occupation, for much depends on the nature of the land itself. Consequently, recovery of possession through self-help by the paper owner in order to 'stop the clock' must also be such as to demonstrate a retaking of custody and control of the land.

---

65   This is so even if the proceedings are not possession proceedings, provided that the court has determined that the paper owner has title: *Higgs* v. *Leshel Maryas Investment Co Ltd* (2009).

66   *Moran.*

67   *Markfield Investments Ltd* v. *Evans* (2001).

68   Note, however, the decision in *Colchester Borough Council* v. *Smith* (1992): see section 12.2.3 below.

69   Although decided under the LRA 2002, the case concerns the general principles of adverse possession.

4   Permission given by the paper owner, even if unwanted and unasked for, may in some circumstances stop the limitation clock. Clearly, if the permission is accepted by the adverse possessor this is sufficient. However, as BP Properties Ltd v. Buckler (1987) and Smith v. Molyneaux (2016) decide, an unacknowledged permission, given unilaterally by the paper owner, may stop the clock if it indicates that the adverse possessor no longer has an intention to possess the land. Clearly, this is unusual and the facts must be sufficiently robust to allow the court to infer that the unacknowledged permission destroys the claim of adverse possession.

12.2.3   The effect of a successful claim of adverse possession in unregistered land

This section deals with the effects of a successful claim of adverse possession on land of unregistered title: that is, when the evidential base of adverse possession has been proved and the limitation period has expired. In these cases, the effects of a successful claim of adverse possession vary according to the proprietary interests of the parties involved. In particular, the effect on tenants has attracted attention in recent years.

12.2.3.1   *Effect on the paper owner*

It is settled law that, once the limitation period has run its course in respect of unregistered land, both the paper owner's right to sue and their title are extinguished by operation of statute (section 17 of the Limitation Act 1980). After this date, the conventional wisdom is that no acknowledgment of the paper owner's title, written or otherwise, and no payment, rent or other payment can revive the title.[70] This should be uncontroversial, as it is simply the consequence of the application of the Limitation Act 1980 and an expression of its underlying policy. However, the Court of Appeal has held, in Colchester BC v. Smith (1992), that in some circumstances a written acknowledgment of the paper owner's title by the adverse possessor, given *after* the period of limitation has ended, can be enough to prevent the adverse possessor relying on adverse possession when faced with an action for possession by the paper owner. This interesting decision appears to be based on an application of estoppel, in that the adverse possessor is estopped from denying the paper owner's title by the written acknowledgment, freely given. Surprisingly, the court offers no convincing reason why the Limitation Act 1980 should be ignored in this fashion, or even why the paper owner deserves to benefit from an estoppel: after all, the paper owner has slept on his rights, and why should a court of equity now come running to his aid? Neither does the court offer any reason why Nicholson v. England (1926) can be ignored (where an acknowledgment after expiry of the period was not sufficient to prevent adverse possession) and, in this sense, the decision in Smith might be regarded as per incuriam. However, at present, the Colchester decision appears to be authority for the proposition that a bona fide compromise of a dispute between two persons (i.e. the paper owner and adverse possessor), both of whom had legal advice, should be upheld on public policy grounds, even if the 12-year period of limitation has run. This is supported by

---

70 Nicholson v. England (1926).

the decision in the *Trustees in the Charity of Sir John Morden* v. *Mayrick* (2007), in which the claimant was not permitted to disavow a compromise agreement relating to ownership of land (on the ground that he had in fact completed adverse possession prior to conclusion of the agreement), because he had entered into the agreement freely and had raised no argument based on adverse possession at the time. In other words, a person will be bound by their contract.[71]

12.2.3.2   *Effect on the adverse possessor: freeholds*

The traditional doctrinal position is that a successful plea of adverse possession against unregistered land does not transfer the paper owner's title to the adverse possessor. It operates negatively to prevent the paper owner suing the adverse possessor (or person now in possession: for example, a purchaser from the adverse possessor) and extinguishes the paper title (section 17 of the Limitation Act 1980). There is no conveyance of the land from paper owner to adverse possessor. Moreover, because the adverse possessor is not a purchaser from (or even transferee from) the paper owner, the adverse possessor takes the land subject to all pre-existing proprietary obligations, whether these are registered as Land Charges (i.e. under the LCA 1972) or not. So, for example, an adverse possessor will be bound by the burden of unregistered equitable easements and unregistered restrictive covenants (as well as those protected by entry as a Land Charge) because the adverse possessor can never be 'equity's darling'. Yet, it must be the case that an adverse possessor acquires *something* as a result of a successful adverse possession because the adverse possessor may go on to deal with the land as if it were his own. He may sell it, lease it, devise it (i.e. leave it by will), give it away, grant easements over it and generally do those things that an estate owner might do. In other words, a successful adverse possessor does acquire a valuable asset. How, in practice, does this work?

As noted above, in unregistered land, the adverse possessor does not take, and is not treated as taking, a conveyance from the paper owner. Consequently, the paper owner has a bundle of worthless title documents and the adverse possessor has no proof of title at all. Yet, in practice, an adverse possessor with proof of established adverse possession usually can find a willing purchaser and will convey the land by deed to that purchaser. This new deed will be the first evidence of the adverse possessor's title and first evidence of the title of the new purchaser.[72] Necessarily, of course, the adverse possessor will not

---

71 In the context of adverse possession, this seemingly unobjectionable principle does not recognise that there is also a policy consideration – recognised and effected by Act of Parliament, no less – to the effect that sleeping on one's rights deprives a person of those rights. The judgment in *Smith* fails to explain why a contract between the parties can override the express provisions of an Act of Parliament. Although some commentators accept that, in principle, contracting out of the Limitation Act 1980 should be possible, it is submitted that this should not be permitted, save in the most exceptional circumstances. In the *Mayrick* case, prior to the compromise agreement, adverse possession had not been an issue between the parties and one can see why in those circumstances the court was prepared to uphold the compromise agreement.

72 The purchaser will then use this deed and the pre-existing claim of adverse possession to apply for first registration of title under the LRA 2002.

be able to make out a good 'root of title',[73] but the purchaser may be happy with a statutory declaration of good title, supported perhaps by 'title insurance'.[74] In effect then, a 'new' title is generated by the conveyancing process and this title will be confirmed and guaranteed when the transferee (from the adverse possessor) successfully applies for first registration of title under the LRA 2002.

12.2.3.3   *Effect on the adverse possessor: leaseholds*

The traditional doctrine that there is no conveyance of the paper owner's unregistered estate to the adverse possessor has some unusual consequences in the context of leaseholds. It will be remembered that a successful 12 years' adverse possession against a tenant extinguishes only the tenant's estate, and that the landlord has a further period of 12 years after the end of the original period of the lease in which to eject the adverse possessor before he also finds his title extinguished. This is perfectly proper because, as noted above, time can only run against a person when he has a right to recover land, and a landlord only has such a right when the lease expires. However, while it is true that the original tenant has lost his estate by adverse possession vis-à-vis the adverse possessor, it is also true that the original tenant remains as tenant vis-à-vis the landlord for the entire duration of the original lease.[75] Title is relative. So, during the currency of the lease, the landlord can bring forfeiture proceedings against the original tenant (for, say, non-payment of rent), even though the adverse possessor is in possession of the land under a successful adverse possession. The effect of such forfeiture is to terminate the lease and bring forward the landlord's right to possession of the land and thus bring forward the landlord's ability to eject the adverse possessor.[76] Note, however, that the converse of the rule – that the ejected tenant remains 'tenant' of the landlord – is that the adverse possessor is *not* to be regarded as the tenant, or an assignee of the tenant, so cannot be liable on any leasehold covenants save those enforceable as restrictive covenants under the rule in *Tulk v. Moxhay* (1848).[77]

Although apparently complicated, the picture painted above is quite simple: the adverse possessor has extinguished the tenant's title so that the tenant cannot evict the adverse possessor, but the tenant remains the tenant of the landlord. The difficulties arise when the ejected tenant seeks to manipulate his continuing relationship with the landlord to defeat the adverse possessor. For example, we have just noted that the landlord may forfeit the lease in an action against the dispossessed tenant, thereby bringing forward the landlord's right of action against the adverse possessor. In other words, the

---

73 See Chapter 3.

74 A statutory declaration is a sworn statement of truth undertaken by the adverse possessor. 'Title insurance' is an insurance policy, paid for by the adverse possessor and purchased from a specialist company, guaranteeing compensation if the adverse possessor's title should prove to be defective. It is very common in legal systems that do not have a State-backed guarantee of title.

75 See *Chan Suk Yin v. Harvest Good Development Ltd* (2005), per Lord Hoffmann, giving judgment in the Hong Kong Court of Final Appeal.

76 In which proceedings the adverse possessor has no right to apply for relief, having no rights under the lease – *Tickner v. Buzzacott* (1965).

77 See Chapter 8.

landlord does not have to wait until the lease term has expired to bring an action against the adverse possessor because he has terminated the lease in virtue of his rights as landlord. What, however, if the tenant surrenders his lease to the landlord, despite having 'lost' title vis-à-vis the adverse possessor? Does this also terminate the lease and bring forward the landlord's right of action against the adverse possessor? In unregistered land, *Fairweather* v. *St Marylebone Property Co Ltd* (1963) provides a clear answer. In that case, a tenant against whom adverse possession had been completed successfully surrendered the lease to the landlord, and the House of Lords held that this was effective to terminate the lease: the lease was brought to an end by a person (the ejected tenant) who still had an estate vis-à-vis the landlord. Moreover, given that the lease was now terminated, the adverse possessor had no right to remain on the land in the face of an action by the landlord, because the landlord's right to possession was now active. As a matter of strict logic and theory, this is difficult to fault. However, on a common-sense view, it is difficult to see why the ejected tenant should have the power to surrender a lease that, to all intents and purposes, is an empty shell. The inequity to the adverse possessor is even more apparent if the landlord, after having evicted the adverse possessor, regrants a new lease to the ejected tenant![78] Despite powerful criticisms of this rule judicially and academically, it now seems likely that it will not be overruled. Of course, it applies only in the context of unregistered title and unregistered title is rapidly decreasing in significance.

12.2.4 The substantive nature of the adverse possessor's rights prior to completing the period of limitation in unregistered land

Pending completion of the period of limitation in respect of unregistered land, the adverse possessor is taken to have certain rights in the land, even though these can be completely defeated by the paper owner recovering possession within the limitation period. In the case of *Turner* v. *Chief Land Registrar* (2013), it was important to determine the nature of an adverse possessor's rights pending completion of the relevant limitation period in order to determine if he could apply for a caution against first registration of title.[79] The Adjudicator to HM Land Registry determined that such an adverse possessor

---

78 Before the LRA 2002 made comparisons between registered and unregistered land meaningless, the position in registered land under the LRA 1925 was different from that pertaining in unregistered land. In *Central London Commercial Estates Ltd* v. *Kato Kagaku Ltd* (1998), the ejected tenant surrendered its lease to the freeholder, and the registered title to that lease was closed. The freeholder sought to evict the adverse possessor before the original period of the lease had expired. However, the court held that the effect of section 75 of the LRA 1925 (which was then operative) was to ensure that the tenant's original interest was held on trust for the adverse possessor, and that the tenant could not surrender after the period of limitation had run. In effect, the court held that the tenant's interest in the lease actually did pass to the adverse possessor, and the adverse possessor could remain on the land for the remainder of the term. Sedley J goes so far as to say that there was, in reality, a statutory conveyance of the original lease with benefits and burdens intact.

79 This would warn him if any person attempted to first register title to the land he was in the process of adversely possessing.

had 'a legal estate' in the land and on appeal the court indicated that this must have been a fee simple absolute. In consequence, he could not register a caution,[80] but the important point is the confirmation that even an adverse possessor in the process of acquiring title has a valuable property right. Thus, an adverse possessor awaiting completion of the period may transfer such rights as they do have (e.g. two years' worth of possession, ten years' worth etc.) to another person either by will or inter vivos (Asher v. Whitlock (1865)). The period so transferred may then be added to any period successfully completed by the legatee/assignee of the adverse possessor's rights in order to make up a total of 12 years' worth of adverse possession. The same is true if one adverse possessor dispossesses another: as where the paper owner A is dispossessed by X for five years, who in turn is dispossessed by Y for seven years. In such, a case, the current adverse possessor (Y) is able to claim the combined period of adverse possession (X + Y) in order to defeat the paper owner.[81]

12.3   Adverse Possession under the Land Registration Act 1925

If the land is registered title, but is governed by the LRA 1925 (i.e. adverse possession was completed before the entry into force of the LRA 2002)[82] the same limitation period applies as in land of unregistered title; that is, usually adverse possession of 12 years. Similarly, the same principles apply when considering whether the paper owner has managed to stop the clock of limitation. This means that a person who has completed 12 years' adverse possession before 13 October 2003 (the date of entry into force of the LRA 2002) is entitled to be registered as proprietor of the land.[83] Prior to the 2002 Act, in such cases (i.e. completion of the 12 years), the land was held on trust by the registered proprietor for the successful adverse possessor, but this trust no longer exists and has been replaced by the entitlement to be registered.[84] This entitlement to be registered is enforceable against a purchaser of the land from the current registered proprietor if the adverse possessor is in discoverable actual occupation of the land so as to be able to claim an interest which overrides within Schedule 3, paragraph 2 of the LRA 2002.[85] If the

---

80 A person with a fee simple absolute cannot register a caution against first registration – section 15(1) (a)(i) LRA 2002 – because they are to be encouraged actually to first register their title.

81 In a contest between the adverse possessors, the current possessor can claim only that time which has elapsed since dispossessing the previous possessor.

82 For example, Dyer v. Terry (2013).

83 Schedule 12, paragraph 18 of the LRA 2002. The title of the former owner is extinguished and cannot be revived by later registration, Crosdil v. Hodder (2011), before Deputy Adjudicator McAllister.

84 Schedule 12, paragraph 18 of the LRA 2002. The 'trust' concept arises from section 75 of the LRA 1925, but that is repealed.

85 Sections 29 and 30 of the LRA 2002.

transferee is not a purchaser, the right to be registered is binding under the basic priority rule found in section 28 of the LRA 2002.[86]

Importantly, if the adverse possessor had not fully completed 12 years' adverse possession before the entry into force of the 2002 Act, his situation is governed by the scheme of the 2002 Act. This is so even if the period of adverse possession was nearing completion on the day the Act entered into force. For example, if a claimant had completed 11 years' adverse possession on the day the LRA 2002 entered into force, they do not acquire a right to be registered with the title when 12 years have passed. In all such cases, the period of adverse possession (being less than 12 years on 13 October 2003) may count for the relevant period under the LRA 2002, but as we shall see this is very far from giving them any right to title of the land. Consequently, the traditional rules of adverse possession will apply to registered land only in so far as the 12-year period of limitation is fully completed before 13 October 2003.

12.4   Adverse Possession under the Land Registration Act 2002

Most of the case law in respect of adverse possession deals with either land of unregistered title or claims to adverse possession under the LRA 1925, although we are now seeing some cases decided under the LRA 2002.[87] However, while the law concerning how adverse possession is established applies just as much to registered land as it does to unregistered land, the scheme for regulating the *effects* of adverse possession on land whose title is registered is now radically different, having been modified substantially by the LRA 2002.[88] This scheme, which is fully in force, will govern the vast majority of claims of adverse possession in the future. It is premised on the premise that a State-guaranteed title, readily provable from a title register, should not be lost because of the 'mere' possession of a stranger, irrespective of how long that stranger's possession has lasted. This is the natural consequence of 'title by registration'.

12.4.1   The basic principle

Under the LRA 2002, there is no period of limitation against a registered title and no sense in which a registered proprietor can lose title *merely* because another person has adversely possessed the land for a fixed period of time (section 96 of the LRA 2002). Consequently, even if factual possession plus an intention to possess is established, no

---

86 If an adverse possessor who is entitled to be registered (having completed 12 years' adverse possession before the entry into force of the LRA 2002) does *not* have priority over a purchaser (i.e. they are not in discoverable actual occupation so as to trigger an overriding interest), they lose their claim. Note, however, that it has been argued that the adverse possessor in this position may seek rectification of the register, but this would rather seem to defeat the point of the priority rules found in sections 28 and 29 of the LRA 2002.

87 These are often decisions of the registration division of the Property Chamber of the First Tier Tribunal hearing applications about the application of the LRA 2002.

88 Note, however, that even under the LRA 2002, the old limitation period applies in respect of a claim by one squatter to have ousted another squatter. This must be so as the ousted squatter has no registered title.

period of possession of itself can deprive the registered proprietor of his title. However, the 2002 Act recognises that claims of adverse possession are a fact of life and that merely removing a period of limitation will not stop disputes between persons over title to land. Consequently, in place of a limitation principle per se, the 2002 Act establishes an application procedure whereby the adverse possessor may apply to the registrar to be registered as proprietor of the title and this application then triggers the statutory scheme spelt out in Schedule 6 to the Act. Consequently, the onus of making a claim to a registered title shifts to the adverse possessor and the registered proprietor need do nothing to maintain his title save take action when (and if) the adverse possessor applies for registration. A registered proprietor does not, therefore, have to remain vigilant in the vindication of his title but can rely on this new system to alert him to any adverse claim, a claim to which he can then respond to safeguard his interest.

12.4.2   The statutory scheme

Under the 2002 Act, where a person has been in adverse possession for at least ten years,[89] ending on the date of making an application,[90] that person may apply to the registrar to be registered as proprietor. It is a precondition to making such an application that ten years' adverse possession actually has occurred (and is occurring on the date of making the application),[91] so that a registered proprietor who loses his title under this scheme may nevertheless have the register rectified in his favour and recover title if the factual basis of the claim of adverse possession proves to be false – Baxter v. Mannion (2011).[92] If the registrar takes the view that the application discloses an arguable case for registration,[93] a notice will be sent to the current registered proprietor (and certain other persons such as those with a mortgage or lease over the registered title: Schedule 6, paragraph 2 of the LRA 2002). On receipt of this notice, the registered proprietor (and others receiving the notice) has the choice of three responses, but failure to respond at all will mean that the adverse possessor is registered with title.[94] Option one is that he may

---

89 Thus, there is a ten-year threshold, but it is not a period of limitation, merely the point after which an application can be made. The existence of adverse possession for ten years is to be assessed by reference to the traditional principles explained in Pye v. Graham and discussed above in the context of unregistered land – Schedule 6, paragraph 11 of the LRA 2002.

90 Schedule 6, paragraph 1 LRA 2002.

91 Crosdil v. Hodder (2011) before Deputy Adjudicator McAllister. Thus, unlike the position in unregistered land and under the LRA 1925, an adverse possessor who quits the land cannot make an application, even if having completed ten years.

92 In this case, the registered proprietor failed to respond to the notice sent by the registrar and hence initially lost title; see below.

93 That is, that adverse possession under the substantive law arguably has been established. The registrar is likely to reject applications only in the most obvious cases.

94 See the preliminary issue in Baxter v. Mannion. Consequently, the scheme assumes that the registered proprietor actually receives the notice from HM Land Registry. If the address for service is the registered land itself, there is a danger that the adverse possessor will destroy the notice and so the proprietor may never be warned! This is a primary reason why registered proprietors should avail themselves of the opportunity of lodging more than one address for service of notices with HM Land Registry. If possible, this should include an email address.

consent to the application, in which case the adverse possessor will be registered as proprietor. No doubt, this will not be commonplace, but an example is provided by *Balevents Ltd v. Sartori* (2011).[95] The second option is that the registered proprietor may object to the application. If he objects, the application for registration cannot be finalised until the objection has been dealt with. In the absence of a negotiated settlement, the matter may be referred to the registration division of the Property Chamber of the First Tier Tribunal for decision. The nature of the objection is likely to be that the factual basis of the claim of adverse possession is false. However, even if there is doubt about the factual basis of the claim, the registered proprietor is likely also to serve a counter-notice (see option three, considered below), because the counter-notice procedure allows the registered proprietor to defeat the application *whether or not* the factual basis for the claim of adverse possession exists. Consequently, this second response, simple objection by the registered proprietor, is likely to occur only if the registered proprietor clearly can defeat the factual claim for possession or is unable to plead the benefit of the 'two-year rule' (option three) considered below.[96]

The third option open to the registered proprietor, and the most likely to be pursued, is to serve a counter-notice (either with or without an objection under option two). This option is triggered by ticking the relevant box on the form sent by the Land Registry. It is a simple procedure. This counter-notice requires the registrar to deal with the application under paragraph 5 of Schedule 6 to the 2002 Act.[97] In essence, this means that, irrespective of whether the factual basis for adverse possession is made out, the adverse possessor *cannot* be entered as the new registered proprietor unless any one of three exceptional grounds is made out. Moreover, and most importantly, assuming none of these grounds is made out, the registered proprietor will then have a further two years following the application by the adverse possessor to recover possession of the land. Recovery of possession during this two-year period of grace is as of right – i.e. simply because he is the owner – and is available irrespective of how long the adverse possessor has actually been in possession. If the registered proprietor does not so recover within these additional two years – possible, but unlikely – then the adverse possessor may reapply at the expiry of the two-year period and he will be entered as proprietor of the title.[98]

Clearly, this new scheme will have a dramatic effect on the frequency and success of claims of adverse possession. In essence, a registered proprietor will receive notice of any application by an adverse possessor to become the new proprietor and (putting aside consent, simple objection or failure to respond at all), unless one of the three exceptional

---

95 The paper owner was a local authority and the case involved a small strip of land. The dispute was over which person was in adverse possession.

96 This may be because the adverse possessor can claim the benefit of one of the exceptions to the two-year rule.

97 Following *Hopkins v. Beacon* (2011), the registrar should treat the registered proprietor's response as raising an objection and requiring the application to be dealt with under Schedule 6, paragraph 5 if a reasonable registrar would have reached that conclusion. Thus, the registered proprietor's failure to indicate clearly that this was the course of action he desired is not fatal.

98 In such a case, the adverse possessor takes the land subject to any interests affecting the estate, except any registered charge (unless registration is because of the exceptional situations outlined above): Schedule 6, paragraph 9 of the LRA 2002.

grounds is made out, will have two years from that date to recover possession by normal court action. This court action for possession will be successful simply by reason of the paper owner proving his title. No further reason need be given. It will require the minimum of effort and only the most idle, incompetent or uninterested proprietors are likely to fail to recover possession during the two-year period of grace. Moreover, this process will apply whether the adverse possessor applies for registration after ten years or 110 years: there is no period of limitation. So, if the adverse possessor makes no application for registration, or does so and is evicted (assuming the exceptions do not apply), the registered proprietor is safe. This explains why landowners with large and diverse land holdings – such as local authorities – are applying for first registration of title. It offers considerable protection against the claims of adverse possessors.

12.4.3   The exceptions

Given the robust protection offered to a registered proprietor by the LRA 2002, it is clear that most disputes will now concern the meaning and scope of the exceptions listed in Schedule 6 to the Act. This is likely to be the real battleground. After all, if a registered proprietor can evict an adverse possessor within two years of the adverse possessor's application for registration even if the factual basis of adverse possession exists, plainly the adverse possessor will seek to rely, if at all possible, on the exceptions. It is only if the adverse possessor is able to establish adverse possession according to the substantive law *and* is able to rely on one of these exceptions that the adverse possessor stands any realistic chance of being registered as proprietor consequent upon his application.[99]

The exceptional cases are listed in Schedule 6, paragraph 5 of the LRA 2002. These are: first, where it would be unconscionable for the current proprietor to dispossess the adverse possessor because of an estoppel and the circumstances are such that the adverse possessor ought to be registered; second, where the adverse possessor is 'for some other reason' entitled to be registered as proprietor; or, third, where there is a boundary dispute concerning adjoining land and for at least ten years of the adverse possession the applicant reasonably believed the disputed land to be his, provided that the disputed land had been registered land for more than one year prior to the application.

12.4.3.1   *Exception 1: estoppel, unconscionability and 'ought to be registered'*

This first condition imports substantive principles of proprietary estoppel into the law of adverse possession. This is perfectly consistent with the use of estoppel as a remedy for unconscionable conduct. It suggests that, as well as establishing adverse possession (factual possession and intention) for at least ten years existing on the date of the application, the applicant must also show that he has detrimentally relied on some assurance by the registered proprietor in circumstances in which it would be unconscionable for the assurance to be withdrawn. The two examples given by HM Land Registry are where the squatter has built on the registered proprietor's land in the mistaken belief that he was

---

99 Of course, the adverse possessor will also be successful if the registered proprietor does not respond to the notice, consents to the application or fails to recover possession within two years.

the owner of it and the proprietor has knowingly acquiesced in his mistake, and where neighbours have entered into an informal sale agreement for valuable consideration by which one agrees to sell the land to the other. The 'buyer' pays the price, takes possession of the land and treats it as his own, but no steps are taken to perfect his title by registration and there is no binding contract. This illustrates that it is envisaged that estoppel may be used when the 'assurance' is both express and implied by acquiescence, and where it supports a failed contract.[100] Obviously, given the flexible nature of estoppel and the reluctance of courts to 'pigeonhole' cases – see Chapter 10 – it remains to be seen whether this is a wide or narrow ground for gaining title by adverse possession. In this regard, two further points may be made. First, if a squatter can rely on estoppel per se, why would they wish to claim adverse possession at all? As we know, estoppel itself is a sword capable of attacking the proprietor's title and it is not immediately obvious why an adverse possessor would wait ten years and choose to tie his estoppel to a claim in adverse possession. Perhaps it is because a successful estoppel claim by itself does not guarantee that the claimant will acquire title – see *Jennings v. Rice* (2003)[101] – whereas an adverse possession/estoppel claim within Schedule 6 could do so.[102] Nevertheless, given the overlap, there is an obvious need to reflect carefully when advising an adverse possessor who might also be able to claim estoppel. Second, Schedule 6, paragraph 5(2) does *not* say that an adverse possessor will be registered as proprietor if they can support the possession claim by an estoppel. In addition, the applicant must establish that they 'ought to be registered'.[103] Does this mean that the court has a discretion to refuse registration to an applicant even though he has made out ten years' adverse possession and has established an estoppel? If so, on what basis will a refusal be given, especially because by definition the paper owner must have behaved unconscionably for an estoppel to exist in the first place? Further, if there is a refusal to register the adverse possessor despite at least ten years' possession and an estoppel, can the adverse possessor then pursue an independent claim in estoppel for the same, or a different, remedy? Clearly, the exact scope of this exception will need to be clarified judicially.

12.4.3.2   *Exception 2: the squatter is for some other reason entitled to be registered as the proprietor*

This appears to be something of a 'catch-all' condition and its unspecific nature makes it ripe for use by adverse possessors who fear that the registered proprietor may simply take advantage of the two-year period of grace. The examples provided by HM Land Registry are where the squatter is entitled to the land under the will or intestacy of the deceased proprietor, and where the squatter contracted to buy the land and paid the purchase price, but the legal estate was never transferred to him.[104] Indeed, in both of these examples, the applicant need not rely on adverse possession at all to establish title and it

---

100 Assuming, of course, that this is not an attempt to avoid the statutory rules requiring contracts to be made in writing and that there is unconscionability.

101 Discussed in Chapter 10.

102 For example, where the estoppel is merely incidental to the claim and would not give title on its own.

103 Schedule 6, paragraph 5(2)(b).

104 The squatter–buyer is a beneficiary under a bare trust.

raises the question why a claimant would need adverse possession where he was for some other reason 'entitled' to be registered. The provision was examined briefly by tribunal judge McAllister in *Crosdil v. Hodder* (2011), who also noted that both of the Commission's examples were 'instances [where] the claimant or applicant can obtain a remedy without having to rely on adverse possession' and thus she concluded that the exception was to be interpreted narrowly and should not be used to support adverse possessors on a broad view of entitlement. Perhaps the point is that, absent adverse possession, a person 'entitled' would have to make an application for rectification of the register against the proprietor under Schedule 4 of the 2002 Act, and perhaps such an application for rectification might be refused. Hence, perhaps the intention is that, where adverse possession supports an entitlement, the claimant can avoid the limits on the power to rectify the register[105] by using the route of adverse possession.[106] Again, the scope of this exception is not immediately obvious.

12.4.3.3   *The boundary exception*

The third exception reflects the reality of living in a country where the exact boundary line between adjoining land may be uncertain or may have been altered over time without any formal transfer of land between neighbours. It preserves the valuable role of adverse possession as a practical solution to often intractable and bitter boundary disputes.[107] As HM Land Registry indicated in one of its earlier Guides to the Act:

> the condition may be useful in situations where the boundaries as they appear on the ground and as they are according to the title plan do not coincide, for example: where physical features suggest the boundary is in one place but according to the title plan it is in another; or where the dividing walls or fences on an estate were erected in the wrong place and not in accordance with the plans in the title deeds.[108]

In other words, the exception represents a common-sense view of land ownership and title registration and it is likely to be the most commonly used of the three exceptions. Although Schedule 6 does impose four conditions before a claim of adverse possession may be successful under this exception,[109] it is the only one of the exceptions where the claimant may acquire a title *simply because* he has adversely possessed the land, in the sense that there is no need to rely on some additional property law doctrine.

Three of the four conditions for this exception are factual and simply need to be proved in the normal way – that the land of the applicant is adjacent to that to which the claim relates, that the exact boundary has not been determined and that the land

---

105 See Chapter 2.

106 There is some evidence to support this as it appears that the 'other reason' exception can be used where an adverse possessor has established a complete claim before 13 October 2003 and so appears outside the scheme of the LRA 2002, but has failed to apply properly for his 'entitlement' to be registered (section 12.3 above), usually by using the wrong form. In this case, the 'other reason' is that they should never have been within the LRA 2002 in the first place!

107 See e.g. *Zarb v. Parry* (2011).

108 Land Registry Practice Guide No. 4, 2008. See now the updated version of guide No. 4, April 2016.

109 Paragraph 5(4).

(the estate) to which the application relates has been registered for more than one year. The fourth condition is different and might prove to be problematic. It is whether 'for at least ten years of the period of adverse possession ending on the date of the application, the applicant (or any predecessor in title) reasonably believed that the land to which the application relates belonged to him'. This is meant to ensure that an adverse possessor can succeed only if they mistakenly and reasonably believe the land to be theirs, rather than being engaged in deliberate theft of it. See, for example, *Zarb* v. *Parry* (2011), where the Court of Appeal held that the applicants' belief in their ownership was reasonable and so they succeeded in establishing title under the boundary exception. Likewise, in *IAM Group* v. *Chowdrey*, the court held that it was the claimant's belief that had to be 'reasonable', not that of his solicitors and that being told that the land was not his did not make his belief unreasonable. However, as recognised in *Zarb*, the scope of this condition is uncertain. For example, does it require a reasonable belief for *any* ten-year period before the application is made (the view of the tribunal judge in *Crosdil* v. *Hodder*) or must that belief persist for ten years *up to* the moment of the application making it much more difficult to rely on the exception (suggested by Arden LJ in *Zarb* v. *Parry* and possibly adopted by the Court of Appeal in *IAM Group* v. *Chowdrey* (2012))? Can the claim be defeated if the adverse possessor becomes aware before applying for registration of the registered owner's objection to their assertion of title – so that his belief could become unreasonable – and what should the adverse possessor do if he does become aware? Might the adverse possessor in such circumstances be best advised to make an application as soon as they are able, for fear of falling outside the exception?[110] This uncertainty generated by these unresolved issues is of some concern given that the 'boundary exception' is likely to be the most relied on in practice.[111]

As is apparent, the intention behind these three exceptions is to ensure that the adverse possessor is registered as owner when, in a broad sense, he 'deserves' to be and has supported this by ten years' adverse possession. As noted above, the expectation is that normally the registered proprietor will either object to the application in its entirety or simply utilise the two-year period of grace. The exceptions are meant to be truly exceptional. However, it is not fanciful to suppose that we may well see 'sympathetic' interpretations of these exceptions so as to permit adverse possession of registered land in a wider range of circumstances than is really intended by the 2002 Act. This remains to be seen, but it may well be that not all judges share the view that claims to adverse possession should be strangled under the regime of the LRA 2002, especially if e-conveyancing does not become a reality. What is clear, however, is that the LRA 2002 scheme as a whole means the end of one of the last operative feudal elements of English land law. Possibly, we should not lament it. On the other hand, we must also ask

---

110 *Zarb* v. *Parry* (2011). In *Crew* v. *London & Continental Holdings* (2016) the Tribunal thought that the 'reasonable belief' rule meant either reasonable belief for any 10 year period before the application, or an application within a reasonable time of the 10 year period of reasonable belief ending. Otherwise, hardly anyone would succeed under this exception.

111 In its 2016 Consultation Paper, the Law Commission suggest that the adverse possessor may have held the reasonable belief for any period of ten years and not necessarily at the date of application, but propose by way of clarification and amendment that the possessor must apply within six months of that reasonable belief ending. It is not clear whether this will become law.

whether the scheme of the LRA 2002 will do anything to encourage negligent or uninterested landowners to make the most of their precious resource called 'land'. Prior to entry into force of the LRA 2002, a landowner had to be attentive to his estate and failure to use his land meant that others could acquire title to it and, perhaps, use it more beneficially (see *Lambeth LBC v. Ellis* (2000) and *Purbrick v. Hackney LB* (2003)). After the entry into force of the LRA 2002, a landowner with registered title can sit back and wait for the registrar to inform him that his land is subject to another's claim and then he can – usually – evict at any time within the next two years. Then he can sink back into slumber.

12.4.4 Effect of registration of the adverse possessor under the Land Registration Act 2002

If the adverse possessor is successful and is registered as proprietor, he takes the land subject to any interests affecting the estate, except any registered charge, save that, if registration is the result of the operation of one of the three exceptions, he takes the land also subject to any registered charge.[112] The difference arises because the registered chargee – a bank or other lender – that holds a mortgage over the land will have been served with a notice and so could have requested that the application be dealt with under the two-year rule if it wished to preserve its security. Consequently, it can hardly object to the loss of its charge if, having been served with notice, it fails to take action to evict the adverse possessor. However, if the adverse possessor is registered as a result of one of the exceptions, by definition the mortgagee will have been unable to take advantage of the two-year rule and will not be able to challenge the registration. Thus, it is entirely appropriate that the adverse possessor in those circumstances should take the title subject to all incumbrances, including the mortgage.

12.5 Chapter Summary

12.5.1 The traditional principle of adverse possession: the limitation of actions

The ability of an adverse possessor (or 'trespasser') to acquire a better right to the land than the paper owner is based on the principle of limitation of actions. This means that a person (e.g. the paper owner of the land) may be 'statute-barred' from bringing a claim against the adverse possessor to recover possession of the land after the period of limitation has passed. In this sense, adverse possession operates negatively: it prevents an estate owner from suing on his rights and operates to extinguish his title. These principles will continue to govern cases in relation to unregistered land and registered land where the period of adverse possession is fully completed before 13 October 2003, the entry into force of the LRA 2002. There is a new scheme for cases falling under the LRA 2002.

---

112 Schedule 6, paragraph 9 of the LRA 2002.

12.5.2   The limitation period under the 'old law': unregistered land and registered land where adverse possession is completed before 13 October 2003

In most cases, where a limitation period is applicable at all (i.e. not in respect of registered titles under the LRA 2002), that period will be 12 years from the moment of adverse possession by the claimant (section 15 of the Limitation Act 1980). If the current paper owner is a tenant of the land under a lease, the period of limitation against the tenant is 12 years. The period for the landlord is also 12 years, but does not start to run until the original term of the tenancy has ended (Schedule 1, paragraph 4 of the Limitation Act 1980). There are longer limitation periods for special situations; e.g. involving Crown land.

12.5.3   Adverse possession under the Land Registration Act 2002

There is no period of limitation. The adverse possessor may apply for registration of title after ten years' adverse possession and this triggers a notice to the registered proprietor. In all but three exceptional cases, the registered proprietor will have a further two years to remove the adverse possessor simply by asserting his title.

12.5.4   The substantive law: an intention to possess

The requirement that the adverse possessor must 'intend' to possess the land adversely to the exclusion of all others to some extent is artificial. For example, some adverse possessors may appreciate fully that the land is not theirs and act deliberately to exclude the world; others may believe honestly that the land is theirs already, and so do not for one moment think they are excluding the 'true' owner; others still may have formulated no intention at all, but simply treat the land as their own because it is there. In other words, we are not looking here for 'intention' in the traditional legal sense of a *mens rea*, either objectively or subjectively established. What is required is evidence that the adverse possessor, for whatever reason, had an intention to possess the land and put it to his own use, whether or not he also knew that some other person had a claim or right to the land.

12.5.5   The substantive law: physical possession

As well as demonstrating an intention to possess the land, the adverse possessor must also demonstrate a physical assumption of possession. Before the decision in Pye, there was doubt about the circumstances in which possession could be deemed to have been taken and when it also was 'adverse' to the paper owner. However, in Pye, Lord Browne-Wilkinson explained that:

> much confusion and complication would be avoided if reference to adverse possession were to be avoided so far as possible.... The question is simply whether the defendant squatter has dispossessed the paper owner by going into ordinary possession of the land for the requisite period without the consent of the owner.

In other words, we should not seek to over-conceptualise what is 'adverse' and what is not, but ask ourselves the simple, ordinary question: is the claimant in possession of the land without the permission of the landowner?

12.5.6 Stopping the clock of limitation in unregistered land and registered land governed by the Land Registration Act 1925

A successful action for possession will necessarily 'stop the clock', as will an acknowledgment of the paper owner's title in writing, the payment of rent (sections 29 and 30 of the Limitation Act 1980) and possibly physical repossession of the land by self-help or the unilateral giving of possession. Once the limitation period has expired (where applicable), both the paper owner's right to sue and his title are extinguished by operation of statute (section 17 of the Limitation Act 1980). After this date, the conventional wisdom is that no acknowledgment, written or otherwise, and no payment of rent or other money, can revive the paper owner's title: *Nicholson v. England* (1962), but see *Colchester BC v. Smith* (1992). The same principles can stop the ten-year period under the LRA 2002, although that is not likely to be necessary in order to defeat the adverse possessor's claim.

12.5.7 The effect of a successful claim of adverse possession of unregistered land and registered land governed by the Land Registration Act 1925

On the paper owner generally: successful adverse possession prevents the paper owner suing and effectively extinguishes his title (section 17 of the Limitation Act 1980). *On the adverse possessor in unregistered land*: conventional wisdom is that a successful adverse possession does not transfer title to the claimant. The claimant may sell or otherwise deal with the land because the absence of title deeds is dealt with by appropriate conveyancing devices (e.g. statutory declaration, title insurance). *On the adverse possessor in registered land governed by the LRA 1925*: the paper owner will be the registered proprietor but the adverse possessor is entitled to be registered.

On the adverse possessor claiming against a tenant: in unregistered land, it seems the displaced tenant remains in a relationship with his landlord and can surrender his lease, so allowing the landlord to take early action against the claimant to evict. In registered land under the LRA 1925, authority suggests that the adverse possessor steps into the shoes of the tenant when he is registered (*Central London Commercial Estates Ltd v. Kato Kaguka Ltd* (1998)), so allowing the claimant to remain in possession for the remainder of the tenant's full term and even to enjoy rights granted to the tenant – such as the right to extend the lease.

12.5.8 Adverse possession under the Land Registration Act 2002

Under the new scheme, there is no period of limitation and no sense in which a registered proprietor loses title merely because another person has adversely possessed the land for a fixed period of time (section 96 of the LRA 2002). The onus shifts from the paper owner to the adverse possessor. Where a person claims to have completed at least ten years' adverse possession ending on the date of application (and this is to be assessed by the traditional rules: Schedule 6, paragraph 11 of the LRA 2002), that person may apply to the registrar to be registered as proprietor. This application will trigger notice to the current registered proprietor (and certain other persons: Schedule 6, paragraph 2 of the LRA 2002). If the registered proprietor does not respond, the adverse possessor is registered. Usually, the registered proprietor responds and then has three options: consent, objection or to ask for the application of the statutory two-year rule. The adverse possessor cannot then be entered as the new registered proprietor (assuming no consent) unless either of three exceptional grounds is established (estoppel where the adverse possessor ought to be registered, or where the adverse possessor is 'for some other reason' entitled to be registered as proprietor, or where there is a boundary dispute). During the two-year period, absent the exceptional circumstances, the proprietor may evict the possessor simply by proving title. If the adverse possessor is not evicted during the two-year period, he may reapply for registration and must be so registered.

Further Reading

Cooke, E, 'Adverse possession, problems of title in registered land' (1994) 14 LS 1.

Dixon, M, 'Adverse possession and registered land' [2009] Conv 169.

Dockray, M, 'Why do we need adverse possession?' [1985] Conv 272.

Fox, L and **Cobb**, N, 'Living outside the system? The (im)morality of urban squatting after the Land Registration Act 2002' (2008) 27 LS 236.

Harpum, C, '*Buckinghamshire County Council* v. *Moran*' [1990] CLJ 23.

Harpum, C and **Radley-Gardner**, O, 'Adverse possession and the intention to possess: A reply' [2001] Conv 155.

Tee, L, 'Adverse possession and intention to possess' [2000] Conv 113.

Human rights and property law

Dixon, M, 'At the sharper end' [2011] Conv 335.

Gray, K, 'Land law and human rights', in Tee, L (ed.) *Land Law: Issues, Debates, Policy*, Cullompton: Willan, 2002.

Griffiths, G, 'An important question of principle: Reality and rectification in registered land' [2011] Conv 331.

Halstead, P, 'Human property rights' [2002] Conv 153.

Howell, J, 'The Human Rights Act 1998', in Cooke, E (ed.) *Modern Studies in Property Law*, Vol. 1, Oxford: Hart, 2001.

Now visit the companion website to:

* test your understanding of the key terms using our Flashcard Glossary;

* revise and consolidate your knowledge using our Multiple Choice Question testbank.

www.routledge.com/cw/dixon

Index